THE UNCOMMON DEFENSE AND CONGRESS, 1945–1963

A Publication of the Mershon Center for Education in National Security

THE UNCOMMON DEFENSE AND CONGRESS, 1945–1963

By Edward A. Kolodziej

OHIO STATE UNIVERSITY PRESS

To Antje

PREFACE

This study investigates Congress' use of its power of the purse to influence military force levels, weapons systems, and strategic policy between 1945 and 1963—the Seventy-ninth through the Eighty-seventh congresses. It not only describes how Congress has participated in shaping defense policy, but also analyzes and evaluates the actual decisions of Congress as they have been recorded in its review and passage of the annual appropriations bills for the defense establishment.

Part I introduces the major theoretical dimensions of the study. Part II describes congressional action. The historical account is necessarily detailed, for Congress' influence on military policy is primarily felt through its review and rearrangement of the myriad of budgetary figures that the executive branch annually presents to it for confirmation. Attention is concentrated on major appropriations measures. Appendix A lists them. The number of bills which are examined is considered sufficiently large and extends over a long enough period of time to permit observation of the changing character of Congress' approach to, and impact on, defense policy.

Part III fashions out of the historical material of Part II a role which Congress can, and should, play in strategic policy through its power of the purse, and evaluates congressional decisions and actions since World War II in terms of the criteria that are presented. Chapters VIII and IX specifically outline a new intellectual approach to strategic policy for Congress and suggest ways to implement it.

The study departs from much of prevailing thought and opinion about the role of Congress in defense and foreign policy. It draws a picture of Congress' exercise of its purse power that, while not complimentary in many respects, contrasts with the commonly expressed view that Congress has contributed little of benefit to defense policy since 1945. It also argues that Congress can assume a more positive, active, and informed role in strategic policy, and, accordingly, that the effectiveness of United States strategic and foreign policies can be improved. The analysis indicates further that the defects of Congress' participation in strategic policy through its handling of military appropriations stem both from the shortcomings of its collective intellectual grasp of the relation of military force to foreign policy and from the political process by which defense policy is made in Congress.

A realistic statement of what Congress' role should be in national security must be rooted in the knowledge of the role that it has actually played in defense policy. A discussion and evaluation of the congressional defense policy process abstracted from the strategic problems which Congress must resolve are of limited value. The character of these problems, in their range and complexity, and the response of Congress to them must be understood first. Only after these elements have been grasped more clearly can Congress' policy processes be meaningfully assessed. Congressional action on the annual defense appropriations bill will be placed, therefore, in the larger context of the efforts that the United States has made and the difficulties that it has had to face in raising, organizing, and using military force to protect its security interests and to achieve its foreign policy objectives. In this connection, the organization, procedures, and power relations of Congress' policy process will be treated largely in terms of the effect that they have on the decisions that Congress makes—or fails to make—in strategic policy formation.

Congress is one of the nation's principal instruments of popular rule. Its strengths or weaknesses chart the health of democracy in

America. We need to know if Congress is performing its duties well. We need criteria of contemporary relevance by which we assess its actions and decisions. We need standards to evaluate its organization and procedures. This study is keyed to these purposes, particularly insofar as Congress' power of the purse is concerned. Congress' power over federal funds is its most important lever over military policy. The defense budget, presently representing over half of the federal government's expenditures, has an enormous impact on the nation's foreign policy objectives and on its domestic political and economic life. The success or failure of Congress to use its control of the purse to significant and salutary effect in defense policy is an index of its over-all contribution to the nation's strategic posture and of its utility as an instrument of democratic government.

The study is primarily based on the open record of Congress that is revealed in massive and formidable detail in the hearings, reports, and floor debates on the annual defense appropriations bills. To supplement these sources, interviews were conducted in Washington on a number of occasions. In different form, parts of this study have appeared in the March, 1963, issue of the *Western Political Quarterly*, the winter number of *Orbis* in 1964, the October, 1965, issue of the *Review of Politics*, and the winter, 1966, number of the *Virginia Quarterly Review*. I am grateful to the editors of these journals for the use of this material.

E. A. K.

ACKNOWLEDGMENTS

This book could not have been written without the assistance of a large number of people. I am particularly grateful to Professor Robert E. Osgood, director of the Washington Center of Foreign Policy Research, and Colonel Charles H. Donnelly, senior specialist in national defense of the Legislative Reference Service of the Library of Congress. Their careful readings of the manuscript and their equally thoughtful comments are deeply appreciated. Others who read all or parts of the manuscript in one form or another and who offered valuable criticisms include Robert Lamson, Joseph Whelan, and Rick Tarr. I am also in debt to Professor William W. Kaufmann for his helpful comments on Chapter VII.

My associates at the Mershon Center for Education in National Security, Willard Barber, Louis Higgs, Stanley Michalak, Jerome Slater, and Alden Williams, were always available to lend support. Whatever merit Chapter VIII may have is due in large part to their comment and criticism. I feel obliged to single out Stephen Xydis, another of my Mershon associates, for special thanks. Our daily conversations sharpened my thinking and generally helped to improve the final product.

A number of congressional staff members and legislators deserve mention, too, but in deference to their wishes, they shall remain anonymous. They gave freely of their time in patiently answering my many questions. Help of a more general, but important, nature was provided by John J. Kennedy and C. Herman Pritchett. The active encouragement of my colleagues of the Department of Government and Foreign Affairs of the University of Virginia, while much of this study was being prepared, was a source of continued inspiration and support.

My former associates at the Legislative Reference Service, where I spent two fruitful years as an analyst in national security, were helpful in gathering materials or in suggesting relevant items or lines of thought. William C. Olson, chief of the Foreign Affairs Division, generously offered advice and aid as did his predecessor, W. Howard Wriggins. I also appreciate the assistance of Mrs. Eilene Galloway, who often, at expense to herself, furnished me with information and insights about Congress and military policy. Discussions with Andrew Westwood and David Tarr, while sometimes heated, always proved stimulating and enlightening. Last, but certainly not least, especially if the biblical injunction that the last shall be first is remembered, I am deeply in debt to Reno Conti, who could always be counted upon to provide needed data quickly to lighten my research burdens.

My early research was made possible through financial aid furnished by Charles Hardin, who initially opened to me the possibility of exploring my interest in American military and foreign policy through a study of Congress' operations in these areas. Grants from the Wilson Gee Fund of the University of Virginia allowed me to conduct research and interviews, free from teaching responsibilities, during the summers of 1963 and 1964. The University Research Committee at the University of Virginia also paid for some typing services.

The publication of the study at this time was substantially expedited by the post-doctoral fellowship granted me by the Mershon Center for Education in National Security of Ohio State University for the academic year 1964–65. The study has grown quickly to maturity as a result of the financial and administrative assistance afforded by the center. The able and energetic director of the Center's Social Science Program, Edgar S. Furniss, Jr., has created a salubrious intellectual climate in which scholarship on problems of security and foreign policy can prosper. I should also like to acknowledge the generosity of the administration of the University of Virginia for allowing me a leave of absence to accept the Mershon fellowship.

My wife Antje cheerfully performed yeoman work in reading and editing the manuscript in its sundry versions. She also helped in proofreading the final text for publication and the galley sheets. Her keen eye and critical mind caught a host of stylistic and substantive errors. Her larger contribution, however, was the patience and forebearance which she continuously displayed throughout the four years during which this study was researched and written.

Notwithstanding the help that I have received from so many kind and generous people, I alone am responsible for the accuracy of the facts and the merit of the opinions which appear herein.

E. A. K.

CONTENTS

TABLES

PART I

AMERICAN GOVERNMENT AND STRATEGIC POLICY

I

INTRODUCTION

"There can be no grosser mistake," wrote Sir Henry Maine almost a century ago, than "to have an impression that Democracy differs from Monarchy in essence. . . . The tests of success in the performance of the necessary and natural duties of a government are precisely the same in both cases." [1]

The point Maine was making in part—and the part in which he was basically correct—was that in matters of national security and foreign policy all nations essentially confront similar problems vis-à-vis each other. How they are governed is an entirely separate, though obviously a closely related, matter.

Every nation attempts to influence others, through a variety of means, to protect and to promote its interests and objectives. Where persuasion fails or when other means prove unavailing, each is compelled to accept the loss of some desired value that is in dispute or to resort to military force to assert its will. The absence of a basic sympathy among nations or of a commonly held legal or moral code that can be invoked to resolve differences among them compels each nation to use, or to threaten to use, force on many occasions to secure its vital interests and objectives. Aggressor and defender alike, whatever the character of their governmental regimes, must formulate a national strategy which includes provision for military force: it is an imperative thrust on each nation. Every nation, however governed, must successfully cope with the threshold problem of force in international relations. Failure can prove fatal to its goals, its prestige, or, worse still, its independence.

Maine understood, too, that a democracy has to resolve internally its strategic problems in ways that largely do not concern non-democratic regimes. Like other regimes, a popular government faces the imperative of supporting the nation's security and foreign policy objectives with adequate force; but unlike these others, it also confronts the problem of generating a sufficient majority within the nation both to legitimate and to sustain its policies over the long run.[2] Neither set of imperatives can be ignored without jeopardizing popular rule itself. A representative government ultimately depends on the authority of the people for whom it acts in foreign affairs. It cannot impose its policies at will, whatever their merit, nor command with impunity the human and material resources needed to effect them. Periodic elections verify whether the government's policies and its political leaders enjoy the confidence of the electorate. Non-democratic regimes—whether oligarchies, monarchies, or tyrannies—do not face an electoral test based on universal suffrage.

Much of Maine's distrust and even contempt for democratic rule was rooted in his pessimistic view of the ability of a democracy to take adequate and timely steps to defend itself and its interests. Consent would be lacking, he felt; or if it were activated, it would be so too late. Events since Maine wrote have lent more than a little confirmation to his pessimism—enough that even many of the friends of popular government worry and despair over its prospects.[3] The experience of the interwar period is particularly relevant. The fall of France and the Third Republic in 1940, as well as the slow and ineffectual efforts of the Western democracies to stem the fascist advance across Europe, appeared symptomatic of a deeper malaise—

4

of a more profound incapacity of democracies everywhere to marshal their resources and wills when confronted by massive internal and external threats to their very way of life. A yawning gap developed between the defense policies supported by a majority of voters and elected officials and the actual policy and action requirements of the strategic imperatives confronting these popularly governed nations.

The United States rescued the Western democracies when it intervened, however belatedly, in World War II. Its leadership in the postwar period preserved democratic rule in western Europe and extended it to the Far East, particularly to Japan. Whether popular government will survive the future continues to depend largely on what the United States does. The fate of democratic government and the conceptions of justice and liberty on which it rests will be determined, in large measure, by how well the American government and the American people respond to what must be done to sustain American strength and influence in the defense of these values. Can, indeed, the gap between the imperatives of national security and foreign policy, on the one hand, and the imperatives of popular consent, on the other, be bridged? Once bridged, can they be maintained? No conclusive answer can be given. Each generation must answer these questions anew, in terms of its own conditions of life, through the foresight and imagination of its political intelligence, the stamina of its collective will, and the strength of its governmental institutions.

In this introductory statement it might be well to outline the major aspects of popular consent that underlie the determination of United States security and foreign policy; to describe the principal powers and responsibilities of American governmental agencies involved in strategic planning and operations; to sketch the justification for these institutional arrangements; to place these governmental institutions within the context of contemporary international relations; and to define, specifically, the scope and focus of this inquiry.

CONSENSUS REQUIREMENTS OF STRATEGIC AND FOREIGN POLICY

The American Constitution sets more exacting and more taxing consensus requirements in security and foreign policy–making and operations than do most other democratic systems of government. It does this in two fundamental ways. First, it divides the powers of the government and proliferates agencies which are to exercise these powers; second, it deliberately fragments the American electorate which expresses its will at the polls *in locale* and *over time.* Neither the government nor the people are unitary bodies within the American Constitution. If the nation is to act legitimately in common effort in foreign affairs, consensus must be effected among the parts into which the government and the people are divided. Building a consensus is an enormous task; maintaining it over time or redirecting or transforming it to meet new situations, a never ending one.

The powers of government are allocated vertically to a federal government and fifty state governments and horizontally within the federal government among three legally coequal branches. Some powers are exclusively assigned either horizontally or vertically. Most powers, however, are overlapping or are shared, as in the case of appointments to federal positions, including military ranks, which require the recommendation of the President and the advice and consent of the Senate. The significance of the principles of federalism and the separation of powers is obvious enough. A system of institutional checks and balances results both vertically and horizontally. The state and the federal governments check each other, as do the Congress, President, and the courts within the national government. Officials occupying posts in each of these agencies are armed with public authority to protect themselves against the extension of power of other agencies. Their formal authority, moreover, is reinforced by their personal interests in preserving the governmental power that

6

they have against the encroachment of others. The Constitution underwrites the view of *The Federalist Papers*, No. 51: ambition is pitted against ambition, and the interests of office holders at all levels of the government are harnessed to the constitutional guarantees of their offices.[4]

These divisions are clearly reflected in the military clauses of the Constitution. Congress is invested with most, but not all, of the important military powers allocated by the Constitution. It has the power:

To declare War . . .

To raise and support Armies . . .

To provide and maintain a Navy . . .

To make Rules for the Government and Regulation of the land and naval Forces . . .

To provide for calling forth the Militia to execute the Laws of the Union, suppress Insurrections, and repel Invasions;

To provide for organizing, arming, and disciplining, the Militia, and for governing such parts of them as may be employed in the service of the United States . . . [and]. . . .

To make all Laws which shall be necessary and proper for carrying into Execution the foregoing Powers. . . .

These powers are supplemented by an additional grant of authority to Congress to lay taxes "to pay the Debts and provide for the common Defence . . . of the United States."

While Congress possesses the primary sources of constitutional authority for the organization and supply of the military establishment, the President is also invested with important constitutional powers. He is assured a crucial role in military policy–making by being made "commander-in-chief of the army and navy . . . and of the militia . . . when called into the actual service. . . . " Congress sets the size and determines the composition of the armed

7

forces, but the President is principally responsible for their actual direction. The President is also granted the power to appoint all officers of the United States, subject to the advice and consent of the Senate. These military powers are enhanced by the President's position as chief executive, which establishes him as head of the huge and sprawling federal bureaucracy, and as the principal organ of the nation's foreign relations.[5]

The states, too, retain some power over military policy, although its actual significance for over-all strategic policy has been increasingly curtailed during this century.[6] State authority extends principally to the organization and training of the militia or, as it is now known, the national guard. The states are given the right to appoint officers and to train their militia forces according to the discipline prescribed by Congress. These overlapping powers were aimed at protecting the right of the states to raise military forces. These provisions, therefore, made the military clauses an intrinsic part of the federal system, not an exclusive concern of the central government. The clauses themselves have drawn the process of militia policy development into the vortex of the political conflicts generated by the federal system. Militia or reserve policy has not been simply a product of a strategic design laid down by the federal government. It has more often been the residual element of the power struggle among rival interest, attaching themselves to, and working through, state and federal instrumentalities.[7]

In exercising its military powers, the government of the United States, considered horizontally and vertically, almost always requires the co-operation and co-ordination of at least two agencies, each possessing its own source of governmental authority. Militia policy presents the extreme case: it may require appeal to as many as fifty-three instrumentalities—the President, Congress, the fifty states, and, where constitutional rights are at issue, the federal courts. More important for our purposes here, a high degree of consensus is needed between the President and Congress if the federal government is to discharge its primary responsibility for defense against foreign aggression and for advancing national purposes abroad. The security and foreign policy functions of the central government can be executed smoothly and efficiently only when these two branches have agreed upon common policies and approaches. Neither can act autonomously for long without the assistance of the other or without conflict. Each depends on the power of the other to fulfil its separate and joint responsibilities. The President cannot organize an armed force without congressional approval, nor can the Congress authorize military positions which rival the President's power as commander-in-chief. As will be seen more clearly in Part II, the costs of co-operation and co-ordination between Congress and the President for the sake of effective strategic policies come high. They must be paid for in the hard currency of compromise and bargaining, in continual and often painful consultation and negotiation.[8]

But even such appeals may not yield desired results. The elaborate system of electoral compartmentalization established by the Constitution complicates the inherently arduous task of achieving a consensus on strategic policy that is sufficiently stable and informed, yet flexible enough to meet a wide spectrum of evolving foreign challenges. Even if the electorate were capable of deciding difficult strategic issues in cases of disagreement between the President and Congress, the prevailing electoral system which the Constitution establishes deliberately impedes the simple and unambiguous expression of majority sentiment of the electorate. The Constitution divides more than governmental power and functions among a number of institutions: it also divides the electorate in locale and over time.

At the federal level, not one, but three sets of officials are elected to exercise separate and overlapping governmental powers. Each rests on a different electoral base and tends to reflect and foster different interests, objectives, and perspectives. As a general rule, the President and the vice-president, the only nationally elected officials, are inclined to emphasize a national point of view; the Senate and

House, elected on a state and local basis, tend to stress their more narrowly oriented constituencies. At any one election, a voter may be called upon to express himself on a number of different candidates and issues which are related to different horizontal and vertical divisions of the government. During presidential years, he is asked to register his vote on a bewildering number of state, local, and national issues and for a host of state and local candidates. The political image cast by the electorate is bound to be refracted and confused.[9] The contradictions and compromises inherent in the simple "yes" and "no" answers registered by the voter as he casts his ballot in terms of local, state, and national issues, let alone those stemming from his social, religious, class, or party preferences, find varied expression in and through the divided institutional arrangements outlined in the Constitution. The electorate speaks through a number of institutional tongues, each with its own language, style, and nuances of power and purpose.

Any one election may settle little or nothing. It is likely to produce even more ambiguity and uncertainty in policy-making. Political conflict among governmental officials occupying posts in different agencies of the government may be increased as segments of the electorate secure control of some elements of governmental authority and press their particular interests and views through them. Under these circumstances, the problem of building a consensus that can support an effective strategic posture is rendered more acute, and perhaps completely intractable, on some or all strategic issues.

The system of staggered elections required by the Constitution compounds these difficulties. Only part of the electorate is engaged in any federal election. Congressional by-elections neglect two-thirds of the Senate and the President and vice-president. Presidential elections, while they include the election of a new House, again leave two-thirds of the Senate intact. Meanwhile, state and local elections are conducted at intervals that may or may not dovetail with federal elections. Only parts of the passing political moods and

10

attitudes among the electorate are recorded, albeit vaguely and confusedly; others must await other elections to find an outlet. The sheer number of these elections may also sap a nation's capacity to meet its foreign policy imperatives. Elections inevitably tax and divide the public's time, energy, and attention when order and consensus are perhaps most needed at home; the regularity and staggered spacing of elections reinforce these shortcomings. They may be held at perilous moments in the nation's life, during wartime or under tense international conditions. For these reasons, the British Parliament suspended national elections during World War II. The United States does not possess the same flexibility, since the Constitution prescribes that federal elections be held at defined intervals. The movement of celestial bodies, not political issues, determines when American elections will be conducted.

THE MILITARY POWERS: RATIONALE

Authority to organize and use force.—The military clauses of the Constitution are, of course, neither arbitrary nor contradictory. They are parts, not the whole, of the Constitution and are subordinate to its higher purposes. Security is only one of the goals of the Constitution and the political order that it establishes. Individual freedom and justice are its highest aspirations. The military clauses are fashioned to protect and advance, not to nullify, these ends under changing conditions of domestic and international life. The military powers granted by the Constitution to the government are parts of an over-all solution to the more general problem of balancing the need for a strong government able to rule and discharge its assigned functions, and the equally compelling desire to prevent that government from becoming so powerful that it threatens the liberty and rights of the people. *The Federalist Papers*, No. 51, states this dual problem simply and clearly:

11

In framing a government which is to be administered by men over men, the great difficulty lies in this: *you must first enable the government to control the governed;* and *in the next place oblige it to control itself.* A dependence on the people is, no doubt, the primary control on the government; but experience has taught mankind the necessity of auxiliary precautions.[10]

As for the first part of the problem posed by *Federalist* No. 51, the federal government is granted sufficient military power to maintain itself and to achieve the objectives intrusted to it. The proposals of Elbridge Gerry and Luther Martin at the Philadelphia Convention to write specific limitations into the Constitution on the size of the nation's armed forces were rejected.[11] The view presented with most clarity by Alexander Hamilton in the *Federalist* was adopted instead:

The circumstances that endanger the safety of nations are infinite, and for this reason no constitutional shackles can wisely be imposed on the power to which the care of it is committed. This power ought to be co-extensive with all the possible combinations of such circumstances; and ought to be under the direction of the same councils which are appointed to preside over the common defense.[12]

Since it was impossible to predict what kind of military force would be necessary to cope with future military threats which one or more foreign governments might pose for the union, limitations on the central government's power to raise an army and navy were abandoned.

The central government's power to tax was also broadly defined and tied directly to its military powers. Without strong taxation powers, the national government would be helpless in its attempts to organize armed forces or to supply them with needed materials. Hamilton again cogently expressed the thinking underlying the taxing powers granted to the federal government:

As duties of superintending the national defense and of securing the public peace against foreign or domestic violence involve a provision for casualties and danger to which no possible limits can be assigned, the power of making that provision ought to know no other bounds than the exigencies of the nation and the resources of the community.[13]

The Constitution assigned the federal government sufficient authority to raise and employ forces which are powerful enough to provide for the common defense and to foster American political objectives abroad. In other words, the federal government, composed of the Congress and the President, was granted enough authority to elicit the human and material sacrifices needed to attain these ends. Or, in the shorthand of *Federalist* No. 51, the national government was given adequate authority "to control the governed" in defense and foreign affairs.

The control of military force.—The Constitutional Convention was no less concerned with the other aspect of the general problem which *Federalist* No. 51, implicitly posed—the control of the military powers with which the federal government would be invested. Delegates at the Philadelphia meeting were aware of the dangers that the standing armies held for republican governments. The delegates knew that building a military establishment, however necessary it might be, inherently raised a number of critically important derivative difficulties. They understood that a standing army might overthrow the political order which constituted it; that civilian groups might secure control of the armed forces in order to undermine the legitimate political authority of the state or to oppress other groups; or that the fundamental values of the political community might be distorted or irreparably warped in its preparations for war.[14] The delegates knew, too, of the long struggle between the English Crown and Parliament over the control of the army and of the writings of

Locke, Montesquieu, Coke, and Blackstone which warned against the dangers which a standing army presented to the freedom of a political community. James Madison eloquently voiced the fears of many delegates when he later wrote:

> Not the less true is it, that the liberties of Rome proved the final victim to her military triumphs; and that the liberties of Europe, as far as they ever existed, have, with a few exceptions, been the price of her military establishments. A standing force, therefore, is a dangerous, at the same time that it may be a necessary, provision. On the smallest scale it has its inconveniences. On an extensive scale its consequences may be fatal. On any scale it is an object of laudable circumspection and precaution. A wise nation will combine all these considerations; and, whilst it does not rashly preclude itself from any resources which may become essential to its safety, will exert all its prudence in diminishing both the necessity and the danger of resorting to one which may be inauspicious to its liberties.[15]

The most compelling apprehension among the convention delegates was rooted, not in their reading of the past, but in their own experience with British and Hessian troops, who had always been an onerous social and economic burden on the colonies. The quartering of troops with private citizens provoked innumerable disquieting incidents among the populace, out of which a large backlog of resentment accumulated over the years. The British and Hessian troops, too, established a long record of intimidation against the colonists in exercising the English Crown's authority. Worst of all, they had been the major obstacle to American independence. They symbolized the oppressive constraints and injustices of Crown rule. The victorious colonists were hardly prepared to replace one coercive military establishment with another, even one of their creation.[16]

The Constitutional Convention settled the problem of controlling the organization and the use of force by the federal government in much the same way that it resolved the general problem of relating the government to the people—through the separation of powers and federalism. While the national government was given sufficient military authority to achieve those objects which it was assigned, that authority was divided among a variety of officers and governmental bodies which were relatively independent of each other.

The separation of powers was to achieve two objectives. First, the exclusive sharing and division of governmental authority between the President and Congress firmly established the principle of civilian primacy over the military establishment. No military official would be empowered to act on his own authority; he would be ultimately responsible to elected civilian authorities and would serve at their pleasure. Second, the separation of powers provided a formidable barrier to any civilian group which might wish to employ the national government's military power for its own advantage to the detriment of other segments of the political community. The conflict between king and Parliament reminded convention delegates that there was as much to fear from the improper use of military power by civilian authorities as from the possible usurpations of the military establishment itself. Since the election of the President, the Senate, and the House of Representatives rested on different electoral bases and since each of these governmental units served for varying lengths of time, it would be very difficult for any group to acquire the control of the federal government and the nation's armed forces. The system of checks and balances would immediately come into operation. Nor would a conspiracy among government officials to oppress certain individuals or groups in the nation be successful. Before the government could be completely transformed in personnel, four to six years would have to elapse. This would furnish enough time for the exposure of conspiratorial intent among legislators or officials of the executive branch.[17]

The federal principle buttressed these precautions against the improper use of force. The members of the Philadelphia gathering were certain that the federal system of government would inhibit the abuse of military power and check the power of a standing army. Thus, the states were given the right to command militia forces, to train them according to the discipline prescribed by Congress, and to appoint officers. A strong militia in the hands of the state governments would presumably hinder federal encroachments on state authority and on individual liberty, and would counter any illegal designs of a standing army.[18] As an additional obstacle to military dictatorship, the Second Amendment was adopted to secure the right of each citizen to keep and bear arms.

MILITARY POWERS: HISTORICAL JUSTIFICATION

The Constitution ratified in 1789 provided a delicately balanced formula by which the nation could both raise adequate military forces to support national objectives and minimize the danger of usurpation by the military establishment or by civilian officials. America's experience throughout the nineteenth century and the early part of the twentieth seemed to reveal the genius of these constitutional arrangements. The geographical isolation of the United States, the balance of power in Europe, and the fortuitous dominance of the British fleet until World War I insulated the New World from foreign influence and invasion. Freed from having to participate in the power struggles of Europe, with all of their inconclusive compromises, limited successes, and exhausting frustrations, America could concentrate its attention and energies on domestic issues. It could guide its foreign policy by Washington's simple advice of avoiding entangling alliances and could direct itself to its more immediate interest in continental expansion. Here, too, America seemed exempt from the ignoble competition for power incident to European politics. Except for isolated resistance from Indian tribes and from the hapless Mexicans in 1846, the United States rapidly

16

expanded from the Atlantic to the Pacific coast in less than a century. In its relations with other nations, the United States solved the problem of harnessing enough military power to achieve its national objectives almost by default.[19] Gaps between the military and foreign policies pursued by the federal government and the support that they required from the electorate in terms of military capabilities were rarely great or prolonged. Where they appeared, as in the War of 1812, they never really raised the question of national survival as acutely and as fundamentally as they do today.

The derivative problem of controlling military power was likewise resolved easily. The assumption of the Philadelphia Convention that Congress would not be supplied with sufficient cause to raise and maintain a large standing army capable of threatening personal liberty seemed verified by American experience. There was little to fear from a standing army and navy which would be usually limited in size and bereft of political power or support. Even Hamilton, who was committed to a powerful armed force,[20] could not "conceive a possibility that dangers so formidable can assail the whole Union, as to demand a force considerable enough to place our liberties in the least jeopardy. . . . "[21] America's geographical isolation and the long travel time between the Old World and the New World would make a large standing army unnecessary. The navy, not the army, would be the nation's first line of defense; and, happily, that branch of the service allegedly presented a lesser danger to popular government. Again, argued the *Federalist*:

> It must, indeed, be numbered among the greatest blessings of America, that as her Union will be the only source of her maritime strength, so this will be a principal source of her security against danger from abroad. In this respect our situation bears another likeness to the insular advantage of Great Britain. The batteries most capable of repelling foreign enterprises on our safety, are happily such as can never be turned by a perfidious government against our liberties.[22]

17

For most of American history, the Framers' assumptions seemed correct. Except for the Civil War, Congress during the nineteenth century was not moved to maintain a large army for very long. During periods of stress, Congress followed a pattern of raising armed forces and of delegating many of its immense powers to the President. With the passing of each emergency, it characteristically reassumed its delegated powers and subsequently reduced the size of the military establishment. The army of 10,000 men authorized at the close of the War of 1812 was permitted to dwindle by 1821 to 6,183 officers and enlisted personnel. The Mexican War brought about a hurried expansion to 12,000 men, but a subsequent retrenchment drive cut the army by one-third. At the start of the Civil War, the Union's military forces were in a deplorably low state: only 16,000 officers and men were in service. After this crisis had passed, Congress reverted to its policy of a minimum army given minimum duties, like Indian-fighting on the frontier or garrison-tending, to perform.[23] The Spanish-American War and World Wars I and II resulted in a temporary enlargement of the nation's military forces. But again, after each conflict, they were quickly demobilized, only to be hurriedly rebuilt in the face of a new foreign confrontation.

Civil control over the military establishment was also maintained by simply isolating the officer corps and service personnel from other citizens, with the exception of a few detachments which guarded coastal installations or served at the War Department in Washington.[24] This policy of isolation continued throughout the nineteenth century and can be traced to World War II. Until 1890, the army was spread along the frontier to fight Indians. After the Spanish-American War, many military officers and men were transplanted to overseas areas in the Philippines, Cuba, or Central America. Naval officers were no less divorced from the mainstream of American life when they spent long periods of time at sea or at foreign stations.[25] Indeed, there is evidence today that the military profession is still socially isolated from the other major social groups in society.[26]

THE UNCOMMON DEFENSE AND AMERICAN INSTITUTIONS

Sketch of a new world.—The revolutionary changes in the domestic and world environments over the past half-century have overtaken the assumptions about political life which were held at the founding of the Constitution and which informed and shaped much of America's response to international relations until World War II. The United States can no longer maintain the posture of isolation which President George Washington prudently advised during the nation's formative years. The traumatic shocks of three armed conflicts—the Spanish-American War, World War I, and, especially, World War II—have decisively shattered whatever illusions remained of American insularity. The cold war, following in the wake of the collapse of the Axis powers, confirmed the experience of these three military engagements. Since 1945, the United States and the Soviet Union and, increasingly since the 1950's, Communist China have been pitted against each other in some form of actually or potentially dangerous military conflict, either directly or through proxy powers, in such diverse areas as Greece, Berlin, Korea, the Formosa Straits, Lebanon, Cuba, the Congo, Laos, and South Vietnam. These repeated clashes have raised into question the capacity of the United States to preserve its way of life and its independence. The preservation of American democracy and the success of American security and foreign policy are by no means self-evident or self-fulfilling, as they might have once appeared. The United States cannot concentrate solely on its continental hegemony and retreat behind the geographical confines of its jurisdictional sovereignty. Its interests, commitments, and responsibilities stretch around the globe. The exercise of its military power must similarly be world-wide in scope.

New international problems affecting American objectives are constantly emerging; they add an expanding number of novel issues to the ones already confronting American strategic planners. As former colonial peoples achieve nationhood, they must be internally stabilized and integrated into the world community. The demand of peoples everywhere for higher economic standards and an end to racial barriers must be satisfied. Clashing ideologies must somehow be resolved before the world stumbles into a nuclear holocaust. On every important front—scientific, technological, military, economic, social, political, and ideological—the United States is being put to trying tests.

For the first time since the founding of the republic, the United States is confronted with the task of devising a truly national strategy during relative peacetime which will co-ordinate its power resources, both military and non-military, in order to maintain its security and to achieve its long-range political goals. As one part of its over-all strategy, it must develop a plan for the rational use of military force to support its policy objectives. The existence of massively destructive weapons makes the formulation of such a military force a more pressing concern today in any previous period.

The question whether to maintain a small standing army or to rely principally on the militia during wartime is now academic. The overriding importance of military power in international relations makes it imperative that the United States continue to operate a large and varied military establishment. Since World War II, military considerations have had a powerful impact on the economy and the educational system of the United States. Military defense budgets, totaling in the 1960's over $50 billion annually, have had a profound effect on the domestic political life of the nation as well. The loss of a defense contract or the closing down of a military base can precipitate a crisis in many American locales dependent on these activities. ROTC programs can be found in hundreds of American universities and colleges throughout the nation. It is not surprising, either, that military personnel participate increasingly at all levels of national policy-making which in some way possess a military dimension. Few important segments of national life, ranging from civil rights to agriculture and water policy, are free from some military aspect. Many military officers, like Generals George C. Marshall, Douglas MacArthur, and Maxwell Taylor, as well as Admirals Alan Kirk and William Leahy, have held important political posts at home and abroad. Moreover, the role of the military in foreign countries has grown considerably since 1940, a trend that is likely to continue into the distant future. The United States is presently allied with over forty countries in eight separate collective defense arrangements.[27] American treaty commitments to NATO involve hundreds of thousands of troops in overseas bases and a system of military-political collaboration among nations that is without parallel in European and American experience. The number of American treaty entanglements necessitates the active participation of military personnel in their implementation. The magnitude of the security problem has necessitated the maintenance of a massive, world-wide military establishment.

Many observers have been gravely troubled by these developments. They have voiced fears that the growth of the military establishment and the defense industry to support it have weakened civilian control and undermined basic liberties. A number envision the rapid movement toward a "garrison state" in the United States. "Specialists in violence" (military and police officers) would predominate in such a state; the internal power pyramid would be steep and pointed, with power centered at the top; economic production and scientific investigation would be geared to military consumption; and the lives of the citizen population would be strictly regulated and militarized.[28]

Others already see the insidious presence of a political-industrial-military power elite which controls the nation's policy-making and manipulates popular opinion to its advantage.[29] In a popular study that has become a minor bestseller and a choice of a national book club, Fred J. Cook stridently argues that the so-called ultra-conservative classes, composed essentially of the groups who are parts of the power elite, "have led us into an age of social upheaval and revolution, obsessed by a paranoid phobia of change and revolution." [30] He offers the sweeping conclusion that

> America has changed, without any general popular recognition of the fact, from a peace-loving and isolationist democracy into a Warfare State whose real intent, avowed on many occasions and in high places and low, is not the preservation of peace and law and order in the world, but the extension of our capitalistic system throughout the world at the expense of the communist system. [31]

Anxieties about the impact of the nation's growing military power on its domestic life have not been the exclusive concern of pamphleteers. Prominent national political leaders have persistently expressed fears about a military take-over, or they have spoken in the idiom of the gradual loss of civilian control over the military. The defense reorganizations of the post-World War II period have reflected congressional disquietude over the seeming inordinate concentration of military power. [32] In opposing the National Security Act of 1947, which completely revamped the defense establishment, Senator Edward Robertson of Wyoming argued that the intent of the bill was "to create a vast military empire, one in which ambitious men will wield greater power over the Military Establishment than has ever been heretofore granted to non-elected individuals, and one which will wield untrammeled power over the entire social and economic structure of the nation." [33] Even the bill which was passed over Robertson's objections was careful to divide the military organization into three service branches to guard against the development of a unified military staff[34] and, incidentally, to preserve congressional prerogatives in reviewing the military establishment's policy and operations.

The Hoover Commission of 1949 was equally disturbed about the issue of civilian control. Its report on the National Security Organization noted that one of the major reasons for its recommendation to bolster the "means of exercising civilian control" over the military was to "safeguard our democratic traditions against militarism." [35] Over a decade later, though in a different context, the same concern for civilian control and for democratic liberties was re-echoed by President Dwight D. Eisenhower. In his final address to the nation as chief executive, he warned against "the acquisition of unwarranted influence, whether sought or unsought, by the military-industrial complex." [36]

These growing apprehensions about the profound changes occurring in the domestic and international environment of the United States reflect an anxious uncertainty about the quality of the American people's understanding of their contemporary situation, about the military and strategic imperatives pressing on them, and about their and their government's capacity to cope with them. They cast doubt, too, on the traditional interpretations of the proper relations between governmental instrumentalities at the national level and between the government and the people which were first set down in the Constitution in 1789. The question continually urges itself upon the political consciousness: Are the American people and their institutions equal to the demands placed upon them?

In this regard it is relevant to remember that the institutional framework erected to settle the two aspects of the general problem stated by *Federalist* No. 51—the relation of the government to the people and the protection of the people against an all-powerful government—was meant to endure beyond the formative years of the republic. The Framers of the Constitution were establishing a more perfect union for the future, not merely for their own time. The indefinite character of the war powers given to the federal government and the imprecise way these powers were subsequently divided between Congress and the President testify to this intent. The Philadelphia Convention constructed a union which could meet unforeseen military threats to the nation's security and foreign policy objectives, while keeping the

23

control of military power in politically responsible hands. Future generations, facing entirely different issues and changed international circumstances, could act through a sufficiently flexible constitutional structure which would permit the expansion and contraction of military power wielded by the federal government when the public welfare might dictate such a course of action. The Constitution was not intended as a catalogue of rigid relations and powers that could not be periodically reassessed. The amendment procedures of the Constitution serve as a clear reminder that each generation possesses the opportunity—indeed, is charged with the obligation—of reinterpreting, in terms of its historical experience and unique problems, the ideals and governmental arrangements traced within the Constitution.[37]

REASSESSING THE ROLE OF CONGRESS

The power of the purse and security policy.—There is a pressing need today to re-evaluate and reformulate the role of the nation's governmental institutions in strategic and foreign policy in terms of contemporary conditions of international life. This study seeks to aid this process of reinterpretation. It focuses on Congress' use of its power of the purse to raise and support the nation's armed forces since World War II. Clarification of the role that Congress has played in military policy through its control of federal funds will assist in defining the proper role that it can—and should—play in strategic policy.

For purposes of this study, military strategic policy will encompass the following basic elements: the determination of the security and foreign policy goals sought by the nation; the assessment of the military threats to the achievement of these goals; the formulation of plans to meet these threats; the determination of force levels and weapons systems to carry out accepted plans; the allocation of scarce time, human, and material resources to raise needed military forces to effect strategic plans; and the formulation of declaratory policies

24

for the use of military force. The terms "defense" and "military strategic policy," or simply "strategic policy," will generally be used interchangeably. They will refer either to all of the major logical components indicated immediately above or to one or more of them: the context in which a term is used will indicate the extent of its applicability. "National strategic policy" is a broader term, covering both military and non-military elements, including most especially foreign economic assistance, propaganda and information, and diplomacy. The term refers to the over-all plan for using the nation's power resources to achieve its security and foreign policy objectives.[38]

It should be recognized that, while military and national strategy primarily refer to a foreign policy sphere, neither is viewed apart from the domestic political environment. As Part II indicates, the theoretical distinction between domestic policy, on the one hand, and security and foreign policy, on the other, breaks down in operation. Resources to achieve domestic, foreign, and security goals are limited. Their allocation demands the establishment of priority schedules that cannot be realistically constructed unless these goals and the means to obtain them are related to each other within a common policy framework. The budgetary process can potentially furnish this common framework for weighing goals and available resources.

The defense budgetary process in Congress is a part, therefore, of this larger sphere of political activity. While a full treatment of the domestic considerations which influence military strategic policy are beyond the scope of this study, they are kept generally in mind throughout. Thus, within the context of these larger congressional responsibilities, this study seeks to define the role which Congress can, and should, specifically play in military strategic policy through its power of the purse under the novel economic, political, military, and technological conditions of contemporary life.

Congress is viewed as an instrument of popular government. Both the House and the Senate are seen to share a common and collective responsibility to provide for national defense and for the military

25

support of the nation's foreign policy goals. The military and money powers which have been mutually invested by the Constitution in both houses imply these duties. The Senate and House must act together to declare war, to raise and support an army, to provide for a navy, to make rules for the regulation of military forces, and to legislate for state militias. The view of Congress adopted here distinguishes also between Congress as a whole and its agents—the large number of official and non-official (largely political) committees and subcommittees which actually wield most of the powers which are assigned to the House and the Senate. If these agencies are to remain responsible, they must be subject to the direction of that house of Congress in whose behalf they act. The existing organization and procedures of Congress are viewed from the point of view of their contribution to the realization of Congress' responsibilities under the Constitution. They are neither seen as divinely ordained nor as beyond the pale of change or criticism, notwithstanding the entrenched interests and traditions that may in fact protect them against abolition or reform. This study hopes to shed light on how these groups have served both the Congress as a whole and the nation.[39] These include especially the defense appropriations subcommittees and, since 1961, the armed services committees, which are, as a group, most directly concerned with the annual budgetary process for the military establishment.

Congress is not viewed simply as a medium for interest group rivalry or as a "different battlefield" for the group struggle.[40] These insights, while critically important to an understanding of congressional activity, must not be allowed to obscure a clear perception of Congress' institutional duties in the area of military strategic policy development. Congress is above all else a vehicle by which the American people govern themselves; it should be judged accordingly, in terms of the contemporary requirements of public policy, including the nation's use of military force.

Power of the purse and civil-military relations.—The derivative problem of civil-military relations is not treated directly, but through Congress' approach to the substantive strategic problems which have developed since World War II. The problems of civilian control over the military and of the alleged growth of militarism or of a military-industrial complex in the United States are considered of less pressing concern today than the more basic issue of relating the nation's military power resources to the achievement of its policy objectives. It will be seen more clearly below that the military leaders of the nation do not conform to any one particular description, that there are many "military minds" and no one hard-cast product can be attributed to a majority of the officer corps, that military leaders often disagree among themselves on basic military strategy, and that coalitions made up from both ranks will be found on different sides of a strategic issue.[41]

These observations are not meant to deny the validity of the problem which a military establishment poses for a democratic nation. Events in France in 1958 which led to the creation of the Fifth Republic[42] and the political activities of military officers in South Korea, Pakistan, and Turkey indicate the decisive effect which military power can have on the internal life of a nation.[43] Yet the political conditions prevailing in these countries cannot legitimately be transferred to the United States in interpreting its specific situation with respect to civil-military relations. Presently, and in the immediately foreseeable future, there is far less reason to fear a coup d'état or, more realistically, undue military influence in public policy formation, than the various military and non-military threats which are presented by the Soviet Union, Communist China, and by other trouble spots around the world.

The problem of civil-military relations as it is found in the United States does not arise essentially out of domestic circumstances. This problem is derivative, stemming from the cold war and the revolutionary developments in the world of this century. Its resolution

27

depends ultimately on the response to the substantive military threats confronting the nation. If the Congress and the President and those appointed to political office can play important and effective parts in military and non-military strategic policy, the problem of controlling the military establishment and of preserving free governmental institutions will be largely settled.

The effective participation of political officials is, of course, complicated by the immense proportions and implications of the strategic issues facing the nation and the need for technical expertise to meet them. The knowledge and training of military officers must be integrated into strategic policy development and operations. Military professionals must play a critical role in shaping the nation's military initiatives and its responses to the moves of hostile powers. Seen in this light, the submission of the military to civilian authority is only one aspect of the problem of civil-military relations, and a lesser one at that. The problem of the military establishment is a task of co-ordinating its activities and opinions with those of the civilian branches of the government, more than it is a job of simply subordinating itself to civilian rule.

There are difficulties here, too. For there are two facets to civil authority—bureaucratic and political. Civil-military relations imply both. The military establishment must be related to the huge, sprawling civilian bureaucracy, which is no less concerned with strategic and foreign policy problems. Perhaps the most pressing problem to be solved is the integration of the officer corps with the army of scientists and technicians who are engaged in relating modern scientific and technological knowledge to warfare. Defense budget proposals for this research, development, and testing already exceed $7 billion; and expenditures for these items are approximately equal to all federal spending for health, welfare, and labor.[44] In the first instance, the question of civil-military relations requires that these two sets of civilian and military bureaucrats be related to each other within the same agency, as in the Defense Department, or between

28

agencies, as the Defense Department and the Arms Control and Disarmament Agency, the State Department, or the Agency for International Development. In the second instance, these civilian and military bureaucratic structures must be brought under the control of the elected and appointed political officials who head them.[45]

The pertinence of the traditional civilian-military dichotomy is often overstated. It is overshadowed by the larger problem of making both the civilian and military bureaucracies responsive to politically elected or appointed officials. This critical issue was brought to the surface in 1962 during the discussion of alleged "muzzling" of the policy views of military officers by the political leadership and civilian review officials of the Defense and State departments. In an exchange between Representative Porter Hardy, a leading member of the House Armed Services Committee, and Secretary of Defense Robert S. McNamara, the defense secretary sketched the wider dimensions of maintaining political control in the hands of politically responsible officials over civilian and military career personnel:

> Mr. Hardy: There has been some suggestion . . . about permitting the military to just go off and spout off without considering . . . civilian control. I certainly don't want to get myself in any such category as suggesting that. . . .
>
> But what bothers me a little bit is what civilians are doing to control.
>
> Now, if I could be pretty sure that the controls are going to be pretty close to the top in either Defense or State, I wouldn't be particularly apprehensive. But if some of the people at a lower level in the Department of State are telling the military what they can or can't say, it worries me a little bit. Can you give us any reassurance on that?
>
> Secretary McNamara: . . . Let me say first that I really—and I believe and feel this very deeply. I really don't think the question of civilian or military control is involved here at all . . . I know that this is frequently tagged as an issue, but I honestly don't believe it is. . . .

The problem is one really of . . . management and leadership direction. It isn't a question of civilian versus military. It is a question of where policy is going to be established—way down underneath or at the top. And I think that we would all agree that if we are going to have unity in a large complicated organization, the policies must be established at the top.[46]

An effective system of civil-military relations must first be founded on a closely co-ordinated and co-operative relationship in strategic policy between the President and the Congress, the principal political branches of the federal government. This most basic relationship, in turn, must rest on a common understanding of, and an agreement on, strategic policies and methods that can meet the nation's military and foreign policy problems without destroying the fundamental ideals and objectives on which the American democracy rests. Over the long run, only this kind of political consensus can furnish an adequate basis for the political control of the civilian and military bureaucracies. What is to be attained is more than the control of the military officer corps and their civilian counterparts. What is to be achieved are those objects which have been assigned to the federal government—security, solvency, and the liberty and general welfare of the public. These overriding objectives hinge critically on the quality and merit of the political policies, decisions, and leadership of the President and Congress. The ultimate test of control exercised by elected officials is the character of these political factors and their relevance in resolving the nation's strategic problems. Civilian control of governmental officials, whether military or non-military, is vain unless it is informed by strategic realities and is based on them.

PART II

PEACE WITHOUT POWER:
THE DISENCHANTMENT I, 1945–1947

World War II—Fall of Czechoslovakia

II

THE OVER-ALL SETTING

The United States emerged from the tumult and chaos of World War II as the most powerful nation in the history of the world. American interests stretched around the globe, from the center of Germany on the west, to Japan and China on the east, to Latin America on the south. The American people had not envisioned this revolutionary outcome of the war, nor had they clearly perceived it in the conduct of the war. Nor, understandably, did they immediately comprehend the new modalities of American power in the aftermath of the Japanese surrender in 1945.

The assimilation of the experience and significance of World War II into the intellectual and emotional mainstream of American life came later, and was consummated, less as the product of a self-generated, theoretical understanding of the postwar international environment than as the gradual result of a slow accretion of specific reactions and improvisations to check unceasing Russian pressures on American frontier positions around the world. The long, painful, often frustrating, years of the cold war were primarily responsible for shaking most Americans loose from their tenaciously held illusion of United States insularity. The daily test of the cold war slowly disciplined the thinking and emotions of most Americans in what, from the vantage point of years, is now understood to be the obvious lesson of World War II: that the vital interests of the United States, indeed its ultimate survival, independence, and destiny, depend critically on how it uses its enormous military, economic, and political power.

But more was at stake than American interests at the end of World War II. The peace of the world hinged on the exercise of American power. The defeat of the Axis Powers created an unprecedented power vacuum that only the United States among the non-communist nations could fill. World War II exhausted England and France and largely collapsed their empires. Only the United States could maintain world order and organize the recovery and rehabilitation of the war-devastated areas of the world. America, too, was the only power capable of countering Russian expansionist designs and of containing Russian political dominion within the geographical boundaries occupied by the Red Army. Only American military forces, bolstered by their possession of the atomic bomb, could forestall the Red Army's complete sweep across the European continent and eventually across most of Asia. It was not too much to say that the freedom and prosperity of over half the world were inextricably tied to United States power, as both are still today. Never had American foreign commitments and responsibilities been so extensive. Never in the history of the Western world, which encompasses the Roman and British empires, had so many men depended so crucially on the decisions and actions of one people.

The presence of millions of American soldiers abroad in 1945 symbolized American primacy and its world-wide interests, commitments, and responsibilities. Just as clearly, however, the reckless speed of American demobilization symbolized both the inability and unwillingness of most Americans either to recognize or to accept the nation's radically altered position. Even before the surrender of Japan, the legislative and executive branches of the government were responding to public clamor "for the discharge of the millions of men in service."[1] A proud and triumphant military force of over twelve million men at the close of World War II had dwindled to less than a million and a half by the outbreak of the Korean War. The army was hit hardest, shrinking from 8.3 million to 593,000, hardly more than a constabulary force.[2] The rate of demobilization, as General George C. Marshall told a special joint meeting of Congress in 1945, was "determined by the transportation facilities and by the availability of trained personnel to carry its administrative requirements out."[3] It had no relation to the future needs of the army, nor to the strategic requirements of American political interests and foreign obligations.

World War II thrust the leadership of the non-communist world on the United States, although it was not consciously sought nor actively desired. For most Americans, therefore, it seemed to be more a prescription of fate than an act of willed intention that moved the United States into its singular position on the world scene in the middle 1940's. No new doctrine of manifest destiny rationalized or promoted the expansion of American interests. The history of the cold war can be written largely in terms of the American people's slow and tentative intellectual grasp of the responsibilities of world leadership and their reluctant, often contradictory, adjustment to its full implications, a hesitancy of mind and spirit that has yet to be fully overcome. We now look at one important phase of that history— Congress' use of its power of the purse to influence and shape military strategic policy. If it should appear that Congress' actions are contradictory, they can be fully understood only as a part of this more inclusive backdrop which Congress both helped to shape and was shaped by in return.

To a marked degree, Congress' action on the President's military appropriations bills in the immediate postwar period mirrored the nation's vacillating mood toward, and its dim understanding of, America's new role in the international environment. Most congressmen, like most Americans, longed to return to the seeming calm, the normalcy, and the predictability of the prewar era. It was in this frame of mind that Congress and the appropriations committees consented to—even spurred—the rapid demobilization of the nation's military forces. Congressional participation in strategic decision-making reflected the nation's deeply felt desire for at least a brief respite from the unsolicited responsibilities of international leadership. To be sure, Congress approved a $400 million aid bill to Greece and Turkey. It also agreed to Point Four, the Marshall Plan, and NATO. Yet the dominant tone and basic direction of American politics after World War II were pre-eminently domestic. Only the shock of the North Korean attack would force the nation, the Congress, and the Truman administration into a fuller realization of the exacting military requirements of international leadership under cold war conditions.

Between 1945 and 1950, Congress' pattern of examination of the military departments' appropriations requests closely resembled its prewar approach to military policy. Congress concentrated principally on an item by item review of military spending, and it reintroduced its traditionally employed standards of economy in spending and efficiency in administration into its deliberations on the defense appropriations bills.[4] It interested itself essentially in the *how*, and not in the *why*, of military spending. Largely ignored were the many interacting and seemingly intractable relations between the nation's actual and potential military power and, correspondingly, its subtly shaded spectrum of foreign policy goals that, to be supported, required different kinds of military power for varying political contingencies. In its consideration of the annual appropriations bills for the military services, Congress markedly failed to define for itself the over-all foreign policy objectives of the nation; to determine the possible threats to the achievement of these policy goals; to identify both the most serious and the most likely contingencies in which military force might have to be used to protect American interests and policy objectives; to relate the plans, force levels, and weapons systems

36

underlying the President's appropriation requests to meet these various contingencies; to explore what might possibly be more feasible military and non-military alternatives to the administration's proposals; and to assess the political willingness and economic capacity of the American people to support these plans.

Congress reviewed the President's defense proposals within an intellectual framework that was largely disassociated from the military strategic imperatives facing the nation. Although the United States found itself challenged in Iran in 1946, in Greece and Turkey in 1947, in Czechoslovakia and Berlin in 1948, in China in 1949, and, finally, in Korea in 1950, there was little or no attempt in Congress to determine how the annually proposed military budgets would specifically meet various kinds of communist probes in these and other areas of the world. Hearings and debates on strategic policy were perfunctory when compared with the enormous time and effort which was exerted, especially in the House, in reviewing the itemized estimates of the military departments. The Korean War merely dramatized what was the overriding characteristic of congressional action on the budgetary requests for the armed forces. It offered visible proof that Congress had repeatedly consented to military policies, force levels, and weapon systems that could not support the nation's policy objectives, interests, and commitments. The nation's military power and foreign policy were clearly out of joint.

Where Congress did strike a connection between the nation's military power and its foreign policy objectives, the connection was either only tangentially or partially related to the nation's over-all strategic problems. That is to say that in those instances in which Congress actually analyzed the administration's defense proposals it primarily concentrated on specific hardware items. It pressed the administration to accept more air power for the navy or more strategic striking power for the air force in the form of a seventy-group force. Never was there any concerted attempt in the appropriations process to relate the suitability of these military capabilities to the full range

37

of the nation's foreign policy goals and strategic challenges. Military policy and foreign policy making in Congress generally proceeded independently of each other. In addition, Congress uncritically accepted, and therefore unnecessarily restricted itself to, the budgetary framework established by the executive branch for defense spending. Congress never directly questioned the Truman administration's $15 billion ceiling on military spending that prevailed during the postwar period until the Korean War and that, ironically enough, was never reached. There was widespread agreement that the economy could not afford a greater defense effort. Congress neither tested this assumption nor explored the strength of the American people's willingness to support various levels of defense expenditures. Congress essentially abdicated its leadership responsibilities. While its record was perhaps no worse than the executive branch's, it was no better when it might well have been.

THE DOWNWARD MILITARY SPIRAL BEGINS: FY 1947

War Department demobilization.—The military services introduced their appropriation requests to Congress in two separate bills. The War Department, including the army and air force, recommended appropriations of $7.1 billion for FY 1947; in another bill the Navy Department requested $4.3 billion.[5] Expenditures for all federal activities were set at $35.8 billion. Of this total, 42 per cent or $15 billion was allocated for occupation, demobilization, and defense. The War and Navy departments were expected to spend $13 billion for these purposes. This sum sharply contrasted with the $80 billion spent by the two departments during fiscal 1945, the high point of wartime expenditures.[6]

In presenting the War Department's money bill to Congress, Secretary of War Robert Patterson and army officials emphasized the army's occupation duties. Millions of people in Germany and Japan and in previously held enemy territories had to be fed, clothed, and

38

sheltered; and a rudimentary system of order had to be constructed and maintained. These manifold problems were expected to absorb most of the army's financial and personnel resources in fiscal 1947. Little time or serious attention was, or could be, devoted to the problems of a post-hostilities army or to postwar political developments abroad. Even if army planners had wished to focus on these longer-range considerations, the army's drastically curtailed $5.3 billion budget and its projected military manpower reductions to 1.1 million men, including air force personnel, by the end of the fiscal year precluded any realistic planning for future military contingencies. Army leaders concentrated their efforts on the urgent tasks of occupation. There was little else that they could do.

The air force, although still nominally under the authority of the army, did not feel itself so confined. Largely relieved of occupation duties, air force officials were freed to focus on developing an expanded role for air power in the future defense of the nation. The congressional hearings on the first postwar air force budget set the tone and direction for subsequent air force presentations in later years. In these hearings and in countless other exchanges between air force and congressional officials the Douhet doctrine of strategic bombing was repeatedly hammered into the sympathetic ears of congressional leaders until it almost completely pre-empted the thinking of Congress about military strategy. The air force, of course, reshaped and reformulated Douhet's gospel to fit an American audience, but the message was basically the same. An overwhelmingly superior strategic bombing capacity would deter aggression, and if deterrence failed, it would destroy the enemy's military forces, his homeland, and his will to fight. Air power, not sea power, was to be America's first line of defense—and offense. Strategic bombing was heralded as the quick, relatively inexpensive, and ultimately decisive means to victory in any future war.

General Carl Spaatz outlined the air force's strategic doctrine to Congress. "Advances in reach, speed, and destructiveness of air power, with its impact on geography" exposed the United States to attack

39

from any point on the globe for the first time in its history. The answer to what Spaatz termed a "new strategic situation" was to be found in "the decisive role of air power in World War II." "In modern war," Spaatz argued,

> any nation losing command of the air approaches to its vital areas is in serious peril. Defense against air attack is difficult. . . . The surest defense will be our ability to strike back quickly with a counter offensive, to neutralize the hostile attack at its source, or to discourage its continuance by striking at the vitals of the aggressor. Only air power has the reach and speed.
>
> . . . .
>
> The first requirement of the peacetime Air Force is a combat force-in-being; ready for immediate employment; thoroughly trained; well equipped; wisely disposed on strategic bases, and capable of rapid concentration. . . .
>
> . . . .
>
> In the future, unless our initial effort is more substantial than in World War II, we may lose the war in the air, and with it lose all chance of victory. Had this country possessed in the thirties a more adequate Air Force, the story would have been different. There might not have been a war at all.[7]

To support its strategic design, the air force asked for seventy combat air groups, composed of a force of 400,000 men and an inventory of 21,000 planes. Also recommended was an appropriation of $400 million for the procurement of 1,020 airplanes. Of this total, 160 were to be heavy bombers; 526, fighter interceptors. An additional $185.5 million was projected for air force research and development. The total amount requested for all air force activities was $1.2 billion.

These recommendations were not supported by any specific analysis of how a seventy-group air force would cope with different, often discreet, political developments around the world in which American interests might be assailed. Air force officials generally assumed that a larger air force would be sufficient to meet most contingencies in which American military power might have to be exercised. Neither this assumption nor the precise reasons why seventy air groups were considered an optimal force was challenged in Congress' examination of the air force's presentations. Air force planning proceeded independent of any definite perception of how a seventy-group force would support the full spectrum of American policy objectives and political commitments; how the air force would defeat the Red Army if it should sweep across Europe without devastating the European Continent; how it would save China from communist domination; or how it would deal with the political unrest provoked by World War II in such diverse areas as India, Malaya, Iran, and Palestine. Just as significantly, air force requests, much like those of the army and navy, were based on calculations that largely ignored the contributions of the other services to national defense. Even stranger was the fact that few in Congress or in the executive branch discerned this fractured and dichotomous approach to military strategic planning to be disconcerting or alarming.[8]

The House Subcommittee on War Department Appropriations was the first congressional group to review the budgetary requests of the army and air force. It adopted a very narrow role for itself, concentrating its attention on internal administrative problems of War Department economy and efficiency. Little of its questioning dealt with underlying political justification for the War Department's proposed activities. The subcommittee approved, almost mechanically, most of the features of the administration's military proposals. The bulk of the subcommittee's interrogations centered on projected expenditures for such specific items as hospital beds and mess hall utensils. Subcommittee members continually emphasized the need to minimize waste and duplication in armed service operations. Representative Albert Engel expressed the dominant concern of his colleagues when he said, "I want to obtain all the national defense I can. . . . I want to get a dollar's worth of national defense for every dollar we are spending." [9]

The subcommittee's announced intent was to leave the settlement of military policy issues to the President and the War Department. Once a plan was devised for the use of men and material in the executive branch, the subcommittee would enter the picture to check whether the amount of money being spent was "the minimum required." "I believe," began Representative Engel,

> . . . that the President ought to formulate a plan setting forth the peacetime strength of the Army and Navy, with the spheres of operation of the Army and the Navy and who is going to do each individual job; which branch will operate the land-based planes, just where the Navy stops and the Army begins and where the Army stops and the Navy begins.

> Mr. Mahon: I agree . . . and I feel that before the Army and Navy budgets are presented to the Congress they should be gone over by some kind of a joint group so there will not be any duplication in the waste of manpower [sic] and the amount of money should be brought to the very minimum required. [10]

But the subcommittee could not escape its broader responsibilities for defense so easily, even on its own terms. The starting point for an inquiry into the efficiency and economy of army operations should logically have been placed at the planning stages of the proposed military programs. Once a course of action had been adopted, millions of dollars might be spent before a decision was reached to revamp or abandon the program. Most legislators were not disposed to speculate about the projected economic feasibility or political benefits of any one proposed program. It was easier to compare the yearly operations of ongoing programs than to face the immediately less pressing, but more important, question of what the nation's future military needs might be. It might have proved more economical in the long-run to have actually increased the appropriations for the armed services beyond the President's request. War destroys a nation's human and material resources. A timely expansion of military forces might preclude their increase later at greater cost at the outbreak of hostilities. Adequate forces in being might well prevent the eruption of open conflict or might conceivably limit its magnitude in the initial stages before it developed its own logic and momentum.

Most important of all, there was almost no inclination within the subcommittee to question the foreign policy objectives which presumably animated the President's defense budget. The subcommittee could not determine the economy or efficiency of the armed services unless it explored the ramifications of this vital question. Efficiency and economy in government is almost meaningless unless it is hinged to political purposes. Only once in the published hearings did the subcommittee reveal to itself—and then only briefly—the paucity of its basic orientation to the military budget. The occasion was an exchange of opinions over the occupation policy of the United States:

Mr. Engel: Do you suppose that Germany, regardless of how long we occupy Germany, regardless of what we do, is going to try to get back the whole of Germany? Isn't it natural for them to do that?

General Handy: Yes, sir; it would appear so. . . .

Mr. Engel: There is no question about what Russia intends to do with some of the territory she has taken from Germany. There is no question about what she intends to do about the territory she has taken from Poland. The question is, will that bring about peace? Aren't we going to be up against the same question in Germany regardless of how long we occupy it or what we do?

General Handy: You are getting me in pretty deep water.

Mr. Engel: I will not ask you to answer it. We will let the question answer itself.

Mr. Norrell: *Maybe we had better get back to the budget.*[11]

The subcommittee heeded Norrell's injunction, and went "back to the budget." The issue of American presence in Central Europe was set aside as quickly as it had been raised.

The subcommittee reached its decisions on the War Department's bill about a month after its hearings on the measure had begun. The subcommittee report, submitted through the House Appropriations Committee, accepted the army's projected reduction in military strength to 1.1 million, including the air force's program of 400,000 men. With only one exception, dealing with the army's relief activities, the report took no substantial issue with the administration's proposals. The House report was largely drawn from the testimony of Major General George Richards, budget officer of the War Department.[12]

The recommended War Department budget for FY 1947 totaled approximately $7.1 billion, $117 million below administration estimates. The air force received its requested $1.2 billion, while the army secured the balance. The principal cut was made in proposed funds for subsistence aid to the people of occupied areas. One hundred and fifty million dollars were slashed from the original estimate of $500 million.[13]

The committee report also emphasized the interest of many legislators in military research and development and, particularly, for swift development of new airplane designs. Committee members "held the firm opinion that America must not lag behind in this tremendously important field."[14] The committee granted the War Department's appeal for $281.5 million for research and development. Most of this amount—$185.5 million—was to be spent by the air force. Underscoring its interest in the military strategic importance of nuclear weapons, the committee added $175 million to the administration's requests for atomic services.[15]

Representatives John Kerr and Albert Engel, respectively the ranking Democratic and Republican members of the Subcommittee on War Department Appropriations, dominated the House proceedings on the military budget. Their presentations encountered little opposition from the other members of the lower chamber, nor did it occasion a general debate of the political objectives that the administration hoped to achieve through the maintenance of its proposed level of armed might. Discussion moved erratically, centering first on one and then another small or tangential point. Representative William A. Pittinger was interested in the creation of an inspector general of the army directly responsible to Congress. Mrs. Edith Rogers of Massachusetts expressed concern about appropriations for paraplegics. The military budget was finally passed without change and sent to the Senate. Only a month and a half elapsed between the War Department's submission of its $7.1 billion estimates and the House's final approval of them.[16]

Senate action on the bill was marked by considerably more haste. The Senate Subcommittee on War Department Appropriations held three days of short hearings before it presented its report. It recommended $7.6 billion for the War Department, an increase of $500 million over the House's limit. The Senate restored all of the House cuts, including an additional $250 million for military housing.[17] The Senate passed the bill, accepting the committee report with only the briefest examination and discussion.[18] The entire process took one week.

Final passage was delayed because House conferees vigorously opposed a Senate provision which would have permitted the secretary of war to transfer appropriations between accounts up to 10 per cent of the original grant. The House finally accepted a 4 per cent clause. Other differences were more easily compromised. The air force received its suggested $1.2 billion, while the army was granted $6.1 billion. Of this amount $5.3 billion was earmarked for military activities. The remaining $800 million was divided between atomic service and the relief of peoples in occupied territory.

Navy demobilization.—Congress' examination of the navy appropriations bill seemed radically different from its review of the War

Department's requests. Personality differences were obvious enough. Now admirals, not army officers, justified the administration's budget, and they appeared before special Navy Department subcommittees in the House and Senate which differed outwardly in attitude and composition from their War Department counterparts. More significant, however, was the seeming clash of substantive policy proposals, not simply personalities, that characterized congressional discussion of the navy's estimates for FY 1947. Sharp conflicts arose between congressional committees, between individual congressmen and the President, and between the Navy Department and the Budget Bureau over navy force levels. The principal sources of dispute were the number of men to be kept in uniform, the composition of naval forces, and the size of the active fleet.

These differences were deceptive. The navy appropriations bill that emerged from Congress bore a close resemblance to the product of Congress' War Department deliberations. More clearly than through a scattering of angry congressional charges of presidential neglect of navy power, the $4.1 billion navy budget that Congress passed demonstrated that most legislators were agreed that the navy should return eventually to prewar levels.

Controversy centered around two conflicting navy plans. In Plan 1-A, the navy outlined a postwar force of 558,000 men, organized around an active combatant fleet of 1,079 ships and 12,000 planes. A $6 billion appropriation for FY 1947 was needed to finance these force levels. President Truman and his budgetary advisers, however, rejected the navy's initial estimates and ordered downward revision in its planning by more than $2 billion. Plan No. 2 was subsequently issued. It called for a fiscal year-end force of 494,800 men and an active combatant fleet of 965 ships, 114 vessels less than Plan 1-A. Naval aviation was reduced too, by 3,600 planes. Airplane procurement was set at 1,359. This represented a difference of 380 planes from the 1,739 planes envisaged by Plan 1-A. Both plans were to operate the active fleet with a force of 70 per cent of wartime complements. Reserve and inactive fleets were to be maintained respectively, at 30 and 10 per cent of normal wartime strength.[19]

Navy estimates totaled $4.3 billion, including a request to transfer $500 million from the naval stock fund to augment direct appropriations. Of this amount, the Bureau of Aeronautics was to receive $595 million as well as an additional $275 million in new contract authorizations for aircraft procurement.[20] The navy would be built around carrier forces.

Despite a reduction of strength, the navy's primary role in national defense allegedly remained the same—pre-eminent. "So long as men and material must be transported by sea, ships will be required, and, concomitantly, a Navy adequate to keep the sea lanes safely open," said Navy Secretary James F. Forrestal.[21] Enemy aggression abroad or a nuclear air attack against the United States would be principally countered, not by an air force strike against the enemy's homeland, but by strong naval forces which would advance America's forward lines of resistance and project its military power overseas.[22] The Chief of Naval Operations (CNO), Admiral Chester Nimitz, amplified Forrestal's opening remarks and sketched the functions that the navy would perform. It would transport troops to overseas positions; it would provide, through the carrier fleet, a mobile tactical air force capable of destroying specified targets and, in combination with other surface ships, gunfire support for amphibious landings; submarines would supply a powerful offensive force to secure United States dominance of the sea; and antisubmarine and reconnaissance ships would cover the approaches to American ports and guard vital supply lines at sea. "The operating force plan for 1947," Nimitz summarized,

> has been prepared . . . with due regard to the requirements of our postwar national economy and to the necessity for accomplishing the peacetime tasks of supporting the foreign policy of the United States and supporting the occupation forces overseas. . . . It includes sufficient force in each ocean to meet commitments to the United Nations Organization and to the regional organization for the peace of the Western Hemis-

phere. *It is sufficiently flexible to permit rapid readjustment to changing conditions.*[23]

The flexibility of naval planning was precisely the issue of concern. It was too flexible. The changing conditions to which it was readjusted were determined more by budgetary constraints than by strategic imperatives. Nimitz' presentation was too all-purpose. It could have justified either Plan 1-A or 2 or any other plan that the navy might have proposed. There was no precise linkage between navy planning and probable military conflicts abroad. Plan 1-A undoubtedly was potentially more capable of supporting United States policies than Plan 2 simply in terms of the force levels that each contemplated. By the same token, a navy twice as large as the Plan 1-A force presumably would have been even more prepared to advance American objectives. Still, the justification of any navy plan had to rest on a projection of its political consequences abroad and, relatedly, of its impact on shifting international power positions that affected American interests. The navy did not present its estimates in this more complicated, yet more relevant, framework. Like those of the army and air force, navy requests disregarded the contributions of the other services to national defense and to an over-all plan for American postwar foreign and military operations. The fault, of course, did not lie entirely with the military services. Governed principally by budgetary, not foreign policy considerations, the services filled the political vacuum in which they operated with elaborately developed plans and detailed requests for equipment and trained personnel, guided largely by their own inflated conceptions of their particular roles in a future war.

Within its sphere, Congress did no better. There is little evidence of any serious congressional attempt to encourage the services to co-ordinate military planning or to agree on a clear division of military functions. Congress accepted the services on their own individualistic terms. The War and Navy department budgets essentially represented two streams of disparate experience for Congress, although both bore on the question of military support for American foreign interests and commitments. The situation was much the same in the executive branch when the military budgetary streams were joined only briefly, albeit perfunctorily, as they passed through the Budget Bureau. Once in Congress, an appropriation bill for a military department continued within its own defined path that conformed to the long established traditions and folkways of Congress' review of defense appropriations and expenditures. Congress' examination of the navy's budget for FY 1947 provided no fundamental change in this basic pattern. It emphasized again Congress' hesitancy to focus on military and foreign policy problems. While the House and Senate subcommittees on naval appropriations took exception to the administration's reduction of naval power, their criticisms of administration policy turned more on a comparison of specific manpower and hardware items of Plans 1-A and 2 than on an analysis of the military support that various levels of naval power provided for the nation's defense.[24] Only a handful of congressmen appeared to be aware of the weaknesses of Congress' and the executive's decision-making in defense. A brief discussion between Secretary of War Robert Patterson and Representative Albert Engel during the hearings on the War Department money bill suggested the dimensions of these shortcomings:

Secretary Patterson: There is no way you can get here in this subcommittee or in the other one [the Subcommittee on Navy Appropriations] an over-all view of the national defense. You ask me questions about the Navy, and I say I do not know, and I do not.

Mr. Engel: I wondered whether you did or not.

Mr. Patterson: I do not. . . . No; you have to operate in the dark.

Mr. Engel: There are two arms of national defense, and two subcommittees on appropriations handling primarily the appropriations for the two arms of our national defense. We [on the War Department Appropriations Subcommittee] are handling the Army arm on the one hand and the Subcommittee on Navy Appropriations is handling the Navy arm, and the one hand does not know what the other hand is doing, and it never has since I have been here.[25]

Representative Harry Sheppard, chairman of the naval appropriations subcommittee, presented the findings of his group to the House. Following the pattern previously adopted in the House hearings the report compared Plans 1-A and 2. One of two courses of action appeared feasible. An appropriation of $2 billion could be provided to implement Plan 1-A, or the force levels of Plan 2 could be approved on the condition that the active fleet would operate at maximum personnel strength rather than at the administration-proposed complement of 70 per cent. Reserve and inactive fleet personnel strength would also be increased from a 30 and 10 per cent peacetime basis, respectively, to a 100 per cent wartime level. Cost of the expanded reserve plan would be $133.8 million or $55 million more than the original budget estimate. The marine corps would be given $12 million more than it had requested to train 60,000 ground and air reserve personnel, doubling its initial proposal of 30,000. The appropriations committee concluded "that the interests both of national security and the national economy will be sufficiently served by the adoption of the latter of the above alternatives."[26] The total cost of the revised congressional plan for the navy was estimated at $4 billion. The navy was also authorized to transfer $500 million from its stock fund to its general accounts. Total naval appropriations stood at $4.6 billion. The committee's recommended outlay for naval power was $374 million greater than the Budget Bureau's estimates.[27] Much of this increase, however, rested on an accounting manipulation. Actual navy strength was not appreciably bolstered.

The House Appropriations Committee also recommended a slightly expanded military research and development program. It found that the funds provided under Plan 2 were "insufficient to permit the Navy to devote the necessary energies to perfecting known principles of scientific and technical design and to pursuing fields of pure research. . . . "[28] Almost $40 million was added to the original estimate for these purposes. Although the bulk of the $250 million for research and development was earmarked for naval aviation, no comparisons were made between the navy and air force research programs to minimize waste and duplication or to pinpoint possible gaps in planning.

Procurement for ships and planes formed the final significant phase of the committee report. It recommended $350 million for the construction of seventy-two combatant ships.[29] No change was advised in the number of aircraft to be procured under Plan 2. Only the navy's funding program was revised. The committee rejected the navy's request for $275 million in contract authorizations for airplane procurement, arguing that this method of financing confused "the public mind as to the true fiscal status of the Government."[30] It substituted a direct appropriation to the Bureau of Aeronautics of $200 million which, when combined with two other small items, raised the navy's aircraft procurement estimates from $595 million to $806 million. While the navy's direct appropriations were sizably increased, its total new obligational authority actually decreased by three-quarters of a million dollars.[31] These budgetary changes accounted for most of the differences between the administration's funding estimates and the final House bill.

House debate on the navy bill was charged with bitter denunciations of the administration's naval reduction. Clear differences were openly registered within Congress and between legislators and various agencies of the executive branch. The debates on the navy's estimates revealed a surprising lack of communication and co-ordination between the Naval Affairs Committee and the Subcommittee on Navy Department Appropriations. Nor was the confusion restricted to these two groups. It marked the open policy disagreements between the Navy Department, on the one hand, and the Budget Bureau and the President, on the other.

At the start of the House debate, Representative Carl Vinson, chairman of the Naval Affairs Committee, voiced his committee's unanimous opposition to the navy cutback outlined in Plan 2. He rested his argument on House Resolution 80 of October, 1945, which had set naval strength at 1,079 major combatant ships and 500,000 men.[32] This unanimously approved resolution had been the basis of Plan 1-A. Failure to reach its projected levels, Vinson complained, indicated that congressional power over navy policy was being usurped. "It is up to the American Congress to say what shall constitute the United States Navy," he asserted.

> Has the time come when you, the representatives of the people, sit here merely to be Charlie McCarthys for the Bureau of the Budget. . . .
> The facts show conclusively that the minimum requirement for the national security is a Navy of the size covered by the budget submitted by the Navy Department. We occupy the position as the greatest Nation of this world, with more at stake than any other people on this earth, and with the greatest coastline to defend. The Navy said the minimum we could get by with was what the Congress had approved as the size of our postwar Navy.[33]

Representative Sterling Cole of New York supported Vinson. He insinuated that President Truman was personally opposed to a large navy. "Plan No. 1 . . . was a Navy Man's Navy, and was approved by the Joint Chiefs of Staff," he remarked. "Plan 2 . . . is a financial man's, a Budget man's, a drugstore man's, or whatever the budget officer may have been who passed upon these requisitions [sic]—it is his type of Navy. . . . "[34]

But what factors—political, economic, military—determined the minimum navy that the nation "could get by with"? Neither Representative Vinson nor Representative Cole defined them. The navy's Plan 1-A was taken as a point of departure. The upshot was that, while the House Naval Affairs Committee may not have been the Charlie McCarthy of the Budget Bureau, its denunciation of Plan 2, through Vinson and Cole, came dangerously close to suggesting that it had transformed itself into a mouthpiece of the navy. Vinson's analysis of the nation's postwar naval requirements, however, did not surpass the navy's dubious presentations in clarity or in breadth.

There was something of a paradox, too, in Vinson's counterproposal to the House Appropriations Committee report. In contrast to his attack on Plan 2, his substitute motion was quite modest. Curiously ignoring the large cuts in navy personnel, he concentrated on raising the number of major combatant ships above the Plan 2 level of 965 vessels. He noted a difference of 114 ships between the size of the fleet embraced by House Resolution 80 (1,079) and Plan 2. He conceded thirty-four of these—six to atomic testing and twenty-eight to abandoned construction. He offered an amendment to increase naval appropriations by $32 million in order to berth the remaining eighty ships for immediate use in case of a national emergency. Members of the Navy Department appropriations subcommittee objected to Vinson's motion, maintaining that the House bill already carried enough funds to berth the disputed vessels. To everyone's embarrassment, both Vinson and the members of the naval appropriations subcommittee cited the same Navy Department officials to support their respective claims over the availability of funds for berthing naval ships. House members following the debates on the floor were helpless to decide between the positions. They were even less prepared to give a convincing answer to the question of postwar naval policy. Representative Ross Rizley perplexedly asked:

When one committee of this House says that those in charge of naval affairs tell one story, and on the other day tell such distinguished men as the Chairman of the Naval Affairs Committee another story, what is the average member of the House who is not a member of either committee to rely upon? Has it come to the place in this country [sic] where everyone is making double talk out of one side of his mouth at the same time? [35]

Vinson admitted that the matter was "worse than confused," and subsequently withdrew his amendment after repeated assurances that the eighty ships in question would be properly berthed. With only one minor change in wording, the House accepted its committee's report, and the bill passed to the Senate without a record vote.

Senate hearings on the navy bill lasted a short week, contrasting with House investigation that gathered over two thousand pages of testimony.[36] The Senate adopted the posture of an appellate court and restricted itself mainly to the findings of the House. The navy's Bureau of Aeronautics received the most sympathetic reception. Admiral Harold B. Sallada, chief of the Bureau, told the Senate appropriations subcommittee that the House's revision of the finance program for naval aircraft would cost the navy $75 million and would curtail navy aircraft procurement in FY 1947. The 1,379 airplanes which had been projected would have to be cut to 1,087, a reduction of 272 units.[37] General Alexander Vandegrift, commandant of the marine corps, testified that the House's $12 million increase of the marine reserve program could not be efficiently spent unless Congress guaranteed larger appropriations in subsequent years for this purpose.

Neither the Senate nor the House was prepared to guarantee the marine corps or any other phase of the military program before them. The Senate Appropriations Committee report, offered by Senator John Overton, recommended no substantial changes in the force levels approved by the House. Marine reserves were to return to the strength levels of Plan 2. The Bureau of Aeronautics received a token increase in its accounts.[38]

Senate debate was perfunctory and unsystematic even when compared with the House's chaotic review of the navy's requests. The Senate did not consider the adequacy of the navy budget, nor the postwar requirements of naval power in a rapidly changing international environment. No comparison was made between Plans 1-A and 2. Almost half of the Senate's deliberations centered on the navy's proposed shutdown of its ordnance plant at Newport, Rhode Island, and the transfer of its activities to a new installation at Forest Park, Illinois. Senator William Green of Rhode Island, fearing a loss of jobs in his home state, objected to the navy move. But his amendment to stop the navy action failed, and the Senate Appropriations Committee's report was upheld.[39]

Much of the balance of the Senate's interest in the navy program was absorbed by the issue of time-study methods in navy yards. For thirty years, naval appropriation bills had carried a clause forbidding the introduction of such procedures into naval construction projects. At the behest of the Navy Department, the Senate Appropriations Committee recommended the deletion of this provision in the FY 1947 bill. In a narrow twenty-eight to twenty-six vote, with forty-one senators unrecorded, the upper house once more upheld its committee's recommendation.[40] A few moments later the Senate approved a $4.1 billion appropriation for the Navy Department.

Just as the Senate prepared to turn to other business, Senator Brien McMahon secured the floor to comment on the Senate's recent action. He sternly rebuked his colleagues' hastily considered decision on the navy's proposals. "Mr. President," he said,

> . . . I do not suppose there is a Senator on the floor who can conscientiously say that he knows within a billion dollars whether this appropriation is right or not. I have read the hearings; I have read the committee report—which does not amount to anything—I have read the bill, and frankly, I have not the slightest idea whether $4,100,000,000 . . . is the correct

amount the Congress should appropriate for the Navy during the coming year.

. . . .

As I looked through the hearings I read what the admirals said. What else would we expect to hear from admirals except demands for all the money they think Congress will appropriate? I don't blame them—that is their business, but it certainly is our business to double check them, and we have not the facilities for doing it.

I say to Senators that they have sat here today and, by a voice vote, put through a $4,100,000,000 appropriation, and they really do not know very much about it. They do not know whether the battleships which are carried in the appropriation bill are worth anything or not, and they have not had any advice except from the admirals. That observation applies from the first page of the bill to the last.[41]

Senator McMahon's criticism was as sharp as it was perceptive. But congressional understanding of defense policy was to get worse before it got better.

THE NATION TURNS INWARD: FY 1948

President Truman's State of the Union message in 1947 returned to the prewar order of priority between domestic and foreign policy. Attention focused on settlement of labor-management disputes, extension of economic and social welfare, economic growth, and reduction of the $275 billion federal debt. "If we are to fulfill our responsibilities to ourselves and to other peoples," the President observed, "we must make sure that the United States is sound economically, socially, and politically." [42] The argument was traditional, but for that very reason was the more compelling to a nation and Congress whose principal interests and cares since the War of 1812 had been domestic in origin and significance. The bitter economic controls and the physical and spiritual exhaustion of World War II also had had their effect. They reinforced the nation's historically conditioned tendency to emphasize domestic problems at the expense of its now enormous, but yet dimly perceived, international interests and responsibilities.

American foreign policy rested on the assumption (and hope) of continued big power co-operation within the framework of the United Nations. This assumption largely controlled official American policy until the fall of Czechoslovakia in February, 1948, despite accumulating signs of Soviet aggressive intent, including the installation of communist regimes in eastern Europe, the support of the Greek communist rebellion, Russian pressures on Turkey and Iran, and the collapse of five meetings at the foreign minister level between September 1945 and October 1946. President Truman depreciated the significance of these unsettling developments in his State of the Union address: "Whatever differences there may have been between [the United States] and the Soviet Union . . . should not be allowed to obscure the fact that the basic interests of both nations lie in the early making of a peace under which the peoples of all countries may return . . . to the essential tasks of production and reconstruction." [43] The President, however, hedged his optimism with the cautious observation that the United States was living "in a world in which strength on the part of peace-loving nations is still the greatest deterrent to aggression. . . . When a system of collective security under the United Nations has been established, we shall be willing to lead in collective disarmament, but, until such a system becomes a reality, we must not again allow our weakness to invite attack." [44]

If the President had had any anxiety about Soviet imperialist intentions, they were not reflected in his military budget for FY 1948. Expenditures for the War and Navy departments were scaled downward by approximately $2 billion to a little more than $11 billion— $6.7 billion for the army and air force and $4.4 billion for the navy. War Department estimates totaled $6 billion, $5.7 billion in direct appropriations and the remainder in contract authorizations. The navy requested $3.5 billion in appropriations, $170 million in aircraft contract authority, and permission to transfer $164 million from certain established accounts.[45] Lower appropriations indicated still lower expenditures in future years.

The War Department restates its case.—The army remained primarily concerned with its occupation and rehabilitation responsibilities in FY 1948. What was novel about the army's presentations before Congress was its more sustained emphasis on the possibility of surprise attack and the corresponding need for forces in being. "It is certain that, if war comes again," stated Brigadier General George A. Lincoln, chief of the army plans group, "we will not have the time to mobilize we had from 1939 onward. Adequate forces in readiness must be immediately available and there may be little warning."[46] Army Chief of Staff General Dwight D. Eisenhower later echoed this view in the House hearings.[47] This position also formed one of the driving forces behind the administration's recommendation to Congress that it adopt universal military training (UMT) to maintain a minimal level of national readiness for war. "In case of another major war," explained General R. S. McLain,

> the pattern would probably take the following form: First, the blitz using all modern means. If this should succeed the war would be over. It would be hopeless to carry on by underground means. If the blitz, however, is stopped, the second phase would be a softening-up phase in which bases, industries, and ports would be bombarded. The final phase would be a struggle between complete teams, air, sea, and ground, in which the accompanying attrition would finally point to the victor.[48]

The air force, while it, too, hammered at the themes of surprise attack and swift victory, minimized the second and third phases of any future global conflict. It implicitly downgraded the role of the army and the navy, and emphasized its own importance. "With the advent of new weapons," argued Air Force Chief Carl Spaatz, "it is reasonably certain that war will come with less warning and with greater destructiveness and the decision may be reached in a much shorter time than in . . . the past." [49] The principal new weapon was of course the atomic bomb, and the new weapons system was the bomb plus the air force's long-range bomber—the B-29 in 1947 and, in a short while, the B-36. Only a powerful air force could deter the enemy attack that was anticipated over America's arctic frontier. The test of such an air force, Spaatz suggested, was its ability to "provide a long-range striking force in instant readiness and [sic] with the power and capacity to destroy the storehouse of enemy weapons and thereafter to reduce the enemy's industrial capacity and war-making potential." [50]

These army and air force sketches of the future conflicted with the administration's predominantly sanguine interpretation of increasing Soviet intransigence. The service positions implicitly cautioned against a military cutback. Yet neither the Congress nor the nation was sympathetic to an increase in defense appropriations. "A $275 billion national debt," as one perceptive commentary observed, "was felt to require a very careful scrutiny of any proposals that would increase the tax burden." [51] For its part, the Truman administration itself was unwilling to recommend an unpopular and expensive outlay for the military in what was officially recognized as a time of peace. As early as August 2, 1946, with an eye toward holding down appropriation requests for FY 1948, the President ordered a stretchout of defense expenditures, including funds for aircraft procurement and research and development. [52]

The army and the air force originally asked the War Department for $10 billion. [53] Trimmed to $8.4 billion by the secretary of war, this latter sum was subsequently reduced in the Budget Bureau to $6 billion, composed of $5.7 billion in direct appropriations and the balance in contract authority. The air force's renewed request for seventy groups was again denied in the War Department. A force of fifty-eight groups was authorized at full strength and twelve at skeletonized levels.[54] The Budget Bureau's reductions cut this force to fifty-five limited strength groups and fifteen skeleton elements for FY 1948. The air force was permitted to submit an $850 million appropriation as well as contract authority of $280 million. Of these amounts, $440 million was assigned to the purchase of 932 airplanes, less than the attrition rate of aircraft in air force inventories.[55] Personnel requirements were curtailed to 364,000 in the first half of FY 1948 and 386,000 in the second half.[56] Army strength suffered a slight reduction, too. Its average strength for the first half of the fiscal year was pegged at 706,000 and at 684,000 in the latter half. Appropriations for this force came to $4.9 billion. The procurement program was negligible.[57] These reductions prompted General Eisenhower to complain to the Senate

> that the War Department budget . . . represented an extremely close-cropped national security program. . . . The War Department budget already reflected the following drastic curtailments: No modernization program in the ground Army. A severely curtailed modernization program in the Air Forces. Reduction of occupation forces to a bare minimum. Reduction of civilians below firm requirements. Reduction of the Air Force 70 group program to 55 groups. Delayed research and development projects. Severely curtailed Reserve, ROTC, and National Guard programs.[58]

Congress wields an economy ax.—Having gained control of the Eightieth Congress, the Republicans commanded majorities on the War and Navy Department appropriations subcommittees of both houses for the first time since 1932. Now the incentives of partisan advantage joined with the already strong bipartisan pressures for a reduction in governmental expenditures and a relief from wartime economic controls. Led by Representative Albert Engel, the Republican-dominated House military appropriations subcommittee pressed with new resolution to pare the War Department's budget. Representing the largest departmental element of the government's spending program for FY 1948, it was the obvious target of congressional scrutiny. The House subcommittee probed painstakingly through the War Department requests. Witnesses were repeatedly asked to suggest cuts in the administration's proposed $6 billion appropriation. Almost invariably they replied that the War Department estimates were "stretched pretty close to the elastic limit." [59] Supplemental hearings were held to wear down the resistance of administration advocates. The move proved unavailing.

Blocked on one front, the House subcommittee shifted its economic offensive to the House floor where administration strength was minimal. "Cutting our expenses and meeting our obligations," said Representative John Kerr, Engel's Democratic counterpart in the subcommittee, "is the most serious duty that ever confronted us." [60] Other subcommittee members agreed. Representative Harve Tibbott warned against impending national bankruptcy unless the government reduced spending, and Representative Francis Case complained that the subcommittee had not received adequate newspaper coverage of its budget-cutting efforts.

The House report reflected these sentiments. It recommended a $475 million reduction which was to affect three principal areas. The air force's aircraft procurement estimates were lowered by 10 per cent, and officer and civilian personnel strength were reduced, respectively, by 20,100 and 75,000. These manpower decreases were designed to align officer-enlisted personnel and civilian-military personnel ratios with prewar levels. "Despite the fact that the budget before us should be based on a principle that tends toward a peace time Army," the report noted, "it contains 13.5 percent officer personnel or almost 3 percent more than that of the wartime peak."[61]

The committee also felt that the proposed War Department ratio of one civilian to two soldiers was "a considerable increase over the prewar civilian ratio" of four to one.[62]

Much of the dynamics of developing global conflict between the United States and the Soviet Union was squeezed through an assortment of personnel ratios. What were essentially management techniques for the efficient utilization of personnel were substituted for strategic policy-making. An assessment of the nation's defense posture was transformed into a comparison of prewar and postwar personnel policies. Ignored were the rising number of Russian-American clashes in western Europe, the Middle East, and China. The neglect was conspicuous. For the Soviet-American confrontation in Iran was still fresh in the memory of official Washington;[63] reports from the Far East increasingly indicated the gradual collapse of the Chiang Kai-shek regime; and only two months had elapsed since President Truman's dramatic appeal to Congress for $400 million aid to Greece and Turkey, to stem communist encroachments. For the majority of subcommittee members, these enlarging areas of conflict posed no immediate threat to the United States.

Representative George Mahon was the sole subcommittee member to object to the House report.[64] He offered an amendment to restore the 10 per cent cut in the air force's procurement fund. Latest air force figures indicated that a rising price level would cut its actual procurement from 942 to 749 planes. The subcommittee's 10 per cent reduction would further lower procurement to 561 planes.[65]

The Mahon amendment provided a leaven in the fermenting House opinion over the issue of declining air power strength in the face of a growing prospect of war with the Soviet Union. During the House debate, Russian airplane production was alleged to be three times that of the United States. In what was to become a prophetic pronouncement a decade later, Representative Mendel Rivers asserted that the United States lagged behind Russian "know-how on guided missiles . . . [and] on jet-propelled airplanes."[66]

Others, like Representative John J. Rankin, were even more out-spoken:

> We are faced with the greatest crisis in world history; we need not 'kid' ourselves. Communism is making war on the United States. . . . I say we should have the strongest air force on earth. We should keep the atomic bomb, and I am in favor of turning it back to the military authorities, keeping a supply of bombs on hand, keeping planes equipped to distribute them and aviators trained to operate them, keep our Air Force ahead of any other Air Force on earth, because you are dealing with a savage force that does not recognize anything on earth but force, or power.[67]

These arguments, along with Engel's withdrawal of opposition to Mahon's proposal, influenced the House to restore the air force procurement funds to their original level. For the moment the rising tide of congressional sentiment in favor of a larger air force subsided. It would, however, swell again in size and intensity in succeeding years, rising to an unexpected crest in one year, only to fall, unpredictably, to a new low in another.

After brief hearings and hasty floor consideration, the Senate restored 12,500 officers and approximately 35,000 civilian employees to the War Department bill. It also overruled the House's curious $80 million cut in the air force budget which would have seriously hampered its operations by reducing its gasoline supplies. The air force's cash appropriations were raised to $858 million, slightly more than the War Department request. Contract authority for aircraft acquisitions was also nearly doubled over the House approved figure.[68] Enough funds were furnished to purchase 1,100 airplanes and to support fifty-five air groups. However, Senator Cabot Lodge's amendment to add $613 million to the War Department appropriations fund to build a seventy-group air force was defeated. The bill passed after brief discussion of stop watch procedures on War Department projects, a ceiling on civilian employees, and the secretary of war's authority to transfer appropriations.[69]

The conference committee quickly resolved the House and Senate differences. The air force received almost the entire $850 million that it had requested and an increased contract authorization of $430 million. The army was forced to absorb a $200 million decrease, its appropriations totaling $4.65 billion.[70] The conferees struck 58,371 civilian employees and 13,650 officers from the War Department payroll.[71] Despite congressional disclaimers that these cuts did not affect War Department programs, they resulted in cutbacks in army and air force research and development. The Senate's insistence on lower personnel reductions than the House's initially approved levels prevented greater slippages in these areas. A major casualty of these congressional reductions was the air force's budding intercontinental ballistics missile (ICBM) program. The air force's missile budget was cut from $29 million to $13 million in FY 1947. By June 1947, all major ICBM contracts were cancelled. Long-range missile research was to remain in an arrested state of development until the early years of the Eisenhower administration when it would be finally placed on a continuing and high priority basis.[72]

The decrease in army funds, the Mahon and Lodge amendments, and the House's brief, but revealing, debate on air power—all were significant and symptomatic. They indicated the gradual crystallization of a new congressional consensus on military strategic policy. The threat of increasing Soviet expansionism could not be ignored much longer. Since a general war with the Soviet Union was recognized as the most immediate and likely military threat, the air force's forcefully presented seventy-group formula and its strategic bombing concepts—which, incidentally, the army had come very close to accepting in 1947—appeared increasingly persuasive to an ever larger number of legislators. Strategic air power would either checkrein Soviet imperialist moves or would destroy the Soviet Union's economic and military capacity to carry on a war against the United States.

The Soviet homeland would be attacked immediately, with devastating results. The Russian people's will to fight would allegedly be destroyed beyond any hope of repair.

Buttressing these doctrinal arguments were a number of decisive economic and budgetary considerations. Neither Congress nor the President was willing to abandon the $15 billion ceiling on annual defense expenditures, a limitation that was to prevail until the Korean War. Moreover, widespread congressional demands for tax reductions which reached a heightened proportion in the Eightieth Congress effectively neutralized any congressional pressures that might have been marshalled to expand the nation's military forces. President Truman vetoed two congressionally initiated tax decrease bills in 1947, had another passed over his veto in 1948, and failed in his attempt to increase taxes by $4 billion in 1949.[73]

The upshot of these doctrinal and budgetary factors was becoming gradually clearer. Whether implicitly or explicitly understood by a majority of legislators, they were leading Congress to a hard choice with respect to the size, composition, and readiness of the nation's military establishment. The pressures in Congress for lowered defense expenditures, increased private spending capacity, and more air power pointed inescapably to a reduction in army and navy new obligational authority. This was precisely what Congress had accomplished in passing the FY 1948 War Department bill. The navy appropriation bill for FY 1948, discussed below, was also to reflect Congress' slow withdrawal of political support from naval power. Beginning in 1947, the navy, like the army, had its appropriations requests cut in each fiscal year until the North Korean attack in 1950. As Congress' appropriations support for the army and navy decreased, its aid to the air force increased, although never so much in any one fiscal year that the total of appropriations granted by Congress exceeded the President's over-all budgetary estimates.[74] As early as 1947, the consensus in Congress was polarizing around the air force's seventy-group proposal.

65

The navy's day in Congress.—The developing political support for more air power paralleled the evolution of postwar naval doctrine. The experience of World War II prompted a new and heightened appreciation of air power among professional navy officers.[75] The carrier had replaced the battleship as the navy's principal weapon system. The navy's FY 1948 program reinforced this trend and included twelve medium and large aircraft carriers in the active fleet. Only one battleship remained. Forty per cent of the navy's general line officers were listed as aviators. Admiral Arthur Radford, deputy chief of naval operations, outlined the navy's growing air power commitment "as a key weapon of its fighting strength." [76] Naval air units allegedly provided "the most mobile air force in the world . . . they could support . . . the economic and political interests of the nation in almost all parts of the world; and . . . in the event of war they would bear the brunt of air fighting against short-based aircraft while . . . national mobilization [was] in process. . . . " [77]

The navy's actual hardware requests for FY 1948 did not match its newly announced accent on air power. Only 579 new planes were projected.[78] This sum was far below the 2,115 aircraft needed annually to replace those lost to attrition or obsolescence.[79] Acquisition of aircraft in FY 1947, moreover, had not reached expected levels. Instead of the estimated 1,359 new aircraft to be purchased, only 1,063 were actually acquired. The House $75 million cut and a rising price level kept deliveries down. Gaps between new purchases and operational and inventory losses were to be filled by depleting existing aircraft in storage and not by increased procurement. Major combatant ship operations were also reduced. Twenty-seven vessels were cut from the previous year's total of 965.[80] A conspicuously small $9.7 million was requested for a new ship construction program that would finally cost $122 million by the early 1950's.[81]

Naval personnel strength, including the marine corps, was to drop also. Average naval strength was set at 471,000 for FY 1948, to be composed of 425,000 enlisted men and 46,000 officers, approximately

30,000 fewer personnel than in FY 1947.[82] Marine corps strength that had operated approximately at average levels of 100,000 enlisted men and 8,000 officers was to be slimmed down to 90,000 and 7,500 respectively by the end of FY 1948. Actual year-end totals were estimated at 85,000 enlisted and 7,000 officer personnel. This force was but a dim shadow of the 485,000 peak which had been reached at the height of World War II.[83]

The navy program, given so sympathetic a hearing in 1946, experienced rougher treatment at the hands of the Eightieth Congress. Part of the explanation lies in the shift in party power resulting from the Republican victory in 1946. Representative Charles Plumley replaced Harry Sheppard, a self-confessed "Big-Navy" man, as chairman of the naval appropriations subcommittee. During his term as chairman, Sheppard had at least avowed that the "first" responsibility of the subcommittee was "to see that our Naval Establishment is sufficient in size and possessed of the modern tools of its trade . . . to carry its share of the national defense . . . under any future contingency." [84] To be sure the announced primary responsibility of the subcommittee was actually subordinated in its FY 1947 proceedings to its "other serious duty" which, in Sheppard's words, was "to see that the taxpayers' dollar brings a return of 100 cents. . . . " [85] A proper set of priorities was thus maintained in rhetoric, if not always in fact. Plumley, however, swept away even this rhetorical restraint in his remarks opening the House's hearings on the navy's FY 1948 requests:

> During the war. . . . Congress was forced to be very liberal in its response to the requests of the armed services for money since we realized that anything that would shorten the war . . . would save American lives.
> That atmosphere of crisis is now over. We now must return to good business practices as of peacetime . . . in which economy and efficiency are the keynotes. It is important to insure the stability and the strength of our country and the world that

the expenditures of this Government be curtailed so that we can start making a reduction in the huge national debt which accumulated during the conduct of the war and try to balance the budget, to the end that eventually the burden of the individual taxpayer may be reduced.[86]

Congress' main job was to curtail governmental spending, not to search for areas, such as national security, where greater over-all expenditures might be advisable, or to question the adequacy of the President's defense policies. Plumley's point of view prevailed. Except for the presentations of the secretary of the navy and the chief of naval operations, there was little reference in the lengthy House hearings to the deteriorating international situation to which the navy's program was presumably addressed. Congress reviewed the navy budget largely outside the military-political context that it was designed to influence in support of American overseas interests.

The House Appropriations Committee's report, although written in the wake of President Truman's appeal for assistance to Greece and Turkey, focused unwaveringly on what was conceived to be the alarming size of the navy's budget. The committee's oversight was all the more incredible in light of the fact that the American presence in the Mediterranean was primarily exerted through naval power.[87] The $4.7 billion cut from initial navy estimates by the secretary of the navy and the Budget Bureau did not impress the committee. The $3.5 billion which was requested was still considered too much. The committee recommended an additional cut of 10 per cent. Navy and marine corps personnel accounts were most seriously affected, sliced by $94 million and $20 million in each instance. The bureaus of Aeronautics, Ordnance, and Ships were also asked to sustain reductions amounting to approximately $160 million. Almost $400 million was shaved from the navy's estimates. All major appropriations were cut; no categories, however small, were raised.[88]

Representatives Plumley and Sheppard divided a brief, two-hour rule to debate the navy bill. Plumley was particularly gratified by the time limit, for it precluded extensive amendment of the bill that might have restored the navy's original estimates. "To be perfectly frank with the House," Plumley candidly asserted, "inasmuch as prolonged debate involves a greater expenditure of money. . . . I am in agreement that the debate be limited to two hours." [89] Some of Plumley's Democratic colleagues on the naval subcommittee, however, were not as convinced of the advisability of limiting debate on a $3.5 billion budget or of cutting the navy's estimates.

Representative Sheppard reiterated his plea of a year before for a naval force "to meet any eventuality that may ultimately develop." [90] He reserved his support of the appropriation committee's recommended reductions until the navy should have had enough time to analyze their program effect. Democrat Albert Thomas, another subcommittee member, went further. He attacked the proposed navy reduction for military personnel which, when combined with a $32 million miscalculation by the Budget Bureau that had recently been uncovered, threatened to lower average naval enlisted strength in FY 1948 from 425,000 to 355,000. The marine corps, moreover, would suffer losses of 1,000 officers and 11,000 enlisted men. Thomas criticized, too, the small size of the navy's research and development program. To rectify the committee's action, he offered amendments to raise naval personnel funds by $126 million and a number of other navy items by $154.5 million. But these moves were decisively defeated. Plumley's, not Thomas', views on naval spending reflected dominant House opinion: "I want to tell you [Representative Thomas] something you should bear in mind," Plumley admonished, "that this was a unanimous report of the subcommittee and a unanimous report of the Appropriations Committee. Everybody present voted for it. Now, you can kick and buck and haul as much as you want to, but you are sunk." [91]

Representative Plumley's imagery was apt. The navy was slowly sinking. In testimony before the Senate naval subcommittee Admiral T. L. Sprague, chief of naval personnel, testified that the House reductions which included a 7 per cent decrease in military pay would result, as Thomas had predicted, in a navy of 355,000 enlisted men and 42,000 officers. Revised funding estimates revealed that even if the Senate restored the Navy's original budget requests, they would provide only 395,000 enlisted men and 43,000 officers, approximately 25,000 less than the personnel totals that had been originally recommended for naval operations in FY 1948. The marine corps grudgingly accepted the House cuts in its enlisted personnel, but requested restoration of officer levels to 7,000 rather than the House-approved 6,760. The navy agreed, too, to accept a 5,793-plane naval air program, abandoning its initial projection of 6,130. Important was the fact also that $37 million was needed over the House's approved sums to cover even this scaled down operation.[92]

The hurried week-long Senate hearings made it impossible for the navy to assess the full effect of the $400 million diminution in its budget. The Senate's examination of the navy budget was correspondingly cursory and superficial. The Senate subcommittee was compelled to rely on navy estimates that were themselves hastily assembled. Fortunately for the Senators on the naval subcommittee, the navy presented two sets of figures. One set was labeled "must" appropriations and totaled $176 million; the other was considered desirable and was raised to $300 million. The Senate Appropriations Committee and the full Senate seized on the lower figure as a satisfactory compromise between the positions of the navy and the House. Except for an unsuccessful attempt by Washington Senator Warren Magnuson to increase funds for the Bureau of Ships that would spend money in Washington shipyards, the navy bill slipped through the upper house without debate and with surprisingly little interest being demonstrated in it.[93] The House conferees, satisfied that the navy would resist any further retrenchments, accepted the Senate's restorations of the navy's "must" appropriations. The final bill totaled $3.3 billion, $200 million less than the Navy Department had requested.[94]

PEACE WITHOUT POWER:
THE DISENCHANTMENT II, 1948–1950

Fall of Czechoslovakia—Korean War

III

SELF-CONTAINMENT OF CONTAINMENT

The communist coup d'état in Czechoslovakia of February, 1948, dealt a decisive blow to the major assumptions upon which American foreign policy had been erected since the closing years of World War II. For three years, the Truman administration had vainly tried to maintain the position that American and Soviet interests were basically compatible. What policy rifts existed were officially recognized as being transitory and susceptible to resolution. Patient negotiations with the Russians would eventually yield a settlement on postwar differences. Even in his call for aid to Greece and Turkey, President Truman clung tenaciously to the retreating hope of big power co-operation through the United Nations. Carefully he refrained from identifying the Soviet Union as the principal source of friction in the Mediterranean. He merely referred to sinister "foreign pressures" which were undermining the stability of the area. To the extent that it could be, the behind-the-scenes debate within the executive branch over American-Soviet relations was also kept hidden from public view.[1] It was in this connection that George Kennan, who was a key administration adviser on Soviet policy, published in 1947 his "Sources of Soviet Conduct," in *Foreign Affairs,* under the pseudonym of a "Mr. X."[2] Kennan's celebrated article sketched what was soon to be dubbed the strategy of containment to stop Soviet expansionism.

Until the fall of Czechoslovakia, the administration had publicly resisted embracing the Kennan position. Czechoslovakia's loss to the West, however, transformed the strategic debate. The President overruled the argument championed by Commerce Secretary Henry Wallace and others that greater concessions and security guarantees to the Soviet Union would pacify it. It was now assumed that the Soviet Union had long-term expansionist intentions and that additional concessions would only encourage the Soviet Union's seemingly limitless appetite for power. In a dramatic appearance before a joint session of Congress on March 17, 1948, President Truman openly charged for the first time that the Soviet Union had "not only refused to co-operate in the establishment of a just and honorable peace, but—even worse—[had] actively sought to prevent it." [3] The Soviet regime was indicted for its frustration of postwar Allied negotiations, its failure to honor its treaty agreements, its obstructionist tactics in the United Nations, and its imperialism in Eastern and Central Europe. The President censured communist pressures on Finland, Greece, and Italy, and lamented "the tragic death of the Republic of Czechoslovakia." [4] In answer to the newly developed Soviet challenge, the President, while reaffirming American support of the United Nations, recommended three courses of national action to Congress: the speedy enactment of the European Recovery Program (ERP), the acceptance of universal military training, and the temporary re-enactment of selective service legislation.[5] "The message was, and was widely assumed to be," as Walter Millis has observed, "a ringing call for a serious effort at military rearmament to meet an [international] situation that had been deteriorating alarmingly in the preceding weeks." [6]

But the administration's proposed military policies in the remaining years before the Korean War never equaled its bold pronouncements. The President's request for UMT and a renewal of the draft were, in retrospect, more like political ploys than calculated parts of a comprehensive military plan to counter Soviet aggressive moves. Revival of

72

the draft, while necessary "to maintain [the] Armed Forces at their authorized strength,"[7] would have merely brought them to the established levels of 1946. UMT did not promise more, either. For at the very moment that its statement of the military and international situation was gravest and had the most moving effect on Congress and the public to accept UMT, the administration lacked a plan for a revamped military structure into which UMT would be fitted. Even the President's request for a readoption of selective service was hurriedly formulated and was not tied to any definable budget increase.[8]

The cumulative effect of the four major appropriations bills which the administration recommended to Congress before the outbreak of the Korean hostilities—the Supplemental Appropriations Bill for FY 1948 and the military appropriations bills for FY 1949, 1950, and 1951—had the ironic effect, not of expanding, but of contracting the size and operational readiness of the military establishment. While the nation's armed forces shrank, communist pressures on the West and on the United States mounted as a result of the loss of China, the Berlin Blockade, the Soviet explosion of a nuclear device in September, 1949, and widespread communist guerrilla activities throughout Asia, including such diverse areas as French Indo-China, the Philippines, and Malaya. In his famous "Mr. X" article, Kennan had recommended that the Soviet Union be "contained by the adroit and vigilant application of counter-force at a series of constantly shifting geographical and political points, corresponding to the shifts and maneuvers of Soviet policy. . . . "[9] Some of the economic and social facets of Kennan's strategic design were realized in ERP, Point-Four,[10] and the aid program to Greece and Turkey. The same cannot be said of the military aspects of containment for the years before the Korean War. In their planning the services primarily emphasized the contingency of total war which, nevertheless, neither they nor their civilian heads believed to be very probable in light of the United States atomic capability and the prevailing assessment of Soviet intentions and capabilities. The probability of lesser conflicts between East and West were generally considered even less likely. The State Department Policy Planning Staff under George Kennan was the principal organizational dissenter from this view. Kennan's group envisaged lesser military conflicts than total war as very likely to occur. The administration and Congress never fully confronted this range of argument. The military prowess of the communist world did not negate containment as a strategic posture. The defect lay more in the budgetary and, to a slightly lesser extent, in the military doctrinal constraints which operated within the executive and legislative branches. They precluded the world-wide implementation of containment. Budget ceilings and air force strategic doctrine combined to force the Truman administration to accept an operational strategy that relied principally "upon the deterrent effect of a strategic air strike which the United States could mount if the Soviet Union invaded western Europe." [11] From a military-political point of view, containment was self-contained.

THE CHIMERA OF REMOBILIZATION: SUPPLEMENT TO FY 1948

Balanced forces vs. air force superiority.—The supplemental National Defense Appropriation Act for 1948, which the administration proposed about one month after President Truman's appearance before Congress, crystallized the terms of strategic debate in Congress until the Korean War. The strategic debate was narrowed to the interrelated questions of the economic and military feasibility of a seventy-group air force. The struggle over a seventy-group force developed a multifaceted battle among a host of forces within the legislative and executive branches, including, most prominently, James Forrestal, the nation's first secretary of defense, President Truman, the individual armed services, and a shifting array of congressmen and congressional committees. Interest group activity, particularly among aircraft manufacturers, also markedly increased.

Defense Secretary Forrestal was committed to a balanced force concept of military preparedness. The navy and, to a somewhat lesser degree, the army generally supported Forrestal's position. The President was only mildly persuaded by Forrestal's argument. He paid lip service to Forrestal's military recommendations only insofar as they did not conflict with his absorbing interest in balancing the budget which he felt required a $15 billion annual ceiling on defense expenditures. On the other hand, the civilian and military officialdom of the air force, gripped by a fervor and resolve that approached religious commitment, pressed ceaselessly for a seventy-group force. To secure this objective, the air force employed a variety of tactics. Either singly or in combination, air force officials openly defied Forrestal's balanced force proposal before Congress and in the press, challenged the President's spending directives, or recommended the further downgrading of army and navy activities. The President acted as much as an arbiter of these competing positions as a determiner of strategic policy. In this confused arena of rival interests and viewpoints, Congress added its demand for lower taxation and a clamp on military spending.

It is not surprising, therefore, that Congress' consideration of the defense budget proposals after 1948 should have been equally confused and contradictory. Majorities were hastily constructed in one year to support one military policy position, only to crumble and be refashioned to support a conflicting view a year later. Congressional majorities were formed, too, that contradicted each other within the same year and, as the FY 1948 Supplemental Appropriations Bill demonstrated, within the same piece of legislation. Whipped by contending passions—by demands for more air power and for lower taxes and governmental spending, or by clashing doctrinal persuasions, or by considerations of personal and partisan advantage—worried also by the prospect of internal economic collapse, and never fully appreciating the enlarging and diffuse nature of the communist military threat, Congress stumbled from one defense appropriations bill to another, directed only by the crudest and most rudimentary elements of a coherent strategic design. Yet its stops and starts, its desultory movements, and its meanderings were not without their effect. Like the administration, the Congress, too, contributed to the deterioration of the nation's armed force strength, including ironically enough the strategic striking power of the air force. At the onset of the North Korean attack only a dim shadow remained of the once triumphant military force of World War II.

The Forrestal–air force split over strategic policy reached a point of heightened intensity in the first half of 1948. The principal public battlegrounds were the hearings before the Senate Armed Services Committee on selective service re-enactment and the hearings in Congress (six in all) on the administration's appropriation requests for FY 1948 and FY 1949. On March 25, Forrestal told the Senate Armed Services Committee that his request for selective service legislation was tied to the policy of a "balanced strength in manpower" for the armed services.[12] He proposed personnel increases of 240,000 for the army, 63,000 for the navy, and 36,000 for the air force. An expansion in the number of men in uniform was aimed at preparing the nation to fight a full-scale war and—just as importantly—at meeting contingencies of less than total war proportions. A balanced spectrum of military capabilities was more likely, too, to prevent the development of conditions leading to open hostilities or to mitigate their adverse effect on national interests and objectives.[13]

In a later appearance before a House appropriations subcommittee, Forrestal attacked his critics who charged that he was opposed to a seventy-group air force. He did not attack its desirability. His reservations revolved more around the adverse effects that a seventy-group air force would have on the nation's over-all economic and military posture. Forrestal questioned the "extent to which a large additional program of military procurement [could] be imposed upon an already tight and fully occupied production machine without at the same time creating through certain legislative processes . . . pre-emptive . . . power, or, as an alternative, accepting the risks of explosive inflation. . . . "[14] Congress, if it wanted a seventy-group air force, would have to accept distasteful economic controls over the economy in an election year. It would also have to increase funds for the army and navy. The army and navy secretaries confirmed Forrestal's argument that an additional outlay of over $2 billion would be necessary to realize the air force's expanded program.[15] The defense secretary doubted "the wisdom of assuming that our military problems can be solved . . . by expanding the Air Force without regard to the relative requirements of the other forces."[16]

The air force launched a full-scale offensive on Capitol Hill against Forrestal's balanced force proposal. In the Senate selective service hearings, Air Force Secretary Stuart Symington pleaded again for a seventy-group air force. General Carl Spaatz, air force chief of staff, strongly supported Symington's testimony. He countered Forrestal's military personnel recommendations and proposed an increase of 102,000 men in air force strength.[17] The air force position was spelled out in greater detail in the congressional appropriation hearings. Symington contradicted Forrestal's estimate that $2 billion would be necessary to secure seventy air groups. Air force calculations placed the increase at $232 million.[18] To these economic considerations, Symington added the criticism that Forrestal's balanced force concept was at base misguided from the point of view of strategic policy. Whatever the size of the American effort, Symington contended, it would never match the ground forces of the nation's chief potential enemy, the Soviet Union. "It seems to me," Symington began,

when we talk about balance we ought to talk about the balance of our armed forces from the standpoint of the only enemy that we see might be a possible enemy.

With that premise, it seems to me we are already in trouble against 175 [Russian] divisions, and that we are in no trouble from the standpoint of the Navy, because we have the greatest Navy in the world. . . .

.   .   .   .

The only thing we do know is—and I am quoting Secretary [Averell] Harriman, who spent a lot of time in Russia—'The only thing the Russians are afraid of is a great air force' and they are building a great air force just as fast as they can.

.   .   .   .

Therefore, I think it is not a question of whether the Army should have something, because the Air Force has it, or whether the Air Force should have something because the Army has it. That is secondary to what is the best balance to handle our defense situation from the standpoint of our only enemy today.[19]

The air force position which Symington presented was given an added boost by the President's Air Policy Commission (the Finletter Commission) and the Congressional Air Policy Board headed by Senator Owen Brewster. Both bodies recommended the construction of a seventy-group air force at the earliest possible time. The nation, stated the Finletter report, "should build to this force as rapidly as possible and once it is achieved, never permit it to drop below this level."[20] There was still time to build such a force. The report predicted that no hostile power would have substantial numbers of atomic weapons in production before 1952.[21] The congressional group studying the nation's air power was equally emphatic about the need for a seventy-group force. In recommending an air force program of seventy groups, it concluded "that the capability of the United States most likely to discourage an aggressor against attack upon this Nation, most effective in thwarting such an attack if launched, and most able to deal out retaliation to paralyze further attack, is air power."[22]

Unwittingly, too, Forrestal and the President aided the air force crusade. In early April, 1948, the administration sent the FY 1948 Supplemental National Defense Appropriations Bill to Congress. In a move to gain lead time, the bill permitted the air force and the navy to let contracts for aircraft procurement before FY 1949 funds became available. Obligations that would be incurred would be technically charged to FY 1948 appropriations. The air force was to receive $1.47 billion in cash and contract authority. The navy was assigned $903 million. The $2.38 billion request included items which were parts of Forrestal's desired $3.481 billion supplemental request for FY 1948 and 1949. But the consolidation of aircraft procurement funds into a separate bill distinct from the regular appropriations requests for the military establishment accented the seventy-group issue. Forrestal had been subtly drawn into the role of stalking horse for the air force before Congress.

Congress turns to air power.—Although each protagonist in the strategic debate in the executive branch—Forrestal, the President, and the armed services—found ready advocates in Congress, the strongest and most persuasive congressional forces were enlisted in the ranks of the air force. The two major exceptions were John Taber and Walter Andrews, the respective chairmen of the House Appropriations and Armed Services committees. Taber had confided to Forrestal that he "was highly critical of the Air Force presentation of figures and of their overstatement." [23] Andrews registered his dissent from the air force during the debate on the supplemental bill when he attempted, unsuccessfully, to marshal support for Forestal's balanced force concept.[24] He faced stiff opposition from his own committee. Representative Carl Vinson, ranking minority member of the Armed Services Committee, raised the ominous specter of a mass Russian Army of 175 divisions overwhelming a numerically inferior American armed force. Air power was the great equalizer. "In the air [the United States is] capable of competing with the Russians—and they are capable of competing with us. Preponderance of air power is in the balance. It is this element in which the decisive struggle is likely to take place. . . . " [25] Other legislators joined the seventy-group chorus. Some emphasized the findings of the Congressional Air Policy Board and the Finletter Commission or voiced worry over the future possibility of Russian possession of the atomic bomb. Going further, some legislators looked upon the air force as a kind of super-law enforcement

79

agency, a supranational police force. The air force, asserted one congressman, would play a prominent role in leading "the world vigilantes in the direction of international law that will bring reorganization and bring the power that will stabilize the world into some system of law." [26]

In the face of concerted House pressures, Taber reluctantly offered an amendment to increase air force appropriations by $822 million. Complained Taber: "I believe that the best airplanes will be procured after a detailed hearing on the part of the Committee on Appropriations as to the needs of the service. But that seems impossible with the present feeling in the House." [27] The sum that Taber proposed was $100 million below the amount originally requested by the air force for its seventy-group project, but it was accepted with little grumbling. A unanimous vote of 115 to 0 underlined the House's support for the amendment. The final bill passed by a lopsided 343 to 3 vote.[28] The Senate concurred a short time later.[29]

There is little indication that a majority in Congress understood the doctrinal and budgetary implications of its vote for a seventy-group air force. Air power would be decidedly useful in a war with the Soviet Union. But would a larger air force prevent such a war? How, too, would the United States respond to a less than full-scale Soviet attack against Europe or the American continent? How would it stem increased communist pressures by non-Russian military forces? What use would strategic air power be in the jungles of the Philippines and Malaya? These difficult questions were neglected in Congress' deliberations on the supplemental bill. The focus was almost exclusively on long-range air power. The broader aspects of America's strategic problems were obscured. Representative John Rankin's remarks during the House debate on aircraft procurement for the air force embody the deep contradictions and startling strategic myopia which characterized much of the air power debates:

This movement to increase our Air Force is to me the most encouraging step that has yet been taken on this floor. We have reached the time when our Air Force is the first line of defense. The next war will be an atomic conflict. It will be fought with airplanes and atomic bombs. *It may mark the end of our civilization. I shall vote for the top amount offered here [of $822 million].*[30]

The airplane procurement bill had dramatized the growing possibility of total war with Russia. Conjured up in the congressional debates were horrible visions of Russian sneak attacks, of atomic bombings, of armed hordes of half-civilized Russian soldiers sweeping over a numerically weaker West. The answer to the Soviet menace seemed simple: a large strategic air force equipped with atomic weapons. Said one representative: "Machines, not men [will] win the next war."[31] One grand gesture—an increase of $822 million in the air force budget—would resolve the nation's security problems.

The budgetary gesture may have been grand in form, but it was something considerably less in substantive effect. Taber had cleverly inserted what Defense Secretary Forrestal later called a "hooker" into the supplemental bill. The act authorized the President to spend the added air force fund only after he had made a finding as to its "necessity." It also extended the time over which the $822 million could be spent. Since the President opposed the air force increase, Taber's "hookers" in effect nullified any significant stepup in air force strength.[32]

REACTION AND COMPLACENCY: FY 1949

Army and air force presentations.—Congress' examination of the regular FY 1949 military estimates sharply contrasted with its intense debates over the $822 million increase in air force appropriations.

Like a second-run film, the appropriations melodrama of the previous year was replayed. A vigorous, economy-minded House, led by Representatives Engel and Plumley, made large cuts in the military budget estimates for the army and air force; a sympathetic, but time-pressed Senate, hastily repaired what damage it could in a few days of improvised hearings on the House bill; and finally a compromise was struck between the House and Senate which would again sap even more strength from the nation's armed forces. In a letter to General George Marshall, Forrestal suggested the altered attitude on Capitol Hill and in the nation. He was worried that a temporary slackening of tension with the Soviet Union had combined "with the political stresses of an election year . . . to produce a dangerous complacency on the part of certain elements in the country." [33]

Congress reviewed a revised FY 1949 budget request in the aftermath of the President's March 17 address. Army and air force average man-year strengths were to expand by 135,000 and 54,000 respectively. Table 1 summarizes the differences between the initial and the supplemental personnel increases which grew out of Forrestal's $3.481 billion partial rearmament program. The army would be gradually expanded to 790,000. These increases would aid in overcoming army shortages which, according to the testimony of General Lawton

TABLE 1*

MILITARY PERSONNEL, FISCAL YEAR 1949, AVERAGE STRENGTH
(MAN-YEARS) FOR THE ARMY AND THE AIR FORCE

	Regular Estimate	Supplemental	Man-Years Increase
Air Force	362,290	416,084	53,794
Army	560,000	695,200	135,200
Grand Total	922,290	1,111,284	188,994

* Source: HSAC, *Hearings, Military Functions, National Military Establishment Appropriations Bill for 1949*, 80/2, 1948, Part 3, p. 1316.

Collins, included 24,000 in Europe, 57,000 in the Far East, and 51,000 in the United States.[34] A modest $157 million was also included in the army's requests for modernization.[35]

The air force, having scored what appeared to be a significant victory over the secretary of defense, the Budget Bureau, and the President in the supplemental appropriations bill for FY 1948, pressed to solidify its gains. It forced Forrestal in the FY 1949 bill to accept a sixty-six–group operating force. Forrestal reluctantly agreed to the addition of eleven air groups over the fifty-five–group force of FY 1948 only because the expansion would be achieved by taking wartime B-29's out of storage. The air force accepted the sixty-six–group compromise although it fell short of its seventy-group objective. The remaining four groups which were involved were basically tactical forces for ground troop support, an area of secondary importance for the air force. To operate the sixty-six–group air force, the average strength was estimated to climb by almost 54,000 average man-years. Terminal strength was set at 444,500.[36]

Economy wave sweeps Congress.—The House Appropriations Committee approached the military budget skeptically. Almost $650 million was cut from the $7.2 billion requested by the army and air force. The army sustained the largest cut of $615 million.[37] The committee, while disclaiming any intention to reduce the size or effectiveness of the army, noted that it was "the habit of the services to estimate their fund requirements generously in order that they may be able to meet all contingencies." [38] Reminiscent of Representative Plumley's attitude toward the navy budget of the year before, the report tendered by Representative Engel to the House observed that a policy of meeting all contingencies was only

> a sound policy to follow during actual warfare. . . . There is no sound reason why the Army cannot be administered during peacetime with more regard for dollars than apparently is the custom or intent [of the Army]. The reductions imposed by the

committee are for the purpose of bringing the funds provided into budgetary relationship to services to be paid for and supplies and equipment to be purchased. If emergencies requiring additional funds arise the Congress will be in session in ample time to make provisions therefor.[39]

If the budget was inflated by assumption, Congress' major—its almost exclusive—duty was "to let the air out." Although no one could gainsay that the appropriations committee should strip unnecessary items from the defense budget, its preoccupation with this task deflected its attention from the important question of whether the army was strong enough to uphold the nation's diplomatic position. The committee report made no mention of the fall of Czechoslovakia— the spark that had ignited the rearmament drive; of communist encroachments in the Balkans; or of the weak United States military posture in the Far East. Passed over, too, was General Hodge's ominous report from Korea which warned that the "dangerously low troop strength" of his command was "a definite political liability" and that his present strength was "well below a safe level for the performance of [its] mission."[40] At a minimum it would have appeared reasonable to expect the committee to justify its recommendations to the House by some reference to the international scene. The committee brushed aside its potential critics with the crisp observation that the military services padded their budgets to meet all contingencies.

But what contingencies would the military budget meet; and if an emergency struck, would the Congress have enough time to assemble to provide needed funds and authority to the armed services? The nation may not have been at war, but it certainly was not at peace with the communist world. There was no easy way to know when, where, or in what proportion a military or political crisis might explode in the world. In such situations legislative fiat would hardly be a substitute for trained and organized military forces. The problem would only be heightened in the case of war. No amount of swift legislative mobilization would stem a communist military strike against American interests. On the other hand, adequately trained and equipped forces in being might preclude a military conflict in the first instance or mitigate its adverse effects once it had erupted.

Notwithstanding the committee's protest that it did "not propose to reduce the size of the Army below numbers estimated by the military authorities as requisite or the amount of equipment and supplies necessary to maintain such an Army," [41] its reductions pointed in this direction. The army was prepared to accept only about $100 million of the House cuts in its reclama request to the Senate. Some 70,000 civilian employees were to be dropped from the army's rolls. Army Secretary Kenneth Royall testified that two of the army's planned eighteen divisions would not be ready to fight if war came in the next year. Many units, including some in the air force, would lack adequate weapons and material support. Specifically eliminated were funds for rifle ammunition, assorted air force rockets, 142 light tanks, and 133 armored utility vehicles.[42]

A harassed Senate, meeting a scant two days, hurriedly processed the military budget. On the advice of the military services, it hastily restored $330 million to the House bill. This was about half of the amount that the House had reduced. The House conferees generally accepted the Senate version, and the army and air force received an appropriation bill of $6.7 billion, about $500 million less than the administration had recommended. The air force, however, received most of its requested $1.2 billion.[43]

The navy's rearmament program.—The navy was slated to share in Forrestal's rearmament scheme. Its flush-deck carrier, the "United States," was the most significant feature of its expansion program. When completed, the "United States" would be the largest of its class. "I cannot tell you," said Navy Secretary John Sullivan, "how very, very important everyone in the Navy feels that this [carrier]

85

is."[44] Chief of Naval Operations Louis Denfeld affirmed the importance of the carrier to the navy's view of its strategic role. "The fleet which we maintain today," said Denfeld, "is essentially an air striking force. . . . A surface-to-surface battle is not much in our thoughts these days, and we are left free to concentrate on surface-to-air . . . probabilities. . . . "[45] Total cost of the anticipated carrier was initially estimated at $124 million, requiring two years to complete. The navy felt so strongly about its carrier program that it was prepared to stretch out or cancel construction of thirteen other partially completed vessels to make $307 million available for the "United States."[46]

To round out the navy's limited expansion, total operating aircraft was to grow to 10,713. Average strength during FY 1949 would be around 9,000 aircraft, a significant increase over FY 1948. Cost was stated at $617 million, which the navy considered a down payment on its projected 14,500-plane goal.[47] Personnel strength was set at 460,000, composed of 410,000 enlisted and 50,000 officers.[48] The marine corps was stabilized at a little over 91,000.[49] Cost of the navy program topped $3.9 billion.[50]

The naval subcommittee held long hearings on the navy bill. Under Representative Plumley's direction the subcommittee again steered clear of hazardous military-political issues.[51] The appropriations committee's report which Plumley submitted to the House epitomized his subcommittee's narrow budgetary concern. The report compared navy expenditures and appropriations between 1947 and 1949. The committee presented a table which showed that in 1947 the actual cost of the navy exceeded appropriations by $1.9 billion; in 1948 the excess cost over appropriations was $1.2 billion; and it was estimated that in 1949 the excess would be $1.3 billion. "This is a matter of grave concern," noted the committee report, "which the Congress should be prepared to consider in the near future."

> We must have in mind the question of whether we are going to continue even larger appropriations to maintain the same size

Navy, or whether we can safely maintain our place in the world with a smaller one. It is to be hoped that the world situation will soon stabilize so that we will have a better idea as to the exact future requirements.[52]

The issue of America's precise responsibility to stabilize world conditions was not raised, nor was an inquiry conducted to determine the kind of naval power which would be required to produce an ordered state of international relations.

The House overwhelmingly approved the appropriations committee's naval bill. Representative Carl Hinshaw, member of the Armed Services Committee and the chairman of the Combat Aviation Subcommittee of the Congressional Aviation Policy Board, raised the only important dissent. He questioned the cost of the carrier program which required a considerable number of supporting ships to make it operational. He wondered, too, about its military usefulness. The carrier could handle only a small number of strategic-type aircraft of limited range. It was vulnerable to attack and sinking. There was doubt whether airplanes that were launched from its decks during combat would be able to return to it.[53] Hinshaw proposed that before Congress adopt the carrier program, it should be submitted to a board "of relatively disinterested persons for a decision as to whether or not it was a thing that was feasible before the construction was entered upon."[54] Although nothing came of Hinshaw's remarks, they were an augur of the looming rift between the navy and air force over United States military strategic policy. Hinshaw had in effect fired the first shots of a strategic debate that would culminate in the B-36 hearings of the House Armed Services Committee and the "Admirals' Revolt" of 1949.

The Senate naval subcommittee was handicapped in its review of the navy bill in much the same way that its counterpart had been in its examination of the army and air force requests. Only two days were assigned to the Senate hearings.[55] There was no time to study either the budgetary or the economic or the foreign policy implications of the navy's proposed expenditure program. Nor was there enough time to weigh the virtue of the House's more deliberative action. The Senate Appropriations Committee accepted about $125 million of the navy's $191 million reclama requests.[56] Over the mild protests of Senator Tobey, who balked at increasing the House version of the navy bill, the Senate concurred in its committee's recommendation without protest. A House-Senate Conference Committee finally agreed to a $3.75 billion appropriation for the navy, a sum which was closer to the House's initial determination.

Despite the reductions in the appropriations bills of the armed services for FY 1949, the larger implication of Congress' action was that it had lent some political support to a partial rearmament program. Unfortunately, its support would be temporary, for its enthusiasm for rearmament was based on shaky grounds. It was too narrowly focused on air power. Congress could not be persuaded that forces in being of all types were needed as a check against a variety of conceivable communist military actions against United States interests. While Forrestal had succeeded in convincing Congress that more arms and a re-enactment of selective service were needed in the wake of the March crisis, he had failed badly to harness congressional political support for his balanced force concept. As the battle over the FY 1950 budget would make clear, more arms tended to be equated with more air force striking power. Even where air power was at issue, Congress' willingness to underwrite a seventy-group program was suspect. Taber's "hookers" cast doubt on the constancy of Congress' commitment to an expanded air force. The next two years would witness a congressional reversal of policy on air power. Congress would increase air force funds sizably in FY 1950 only to withdraw its political succor in FY 1951. Its attention to and concern for the evolving military factors of the cold war shifted unpredictably from year to year. Domestic politics was also having an adverse influence. In 1948, in the midst of a bitterly contested presidential election, congressional thoughts turned instinctively to problems of partisan conflict and personal political campaigns for re-election. Domestic economic issues loomed larger on the political horizon. There was, too, a brief relaxation of Soviet pressures on the United States. All of these elements had a depressing effect on congressional interest in military and strategic problems, an interest that had never been strong and sustained.

The budgetary schizophrenia displayed in Congress was no less apparent in the executive branch. President Truman had agreed to Forrestal's $3.481 billion supplement (which the Budget Bureau actually slashed to $3.1 billion), but he "was willing to submit this supplemental on one condition—that the Armed Forces did not spend it!" [57] "Specifically the President's condition," Forrestal wrote, "was that administratively we do not, in the next eight months, create a military structure which would require in excess of approximately $15 billion for the next fiscal year [1950]." [58] And even if Taber had not inserted his "hooker," the President was ready to announce that the $822 million would not be spent to speed the air force toward its desired seventy groups. An executive directive published in the middle of FY 1949 instructed the three services to hold their expansion programs within such limits that the proposed fiscal 1950 budget would not exceed $15 billion. No sooner had rearmament begun than a retrenchment policy was instituted. Gains of approximately 170,000 men in uniform during FY 1949 were to be temporary. At the outbreak of the Korean War, the United States would find itself at about the level it had reached before Forrestal's rearmament program had been tentatively initiated.

MILITARY RECESSION: FY 1950 [59]

Unification through budgetary determination.—In his budget message to Congress in 1949 President Truman optimistically noted that "the recommendations for the National Military Establishment for the fiscal year 1950 mark a beginning toward a national defense program in which our air, naval, and land forces plan and operate as a team under a unified strategic concept." [60] The observation was misleading. Nothing of the sort had occurred. There was of course new decision-making machinery through which unified strategic planning, programming, and budgeting could be effected. The National Security Act of 1947 had created a secretary of defense with authority to "exercise general direction, authority, and control over" the military departments, a Joint Chiefs of Staff, a Central Intelligence Agency, and a National Security Council—all of which were to bring cohesion and unified direction to the military establishment. The budgetary process was tightened also. The FY 1950 budget marked the first time that the annual appropriation estimates of the armed services were considered as a whole by the Joint Chiefs of Staff and the secretary of defense and presented to Congress in a single bill.

These organizational mechanisms by themselves were unable to bridge the yawning gaps between the secretary of defense, the military services, and the President over the question of the size and composition of the military budget or to settle the enlarging differences over strategic doctrine that were brewing within the newly formed Defense Department, particularly between the air force and navy. The House Appropriations Committee report on the FY 1950 budget came closer to the truth. "It would be pleasant," said the report,

> if . . . the Congress could be assured that the numerous problems of unification had been solved. Such is not the case. . . . A radical readjustment of the thinking of the military is required and while the strong currents of dissension and controversy are not defended, they are easily understandable. . . . The problems are many . . . but [the military] establishment . . . should find it possible to perfect its own unification. The nation will expect no less. The interests of economy, efficiency, and security demand it. The foremost thought in the minds of the members of the committee is to provide through this appropriation a bal-

anced military force sufficient to keep the peace and within the range of the financial capacity of the taxpayer.[61]

The President was no less concerned with the financial capacity and political willingness of the citizen to pay more taxes. In the midst of the crisis over Czechoslovakia, he had set a ceiling of $15 billion on defense spending for FY 1950, a step designed to curb inflationary pressures in the economy. The President could have asked for increased taxes or economic controls to cope with inflation, but he was convinced that these courses were not economically or politically feasible. The consensus in Congress had also settled on a $15 billion ceiling. The President felt that the administration would incur serious political disfavor if it pressed for greater military expenditures. Budgetary ceilings were, therefore, laid down, although the nation could have certainly afforded more money for defense. Military requirements were cast in the confining economic and budgetary molds fashioned by the chief executive. The military services were unified less by a common set of strategic concepts than by the shared experience of having had to shape their respective budgets to conform to the President's spending ceiling. Unity achieved on these Draconian terms would necessarily be superficial and short-lived. Strategic policy-making within the executive branch was essentially reduced to a mean and bitter struggle among the individual services for as large a share as possible of the President's $15 billion allowable expenditure total.

The JCS originally submitted a $30 billion budget to the secretary of defense for FY 1950. It was based upon the unilateral plans and statements of requirements of the individual services. At Forrestal's behest, the JCS established a three-man board, composed of the highest ranking budget officers of the three services, to pare the budget. The McNarney Board arrived at a $23.6 billion figure. Forrestal pressed his Chiefs further. He wanted them to spell out the military implications of the President's $15 billion budget limit in terms of the over-all capacity of the services to meet various military situations. As Millis observes, Forrestal wanted

> . . . simply to bring out the absurdity to which the presidential ceiling led . . . in functional terms. Only so could they [the Joint Chiefs] provide him with anything with which to argue against the Budget Bureau. On the $15 billion limit they could 'certainly' mount an air offensive from Britain; but that was all they could do, and in that case all the rest of the Military Establishment became useless. The result was an obvious absurdity—unless, as Gruenther [Forrestal's informal aide] added, 'you are willing to gamble on that the air offensive—that it will bring the end of the war.' [62]

But the military chiefs rebuffed Forrestal's entreaties.

Acting on his own, Forrestal whittled the JCS's recommendation to $16.9 billion and suggested that the President raise his budget ceiling slightly to accommodate this higher sum. The President refused, holding firmly to his demand that an appropriation bill be hammered out that would not lead to defense expenditures beyond $15 billion. The President fixed a $14.2 billion limit on new military obligational authority which included a contingent item of $830 million that was earmarked for UMT if the Congress would finally implement it.[63] An appropriation request of this size would hold defense spending to the President's determination.

In his appearance before the House Armed Services Appropriations Subcommittee, Forrestal defended President Truman's spending ceiling before a sympathetic Congress which was already "'shocked and disturbed' by the 'tremendous' sums involved." [64] He kept silent about his attempts to free the Defense Department from the chief executive's budgetary strait jacket. Forrestal said that his department recognized "the clear necessity imposed upon the President to formulate a comprehensive plan for the Government as a whole, and for the National Military Establishment as one segment thereof." [65] The $30 billion budget of the jcs was based on purely military considerations. "It was a statement of what [the nation] would need if [it] were going to war, but it was not in any sense a request for funds." [66]

Forrestal further pointed out that the budget presented to Congress was "designed to maintain a military posture for the preservation of peace. It was not a war budget." [67] It would sustain an armed force of 1,616,000 during FY 1950. The army would receive 667,000 men, the largest share; the navy, 527,000, including the marine corps; and the air force, 412,000.[68] This force represented the approximate level of uniformed personnel in the armed services at the beginning of the fiscal year. The personnel expansion program that had been announced in the spring of 1948 was quietly abandoned. What is more, congressional cuts, together with subsequent presidential directives, reduced this force further to 1,460,000 by the outbreak of the Korean War. The FY 1950 military budget, while ostensibly a peace budget, would be unable to keep the peace.

The services present their requirements.—Still ignoring Forrestal, the air force restated its opposition to the defense secretary's balanced force concept. To be sure, much of the sting of the air force's previous attack on the administration was absent from its presentations to Congress. Forrestal and Truman had at least temporarily squelched open service challenge to their policy directives before Congress. General Hoyt Vandenberg, air force chief of staff, confined himself to the oblique criticism that a $15 billion defense budget could adequately prepare the United States militarily provided that the air force would be granted the lion's share of the military budget.[69]

The army, perplexedly, went along with the air force's assessment of strategic policy, although it stood to gain most from Forrestal's countervailing view. Army strategists concentrated on the possibility of a third world war. Other forms of military conflict were discounted or minimized. With the prospect of global military struggle uppermost in its thinking, the army voluntarily subordinated its position to that of the air force. Central to the argument of both services was the need for an immediate launching, as Army Chief of Staff Omar Bradley stated, of a "strong retaliatory blow [in the wake of an enemy strike against the United States] aimed at the crippling of the enemy's industry, national prestige, and morale." [70] The remaining two phases of the war would be fought in classic World War II terms, but on an even grander scale. The army would be the protagonist during the later phases of the war and would be responsible for bringing the war to its climax and successful denouement. The army was almost hopelessly captive to air force doctrine, a situation occasioned by the air force's persuasive and confident statement of its position and by the army's continued distraction by its occupation duties. The army's commitment to air force strategy, even a revised strategy that sketched a broad army responsibility for the latter phases of a general war, had the inevitable effect of undermining the validity of the army's initially large personnel and material requests. The air force would gain time for army mobilization. A ready force in being was not needed. If the budget was tight and total war was the likely military contingency facing the United States, first priority would have to go to air power. Even if the army was unable to grasp this logic, the administration and Congress had no trouble in doing so.

The army and air force agreed, too, on the scope of the navy's responsibilities in any future world-wide conflict. The navy was cast in the unglamorous role of providing logistic support for its sister services. [71] This view bore no resemblance to the navy's image of itself. With one eye on the air force, Admiral Louis Denfeld, chief of naval operations, warned against placing the nation's "entire reliance on the success of any one plan or weapon to the exclusion of providing means to carry on the war in case that one plan or weapon is less decisive than hoped for." [72] What would prove decisive? A strategic-striking air force was not enough. A powerful, nuclear-strike navy was also needed, a navy strong enough to "launch a swift and powerful counterblow . . . to destroy the enemy's capacity to mount and sustain offensive operations." [73] Naval air power was the key. Because it would be widely deployed and mobile, Denfeld argued, it could strike at any part of the world. It could also subtly discriminate among targets—what air force power was not completely equipped to do—and, consequently, could limit both the geographical area and duration of a war. "For these reasons," Denfeld observed, "naval power, and in particular naval air power, can make, and will make, an indispensable contribution toward that initial stemming and containment of the enemy upon which so much depends." [74] It was wrong to weigh the nation's air strength solely in air force strength. Affirmed Denfeld: "There is a tendency . . . to reckon this country's air power in terms of the air force alone; actually this country's air strength is the total strength of air force . . . and naval air power and each . . . contributes substantially to the effectiveness of the other." [75] The navy's air arm complemented—it did not compete with—the air force.

While the navy also focused on the possibility of a third world war, it differed radically from the air force–army conception of its mission in such a struggle and in its vision of what would be the probable scope, intensity, and character of future global military operations. But so long as the navy was allowed to build its super carrier, these differences in outlook and strategy were allowed to remain hidden. The cancellation of the super carrier program would force these conflicting points of view to the surface. Each of the services was approaching a breaking point where any additional budgetary restrictions would threaten its very survival as a viable military instrument. The air force in 1948 felt that it had already dangerously approached this point and would feel so again. The navy was also on the verge of a break with the political officialdom of the executive branch. The break would come soon, with considerably more divisive effect than any previous break in service ranks.

A premonition of developing strife among the services over strategic policy was dimly sketched in their force levels requests to Congress for FY 1950. Each service chaffed under the President's budgetary restrictions. Each was compelled to submit personnel, procurement, and operational estimates that were half as much as each actually desired. In every case, wide gaps appeared between the grand strategic thinking of the services and the hardware and manpower requests that each was allowed to present to Congress.

The disparity was most apparent in the army's justifications. It had projected a 900,000 force in 1948 at the initiation of Forrestal's rearmament drive. To build toward this goal, an army of 790,000 men was to be reached by the end of FY 1949. This goal was reversed downward when the Budget Bureau apportioned $62 million less to the army than it had expected. Congress further hampered army expansion with its own $82 million cut for FY 1949.[76] Hope of raising the army to the 900,000 figure was finally squashed by an executive order which directed the army to hold its military personnel to levels that would conform to a force of 677,000 men at the end of FY 1950.[77] Dutifully, the army complied with these constraints which included, additionally, a minimal authorization to request $246 million for new procurement. The bulk of the army's buying program was keyed, not surprisingly, to its antiaircraft mission. The army was preparing to meet an enemy aerial assault against the United States.

The air force was equally unsuccessful in its drive toward its announced objective of seventy groups and a personnel end-strength of 44,500. The Truman administration allowed the air force a forty-eight–group force to be supported by 412,000 men at the end of FY 1950.[78] In addition, new procurement was placed at 1,668 new aircraft. Air force officials complained that this number would modernize only forty of its forty-eight groups. More money would be needed to make up the difference and advance to the sacrosanct seventy-group force.[79]

The navy's new obligational requests were down by about six hundred million dollars when compared with FY 1949. The navy presented its request largely in terms of the adverse effect of the

President's reductions on its planning and operations. The navy's tack became so confusing to the House appropriations subcommittee that Chairman George Mahon stopped Admiral A. M. Price, chief of the Bureau of Aeronautics, and pointedly asked him whether he had come to defend the budget or to bury it.[80] The navy's frustration was embalmed in the shrunken budgetary figures that it offered to Congress. All of its principal appropriation requests were lowered by the administration. Naval personnel was scheduled to decline to a fiscal year-end strength of a little more than four hundred thousand, approximately fifty thousand below the estimates of FY 1949. The marine corps was to lose about ten thousand of its personnel and to drop below eighty thousand. Rollbacks were ordered in shipbuilding and airplane procurement. The navy had to pledge another $57 million to protect its flush-deck carrier program at the expense of other ship construction.[81] New aircraft procurement was set at a startlingly low level of 843 planes. The navy projected an 846-plane deficit in first-line operating aircraft which would have to be met through utilization of obsolescent equipment.[82] Total operating aircraft available was cut to 7,783 for FY 1950, nearly three thousand planes below the preceding fiscal year.[83]

Congress turns to the defense bill.—For the first time in the history of the appropriations committee, only one subcommittee was assigned the task of reviewing the military budget of all the services. The five-man subcommittee on armed service appropriations, headed by George Mahon, handled the entire complex military appropriations bill. Under Mahon's direction, the subcommittee, while still largely occupied with the detailed estimates of the services, demonstrated for the first time since the 1946 navy hearings a glimmer of interest in the military and foreign policy considerations underlying the defense budget. The subcommittee made an effort, where little had been made before, to determine how the military budget had been adopted and to explore the strategic reasoning guiding its development. There was some vocalized feeling among committee members that the sub-committee could not rationally approve the President's budget unless it was clearly apprised of the different steps by which the military budget had been formulated. All three services were asked to describe how their part of the Defense Department budget had been adopted and the military considerations guiding its formulation.[84]

Carl Vinson, chairman of the House Armed Services Committee, was also invited to present his views. Vinson rejected the President's budget as the sole standard of the nation's defense needs. He contrasted the jcs's budget recommendations which were allegedly "exclusively military in nature" and the President's defense proposals which he suggested were "compounded of a number of *extra* military considerations." [85] Vinson recommended a $16.9 billion budget which approximated the initial representation of the jcs to Forrestal. The army would have been expanded to slightly more than seven hundred thousand; and its procurement program for antiaircraft equipment, doubled. The navy was to grow to a force of 555,000; 50,000 more than the President had envisaged. Vinson found "nothing in the international situation to indicate that so severe a reduction in the strength of the army and navy [as the President had proposed was] . . . warranted." [86] The air force was to receive $800 million more to aid its quest for the illusive seventy-group force.

Unfortunately neither Vinson nor the appropriations subcommittee sustained their seemingly new departure in Congress' analysis of the defense budget. Vinson did not justify his $16.9 billion budget in concrete military or political terms. By and large he relied on such vague phrases as "the international situation," or he appealed to the authority of the jcs to which, as he emphasized, the Congress "must look, and to whom the President must look, for the most authoritative advice on our national defense requirements." [87] Vinson did not specify the contingencies which would be met by an added $800 million expenditure for the air force. He largely overlooked the differences between his and the President's budget in terms of the army's capacity to discharge its anticipated duties in the second and third phases of a general conflict with the Soviet Union—if, indeed, that was the principal problem facing the United States. He simply accepted the JCS opinion that it needed $16.9 billion. He might well have asked what the services could have done with the $30 billion that they had originally advanced or the $23.6 billion that the McNarney Board had agreed upon.[88] But, to Vinson's credit, he publicly aired what most of his congressional colleagues and the President were neglecting: that the rationale underlying Forrestal's partial rearmament program had not been overtaken by any diminution of the external threat to the United States. Vinson's principal shortcoming was more his failure to articulate this point adequately than his inability to sense the possible military implications of a progressively hostile and uncertain international environment.

The Mahon subcommittee hearings were as disappointing as Vinson's testimony. Despite its auspicious beginning, the subcommittee quickly turned to its established approach to the military budget. The President's budgetary ceiling was adopted as the major premise of the hearings. Convinced that a higher military spending level than $15 billion would bankrupt the nation, the subcommittee searched for itemized economies in the military estimates. As one acute observer correctly notes, the subcommittee did not "secure, first, information about the kinds of military problems the services were likely to confront, and, second, information about the consequences for their ability to meet those problems if this, that, or some other sum of money was made available."[89] This information was needed if the subcommittee were to judge the merit of the President's defense budget or to suggest alternatives to it. It had to reach some determination on the likely impact that an increase, decrease, or a shift in spending priorities of the FY 1950 military budget might have on the behavior of potential enemies and on the nation's prospects in achieving its foreign policy objectives. These questions, unhappily, were glossed over.

99

In its report, the House subcommittee asked the House to cut $123 million from the army's budget. The subcommittee's attitude toward the army was clearly, albeit painfully, expressed in the opening sentence of its presentations to the full House. "The Army," remarked the unanimously agreed upon report, "does not have a spectacular role in the National Military Establishment, but this fact in no way diminishes the importance of the Army to our national security." [90] The afterthought on the army's importance was hardly consoling to army officials. The subcommittee's cuts did not erode the personnel level determined by the administration. Procurement and ordnance activities were principally affected. The navy received all but $33 million of its requests. The subcommittee raised no criticisms or questions about the administration's plan to shrink army, navy, and marine corps strength or naval airplane procurement and operations.

The air force received considerably more favorable though not more enlightened assistance from the House group. Actively led by Mahon, the subcommittee recommended an $800 million increase in air force funds. The added spending power was keyed to an air force of fifty-eight groups. Personnel was to rise, too, to an average of 440,000 during the fiscal year. Curiously, the subcommittee made no effort to justify its extraordinary action on military grounds. That was left to the House debates. It accepted the seventy-group concept as an obvious defense necessity and one which, from the viewpoint of domestic affairs, would be economically and politically feasible. It was the intent "of the [appropriations] committee to provide the air force with the means to maintain a steady program, one that the Congress and the country can and will consistently support." [91]

Mahon summarized his subcommittee's report to the full House.[92] He stressed that bombers carrying atomic devices could strike any nation that might attack the United States. That awesome power of devastating retaliation would serve as the most effective deterrent to war. "There would have been no Pearl Harbor in 1941," reasoned Mahon, in justifying higher spending authority for the air force, if we had been prepared to strike a quick and deadly blow at the vitals of Japan and Germany. We greatly diminish the likelihood of world war III when we prepare ourselves to strike a quick and deadly blow at the very heart of the potential enemy. * * * The only force under heaven that can now deliver the quick and devastating blow is the United States Air Force. So I say without hesitation that our first line of defense is the Air Force.[93]

Mahon was essentially agreeing with what implicitly had become the administration's military strategy. He and a majority of the Congress differed not so much on the validity of that strategic posture as on the administration's execution of it. If air power was to be the nation's answer to growing Russian power, then it followed that the air force should be given the wherewithal that it insisted was needed to discharge its projected mission in a total war. The President simply had not gone far enough. It was Congress' responsibility to seize the initiative and provide the necessary funds.

The appropriations committee's generosity was more apparent than real. The House debates revealed what the committee report left silent, namely, that the $800 million given to the air force had been earmarked as a contingent item in the defense budget for UMT. At the moment when the committee was granting the air force increased funds, it was in effect applying the coup de grâce to the President's $830 million to UMT. The committee did not openly state that this was the upshot of its action. Nor did it indicate precisely the reasoning which had led it to increase air force appropriations. The defense subcommittee hearings did not identify the distinguishing features of the administration-sponsored forty-eight air force groups for FY 1950; the air force's March, 1949, suggestion that fifty-seven groups be operated in FY 1950; the committee's recommended fifty-eight–group force; or the longer range seventy-group plan. Representative Robert Sikes' attempt to indicate these differences did not prove suc-

101

cessful. An actual comparison has to be fitted together from a number of disparate sources which were not specifically brought together by the House military appropriations subcommittee. Table 2 compares these differences.

TABLE 2*

COMPARISON OF AIR FORCE GROUPS AT 48-, 57-, 58-, AND 70-GROUP LEVELS

| GROUPS | STRATEGIC BOMBER | | LIGHT BOMBER | RECONNAIS- SANCE | TACTICAL FIGHTER | TROOP CARRIER |
	Heavy	Medium				
48	4	10	1	7	20	6
57	4	14	2	7	23	7
58	4	14	2	7	24	7
70	4	16	5	10	25	10

* Source: Table 2 is drawn from the following: HSAC, *Hearings* Military Establishment Appropriations Bill, FY 1950, 81/1, 1949. *passim.*; H. Rept. 417, 81/1, 1949, pp. 30–31; and Warner Schilling (ed.), *Strategy, Politics, and Defense Budgets* (New York: Columbia University Press, 1962), pp. 74–79, including citations which are noted therein.

So far as strategic bomber groups are concerned, there is a difference of only six groups between the forty-eight and seventy-group–programs and four between the forty-eight–group proposal and the remaining force level plateaus. Heavy bomber groups remained the same in each instance. Actual strategic bomber procurement at the forty-eight–, fifty-seven–, and fifty-eight–group figures would have been approximately the same. In no instance was there any plan to procure more B-36 bombers, the air force's principal strategic delivery weapon. The four medium bomber groups which would have been added in the fifty-seven–group and fifty-eight–group recommendations would have primarily been an organizational and not operational change. Large-scale bomber procurement was not contemplated. Additional air force appropriations were to be largely allocated for tactical and troop support aircraft. A budget officer explained that the decision to spend increased grants on these smaller aircraft had been taken because the air force had already "augmented [its] bomber program and [its] strategic striking force to the extent possible in the production schedules. . . . "[94] Air Force Secretary Stuart Symington confirmed this testimony.[95]

The appropriations committee report avoided any clear-cut appraisal of what an added $800 million would buy for the air force and why the purchase was necessary on strategic grounds. The committee's fifty-eight–group proposal would have added only one *tactical* fighter group to the air force's fifty-seven–group suggestion. The "20 bombardment groups" which the House report noted, while equaling the number envisaged in the seventy-group concept, actually included two light bomber groups designed to assist ground troops. Consequently, the additional sums recommended by the appropriations committee and supported in such ringing words by Mahon in terms of their application to strategic bombing would purchase very little actual strategic capability. That most members of Congress were similarly, if not even more, confused about the implications of the $800 million increase is indicated in the remarks of Representative Clarence Cannon, chairman of the appropriations committee, during the debates on the military appropriations bill. In criticizing the navy's carrier program Cannon argued that the House should put "money in the only place that counts, and that is on long-range, land-based bombers."[96] Cannon based his support for more strategic air power on the assumption that a third world war would be short, precluding any need to spend larger sums on army or navy preparedness. Nevertheless, the bulk of the air groups which Cannon advanced—about six out of ten—were earmarked at the time he was speaking for ground support activities. Cannon's obscure grasp of the implications of his vote for more strategic air power suggested Congress' collective confusion on this question. Both houses of Congress eventually followed Cannon's recommendation and voted more air force funds. The surface irony of course was that, if Congress' will had been implemented, its increase would not have yielded more long-range bomber power. The irony intensified in effect when President Truman impounded most of the Congressional increase soon after the passage of the FY 1950 appropriation bill.[97] The increased funds would lie fallow in the budgetary vineyard. The tactical air power that it would have produced would be painfully missed in the course of the Korean War which was to erupt in less than a year.

Encouraged by the favorable atmosphere in Congress surrounding air power, navy partisans in the House pressed what they thought to be an advantage and demanded more naval air power. Vinson admonished that he was "at a loss to understand how [Mahon could] reconcile his views [about the future of air power] with the action of [his] committee in reducing naval aviation. . . . "[98] Vinson's plea for an enlarged naval air force rested on three political factors: increasing Soviet intransigence and military power; the United States deteriorating position in the Far East, particularly in China; and its increasing military responsibilities throughout the world under NATO.[99] But these and other buttressing arguments failed to move the House. A $300 million amendment to increase naval air power was defeated.[100] Leading the counterattack, Cannon argued that more naval air power, transported by large carrier fleets, was highly vulnerable and that, in the final analysis, it duplicated the air force's strategic missions. More naval aircraft power would be a waste of resources.[101] The navy, agreed Republican Representative Albert Engel, was merely "empire building."[102] Following the defeat of the naval amendment, the appropriations bill for the entire military establishment cleared the House with only one dissenting vote.[103]

In a week of hearings, the Senate again hurriedly examined the House's action. It had heretofore been its general lot to raise the appropriations for the services after severe House cuts. The situation was now reversed. The Senate military appropriations subcommittee was unsympathetic to any increase in defense appropriations. The report of the appropriations committee, while paying a tribute to its "paramount" duty to protect the nation's security, admitted that it "was guided principally by the recommendations of the President. . . . "[104] The admission was damning. Operating within this frame of mind, the members of the military appropriations subcommittee were not disposed to explore the strategic validity of the President's budget, the economic and political assumptions on which it rested, and its relation to the other domestic and international aspects of the President's budget.[105]

Holding the line on expenditures was the major preoccupation of most senators. Secretary of Defense Louis Johnson's boast that a billion dollars could be saved in the Defense Department "by cutting out wastage, duplication, and by cutting down unnecessary civilian employment"[106] warmly gratified the Senate defense appropriations group. It was so impressed by Johnson's sincerity that it convinced the Senate to authorize the newly installed defense secretary to reduce defense appropriations up to $434 million "whenever in his discretion such action would not jeopardize the national security."[107] This was an extraordinary delegation of authority to the executive branch. If the Senate's action had been upheld by the House (which it was not), it would have provided the President with an even freer hand to set ceilings on defense spending and force structure and to determine strategic policy. The Senate was voluntarily withdrawing from participation in these decisions.

Prevailing opinion in the upper chamber adopted the appropriations committee's report, siding thereby with the President who opposed any increased spending and, concomitantly, a seventy-group air force. The handful of senators who opposed deletion of the air force increases were buried in a forty-nine to nine vote on the committee report.[108] Chairman Elmer Thomas of the Senate Armed Services Appropriations Subcommittee summarized the predominant feeling of his colleagues: "I must be guided first by the Commander in Chief of the Nation. He is in a position to get the best advice in the world, and he does get that kind of advice. He has at his call all the experts of America, and he can bring in experts from other places to advise him as to what should be done."[109] What Thomas neglected was the painful fact that the experts disagreed. The JCS had proposed at least three different budgets based on different strategic projections. Followed to its logical conclusion, Thomas' line of reasoning would have exempted Congress from the onerous but necessary task of assessing the adequacy and the relevance of the President's defense proposals to the nation's foreign policy objectives.

The appropriations bills passed by each house differed widely. Two conference reports were issued and over a month of negotiations were held before these differences, amounting to 100 amendments, were resolved. Principal disagreement centered on the air force provisions. In the midst of their bargaining with the Senate, House managers secured a decisive 306–1 vote in favor of their appeal to the House to stand firm on the air force issue. Faced with the reinforced House mandate for air power, the Senate conferees withdrew their opposition. Senator Thomas asked the Senate to go along with the House. He told his colleagues that the President had finally relented on the question of raised appropriations for air power. He intimated, however, that the House victory would be empty because the President very likely would not spend the money. "I leave the impression," Thomas confided, "that if the money is appropriated it may not be used."[110] Assured by these veiled remarks, the Senate accepted the air force increase.

The final military bill signed by the President carried $12.95 billion in appropriations and $2.67 billion in contract authorizations. Each of the services received an approximately equal share of these funds. The Senate's $434 million grant of discretion to the secretary of defense was deleted at House insistence. Instead, the two houses applied a cut of $239 million themselves. The army was granted an average of 677,000 uniformed men for FY 1950, but was denied $200 million in supporting personnel funds. The navy was similarly stripped of funds. Naval personnel support was reduced from an expected 527,300 men to 499,000. No additional aid was assigned to naval shipbuilding, ordnance, or air power. The Senate blunted some of the House drive for a larger air force. The final bill provided merely 5,000 more air force personnel than had been requested,[111] enough to throttle further agitation in Congress for more air power yet too few to be realistically applied to a seventy-group program.

MILITARY DEPRESSION: FY 1951

Background to strategic reassessment.—The administration's tactical successes in Congress were to prove transitory. It would soon be compelled to revise its economic and military thinking. Not that Congress would force any change. Rather, a number of internal and external developments were quickly overtaking the assumptions on which the Truman administration's strategic policies rested. Two months before Congress formally passed the FY 1950 military budget, the Soviet Union exploded its first atomic device, approximately five years ahead of the schedule predicted by the Finletter Commission. The American nuclear monopoly was ended. The United States and the world would have to adjust to an entirely new phase of the cold war. Within a decade, the balance of terror that Churchill had referred to in the late 1940's would be a reality of international politics. Moreover, a few months after the Soviet atomic success, the Chinese Communists completed their conquest of the Chinese mainland. American hopes for a free and friendly China were dashed. In Europe, the prospects for the West did not appear much brighter. The Berlin Blockade was ending, but over-all Soviet intransigence was growing. The military and economic aid program to Europe had been only recently launched. It had not yet worked its stabilizing effects on the social and political fabric of European life. In the meantime, the United States faced the problem of defending Europe and, similarly, Asia against communist military action.

At the behest of the State Department's Policy Planning Staff, a broad review of American strategic policy was initiated in the summer of 1949. After a lengthy gestation period, State-Defense Department co-operation produced a policy paper—NSC 68—which urged a radical shift in American policies, particularly in its military posture, to cope with the new realities of communist power. The report, which was sent to the President less than three months before the Korean War, recommended a gradual military expansion to meet both all-out or limited conflict situations with communist powers. It did not flinch from the economic and budgetary implications of its assessment. It recognized that at least a doubling of the defense budget would be necessary. "An even higher figure, $50 billion," notes one commentator, "was considered a reasonable guess." [112]

But almost a year before these recommendations could be placed before the President or be absorbed by the policy process, a "revolt" against the administration's operational strategy was taking shape within the Navy Department. Budgetary restrictions on naval spending had already strained navy morale to the breaking point. Defense Secretary Louis Johnson's cancellation of the flush-deck carrier, the "United States," on April 23, 1949, proved the final blow. Supported by the army and air force chiefs of staff, Johnson overrode strong, in some cases, passionate navy appeals in behalf of the super-carrier on the grounds that it duplicated the air force's strategic mission. The navy stood nearly unanimously opposed to the secretary's decisions. Navy Secretary John Sullivan tendered his resignation immediately. In his letter of withdrawal to the secretary of defense, Sullivan, charged that Johnson had "drastically and arbitrarily" restricted "the operational plans of an armed service without consultation with that service." [113] The accusation was very nearly true.

The officer corps of the navy felt the defense secretary's action even more acutely. The demise of the flush-deck carrier convinced most naval officers that naval air power was being deliberately curtailed—perhaps even being nibbled to death—and, concomitantly, that the navy itself was being gradually subordinated to the dictates of its sister services. The navy's organizational independence and integrity, its parity with the other armed branches, and its strategic viewpoint appeared to be in mortal danger. Throughout the spring and summer of 1949, the professional navy marshaled its force for an attack on the administration's strategic policies. But the focus of its assault was not the President or the secretary of defense. The air force was singled out as the principal enemy. The supercarrier was crucial to the navy's future. The air force's incorrigible opposition to the flush-carrier and its strategic bombing concepts which relegated the navy largely to logistics operations made it the natural target of naval enmity.

Reports began to reach congressional offices from anonymous navy sources that the air force's B-36 bomber was not only incapable of carrying out its assigned mission but had also been procured through a questionable exercise of influence. The House Armed Services Committee investigated the navy's charges and found them to be false. The committee disclosed that a certain Mr. Cedric R. Worth, a naval civilian employee, had been largely responsible for spreading the falsely incriminating charges against the air force.[114] The navy's failure to have its position publicly vindicated, compounded by the announcement that the secretary of defense planned to cut $353 million from navy expenditures during FY 1950, impelled one member of the navy officer corps, Captain John Crommelin, to hold a news conference in which he accused the Joint Chiefs and the secretary of defense of undermining the navy. Crommelin's accusations prompted a reluctant Vinson to reopen the B-36 investigation and to expand it into a general examination of the unification and strategy of the armed services. Nevertheless, it was the navy which induced Congress to consider strategic policy, and not the other way around.

The navy presented a many-sided attack on the B-36 and the strategy that it symbolized. Admiral Arthur Radford, an experienced naval aviator and commander of the Pacific fleet, led the navy's forces. He discounted the air force's evaluation of the B-36. Radford charged that the B-36 was "a bad gamble with national security." [115] It was too large, slow, and ponderous a delivery vehicle to avoid destruction by enemy antiaircraft and fighter defense forces. Radford assembled an impressive array of naval air specialists who attested to the B-36's vulnerability. The B-36, the navy experts agreed, would fail in its assigned strategic mission or would discharge it at an unacceptable cost. In his testimony, Radford also indicated, though somewhat more confusedly, that the technical weaknesses of the B-36 suggested the defects of the military strategy which nourished its development. Observed Radford:

> The United States is not sound in relying on the so-called strategic bombing concept to its present extent. This concept is symbolized by the B-36 delivering the atom blitz. In the minds of our citizens this fallacious concept promises a short cut to victory. Our citizens must realize that its military leaders cannot make this promise—that there is no short cut, no cheap, no easy way to win a war. We must realize that the threat of instant atomic retaliation will not prevent it, and may even invite it. We must realize that we cannot gamble that the atom blitz of annihilation will even win a war. We must realize if war is forced upon us, we must win it, and win it in such a way that it can be followed by a stable, livable peace. [116]

Rear Admiral Ralph A. Ofstie, who followed Radford's team to the stand, focused the political and military shortcomings of the air force's and, by implication, the administration's operational-strategic policies. "The greatest defect of the present concept of strategic bombing," Ofstie began, "is its contradictory relation to fundamental ideals, policies, and commitments of the United States." [117] Strategic bombing could not defend Europe against a Soviet attack. It could not quickly destroy the military capacity of the enemy, protect forward bases, or command the seas. Europe could be liberated, Ofstie hinted, but only after first being decimated. Ofstie found strategic bombing in conflict with traditional American policies which sought to ameliorate the destructive effects of war. Atomic bombardment threatened to undermine "those standards of morality which [had] been a guiding force" in the American democracy.[118] It unavoidably included the "wholesale extermination. . . . [and] the random mass slaughter of men, women, and children in the enemy country."[119] Nor could it prevent the demolition of the physical structure of civilization. In the wake of an atomic attack, the social, economic, and political fabric of the world would be irreparably rent. The concept of "instant retaliation," warned Ofstie, created the "illusion of power and even a kind of bomb-rattling jingoism."[120] Prophetically, he concluded:

> The idea that it is within our power to inflict maximum damage upon the enemy in a short time without serious risk to ourselves creates the delusion that we are stronger than we actually are. This, in turn, becomes a constant temptation for policy makers to overcommit themselves, to make commitments actually impossible to fill.
>
> In recent weeks we have been made aware of the fact that we are not alone in our possession of the atomic weapon, which had been the basis of this illusory strength. Perhaps now more prudent and realistic policies will get the attention which they deserve.[121]

For all its trouble to present a different strategic view to Congress and the public, the navy received little in return. The President was determined to bring it into harness. Discipline again was restored when the services presented their FY 1951 budgets to Congress. Discussion of the B-36 embroglio was conspiciously absent from the appropriations review. The abrupt departure of Admiral Louis Denfeld as chief of naval operations stood as an example to other potential recalcitrants in the military establishment. Most legislators

111

appeared relieved that the administration had brought the services under temporary control.

Budgetary policy in search of a strategic design.—The prudence and realism to which Admiral Ofstie referred were scarce items in Washington in December, 1949, when the FY 1951 budget reached the White House for decision. Domestic economic considerations again largely shaped the military budget. A meeting of the service secretaries, the secretary of defense, the JCS, the President, and the director of the Budget Bureau produced a $13 billion spending ceiling on the military establishment during FY 1951. Aided by Secretary of Defense Louis Johnson and General Dwight Eisenhower, the JCS allocated the available funds among the services. Simultaneously, FY 1950 programs were rephased to produce a gradual drop-off in personnel strength by June 30, 1950.[122] Despite scattered congressional objections,[123] this action was taken even before Congress had approved the FY 1950 defense program which rested on different expenditure assumptions. The effect of these personnel reschedulings was to reduce armed force strength from about 1.61 million at the end of FY 1949 to 1.46 million a year later. The army and navy were to absorb 80 per cent of these cutbacks.[124] Military expenditures were being decreased in the face of the Soviet atomic explosion and the expression of Soviet naval and aircraft procurement, the consolidation of Soviet conquests in eastern Europe, the enlarging Soviet military threat to western Europe, the Red Chinese victory, and, correspondingly, the resulting increased communist armed threat to Southeast Asia, particularly to Indo-China, Korea, Malaya, and the Philippines. Strategic and budgetary policies were neither allies nor friends. They were essentially strangers to each other.

In a number of important senses, too, the President's military budget was even unrelated to the strategic picture which the administration drew for popular consumption. Although the mainstay of the administration's military posture, the air force was to be kept at around FY 1948 levels, while the army and navy were to shrink in manpower and material resources. The administration stressed the need for more reserve units, planning for industrial mobilization, the accumulation of critical war materials, and research and development—all elements of a mobilization strategy. A deterrent or forward strategy, capable of applying discriminating forms of military power when and where needed to bolster American interests was implicitly rejected because of the high immediate and continuing costs of such a program. From a narrow perspective, the FY 1951 budget would, indeed, in the words of President Truman, "provide for balanced land, naval and air forces" and a base for rapid expansion of the military strength of the nation in time of stress.[125] But would it forestall aggression? The administration's flight from military responsibility for the sake of a questionable economic stability overlooked the obvious rule of thumb that a domestically balanced military force and a ready industrial base for mobilization could be secured at a level which was less than adequate to preclude armed aggression. Keynes had demonstrated that savings and investment could be brought into equilibrium without the realization of full employment. The Korean War would show that the domestic consensus on defense policy might also achieve equilibrium, but one keyed to a level of military preparedness that would be insufficient to deter enemy expansionism through military force.

The services voiced no open criticism of the President's budgetary decisions. Air Force Secretary Symington stoutly defended the President's balanced budget policy, while resigning himself to the President's order which impounded most of the added appropriations which Congress had authorized for the air force in FY 1950. Service spokesmen did not depart very far from their assigned task of presenting the Budget Bureau approved estimates for their services. Surprised by the show of unity among the services, Representative Engel remarked that it was the first time in his long congressional service, which extended through three secretaries of war, two secretaries of the army, and five chiefs of staff, that he had "ever seen the Army, the Navy, and the Air Force rather meekly accept the cutting of costs." [126] Secretary Johnson added more gloss to service unity when he submitted testimonials from the JCS, affirming the nation's high state of military preparedness. [127]

The army defended a modest $4 billion budget. Average strength for FY 1951 was placed at 540,000 men, a loss of about 37,000 from the previous year's total. More intensive training would compensate for a lack of numbers. To support its personnel, a limited army modernization program was announced, pegged at a level slightly above fiscal 1950. These harsh facts of eroding army strength contrasted sharply with the glowing picture of army preparedness that General Lawton Collins, army chief of staff, painted for Congress:

> We have units that are ready to move right now in case of aggression; we have the best men in the Army today that we have ever had in peacetime, and although we have a number of critical equipment problems yet to solve, I can assure you that our troops, with the equipment that they have, would give a good account of themselves, if we were attacked. The recent reductions in our occupation commitments have enabled us to concentrate more of our efforts upon strengthening the combat units which form the hard core of our fighting force. We are giving our divisions and other combat units more officers and men, some items of better weapons and equipment, and improved training under field conditions. [128]

It was becoming progressively difficult to discover where reality ended and hope—and fantasy—began.

The navy was equally cowed before Congress. Naval officers carefully proclaimed their support of the President's program. Admiral Louis Denfeld's dismissal as chief of naval operations provided an instructive example of what fate awaited military dissenters. Naval spokesmen manfully defended the administration's reductions in all major categories of navy strength—i.e., naval and marine corps personnel, aircraft and ship construction and operations, and ordnance procurement. Admiral Forrest Sherman, Denfeld's replacement, confined himself to the feeble warning that the one billion dollar reduction in the navy's new obligational authority for FY 1951 would necessitate increased appropriations in later years.

The table below summarizes the navy's gradual shrinkage between 1949 and 1951 in terms of ship and aircraft operations. Major combatant ships—to be manned at 33 per cent of wartime complements—were set at 239 for FY 1951, a drop of 54 ships over three years. In

TABLE 3*

COMPARISON OF SHIP AND AIRCRAFT OPERATION FOR THE NAVY
AND MARINE CORPS FROM 1949 WITH ESTIMATES FOR 1951*

Types	1949, Appropriated	1950, Appropriated	1951, Proposed
Ships			
Attack carriers	11	8	7
Light and escort carriers	10	11	8
Battleships	1	1	1
Cruisers	31	18	13
Destroyers	160	170	140
Submarines	80	80	70
Total, major combatant ships	293	288	239
Aircraft			
Navy and Marine Corps (operating)	8,035	5,598	4,389
Navy and Marine Corps Reserve (operating)	2,678	2,185	1,844
Total, operating	10,713	7,783	6,233

* Source: HSAC, *Hearings, Department of Defense Appropriations, FY 1951*, 81/1, 1950, Part 4, p. 1734.

the same period, naval aircraft operations dwindled almost to half. Average personnel for the navy and marine corps was to be cut 40,000 below FY 1950. Year-end strength was to settle at 373,303 in the navy and 71,862 in the marines. The cancellation of the "United States" signaled larger naval aircraft decreases. FY 1951 estimates, based on lower operating aircraft levels, projected a procurement program of 817 new airplanes. This left the navy with a deficiency of 530 planes for the year. Again second-line inventory equipment was to be impressed into service to bridge the gap between the requirements advised by the Bureau of Aeronautics and the administrative stipulations of the Navy and Defense departments. Admiral Price, chief of the Aeronautics Bureau, reiterated his prediction of a year before that a procurement program of 817 planes "would result in a progressive reduction of aircraft operating inventory to less than 3,000 aircraft" in the early 1950's.[129]

No less than her sister services, the air force was ordered to operate at depressed levels. With its $4.64 billion cash budget and $600 million in contract authorizations, the air force was expected to maintain its FY 1950 force of forty-eight groups. It was an expectation beyond realization. The FY 1951 aircraft procurement program of 1,383 planes, while higher than the 1950 procurement of 1,250 planes, was 2 million airframe pounds less in weight. Actual requirements for a forty-eight–group capability called for 2,000 new planes each year and an additional $200 million over the earmarked $1.35 billion for aircraft purchases in FY 1951. Two billion dollars was estimated as the breaking point for the retention of a modernized forty-eight–group force. The administration's lowered spending authorizations were unmistakably driving the air force to a forty-two–group level.[130]

Congressional anxiety, then acquiescence.—An anxious concern for the adequacy of the administration's projected military program coursed below the surface of the House hearings. It was reflected in a number of ways. The House defense groups investigated the process and the reasoning which produced the President's budget. For the first time in the subcommittee's history, the Budget Bureau director was invited to present his view. As Chairman Mahon correctly recognized: "If [the defense budget] is submitted on a fallacious basis, then we cannot afford to put much reliance in it. To put reliance in an ill-conceived program might imperil the safety of the country."[131] In his brief appearance before the subcommittee, Budget Director Frank Pace described in tired detail how the military budget was prepared. He was not much help. He steadfastly refused to accept responsibility for the adequacy of the military power provided in the President's money recommendations. He insisted that the Budget Bureau operated "only as a staff arm of the President."[132] All final decisions and accompanying responsibility on defense questions belonged to the chief executive and, by extension, the Department of Defense. The Budget Bureau advised solely on the fiscal implications of the military budget. Pace's remarks did not enrich congressional knowledge of budgetary procedures, nor did they reveal the broad influence of the Budget Bureau on defense. The appearance of the budget director ended on the expressed hope of closer liaison between the defense subcommittee and the Budget Bureau in future years. The hope is yet to be realized.

Secretary of Defense Johnson was also asked to return with his principal civilian and military advisers to discuss the strategic policies underlying the Defense Department's budgetary requests. No new insights or disclosures were presented. Johnson reheated his previous testimony and served it again to the subcommittee.[133] A smaller defense budget, asserted the defense secretary, would actually result in increased military efficiency. The savings that would be recovered could then be reapplied to other useful military programs.

Some subcommittee members, unable to share Johnson's optimism, solicited repeated assurances from service witnesses about the military establishment's preparedness for war.[134] The solicitation bordered on the pointless and ritualistic in the wake of the defunct B-36 hearings

117

and the pressures for economy that were operating in both branches of the federal government. The military could hardly be expected to speak candidly about military readiness in open congressional sessions. A bemused House subcommittee chairman finally blurted out:

> I do not want to be unduly critical of the military, particularly since I realize the military is not always the one who writes the ticket, but we talk about war plans and we do not seem to make them realistic.
>
> For example, since this committee reported the general appropriation bill for the House last year there has been almost a complete loss of China and a transfer from friendly hands to Communist hands, or unfriendly hands, at least for the present.
>
> Russia has exploded an atomic bomb.
>
> The ordinary layman would think that this would increase the power which might be arrayed possibly against the United States, and possibly would call for larger preparedness on our part to meet a possible emergency. It might be more, perhaps, to prevent it from arising than anything else.
>
> Yet the military, with all their planning, come in with a lesser budget.[135]

Mahon's plaintive remarks were more in the form of a footnote to the hearings than a prologue to a critique of American strategic policy. Yet Mahon's observations were revealing. He was evidently aware, as some of his colleagues were also, that it made little sense to reduce the army by 40,000, while increasing military commitments abroad. Others perceived, too, that naval and air force air power was being whittled away by administrative decree. Still little was done in the hearings to pinpoint the areas of widening disparity between American military power and its foreign obligations. Even less was attempted in the appropriations committee report. The committee simply rationalized the army's receding strength. Lessened occupation responsibilities—the army's occupation in Germany had terminated in

September, 1949—and allegedly greater army firepower, mobility, and improved training would balance off troop reductions. While the report conceded the army's inability "to sustain a counter-offensive as could a large force," it accepted the administration's "calculated risk measured by a comparison of . . . [the nation's military] capabilities of the potential enemy." [136] These "calculated risks" also shaped navy and air force estimates. Of course every military budget carried "calculated risks." The problem was to determine the degree of calculation that went into the budget in the first instance and the degree of probable risk that was anticipated. The defense appropriations group did not approach its problem in these terms. The report did attack the President for having impounded slightly more than $730 million in air force funds during FY 1950. Still it could muster only irritation. In behalf of the air force, the report meekly advised "a restudy and revaluation of military strength projected into future years." [137] The navy's air program was quietly passed over.

What doubts appropriations members may have had about the adequacy of the nation's military strength tended to be resolved by four widely held positions. Foremost was the argument that the defense budget could not be pushed much beyond a prescribed limit. By FY 1951 the previously established $15 billion budget barrier was lowered to $13 billion. "Thirteen billion dollars is too much for a peacetime budget," one ranking subcommittee member explained. "It is not enough for a wartime budget; but it is all our economy can stand." [138] While many legislators sincerely feared an economic crisis if the budget were expanded, many similarly felt that the $13 billion ceiling was the highest politically feasible level of expenditures that would be accepted by the voting public. Justifying the spending limit merely obfuscated the political responsibility of the appropriations committee and the President to balance economic capabilities with strategic need. The argument that the President's defense spending proposal "was not a wartime budget" implied that more money could be spent. The obstacle was thus more political than economic.

Members could reasonably argue the second point, too, that opposition to the President was futile anyway. He had impounded congressional increases before; he would again. There was little partisan advantage in raising defense expenditures since the Democrats controlled both houses of Congress. Criticism for the sake of criticism seemed vain. Republican critics were even less inclined to challenge the President because, as a group, they tended to be even more convinced than their Democratic colleagues that the nation was spending itself into ruin. Consequently, a worried or tired legislator could simply absolve himself of responsibility for military policy. If the defense budget proved too low in a future emergency, the President, not Congress, would be at fault. Military policy, asserted ranking Republican Albert Engel, "is the responsibility of the Chief Executive and not mine." [139] Some Democrats were prone to the same argument. Senator Elmer Thomas had stated essentially the same position during the debate on the FY 1950 budget.[140] In this instance, Thomas was supporting the President. The effect of his posture was nevertheless much the same as Engel's. Agreements and disagreements on strategic policy did not neatly follow party lines. Both parties could claim members who were equally reluctant to engage their intellectual capacities and to invest their limited political power resources in wrestling with the nation's strategic problems.

Moreover, if the first two positions appeared untenable, congressmen could fall back to yet a third area for protective cover. There was no need to worry about the level of defense expenditures under almost any circumstances since, as the House appropriations group pronounced, in 1949: "If emergencies requiring additional funds arise, the Congress will be in session in ample time to make provisions therefor." [141] The fourth position, discussed below, was stated by Mahon during the House deliberations on the FY 1951 defense estimates. It should be emphasized, however, that an individual congressman was likely to abandon any one of these positions under differing political conditions or under the prompting of varying political attitudes and motives. The arguments, not the adherents, tended to remain constant.

The appropriations committee report on the FY 1951 budget did not pass the House completely unscathed. Again Armed Service Chairman Carl Vinson led a minor assault against the President's program. He was joined by a varied array of other congressmen, including Representative Charles Plumley, one of the two Republicans on the House defense appropriations subcommittee. Vinson found Secretary Johnson's "economy scalpel [had] not only carved away some service fat but [had] cut—deeply in some areas—into the sinews and muscles of the armed services." [142] Plumley, resorting to another cadaverous image, charged that "the effectiveness of the economies proposed by . . . Johnson . . . [were] comparable to those accomplished by the man who cut his wife's throat to stop her nose bleed." [143]

Closer inspection of these accusations revealed that they were not as extensive as they had initially appeared. Vinson and his supporters were primarily upset about the curtailment of air power during Johnson's tenure in office. The arguments they raised were replays of the debates of the previous year. Only passing mention was made of the weakening strength of the army and navy.[144] The principal attack on the administration was its failure to carry out the 1950 aircraft program and, especially, its continued refusal to go beyond a forty-eight–group air force. Vinson also objected to the gradual depletion of the navy's air strike capability. Encouraged by Vinson's sharp words, other congressmen exhorted their colleagues to amend air-power estimates upward. Plumley hit at Johnson's decision to stop construction on the supercarrier, the "United States." [145] Yet in all of these rebukes there was no hint that economic assumptions upon which the defense budget ostensibly rested were unjustified.

Mahon answered Vinson's attack. He adopted a paradoxical line of rebuttal. Mahon now found himself relying on the same arguments that he had opposed the year before in pressing for an increase in air force appropriations. Mahon argued that "the thing that [made] America the foremost leader of all the world . . . [was] America's industrial potential, America's capacity to fight back and continue to fight back until victory had been achieved."[146] This position, which implicitly defended the President's defense spending ceiling, was tantamount to a rejection of the evolutionary development of strategic thinking since World War II. Industrial potential, not forces in being, was the basis of the United States deterrent strength. A year before Mahon had assigned deterrent responsibility to the air force.[147] Now Mahon was suggesting that those who would increase the military budget were simultaneously destroying America's deterrent. In the light of the Soviet Union's possession of the atomic bomb and its developing long-range bomber fleet, Mahon could not have chosen a poorer time and occasion to pose this argument.

The appropriation committee leaders held the trump cards in the House debate. Supplemental hearings held after the General Appropriations Bill had come to the floor brought requests for increased funds for the three services from the secretary of defense.[148] Toward the close of the House debates, Mahon introduced a long series of amendments which, for the most part, raised different appropriation categories. None of them met opposition in the House. Three were especially important. The first two dealt with aircraft procurement. The navy received $100 million and the air force $200 million in increased contract authorizations. A third amendment added $50 million to the navy's antisubmarine warfare campaign.[149] The introduction of these measures blunted further criticism of the administration's program. When the amended bill finally came to a vote, it passed by an overwhelming majority—362 yeas to 21 nays, with 45 not voting.[150]

The appropriations bill passed to the Senate on May 10. Breaking with usual procedure, the Senate hearings had begun before the close of the House investigations. The added investment of time served no fruitful purpose in this instance. The committee report, which generally called for higher appropriations for the Defense Department than the House had advised, was presented to the Senate on July 8, two weeks after America's entry into the Korean War. There was almost no discussion of the bill on the Senate floor. The administration revised estimates of $13.3 billion in cash, now including $300 million in public works requests, and $1.4 billion in contract authorizations passed the Senate. The conference report was similarly passed without incident or dispute. The Senate's position carried on fifty-nine out of sixty-nine cases of disagreement.[151] Everyone knew that the Defense Department authorizations were inadequate. By the President's own admission, the armed services were operating on a peacetime budget. The country was now at war. A radical revision of strategic plans, military forces, and budgetary thinking was urgently needed.

THE KOREAN WAR:
TURMOIL AND TRANSITION, 1950–1953

IV

OVER-ALL SETTING AND DEVELOPMENT

The North Korean attack compelled a radical revision of the Truman administration's perception of the Soviet threat. NSC 68, completed shortly before the outbreak of hostilities, had already recognized the growing strength of communist military power and had recommended an expansion of American military might. The Korean War transformed the assumptions of NSC 68 that communist nations might use force to secure their objectives into hard and unpleasant realities. The Soviet threat had heretofore been interpreted principally as a problem of protecting allied nations against internal political subversion and of withstanding outside pressures against the free world's allegedly vulnerable economic system. The Marshall Plan and Point Four were cast in this view. Both were designed to stabilize the economic and political life of western Europe and of the major underdeveloped nations outside the communist camp. The military action in Korea added entirely new and ominous dimensions to this simpler understanding of communist intentions and capabilities. In an address to Congress on July 19, 1950, President Truman made it "plain beyond all doubt that the international Communist movement . . . [was] prepared to use armed invasion to conquer independent nations." The United States, he went on, "must therefore recognize the possibility that armed aggression may take place in other areas." The communist decision "to use arms to gain its ends" had produced a fundamental change in the "estimates of the military needs of the United States."[1] The nation would have to rearm.

But how, at what rate, and to what level should the rearmament proceed? Where should these forces be deployed? What should be the long-run size and pattern of defense expenditures? What role should America's allies play in the rearmament effort? What forms and amounts of aid should the United States provide non-communist countries? How should fiscal and economic policies be integrated with strategic and non-strategic programs?

The Korean War years between 1950 and 1953 roughly mark a period of confused and anxious searching, principally within the executive branch, and, to a considerably lesser extent, within Congress, for answers to these pressing questions. The major outlines of a new strategic posture did not crystallize until the presentations of the FY 1952 and FY 1953 budgets. While all of the budgets during this period called for an expansion of army and navy strength and for greater forces in being, their larger effect was to increase sizably the nation's strategic nuclear striking forces. The New Look policies of the Eisenhower administration did not constitute as radical a departure from previous strategic thinking as the Republican administration was to suggest to the American voter. The seeds of the New Look were planted in the last few years of the Truman administration. After thrashing about for almost four years, the Truman administration and, more decisively, the Eisenhower administration settled upon the uncomplicated and not novel formula that more— indeed, much more—strategic air power was needed to deter communist aggression than had previously existed. SAC bombers, bolstered by nuclear equipped carrier strike forces, were to be the key to strategic superiority over the Soviet Union. Despite the limited war in Korea, the Truman and Eisenhower administrations increased the nation's reliance on nuclear delivering air power. Other forms of military force were progressively discounted. The slide downward, while slow during the later stages of the Truman period, quickened in pace after the Republican takeover in 1953.

The Korean expansion of the armed services, particularly the air force, inevitably led to the abandonment of the $15 billion ceiling on defense spending. It was replaced eventually by a new upper limit on military expenditures that slowly crept from approximately $35 to $40 billion annually during the 1950's. Actual military spending each year between FY 1952 and FY 1960 averaged $39.3 billion.[2]

Congress played a small part in this transition process. The Korean War confused and distracted most legislators. It was against this backdrop that it may be said the Truman administration served its successor. It conditioned a perplexed and distracted Congress to accept a new defense spending plateau and to support with some enthusiasm what was to be finally hailed as a strategy of massive retaliation. The Eisenhower administration was to build its New Look policies on this developing consensus in Congress. Yet congressmen were no more certain of the merit of the higher defense spending level of the 1950's than of the pre-Korean War figure of $15 billion. The new upper limits on defense expenditures were accepted without a thorough exploration of the capacity of the economy or the nation's present and future military needs. Nor did the Congress demonstrate any deeper understanding of the military strategic issues facing the United States than it had before. The Korean War and the Soviet explosion of an atomic device did not shake Congress' simple faith in the redemptive force of nuclear weapons. These developments seemed almost to spur Congress' collective commitment to nuclear doctrine, much like the renewed act of faith that a sinner makes who, having returned again to the fold, is convinced that the evils which have been visited upon him stemmed less from any omissions on his part than from his lack of sufficient faith. Nearly a decade would be required before any sign would appear that the Korean experience and the recognition of growing Soviet military strength had been assimilated emotionally and intellectually into the slow moving stream of strategic thinking in Congress.

After the initial shock of the North Korean attack had worn off, Congress reverted to its traditional concern with economic stability and efficiency in defense spending and administrative management. Politically habituated to emphasize these issues, Congress easily turned to them. They seemed more tractable, or were perceived to be more amenable to understanding and determination, than the seemingly obscure processes and arguments of strategic planning and operations that were in almost incessant ferment and flux. It was difficult for many congressmen, and for the American people, to resign themselves to the idea that a single enemy nuclear strike could prostrate the United States. It was hard to grasp that at the outbreak of a general war there would be little or no time to transform economic power into military might; an effective military machine could not be quickly organized after the devastation resulting from an enemy nuclear attack. The Korean experience notwithstanding, the point was not fully appreciated immediately that actual forces in being could more effectively deter various forms of communist military aggression than potentially mobilizable military power. A congressional majority reluctantly abandoned the World War II precept that the military establishment was simply the spearhead of the industrial economy, which would ultimately decide any military struggle with the communist world. Almost three years after the Soviet detonation of a nuclear bomb, leading members of Congress could still be heard energetically pressing this argument.[3] So long as the economy remained strong, even a blunt spear, as it were, would be an adequate deterrent. And, expectedly, a strong economy was generally defined in terms of a stated level of defense spending.

Where Congress did focus on strategic matters, its attention was once more narrowly confined to the actual hardware items and operational readiness of the nation's strategic air power and nuclear weapons. Presidential-congressional conflicts over military policy in the 1950's principally concerned the nation's strategic strike forces. The Truman administration largely escaped congressional criticism of its long-range air-power programs. All of the services, including the air force, were undergoing substantial and rapid expansion during this period. Attacks on the President's defense proposals would have been pointless in this bullish atmosphere. A more discernible, though not always consistent, pattern of congressional criticism of the chief executive's alleged failure to build an adequate nuclear deterrent developed during President Eisenhower's term of office. Congress lent credibility to these verbal assaults, particularly after the flight of the first Sputnik, by increases in the administration's requests for long-range air power, missiles, and continental defense, or for all three during a single fiscal year.

During the years of the Korean action, however, the task of identifying a wider and more inclusive spectrum of contingencies under which American military force might have to be engaged was neglected. So also did Congress fail to analyze the President's defense proposals in terms of feasible alternatives. Congress was swept along by the tidal wave of frustrated hopes, fretful projections of an uncertain future, and feverish activity that the Korean War produced within governmental circles, especially within the military establishment, and within the larger political and economic spheres of the nation. Thousands of World War II veterans were reactivated. Military forces expanded rapidly. Industry rushed to retool for war. Bewildered perhaps by this hurry and upheaval, Congress abdicated its leadership responsibilities in shaping strategic policy. There is little wonder that it did. As a body it was unable to understand or to cope with the new dimensions of the Soviet threat on its own terms. Unable to counsel and guide the nation or itself, it failed during this period to discharge its responsibilities to the executive branch in examining the spending recommendations of the military services. The defense spending ceiling set by the Truman and Eisenhower administrations, which were in some measure a response to congressional expectations and pressures, essentially defined the scope and direction of the defense debate in Congress for the greater part of a decade.

MEETING THE ENLARGED COMMUNIST MILITARY THREAT: SUPPLEMENTS TO FY 1951

Executive branch response.—The President and his leading advisers on foreign affairs interpreted the Korean aggression as only one part of a broader and more pervasive communist military threat to the United States global position. During the remaining months of 1950, the President ordered a host of other changes in United States military and foreign policy. American forces in the Philippines were strengthened and military assistance to aid the French in their fight against communist-led insurgents in Indo-China was stepped up. The Seventh Fleet was dispatched to Formosa to assure that the island would "not become embroiled in hostilities disturbing to the peace in the Pacific." [4] The deployment of the Seventh Fleet into the Formosan Straits, although primarily motivated by a desire to keep the war in Korea limited, marked a basic shift in American policy toward the Chinese Nationalists, indicating an increased United States commitment to the Chiang Kai-shek regime. The trend of American disengagement in the Far East was temporarily reversed, and the American people found themselves plunged once more, now more deeply than before, into the center of the Chinese Civil War.

But the administration's major concern was trained not on China or Korea, but on the Soviet military threat to western Europe. Deprived of the American nuclear deterrent, NATO posed no special difficulty for the Soviet Union in the summer of 1950. Its handful of poorly equipped, loosely organized, and haphazardly deployed divisions faced an impressive Russian force of 27 divisions, backed by approximately three times as many quickly mobilizable divisions in eastern Europe and the Soviet Union. Hurried discussion within the executive branch, principally between State and Defense Department personnel, yielded a four-point program of increased financial aid to Europe, the commitment of American ground troops to the Continent, a supreme commander for all NATO forces, and strong American backing for German rearmament. These proposals were placed before the NATO members meeting in New York in September 1950,[5] and were favorably received. The $1.2 billion foreign military aid bill for FY 1951 was greatly increased when in July, 1950, the President presented Congress with a $4 billion request to bolster allied military forces. Significantly, too, as one commentator notes, "over the last six months of 1950 deliveries of material to [America's] MDAP allies doubled, despite the pressing demands in Korea for war material."[6] In his July message to Congress, President Truman summarized the rationale underlying these multiple political, diplomatic, and military moves:

> It is apparent that the United States is required to increase its military strength and preparedness not only to deal with the aggression in Korea, but also to increase our common defense with other free nations.
> The increased strength which is needed falls into three categories:
> In the first place, to meet the situation in Korea, we shall need to send additional men, equipment and supplies to General MacArthur's command as rapidly as possible.
> In the second place, the world situation requires that we increase substantially the size and material support of our armed forces, over and above the increases which are needed in Korea.
> In the third place, we must assist the free nations associated with us in common defense to augment their military strength.[7]

The President's congressional address also prefaced his submittal of the first of three large Defense Department supplemental appropriations bills during FY 1951 to implement his three-part strategic program. These supplemental measures may be viewed in two ways.

Considered individually, each represented a discreet administration reaction to the evolving communist military threat. The First Supplemental Appropriation Bill for 1951 was quickly erected on the assumption of an early and favorable settlement of the Korean War. Defense Secretary Johnson spoke optimistically in terms of a six to eight month war.[8] Continued bitter fighting extended the projected termination date for hostilities. The Second Supplemental Bill, sent to Congress on December 1, was built on the premise that the Korean War would conveniently end at the close of the fiscal year. This calculation did not include the possibility of Communist Chinese entry into the war. Before Congress could pass on the measure, Chinese troops were massed against United Nations forces. Like the two previous military functions bills, the Second Supplemental proved inadequate even as it was being proposed.[9] In spite of its defects, General George Marshall, who had recently replaced Louis Johnson as secretary of defense, asked Congress' approval of the supplemental request. A third supplemental was hastily assembled and submitted to Congress in the first half of 1951.

Viewed as one continuing administration action, however, the supplemental bills for FY 1951 broke with previous military and economic planning and programming and initiated a defense build-up that continued into the Eisenhower administration. The nation's military power was not prepared for a limited, conventional war on the Korean model in June, 1950. War, if it came, was to have been triggered by a direct Soviet attack in western Europe, a contingency that seemed remote in light of the American superiority in nuclear weapons and long-range delivery systems. The army and navy, consequently, were permitted to deteriorate. General Omar Bradley, chairman of the Joint Chiefs of Staff, told David Lilienthal, chairman of the Atomic Energy Commission, "that . . . [the military] had no reserve except the A-bomb in the event of aggression against us any place in the world. . . . We had, it seemed to me, falsely relied upon the security of merely a stockpile of A-bombs."[10] The Korean conflict confirmed Bradley's judgment. The Russian development of an atomic bomb and the subsequent gradual diminution in credibility of the American nuclear deterrent reinforced it. The FY 1951 supplements that were presented to Congress may be viewed as part of a broader program for the orderly expansion of land, sea, and air forces above the estimated Korean requirements in order to bring America's military power, at least momentarily, into line with its widened perception of its political commitments abroad. The Korean War acted as a catalyst for the implementation of the strategic view that was outlined in NSC 68. General Bradley had already suggested the broad perspective and the recommendations for a long-term military buildup that were embodied in NSC 68 in a popular magazine article that appeared nine months before the Korean War began. "Our way toward security lies not in any sudden burst of activity," the General wrote, "but in the steady, unwavering purposeful application of energy over a long period of years. . . . We are in for a *long pull*." [11] Bradley's "long pull" concept would be the slogan of the 1950's, appearing also under the banner of the Truman administration's FY 1953 "stretch out" or the Eisenhower administration's "long haul" of FY 1954 and after. Although the supplemental appropriation bills were clearly improvised in great part, they reflected a more comprehensive and integrated approach and understanding of the nation's strategic position than had hitherto animated American foreign policy thinking. To a considerable extent, "rearmament was based on a plan, which was more than simply a military reaction to a particular military move." [12]

Under the pressure of a concerted military threat, the administration temporarily cast aside the fetters that hamstrung its economic thinking. Dire warnings of impending economic disaster, if the government were to spend more money than some fixed budgetary amount, were ignored. New faith was placed in the nation's economy that had only recently been pictured on the threshold of complete breakdown. Table 4 compares FY 1950 and 1951 cash appropriation requests for each of the services and for the Office of the Secretary of Defense. The two most significant columns are 1 and 6 which compare military appropriations before and after the outbreak of the Korean War. Appropriations jumped almost 400 per cent during this short period. Largest immediate gainer was the army. Large grants for the other services underlined, nevertheless, the initially balanced character of the military program presented to Congress for its consent. Cash appropriations of $48.26 billion for FY 1951 exceeded the total amount of spending authority granted to the defense establishment in all of the years after World War II.

TABLE 4*

COMPARISONS OF CASH APPROPRIATIONS FOR THE ARMED SERVICES
FOR THE FISCAL YEARS 1950 AND 1951
(Discrepancies in totals due to rounding)
(In Billions)

	FY 1950	Basic Appropriations, FY 1951	First Supplemental	Second Supplemental	Third Supplemental	Total FY 1951
Defense Department	0.2	0.4	0.3	0.05	...	0.69
Army	4.5	4.1	3.2	9.2	2.85	19.26
Navy	4.4	4.1	3.7	3.0	1.64	12.46
Air Force	4.2	4.6	4.6	4.6	1.90	15.85
Total	13.3	13.3	11.7	16.85	6.39	48.26

* Sources: H. Doc. 120, 82/1, 1951, p. 20; and HSAC, *Hearings, Fourth Supplemental Appropriation*, 82/1, 1951, pp. 31–32.

For a short time at least, defense budgets would be primarily shaped by military estimates of strategic requirements rather than by hardened budgetary ceilings. Said Under Secretary of Defense Robert Lovett to a House appropriations subcommittee in defending the Second Supplemental Bill, "We have tried this time . . . to use military needs as the principal item of . . . concern rather than to apply an arbitrary dollar ceiling and try to fit . . . [armed service] needs to it; that is, to deal with this budget estimate from the point of view of national security which is our primary concern." [13]

Lovett's rhetoric soon surpassed its effect. The reoriented point of view that he described did not prevail much beyond the FY 1952 budget. A hedge against a future cutback in defense was implicit in the initial rearmament program itself. A military buildup did not mean full or immediate mobilization. The administration resisted such proposals fearing that a mass-produced output of military goods would unbalance the economy and exacerbate already strong inflationary pressures. Supporting these arguments was the view that the maximum year of military danger vis-à-vis the Soviet Union was 1954. Rapid defense expansion, if completed at an earlier date, would be wasteful.[14] "This is not a war or a full mobilization budget," summarized Under Secretary of Defense Lovett:

> It is an initial step in a planned 4-year effort to restore our military posture in order to give us some measure of security against disaster and to put us in a better position to meet our obligations internationally. It is designed to provide a deterrent against aggression and to provide a base from which rapid build-up can be attained in case of all-out war. But it is obviously not a war-footing budget request. That would involve hundreds of billions of dollars. This aims at the creation of a Defense Establishment which can be maintained over a substantial period of time without excessive strain while providing the essential quality of quick build-up from a sound base.[15]

As the Korean War receded in importance, emphasis again shifted to the maintenance of a "sound base" that became identified, as before, with a defined budgetary spending level that rested not so much on an assessment of the nation's economic capacity to support various stated military programs as on a judgment as to what was, domestically, politically feasible and desirable.

The FY 1951 supplements placed highest priority on military personnel and procurement expansion. Table 5 indicates the personnel increments of each supplemental bill, the projected year end totals for the armed services, and the estimated average man-years. Column 5 summarizes the end strength contemplated by the four appropriation bills passed for FY 1951. All of the services increased their personnel strength. Ground forces expanded more rapidly both in numbers and in rate of growth. Army end-strength was to stand at two and one-half times the size projected in the original defense appropriation request for FY 1951.

TABLE 5*

MILITARY STRENGTH ESTIMATES FOR FISCAL YEAR 1951

	Basic	First Supple-mental	Second Supple-mental	Fourth Supple-mental	Total End-Strength	Average
Army	631,900	204,000	429,000	287,000	1,551,900	1,087,000
Navy	376,501	203,304	104,067	51,128	735,000	558,513
Marines	74,437	63,576	28,142	37,874	204,029	156,407
Air Force	416,000	132,314	102,781	198,905	850,000	546,712
Total	1,498,838	603,194	663,990	574,907	3,340,929	2,448,632

* Sources: Columns 1, 2, and 3 are found in the following: H. Rept. 3193, 81/2, 1950, p. 22. The last three columns were compiled from various pages of the following document: HSAC, *Hearings, Fourth Supplemental Appropriations Bill, FY 1951*, 82/1, 1951, pp. 69, 601, 639, and 663. The Fourth Supplemental Bill was actually the third appropriation supplement made for the Defense Department in FY 1951.

The three supplemental appropriation bills heralded a long overdue procurement program. Following World War II modernization and replacement of armed service equipment was negligible when measured against the needs of the Korean conflict. Surplus war stocks, which soon became useless or obsolete, furnished the bulk of the weapons supplied to the services. As the years wore on, the gap widened between the kinds of weapons that composed the arsenal of the military branches and the kinds of military equipment that they were likely to face in combat.

The army was understandably the largest benefactor of the expansion drive. Funds available to the Army Ordnance Department jumped from $637 million in the regular FY 1951 budget to almost $7 billion. The Second Supplemental Bill alone added $4.0 billion to ordnance activities, twice as much as the previous three yearly defense appropriations. Ammunition purchases predominated. Heavy investments were made in light, medium, and heavy tanks. The demand was so great that many tanks were placed into combat without a test-run. Other important heavy items included personnel carriers, jeeps, mobile artillery, and antiaircraft weapons. A wide assortment of smaller arms, including the 3.5-inch bazooka which could pierce the heavy-armored Russian tanks operating in Korea, were also incorporated into the army's procurement program.[16]

The navy recommended 192 new ship constructions in the three supplemental bills. The majority of these new ships were landing craft and mine sweepers. There was some mention of a new aircraft carrier along the lines of the one which had been rejected by the secretary of defense in 1949, but no action was taken. The ship conversion program similarly emphasized small naval craft. Needed warships were to be acquired from the navy's large reserve fleet. Major fighting ships in operation quickly rose from 243 to 323, and total active naval vessels were increased from 683 to 1,044.[17]

Increments in air force and naval aircraft procurement and operation rounded out the augmented military force levels. The navy planned to maintain over 8,000 planes by June 30, 1951. Almost 2,000 new airplanes were added to the navy's fleet. The air force, with forty-eight incomplete groups, gradually expanded its requests in each supplemental bill to eighty-seven groups. The seemingly impregnable barrier of seventy groups was finally breached. Appropriations for new construction and related procurement multiplied four times during FY 1951. More than five thousand new airplanes were to be bought for the air force's arsenal during the fiscal year. Navy procurement, while placed at a lower level, was still substantial when compared with its previous aircraft procurement program.[18]

Congress and rearmament.—The discussion so far has necessarily centered on the thinking and actions of the executive branch. Congress did not exert an important influence over the course of military policy development during this period. Certainly it did not press its appropriations power to shape the military views of the administration. The Korean hostilities further weakened congressional influence over military policy as the legislative branch was swept along by the tide of war. President Truman had not consulted Congress or its leaders before ordering American troops into battle. Once American lives were committed, a majority in Congress could do little else except close ranks behind the President and acquiesce in his military and economic policies until the crisis had passed.

Few in Congress immediately understood the Korean War and the changed nature of the communist challenge that it implied. Stopping the communist aggression in Korea was generally approved. Most legislators agreed that a line had to be drawn somewhere against further military expansion.[19] Yet the specific reasons for America's involvement in a conventional war on a tiny peninsula over 5,000 miles away seemed beyond the comprehension of most legislators. Like the rest of the nation, Congress struggled simply to keep itself abreast of the rapidly changing events. The appropriations committees of both houses were in almost continuous session from January 1950 to August 1951. The many doubts about pre- and post-Korean War economic and military policies were provisionally resolved as similar misgivings had been during World War II. The

Congress turned for counsel to the nation's military experts who now spoke, albeit temporarily, with a united voice.

With little hesitation the appropriations committees of both houses consented to the administration's massive military buildup and to its equally extensive appropriation requests. No major economic or military recommendation was either disputed or denied. Limits on personnel authorizations were suspended. Only one noteworthy assertion of congressional independence was displayed in its consideration of the three supplemental defense appropriation bills. It came in the midst of the Senate floor debates on the Second Supplemental Bill. A Republican-inspired amendment to decrease civilian war relief funds for Korea by $50 million carried over the appropriations committee's report.[20] Neither house was inclined to overturn any of the major proposals issuing from the executive branch. The mood of Congress—and especially of the House Subcommittee on Defense Department Appropriations—was one of searching inquiry to determine whether the money estimates of the armed services were sufficient to carry out the programs outlined by them in the hearings.[21] It was with a sense of relief that House Appropriations Committee leaders could quote General Bradley as saying, "that the forces requested . . . [were] considered adequate for the emergency situation" and that the Joint Chiefs of Staff would "inform the Congress as quickly as possible of any necessary revision in . . . [military] requirements. . . . "[22] In effect, Congress would be told of changes in military policy and requirements after they had been decided elsewhere. There were few congressmen who voiced any concern about the almost total reliance of Congress upon the advice of military leaders for strategic policy direction. Representative Mahon, in summarizing the First Supplemental Bill before the House, readily admitted his subcommittee's dependence on the Joint Chiefs of Staff:

The choice that has been made [about the nation's defenses] has been the choice of the President of the United States, the Department of Defense, and the Joint Chiefs of Staff. We of the Appropriations Committee in presenting this bill have not undertaken to override the recommendations of the President and the Joint Chiefs. We have accepted their recommendations as the very best possible source of guidance in this critical world situation.[23]

There was no assuring note in Mahon's remarks about Congress' ability to deal with the new condition of international life created by the Korean War. Confidence in congressional budgetary omniscience, voiced three years earlier by Representative Charles Plumley at the opening of the naval appropriation hearings of the Eightieth Congress, was gone.[24] The three supplemental bills provoked very little discussion in either house. Committee examination of the defense estimates was swift, if not always careful. The $17 billion Second Supplemental Bill swept through the House two weeks after its submission. A week later the Senate approved the measure. The other two supplements required one month each to go through Congress. Under pressure from the executive branch and distracted by the deteriorating United Nations military position in Korea, the appropriations committees generally relaxed their demand for detailed budgetary information. "The committee has approved the request for funds as presented," a House committee report admitted, "realizing that the circumstances under which the requirements are presented does not give to either the departments or the Congress sufficient time or information upon which to base the usual careful consideration given to requests for appropriations." [25] Over $48 billion in cash appropriations were granted to the Defense Department. Whatever inhibitions the President and the secretary of defense may have experienced in using these funds or in deploying American troops abroad were self-inspired. They were neither dictated nor apparently influenced in significant degree by Congress. The legislative will was hostage to the exigencies of the moment which were beyond its immediate capacity to control.

139

CONTINUED BUILDUP: FY 1952

A temporarily broader military stance.—The Truman administration's broadened military program first took shape during the hearings on the Second Supplemental Bill; assumed a more refined state during consideration of the Fourth Supplemental measure which was presented to Congress in early spring of 1951; and finally crystallized, though only for one brief year, in the Defense Department budget for FY 1952. Five basic military requirements were recognized: (1) the maintenance and supply of forces in Korea; (2) the modernization and expansion of the armed forces to a total of 3.5 million men at the end of the fiscal year; (3) the provision of equipment for training purposes and for reserve components; (4) the production of military items for allied countries; and (5) the buildup of a production base and material reserves against the contingency of a full-scale war.[26] Cost of the five-point program was estimated at $62.1 billion. The army and air force were to receive approximately $20 billion each; the navy's allotment totaled about $5 billion less. The balance of the funds were earmarked for public works projects, the liquidation of former contracts, and the administration of the Office of the Secretary of Defense. New obligational authority was placed at $60.7 billion. This was four times the "absolute maximum" of fiscal 1950 for the military establishment. Almost 50 per cent of the $60 billion was directed toward the acquisition of hard goods—aircraft, ships, tanks, artillery, ammunition, and similar items needed to equip the armed forces.[27]

In keeping with the new emphasis on strategic over fiscal imperatives, the military budget was based primarily on the military requirements set down by the Joint Chiefs of Staff. By comparison with previous years, the influence of the Budget Bureau was slight. Also, budgetary ceilings were not applied during the formulating phases of the defense budget. The services were permitted to determine

140

their needs in view of their understanding of the strategic situation facing the United States. Secretary of Defense Robert Lovett, who had replaced General George C. Marshall, assured a worried Congress that the force levels and weapons systems proposals presented by the Defense Department were the same agreed upon by the Joint Chiefs.[28] The congressional hearings corroborated Lovett's assurances that the civilian leaders of the executive branch had deferred to the decisions of the military heads of the services. The service chiefs confirmed the military recommendations which were embodied in the appropriations bill.[29] They refrained, too, from criticizing each other's appropriations requests to Congress, focusing instead on their respective service requirements. A huge $60 billion budget provided a momentary respite in interservice rivalries. All of the services participated in the defense boom. The realization of Forrestal's vision of a balanced military force appeared finally to be in sight. Temporarily, the nation's dependence on its atomic arsenal, compared with its pre-Korean War strategic posture, was being reduced. While the air force would continue to provide the nation's long-range nuclear punch, the army and navy would furnish other, less devastating but more subtly shaded forms of military power that would correspond more readily and commensurately to the nation's divergent foreign policy interests or objectives. It was in this strategic context that President Truman made the controversial political decision to dispatch four American army divisions to western Europe as a part of the developing NATO ground army.[30] The presence of American troops in Europe symbolized American commitment to its NATO allies and acted as a stimulant to complementary European contributions to a unified NATO force under the direction of General Dwight D. Eisenhower, President Truman's choice to be the first commander of SHAPE. The four divisions represented the first instalment on the American commitment to the newly adopted forward strategy for Europe. America went beyond a determination to liberate a conquered continent. Western Europe would be defended at its frontiers.

141

Army strength was programmed at 1,552,000 men for FY 1952. Average strength was to be 20,000 under this figure, two and one-half times the size of the pre-Korea army.[31] Procurement requests paralleled these increases. In the FY 1950 army budget, only 7 per cent of the army's budget ($273 million) was earmarked for hardware items. In FY 1951, this figure rose to 42 per cent and climbed further to 46 per cent in FY 1952. Cash amounts for these two years were recorded at $8.2 and $9.5 billion respectively.

These large outlays for personnel and procurement, comprising the bulk of army expenditures for FY 1951 and FY 1952, were aimed at quickly repairing the neglect of the preceding half decade. The President and Congress shared a great deal of the blame for the army's low state of military preparedness before the Korean War. Executives branch budgetary ceilings impeded army modernization. Congress, in turn, had too easily accepted the administration's reduced appropriations requests without exploring the implications of these cutbacks. What is more, Congress had slashed ordnance requests between 1947 and 1950 well below the minimal amounts recommended by the army. Army modernization was strangled. The replacement rate of obsolete equipment was negative.

The navy's submissions were similarly directed to rectify past oversights. An average of 558,000 naval officers and men in FY 1951 would rise to approximately 785,000 a year later.[32] New ship construction totaled 113, including the first nuclear-powered submarine, the "Nautilus," and a flush-deck carrier, the "USS Forrestal." When added to the active fleet, these new ships would bring operating levels to 1,116 vessels. A little over 400 of these were major combatants which were to be maintained at 85 per cent of wartime authorizations.[33] Aircraft procurement paralleled these increases. The navy proposed a $3.6 billion appropriation for 4,000 new airplanes.[34]

The "Forrestal" carrier was the most prominent feature of the navy's FY 1952 recommendations. The "Forrestal" reasserted the navy's claim to importance in the nation's defense structure. The navy had argued in 1949 that the United States should not adopt a one-weapon strategy or depend on any one service. Francis Matthews, the secretary of the navy, essentially re-echoed this argument in his semi-annual report to Congress: "It was realized early," he said, "that we cannot safely place reliance on any single weapon or weapons system, but must carry relatively a 'full bag'—must keep them versatile and adaptable to any situation." [35] These general remarks were subsequently followed by a concluding appeal for more aircraft carriers. Weapons flexibility for the navy, the intimation was clear, meant not only the air force's long-range bomber capabilities, but also a fleet of "Forrestal" carriers. Based allegedly on world conditions at the time of the report, the navy estimated it would require a minimum of twelve "Forrestal" carriers to fulfil its primary mission, loosely defined as the control of the seas. [36] The command of the seas also required offensive strikes against enemy shore installations and could conceivably include strategic assaults against enemy population centers. Breaking a nation's will to fight would *ipso facto* yield control of the seas to the victorious power. The navy's carrier fleet and the air force's Strategic Air Command were in close competition again.

The air force found the competition tolerable because it, too, was rapidly enlarging its strength. General Hoyt Vandenberg, air force chief of staff, emphasized the nation's need for strategic striking air power. "Our aim is still to build the Air Force as a deterrent to war," Vandenberg testified. "We must maintain a force of such demonstrable strength as to make any aggressor consider war an unprofitable way to attain his world wide aims; or, in case of a miscalculation by the enemy, to protect the nation against defeat." [37] Vandenberg cited the Soviet Union's swelling atomic stockpile and its developing long-range bomber capability as additional reasons for "a concentrated and increasing effort." [38]

Other air force officers spelled out the implications of "a concentrated and increasing effort." Despite its Korean responsibilities that were overwhelmingly concerned with tactical ground support and air

143

control, the air force doggedly clung to its strategic bombing pre-conceptions. Its highest priorities were still placed on long-range manned delivery systems. The Korean experience did not materially affect the air force's statement of its aircraft requirements. The largest segment of its $11 billion aircraft procurement program was keyed to strategic aircraft which were to form the heart of its newly projected ninety-five–group program. To man this force, air force personnel was to jump from 787,000 on June 30, 1951, to 1,061,000 a year later. Average strength for the two years was reckoned, respectively, at 595,000 and 925,000. The pre-Korean American nuclear deterrent would be regenerated by the acquisition of more, and bigger, bombs and bombers and a large increase in uniformed manpower.[39]

Congress examines the defense bill.—The House and Senate defense subcommittees were given approximately a month and a half to examine the Defense Department's $60 billion budget. The task was hopeless from the start. The subcommittees were not prepared to challenge either the administration's political goals or the detailed appropriation estimates which were allegedly related to their achievement. The House report, the longest that had been written on the budget requests for the military establishment since World War II, devoted two short paragraphs of its 158 pages to the policy objectives of the defense budget bill. Even that discussion was drawn from the testimony of General Omar Bradley.[40] The House report merely annotated the detailed budget estimates sent by the President to Congress. No significant changes were made. The Senate report was equally uninformative with regard to the future military programs of the United States.[41] It was a great deal shorter and conspicuously neglected any discussion of the policies on which the budget rested. It was similarly dependent on the testimony of the civilian and military defense administrators who appeared during the Senate hearings. The two appropriations subcommittees concentrated on the detailed appropriation estimates of the Defense Department but were largely unable to reduce them in any appreciable degree. The President's $57.7 billion appropriation measure was cut to $56.9 billion by Congress, a reduction of approximately 2.5 per cent of the original request.[42]

The sole significant difference between the House and Senate reports was the latter's recommendation of an additional $5 billion over the President's request to speed the air force to its ninety-five–group objective. The Senate's action, while suggesting the development of an independent point of view, actually underscored its dependence on presidential and Defense Department leadership. Its $5 billion increase, first of all, was not formally requested by the air force. The Senate subcommittee had considerable difficulty in inducing the air force to admit that the $11 billion earmarked for airplane construction in the 1952 budget was insufficient for a completely modern ninety-five–group air force.[43] Lacking administration and air force support for its initiative, the Senate subcommittee was forced to compromise its position in conference with the House. A one billion dollar increase was finally approved for aircraft procurement. The navy received one-third of this amount; the air force, the balance. But the initial language of the Senate grant of $5 billion was revealing. It placed wide discretion in the hands of the secretary of defense, after consultation with the Joint Chiefs of Staff and the President, to use the money as he saw fit to increase the air striking power of the nation. The Defense Department gave no indication that the money would be spent, nor was the Senate subcommittee informed of how the extra money would be allocated if the President chose to spend it.

The sheer size of the appropriations bill rather than its strategic content touched off the longest debates on the Defense Department budget since World War II. Even the House broke with usual practice. Its leadership agreed that the bill be permitted unlimited debate. Members of both houses perceived that the days of $15 billion budgets were quickly passing and that the nation faced the prospect of expanded and continued defense spending in future years. Shifting ground from his previous year's stand, subcommittee chairman George Mahon frankly told the House that the defense of the nation was a "long-haul proposition." [44]

The dominant concern of the debates in both houses was the question of Congress' receding capacity to understand and control the military budget and the policies to which it was directed. Early in the debates, Ohio Representative Clarence Brown voiced the pervasive anxiety of many of his colleagues:

> I speak as one of those who is not at all certain just what this bill provides or what all of the items in it means [sic]. I believe, in speaking as I will, that I will perhaps be representing a great portion of the membership of this House, or, at least, that which they are thinking.
>
> I question very seriously that there are many Americans who can comprehend or understand what the huge amount carried in the total appropriation as provided in this bill . . . really means. Certainly, there are few of us here who can read this bill, fully understand it, and know all, or even very much, about it. The report of the Appropriations Subcommittee was made available only a few short hours ago. I do not know, and I do not believe many Members of the Congress, including many members of the Subcommittee on Military Appropriations, for whom I have the highest respect, and who, I realize have worked diligently and hard and long, know whether or not the appropriation items contained in this bill are actually needed, or whether these proposed expenditures are adequately justified. [45]

Like most members of Congress, Brown was unable to suggest where the military budget might be cut without impairing the defense effort. With fighting in Korea at a fever pitch, legislators were reluctant to contest the Defense Department's assessment of its budget. Even Senator Taft, long a foe of the Truman administration and the minority leader of the upper house, restrained his criticism of the defense bill. While he attacked the size of the military budget and warned of impending economic disaster unless government spending were slashed, he offered no alternative to the President's projected expenditure program.

Senator Paul Douglas, liberal Democrat from Illinois, confided that he, too, stood helpless before the defense appropriation bill. His opening statements on the military functions measure captured not only Taft's sentiments but those of a majority of both houses:

> One is awed by the magnitude of the [defense appropriation] figures, and one is almost frightened in dealing with them, because no one wishes to diminish the military effectiveness of the Nation. One is always afraid, if he makes a proposal, that it will affect military efficiency. . . . Our friends in the National Defense Establishment have us at a disadvantage. Because of their advantage of technical military knowledge, they make us reluctant to criticize their budget. . . . We are always afraid that if we vote for a reduction in a given expenditure, not only will our friends in the Defense Department criticize us, but our opponents in our States and congressional districts back home will say, 'When you voted to cut the appropriation, you voted to weaken the preparedness program of the United States.' [46]

Douglas' analysis was compelling. Senate subcommittee chairman Joseph O'Mahoney candidly admitted that neither military appropriations subcommittee wished "to substitute their civilian judgment for the military judgment of the men who, in the democratic process . . . [were] charged with the responsibility for handling . . . military affairs." [47] Errett Scrivner, member of the House Subcommittee on Defense Appropriations, went further. Rationalizing that the appropriations committees did not make military policy in the first place, he washed his hands of responsibility for the military budget. [48]

Contributing to the hesitancy of legislators to question the authority

147

of the military was the lack of information afforded the two military appropriations subcommittees during the appropriations hearings. Subcommittee members complained repeatedly that the Defense Department had not furnished adequate justifications for many of its appropriation requests. All the services, it was felt, had neglected to clearly state their requirements for civilian personnel. Also, witnesses were being sent from the different military departments who were not prepared for many of the questions put to them. One subcommittee member exclaimed:

> The testimony submitted, Mr. Chairman, was . . . in many cases highly unsatisfactory. Time and time again no breakdown was available; fundamental information was not forthcoming.
> Time and time again we were told in effect, "This figure represents our best estimate in the light of experience of the Department's needs for the fiscal year 1952." Witnesses were either unprepared or unwilling to supply simple and essential facts.
> Again and again came the response, "We shall have to submit that later for the record."
> Differing sets of figures were given by different witnesses in respect to the same question.
> Literally hours of the committee's time were needlessly wasted in trying to extract by cross-examination information which should have been readily available.[49]

This plaintive note was sounded throughout the hearings.[50]

Another difficulty confronting the subcommittees was the further introduction of performance budgeting into the presentation of defense estimates. The National Security Act of 1949 had authorized the revamping of the budget structure along functional lines in contrast to the organizational categories which were previously used. Performance budgeting brought about a consolidation of many budget categories, resulting in larger, more inclusive authorizations. Costs were redistributed among a number of new accounts, many previous appropriation listings were dropped and others were added. Many subcommittee members had difficulty in following the changes which had been made in the defense budget.

House and Senate subcommittee chairmen struggled to create the impression that the appropriations committees had not blindly accepted the budget estimates of the Defense Department. Both pointed to the voluminous hearings held by each respective subcommittee. The House hearings totaled over 3,500 pages; the Senate, a little more than half this total. The suggestion was implicitly advanced that the very length of the hearings had produced a thorough analysis of the past performance and the proposed future activities of the Defense Department. One congressman, less swayed by the bulk of the hearings than by the admission of a number of subcommittee members that the armed services had fallen short in explicating their budget presentations, bluntly concluded:

> I am just about convinced that the Congress of the United States has substantially lost control of the affairs of the country. When men . . . [of the House Defense Appropriations Subcommittee] are forced to come into this well and tell us they are unable to get information from the military administrators, that detailed information is not forthcoming, that satisfactory answers to questions are not available, that is something for us to be concerned about.[51]

In more sober and circumspect terms, the House report confirmed these fears:

> The books of justifications presented to the committee in support of the estimates for fiscal year 1952 were most inadequate in that they failed to make clear information required each year by the committee and the Congress before action can be taken on annual appropriation bills. Information by the departments was not set forth in readily comparable form and in a uniform manner. . . . Members were forced to develop from witnesses through long and tedious questioning and from material submitted in addition to the justifications, information

149

that should have been readily available in the books of justifications.[52]

The inadequacy of the Defense Department's "books of justifications"
was itself a final blow to the conceit that the legislative branch was
controlling and shaping military policy. Congressmen pride themselves on their detailed knowledge of military programs. Now they
found themselves hampered not only in securing information about
strategic problems in which their interest was demonstrably secondary
and diffuse, but in acquiring data about matters that were dear to
their legislative hearts—the Defense Department's internal organization and its administrative operations dealing with pay rates, grade
levels, job requirements, and the like.

The sole organized and concerted attack on the varied appropriations for the Defense Department was made by Senator Douglas of
Illinois, who waged a one-man fight against alleged waste, inefficiency,
and duplication in defense management. He offered a number of
amendments to reduce the number of appropriations categories.[53]
While most of them failed, his persistent drum-fire attack prepared
the way for a subsequent Republican amendment to diminish all
appropriations for the Defense Department by 2½ per cent, if
national defense would not thereby be impaired. This meat ax
proposal carried and became part of the Senate bill sent to conference where it was eventually dropped.[54] The House and Senate
versions of the defense budget, being essentially alike, were easily
reconciled.

PREFACE TO FY 1953

One conviction, based more on a vaguely articulated fear rather
than on a clear perception of the political, military, and economic
ramifications of the FY 1952 budget, took hold of a growing number

of legislators. Congressional feeling ran high that defense expenditures would have to be cut radically and rapidly below the $57 billion defense bill for FY 1952 if the nation was to escape economic bankruptcy. "It may or may not be necessary to spend this money," Senator Robert Taft ominously warned, "but we ought not to spend it without realizing that if we are going to continue such a scale of expenditure, we will plunge the country into economic difficulty. . . . We will weaken our whole economic structure."[55] Taft's cautionary remarks presaged a slow shift within the congressional consensus. Military and strategic problems, however important they might be, would have to be shaped in terms of the nation's economic capabilities. In principle there could be no objection to this point of view. What proved suspect was its application in Congress. For neither Congress nor its committees attempted to identify the feasible limits of the nation's economic power to sustain the existing rate of defense expenditures in FY 1952. The appropriations committees might well have appealed to the Joint Economic Committee for reliable estimates of the nation's economic strength. Or, they might have requested guidance with respect to the growth potential of the economy and its developing capacity to translate its evolving strength into operational military power to contain the accelerating size and range of communist military power. None of these moves were made. Crude guesses were relied upon instead.

Buttressing the fear of economic collapse was the feeling, given lucid expression by Senator Paul Douglas, that the Defense Department was guilty of wasting huge sums of money through improper or inefficient management of its budgets. Rumors circulated in Congress about corruption among defense officials in high places. Disclosure of nefarious dealings by some procurement officers and military commanders lent support to these congressional suspicions.

Congress found itself trapped between two forces of darkness. On the one side, it was frightened by the specter of economic disaster as a by-product of military preparedness; on the other, it was oppressed by the possibility of military defeat by the Soviet Union. Slowly and ponderously it began to search for an alternative to the strategy temporarily adopted by the administration.

The Truman administration appeared no less concerned with the dilemma into which its strategic planning had seemingly led it. The administration and controlling majorities in Congress reached the paradoxical conclusion in 1952 that military expenditures would have to be cut to forestall the development of inflation and economic dislocation, when at the same time, intelligence reports indicated that the Soviet military threat to the United States was reaching its peak. The contradiction between the administration's perception of the Soviet military threat and the domestic demand for a diminished response to that challenge would be uneasily resolved by placing increased reliance on retaliatory air forces and nuclear bombing. This shift proved generally agreeable to most congressional members.

Largely ignoring the Korean experience, a strategy based on strategic air power was gradually resurrected. The human and material costs of supporting conventional forces and weapons systems seemed to be too painful a burden for the nation to endure. Air power would allegedly succeed where it had previously failed. At a tolerable cost in men and money, it would strengthen the deterrent capacity of the nation's military forces and render more protection for the nation in the event of a Russian attack.

YEARS OF REAPPRAISAL: THE TRUMAN "STRETCH-OUT": FY 1953

The last year of the Truman administration and the first year of the Eisenhower administration were years of reappraisal of the nation's military structure and requirements. Many of the cutbacks in force levels which were to mark President Eisenhower's term of office were foreshadowed in the FY 1953 budget prepared by his Democratic predecessor. FY 1953 and FY 1954 must be discussed as a unit to be understood. In these years, the Democratic and Republican administrations were separated more by their political rhetoric than by the substance and direction of their respective military proposals.

New force levels announced.—President Truman's FY 1953 defense budget set new and impressive goals for the Defense Department. Planned was an air force of 143 wings,[56] an army of twenty-one divisions, a navy of 408 major combatants and sixteen carrier air groups, and a marine corps of three divisions.[57] Military expenditures were estimated at $52 billion. The President asked for $52.4 billion in new obligational authority, $9.3 billion less than the preceding year. The reduction, explained the President, was "possible because a substantial portion of the obligational authority required to finance . . . military expenditures has already been provided by the Congress."[58]

The hearings revealed another, and even more decisive factor, influencing the reduced defense estimates. The military departments were initially instructed to develop budgets according to their estimate of the nation's military requirements. When these were submitted to the secretary of defense, they totaled $71 billion in new appropriations authority. This sum was needed in order to support an expenditure of $73 billion, exclusive of military assistance programs to other countries, which would have brought the army and marine corps to the readiness goals, described above, by July 1, 1953, and the navy and air force to a state of preparedness of 143 wings and 408 combatant ships a short time later. The secretary of defense, however, pared the Joint Chiefs' recommendation to $55 billion. The Budget Bureau and the President further cut this figure by $3 billion so that military expenditures for the fiscal year would be kept under $60 billion. The justification for this reduction in armed force funds were various, but they were basically fiscal. Defense Secretary Robert Lovett explained that military expenditures had to be curtailed: (1) to release scarce raw materials for use in the civilian economy, the lack of which could lead to widespread unemployment;

153

(2) "to reschedule certain items of equipment in such a fashion as to avoid excessive peaks which might thereafter result in abrupt and permanent shut-downs"; and (3) to prolong "the procurement of certain types of items in those fields in which unusual technological advances give promise of substantially improved weapons within the next two or three years." [59] While the preparedness goals set by the military staff were accepted,[60] the appropriations restrictions established by the secretary of defense and, subsequently, by the President, "stretched out" the period in which readiness was to be accomplished.[61] The FY 1953 budget would merely build toward these goals. It held no promise that they would be reached by the end of the year, nor would they be achieved at the end of FY 1954 when the military threat to the nation's security was to be at its height on the basis of intelligence estimates.

The army was asked to "stretch out" more than the other services. Though beset with increasing responsibilities—including the successful conclusion of the war in Korea, the protection of military bases in the Far East and Europe, the contribution of forces to NATO, the strengthening of United States air defenses, the training and equipping of active and reserve forces, and the maintenance of an extensive research and development program—the army was permitted to ask for only $14.2 billion in contrast to the approximately $21 billion appropriated in FY 1952.[62] The major cause for the drop was the cutback in ordnance procurement appropriations. The Budget Bureau cut the army's $8.6 billion ordnance request to $3.7 billion.[63] Personnel strength, however, was to be kept at FY 1952 levels.[64]

The "stretch out" drive affected the navy, although less severely. Its $16 billion FY 1952 appropriation slipped to $13.2 billion. Unlike the army, it successfully protected its procurement program. The army's equipment purchases totaled 26 per cent of its budget for FY 1953, a slump from the 42 per cent of the previous year. The navy, on the other hand, sustained its purchasing program at 46 per cent. Its future was being built on a more lasting basis. The administration approved a shipbuilding program of 554 new vessels, including another supercarrier of the "Forrestal" class,[65] and an aircraft procurement schedule that would bring the navy's operating fleet from 8,700 to approximately 10,200, still 700 short of the navy's estimated minimum requirement for full modernization of its forces.[66] Navy uniformed strength was to expand to an average of 825,000. The 40,000 increase over FY 1952 was primarily keyed to the newly augmented emphasis on naval air power that was to be the spearhead of its 408 major combatant fleet, a post-World War II high.[67] Communist military successes in Korea pushed marine corps personnel needs upward to an average of 243,700.[68]

The air force alone escaped most of the "stretch out" order. It received permission to request $22.4 billion to support its 143 wing goal. Of this total, 58 per cent was allocated to major procurement, the same percentage marking the FY 1952 budget. $12.7 billion was earmarked for aircraft procurement.[69] While personnel was to remain at FY 1952 levels, personnel totals were to climb to 1.2 million in the two succeeding years.[70] Expansion of air strength principally signified the modernization and growth of the Strategic Air Command. The air force's tactical and air transport and defense missions were slightly enlarged, but these were clearly subordinated in importance to SAC. Leading air force spokesmen preferred to speak of 126 combat wings rather than of the administration's 143 wing total which included airlift wings. The air force did not consider this seventeen-wing force to be properly within its area of responsibility.[71] If cuts had to be made in aircraft procurement, the air force stated that these would be applied to its tactical support units.[72] SAC would be insulated against cutbacks. The nation's strategic air power, argued the air force, would counter Russia's long-range atomic capability and would offset communist superiority in men and military equipment. To twist a Mahanian aphorism, SAC would be the great equalizer. Said General D. N. Yates, air force director of research and development:

In order to most effectively blunt the enemy's capability to continue the atomic bombardment of our Nation, as well as to

destroy his industrial and economic potential to support the war
on land, sea, and in the air, we must be capable of exploiting
our greatest advantage—our stockpile of atomic bombs. We must
provide strategic bombers having range and speed characteristics
capable of penetrating the enemy defense and placing these
bombs on vital targets.[73]

The FY 1953 budget left little doubt that the air force position on
strategic policy had regained much of the ground that it had lost
within the councils of the Truman administration during the early
stages of the Korean War.

Congress contests the military budget.—Congress was hostile to the
President's budget. The major objections were not directly related
to the merit of the strategic policies and analyses underlying the
budget. Few congressmen probed the dimensions of these issues. Even
less were they inclined to offer feasible alternatives to the President's
defense recommendations. The principal concern of most legislators
turned on the size of the defense bill. Some, like the members of
the House Appropriations Committee, felt that there was a great
deal of waste and inefficiency in the military establishment and that
the administration's military program could be achieved at less cost.
Defense Department unobligated funds, totaling almost $60 billion
on July 1, 1952, supported this argument. Others, like the chairman
of the Senate Defense Appropriations Subcommittee, demanded a
limit on defense expenditures to guard against economic collapse.
These viewpoints had been present in previous congressional deliberations on the military budget. The year 1952 differed from others,
particularly since the outbreak of the Korean conflict, in the surprising
force with which these two positions were sounded and the degree
to which they struck responsive chords among many legislators anxious
about their fortunes in the upcoming presidential elections. Rumblings
from the grassroots indicated widespread voter impatience with the
slow and costly progress of the Korean War. The conflict loomed in
early spring as the key issue of the campaign.

156

President Truman's "stretch out" drive unwittingly contributed to congressional antipathy to the continued level of defense spending. The administration's unwillingness to reach the force levels that it set for the military services before 1954, the year of "maximum danger," undermined congressional confidence in the Defense Department's budgetary proposals. If the President found that it was expedient to cut the defense budget without impairing the nation's defense, congressional leaders reasoned,[74] there seemed to be no compelling reason why Congress could not do likewise. The ceiling on defense expenditures encouraged many legislators to believe that the President did not take too seriously his own intelligence estimates of Soviet military strength. The President's "stretch out," therefore, placed the military departments at a distinct disadvantage in making their budget presentations to Congress. Since their civilian superiors had vetoed their initial requests and lengthened the period in which their program goals would be reached, it was difficult to persuade a skeptical House and Senate of the gravity of the Soviet buildup. Congressional doubts about the firmness of the armed service requests were not resolved by Secretary of Defense Lovett's admission that, in cutting defense estimates, the administration was accepting a "calculated risk" that the Russians would not attack the United States.[75] Congress, too, was in a gambling mood in 1952.

Congress' quarrel with the President's defense budget was linked to a number of other heated issues which tended to divide further the two branches of the government on the defense bill. There was the pent up frustration over the seemingly endless series of bitter failures to terminate the Korean hostilities on an acceptable basis. The truce talks at Panmunjom droned on for long, painful months as American casualties mounted. The contentious repercussions of General Douglas MacArthur's dismissal also were still reverberating through Congress. The ably conducted Senate hearings on the United States Far East policies blunted, but did not squash, criticism of the Democratic administration.[76] There was a drift, too, within important congressional circles of both parties not only toward a policy of retrenchment in governmental operations but also towards a corresponding military disengagement in Europe and Asia. These were the essential elements of Senator Taft's *A Foreign Policy for Americans* and former President Herbert Hoover's "Gibraltar" speech.[77] Both men typified the sentiments of many Republican leaders, particularly those within the conservative wing of the party. If the Senate debate of the preceding congressional session concerning the sending of troops to Europe did not succeed in stopping President Truman from ordering American forces to Europe, it did raise into question his authority and, more importantly, force him on the defensive to justify his action.[78] Senator Joseph McCarthy's strident charges of communist infiltration and subversion in the executive branch accelerated the erosion of popular and congressional confidence in the Democratic administration's management of both domestic and foreign affairs. Disputes in Congress over these and other issues transformed the legislative branch into a sprawling battleground on which a host of small and large contests raged, intensified to fever pitch by the inevitable partisan and personal conflicts of the congressional and presidential elections of that year.

The House subcommittee slashed $4.2 billion from the military budget. The army lost $1.7 billion; the navy, $1 billion; and the air force, $1.5 billion.[79] Bristling with criticism, the House report charged the armed forces with mismanagement and recommended numerous changes to improve operations. "A considerable portion of the 1.4 billion dollar reduction . . . " admitted the House appropriations group, "has been made with the specific purpose in mind of enforcing a better job of military management and expenditure. Some way must be found to shock the people in the Department of Defense from top to bottom into the full realization that Congress and the American people will not tolerate flagrant waste in money and manpower."[80]

Over half of the army reductions were in procurement. The balance was largely divided between personnel and maintenance and operations. The $900 million decrease in procurement, while not specifically allocated, was derived, the House report maintained, "from actual application of data made available to the committee and it is not a slash in the dark." [81] The House assertion was doubtless true on its surface, but misleading nevertheless. As the record of the hearings was released, it became clear that the cuts rested on committee decisions that were more hastily conceived and less foresighted than the committee would have had the House believe.

House opposition to the navy budget exhibited one major policy disagreement with the administration. The appropriations committee recommended postponement of the construction of a second "Forrestal" carrier together with 162 smaller vessels.[82] Deferment of the supercarrier would "afford the committee and the Congress fuller opportunity to consider all aspects of the matter in light of certain technical and other developments in the picture." [83] None could gainsay so seemingly rational a plea for more data and a more dispassionate approach to the carrier program. However, there was only a slim possibility that "certain technical and other developments" would actually be examined by Congress, since the inspiration for the carrier's temporary demise was Representative Clarence Cannon, chairman of the appropriations committee, whose implacable opposition to the navy's carrier program predated the Korean War.[84] No amount of new data or reanalysis was likely to budge Cannon. Led by its chairman, the House Appropriations Committee deepened its wound to the navy's pride and pocketbook by the additional reduction of $150 million from the naval airplane procurement fund. Among the reasons which the committee gave for its action was that aircraft funds would not be needed with the deletion of the carrier.

Even the air force, long the darling of the House appropriations unit, could not escape its wrath. Of the $1.5 billion taken from its appropriation request, $730 million was lost from the procurement program; $600 million from maintenance and operations; and $150 million from personnel. Curiously, the House committee did not

159

wish "that the number of aircraft to be procured . . . [should] be reduced."[85] Nor did it desire that air force personnel requirements be reduced by "one single person."[86] It expressed the hope "that by efficiencies and reductions in cost additional aircraft may be procured for the same money."[87] This same reasoning was applied to maintenance and operations and generally to the entire air force budget.

The committee cut was only the first phase of the battle of the budget in the House during 1952. While a few legislators registered concern over the severity of the House Appropriations Committee's reductions[88] and while others cautioned against more appropriations curtailments,[89] the report received little criticism on the House floor. A majority of the House chopped even deeper into the defense estimates. A series of amendments produced another $500 million in reductions.

One House amendment merits special attention. Representative Howard Smith of Virginia offered an amendment to limit Defense Department expenditures to $46 billion in FY 1953. Limitation on defense outlays was to diminish by $5 billion the over-all budgetary deficit of $14 billion projected for FY 1953. Smith and others argued that the expenditure limitation would further reduce waste and would finally give Congress control over the military budget. Amendment supporters held that their motion would not force any reductions in the defense budget. The military services would still be authorized to bring their unobligated balances forward, though a sum greater than $46 billion could not be expended during the fiscal year.[90] The amendment split the House Military Appropriations Subcommittee and cut across party lines in the lower chamber. Spurred by a coalition of Democrats and Republicans, the amendment carried by a wide margin.[91]

The Senate hearings concentrated heavily on the House slashes. The hearings were roughly divided between a Defense Department attack on Section 638—the Smith amendment to the House bill—and a plea for restitution of the funds cut by the House. The two issues were separate because the House limitation on military expenditures and its paring of Defense Department requests, if sustained, would have had two entirely different effects on strategic policy. The House, in its enthusiasm for lowered defense costs and greater efficiency in the Defense Department, had made numerous cuts in defense appropriations while only vaguely aware of the policy implications of its decisions. The Senate hearings built to this conclusion.

The Smith amendment had the broadest and most adverse effect on military planning. All leading defense officials vigorously opposed the House expenditure limitation.[92] The principal burden of the House ceiling fell upon the defense procurement program. Personnel and maintenance costs could not be lowered because they were relatively fixed factors. Secretary of Defense Lovett estimated that the $18.9 billion projected for payment of major weapons in 1953 would have to be diminished by one-third if the Senate agreed with the House position. This cutback would force the cancellation of a large number of established contracts, an increase in prices for a wide assortment of end-items, and substantial losses of time and human resources. Threatened by disruption, too, was the delicately balanced production base on which the administration's defense policies depended.

The irony of the Smith amendment was that Congress would lose even more of what little influence it enjoyed in shaping the military budget. The secretary of defense would exercise power usually reserved to Congress. Under a general expenditure limitation, the secretary of defense could execute a disbursement program at variance with the defense program approved by Congress. The Smith amendment was tantamount to a nullification of elaborate and lengthy hearings conducted by the defense appropriations subcommittee.

One of the most important features of the hearings is the opportunity they provide the Congress for review of the future policies of the administration in power. The latter is constrained to reveal the different courses of action to be undertaken during the year. The

161

legislative arms of the government can then hold the administration and its agents responsible for policies described during the hearings. The Smith amendment effectively voided many of the formal and informal agreements reached between officials of the two branches of government. The secretary of defense was granted the broad and unspecified mandate of spending the $46 billion permitted for FY 1953 according to his own conception of what military capabilities the nation required without prior review by Congress.[93]

Disruption of armed force plans was no less apparent as a result of the expenditure limitation. The services hastily composed a priority list of items which each would recommend dropped from 1953 schedules if the Smith motion were incorporated into the final defense bill. Only the highlights can be given here because of the far-reaching ramifications of the expenditure ceiling. The army estimated a loss of over 3,000 medium tanks, a variety of cannons and combat vehicles, and a reduction in motor fire control equipment. It concluded "that many units would not even have an initial supply of modern equipment and that in case . . . [the nation] became involved in a major combat operation, there would be no stocks available to replace combat losses." [94] This situation raised serious doubts about the United States ability to maintain troops in Europe and the Far East.[95] The navy expressed distress about delays in its shipbuilding and conversion program and in aircraft procurement. Work on 78 ships and over 500 planes would be deferred.[96] The air force would suffer a loss of modern aircraft for ten combat wings and delayed delivery of at least three thousand planes over an eighteen-month period. Of the 126 wings which were recommended, only 104 would be equipped for combat at the end of the fiscal year. Personnel losses would also total over 90,000.[97]

Specific House cuts had a separate, but equally grave, effect on the Defense Department's program. While the House appropriations subcommittee accepted the administration's force levels, it insisted that they could be allocated at less cost through more efficient management, without sacrificing their rate of development. Unless the armed services were again inflating their estimates before the Senate defense appropriations subcommittee, the House was, quite inconsistently, accepting the administration's military program, and the time limits within which it was cast, without simultaneously providing the funds to realize those force level goals. All the services faced substantial personnel losses if the House bill was adopted. This was true, despite the insistence of the House Appropriations Committee that it was not its intention to lower personnel strength, particularly for the air force.[98] The House assurance that it would provide the air force with supplemental funds took little account of the advanced planning and lead time required to effectively increase the uniformed personnel of the armed forces on an orderly and efficient basis. Supplemental appropriations could not be used as a faucet which could be turned on and off to produce differently stated force levels when they would become desirable.

The adverse effects of the House-induced reductions were even more apparent within the area of hardware procurement. The army doubted its ability to maintain troops in the Far East and Europe on the basis of the House bill.[99] The navy, already distraught over the loss of its carrier, pointed out that it was separate from its airplane requests. The House simply assumed a connection and reduced navy aircraft purchases by $150 million. The target date for the air force's 143-wing program was pushed back as a result of the House's action to 1957. Contrary to congressional expectations, aircraft reductions would amount to almost seven hundred airplanes from the original 1953 estimates of 7,573 planes.[100]

The dichotomy between the House's action and its expressed intention to maintain military strength indicates that the House members of the defense appropriations subcommittee did not fully grasp the policy implications of their decisions. Their desire for economy and lower defense expenditures led them to make cuts which seriously affected the military program for FY 1953. The cuts, while something more than "a slash in the dark," were something less than, "derived from the application of data made available to the committee," [101] as the House report wished to suggest.

The armed services did not face a sympathetic Senate appropriations subcommittee. Unimpressed by the services' arguments, the Senate subcommittee recommended an additional reduction of approximately $500 million from the defense budget.[102] Hardest hit was the air force, though the Senate Appropriations Subcommittee approved the air force's 143-wing program in principle. An additional $40 million was deleted from aircraft procurement. The subcommittee explained that its action was directed at the curtailment of spare parts, and not planes. Without comment, another $100 million was subtracted from related procurement other than aircraft.

The subcommittee did grant the navy its carrier. "The Department of the Navy," its report stated, "should be authorized to exercise its own judgment with regard to this priority."[103] Also replaced was $100 million for naval aircraft procurement. While the Senate subcommittee refused to give the army and navy more funds to absorb the added costs of a recently passed military pay raise,[104] it struck the Smith amendment from the House bill and later successfully prevailed upon House members to accept its position.

The Senate quickly agreed to its committee's report. With one minor exception, committee amendments were accepted en bloc.[105] To assure the air force of 126 combat wings, Senator O'Mahoney asked the Senate to grant $11 billion in contract authority and $4.7 billion in cash for aircraft purchases. This motion easily passed, seventy-nine to zero having been given a powerful boost by Senators Richard Russell and Lyndon Johnson, leading members of the Senate Armed Services Committee.[106] Senators Paul Douglas and Wayne Morse again attacked the large spending measure of the Defense Department, but their amendments to slash the military budget failed. With two-thirds of the Senate voting, the measure passed sixty-six to zero.[107]

The mixed motives leading to the Senate subcommittee's reductions cannot be easily delineated; yet the hearings revealed one overriding consideration—the demand for a balanced budget. A deficit reaching as high as $14 billion was predicted in some circles. "Now why can Congress not make a cut," asked Chairman O'Mahoney, "when it is borne in mind that the balancing of the budget is the first line of defense?" [108] For O'Mahoney and other members of the appropriations subcommittee, the anticipated adverse economic effects of an unbalanced budget posed a clearer and more immediate danger than the potential Soviet military challenge. Shortly before the armed services formally presented their requests to the subcommittee, its chairman and ranking minority member set the tone for the hearings:

> Senator O'Mahoney: . . . When all is said and done, the economy of the United States is the basis for the maintenance of freedom in this world. As I have said before, it seems to me the economic front is the real fighting front in the whole international crisis. . . .
> Senator Ferguson: I would like to say one word. As the chairman said, I think the committee is looking at this matter, in the light of first things first in our defense, and we appreciate, if we are going to deter our enemies and those who will be our enemies we cannot do it alone by machine and military might; we have to do it by a sound economy at the same time. The fact that we have a lot of tanks and so forth will be of little value to us, and, therefore, we must determine the certainty of the economy first, because if we lose that battle, it appears to me that our enemy will find that we are much weaker than indicated by the amount of the machinery that we have.[109]

The Senate, like the House, consoled itself in the thought that the military establishment had already been given sufficient funds, reflected by their large unobligated balances, to build to the force strength they wished. Granting an adequate military deterrent on the basis of the existing funds controlled by the Defense Department, it was possible to argue the feasibility of a diminution of the defense budget, especially since the possibility of a tax increase during the election year had been previously ruled out by the chairman of the Senate subcommittee.[110] Senator O'Mahoney noted the refusal of the House Ways and Means Committee to approve the additional tax measures which had been requested by the President. This action precluded any Senate move to increase defense appropriations or even to sustain the lower-pitched reclamas of the military departments. A majority in the upper chamber was determined to close, however slightly, the yawning gap between government revenues and expenditures.

No serious disagreements separated the House and Senate conferees. The Senate division of funds as well as its insistence that the navy be allowed to build another "Forrestal" carrier was largely adopted. The Senate conference members, although they abandoned the O'Mahoney amendment, succeeded in blocking any further reduction in the air force's original estimates for aircraft purchases. A total of $17.7 billion was permitted. Summarily, a budget of $46.6 billion was passed, $4.3 billion less than the administration had requested. The army shouldered half this latter reduction; the other services divided the remainder of the cuts in approximately equal shares. Credit for the "stretch out" must be assigned to the administration. The congressional parsimony assured the implementation of that policy.

THE EISENHOWER "STRETCH-OUT": FY 1954

Eisenhower attacks Truman.—President Eisenhower's early speeches indicated two major criticisms of the Truman administration's defense policies. First, he charged that they were militarily unsound. They were tied too rigidly to a period "of maximum danger" and a fixed notion of the communist military threat, although the communist challenge was continually undergoing significant shifts and permutations. The Truman "readiness" approach, as it was sometimes called, created an inflexible military establishment which was unable to adapt rapidly to new strategic conditions. Planners took refuge in magic-numbered force-level goals, while insisting, Eisenhower noted, that the latest change was "final, definitive, and unchallengeable. . . . " [111] The communist military challenge could not be keyed to a fixed date. Since it was evolving in direction and content, it had to be met over "a long haul." Episodic military planning resulted simply in an unbalanced military capability. "Instead of trying carefully to balance your program," Wilfred McNeil, Eisenhower's defense comptroller testified, "you tended to create imbalances in the [military production] program because some of the easiest to procure items were secured first and some of the more difficult, but important, items could not be accomplished by the planning date which had been set." [112] Small firearms were quickly stockpiled, but heavy bombers and teams of highly trained technicians—which were considered to be the decisive elements of military preparedness—were neglected or remained in short supply. Deliveries of goods were often poorly phased and unco-ordinated. Delays and bottlenecks inevitably resulted. Worse still, Eisenhower also accused the Truman Defense Department of having de-emphasized innovation in weapons design as a result of its unwarranted concentration on immediate and short-term preparedness. "Today three aircraft with modern weapons," President Eisenhower said, "can practically duplicate the destructive power of all the 2,700 planes we unleashed in the great breakout attack from the Normandy beachhead." [113] There was no need, the Republican chief executive implied, for heavy reliance on manpower. Even before Eisenhower assumed office, it was becoming apparent that an attempt would be made to replace manpower with machines and technical know-how without any loss—indeed, with the anticipation of an increase—in firepower.

But Eisenhower's heaviest assault on the defense policies and programming of the Truman era was made on economic, not military, grounds. Throughout his early addresses, the President stressed the economic pitfalls of the cold war. Of these, easily the most fearsome was deficit spending. "Under the former administration," Eisenhower observed apprehensively, "expenditures for the future were so scheduled as to reach their peak during 1954 and 1955. . . . " Despite the fact that these were "precisely the years when . . . Federal revenues . . . will fall sharply downward."[114] The chief executive pledged his administration to balanced budgeting and, by implication, to lowered governmental spending. It was widely felt within the incoming administration that, unless the size and rate of defense expenditures were reduced or, at least, stabilized, a ruinous inflation followed by stifling governmental controls was likely to occur. The prospect of internal economic disintegration or regimentation or both tended to be viewed as more immediate and fundamental problems than external military dangers. "We must see, clearly and steadily, just exactly what is the danger before us," warned President Eisenhower:

> It is more than merely a military threat. It has been coldly calculated by the Soviet leaders, for by their military threat they have hoped to force upon America and the free world an unbearable security burden leading to economic disaster. They have believed—and, in fact plainly said—that free people cannot preserve their way of life and at the same time provide enormous military establishments. Communist guns, in this sense, have been aiming at an economic target no less than a military target.
>
> . . . .
>
> [Our] defense must, first of all, be one which we can bear for a long—and indefinite—period of time. It cannot consist of sudden, blind responses to a series of fire-alarm emergencies, summoning us to amass forces and material solely on the theory that we can point to a D-day of desperate danger, somewhere in the near future, to which all plans can be geared.
>
> To watch vigilantly on the military front must never mean to be blind on the domestic front. In our present world—in this kind of prolonged tension and struggle—a crippled industry or

a demoralized working force could be the equivalent of a lost battle. Prolonged inflation could be as destructive of a truly free economy as could a chemical attack against an army in the field.[115]

The revised defense budget which President Eisenhower submitted to Congress in early May for FY 1954 was designed to remedy the military and, especially, the economic shortcomings of the postwar Democratic budgets. All of the service budgets were cut below the level approved by the Truman administration. Table 6 compares the Truman and Eisenhower defense budgets. Truman had recommended new appropriations of $40.7 billion, a drop of $6.5 billion from FY 1953. Eisenhower cut this total further by almost $5 billion and suggested a military budget that was $11.4 billion less than that for the preceding fiscal year.

TABLE 6*

SUMMARY OF APPROPRIATIONS FOR FISCAL YEAR 1953 AND BUDGET
ESTIMATES FOR 1954 AND THE REVISED ESTIMATES OF
THE EISENHOWER ADMINISTRATION FOR 1954

Appropriations	Appropriations, 1953	Budget Estimates, 1954 (Truman)	Revised Estimates, 1954 (Eisenhower)
Office of Secretary of Defense ...	0.4	1.0	1.0
Department of the Army	12.9	12.1	13.7
Department of the Navy	12.9	11.5	9.8
Department of the Air Force	21.0	16.1	11.3
Total	47.2	40.7	35.8

* Source: S. Rept. 601, 83/1, 1953, p. 2.

The air force ostensibly suffered the largest cuts of $5 billion. The Eisenhower administration requested an air force of 120 wings. Between 110 and 114 wings were to be made ready by the end of

FY 1954. The interim goal of 120 wings was to be accomplished some time during FY 1956, almost a year after the original Truman recommendation of 143 wings was to have been completed.[116] Personnel strength was likewise reduced to balance the lower-keyed Eisenhower air force program. Beginning 1954 strength was set at 980,000; end strength, at 960,000, for a man-year average of 970,000—almost 100,000 below the total envisioned by the Truman planners.[117] Over-all, the Eisenhower administration was prepared to cut approximately 300,000 men from the military payrolls.[118] Nonetheless, the highest spending or actual expenditure priorities within the reduced Eisenhower budget were assigned to air power. Its slice of the appropriations pie was to become, and to remain, the largest of the three services: only the pie was to be appreciably smaller.

The army seemed to have gained $1.6 billion. The rise was more apparent than real. The Eisenhower defense team had actually reduced the army budget by more than $1 billion and, in turn, added $2.5 billion to cover Korean War costs which had been treated in a separate supplemental appropriation bill by the Truman administration.[119] Army personnel was expected to drop from 1,553,000 men in FY 1953 to 1,423,000 at the end of FY 1954. An additional 51,000 army officers and enlisted men were also to be released, if hostilities in Korea ceased.[120] Sizable reductions in procurement accompanied these slashes.

The navy was asked to absorb a $1.7 billion decrease. Naval personnel would fall from 793,000 to 745,000 by the end of the fiscal year.[121] Marine corps strength would slip by approximately 20,000, closing the year with a force of 230,000.[122] The active fleet was reduced by seventy ships from the Truman budget.[123] While the navy was permitted to place requests for 162 new ships, including a third "Forrestal" carrier, its aircraft program was slashed by $2 billion. The navy estimated that it faced a deficiency of 1,300 modern planes by December, 1955, about twice the deficiency that the Truman budget would have produced.[124]

President Eisenhower's revised budget was presented to Congress as an "interim" measure. The administration pleaded for time, in the words of Defense Secretary Charles Wilson, to take "a new look at the entire defense posture." [125] The Truman force-level goals were not necessarily being rejected. Already a new team of service chiefs was being assembled to review the nation's strategic position. The spring announcement of the President's revised military budget was accompanied by the resignation of General Hoyt Vandenberg as air force chief of staff. By summer, all of the members of the Truman Joint Chiefs of Staff were replaced by Eisenhower appointees. The Eisenhower military chiefs, Secretary Wilson explained, would "consider all aspects of defense—strategic plans, forces, missions, weapons readiness levels and mobilization reserves, both stockpiles of material and capacity to produce. This will provide the basis for the FY 1955 budget. The current force plans are subject to whatever change may be indicated by this forthcoming review." [126] The revised FY 1954 force levels were merely tentative directives which would be abandoned, revised, or continued after the "New Look" had been completed and its results duly ratified by the Eisenhower Joint Chiefs.

The FY 1954 cuts pointed to the road that the administration was likely to take. President Truman's outgoing prophecy that the annual defense expenditures would be stabilized at a level "in the neighborhood of 35 to 40 billion annually" would be realized under the Eisenhower regime. The Truman "stretch out" and "long pull" gradually were being transformed into the Eisenhower "long haul."

Congress focuses on air power reductions.—The enormous size and range of the Eisenhower defense budget, touching all aspects of American domestic and foreign policy, were reduced in Congress to one major problem: the "interim" goals of 120 air force wings. Army and navy estimates and the complicated policy questions that they raised were passed over in Congress. But not the air force budget. As in the past, congressmen responded heatedly to a presidential proposal to throttle air force expansion—even for a year. The Truman-inspired objective of 143 wings replaced the seventy-group goal as the new standard for air power proponents. Much of the emotional zeal and salvational fervor that had animated the pre-Korean War movement for more air power was revived and directed at the new target goal. President Eisenhower's reminder that "a reasonable defense posture is not won by juggling magic numbers" [127] influenced few congressional air force advocates. The question of whether 143 Truman wings were as good as 120 Eisenhower wings was a concrete, seemingly definable issue on which most legislators could feel sufficiently certain that they could express an honest and reasonable opinion. Controversy in Congress over the question spilled over into the press, radio, and television and swelled into a national debate over the nation's air power strength. (Arthur Godfrey even used his early morning TV program to press for a larger air force.) While partisanship accentuated the issue, party lines were more weakened than strengthened over its resolution. From the point of view of civil-military relations, legislators, military and civilian administrators, and the President and his political aides found themselves opposing each other over the air-power problem in loosely aligned coalitions.

Dispute in Congress centered exclusively on the comparative adequacy of the Truman and Eisenhower air force estimates to support a deterrent and retaliatory strategy. There was no questioning during the long hearings and floor discussions in Congress of the strategic posture itself. No one publicly questioned the nation's increasing dependence on nuclear weapons that was already sharply outlined in the FY 1954 budget. This debate suffered, too, from its superficial analysis of a nuclear strategy. Ignored were the multiple and interrelated psychological and political dimensions of nuclear planning and diplomacy, involving such problems as United States relations with its allies and neutral countries, the credibility of a

172

nuclear deterrent in the face of the developing Soviet atomic capacity, American bases abroad and the political arrangements that they would imply, and the effect of an expansion of nuclear arms on the buildup of conventional forces within a contracting budgetary framework. The justification for the rapid American and Allied abandonment of the Lisbon goals of 1952 that envisioned an integrated NATO ground force of ninety-six divisions received scant attention despite its adverse effect on a forward strategy in Europe. The Korean experience of limited war and circumscribed political objectives was depreciated. The defense of Europe and, indeed, the remainder of United States interests around the world were capsulized in Congress in a debate over the physical capacity of the nation's nuclear deterrent. The focus, by and large, was on the hardware items that would compose the deterrent.

Outgoing Air Force Chief of Staff Hoyt Vandenberg led the attack on the administration's air power proposals. He argued "that an Air Force of no less than 143 wings . . . was the minimum force which can assure the ability of this Nation to resist success-fully an all-out Communist attack."[128] The 143-wing concept had been a direct response to four factors: the explosion of an atomic bomb by the Soviet Union in 1949; the communist invasion of South Korea and the subsequent entry of Communist China into the war; the formation of NATO; and, most importantly, "the calculation by the Joint Chiefs of Staff that by the middle of 1954 the Soviet Union would be able to launch an all-out atomic attack on the United States." [129] The general saw no change in this strategic picture of Soviet military intentions and capabilities to warrant a departure from 143 wings. Acceptance of 120 wings, even for a short time, was tantamount to a reduction in force levels. He quoted from a March letter of the Joint Chiefs of Staff to Defense Secretary Wilson which took the position that "any reduction of the program of 143 wings to be attained as soon as practicable after fiscal year 1954 would increase the risk to the national security *beyond the dictates of national prudence.*"[130] The JCS had been excluded, the general contended, from the decision to suspend the 143 wing program. His testimony charged that the Eisenhower administration was jeopardizing the nation's defense posture in its haste to balance the budget.

Defense Secretary Charles Wilson, aided by Assistant Defense Secretary Roger Kyes and Defense Comptroller Wilfred McNeil, presented the administration's case before the military appropriations subcommittees. Wilson derided Vandenberg's criticism of the Eisenhower budget. He parried with his own supporting quote from a Presidential address:

> We did not set any fixed sum of money to which our defense plans had to be fitted [President Eisenhower said]—We first determined what is truly vital to our security. We next planned ways to eliminate every useless expenditure and duplication, and we finally decided on the amount of money needed to meet this program.[131]

Wilson's answer was not sufficient to silence congressional doubts. If the administration was so determined to maintain the military security of the nation, it was hard to understand why it did not consult the JCS about the proposed armed service cuts and especially about the air force reductions. The Truman Chiefs were not prepared to defend a scaled-down air force. The President's reassuring words also did not explain away the letter of the Director of the Budget Bureau to the secretary of defense which suggested that defense spending be reduced in order that "the administration's stated policies and budget objectives"—i.e., a balanced budget—would be reached.[132]

The secretary of defense admitted he had initially asked the JCS to state what force levels could be reached if the budget were balanced by reducing defense spending. The secretary's action did underline the administration's search for a formula which would balance the budget and maintain military preparedness without substantially increasing taxes. Although the report of the service chiefs was not fully accepted, it did influence the Eisenhower administration to continue deficit spending because, as the JCS stressed, "it would not be safe to put . . . [a] money limitation on the military effort of the nation." [133]

Air Force Secretary Harold Talbott chimed in with the argument that, conceivably, a larger air force than the Truman 143 wings might be constructed after the "new look" had been completed. The revised FY 1954 program would not sacrifice time and human and material resources. [134] Shorter procurement lead-times would allegedly make it possible to review the nation's military posture and expand quickly if that proved advisable. [135] Wilson added the point that the air force had not been able to spend the money that it had already received. Slippages in production had occurred in each year since the beginning of the Korean War. [136] He pictured the $5 billion decrease in air force requests as the statistical result of a budget review conducted by his office which ascertained how much money could be spent by the air force in FY 1954, without incurring peaks or slippages in production. Explained Wilson: "So when we said what is feasible to do here and went over the things [i.e., the air force budget], this was the result"—a $5 billion reduction. [137] The opinion of the JCS was not ignored. Secretary Wilson testified that it was merely considered along with other factors. [138]

Democrats George Mahon and Stuart Symington led the attack on the revised air force budget in the House and Senate, respectively. Opposed to them stood a relatively stable Republican majority. No new arguments were introduced during the long debates on the air force wings which had not already been posed during the considerably longer and more intensive Senate and House hearings. The issues were formulated in the same fitful and bewildering way which typified the hearings. [139] The committee reports on the defense bills did not spell out the military-political issues raised by the defense cutback. [140]

Much of the Democratic case against the air force budget collapsed with the introduction of a letter from President Eisenhower to Representative Errett Scrivner, manager of the Republican half of the congressional debate. The President took full responsibility for the revised budget and the military goals that it contemplated.[141] This undercut Democratic attempts to drive a wedge between the secretary of defense, the Budget Bureau, the defense comptroller, and the President.[142] Other Democratic forays aimed to discredit the President's military reputation for having approved the meager pre-Korean $15 billion budget and for having failed to support a seventy-group air force.[143] Neither house was persuaded to override the President or its respective appropriations committee's report. A Democratic-sponsored amendment in the House—to increase air force appropriations by $1.175 billion—and a Senate motion—to expand airplane procurement by $400 million and modestly to increase air force personnel—were defeated by comfortable margins.[144] A House Democratic move to have the defense bill recommitted also proved abortive.

There were few differences to resolve in conference, since both houses had reached almost the same conclusions about the sum to authorize. Congress cut an additional $1.3 billion from the already reduced military appropriations for FY 1954. The army's estimates suffered most, an augury of deeper reductions to come. The army lost almost $700 million in its passage through the House and Senate, while the navy and air force in turn suffered appropriations reductions of approximately $350 and $130 millions.[145] The Eighty-third Congress did not dispute the programs of these services, but, like its predecessors, it felt that they could be accomplished with less money.

Recapitulation.—The FY 1954 budget struggle was unique in that it brought into sharper focus a number of characteristics of defense policy-making that had been operating under varying circumstances throughout the Democratic-controlled postwar years. First of all, it pointed up the leading role which the administration and, particu-

176

larly, the President plays in defense policy formation. In 1953, the new President had won a clear-cut victory over a strong and determined group in Congress. Victory, now achieved by a Republican President, underscored the immense prestige and power of the executive branch in determining military policies. President Truman, Eisenhower's immediate predecessor, had been equally successful against an equally determined Congress which had opposed his air force policies. As in preceding years, moreover, the terms and objects of congressional debate over the nation's defense posture and its air power capabilities arose out of pre-existing differences within the administration. In 1949, the navy had stimulated the controversy over the air force's B-36 bombers; in 1953, the out-going air chief of staff challenged the secretary of defense and, indirectly, the President for their reduced combat wing proposals. Congress' role in determining the defense budget was principally confined to a review of the administration's military policy recommendations, both in cost and adequacy.

In the midst of these differences over military requirements emanating from the executive branch, Congress, theoretically, had an important part to play in defense preparations. It was in a constitutional and political position to provide a forum from which the many differences within not only the military establishment but also within the entire executive branch could be aired. If it had chosen, it could have contributed to a definition of the major military policy alternatives open to the nation and the political implications of each. This traditional task, though no less useful for that reason, would have served to instruct the members of the Eighty-third Congress and, more important, to make clearer to the American public the major military problems facing them. Congress' success in defining the crucial military issues for public debate and discussion was lean, indeed. It concentrated too much of its attention and energies on air power—primarily strategic air might—and, in large part, uncritically accepted the other features of the administration's proposals. It did not relate various military capabilities to the variety of remote and immediate military contingencies which might threaten the nation's security interests. It is reasonable to expect that a reduction in manpower while fighting was still heavy and heated in Korea should have provoked some congressional debate.

The open record of Congress' review of the defense bill was also strangely silent on the question of whether bigger bombs and bombers were sufficient to deter or counter a possible Soviet attack against the United States. Nor did Congress extensively explore the possibility that indirect forms of communist aggression in the peripheral areas of the world or internal subversion within nations friendly to the United States might not be deterred by atomic weapons. The fall of Czechoslovakia, the Berlin Blockade, communist uprisings in Korea, Indo-China, Greece, the Philippines, and Malaya provided examples of indirect and ambiguous challenges to American interests which, in fact, were not met by threats of nuclear holocaust. The growing Soviet neutralization of American nuclear power—already recognized in NSC 68—accented the problem of preventing or limiting communist expansion in Europe as well as in the gray areas of the world. These contingencies took on a more pressing and immediate importance than the long-range one of deterring a clear-cut, Pearl Harbor–like assault. Despite the likelihood of limited and ambiguous war being waged against the United States, the nation's legislators gave little pause to examine the defense budget in terms of its ability to provide the necessary military capabilities to cope with these varied challenges.

The more narrowly oriented air power discussion was not significantly more thorough or ordered. The strategic issues underlying the Truman-Eisenhower budget were haphazardly articulated in committee investigations. A coherent argument for or against the 120-wing concept has to be pieced together from widely scattered and loosely connected sources stretching across six cumbersome volumes of House and Senate hearings. The House report obfuscated the air power issue; the Senate report ignored it. The House Appropriations

Committee's blandly worded conclusion "that the course being followed by the new administration is sound and reasonable" did little to enlighten other members of Congress or the public about the many disputed aspects of the President's air force recommendations.[146] Differences of opinion among appropriations members were compromised in committee markup of the defense bill. For the sake of unanimity, the crystallization of political disagreements over the defense bill was reserved, as it had been in the past, for the floor debates where political maneuvering and discussion were severely limited. As in preceding years, most legislators did not possess any clear notion of the consequences or implications of their approval of the President's 120-wing air force or, more generally, of the entire Defense Department bill. The appropriations committees and their defense subcommittees had prepared neither themselves nor the Congress for such a determination.

NUCLEAR PLENTY AND MILITARY WEAKNESS, 1954–1957

V

THE NEW LOOK IS UNVEILED: FY 1955

Background to the presentation.—The New Look military policies, first announced in President Eisenhower's budget for FY 1955, were heralded as a radical departure in defense strategy. Through a revision of prevailing strategic doctrine and force structure, more security would be bought at less cost. The claim was not to be taken lightly. One of the nation's leading generals in war, now a peacetime President, had made it. There was the fact, too, that more than a year of intensive preparations and argument had gone into the making of the New Look. Months before he assumed office, President Eisenhower assembled the nucleus of his military and political leadership corps to begin work on reassessing and reformulating the nation's defense policies.[1]

Shortly after the November elections, President Eisenhower went to Korea. His trip fulfilled a dramatic promise, made in the final stages of the presidential campaign, to inspect the fighting there at first hand. The visit was also part of a larger commitment, implicit in the election pledge, to end the conflict as soon and as honorably as possible. The chief executive started off for the Far East by plane, accompanied by Charles E. Wilson of General Motors, his designate as secretary of defense. On the return trip from Korea, the group was joined at Guam by a group of presidential advisers that had been flown from Washington. Among them were John Foster Dulles and Joseph M. Dodge, Eisenhower appointees to the posts of secretary of state and director of the Bureau of the Budget, and George M. Humphrey, who was designated to head the Department of the Treasury. Admiral Arthur W. Radford, commander in chief of the Pacific fleet was also present, having met the presidential party at Guam. This group boarded the cruiser "USS Helena" en route to Hawaii. A series of informal round-table discussions was held on the three-day voyage. A wide range of subjects was covered, including the Korean War, the most pressing problem facing the new administration, price controls, communist strategy, especially in Asia, and the President's Inaugural and State of the Union messages.[2]

These meetings personally acquainted the leading members of the Eisenhower administration with each other, some for the first time, and furnished a forum for an exchange of public policy viewpoints. The "Helena" sessions similarly provided President Eisenhower with an opportunity to state his position. The leisurely pace aboard the ship and the freedom that it afforded from the political pressures of the mainland served their purposes admirably.

The President-elect sketched his understanding of the over-all strategic problem confronting the nation and his administration. For him, the overriding problem was solving what he called "'the great equation' of maintaining indefinitely a strong military force without bankrupting the country in the process."[3] The President's simple and direct statement of the nation's key strategic problem set the terms and defined the tone of the discussions which were to continue through the first year of his administration in the effort to construct the New Look.

The "Helena" excursion, moreover, permitted President Eisenhower to evaluate his advisers. One development, closely linked to the "Helena" meetings, was the appointment later of Admiral Arthur W. Radford as chairman of the Joint Chiefs of Staff. Admiral Radford made a favorable impression on the President and his company. Mr.

Wilson had been instrumental in inviting Radford, whom he was eyeing for the post of chairman. President Eisenhower agreed to Radford's appointment despite his activist role in the "Admirals' Revolt" of 1949. The appointment was to prove fortuitous. Radford soon emerged as the administration's most energetic and effective advocate within the JCS.

Contrary to journalistic representations at the time, the "Helena" meeting did not produce a new strategic design. Serious conversations about defense policy were held, but they did not crystallize a tightly knit or detailed strategic plan of action. The discussions were general in scope and were not guided by an articulated intention to produce a concrete set of legislative proposals or a priority list of administrative actions in order to redirect immediately the strategic course which had been fixed by President Truman. Unlike Athena, who supposedly sprang fully developed and mature from Zeus' head, the New Look required a longer and more turbulent gestation period. Over a year of often fretful discussion and frustrating compromise among Eisenhower defense officials was needed before the New Look was ready for presentation to Congress. The importance of the seminal "Helena" meetings was to set this process of strategic and fiscal re-evaluation into motion.[4]

To assure a fresh military analysis, President Eisenhower appointed a new set of military chiefs in mid-spring. The house cleaning, while advised on strategic and administrative grounds, was also spurred by domestic political considerations. Senator Robert Taft, Eisenhower's principal opponent for the Republican nomination in 1952, had clashed repeatedly with President Truman's military chiefs since the outbreak of the Korean hostilities. Against his personal inclinations and professional judgment, soft-spoken General Omar Bradley, chairman of the Joint Chiefs of Staff, had in effect permitted himself to assume the role of stalking-horse for the Truman administration in order to draw off opposition attacks on the administration's defense policies. In a series of widely publicized speeches, Bradley had pointedly countered Taft's criticisms of the troops-to-Europe decision and the administration's conduct of the Korean War. Bradley's exposure to the partisan struggle for power compromised the virtue of his military advice in the eyes of many Republicans, and personally irritated Senator Taft, who incurred the brunt of Bradley's attacks.[5] Since the chiefs were tied so closely to the Truman administration's defense policies, they were swept out of office along with their civilian heads in the Eisenhower landslide.

President Eisenhower's new appointees included Admiral Arthur W. Radford, as chairman of the Joint Chiefs of Staff; Admiral Robert B. Carney, commander in chief Allied Forces Southern Europe, as chief of naval operations; and General Matthew B. Ridgway, supreme allied commander in Europe, as army chief of staff. The appointments were made public on May 12. General Nathan F. Twining, vice chief of the air force, had been announced as the replacement for recalcitrant General Hoyt Vandenberg a week earlier. President Eisenhower directed his new appointees, "to make a completely new, fresh survey" of the nation's military capabilities, in light of its global commitments.[6] They were to review all facets of military policy in terms of Eisenhower's "great equation." They were to examine service roles and force levels, weapons systems, and deployment. These factors were to be related in turn to fiscal policy.

The chiefs completed their first report in early August, shortly before they were to assume office. The JCS paper which they produced was unanimously agreed upon. It presented a general statement of strategic principles and guidelines and set the framework for more detailed future discussions. The service leaders identified continental air defense and creation and maintenance of long-range strategic strike forces as the nation's two most important strategic problems. To these the JCS added the points that the United States increase the mobility of its armed forces to maximal levels, that the efficiency and readiness of its manpower reserves be improved, and that service roles and missions remain intact. The chiefs were generally in accord, too, on the question of military deployment. American forces were considered to be over-extended and some kind of retrenchment was indicated. Withdrawal of forces from Japan and Korea offered one possibility. Defense of forward areas was to be the primary responsibility of indigenous troops, backed by United States air and sea power.[7]

This first instalment on the New Look did not address itself to a definition of the specific force levels for FY 1955, although budgetary guidelines were needed immediately. The budget cycle, largely separated from the strategic analysis that was being undertaken throughout the executive branch, was moving swiftly along on its own track, controlled by its own inner directed procedures and organizational demands, toward the annual December deadline when the final estimates for the fiscal year would have to be completed for presentation to Congress. The new chiefs were pressed by the secretary of defense (who in turn was being urged by Budget Director Dodge) to propose hard and fast figures for FY 1955 even as the long-range strategic survey proceeded.[8]

On October 2 the chiefs submitted their recommendations to Secretary Wilson. They advised retention of the FY 1954 force levels, with an increase of about one hundred thousand men for continental air defense. This would have produced an armed force of 3.5 million men, almost one hundred and fifty thousand more than the ceiling of 3.36 million men set by the National Security Council on April 29. This limit—or target goal, as the Eisenhower administration preferred to call its personnel and budgetary ceilings— had been established to keep defense expenditures under the $40 billion mark for FY 1955. Under the October JCS plan, the army would be increased slightly to 1.5 million and organized into twenty divisions. The navy would begin work on a third "Forrestal" carrier and would maintain an active fleet of 1,163 ships. Navy and marine corps personnel would stand at about the 970,000 figure projected in the NSC paper on military personnel. The air force would expand

184

from 114 wings to 120 wings, with a proportionate increase in its manpower totals. The cost of these forces was estimated at $42 billion in expenditures and $35 billion in new obligational authority. This authorization request was $500 million more than Congress had appropriated for FY 1954 and $5 billion over the $30 billion target goal that Dodge had indicated to Wilson would be desirable from the point of view of the administration's fiscal policies.[9]

The JCS had resisted the pressures around them to recommend force levels that would cut defense spending, although they emanated not only from Dodge's office but also from Secretary of the Treasury George Humphrey and from the President himself. The chiefs stood firm, basing their decision to hold the line on force levels on three general grounds: the continued, and reportedly increasing, magnitude of the communist military challenge; the undiminished number and extent of the nation's world wide commitments; and the absence of any settled policy on the use of atomic weapons in future military conflicts.[10] The Korean War had ended, but hostilities might erupt at any time. Political unrest was spreading throughout other parts of Asia, particularly in French Indo-China. The Soviet explosion of a thermonuclear device on August 12, 1953, added to the communist military threat. More personnel would also be needed to discharge the United States NATO obligations and to expand United States air defense capacity. In light of these factors, military personnel could not be reduced unless perhaps, the JCS implicitly hinted, a basic decision might be made with respect to the use of atomic weapons. On the basis of such a decision, the number of contingency plans that would have to be implemented could in effect be compressed, for nuclear weapons might be able to do a variety of military jobs.

The first budgetary crisis over these force level recommendations occurred on October 12 at a meeting of the National Security Council. Wilson and Radford presented the JCS force estimates and the costs that they would incur. The $35 billion defense budget which was outlined fell on incredulous ears within the NSC. The economy bloc, led by Humphrey and Dodge, expected a reduction in defense spending as a result of the end of hostilities in Korea, the increased operating efficiencies that Wilson had allegedly introduced, and a streamlining of military support personnel. Humphrey urged that efforts be made to incorporate the "new weapons" which were available to the nation in order to develop a more effective as well as a less costly strategic posture. Searching for a middle ground, Radford held out the previously stated JCS hope that defense costs could be lowered if a basic decision could be reached on the use of atomic weapons. The military services would then know what kind of war they were preparing for and the kind of weapons that would be available to them. Reductions in manpower could be compensated for by an increase in nuclear fire power. Wilson and Radford were advised to "refine" the JCS force recommendations. The implication was clear that they should be revised downward. The conservation of resources was to be given most weight within Eisenhower's equation of military needs and budgetary possibilities.

Against this backdrop the denouement of the strategic side of the New Look reappraisal was played out on October 30 when President Eisenhower approved NSC 162/2. This document provided the basic statement of the New Look's strategic design that was publicly announced in January, 1954. The principal significance of the paper was its determination to the JCS that the services could plan to use tactical and strategic nuclear weapons in future military conflict whenever it would be to the advantage of the United States. The decision was of fundamental strategic importance. The Truman administration had never arrived at a clear position on the use of nuclear weapons. Now, the nuclear Rubicon had seemingly been crossed.

Despite the wide spread changes in military planning and operations that NSC 162/2 would effect, its immediate import was primarily budgetary. "The intent of this decision," notes one well documented study, "was to foreclose any of the services—in particular the army—from generating large requirements for manpower and conventional equipment based on an assumption that large-scale conventional war was possible." "Henceforth," as one analyst notes, "any wars larger than small 'brush fire' or 'border incidents' were to be considered nuclear for planning purposes." [11] The administration's subsequent directed verdicts on manpower and budgetary reductions for the services would turn essentially on its high assessment of the effectiveness of nuclear weapons of all types as a substitute for manpower. Given a constrained budget framework, this evaluation in effect determined the time and resource priorities that would be assigned to various weapons systems. It also defined the rate and character of the phase-down in forces in being throughout the middle 1950's.

The task of cutting the JCS's recommendations to conform to the reduced resources that were to be devoted to defense fell then to a special committee within the Department of Defense. The Everest committee, named after its chairman, Frank Everest, director of the Joint Staff, was established by Wilson on October 16 and charged with the responsibilities of recommending a strategy that would conform to NSC guidance and of sketching the size and shape of the military services for the period between 1955 and 1957. Wilson set down a personnel limit in the neighborhood of 2.5 to 3 million to be reached by the end of FY 1957. The Everest group reported on December 1. Reflecting the growing disagreements among the services over the priorities that should be assigned to competing force levels and weapons systems, within the constrictions of the Eisenhower budgetary limitations, the committee produced four separate papers. The one major agreement was on the military manpower goal for FY 1957 of 2,750,000. Negotiations among the JCS, Radford, and Wilson in early December finally yielded agreement on a force of 2,815,000, including a million man army. This amounted to an increase of 65,000 of which the army was to secure 50,000 and the marine corps the remainder of 15,000. [12]

JCS agreement on these force levels, however, was based on a number of tenuous and delicately balanced assumptions. A change in any one of them threatened to disrupt JCS harmony on military policy as well as the working relations and mutual expectations of the Joint Chiefs and their civilian superiors. The most crucial assumption was "that the requirement for significant U. S. forces in Korea would shortly cease." [13] To this supposition were added these others: the stabilization of the Korean political situation, the enlargement of German, Korean, and Japanese armed forces according to an orderly schedule, the cessation of hostilities in Indo-China, and the erection of viable political institutions for the area, the ratification of the European Defense Community, and the maintenance of the international order against further deterioration. There was the implicit understanding, too, that the 2.8 million figure would be annually evaluated. How the military services would be phased down in strength to meet the FY 1957 projection was not specifically determined. This would be settled, at least initially, in terms of the resource limits that would be set out in the FY 1955 budget.

The two out-of-phase processes of long-term strategic appraisal and budget formulation for FY 1955 crashed headlong into each other in early December. Signs that they were heading on a collision course had appeared throughout the year as the two processes brushed lightly past each other first at one point and then at another. Their merging, however devastating or disruptive the immediate impact, could no longer be postponed. The day of reckoning arrived on December 5 when the services submitted their FY 1955 estimates of $35.9 billion, almost $6 billion more than the target figure hoped for by the President, his budget director, and his irrepressible secretary of the treasury. About a day or so later, Secretary of Defense Wilson, with presidential approval, ordered a 10 per cent reduction in army, navy, and marine corps manpower. Less than a week later, the President directed the army to reduce even further to a level that was approximately 300,000 below the April NSC guidelines and 117,000 below the figure tentatively agreed to by Wilson on December 9 when the completed New Look report of the JCS reached his desk. In two days the JCS estimates for a military establishment of 3,128,000 men at the close of FY 1955, including an army of 1,281,000 were slashed to a little over three million, with an army total of 1,164,000. Wilson had capitulated to the economy forces within the administration in accepting a speedier reduction of the army, which was now being ordered to retrench during FY 1954 and FY 1955 to three quarters of its active strength. On December 15, at a meeting of the NSC, the President approved these various force level changes for FY 1955 and the budget recommendations that they implied. The rest was up to Congress.

The unveiling.—The basic strategic elements of the New Look, along with its force level and budgetary recommendations for FY 1955, were essentially included in the President's message to Congress on January 21, 1954. Table 7 below summarizes the force levels for FY 1954 and 1955. The President announced, first of all, that the nation would henceforward rely primarily on "the full exploitation of air power and modern weapons" as the major deterrent against communist military aggression.[14] "Modern weapons" was the Republican administration's euphemism for tactical and strategic atomic weapons. The principal instrument of this new approach was to be the air force with its long-range bomber forces. The administration planned to build to 137 wings by the end of FY 1957 of which 120 wings were to be completed by June 30, 1955. The loss of six wings from the Truman proposal of 143 wings was to be absorbed by logistics and tactical support aircraft. Air force personnel levels were to rise slightly to 970,000, an increase of 15,000 over the preceding year. The navy's carrier fleet was to supplement the air force's strategic strike forces. Naval air power was assigned top priority and a fourth "Forrestal" carrier was planned. Operating aircraft was set at 9,941. Approximately 2,280 planes were to be delivered in FY 1954 and another 2,760 the following year. The procurement program for FY 1955 called for 1,450 new planes, bringing the navy air arm to 87 per cent

TABLE 7*

	June 30, 1954	June 30, 1955
Major military forces		
Army		
Divisions	19	17
Regiments and RCT's	18	18
Antiaircraft battalions	117	122
Navy		
Warships	409	404
Other ships	717	676
Total navy, active	1,126	1,080
Carrier air groups	16	16
Carrier ASW squadrons	15	15
Marine divisions	3	3
Marine air wings	3	3
Active aircraft inventory	13,285†	13,191
Operating aircraft	9,941	9,941
Logistic support	3,341	3,250
Air Force		
Total wings	115	120
Combat wings	99	107
Troop carriers	16	13
Active aircraft	21,010	22,927
Military personnel and strength (including cadets and officer candidates)		
Army	1,407,000	1,172,700
Navy	741,000	689,000
Marines	225,000	215,000
Air Force	955,000	970,000
Total	3,328,000	3,046,700

* Source: HSAC, *Hearings, Department of Defense Appropriations, FY 1955,* 83/2, 1954, p. 116.

† The discrepancy in total for aircraft inventory with the figures immediately below is to be found in the original table.

of its modernization program by the end of 1956.[15] Cutbacks in over-all naval strength were imposed on support personnel and on smaller ships with conventional fire power. Personnel was to slip to 689,000, about fifty thousand less than the projected terminal strength for FY 1954.[16] Large expenditures for the development and control of atomic energy, a program already initiated under the Truman administration, were sustained.[17]

Second, increased mobility and fire power were to be substituted for personnel in future military conflicts. The fire power would be furnished largely through the introduction of tactical nuclear weapons into the arsenal of the ground forces. This shift had been fore-shadowed in NSC 162/2. Even NATO, the President added, would be "engaged in a reappraisal of strategy and tactics to reflect the prospective availability of atomic and other new weapons." [18] In line with these considerations, a reduction in army strength of three divisions was sketched. The army's seventeen divisions at the close of FY 1955 would be supported by 1,172,000 men.[19] The marine corps was also directed to cut its force levels by 10,000. Machines would replace men.

The forward positions of the free world on the communist frontier would be largely manned by indigenous troops. American forces would be supplemental. Native forces would withstand an initial communist assault until the United States would arrive with its immense air and sea power. American ingenuity and technical know-how were allegedly put to better use on the battlefield in emphasizing these forms of military power than in laying stress on conventional fighting power. A week before the President presented his military budget to Congress, he ordered the withdrawal of two American divisions from Korea. This military disengagement was made possible, the President explained, "by the cessation of hostilities [in Korea], the increased mobility and striking power of . . . air and other combat forces, and by the increasing capabilities of the Republic of Korea forces." [20] To assist the development of what Dean Acheson, President Truman's secretary of state, had called "situations of strength" around the world, military assistance was given priority over economic aid to foreign nations. The administration also looked expectantly toward the rapid creation and incorporation of twelve German divisions into NATO and the acceptance of the European Defense Community by the French National Assembly. American forces in Europe meanwhile would in effect remain hostage to the United States announced intention to employ its nuclear power in behalf of its NATO allies in the event of a Soviet attack. American strategy was tilted heavily in the direction of deterrence, and not defense. Calls for "liberating the captive nations" of Eastern Europe or the "unleashing of Chiang Kai-shek"—prominent slogans of Eisenhower's campaign for the Presidency—were quietly dismissed.

Third, the President acknowledged a significantly greater stress on continental defense, which had received very little in the way of governmental support up to 1954.[21] The Soviet explosion of a thermonuclear bomb in August, 1953, confirmed the need for an extensive air defense system on the American continent. An enhanced capacity for active and passive defense against enemy air attack was also a logical corollary of an enlarged nuclear deterrent posture. An effective internal defense system underwrote the credibility of the American nuclear deterrent and of the United States determination to use its atomic power if necessary. The development of a large-scale air defense system was an open admission that the American homeland was now vulnerable to outside attack. This was the furthest that any administration had gone in admitting the possibility of enemy raids on the United States. In the closing months of its stay in power, the Truman administration had tentatively suggested a move in this direction in the NSC paper No. 141. It fell, however, to the Eisenhower administration to implement this recommendation despite the obvious tax that air defense forces would place on the Defense Department's diminishing resources. All the services were expected to contribute to the construction of the continental defense system. To this end the army was directed to increase its antiaircraft units from 117 to 122 during FY 1955 and to expand its NIKE missile units.[22] Research and development on such items as warning mechanisms, advanced fighter aircraft, and the like were also approved.

Finally, as a hedge against the possibility of a long war, the President pressed the concept of a mobilization base that could be used to put the nation on an effective war footing as soon after the outbreak of hostilities as possible. The accumulation of end-items for the military services was discouraged. The army was ordered to draw on $1.9 billion of previously authorized funds for its procurement purchases during FY 1955 rather than request any new obligational authority. Stockpiling of strategic materials was continued for another year at the prevailing rate of one billion dollars per year. But the bedrock of this mobilization was the announcement of a buildup in personnel and an improvement in equipment and readiness of armed service reserves. The administration's reserve plan, which was submitted to Congress a year later, proposed more exacting training standards for the reserves and their close integration "into the plans for employment of the Active Forces." "We intend," wrote Secretary Wilson, "to introduce into the Reserve Forces to the maximum degree possible the new weapons and techniques continuously being developed by all services."[23] Since reserve forces were cheaper to maintain than regular forces, a strengthened reserve system offered the prospect of quickly mobilizing military forces at less cost to the country.

Rationale of the New Look.—It is of some importance to understand the basic political motivations and intent underlying the New Look strategy. Congress' sympathetic reception and easy acceptance of the Eisenhower defense proposals, despite their many substantive shortcomings and logical contradictions, cannot be fully explained without reference to these considerations. The New Look was more than a strategic doctrine. It was in large part a product of a more encompassing set of factors. In general the New Look was a response to domestic economic and political forces as well as strategic imperatives. Specifically, it was a reaction to the technological revolution that was quickly overtaking military weaponry to the chimerical, yet also expanding, communist military threat, and, most important of all, to the perceptions of Americans as to their world-wide commitments and leadership responsibilities and to their willingness to bear the human and material burdens to discharge them. While an appreciation of these larger forces at work does not excuse the deficiencies of Congress' review of the New Look, the culpability both of Congress as an institution and of the actions and decisions of individual legislators is mitigated to a degree.

The decisive importance of economic factors in shaping the New Look and its associated budgetary recommendations was clearly suggested by Eisenhower's statement of the "Great Equation." It begged its own solution. In stating the problem of national security in terms of the military forces that could be maintained without bankrupting the country, fiscal considerations were implicitly given precedence over all others in determining the operational character of the New Look. The administration's commitment to a balanced budget, decreased governmental expenditures, the reduction of the national debt, and a lowering of taxes on businesses and individuals narrowed the framework within which military policy would have to be developed. It was not an accident, therefore, that a reconstituted tax system which was to leave an additional $7 billion in private hands was closely linked to the President's New Look budget message. The military establishment was pushed and prodded into formulating its requests in light of these fiscal policies. Radford admitted as much when he testified that the Joint Chiefs obtained "prospective national income [figures] over the long pull, . . . eliminated the more or less fixed expenses, and . . . came up with a military program which was adequate for the security of the United States." [24] Ridgway was more blunt and considerably more critical of this procedure. "The force levels provided [for 1955, 1956, and 1957] were not primarily based on military needs," he wrote shortly after his retirement.

"They were not based on the freely reached conclusions of the Joint Chiefs of Staff. They were squeezed between the framework of arbitrary manpower and fiscal limits, a complete inversion of the normal process." [25]

There was no question, either, that the New Look claimed to relieve the material burden of carrying on the cold war. The new reliance on air power and modern weapons was to be the key to decreased defense budget and increased military security. "With the shift in emphasis to the full exploitation of modern weapons," the President asserted, "we are in a position to support strong national security programs over an indefinite period with less of a drain on our manpower, material, and financial resources." [26] The President backed this boast by asking for less new obligational authority than had been enacted during the preceding fiscal year. Table 8 compares the expenditures and appropriations estimates of the Defense Department for FY 1954 and FY 1955 which were presented to Congress.

TABLE 8*

Estimated Appropriations and Expenditures for the Department of
Defense for Fiscal Years 1954 and 1955
(In Billions)

	Expenditures		New Obligational Authority	
	1954	1955	1954	1955
Direction and co-ordination of defense....................................	0.01	0.01	0.01	0.01
Other central defense activities..................	0.44	0.56	0.76	0.55
Army defense................................	14.20	10.20	12.78	8.24
Navy defense................................	11.30	10.49	9.53	9.88
Air Force defense............................	15.60	16.21	11.42	11.21
Proposed legislation..........................	.....	.10	.....	1.11
Total...................................	41.55	37.57	34.50	31.00

* Source: Based on figures taken from B.B., *U. S. Budget, FY 1955*, p. M42. Discrepancies due to rounding.

Expenditures were expected to drop by $4 billion in FY 1955; similarly, appropriation requests were set at almost $3.5 billion less than they had been a year before. The army was to absorb most of the cuts. The navy's spending program held steady. The air force budget rose noticeably to a record peacetime high of $16.2 billion.

The drive for decreased governmental expenditures for defense and non-defense items rested on a yet more fundamental value. It was the faith that a dominant segment of the Eisenhower administration placed in the private sector of the economy. It was widely felt that the decisions of private individuals would yield a greater measure of economic progress and stability for the nation and, by implication, would strengthen the country in its cold war struggle. There was still more than a trace within the New Look of the conviction that the industrial might of the nation would be the decisive element in a future military encounter with the Soviet Union. The nation, indeed, had moved away from a mobilization strategy that had characterized the pre-World War II and pre-Korean War periods, yet influential individuals and groups within and outside the administration continued to act in terms of outdated strategic concepts. Said the President: "We are convinced that more progress and sounder progress will be made over the years as the largest possible share of our national income is left with individual citizens to make their own countless decisions as to what they will spend. . . . Our development, since the early days of the Republic, has been based on the fact that we left a great share of our national income to be used by a provident people with a will to venture. Their actions have stimulated the American genius for creative initiative and thus multiplied our productivity." [27]

The renewed stress on "creative initiative" was intimately tied to another widely held American article of faith. In stressing the use of modern weapons, the New Look appealed to the American penchant to engage its scientific and technical know-how to solve national political and military problems. American brains, not brawn,

196

would win any cold or hot war. Certainly, it was felt, American manpower should not attempt to match the human hordes under the command of communist leaders. Let Asians fight Asians; and Europeans, Europeans. Precious American manpower, in short supply, would be withdrawn within the American laager and used selectively against communist aggression in conjunction with the most powerful weapons that science and technology could produce. Senator Homer Ferguson, in presenting the defense appropriations bill to Congress, expressed much of the administration's point of view when he argued that it was "not in the interest of the United States, or its free world partners . . . to devote too great a share of our young manpower to our standing forces, at the expense of our society and industry. . . . In my opinion, we need our manpower for use in the sciences and in industry, and to assist the manpower of the rest of the world." [28]

The New Look seemed to introduce for the first time a sense of order and stability into military planning. The FY 1955 budget was "aimed . . . at providing a strong military position . . . over the extended period of uneasy peace." [29] The Truman procedure of depending on "several successive assumed fixed dates of maximum danger" and gearing procurement and personnel plans to these dates was abandoned. Stability over the long haul was now possible because there had occurred, the President confirmed, "a great strategic change in the world during the past year [1953]. That precious intangible, the initiative, is becoming ours. Our policy, not limited to mere reaction against crises provoked by others, is free to develop along lines of our choice not only abroad but also at home."[30] If initiative resided in the United States, there would be no need constantly to revise military force levels in response to varying communist military challenges. The United States would presumably do the challenging, if there were to be any at all. Military planning and operations would thus be more orderly, predictable, and efficient.

The speech of Secretary of State John Foster Dulles to the Council on Foreign Relations, delivered only a few days after President

Eisenhower's budget message to Congress, implied that these results would soon be forthcoming. Dulles insisted that the United States would no longer have to react impulsively to Soviet initiatives. The communists, instead, would have to calculate United States moves and shape their policies in terms of them. This shift in the basic strategic posture of the United States and the Soviet Union had been effected, Dulles maintained, when the National Security Council decided to permit the use of the nation's atomic weaponry in future military conflicts of all types, although these might be limited in geographic scope or political value, if the United States would gain a corresponding military advantage. This "basic decision" would not only restore America's strategic pre-eminence in the cold war but would prevent large-scale domestic economic and social dislocation. Said Dulles:

> We need allies and collective security. Our purpose is to make these relations more effective, less costly. This can be done by placing more reliance on deterrent power and less dependence on local defensive power.

> . . . .

> The way to deter aggression is for the free community to be willing and able to respond vigorously at places and with means of its own choosing.

> . . . .

> The total cost of our security efforts, at home and abroad, was over $50 billion per annum, and involved, for 1953, a projected budgetary deficit of $9 billion; and $11 billion for 1954. This was on top of taxes comparable to wartime taxes; and the dollar was depreciating in effective value. Our allies were similarly weighed down. They could not be continued for long without grave budgetary, economic, and social consequences.

> But before military planning could be changed, the President and his advisers, as represented by the National Security Council, had to take some basic policy decisions. This has been done. The basic decision was to depend primarily upon a great capacity to retaliate, instantly, by means and at places of our choosing.

198

Now the Department of Defense and the Joint Chiefs of Staff can shape our military establishment to fit what is *our* policy, instead of having to try to be ready to meet the enemy's many choices. That permits a selection of military means instead of a multiplication of means. As a result, it is now possible to get, and share, more basic security at less cost.[31]

Here were summarized most of the factors that had shaped the New Look. Budgetary and economic considerations were clearly evident in Dulles' references to deficit financing and currency depreciation. His phrase "grave . . . social consequences," while surrounded with more ambiguity, suggested the often stated concern of President Eisenhower and others of his administration that the United States would develop into a garrison state unless economic and social controls were relaxed. The phrase reflected, too, the desire of many Americans in the middle 1950's to be rid of the galling personal burdens, including high taxes and military service, that the cold war imposed. Just as significantly, Dulles' speech reaffirmed America's commitment to its allies and its determination, through a deterrent posture based on selective massive retaliation, to protect them against communist encroachments. Massive retaliation was to meet more than the one contingency of a general war. It was to forestall communist aggression along the entire perimeter of the communist world. Dulles went on to apply the doctrine to Europe and to Asia. He warned that resumption of communist military action in Korea would prompt a "United Nations response which would not necessarily be confined to Korea."[32] "Open Chinese army aggression [in Indo-China]," he went on, " . . . would have 'grave consequences which might not be confined to Indo-china.'"[33]

The New Look touched all the important political bases: small and big wars would be deterred; the military establishment would be streamlined and modernized and the blessings of science and technology incorporated into its weapons arsenals; America's allies would be reassured of American military support; the communists every-

199

where would be put on clear notice that they would pay dearly through a massive retaliatory attack against their homelands if they should commit aggression against the United States or its friends; the government's budget would be balanced, defense spending cut, and taxes lowered; and Americans would be spared most of the grating personal inconveniences and sacrifices of the cold war.

CONGRESS AND THE NEW LOOK

A majority of the Republican Eighty-third Congress had no difficulty in repairing to the New Look standard. Moreover, the Democratic Eighty-fourth, Eighty-fifth, or Eighty-sixth congresses, while more critical of the New Look, did not succeed in departing significantly from it. In its essential conceptual features, the New Look remained intact until the advent of the Kennedy administration in 1961. So also did the budgetary limits on defense spending which the administration annually established. Most legislators resisted proposals to authorize more funds for defense than the President had requested. Their almost instinctive inclination to economize was buttressed by the administration's repeated assurances that the nation's security position was actually improving each year.

While it is true that the administration, especially in the pre-sputnik period, was able to dominate Congress, it was unable to silence or to isolate criticism of its policies. Two different, though somewhat overlapping, sets of opposition forces developed within Congress and, to a degree, within the appropriations process. These forces sought one or both of two general objectives: to modify the administration's strategic doctrine and the nation's strategic posture or to increase defense spending for selected military capabilities such as for air power or for more ground troops. Though each differed in aim and emphasis, both were forged out of the same compound of elements which were principally composed of (1) an increasingly heightened perception of the evolving communist military threat; (2) the inadequacy of the New Look in meeting peripheral risks in Southeast Asia and the Middle East or in supporting the nation's negotiating position in its dealings with the communist bloc; and (3) the proliferation of the number and complexity of the problems and choices that were being forced on Congress by the accelerating rate of the revolution in military technology.

The first set of forces, paradoxically enough, attacked the administration for not having actually implemented its own doctrine of massive retaliation. Criticism was not directed at the strategic design of the New Look but at its low state of operational effectiveness. The nub of the issue was budgetary. It expressed itself in conflict over the adequacy of the air force in terms of the number and quality of its strategic aircraft; the relative strength of American and Soviet air power; the capacity of American air power to deter communist military action, bomber and missile research and development programs; and the dispersal, protection, and warning afforded the nation's strategic strike forces. The Eisenhower proposal to expand continental air defense also prompted numerous clashes within Congress and between Congress and the executive branch over antiaircraft and antimissile programs and over the merits of the army's point defense system as opposed to the air forces's area approach, each based on competing weapon systems and differing deployment and operational patterns.

A second set of forces, composed, in part, of groupings of legislators who favored an increase in the nation's nuclear capability, challenged the very conceptual position of the administration. Influenced largely by army thinking, this bloc of congressional opposition, while conceding the need for strong atomic striking power, insisted, too, on more conventional and tactical nuclear military capabilities. It was argued that deterrence required more than strategic nuclear weapons to operate effectively against the communists and that, if deterrence failed, the United States should be prepared to meet a communist

201

attack on free-world interests with military forces that were proportioned to the geographic scope and political stakes at issue in the conflict. Controversy revolved in large part around the size, readiness, and composition of the army and marine corps, the tactical fire power support supplied to ground troops by sea and air forces, and the mobility and logistics requirements of ground troops, particularly those to be held in reserve on the American continent.

It should be stressed, however, that these counterflows to the main stream of the administration's policies did not develop rapidly or systematically in Congress. While they steadily grew in strength and momentum in the course of the Eisenhower administration, within any one year, when Congress was faced by the task of again passing a specific defense appropriation bill, these streams of criticism ebbed and flowed unpredictably down various channels. The appropriations subcommittees did not abandon their traditional approach to the defense budget. A majority of the membership on both defense subcommittees occupied themselves with the traditional search for economy *within* the framework of the administration's defense budget. Only slowly, imperceptibly, did the subcommittees expand the scope of their interest to include marginal exploration of the wider and more critical questions of the use of different forms of military force, under varying political contingencies, to foster United States policy interests. As they enlarged their purview, they correspondingly exerted greater influence on military policy. This occurred at two related, yet distinct, levels. In combination with other congressional elements, the appropriations subcommittees prodded the administration into strengthening specific parts of the nation's military establishment, principally its strategic air power capability. More subtly and pervasively, they also contributed to the education of that segment of public opinion that was concerned with defense issues. They aided the formulation of a new consensus in Congress that was to support more defense spending, more conventional and atomic fighting power, and a resuscitation of the nation's forward defense posture. But the development of this shift would require the remainder of the Eisenhower administration and would be finally consummated only by a change in the control of the Presidency in 1961. What remains to be delineated are the steps that led from the early and solid acceptance of the New Look in Congress to the slow breakup of the congressional consensus in the years that followed. The pilgrims' progress began with the FY 1955 defense budget.

CONGRESS BLESSES THE NEW LOOK: FY 1955

The congressional hearings on the President's FY 1955 defense budget proved disappointing. Most members of Congress received the New Look sympathetically. Few did so thoughtfully. The administration's assertion that its proposals were radical departures from previous defense policies was accepted by and large at face value. The question of what actually might be the military and political effects of the New Look stirred only a ripple of curiosity within Congress and within the defense appropriations subcommittees. The answer appeared self-evident to most. Only a handful of legislators publicly voiced doubts whether the Eisenhower changes in defense were for the better. Although the administration's policies rested on a jerry-built foundation of tenuous assumptions about the evolution of the international environment, on assorted unarticulated strategic risks, and on crudely imposed budgetary ceilings, they were adopted overwhelmingly as doctrinally valid. Reflecting much of congressional opinion, the appropriations subcommittees were attracted both to the outward simplicity of the New Look on strategic grounds and to its bargain-basement price tag. Disposed to a nuclear strategy whose roots of congressional support antedated the Korean War, the appropriations subcommittees defined their review function narrowly, training the bulk of their energies, as they traditionally had, on securing the same amount of military capacity advocated by the President, but at a lower cost. They conducted no deep probe of the assumptions on which the New Look rested; of its adequacy in light of changing political, military, and technological conditions; or even of the soundness of the administration's plan for implementing its announced innovations. Perhaps the New Look in 1954 might have survived close congressional scrutiny. There is little evidence that it was submitted to an exacting legislative test. The price of the FY 1955 defense budget, not the quality or the quantity of its product, was at issue.

A measure of the weakness of the congressional effort may be discerned by carefully analyzing General Ridgway's presentation in behalf of the army budget. Had the subcommittees closely reviewed Ridgway's remarks, they would have crystallized for themselves and for their colleagues most of the major military issues that were glossed over by the leadership of the Eisenhower administration in its testimony on the defense requests. Only Representative Robert Sikes, a member of the subcommittee on army appropriations, made an intensive attempt to place into the record the principal criticisms of, and policy alternatives to, the New Look that had been generated within the army and within parts of the executive branch generally. The effect of his questioning was slight. The little time at Sikes' disposal and his evident minority position on the subcommittee seriously hampered his efforts. He did succeed, however, in drawing from Ridgway the admission that the New Look would impair army readiness:

> Mr. Sikes: Do you feel under this budget that you have presented, where it proposed to reduce the number of men in the Military Establishment, that the Army will be able to maintain or to increase combat effectiveness above the present level?
>
> General Ridgway: No, sir. I would not think we can increase combat effectiveness. I think all the improvements that are going on all the time will increase the relative combat effectiveness

unit-for-unit, but a reduction in the order of magnitude that we are making will certainly when completed leave us with less combat effectiveness than we had when we started.[34]

This revelation only scratched the surface of the Army's and of Ridgway's discontent. The seeds of army opposition to the New Look lay more deeply embedded in Ridgway's opening statement. Had the subcommittee leadership and majority been interested in pursuing the suggestive implications of his remarks, there might have been initiated a thorough debate of the nation's strategic policies, with the result of strengthening them and their long-run consensual basis in Congress. At a minimum, the Congress and the public would have been better informed. These possibilities were not exploited.

Ridgway candidly admitted that the army budget had been guided "by basic economic and strategic decisions which [had] been made at a higher level."[35] Neither the relevance nor the substantive merit of these economic directives was investigated by the subcommittee. The Eisenhower spending limit on defense, like its military recommendations, commanded the same degree of unquestioning congressional fealty. The conspicuous silence of Congress and the defense subcommittees on so vital an issue prompted one commentator to complain with a measure of exasperation that "no one, absolutely no one, ever, ever questions whether the proposed sum—whether it be $13.4 billion or four times that much—is the proper sum to spend on national defense. In short, no one ever asks the important questions."[36]

Ridgway's ominous conclusion that "the military power ratio between western defensive capability and the Soviet bloc's offensive capability is *not* changing to our advantage"[37] received no special treatment despite its obvious contradition of the administration's claim that it had seized the strategic initiative against the Soviet Union through the New Look. What Ridgway was insisting upon, of course, was the traditional view that a nation's military power should be measured, not by some absolute standard that depended on a nation's own perception of its power, but by a flexible yardstick that marked out the relative strength of the nation vis-à-vis other nations over time. The New Look had turned inward for its standards in assessing the military strength of the United States. The communists were expected to respond to the moves of the United States. Ridgway's conception of the value of military power and its relevance to foreign policy was more fluid and evolutionary in nature and depended on an assessment of enemy capabilities and intentions. For him, nuclear weapons had not halted the qualitative or the quantitative dimensions of the arms race or the political struggle among nations. The larger effect of atomic power was to redirect these military, technological, and political processes along different, and in many ways more hazardous, lines of development. Conventional weaponry would again become increasingly important as a state of mutual nuclear deterrence between the super powers was approached. Representative Sikes, a reserve general in the army, again opened this line of thought and General Ridgway was prompt to supply the appropriate answers:

> Mr. Sikes: If we reach the point that we and the Communists offset each other's atomic warfare capabilities, so that neither side will dare to use those monsters of destruction. . . . will that not leave us at a material disadvantage defensivewise in having reduced the strength of our ground forces?
>
> General Ridgway: I think it could, sir. To me the hypothesis you present would entail a reversion to reliance on what we now term conventional forces and conventional weapons.[38]

The New Look rested in part on the assumption of continued United States atomic monopoly, although that monopoly had already been shattered by the Soviet Union's nuclear explosion of 1949 and its thermonuclear blast of 1953. Only the illusion of an indefinitely maintained American atomic monopoly remained, and the New Look was wedded closely to it.

Ridgway's strongest objections to decreases in army personnel and readiness rested principally on technical and military grounds. He denied that tactical nuclear weapons were a substitute for manpower as the administration had suggested. In his statement he strongly hinted that they would not be available in sufficient quantities to justify the army retrenchment in FY 1955.[39] Sikes forced this issue in his questioning of Ridgway:

> Mr. Sikes: Then those new weapons will not be of particular benefit to you in replacing ground forces during the coming year?
>
> General Ridgway: I think that is a fair statement; yes, sir.[40]

Ridgway would have objected to the army cuts even if these "modern weapons" had been made available, since, as he was to write later,[41] technological innovations in weaponry tended to require more, not less, troops. Complicated weapons necessitated large armies of technicians to maintain and operate them. Greater explosive power on the battle field would produce larger casualties. To compensate for these higher losses and to hold them at minimum levels, an expanded reserve of battle-ready troops and a larger medical service would have to be developed. The introduction of more destructive weapons on the battle field called for a radical change in tactics. Great bodies of troops would have to be dispersed over a large battle area to limit loss of life. They would have to be capable of rapid mobility over a wider battle field area than had heretofore been imagined. The army neither possessed such tactical mobile fire power nor foresaw its provision in the immediate future. Strategic air and sea lift units, capable of supplying and transporting combat troops over long distances, were similarly underdeveloped. Ridgway was skeptical, too, of the administration's plans to upgrade the reserves and its glowing optimism about the integration of twelve German divisions into NATO. He doubted whether either or both could compensate for larger

American ground forces in being. Modern warfare required a faster reaction time than the reserves appeared capable of achieving. So far as the German divisions were concerned, Ridgway did not see how they could become operational for a number of years. Meanwhile the army's thinning forces would have to perform an increasing number of tasks.[42]

The general took pains to describe the world-wide military commitments of the United States, stretching from the NATO countries in Europe to Southeast Asia, and the army's multiple responsibilities in discharging them. His brief analysis barely concealed a rather fundamental criticism of the administration's contradictory military policy, viz., that of disengaging American military might around the world while simultaneously maintaining and even extending the nation's political obligations to defend its allies. Ridgway said:

> I believe that . . . there is an existing requirement for the overseas deployment of Army forces in significant numbers, as well as for the maintenance of forces in the United States to support them. . . . I believe that the presence of United States Army forces in sensitive areas on our security frontiers has contributed materially to such military stability as exists in the world today. . . . " [43]

How the administration's plans for shrinking and redeployment of army forces would overcome these discreetly stated objections was not answered in the course of the hearings. Nor were these questions explicitly pressed.

The Senate's hearings on the defense appropriations bill mirrored those of the House. More effort was spent, for example, on the army's depot accounting system than on the political and military import of the New Look. Special committee investigators were assigned to review the army's allotment procedures. The comptroller of the army submitted a flow chart to the defense subcommittee which summarized in elaborate detail the budget authorizations and fiscal reports for the maintenance and operation of the army general depot in Atlanta, Georgia.[44]

Ridgway, on the other hand, was given short shrift. Senator Burnet Maybank, one of the appropriations subcommittee members, made a small attempt to uncover the reasons behind Ridgway's cool support of the New Look budget. The paucity of his effort suggests the superficial nature of the Senate probe:

Senator Maybank: . . . We read different statements and editorial comment by Secretary Dulles and others which sort of tended in some peoples' minds to think we were sort of leaving everything to atomic power, rather than the regular three branches of services with the unification we put into effect. . . . I read an article today about this leaving too much to atomic warfare. But you are satisfied, and you agree that the Army appropriation would be sufficient under the circumstances that we are up against today.

General Ridgway: I accept this program as sound.

Senator Maybank: I did not ask you if you accept it. I can understand that as a distinguished military man you are, as you said in prefacing your remarks, a career officer will accept orders from above and you accept them, you accept the amount of money and the reduction of the Army [sic]. But you do not recommend that?

General Ridgway: The time for recommendation is past, sir.

Senator Maybank: I understand that, but did you recommend it to the Joint Chiefs of Staff?

General Ridgway: I believe, Mr. Chairman, that I would like to submit to you the propriety of answering particular questions in executive session.[45]

Ridgway was never pressed beyond this point, even in closed session, although he was at the threshold of divulging the many points of disagreement between the army's position and the administration's. In reply to a question on the Senate floor, Homer Ferguson, chairman of the Senate defense appropriations group, revealed that "General Ridgway never asked to make an explanation, nor did the Senator from South Carolina [Maybank] ask him to make one." [46]

The reports of the appropriations committees on the defense bill, like the hearings of both houses, carefully avoided any confrontation of the New Look on policy grounds. The House report was,

> greatly encouraged by the increasing determination on the part of both civilian and military leaders within the Department of Defense to place our military organization on a sound and firm base to which constant improvements can be made in a more orderly manner to give us the required military strength without the waste of taxpayers' dollars.[47]

The Senate report expressed similar satisfaction with the reductions in defense costs. The one anxious note that was struck concerned a reported lag in guided missile development. The Senate committee directed the secretary of defense "to investigate the guided-missile program . . . and to report" his findings by January 15, 1955.[48]

Seized by the economy fever that had already swept through the executive branch, the House and Senate committees agreed to subtract slightly more than one billion dollars from the administration's $29.9 billion budget. The army budget was slashed another $600 million. The navy and the air force were forced to absorb decreases of $200 and $275 millions, respectively.[49] The two chambers later sustained their two committees on appropriations unanimously.

The brief House and Senate debates, each lasting two days, provided little opportunity for New Look opponents to marshal their arguments or their scattered political strength. Administration supporters controlled the direction and the outcome of the discussion by the two chambers. The House invested most of its attention in a host of peripheral military questions, including provision for reserve armories and training,[50] farm product purchases,[51] sports events at military installations to raise funds for charity,[52] United States dependents abroad,[53] medical and dental care of service personnel,[54] the use of the merchant marine,[55] and naval shipyards operations.[56] The longest debate centered on an amendment by Representative Frederick Coudert of New York that would have restricted the President's discretion to deploy troops abroad.[57] The amendment was clearly aimed, as one representative indicated,[58] at precluding, without congressional approval, the dispatch of American troops to Indo-China to forestall the imminent collapse of French rule there. Despite a number of passionate expressions of support for the measure, it failed on a teller vote, 214 to 37.[59]

In his lengthy presentation to the House, Representative Sikes stood almost alone among House members in addressing himself to the gamut of strategic issues underlying the New Look. He may as well have been speaking to himself. His success in rousing the House was as unavailing as his efforts within the defense subcommittee. "The conditions under which the New Look in defense was developed," he observed, "no longer exist." [60] The Western defense posture in Asia and in Europe had noticeably deteriorated. The French were being rapidly pushed out of Indo-China and were dragging their feet in the National Assembly on the question of passage of the European Defense Community. Sikes further argued that nuclear weapons which had not prevented the Korean War would not preclude communist military aggression in the future. He foresaw the likelihood of conventional engagements like Korea and Indo-China increasing as the Soviet nuclear threat expanded. "In this struggle for atomic supremacy," Sikes speculated with rare prescience, "it may not be long until we have reached a plateau where the forces of communism and those of the free world will have neutralized each other in the field of atomic warfare so that each would be fearful of employing such weapons against the other because of the fear of retaliation directed at their homeland." [61] Representative

George Mahon, minority leader of the House defense appropriations subcommittee, expressed similar doubts about the effectiveness of massive retaliation.[62]

Neither Sikes nor Mahon pressed his objection to the New Look to the logical conclusion of introducing amendments to increase defense spending for the army. The economy bloc in Congress simply commanded too much voting power to be overcome by a handful of dissidents in the House. Proposals to increase defense appropriations in the face of a defense subcommittee recommendation to decrease an already shrunken defense budget by an additional one billion dollars were doomed at the outset. Sikes conceded as much in the opening remarks of his presentation. "I would like to point out in the beginning," he announced, "that I have no quarrel with the committee action within the framework of fund limitations which were imposed by the Department of Defense and the Bureau of the Budget. Within that framework we of the committee were in substantial agreement." [63] Sikes' concession effectively blunted the sharp impact that his critique might otherwise have had. Once the administration's money ceiling on defense was adopted, it followed that the strategic air power should receive the major share of funds in the defense bill. All of the services—even the army—admitted the overriding priority that attached to long-range air power. Within the cramped confines of the administration's $29.2 billion budget, there was little room left for army expansion. The high costs of strategic aircraft procurement, maintenance, and operations precluded the sustenance of army strength at even FY 1954 levels. Sikes' criticisms reduced themselves, therefore, to a plaintive bleet of frustration:

> I fear that we may be again placing ourselves in the peaks and valleys system of rapid and costly buildup during emergencies, which. . . . has resulted in great cost, not only in dollars but great cost in lives as well. I feel that I must point out to the

House, as I have done before, that there is no shortcut, no cheap and easy way, to win a war. We cannot coast to victory.[64]

Unpersuaded, the House, like the administration, decided to coast. The Senate came sliding quickly behind, hindered only momentarily by a small band of young insurgent Democrats who launched a vocal assault on the New Look in a last minute attempt to halt the downward spiral in army strength. Senator Ferguson had defended the Eisenhower military budget by comparing it to those that preceded the Korean War.[65] Senators Albert Gore of Tennessee, Hubert Humphrey of Minnesota, and John F. Kennedy of Massachusetts, leaders of the opposition, attacked Ferguson's presentation. They insisted on a relative standard of evaluation that measured American military power in terms of the expanding Soviet military threat and the changed international political condition to which Sikes had also referred. "There does not seem to be any co-ordination between the statements of the Secretary of State and others as to what action the United States would take to prevent the fall of Southeast Asia and these budget figures," complained Kennedy. "It seems to me that they are operating on two entirely different levels. On one level there is the assumption of a long haul without a year of maximum crisis. On the other level there is the assumption that if we are not called upon to take part in military action in Southeast Asia, at least we shall be called upon to join in a collective pact in the area." [66] Kennedy offered an amendment to increase army appropriations by $350 million, which would have been sufficient to maintain it at the reduced FY 1954 level that the administration had programmed. The Senate debate revealed that the intent behind this amendment was to insure more fully the nation's military commitments to its allies, to meet future contingencies such as Korea with military means short of nuclear weapons, and to bolster the United States negotiating position with the Soviet Union. There was the added point that the

213

United States cutback had prompted its allies to follow suit. The indigenous troops on which the administration was counting to man the forward positions of the free world were being demobilized and disengaged.[67] Humphrey summarized these points in his brief, but biting, statement to the full Senate chamber:

> It does not do any good to talk about mass [sic] retaliation. It does not do any good to talk about something going to happen which is not going to happen. We have had our bluff called two or three times in the last month [over American intervention in Indo-China to prevent the French collapse]. We have been defeated at Geneva. . . . The first mistake was made last year, in April 1953, when our officials went to the NATO conference and stated to the European powers that the [military force] objectives could be stretched out over a few more years, and for them to take it easy. I think it is now evident that when we ask to sit down at a bargaining table with Soviet or any other satellites we have to be in a position of strength. I believe we went to Geneva without being in a position of strength. Our representatives went to Geneva after the budget had been cut and there had been put into effect a reduction in the Air Forces, when we were in Geneva with our allies, and we came home defeated. . . . [68]

Despite these arguments, the Eisenhower majority held firm. The Kennedy proposal was defeated in a fifty to thirty-eight division.[69] The New Look had successfully weathered its first legislative test.

THE NEW LOOK FORGES AHEAD: FY 1956

The administration's requests.—The second New Look budget of FY 1956 experienced more resistance in passing through Congress. Congressional receptivity to the New Look had worn slightly thinner in the course of one year. There developed a sharper sense of

214

skepticism among defense appropriations subcommittee members about the merit of the political and military considerations underpinning the FY 1956 defense budget. The hearings and debates on the defense bill evidenced a growing difference of opinion between an increasing number of legislators and the chief executive over the adequacy of the New Look. Part of the explanation for the increased criticism of the administration was personal and partisan; part of it—certainly the larger part—was the outgrowth of a progressively clearer realization that the New Look and its doctrine of massive retaliation were unable to fulfil United States commitments abroad or to stem communist enlargement of its political influence through the use of its military power.

The Democratic victory in 1954 swelled the number of opponents to the Eisenhower military program and brought some of them to posts on the House and Senate defense appropriations subcommittees. The House subcommittee increased its membership from nine to fifteen. Five of the newly appointed Democratic members—Jamie L. Whitten (Miss.), George W. Andrews (Ala.), John J. Riley (S.C.), Charles B. Dean (N.C.), and Daniel J. Flood (Pa.)—actively participated in a review of the administration's armed force recommendations. The Senate subcommittee also struck a more critical attitude than it had demonstrated in previous years.

The setback in Indo-China, where the French had agreed in July, 1954, to a partition of the country, initially prompted the increased tempo and intensity of congressional interest in the adequacy of the New Look. Indo-China had exposed a glaring weakness in American military power. The United States simply did not have sufficient ground forces to intervene effectively. Ridgway estimated that the cost of salvaging the French position "would have eventually been as great as, or greater than . . . paid in Korea." [70] It was a combination of Ridgway's opposition and the reluctance of United States allies, particularly Great Britain, to support an intervention scheme that cooled congressional and presidential ardor despite initial support within the Defense Department, spearheaded by Admiral Radford, to send troops into the Southeast Asian struggle. Commented Ridgway: "In Korea, we had learned that air and naval power alone cannot win a war and that inadequate ground forces cannot win one either. It was incredible to me that we had forgotten that bitter lesson so soon—that we were on the verge of making that same tragic error." [71] The lesson had not been forgotten. It had not yet been fully learned.

Three months after the Vietnamese partition, the Communist Chinese began to bombard the tiny Nationalist island-stronghold of Quemoy just off the China mainland. The administration's response to the Chinese shelling again exposed the impotence of the New Look in meeting attacks on American forward positions. On January 18, 1954, a few days after the FY 1956 budget had been presented to Congress, the Communist Chinese seized the island of Yikiang near Quemoy. Fear grew of a Red attack on Formosa. On January 24, President Eisenhower proposed a resolution to Congress, granting him authority to employ United States armed forces to protect Formosa and the Pescadores. The Formosa Resolution went on to include provision for presidential authority to use military force beyond these islands, presumably incorporating Quemoy and nearby Matsu, if a communist attack on these off-shore outposts were, in the words of the President's message, "recognizable parts of, or definite preliminaries to, an attack against the main positions of Formosa and the Pescadores." [72] The President apologized for the ambiguous extension of authority. "But, unhappily," he said, "the danger of armed attack directed against that area compels us to take into account closely related localities and actions which . . . might determine the failure or the success of such an attack." [73] The Formosa Resolution substituted calculated ambiguity for clarity of intent. Secretary of State John Foster Dulles had spoken of selective massive retaliation as a means of keeping the communists off balance with respect to American military initiatives. He had meant that the communists

216

would be kept guessing about American military moves, and not that the administration would be gripped by an air of expectancy about its own actions.

The administration accentuated the strains within the New Look policies by its insistence on increasing United States military and political commitments abroad while decreasing United States military forces at home and withdrawing them along the communist perimeter. The French defeat in Indo-China precipitated the formation of the Southeast Asia Collective Defense Treaty (SEATO) to buttress the West's sagging position in the area. The pact was signed on September 8, 1954, about the time that the Red Chinese opened their barrage on the Nationalist strongholds off the China coast. SEATO established the rudiments of a consultative framework through which the member states of the United States, the United Kingdom, France, Pakistan, the Philippines, Thailand, New Zealand, and Australia could work to meet communist military action in the southeastern Pacific. On December 2, 1954, three months after the SEATO signing, the United States entered into a mutual defense treaty with the Chinese Nationalists. The bilateral agreement with the Nationalists and the SEATO Pact were parts of a broader collective defense system that included NATO, the Rio Pact nations of South America, ANZUS, and bilateral mutual defense arrangements with the Philippines, Japan, and Korea.

The FY 1956 defense budget provided questionable proof of United States determination to underwrite fully its world-wide obligations and commitments. In presenting his budget to Congress, President Eisenhower announced the recall of five more army divisions from Korea as well as one and a third marine corps divisions. These troop removals were coupled with a budgetary recommendation for FY 1956 to diminish further the nation's forces. The President defended his action on the then familiar grounds that modern atomic weapons had been introduced into the military arsenal and that the mobility of ground troops had noticeably increased. Less troops could be thinly spread around the world without compromising the effectiveness which they had achieved at higher manning levels. These reductions in ground strength did not indicate, the President said, that the nation was placing "undue reliance on one weapon" or was preparing "for only one kind of warfare. . . . " [74] A year before, Admiral Radford had made the same point in his presentation to the Senate Committee on Foreign Relations.[75] The actual force level and spending levels recommended for FY 1956 pointed in the opposite direction. The distance between the administration's announced and operational policies widened. Not only did the nation's military capabilities lag behind its security obligations and the pace of the communist buildup, but its actual military capabilities fell short of the strength claimed by the administration to exist. The administration, therefore, was misleading both the enemy and, less justifiably, itself with respect to the real state of the nation's military preparedness.

A month before the budget was to be presented to Congress and after the army estimates had already been assembled, the President and his secretary of defense revised the army strength figures downward for the remainder of FY 1955 and FY 1956. For the second successive year, the army was ordered to cut its forces to fit the budgetary Procrustean bed ordered by the administration. The budgetary and strategic decision-making processes were again brought violently into temporary congruence as the administration prepared to make its policy recommendations public. The assumptions and decisions of almost a full year of careful planning and programming were hastily revised in less than a fortnight of hectic budgetary reshuffling. Congress had approved an army of 1,172,000 for FY 1955. The revised administration figure was established at 1,101,000—a 71,000 decrease. The FY 1956 totals were slimmed down by an additional 74,000, yielding an army of slightly above a million men. The administration's refusal to allow the army to request procurement authority for the second successive year placed the decreases in army ground strength into even bolder relief. In this connection, the marine corps's personnel levels were lowered at approximately the same percentage as the army's, from 215,000 in FY 1955 to 193,000 at the close of FY 1956.[76]

Favored was navy and air force air power. An estimated two-thirds of the defense budget was devoted to the procurement of delivery vehicles. The navy proposed a fifth "Forrestal" carrier and an added carrier wing. Naval operating aircraft was to rise to 10,061, an increase of about 120 airplanes over the preceding fiscal year. Airplane procurement would add 1,600 new planes to the navy's air arm.[77] The growth of the air force was noticeably greater. To assist it to its 137-wing goal, over $6 billion was assigned to its aircraft and related procurement requests, including a half billion dollars for guided and ballistics missile development.

The administration asked for $32.2 billion in new obligational authority. This sum represented a slight increase in appropriations over the previous year, but it was balanced by an equally slight decrease in defense expenditures for the same period.[78] The army was permitted to request $7.6 billion, a post-Korean War low. This sum was even smaller in real dollars. Almost $400 million of this sum was earmarked for services to be performed for the navy and the air force.[79] The navy was likewise saddled with a more confining budget of $9.2 billion. Air force estimates, in contrast, climbed to $14.8 billion. Its budget nearly doubled the combined budgetary totals of the other services.[80]

Congress and the New Look: Round two.—In striking contrast to their almost muted acquiescence in the New Look of a year before, the members of the defense appropriations subcommittees now pressed administration spokesmen to defend their policies and budget requests. The cordiality of the previous year, while outwardly evident during the hearings, was placed under repeated strains as the legislators moved through the testimony of administration spokesmen. In one heated exchange, Representative Mahon, chairman of the House

219

defense group, reprimanded Secretary Wilson for his discursive answers. In reply to a Republican member of the subcommittee who was defending Wilson's presentation, Mahon said, "It is perfectly all right for him [Wilson] to make an observation, but we do not want to go rambling about and not answer the questions, in order to get on with the hearings." [81] Mahon's impatience reflected more than a temporary exasperation with Wilson's habit of wandering about in his testimony. His outburst came in the wake of a lengthy and abrasive exchange between Secretary of Defense Wilson and Representative Daniel Flood over the administration's justification for reducing military personnel strength. Wilson defended the cuts and accused the services, in his words, of "end running" him to Congress.[82] It was the New Look, not Wilson, that was on trial.

On the Senate side, Senator John Stennis, during his questioning of Secretary of the Navy Charles S. Thomas, expressed the same general anxiety of many of his colleagues over the decreases in military strength:

Senator Stennis: . . . The conditions in the Formosa Straits are certainly not getting better?

Secretary Thomas: That is right.

. . . .

Senator Stennis: If we should go into action on Quemoy and Matsu or Formosa, we would not get any help from any of the Asiatic allies, would we? They have all they can do at home.

Secretary Thomas: That is right.

. . . .

Senator Stennis: We would not get any help from the European allies. Their announced position is no help on Matsu or Quemoy, and it is a question as to whether we would have any on Formosa as far as ground troops are concerned, is that not right? Would you agree to that?

Secretary Thomas: Yes, I will agree to that.[83]

And again a little later in the hearings:

> Senator Stennis: Mr. Secretary, there is a great deal of concern here at this table about the reductions of these mobile forces. . . . It seems to me like it goes back to what we are going to do if we are called on to defend Formosa. As a civilian Secretary, do you not think it will require ground troops on our part on Formosa if there is an attempted invasion there?
>
> Secretary Thomas: Senator, I would still like to stick to my original answer to your question. I think this is a sound program. . . .
>
> Senator Stennis: The inference is that we will not have to use ground troops there. I cannot escape the conclusion on my part that we will have to use them. We always do when we are involved. . . . [84]

This exchange between Stennis and Thomas should not suggest that the hearings had undergone a kind of metamorphosis in one year. There developed no systematic analysis or critique of the administration's strategic policies. The questioning moved along the meandering course of over a generation of appropriations hearings. What was new was not the process of review, but the manifestation of a more acute congressional appreciation of the tenuous assumptions underlying the New Look, of the possible unreliability and effectiveness of the military establishment under a variety of plausible conflict situations, and of a slightly deeper understanding of the limitations of force, particularly nuclear force, in supporting the nation's foreign policy position. Faith in nuclear energy was not being withdrawn in Congress. It was being qualified, and it was simultaneously being placed on firmer, more defensible ground.[85]

Defense Secretary Wilson and Admiral Radford argued the administration's case before Congress. Again the differences between the administration and the army, summarized in the testimony of Admiral Radford, were distributed loosely and unsystematically throughout the hearings. It was unfortunate that the House and the Senate reports did not crystallize the many critical points in dispute. These must be laboriously dredged from the surrounding verbal quagmire.

Anticipating its critics, the administration proposed a new reserve plan which it skilfully represented as an effective substitute for the maintenance of larger and more costly ground forces in being. Closely tied to the military budget of FY 1956, the reserve plan called for the participation of men who would have otherwise been eligible for selective service to attend weekly training drills and annual two-week summer encampments for a period of six years in lieu of their two-year military obligation. These reserve forces were to be kept in a high state of readiness for rapid mobilization. The administration's proposal proceeded through Congress without encountering serious dispute. It is not hard to understand why. The prospect of cutting defense costs without impairing military preparedness was appealing to most legislators. The appropriations committees were particularly sensitive to this argument. For the same expenditure, larger reserve forces could be maintained than active duty personnel. The nation's defense posture, argued administration spokesmen, would not be sacrificed; it would actually be improved.[86] The lobby activities of the National Guard Association and the Reserve Officers Association reinforced the economic attractiveness of the reserve plan. Both organizations, especially the guard group, are deeply rooted in the local politics of the nation and have traditionally exercised strong influence over reserve policy.[87] Many legislators, furthermore, needed little exterior prodding. The ideal of the citizen-soldier still lingered on. The administration's "carrot and stick" techniques combined, therefore, with a firmly based congressional disposition in favor of strengthening the reserves. A majority in Congress was quick to accept the administration's reserve plan despite army reservations about the feasibility of replacing regular troops with larger reserves. Congress happily seized on the administration's assurance that a substitution could be made without lowering defense preparedness.[88]

Other reasons, besides an improved reserve force, were advanced to justify the army and marine corps reductions. The United States would rely on help from other allied countries to supply ground troops for limited war engagements.[89] The increased mobility and fire power of army units and the more efficient utilization of service manpower which was alleged made a reduction in military personnel possible and economically desirable.[90] Buttressing these arguments, Admiral Radford reiterated the administration claim that, "to be prepared indefinitely for both atomic and a nonatomic war on a global basis would require expenditures of such magnitude that it would be staggering for. . . . this country."[91] The country could not—and would not—bear the cost. Ground forces had to be cut to assure sufficient funds for the buildup of air power. The difficulties surrounding German rearmament associated with the repeal of EDC and the powerful opposition of groups within Germany were noted only in passing.[92] As for the increase in army mobility, the army admitted some expansion in its tactical capability but denied any increase in strategic air mobility, the key factor in swift movement to troubled spots abroad. An army report that was buried in the House appropriations hearings observed, "As to the percentagewise improvement in airlift potential in the last 12 months, the answer is there has been none."[93]

These reservations were easily overriden. The administration's case proved too compelling when it assured Congress "that in the event of a drastically worsened world condition additional funds for an expanded military program would be promptly requested. . . . "[94] "It is in the light of this situation," the House report revealed, "that the Committee is approving the military budget substantially as finally submitted."[95] The report noted that some committee members had opposed the "reductions with great reluctance," but these were permitted to stand. The House group recommended an appropriation of $31.5 billion, which was $759 million below the amount requested by the administration; the Senate, more expansive and sensitive to air power needs, proposed a $31.8 billion defense budget, the bulk of the increases being accounted for by an added $200 million administration request for the air force to speed B-52 production.[96]

The defense appropriations bill ran into stiffer opposition on the House and Senate floors. A small group, occupying the bottom seniority rungs of the House defense appropriations subcommittee, openly attacked the administration. Representatives Daniel Flood and George Andrews offered a number of amendments which, if they had been passed, would have essentially maintained the previously approved force levels of FY 1955 for the army, navy, and marine corps. The army and marine corps would have been kept at an end-year strength of 1,172,700 and 215,000, respectively, for FY 1956. The navy would have retained 8,300 more men in uniform than the President had assigned to it. This increase would have made it possible to operate a fleet of 1,061 ships instead of the 1,001 vessels proposed in the budget. Most of this increase in naval ship operation was directed toward small amphibious craft essential to the tactical mobility of army and marine corps units. The administration had cut these ships from its 1956 program, though it continued to speak of the need for quick and efficient deployment of American troops in case of emergency. The Flood and Andrews amendments were defeated, as a similar proposal had been in the Senate a year before. A coalition of Democrats and Republicans joined in repulsing the floor assault. The refusal of George Mahon, the defense subcommittee chairman, to aid the insurgents deprived them of the support that they needed to gain full House acceptance.[97]

The Senate floor fight, on the other hand, provided the first example of a successful congressional attack on an Eisenhower defense budget. Senate members had similarly expressed worry over the effect of the administration's diminution of ground forces. Particularly disturbing were the cutbacks in marine corps personnel. The appeal of the marine corps to most Senators transcended its military utility, however significant that might be. The corps symbolized American preparedness and determination to fight if attacked.

Cuts in army strength could stir, as they had, strong intellectual objections on grounds of rational strategic policy; cuts in the marine corps struck more sensitive nerve endings, including the emotional attachment of the Senate (and the nation) to the corps and the very patriotism of Senate members themselves. Senator Stuart Symington, President Truman's secretary of the air force, led the Democratic majority in the fight to amend the appropriations committee's report upward. He proposed a $46 million increase in marine corps personnel funds to raise the force from 193,000 to 215,000 during FY 1956. In a close forty to thirty-nine party vote, Symington's amendment carried. The other features of the defense bill were not strongly disputed.[98] In conference, the bill emerged closely resembling the President's recommendations. Both houses approved the amended bill of $31.9 billion, approximately $200 million less than the administration had wanted.[99]

The change in marine corps funding indicated a developing mood in Congress that was to become important in the deliberations upon the FY 1957 defense bill. It was another sign of the rising doubts about the New Look program and of Congress' growing interest in deciding for itself what was the actual defense capability of the nation. Legislators were girding themselves to challenge the President on military policy. The FY 1956 budget battle would appear in retrospect to be merely a quiet skirmish before a full-scale offensive, centering on air power, would be launched against an Eisenhower defense budget for FY 1957.

THE NEW LOOK ATTACKED: FY 1957

Except for an increase in funds for guided missile procurement (which topped the $1 billion mark for the first time), President Eisenhower presented very little that was new in his FY 1957 military budget.[100] In his statement before the House, Secretary Wilson echoed the President. He proposed nothing "fundamentally different from that outlined . . . last year." [101] The business of defense would continue on an orderly, stable basis. Peaks and valleys in production would be avoided. Air power would be emphasized. The air force's requests were set at $15.7 billion. The army's budget was half as large at $7.8 billion; the navy, two-thirds as large at $10.0 billion. Combined air force and navy procurement, principally for aircraft, was to cost $6.8 billion. The total budget inched upward only slightly to $34.1 billion, approximately $2 billion above the preceding year's figure.[102] This sum was keyed to a defense spending program of approximately $35 billion.

The musical score had not markedly changed. What little re-arrangement had occurred in the composition of military forces had the effect of further diminishing the role of conventional weaponry. The administration, however, was unable to elicit the same kind of three-part service harmony in support of its recommendations that had been achieved in previous public and congressional performances. The army again sounded an array of dischordant notes in its budgetary presentations to Congress, clashing repeatedly with the administration's policy directives. The publication of General Matthew Ridgway's attack on the New Look in his *Memoirs* and in his widely circulated article appearing in the *Saturday Evening Post* sharpened the dissonant effect of army complaints.[103] Administration leaders might have drowned out the army criticisms if they had not been accompanied in counterpoint by others vocalized by the air force. For the first time since 1953 the air force, too, departed from the role assigned to it in defending administration policies. In contrast to the army, air force officialdom, both military and civilian, whole-heartedly accepted the New Look and massive retaliation. Its objection centered not on strategy, but on the military requirements and budgetary limits set by the administration in implementing its strategic design.

The House and Senate appropriations hearings helped to define the conflicting viewpoints of the army and the air force and of these services and the administration. The somnambulism within the appropriations subcommittees that had marked their previous reviews of the Eisenhower budget was temporarily overcome. The House examination of the FY 1957 budget was particularly searching when compared with preceding years. "I guess sometimes you may feel," Representative Charles Deane told Defense Secretary Charles Wilson, "that when members of the committee ask questions involving policy maybe we are getting out of our field, but actually that is what seems to me to be the purpose of your presence; not to go into detailed information, but to discuss generally speaking overall policy." [104] Other members of the House subcommittee shared Deane's view and were more probing and direct in their questioning and criticism of administration witnesses. Representative Daniel Flood attacked Secretary Wilson's failure to spend the extra money appropriated by Congress for the marine corps in FY 1956.[105] In a masterful line of questioning, Representative Robert Sikes summarized General Ridgway's brief against the administration.[106] Chairman George Mahon's leadership of his subcommittee was cast in the same policy-oriented mold. His questioning was no less sharp. Referring to an article by Secretary of State John Foster Dulles applauding brinkmanship diplomacy, Mahon asked Wilson how he had co-ordinated his department's actions with those of the State Department:

> Mr. Mahon: . . . Secretary Dulles . . . comes out and talks about our dancing or balancing on the brink or the precipice of war three times, stating that this is a necessary art and all of that business, and yet while Mr. Dulles is on the brink, 'ground crew shortage cuts Air Force flights,' and all of these sad stories are given to us. That is no way for the Defense Department to be run, while we are swaying right there on the precipice, Mr. Secretary. . . .
>
> Secretary Wilson: I think that you are overstating one side of the matter.

. . . .

> Mr. Mahon: . . . My question to you, Mr. Secretary, is, 'What were you doing when Secretary Dulles was at the brink, whether it was a bad brink, a little brink, or a medium-sized brink. What was the Defense Department doing specifically at that time?' [107]

Wilson was hard pressed for an answer and the discussion was soon dropped.

The House hearings concentrated on three broad policy issues: the army's case against the New Look; the reported lag in United States missile development; and what the House subcommittee termed the administration's policy of simply maintaining "what is determined to be a sufficient air force equipped with the best modern aircraft to act as a deterrent to any possible aggression" rather than an air force superior to the Soviet Union's "in the overall size . . . and in the numbers of aircraft to be produced. . . . " [108] The 1,200 pages of general House hearings on the defense budget also raised such issues as the role of the JCS in determining military force and budget levels; the process by which the budget was formed; the economic considerations guiding its development; the military forces needed to meet various contingencies; the effectiveness of army and air force management; and the seeming slow pace of weapons systems research. [109]

The Senate hearings were not as comprehensive. They focused largely on the issue of United States strategic air power. [110] This narrowed spotlight was encouraged by the Senate Armed Services Committee's well-publicized and extensive investigation of American air power. [111] The Symington hearings on air power, named after the investigating subcommittee chairman, overshadowed the appropriations review in public importance and had a detectable influence on the defense budget. In large part as a result of the Symington hearings, the shortcomings in the nation's offensive and defensive air power capability became a major issue of the 1956 presidential campaign. Spurred, too, by the partisanship of an election year, the

228

defense review of the Democratic Eighty-fourth Congress was the most searching examination of the nation's strategic posture since the "Admirals' Revolt" of 1949.

The army dissent.—By 1956, the army had hammered its varied criticisms of the administration into a coherent strategic position. Its previous attacks had tended more to be isolated thrusts than parts of an integrated plan of assault on the administration's strategic purpose and design. Now all of its many disgruntlements were codified into a strategic view that contrasted sharply with the administration's official position. The army disagreed with almost every major element of the administration's massive retaliation doctrine. While it conceded the air force's request for strategic retaliatory forces to deter a general war, it denied that such a conflict was likely to ensue as nuclear parity was reached. Limited conflict, requiring the use of large, mobile ground forces, was the more probable kind of war that the United States would be compelled to fight. A condition of mutual deterrence made a policy of avoiding a total war imperative. No rational purpose could be achieved through such a devastating military action. As nuclear parity became a reality, both sides, army spokesmen argued, would make every effort to avoid a general war. This situation placed a premium on conventional and irregular warfare forces, and encouraged the Soviets to use such forms of military power to extend their influence, as they had done in Asia despite overwhelming United States atomic superiority. On the other hand, if a total war were to erupt, the army felt that it would be a long and trying struggle in which all units of the armed forces would be employed fully. A short-war concept was specifically rejected.

Lack of limited war capabilities was viewed as a political liability. Without such strength the nation's military response to a communist non-nuclear attack would be restricted to the possible initiation of an all-out war, ineffectual resistance, or capitulation. None of these options served United States foreign policy objectives. In the first instance, nuclear war would be disastrous; in the latter two cases, the nation would be confronted with a dangerous, conceivably fatal, erosion of its diplomatic position. The lack of large conventional forces deployed in forward areas overseas exposed United States allies to swift defeat, while simultaneously undermining the credibility of the nuclear deterrent. America's allies could not rely on the United States to defend them; they could count only on the possibility of United States liberation after a devastating nuclear war—a war which the United States would hesitate to start since its own existence would be gravely threatened. Such a corrosive frame of mind would encourage America's allies to adopt one or a combination of three postures in a search for security: disengagement from the super-power struggle of the cold war and a posture of official neutrality; an independent program to develop nuclear arms; or integration into a new "third force" as a counterweight to the United States and the Soviet Union.

The army advanced what it termed a "tridimensional" strategy of deterrence, resting on large land, sea, and air contingents. Massive retaliation would give way to measured retaliation. Military responses to Soviet initiatives would be proportioned to the military force, geographical area, and political stakes at issue. The ability to wage limited and conventional warfare would provide American diplomacy with a greater range of choice in the use of force to achieve the nation's foreign policy goals. Army Chief General Maxwell Taylor, who had replaced General Ridgway, presented the core of the army's case:

> I would now like to discuss the need for versatility in the Army as it prepares itself for all types of future war. I am aware of the fact that many students of the world military situation regard only one type of war—the general nuclear onslaught—as being sufficiently important to cause much concern. I do not adhere to that view. I believe that as parity is approximated in numbers and types of atomic weapons between the East and

West, every effort will be made on both sides to avoid the general atomic war. But, at the same time, I cannot believe that the Communist bloc will give up aggression as an instrument of policy. It appears probably by pressure on the soft spots about the Soviet periphery through subversion, guerrilla actions and *coups d'état*; by small-scale wars; and the ever-present threat of their large armies, the Communists will continue to seek an extension of their boundaries at the expense of the West. Failure to respond quickly and effectively to these types of warfare will permit the piecemeal loss of important areas belonging to friends and allies. Such failure would create situations which might expand into the general war that all parties seek to avoid. . . .

As one considers . . . potential trouble spots, one is bound to reflect on the varied requirements for effective military action in these areas. Facts of geography, climate, ethnology and politics would make every case a special problem. They have at least one characteristic in common—any military action therein will be essentially a land operation with a very limited role, if any, for heavy weapons of great destructiveness. To deal with explosive situations in most of these areas, the first requirement is for reliable indigenous ground forces. We should be prepared to reinforce these forces with our own, if and when United States policy calls for active participation.

It is the Army's view that the United States must be capable of deterring general atomic war, and at the same time be capable of deterring a small war, or of suppressing it quickly if it breaks out. . . . After allocating the national resources necessary for deterring general and local war and of winning local war, we should proceed to satisfy the residual requirements for fighting a general war.[112]

To carry out its strategic plan, the army pressed for a sizable increase in its active forces (Taylor thought that an army of twenty-eight divisions, composed of 1.5 million men, would be ideal); a rapid modernization of combat equipment; a larger stockpile of conventional weapons; stepped-up guided missile development for field, antiaircraft, and antimissile purposes; large-scale mobile air and sea transport services; and an expanded tactical air support capability. The FY 1957 budget did not provide for the army's shopping list. Although the army did not fully join the issue, the implication was clear that it was calling either for a larger share of the defense appropriations pie or for congressional enlargement of the pie itself.

Air Force dissent.—The army did not secure redress in Congress despite the sympathetic hearing that it received. The issues raised by the air force, while of lesser theoretical importance, appealed more strongly to most congressmen who, for a decade, had been preoccupied with the task of maintaining United States nuclear striking superiority over the Soviet Union. The air force now charged that superiority was being lost. As early as 1954, shortly after the controversy over a 143 wing air force had been stilled by the Eisenhower administration, reports began to filter into the public press that the Soviet Union was surging ahead of the United States in nuclear delivery capacity and general air power strength. In the May Day celebration of 1954, the first Soviet Bison bombers were sighted. These were comparable aircraft to the B-52. A year later air force officials counted at least twelve of these heavy bombers in flyovers in the Soviet Union.[113] At about this time the American press began publishing items which suggested that the Soviets were also forging ahead in missile development. Joseph Alsop wrote of a Russian engine capable of exerting over 200,000 pounds of thrust and of the production of a two-stage Soviet rocket with a range of 1,500 miles.[114] The *Nation's Business* printed a cautionary article titled "Red Rocket Know-How Matches Ours" in February, 1955.[115] A year later, Senator Stuart Symington expressed the opinion before NBC's "Meet the Press" that the Russians had fired long-range ballistic missiles hundreds of miles farther than the United States had ever tested. "I do not believe the Soviets are ahead of us in the ballistic missile," he said. "They *are ahead* of us. . . ."[116] These reports were made all the

232

more disturbing by the upward revision of intelligence estimates of Soviet missile and aircraft productive capacity.[117]

The resignation of Trevor Gardner as assistant secretary of the air force for research and development lent credence to these signs of rapid Soviet technological progress. Gardner broke with the administration because it refused to lift its budgetary restrictions on air force modernization, bomber production, and, more particularly, on missile development. Gardner predicted that, unless the United States speeded up its missile work, it would soon fall behind the Soviet Union. Leaks emanating from the air force buttressed Gardner's accusations. They indicated a slow down in the planned completion of the administration's announced 137 wing air force.

These reports and charges prompted the Symington air power hearings. After a year of intensive investigation and study the Symington group confirmed the view that the Soviet Union was overtaking the United States in over-all air power capacity and had already assumed the lead in a number of defined areas. The air power committee found that the Soviet Union possessed more fighter and bomber aircraft than the United States and was producing more in each category. The quality of Soviet aircraft was improving, too. It was also moving "at a faster rate than the United States in the development and production of new type scientific weapons and, if present plans and programs of the United States. . . . [were] not changed," the report concluded, "the U.S.S.R. would attain superiority in this field." [118] The Soviets were alleged to be already ahead "in some aspects of ICBM and IRBM" development.[119]

The Symington probe had a decided impact on the course of the defense appropriations hearings. The Senate defense subcommittee was almost totally absorbed in the strategic air-power problem; the House group, while it struggled to gain a broader view of the defense establishment, found itself repeatedly returning to a discussion of Soviet-American aircraft and missile strength. General Curtis LeMay's testimony as commander of the Strategic Air Command outlined the major sources of air force discontent with the FY 1957 budget. There was no doubt in LeMay's mind about sac's deteriorating deterrent capacity, unless it were supported by more funds. Unlike army representatives, LeMay saw no requirement for large conventional forces. A powerful strategic air force was sufficient to deter both big and small wars and assure the strategic superiority of the United States if war should arise:

> Looking at the national defense picture for the next 15 years, we can see a number of enemy strengths of various types . . . but the biggest and the only threat which can destroy the United States and our allies is the Soviet capability to deliver a surprise massive nuclear air attack. So I think that whatever we buy, it must be able to deter that threat before it is applied. If it can deter that ultimate threat, it can deter anything smaller. I know of only one thing which will make us capable of meeting the threat of an all-out nuclear attack as well as lesser threats and that is the clear possession by the United States of an effective strategic nuclear air offensive force in being. . . . We must have a force strong enough in size, so deployed and in such a condition of readiness to guarantee to him that the inevitable consequence of any attack they [sic] might launch will be devastation of his own homeland. Should they be so foolhardy as to miscalculate our capability, this force must be capable of insuring the emergence of the United States as the superior power.[120]

LeMay flatly rejected the army's strategic analysis and its claim for more funds. The air force, not the army, needed more money. To deter the Soviet Union from using its mounting nuclear strike capacity, LeMay recommended the rapid completion of the 137 wing goal. This force would require 1.2 million men by LeMay's calculation, not the 975,000 assigned by the administration. LeMay expressed particular concern over the slippages in B-52 production which were below the planned level of twenty per month. He complained, too, that his $8 billion budget had been sliced to $6 billion. The reduction, he contended, was seriously hampering sac operations.[121]

LeMay stated his position most explicitly before the Senate defense appropriations subcommittee. The House group devoted more time and attention to missile development. In preceding years the subject had been touched upon only briefly. It could no longer be ignored. Mahon voiced the concern of many of his colleagues when he observed at the start of his subcommittee's hearings that Congress was "being warned from time to time that perhaps in the guided missile race and in the race for the intercontinental ballistics missile the United States may be behind. . . . " [122] Gardner was summoned before the House subcommittee to present his views. He told the subcommittee that he "could not in good conscience participate in a program which had a reasonable chance . . . of losing the technological race with the Russians." [123] Inadequate financing and poor management were cited as the principal reasons for the United States slow progress in ICBM's. Instead of the $610 million earmarked for air force research and development in FY 1957, Gardner recommended $850 to $900 million.[124] The budgetary limitation preventing air force expansion to 137 wings was similarly hindering progress in missile development.

Gardner deplored, too, the rivalry among the services for more missile money and status. Interservice struggles were sapping the energy and drive of the missile program. The Nike-Talos wrangle between the army and air force was only one of a number of examples of counterproductive service competition. The meaning of "top priority" had all but disappeared. The ICBM phase of missile work had been granted "top priority" status only in 1955. It shared this priority listing with a number of other missile projects for more than two years.

Mismanagement of the missile program was also losing valuable time in the race against the Russians. In an article that appeared in *Look* magazine shortly after he testified, Gardner added the criticism that the over-all missile program was "something of an administrative nightmare of committees and subcommittees competing with each other for influence and appropriations." [125] Few clear-cut policy decisions emerged from these committee meetings. They tended to compromise differing positions or to suspend decision altogether. They were also time consuming. This administrative tangle was further complicated by the large number of administrative, rather than missile, experts who occupied key posts on various missile projects.

Congress proceeds cautiously.—The appropriations committees did little to resolve the multiple and intertwined problems posed by the army and air force dissents. Their best efforts were exhausted in exploring the United States lack of limited war capabilities, its slow progress in missile research and development, and its equally sluggish advance toward a 137 wing air force. Some action was taken only on the final issue. The others were simply aired in the semisecret committee hearings and left unresolved.

The House joined the Senate in increasing air force funds by $900 million—$800 million for aircraft procurement and the rapid buildup to 137 wings, $100 million for research and development, including funds for missiles.[126] This sum was in addition to the $248 million supplemental request which the House Appropriations Committee members had prodded the administration into making for FY 1957 to step up B-52 production from 17 to 20 a month.[127] A year before, congressional pressure had secured a supplemental request of over $200 million to expand bomber production from twelve to seventeen a month.[128] Congress had less difficulty grasping the need for more long-range bombers against the Soviet Union. Maintaining the quantitative and qualitative strength of SAC had been an established congressional concern since before the Korean War. Pouring more money into conventional forces or into yet undeveloped and untried weapons systems, like ICBM's, did not have the same traditional attraction. The fault was not entirely, or even primarily, Congress'. The air force had conditioned itself and Congress to the pre-eminence of manned delivery systems. A switch in legislative attitude toward missiles could not be made without some executive branch encouragement which was not immediately forthcoming.

236

For all its efforts, the army received no tangible assistance from Congress except an opportunity to present its views. An additional $100 million was carved from its already austere budget. An army budget of $7.5 billion was approved, slightly more than $200 million over the previous year's total. The air force remained the darling of the administration and of Congress, having been authorized a $16.5 billion budget for FY 1957.[129]

The navy's appropriations requests, on the other hand, slipped silently through Congress. The navy stood apart from the army–air force dispute. This was a turnabout from the leading role that it had played in the 1949 strategy hearings. Boasting both limited and total war capabilities, the navy saw little gain in entering the controversy. If the army's strategic position had won ascendancy in Congress, the navy could simply have requested increases for the marine corps and its surface fleet. Likewise, continued air force pre-eminence assured the continuance of the navy's supercarrier fleet which supplemented SAC's strategic striking force.

The Navy Department was permitted to build twenty-three new major ships, including another supercarrier and six submarines, and to initiate twenty-three major ship conversions. It was also given enough money to add 1,468 new aircraft to the 12,000 already in operation. Naval personnel strength was set at approximately the levels which had prevailed in FY 1956. Cost of the navy program was set at $10 billion. Finding little fault with this estimate, the Congress dropped slightly less than $50 million from the navy request.[130]

The final defense appropriations bill that emerged from Congress totaled $34.6 billion, $500 million over the administration's requests.[131] Despite this increase, the total appropriations authorized by Congress for FY 1957 for all items, military and non-military, were still $258 million below the administration's estimates. In no year since World War II had Congress passed more over-all appropriations than the President had submitted for authorization. The significance of the FY 1957 deliberations was the narrowness of the gap between what

237

Congress finally appropriated and what the President asked. The gap was considerably wider in other years. The FY 1953 and FY 1954 budgets produced the largest spread between Congress and the President. These amounted to $8.6 billion and $12.0 billion in each respective year.[132]

THE NEW LOOK RESURGENT: FY 1958

The shell game.—The strategic problems raised in 1956 were no less pressing in January, 1957, when President Eisenhower presented his military budget for FY 1958. They had, indeed, increased in urgency and number in the face of the accelerating technological revolution in weaponry, the Soviet missile successes, and growing unrest in the underdeveloped nations of the world and behind the Iron Curtain. The Suez and Hungarian crises of fall 1956 typified the latter two dimensions of the United States new strategic position.

These novel challenges to American security and foreign policy interests were not made clear to the public in the middle 1950's. The widening spectrum of national strategic issues was reduced during the 1956 presidential campaign to a debate over air power. The Democratic opposition saw more votes in this one issue than in the more numerous and subtle questions of non-nuclear and non-military responses to the cold war. In the midst of the contest for the presidency, one irritated observer complained, "Hard as it admittedly is for the Democrats to talk sense about defense and still hold their audience, they cannot escape their essential responsibility to do so. . . . It is true that strategy is a difficult stump subject and that the apathy of the people is large. But somewhere, sometime, the vicious circle of public indifference and political silence must be broken. . . . "[133]

Neither, of course, was broken. Eisenhower's second resounding victory over Adlai Stevenson, greater than in 1952, strengthened the economy forces within the administration. Far from being repudiated, the New Look was granted an expanded mandate. The smashing electoral success aided the President and the economy group within his inner circle to assert more control over dissident elements within the Defense Department. Their job was made easier because "troublemakers," like Gardner and Ridgway, had left government. Others, who might have followed their lead, were reluctant to expose themselves to the same fate. Once again the administration was able to concentrate on the fiscal and economic aspects of the defense budget. More remarkably, it persuaded a majority in Congress to busy itself with economic considerations, too.

The President recommended a Defense Department expenditure budget of $38 billion for FY 1958, an increase of about $2 billion over the year before. The Defense Department bill requested $36.1 billion in new obligational authority to support an armed force of 2.8 million. This level had been reached during FY 1957 and was to be sustained despite the Suez and Hungarian incidents. Increased defense expenditures were necessitated by rising cost factors in operations and maintenance, guided missiles, reserve forces, and public works.[134] The services would have pushed defense spending upward by at least $10 billion. The estimates that the administration presented to Congress contrasted with the $48 billion that the services had initially submitted.[135]

The army's budget of $8.5 billion would secure seventeen reorganized divisions, nine regimental combat teams, six atomic support commands, and an increased number of missile and antiaircraft battalions. Personnel, however, was scheduled to slip below one million. "This force," General Taylor explained, was "developed in consistence with the view that the Army's primary purpose is to provide deterrent strength for the prevention of war. Every element has been scrutinized to determine that it does in fact contribute to the Army's ability to prevent war, either large or small, *in conjunction with the means available to our sister services.*"[136] Translated in different terms, the army found itself caught between its argument for limited war capabilities and the congressional acceptance of an atomic strategy. Its commanders sincerely felt that the United States needed conventional military forces, but they also knew that the larger slices of the budget pie went to the services which controlled atomic weapons. Therefore, the army, too, would embrace the atom with more fervor and resolution. General Taylor told the House subcommittee that the army divisions were being reorganized into pentomic units, emphasizing greater mobility and firepower based on atomic weapons. Conventional weapons procurement would be reduced as the new weapons were phased into use.[137] Lieutenant General C. B. Magruder, assistant chief of staff for logistics, stressed the reduction of conventional requirements as a result of greater nuclear fire power:

> The Army feels that battlefield atomic weapons of the types now available and becoming available will reduce our requirement for conventional ammunition in a future war in which atomics are used.
>
> . . . .
>
> Some reduction in our requirements of conventional ammunition is justified and our current estimate is that the reduction may total around 25 per cent in the next 3 to 5 years.[138]

Magruder's testimony was inspired by administration constraints on spending. Ridgway's (and Taylor's) view that tactical nuclear weapons demanded more, not less, personnel was overridden by the administration and, in turn, dismissed by Congress.

The navy also wanted missiles and atomic weapons as well as conventional fighting capabilities. It requested $10.5 billion. A supercarrier to be propelled by nuclear energy headed the list of procurement items. Five guided missile destroyers and four nuclear submarines, including three with guided missile launching capability, completed its major combatant ship requests.[139] Over 1,200 new aircraft were to join the navy's air fleet. Aircraft operations were to stand, therefore, at slightly less than 10,000 for the year. The active fleet was set at 983 vessels, a further decline.[140]

Not to be outdone, the air force struggled to maintain its front-running position. Its estimates came to $16.5 billion. The administration had held the increased funds passed by Congress in 1956 in reserve. It succeeded, moreover, in reducing the air force 137 wing goal to 128 wings. The reductions were to affect army operations, not the air force's primary deterrent mission. Cutbacks, primarily in tactical fighter wings, were justified on the grounds that increased ground fire power had correspondingly generated a reduced require ment for tactical air support. Growing allied fighter plane capacity was also expected to offset these decreases in United States strength.[141] At the close of FY 1958, 603 B-52 bombers were to be in operation. This force was to complete the air force's strategic strike force.[142] At the same time, ICBM development would be pressed. Aircraft procurement was placed at $4.2 billion; missile purchases, at $2.0 billion. Each category was reduced slightly from the preceding year.[143]

While the armed services were pressing for more money, the President and his secretary of the treasury gave every appearance of being willing to accept less. Both expressed reservations about the record peacetime budget of $72 billion in expenditures. President Eisenhower suggested his reservations in his State of the Union address: "Through the next four years," he said, "I shall continue to insist that the executive departments and agencies of government search out additional ways to save money and manpower. I urge the Congress be equally watchful in this matter." [144] Treasury Secretary George Humphrey went much further. He told a news conference that there were "a lot of places in this budget [the President's budget] that can be cut." [145] When pressed, Humphrey refused to say where reductions could be made: "I think, well, I don't believe I will do that. We have been all over this with the greatest care and I don't believe it is up to me to start now to point the finger at people to make cuts. . . . " [146] His criticism of the President's budget culminated in his prediction that "unless a way is found to reduce the spending in the future, we will have a depression that will make your hair curl." [147]

The administration's hesitant defense of its own budget had two broad effects on the appropriations committees and on Congress generally. First, congressional confidence in the appropriations estimates of the executive branch, while never firm even when the President adamantly supported his budget, had all but disintegrated after Humphrey's public statements. The services as well as the other agencies of the government faced increased resistance in Congress to more spending, a result that Humphrey probably intended. Legislators were torn between the pronouncements of the President and the secretary of the treasury that the budget was inflated and service demands that their appropriations requests be approved intact. Representative Harry Sheppard, a strong preparedness advocate, articulated the appropriations subcommittees' dilemma in choosing between these conflicting demands:

> It leaves the committee in rather, may I say, a precarious position to listen to a member of the Cabinet [Secretary George Humphrey], who is rather prominent, make a recommendation to the committee, and yet have you gentlemen come up and defend the budget to the assertive degree you have. You are not alone I want you to understand that. The Army took the same general position and the Navy took the same general position you are taking.[148]

Second, the appropriations committees were drawn into a public competition with the President and Treasury Secretary Humphrey to cut the defense budget. Representative Clarence Cannon, redoubtable chairman of the House Appropriations Committee, insisted on Congress' constitutional duty to cut the budget when possible. Secretary Humphrey was summoned to explain his statements. Humphrey, however, provided no more information to the House committee than he had to the press. He continued to play his version of the pitchman's shell game: "There are excessive requests in the budget, but I won't tell you where they are." The House defense appropriations group had its turn with Secretary Humphrey. Its success was mixed. The secretary's verbal sleight of hand generally proved too quick for the defense unit:

Secretary Humphrey: Well, I want to be perfectly frank and fair. . . . We spent hours and hours and hours going over this budget, trying to get the best figures we could get, and these figures which you have are the best figures we can now produce. Now, I think there are a lot of places where we ought to be able to make some cuts.

Mr. Mahon: Tell us one, generally.

Secretary Humphrey: I cannot go through in detail, through this thing.

Mr. Mahon: Just one, Mr. Secretary.

Secretary Humphrey: If I knew where it could be done today, I would do it today. You are going to have hearings. You are going to have people come in. You are a lot of smart men. You may think of some things they have not thought of.

Everything I have thought of, I have done. What I am saying is I think you are a lot of smart people and maybe, you can help a little if you will try, and that we ought to go on and try, every day, to get something done. I have no suggestion to make today.[149]

Congress decides.—The House and Senate defense subcommittees possessed no clear nor corporate idea of how they should examine the defense bill. Compelled to answer the President's call for cuts in spending, most of the hearings and debates on the defense budget turned on the alleged overstatement of budgetary estimates and on the supposed existence of large-scale waste and duplication in defense programming. Attempts to probe below the surface of the money recommendations in a search for the substantive merit of the defense programs advocated by the administration proved abortive. The controlling elements of the House and Senate subcommittee were not prepared to argue with a President who had won a smashing electoral victory only a few months before and who had been largely successful in frustrating previous congressional moves to increase defense spending. Mahon, as chairman of the House defense appropriations group, temporarily accepted the President's lead. The chief executive defined the battleground on defense spending. Mahon confined his remarks to economy within the President's budget. His plea of a year before for more defense preparedness was not voiced again. "Do not tell me," he told the full House instead, "that we could not have a reasonable and adequate defense program for approximately $35 billion a year rather than $38 billion a year, as presently budgeted."[150] Carrying his attack further, he asked the House to sustain his subcommittee's recommendation for decreased defense appropriations:

> We just proposed a little economy. The line is drawn. If we are going to be pushed over and demolished—if we, the legislative representatives of the people today, are going to be overcome and overrun in the attempt to propose a little economy, it will be a sad day for this country—and you know it. No, we have not taken any chances with the defense of our country. We have given officials practically everything they have asked for, and in many instances we have given them perhaps more than they required.[151]

The House subcommittee recommended a decrease of $2.6 billion; the Senate, $1.6 billion.[152] In conference, the House's position predominated. The bill was slashed by $2.3 billion. The army once more bore the heaviest cut—$1.2 billion, although it had made the smallest request. The navy lost $800 million; the air force, about $500 million.[153] The total bill came to $33.7 billion. Half of the

244

reductions were considered paper cuts, like the $5.6 million in army procurement which was not scheduled for obligation until FY 1959. Almost every appropriation category was reduced in some degree.

The Senate and the House reports presented a detailed account of their suggested cuts.[154] Both concentrated primarily on the various appropriations categories making up the defense budget. Their attention, too, was directed at the administration of the Defense Department—motor vehicle operation, housing programs for the services, armed force post exchanges, medical treatment on certain air force bases, small business policy. The House report made some passing mention of the subcommittee's review of administration defense policy, but its remarks were so perfunctory that it was impossible to determine, from reading the report, what military policies the United States would pursue. The same was true of the Senate report. A Russian intelligence officer was very likely more informed about the defense system of the United States than the ordinary congressman.

Lost opportunities.—Congress' action on the FY 1958 defense budget produced, in effect, a scale model of many of the defects of its military budget review during the Eisenhower years. An analysis of its handling of FY 1958 appropriations throws light on many of its shortcomings in understanding of, and in its approach to, defense policy through the appropriations process.

In their heated search for ways and means to cut the defense budget, most legislators lost sight of the purpose of the defense budget—to allocate limited money resources to maximize the security and foreign policy interests of the nation. To reduce the budget became an end in itself. Even in this limited purpose, Congress was to succeed no more than Sisyphus in the lower depths. Since it adopted the administration's military plans and policies, it could hardly cut very much from the defense bill. There was no feasible way to avoid the material costs of a given defense commitment. Congress would spend most of its energies flushing out furtive economies only to be forced a few months later by mounting Soviet military power to appropriate supplemental funds for FY 1958.

Despite the experience of Korea, the defense appropriations subcommittees resisted measuring "cost" in terms of the loss or gain of political objectives—some of which were quite intangible in character, but no less important because of that fact. Cost was largely viewed as economic. To be sure, cutting the defense budget to preserve an allegedly shaky economy was a political act. By no means, however, was it the only indispensable political goal. Even if it had been, the subcommittees would have defaulted here, too. They attempted no investigation of the economic or political feasibility of enlarging defense expenditures. For reasons never explained in the hearings, reports, or debates, defense spending of approximately $35 to $38 billion was accepted as the maximum amount which the United States could afford.

A majority in Congress and the dominant elements in the executive branch agreed that a budgetary limit should be set for defense expenditures. There was no widespread concern expressed in Congress because military policy was being formulated in reverse.[155] It all seemed quite natural. The nation's leaders would first determine in some mysterious way how much the nation could afford to spend. They would then assume that the enemy would conform to this defense spending ceiling and the order of spending priorities which it encompassed. Military programs, therefore, crystallized as a sort of residual element after a budgetary ceiling had been established. Some of the consequences of such an inverted approach were to become disturbingly obvious on October 4, 1957, a short four months after the FY 1958 budget went into operation, when the first Russian satellite was launched.

Two other important issues went largely unexplored during the first session of the Eighty-fifth Congress: the limited war capabilities of the United States and America's progress—or lack of it—in space development. Both issues had been raised a year before and were left unresolved. Congress' preoccupation with economic and budgetary matters in 1957 allowed little time for systematic analysis of these strategic questions. Yet any congressional decision about the adequacy of the defense budget hinged critically on some determination of them and the myriad of subsidiary problems that they implied.

The army had voiced its discontent with the administration's massive retaliation policy in 1956. It had also complained about the lack of air lift, non-nuclear weapons systems, and antimissile and antiaircraft research and development. In 1957, the army got in step with the atomic parade. This change in the army's disposition led Representative Mahon to ask under what circumstances would atomic weapons be used in a future conflict of less than total proportions. The hearings brought to the surface two different views. Notwithstanding the army's gradual switch to atomic weapons, General Maxwell Taylor insisted that the army was "not overly committed in the atomic weapons field." "We must always have these smaller weapons because the big atomic bang would not be applicable to all situations by any manner or means." [156] He subsequently denied the implication posed by two other questions that atomic artillery was a substitute for conventional artillery and that the tank was losing its usefulness in battle.[157] General Taylor's reservations about too great a reliance on atomic weapons in battle had already been presented to administration officials and had been rejected.[158]

Admiral Arthur Radford presented a different, less hedged view of the future use of atomic weapons: "We have said publicly that we are designing our forces to use atomic weapons. That comes pretty close to saying we are going to use whatever weapons are necessary to defend our vital interests." [159] Defense Secretary Charles Wilson also felt "quite certain if we get involved in another war it would be an atomic war." [160]

There was an obvious disagreement between the army's and the Defense Department's positions over what America's response would be to future contingencies requiring the use of force. It was a question of highest importance to the nation to project the probable consequences resulting from the use of low-yield atomic weapons. It was doubtful whether a limited conflict could be kept restricted once they were employed. Their use in Europe, for example, might touch off a general atomic war. Using them in certain areas, as General Taylor suggested, might prove self-defeating. The enemy might be prompted to respond with his own atomic weapons. Employment of nuclears might actually be to the disadvantage of the United States. Too much bang for the buck might be produced. Or, the United States might find itself on an "escalator" with its opponent: as one side used an atomic weapon of low yield, the other might retaliate with one of a higher yield, until both sides would be drawn upward into a mutually destructive nuclear war. The psychological effects of using nuclear weapons, especially against Asians, might deal a heavy blow to American interests, even if a temporary military advantage might be gained. These were merely some of the questions that could have been raised by Congress and were not.

The House Appropriations Committee report tersely stated that the committee had, "of necessity, considered the effect that possible use of such [atomic] weapons might have on our military posture and on the pending budget request for the Department." [161] It is not apparent from the record of the appropriations committee that the issues described above were extensively explored.[162] There was an almost casual acceptance of these weapons by some legislators. Representative Errett Scrivner, a leading member of the House defense appropriations subcommittee, told the House:

> Now, we are talking about A-bombs and H-bombs, we are talking about megaton yield, thousands of times greater than the yield of TNT. One plane today can carry more potential death and destruction by 1 drop in 1 bomb than all of the planes carried in all of the sorties during all of World War II in both the Pacific and the Atlantic. These bombs are expensive. They are explosive, of course. Somebody ought to tell us how much it

is going to cost to deliver a megaton bomb, whether it is an atom bomb or a hydrogen bomb, by missile, by bomber, by carrier, by submarine. Somewhere, some place, there ought to be an answer as to which is the best and the most economical method.[163]

In Scrivner's mind there was no doubt that atomic weapons would be used in a future war. The question of highest importance, therefore, was the determination of the least expensive delivery system. "Cost" was still economic.

The House and Senate subcommittees left undecided the conflict between the army and the Defense Department over air lift. The House did conduct a special session on strategic air lift. The results were meager. Admiral Radford merely reaffirmed his conviction that the United States was equipped with adequate air lift facilities.[164] This position was in striking contrast to the stiffly worded army reply to a House subcommittee inquiry about the army's viewpoint on air lift:

> The Army has submitted its airlift requirements to the Department of Defense. The Department of Defense has determined that the airlift available is sufficient for Army requirements. The Department of Defense determination appears to imply that the Army will receive the necessary priority to meet its needs in airlift.[165]

The House group did not try to reconcile these statements, nor did it plumb the merits of the army's reservations. The economic ceiling on defense spending silently settled the army's guarded request for more funds.

The appropriations committees through their defense units failed to seize the initiative and make a thorough probe of America's space development. There were many signs of Soviet progress in this area. The House committee report noted that the United States was in a "nip and tuck race with Russia" in the field of missiles. It blandly conceded that the United States was "probably behind the Soviet Union in progress made in the perfection of the IRBM." It asserted without proof that the United States was "very probably ahead of the Soviets" in ICBM development. No new alarm was registered over the possible Soviet leadership in the missile race. The committee's remarks reflected a larger lack of concern in Congress or in the nation over America's position in missile development. The two leading members from each party on the House appropriations subcommittee agreed that too much money was being spent on missiles.[166] Yet the report went on to say, "All available information makes it clear that there is no room for complacency among our people in the consideration of our defense program."[167] In a turnabout, committee members from both parties continued to express a low opinion of the Soviet's ability in science and weapons development.[168]

The subcommittees on the defense bill gave only passing attention to another growing problem—service rivalry, particularly in missile research. The House report deplored wasteful competition among the services,[169] but again conducted no investigation of the main sources of conflict, or the extent to which such competition was salutary or destructive to America's best interests. Thoughtful approval of missile funds for the three services depended in large part on an answer to these questions. Outside experts, like Trevor Gardner, who might have thrown light on the missile situation were not consulted directly. Service rivalry was only superficially settled by Secretary of Defense Wilson's memorandum of October, 1956, which restricted the army to missile development in a range of 200 miles or less and assigned exclusive responsibility for the development of an ICBM to the air force.[170] Here again no questioning developed about the possible helpful or harmful consequences which might result from this redefinition of roles and missions.

The appropriations committees were in a position to ask some pertinent questions about the continued emphasis of manned airplanes over missiles. Together, the air force and the navy planned to expend over one-fifth of the defense budget for manned aircraft, while missile research, development, and procurement remained at approximately the levels of FY 1957. A number of defense officials had serious doubts about the military usefulness of bombers over missiles. In approving the defense budget, the Congress, including its military committees, had an obligation to hold the Defense Department to an accounting for the distribution of funds between these two items. The department was left to its own devices, as Congress searched for ways to prune the different parts of the budget within given administrative fiscal policies.

PRIDE PRECEDES THE FALL

For most congressmen the defense bill for FY 1958 seemed to be, in the words of Defense Secretary Wilson, "just right." Over $2 billion had been cut from it. Defense spending would be held to what seemed to be a reasonable $38 billion. The Russian military threat seemed to be diminishing. But not for long. On October 4, 1957, the Soviet Union announced the first successful launching of a satellite into space. The American people were stunned. The United States had been successfully challenged on a battlefield on which most considered her invincible: she had been dealt a smashing technological defeat. It soon became apparent, moreover, that the United States had lost a great deal more in military, political, and psychological advantage. A country producing a gross national product which was less than half that of the United States had been first into space. A shift had seemingly taken place in the balance of power between the United States and Russia. The Soviet Union now seemed to be surging ahead on a wide front: economic, scientific, industrial, military, and psychological. In much the same way that the Korean War changed America's conception of the Soviet threat, sputnik manifested

251

new and previously underrated sources of Soviet power and, by the same token, new threats to the security of the United States.

An analogy between the passage of the FY 1951 and FY 1958 budgets can be drawn. In both instances, a view of a diminished Soviet military threat was accepted. In each instance, the military departments stood opposed to the President and his secretary of defense who wanted to cut defense expenditures. The pressure for economy and curtailed spending proved overpowering in these periods. Ceilings on expenditures were set in both years. For FY 1951, a limit of approximately $15 billion was established; in FY 1958, $38 billion was set as the ceiling on defense spending. Important strategic questions were swept aside. The navy "revolt" of 1949 and the army and air force "rebellions" of 1956 were brought under control in the respective deliberations on the FY 1951 and 1958 budgets. And, in both instances, economic considerations dominated Congress' examination of the defense appropriations bill. Congress was determined in both periods to be as watchful as the executive branch in saving dollars.

Congress and the American people paid heavily for savings in defense expenditures. The cost of sputnik to United States prestige was immense. It was partly technological and scientific, partly psychological, and partly political. It was not susceptible to reduction to simple, concrete budgetary figures. Nevertheless, the respective decisions of Congress and the administration to cut the defense budget were primarily guided by economic and budgetary factors. The budget as a blueprint for the accomplishment of foreign political objectives was not fully perceived. Left to their own resources the defense appropriations subcommittees approached the cold war disproportionately in domestic economic terms: with the narrowly circumscribed mentality of a bookkeeper rather than with the broad vision of public men bearing equal responsibility with the executive branch for the future security of the nation and the success of its foreign policy.

SPUTNIK AND AFTER:
RUMBLINGS OF A NEW CONSENSUS, 1957–1960

VI

THE CONTEXT OF CONGRESSIONAL ACTION

The period between the flight of sputnik and the assassination of President Kennedy—October 4, 1957, to November 22, 1963—frames a number of fundamental changes in defense policy and operations. Basic shifts occurred in strategic doctrine and planning; in military capabilities, including the size, composition, equipment, weaponry, deployment, and combat readiness of military forces; in the scope and pervasiveness of science and technology applied to military problems; and in the organization of the decision-making process of defense policy and operations.

To appreciate the role played by Congress in affecting many of these modifications and innovations in defense policy and the role that Congress can play in the future, it is important to keep in mind, in rough outline at least, the broader policy and process environment in which Congress operated during this period. The changes which occurred in defense policy since the autumn of 1957 were largely influenced, and even determined, by other processes of change—technological, scientific, political, ideological, economic, and military—that were only partly within the capacity of policy makers in the executive and legislative branches to control. To be sure, alterations in national military policy and posture had an impact on these larger processes of thought and action. The gradual emergence of a mutual nuclear deterrent posture between the super powers is a manifest case in point. Yet even this development hinged on countless other developments in other fields. In the final analysis, defense policy, which is responsive to a nation's political goals, tends to be a function of these other processes of change. In the years immediately after sputnik, American defense policy was, indeed, responsive to changes in technology and science and in world-wide political, economic, and military developments.

Technology, science, and strategic policy.—The rapid, accelerating, and cumulative advances in science and technology in the years just before and after sputnik seriously complicated defense policy–making. They strained the capacity of political leaders to decide among an increasing number of competing weapon systems flowing in a continuous stream from the drawing boards of an army of scientists and engineers. Errors in choice could prove serious or even fatal to the nation's power and prestige. They could result in costly programs without producing any tangible defense gains. The Navaho project, for example, cost over $678.8 million before it was scrapped. Not only money but valuable time could be lost on what later might prove to be programs of decisive importance, such as the development of more reliable ballistic missiles or an effective antimissile system.[1]

The 1950's ushered in a period of rapid technological progress. As this technology grew and improved, it forced corresponding reformulations of strategic doctrine. The history of defense policy since sputnik is testimony to the impact of science and technology on strategic policy. It is no accident that Herman Kahn's *On Thermonuclear War* should have appeared early in this period, nor that Kahn should have chosen as the title of his controversial book an amended version of Clausewitz' *On War* which had been published more than a century before in an era, relatively speaking, of static military technology. Kahn's analysis, which imaginatively formulated the feedback relation of science, technology, and strategic policy in terms of projected changes in weapon systems, described in a sense the revolution that had already overtaken defense policy.[2] One result of the rapid changes in weaponry was to redefine fundamentally the problem of choice in defense policy development. The success of defense strategy turned increasingly on the choices that had to be made with respect to the qualitative, not simply the quantitative, composition of the military establishment. The question of how much defense which is defined by hardware items on hand or to be procured, while continuing to be of great importance, was gradually replaced in primary significance by the question of what sort of weapons mix the nation ought to develop out of a wide spectrum of possible combinations. The arms race between the super powers is dominated crucially by these qualitative considerations.

The intimate relation of science, technology, and strategic policy was given concrete expression in the post-sputnik period in countless hard choices involving long-range bombers, scores of proposed missiles, tactical fighters for combat and air superiority purposes, troop and cargo air and sealift vehicles, strategic warning devices, antimissile and antiaircraft systems, nuclear and non-nuclear forms of propulsion, and military space systems. A crude index of the magnitude of this choice process is reflected in the changes that have occurred in missile research and development. In 1960 the Defense Department listed fifty-one missiles and rockets in operation or development;[3] three years later, forty-six were listed, eleven of which were entirely new or substantial refinements of previous missile and rocket programs.[4]

The difficulty of choice proceeded on at least two distinct levels: within a given weapons system category and between rival forms of weapon systems capability. The TFX controversy that burned throughout 1963 and 1964 typifies the first problem; the B-70, the second. Whether the B-70, later renamed the RS-70, should be developed into a complete weapon system as an addition to the nation's expanding missile force was a major source of disagreement among defense policy officials in Congress and in the executive branch. Conclusive answers are not easily found where criteria for choice are lacking as in the case of unproved weapon systems. Yet human, material, and time resources are inherently limited. Threshold security problems must be resolved somehow and within stated time limits. Choices must be made even when all of the knowledge needed to make a decision is not available and where further delay involves too much cost or unacceptable risks. Choices must be made, too, in a political environment in which the participants differ, often basically, over political means and ends. Technical criteria are not the only applicable standards of choice. The respective power positions of the participants in a decision have importance—decisively so where technical criteria are lacking or imperfectly developed. In politics, as Khrushchev once remarked, two plus two does not always equal four.

Politics, economics, and defense policy.—Political and economic developments also had a telling effect on American defense policy. The two super power blocs that had characterized the postwar era began to loosen and break apart. A more fluid and unpredictable international system gradually emerged, a process that still has not worked itself out completely, nor gives sign of doing so in the near future. The communist and Western camps lost much of their previous cohesion. Simultaneously, and closely related to these shifts, peoples who had only recently reached, or were approaching, nationhood began to assert themselves.

The developing split in the communist world, engendered by the expanding rifts between the Soviet Union and China, came as a surprise to most Westerners. The causes of the division were multiple, including ideological, racial, personal, political, economic, and geographic elements. The prospect of healing the separation has grown progressively dimmer since the late 1950's. Communist parties around the world have been forced to take sides in the struggle, widen-

256

ing further the cleavages within the once seemingly smooth and impregnable exterior of the communist world.

The Sino-Soviet split threw into bold relief, too, the growing loss of Soviet control over the satellites on its western frontier. The Hungarian Revolt of 1956, although suppressed along with insurrectionist tendencies in Poland and Eastern Germany, heralded new and looser relations between the Soviet Union and its European satellites. Constraints on Soviet maneuverability in manipulating its satellites became more pronounced and visible to the outside world. The satellites still followed Moscow's lead, but Soviet influence over satellite actions and policies perceptibly receded. Even tiny Albania could openly defy Soviet pressures. The communist parties of Czechoslovakia and Poland could declare their displeasure at the ousting of Premier Khrushchev in 1964 without incurring reprisal from Moscow. Rumania could follow a course of economic disengagement from the Soviet Union. The communist parties of France and Italy could declare themselves independent of Moscow's control. The militancy and solidity of the Communist Internationale which the West had come to accept and act upon slowly disintegrated. These changing relations within the communist world stimulated a reinterpretation in the 1960's of the United States strategic policy.

The re-examination of past policies was complicated by the hot and cold variations in American-Soviet relations in the half-decade after sputnik. A sketch of the history of these relations suggests their volatile and chimeric character. In December, 1957, shortly after the sputnik success, the *New Statesman* published a letter from Khrushchev in which he suggested a meeting between the United States and the Soviet Union to ease world tensions. This accommodating gesture was followed by another less than a half year later when the Soviets announced a unilateral suspension of nuclear testing. But the political climate heated up very rapidly after the spring of 1958. By the fall the Russians announced that they were resuming testing. In November, 1958, Khrushchev demanded an end to four-power control of Berlin. Throughout 1959 tensions over Berlin mounted and receded in an erratic pattern.

Arms control and disarmament negotiations followed a similarly unpredictable course. Premier Khrushchev's mid-September, 1959, visit to the United States created what came to be called "the spirit of Camp David." In November, in the wake of the Soviet leader's visit, Great Britain, the United States, and the Soviet Union (the latter having recently completed a nuclear test series) announced unilaterally the suspension of nuclear testing for the remainder of the year. These events created a heady atmosphere and considerable public babble of coming Soviet-American friendship. The Soviet announcement of January 14, 1960, that it was cutting its armed force by 1.2 million and the proposed Paris summit conference of May, 1960, lent an air of plausibility to these sanguine expectations. However, the U-2 incident in the spring of 1960 abruptly shattered these hopes. The Paris meeting wrecked, the Soviets once more turned their attention to Berlin, applying pressure on an off-again-on-again basis throughout 1960.

On January 6, 1961, Khrushchev made an historic speech in which he reaffirmed that nuclear war between communism and capitalism was not inevitable, but in which he also proclaimed the Soviet Union's support for wars of liberation. Less than two weeks later he reasserted the Soviet Union's determination to sign a separate peace treaty with East Germany. Both announcements indicated an increase in military tensions. Six months later on August 31, 1961, the Soviet Union announced the resumption of atomic testing in the atmosphere. The possibility of reaching a test ban agreement after half a decade of negotiations seemed permanently smashed. Meanwhile, both sides increased their military forces. In October, 1962, the Soviet Union and the United States confronted each other directly over the emplacement of Russian missiles in Cuba. After weathering this crisis, negotiations again resumed in 1963 on a test ban agreement. They moved slowly, as each side alternately rejected the other's proposals. Again the talks appeared headed for dissolution. In a sudden turnabout, however, the Soviet Union agreed to a limited ban on nuclear testing. The dialogue of *détente* once more actively commenced. Since sputnik, relations between the countries have changed almost in sequence with the passing of the seasons, blowing hot and then cold. American military policy reflected these abrupt changes in the international political climate.

Not only changes in the communist world affected American strategic policies. Political developments within the West were similarly reflected in important segments of American defense strategy, particularly with respect to its policy of sharing nuclear weapons. Having grown progressively stronger economically, politically, and militarily, Europeans grew bolder in asserting their interests and their divergent points of view. They chaffed under United States leadership. Opposition to various aspects of American policy and direction developed, though with differing degrees of intensity in all major capitals of the NATO Alliance. France proved most vocal and intransigent. Under General Charles de Gaulle, France sharply focused many of the issues separating the United States and Europe. Most prominent among these were the growing differences over military strategy in NATO and over the credibility and reliability of the American nuclear deterrent. Disagreements turned on questions of the use and control of strategic nuclear weapons, the place of tactical nuclear weapons, and the role of conventional forces. The Eisenhower-Kennedy proposals for nuclear sharing of information and control were essentially responses to European demands for a larger voice in shaping NATO planning and operations. American reaction, moreover, to European claims posed another policy dilemma. To the extent that the United States mollified Europe on the question of nuclear sharing, it increased Soviet fears of a resurgent Germany in possession of nuclear weapons or of access to them within the multilateral framework of NATO. Efforts to secure a viable and comprehensive *détente* between East and West were, therefore, complicated.

The rising strength of the Common Market also opened anew the question of American economic relations with Europe, while heightening the already existing sharp differences in strategic policy. The 1962 Trade Expansion Act was a response to the invigorated European economy as the multilateral nuclear force (MLF) was a reaction to developing European military power and Europe's growing sense of political independence. France's veto of Great Britain's entry into the Common Market in January, 1963, and its recognition of Red China a little more than a year later gave expression to its desire, and the desire of other European nations, to expand their economic power and political influence, even at the expense of the United States. The political, military, and economic resurgence of Europe was, understandably enough, an important effect on the evolution of American strategic doctrine. Defense policy was again shaped in large measure as a means to influence and control the international environment in which the United States acted to achieve its objectives. It was a function of these larger processes of political evolution.

United States strategic policy was confounded further by the rise of former colonial areas to nationhood and by the widespread social, economic, and political upheavals not only among these new nations but also among already established, albeit underdeveloped, states in South America, Asia, and Africa. These revolutionary developments, while a part of the cold war, were independent of it as well. Even without the East-West struggle, American defense policy would have necessarily been seriously influenced by the emergence of the under-developed and semi-developed nations of the world. The internal political stability and economic viability of many of these nations became questionable without American help. The expanded program of communist subversion, whether Russian or Chinese, accentuated the difficulty of assuring domestic order and economic progress. These problems took specific form in the latter 1950's and early 1960's in such widely separated areas as Lebanon and Iraq in the Middle East; Cuba, Venezuela, and Panama in South America; Laos, Cambodia,

260

and South Vietnam in Asia; and the Congo in Africa. The rapid increase in the number of troubled areas affecting American security and foreign policy interests compelled a reorientation of United States defense policy. Gradually, the Defense Department assumed greater responsibility for the military assistance program; military and economic assistance was expanded and accelerated to those nations where internal turmoil appeared immediate and dangerous; new military units—such as the army's special forces—were organized to cope with ambiguous conflict situations; more money was earmarked for research and development for unconventional warfare; and the United Nations was pressed into service by the United States to undertake increased responsibilities in peace-keeping operations.[5]

SPUTNIK AND CONGRESSIONAL RESPONSE

A new consensus: Incipient stage.—Sputnik itself did not produce the changes in defense policy which have been sketched. Its importance was more precisely linked to the catalytic effect that it had on the defense policy process, prompting—then spurring—those concerned or responsible for military security and foreign policy to reassess and reformulate United States strategic policy in terms of the new modalities of international existence. Sputnik dramatized the many new developments occurring around the globe. It symbolized, as it still does today, America's entry into an altered international setting that contrasted radically with what existed at the close of World War II. What became clearer after sputnik was the point, not so obvious to many, that the United States capacity to shape its external environment was limited, and—even more revealing—was growing relatively smaller with the passage of time. In varying degrees, other nations could successfully challenge American power and prestige. To keep pace the United States would have to run harder and faster simply to influence, much less to control and

261

determine, the course and character of the international order to suit its own design.

The final years of the Eisenhower administration mark the beginning of a new consensus in the making of strategic policy. It is a period characterized by sweeping and often profound discussion, debate, and decision on defense policy. Sharp and repeated clashes occurred among policy-makers at all levels and between both branches of the government over defense policy. Individuals and groups, within and outside of the government, stepped up their activity to expand the nation's defense effort beyond the limits set by the administration. The changes that were wrought during the three years of President Kennedy's term of office, when American defense policy did indeed take a new and definable turn, grew essentially out of the ferment of the latter 1950's. Congress stood closer to the center of these controversies than ever before. Not since the strategic debates of the latter 1940's did it play so central a role in shaping and directing strategic policy. Prominent among Congress' forces were the defense appropriations subcommittees of both houses.

Congress, and, in particular, the defense appropriations subcommittees played a useful role in the eventual strengthening of the nation's defense posture in the post-sputnik period. Without congressional aid, many of the salutary changes which were introduced by the Eisenhower and Kennedy administrations might have either proved impossible or might have been seriously hindered in their implementation. Many, too, such as the speed up of the Polaris program, were effectively placed into operation at congressional behest. It is not that Congress and the defense appropriations subcommittees were solely, or even principally, responsible in accomplishing all of the beneficial shifts in strategic policy and operations since sputnik. It is rather that Congress made a positive and significant contribution to effect and to legitimate these changes. Before granting its consent to the President's defense proposals, Congress successfully pressed the administration for more closely reasoned and comprehensive justifications of its defense proposals. Where gaps appeared in defense planning, Congress, acting often on the promptings of the military departments, proposed its own alternatives. In contrast to previous congressional initiatives in military spending, some were adopted. Debate over strategic policy crystallized sufficiently within Congress to become an important element of public discussion, enough to have an appreciable effect on the presidential campaign of 1960.[6] Sputnik forced the issue of national security into the public's consciousness. The Congress and the appropriations subcommittees sustained public interest and deepened public understanding. In the final three years of the Eisenhower administration, Congress came closer to discharging its positive consent functions in strategic policy in relation to the President and to the public than in any other period since World War II.[7]

Congressional impact on defense policy.—Through its review of the Defense Department appropriations requests, Congress made a perceptible impression on the debate over strategic doctrine, on weapons systems procurement, and on defense economics. In 1956, Congress had not called massive retaliation into question. It had only raised doubts about the size and operational preparedness of the nation's long-range strategic striking forces. In the years after sputnik, massive retaliation, including its later, more tempered restatement under Secretary of State Dulles,[8] was openly criticized. The army-navy position which called for more conventional arms was given closer and more public attention, particularly as Congress became sensitive to the difficulties faced by the military establishment in meeting the limited conflict situations in Lebanon in 1958 and in the Formosa Straits. In the Lebanese crisis, the United States thinning non-nuclear fighting power was stretched almost beyond its capacity. One of the most important defense shifts of the Kennedy administration was the renewed emphasis within American military doctrine on the role of conventional forces. Congressional criticism of Eisenhower defense policies prepared the way for this revived appreciation of limited warfare capabilities as a means of effectively projecting American power abroad. Nuclear weapons were not downgraded. They were placed within a larger operational framework. The strategic nuclear deterrent itself would actually be strengthened, congressional critics of the New Look argued, if the number of military options available to the President, including tactical nuclear weapons, would be increased.

Yet it is clear that Congress' contribution to defense policy was not primarily in strategic conceptualization. Its effect on the formulation of strategic doctrine stemmed more from its close attention to its more established concern for the specific force levels and weapons systems proposed by the administration. In these areas, Congress achieved a remarkable record. Over strong administration objections more funds were appropriated for strategic and for limited forces, both for the purchase of end items and to speed completion of existing programs of research and development in these areas.

The significance of congressional action, however, went beyond increasing appropriations within the major annual defense appropriations bills. Its rearrangement and reshuffling of spending priorities indicated more persuasively the impressive scope and depth of Congress' influence on defense policy. Table 9 summarizes the major changes made by Congress within the annual defense bills for FY 1961, the budget preceding the 1960 presidential election in which congressional impact on defense policy was at its peak. Congress cut $1.3 billion from eleven programs within the defense budget for FY 1961 while adding $1.9 billion to sixteen different programs and projects. In the FY 1960 budget $900 million was deducted from eleven programs and an approximately equal amount was added to eight programs. An examination of these programs and projects indicates that most of the disagreements with the executive branch were over strategic policy, turning not only on the amount of offensive striking power, but also on the degree of protection that nuclear forces enjoyed from enemy air and sea attack. The new concern

264

TABLE 9*

CHANGES IN DEPARTMENT OF DEFENSE APPROPRIATIONS BILL
FOR FISCAL YEAR 1961

		CHANGES FROM BUDGET ESTIMATES APPROVED BY		
		House	Senate	Congress
	Additions			
1.	Army National Guard and Reserves	+105.4	+112.9	+110.4
2.	Air National Guard	....	+ 11.3	+ 11.3
3.	Marine Corps	....	+ 40.0	....
4.	Modernization of army equipment†	+207.6	+260.2	+212.6
5.	Air lift	+250.0	+210.0	+200.0
6.	Air defense	+382.9	+167.9	+267.9
7.	Airborne alert	+115.0	....	+ 85.0
8.	Antisubmarine warfare	+207.0	+ 41.9	+107.0
9.	Polaris	+394.0	+394.0	+394.0
10.	Minuteman missiles	+ 47.7	+ 27.0	+ 27.0
11.	Atlas	+136.0	+136.0	+136.0
12.	BMEWS (Ballistic Missile Early Warning System)	+ 35.0	+ 35.0	+ 35.0
13.	B-70	....	+285.0	+190.0
14.	Midas	+ 36.6	+ 26.4	+ 26.4
15.	Discoverer	+ 45.0	+ 33.0	+ 35.0
16.	Samos	+ 33.8	+ 83.8	+ 83.8
	Total additions	+1,996.1	+1,866.5	+1,921.5
	Reductions			
1.	Travel	− 73.1	− 57.4	− 55.8
2.	Transfers of surplus stock fund cash	− 15.5	− 15.5	− 15.5
3.	Communications	− 84.3	....	− 24.3
4.	Departmental administration	− 33.6	− 13.6	− 18.6
5.	Operations and maintenance	− 85.8	− 63.7	− 66.3
6.	Army procurement	−128.0	− 8.0	− 8.0
7.	Procurement generally	−400.0	....	−418.0
8.	Aircraft procurement	....	− 17.8	− 17.8
9.	Aircraft carrier	−293.0	....	....
10.	Air defense	−204.4	−204.4	−204.4
11.	Bomarc	−675.1	−306.1	−431.1
	Total reductions	−1,993.3	−686.5	−1,259.9
	Net change	+2.8	+1,180.0	+661.6

* Sources: C. R., September 1, 1960, Daily Edition, pp. 19528–29.
†Actual army procurement was $158 million due to congressional decreases in other areas.

with air defense and antisubmarine warfare was directly related to the Russian sputnik.

The possibility that the Soviets might achieve parity or even superiority in long-range nuclear power led Congress between 1958 and 1962 to appropriate approximately $3.6 billion more for larger strategic forces than administration officials thought necessary. The greatest sources of friction between the two branches over defense policy were generated, correspondingly, over the size and composition of strategic nuclear forces. Broken down, about $2.7 billion of the increase were for what might be loosely termed offensive-strike or retaliatory weapons, including principally Polaris, Atlas, and Minuteman missile systems, and the B-52, B-58 and B-70 strategic bomber programs. The balance of $914 million was allocated for defense strategic power made up of greater funds for air defense, air and ground alert, antisubmarine warfare (ASW), and early warning and military intelligence systems.[9]

Congressional support for conventional fighting power, while less clear and generous, demonstrated itself also. The army received appropriations from Congress to maintain a force of 900,000 men in FY 1959—30,000 over the President's approved ceiling—and about $825 million in excess of administration requests for army modernization and air lift between FY 1959 and FY 1962. During the later Eisenhower years, the marine corps, too, was extended financial help to be kept at a strength of about 200,000,[10] although neither the marine corps nor the army was maintained at the levels for which funds were available. These increases anticipated, and indeed prepared, the Kennedy changes in defense priorities that resulted in greater expenditures for conventional forces, for the expansion and modernization of the army and marine corps, and for more increased ground force mobility and fire power.

The justification for these increases was not always clearly delineated. Sputnik, of course, played a part, providing tangible evidence of coming strategic nuclear parity and, consequently, increasing the demand for a stronger and more reliable non-nuclear deterrent and defense force. Yet elaborate and incisive analyses of strategic doctrine—such as those to be found, for example, in the annual presentation of Secretary of Defense McNamara to Congress—did not seem to have heavily influenced the thinking and decisions of most legislators who played a part in effecting these alterations. Congress' response to growing communist military might was more rough and ready, linked to specific, identifiable military programs. If army equipment was obsolete, buy new equipment; if the marine corps lacked the personnel to flesh out three legally established divisions, give them more men; if a full division could not be airlifted, purchase more and faster planes. This seemed to be the reasoning.

Congress must be credited, too, with having cleared some of the clouded economic atmosphere within which military policy was formulated under the Eisenhower administration. Congressional pressures on behalf of increased defense spending between 1958 and 1961 tended to have three general effects. They forced the chief executive to anticipate congressional action by proposing increases of his own in defense expenditures. Second, the expansion of old programs and the initiation of new programs had an inevitably upward impact on defense expenditures in succeeding years. As programs were stepped up in tempo and expanded in breadth, new costs were generated. Third, the loosening of the government's purse strings to purchase more military power demonstrated, in sharp contrast to Treasury Secretary George Humphrey's dire predictions, that the economy was strong enough to sustain larger defense expenditures. The 20 per cent increase in defense spending under the Kennedy administration was not greeted by congressional intransigence as in the past. The increase was all but legislated insofar as a consensus of opinion in Congress, sympathetic to an expanded effort in defense, was already prepared by the work of congressional leaders.

It is important to recognize that Congress did not go beyond the over-all spending limits for all federal programs set by the administration. Despite its sizable increases in military appropriations and its multiple manipulations of the defense budget, it never legislated more appropriations than the President requested for all governmental programs in any of the Eisenhower years. In no year since World War II has Congress surpassed the executive's new obligational requests or expenditure projections. Congress has never gone beyond the President's economic and fiscal policies which set much of the framework for strategic doctrine and military preparedness. Its effect on this framework has been indirect. Its inability or unwillingness to deal with over-all fiscal and economic policy has hampered its efforts in shaping military policy. It is no accident, moreover, that Congress made its smallest cuts and its largest impact on defense in 1960, the year in which controversy was most heated between the two branches. It sliced only $211 million from the President's total request for $84 billion for FY 1961. The point here is not that Congress influenced military policy by appropriating more money than the President requested, but that it influenced military policy because it was willing to deal more directly with the economic and fiscal policies underlying the nation's military programs.[11]

The fusion of the policy process in Congress.—The defense appropriations subcommittees contributed to the creation of a new consensus in defense policy. They did not fashion it singlehandedly. Without the supporting and reinforcing aid of other important segments of congressional opinion and power, their efforts could not have succeeded. Sputnik stirred the whole of Congress and its many separate and loosely related policy processes into action. In the wake of the October launching, four distinct investigations were inaugurated to ascertain American progress in air and missile development. The House Post Office and Civil Service Manpower Utilization Subcommittee held hearings on the government's use of engineers and scientists; the House Defense Appropriations Subcommittee examined missile defense expenditures; and the House Government Operations

Information Subcommittee examined charges that excessive secrecy had hampered missile work. Most significant, however, was the investigation of the Senate Preparedness Subcommittee of the Senate Armed Services Committee under the chairmanship of Senator Lyndon Johnson. "We began with a simple—but revolutionary—fact," stated the final report of the preparedness subcommittee:

> It was that for the first time in all history a manmade satellite was placed into an orbit around the earth. . . . The circumstances under which it happened were startling and brought into sharp focus facts which had been known previously but not fully appreciated. . . . There is no evidence that the satellite is a weapon now. But it has two important implications. First, it demonstrates beyond question that the Soviet Union has the propulsive force to hurl a missile from one continent to another. Second, the Soviet Union has gathered basic information about outer space.[12]

The findings of the preparedness subcommittee reflected the new assumptions on which defense policy would proceed within Congress and, in particular, within the defense appropriations subcommittees. The preparedness group concluded that the Soviet Union led in the development of ballistic missiles and in the construction of submarines, many of which could very likely deliver missiles against American cities. The Soviet Union seemed also to be capable of shorter lead-time in weapons development and production, to be rapidly closing the long-range bomber lead of the United States, and, perhaps most foreboding of all, to be producing more scientists and engineers at a faster rate than the United States.[13]

The subcommittee report recognized, too, that "a stage of history," had been reached "where defense involves the total effort of a nation," including the quality of its educational system. It openly conceded that the nation was vulnerable to atomic attack, a point that had been held, by and large, below the surface of national consciousness.

"Even more important is the fact," noted the report, "that there can be no security in the United States or any other country in weapons. The most accurate and destructive missile yet conceived can bring us nothing but a stalemate." [14] How to maintain even that stalemate became the driving force animating congressional activity in defense throughout the immediate post-sputnik years.

Congressional initiative and intervention in defense policy was a persistent characteristic of the later Eisenhower period whereas it had been episodic and desultory before. To be properly evaluated, the activity of the defense appropriations subcommittees must be viewed in the context of this larger congressional setting. The defense appropriations subcommittees influenced this setting, but were even more powerfully stirred to action by it. The penetrating investigations of the Senate Preparedness Subcommittee were only one noteworthy aspect of the increased effort of its parent body in defense. During the Eisenhower years the Senate and the House Armed Services committees had absorbed themselves primarily in the annual authorization bills for military construction and in peripheral issues insofar as strategic policy was concerned involving the reserves, military pay bills, and manpower utilization. The Symington air power hearings were an exception. After sputnik, both committees adopted a more acutely conscious interest in policy questions. "This year in its review of the fiscal year 1959 construction bill," observed the Senate Armed Services Committee, "the committee placed greater emphasis on the major policy areas which create the forces that require the facilities [for defense]. . . . With this in mind . . . the committee wishes to emphasize again that past experience indicates that the committees of Congress cannot avoid making policy decisions when they consider and report this type of legislation." [15]

In the FY 1959 construction authorization bill, Congress authorized the secretary of defense to choose between the army's Nike-Hercules and the air force's Bomarc before initiating the construction of air defense facilities. The secretary was permitted to transfer funds

270

between the two services after he had reached a decision with respect to the two systems. In 1959, the Senate Armed Service Committee successfully prevailed upon the Defense Department to furnish Congress a comprehensive air defense plan. The committee understood that it could not evaluate a specific spending request for military construction unless it possessed a clear conception of the over-all air defense plan that was presumably guiding Defense Department requests for funds.[16]

Other committees, too, actively engaged themselves in defense policy, although their previous interest had been slight or nonexistent. The Senate Government Operations Committee sponsored a comprehensive probe of the organization of the Defense Department and of the more inclusive processes of national security decision-making in the executive branch.[17] The Joint Atomic Energy Committee pressed for more research and development in atomic energy as a power source in the propulsion systems of submarines and airplanes, and it conducted an important study of antisubmarine warfare. The Joint Economic Committee explored the relation of economic power and defense spending and provided useful comparisons between the economies of the United States and the Soviet Union.[18] The House Government Operations Committee aroused public interest, if not necessarily sympathy, in civil defense,[19] and it investigated the organization and management of the nation's missile program.[20] Capping these activities was the creation of two new committees—the House Committee on Science and Astronautics and the Senate Committee on Astronautics and Space Sciences—to maintain surveillance of the government's space programs.

Since all of these activities were largely in the service of an expanded defense effort, they had a decisive impact on the narrower, but crucially important, appropriations process. Those who labored primarily within the defense appropriations process could not be insulated from these congressional activities external to them. Nor did a majority of the members of the defense appropriations subcommittees wish to be. Sputnik set off a political chain reaction in Congress that fused its multiple processes of influence and decision. The various committees of Congress and their responsible leadership corps as well as the elected party leaders of both houses were forced to look beyond the confines of their special interests and responsibilities to see how the government's activities within their purview bore on national security. This fusion process drew the most influential and energetic leaders of both houses into defense policy-making. Senator Lyndon Johnson, as Democratic majority leader of the Senate, as chairman of the newly created Senate space group, and as a chairman of the Senate Preparedness Subcommittee, did much to galvanize Senate opinion in favor of more defense spending. Even the taciturn Democratic Speaker of the House, Sam Rayburn, and the characteristically economy-minded Democratic chairman of the House Appropriations Committee, Representative Clarence Cannon, joined the mounting number of legislators who dissented from administration defense policy.[21] Pressures to do more in defense, partly set into motion by the defense appropriations subcommittees, fed the now swelling congressional stream that was moving in this general direction. Alone, the leaders of the military appropriations groups would not have succeeded in pointing Congress to the task of reformulating its consensus on defense policy. Once aligned with the other leadership elements of Congress, however, the task of re-evaluation and reassessment could grow apace—and did.

Factors underlying congressional initiative.—But what factors explain the heightened interest of Congress in military policy and its increased willingness to intervene in defense matters even to the extent of initiating changes? There were a number of factors at work, none of which separately can furnish a full answer. The shock of sputnik created a mood of anxious expectancy in Congress that sought an outward demonstration of relief. Most legislators quickly came to feel that something had to be done to counter the new Soviet threat. As the 1958 congressional elections, which resulted in a Democratic victory, indicated, their constituents were also inclined toward a stronger defense posture.[22] The President's slow, unruffled reaction to the Soviet menace and his refusal to depart significantly from his previous defense proposals and spending limits appeared out of step with the novel realities of international life which sputnik symbolically ushered to the forefront of national consciousness. The President's calm and unperturbed response to the sputnik launching perplexed and, in some cases, alarmed even members of his own party in Congress. The President's partial abdication of leadership invited congressional initiative in defense.

Quarrels within the Defense Department over strategic doctrine, weapons systems, force levels, and spending levels provided an additional incentive for congressional intervention. If the Defense Department would not set its house in order, many legislators felt obliged to make the attempt. In many cases, too, congressional assistance was openly solicited. The military services repeatedly appealed to Congress by a variety of means to intercede on their behalf after having their requests for more funds denied by the civilian leadership of the executive branch. Inviting congressional assistance was not confined to the military services. During an examination of the nation's air defense system, for example, Defense Secretary Neil McElroy confessed to the Senate defense appropriations group that, in his words, "as far as I am concerned, it would not bother me if you held our feet to the fire and forced us in connection with this budget [on air defense construction]." [23] Congress accepted McElroy's invitation. Both houses asserted themselves, though from opposing points of view, on the Nike-Hercules and Bomarc missile systems.

The high rate of turnover in the civilian leadership of the Defense Department—three defense secretaries in three years between 1957 and 1960—further encouraged congressional intervention. Many legislators, like Representatives George Mahon and Harry Sheppard, had concerned themselves with military affairs longer than most defense officials. As the perception of the Soviet threat grew and as the Defense Department manifested inner doubt and hesitancy in reaching important defense decisions, these congressmen became gradually bolder and more confident in their capacity to shape military policy.

Rapid changes in military technology and the ambiguity of existing technical criteria by which to choose among competing weapons systems also opened the door for Congress to exert its influence. The political power of Congress entered the vacuum that expertise was temporarily unable to fill. Defections among civilian and military leaders within the executive branch urged Congress forward. Army Generals Maxwell Taylor, John Medaris, and James Gavin, each after leaving military service, wrote books, sharply criticizing the administration's defense policies.[24] Taylor's critique proved prophetic. His recommendations eventually became, with congressional blessing, one of the basic blueprints of the Kennedy administration's action in defense.

A word, too, must be said about partisanship. It played some part in the building of a new consensus. The Democrats, in control of both houses of Congress since 1954, found the defense issue could be turned to their advantage in the fight for additional congressional seats and for the Presidency. Under the capable and fortuitous leadership of two Texans, one a protégé of the other, congressional Democrats loosely organized themselves into a "loyal opposition of the majority" in criticizing the Republican administration. House Speaker Sam Rayburn and Senate Majority Leader Lyndon Johnson threw their powerful weight on the scales in favor of the emergent consensus in Congress, and tipped them in a new direction.

In a sense, the Republicans abetted their critics. President Eisenhower personally constituted a civilian group under H. Rowan Gaither, a San Francisco lawyer, to review the nation's defense posture. On November 7, one month after sputnik, the Gaither Committee presented its report to one of the largest meetings of the National Security Council. Over seventy members were present. Despite the pleas of committee members to make their findings public, the President refused to reveal the contents of the Gaither report. The substance of the report and its recommendations were, nevertheless, leaked to the press. The report found the United States in the most perilous position in its history. It described the alarming erosion of American power and prestige in international affairs and noted America's exposure to nuclear attack from Russian bombers and missiles. It suggested that defense expenditures be increased about $8 billion a year over the $38 billion outlay originally scheduled for FY 1958. Another $5 billion for a civil air defense shelter program was given secondary priority. A sweeping reorganization of the Defense Department and increased preparation for limited war were also indicated.[25]

Buttressing these proposals, the Rockefeller Brothers Fund issued a report of its own close on the heels of the Gaither findings. The study recommended increased defense expenditures for an extended period of years, including more funds for mutual assistance and civil defense. It underlined the need for more IRBM and ICBM development, aircraft procurement until missiles became operational, dispersion and greater protection of SAC bases, accelerated research projects, troop support equipment, surface and underwater missile ships, antisubmarine defense, and higher pay scales for skilled officers and enlisted men.[26]

RUMBLINGS OF A NEW CONSENSUS: FY 1959

The administration's program.—The Eisenhower administration faced a difficult political situation as it announced its FY 1959 defense budget. On the one hand, it sought to convey the impression to Congress and the public that the administration understood—indeed, had in some cases anticipated the new dimensions of the Soviet threat and that it was acting effectively to meet it. President Eisenhower's State of the Union Message in 1958 gave every indication of being the prelude to a new and vastly expanded effort in national defense. Sputnik had changed the administration's view of the Soviet Union in three fundamental ways: (1) the United States was made more vulnerable to strategic atomic attack than ever before; (2) the retaliatory forces of the United States were now seriously threatened by possible annihilation from Soviet missiles and bombers; and (3) the over-all Soviet challenge to the United States was more complicated and diverse than had been previously realized. Observed the President:

> We now have a broadly based and efficient defensive strength, including a great deterrent power, which is, for the present, our main guaranty against war; but, unless we act . . . we could lose that capability to deter attack or defend ourselves.
>
> · · · · · · · · · · · · · · ·
> The threat has become increasingly serious as this expansionist aim [of the Soviet Union] has been reinforced by an advancing industrial, military, and scientific establishment.
>
> But what makes the Soviet threat unique in history is its all-inclusiveness. Every human activity is pressed into service as a weapon of expansion. Trade, economic development, military power, arts, science, education, the whole world of ideas—all are harnessed to this same chariot of expansion.
>
> The Soviets are, in short, waging total cold war. . . . [27]

The President called for a bold movement along a number of fronts to blunt Soviet gains. He spoke of Soviet penetration in the underdeveloped areas of the world and suggested an expanded American effort to forestall further Soviet advances. The Soviet achievements in space and their psychological impact on the world were duly noted. More effort would be expended to catch and surpass the Russians. The President advised a number of steps to increase the strength of American retaliatory forces and to protect them against

276

sudden attack. Attention was directed, too, to preparations for possible limited war situations. "We must maintain all necessary types of mobile forces should they be needed," the President noted. "This means further improvement in equipment, mobility, tactics, and firepower." [28] The President left the impression that the United States would not rely on any one weapons system in dealing with the broadened Soviet military threat.

On the other hand, the administration did not wish to depart significantly from its previous limits on defense spending. Nor did it wish to suggest that its defense policies of the pre-sputnik period were defective in any essential respect, particularly in strategic weaponry. The administration struck on a formula that simultaneously provided some redirection in defense policy and preserved a sense of continuity and stability with the past. The formula was embedded in the careful construction of the President's State of the Union address and his FY 1959 budget. In the former, the President intimated that a number of important shifts in American strategic policy, both military and non-military, would take place, while in the latter he stressed instead an orderly evolution from the past. The total appropriations requested for the Defense Department was set at $39.1 billion; expenditures, at $39.8 billion. Both figures were only slight increases over the previous year, although the announced perception of the Soviet threat had sizably increased. Expenditures for weapons, ships, planes, missiles, atomic energy, research and development were set at $21.6 billion, one billion over the comparable FY 1958 figure.[29] In outward appearance the FY 1959 budget bore a strong resemblance to its predecessor of a year before.

The bulk of the Eisenhower shifts in the wake of sputnik had to be found elsewhere. In large measure they were included in a supplemental request for FY 1958 of $1.37 billion that trailed after the President's FY 1959 budget. These funds were earmarked for the acceleration and expansion of SAC dispersal and alert facilities; for the speeded development and procurement of long-range bombers, comprising the Atlas, Thor, Jupiter, and Polaris; and for improved communications and control equipment for air defense. Expenditures for these programs would be charged to FY 1958, not FY 1959. The total recorded spending for both fiscal years would then be more evenly distributed. At the same time, with quick congressional approval of the supplemental assured, top priority defense programs could be speeded to completion. The FY 1958 supplemental was subsequently followed by two other requests. These latter recommendations were for FY 1959. On April 2, 1958, the President submitted an additional proposal for $1.45 billion in new obligational authority;[30] two months later, he asked for another $600 million.[31] While new obligational authority increased by about $5 billion over FY 1958, estimated new spending eventually was set at $1.7 billion for FY 1959. The potential expansion of the Defense Department was significant, not its actual planned growth during FY 1959. Some new turn in the international political climate might make increased defense spending unnecessary. If no change occurred, then it would be advisable to have reserve spending authority to expand the military establishment.

To compensate for increases in missile and heavy weapons procurement, the administration cut further into already constricted programs. The argument which had been effectively employed throughout the New Look was advanced once more to justify reductions in personnel. "The greatly increased firepower of modern weapons and the continuing increase in efficiency," the President noted, "permit a further reduction in number of military personnel."[32] Table 10 summarizes the personnel decreases which were recommended to offset the increased expenditures for procurement, maintenance and operations, and research and development. Army research forces were also scheduled to be reduced. End strength for the army national guard and reserves was respectively set at 360,000 and 270,000 in FY 1959. Army and air force modernization for tactical missions was checked. The administration moved to curtail expenditures of $1.5 billion for "military arms and equipment and aircraft of declining

278

importance, in favor of the newer weapons." [33] Conventional weapons were to give way to missiles, bombers, and atomic weapons.

TABLE 10*

MILITARY PERSONNEL STRENGTHS, FISCAL YEARS 1958 AND 1959
(In Thousands)

| | END STRENGTHS | | |
| | June 30, 1958 | | June 30, 1959 |
	Approved Fiscal Year 1958 Funding	Revised in Fiscal Year 1959 Estimates	
Department of Defense	2,800	2,608	2,525
Army	1,000	900	870
Navy	675	645	630
Marine Corps	200	188	175
Air Force	925	875	850

* Source: H. Rept. 1830, 85/2, 1958, p. 12.

The army was to absorb the largest reduction in personnel. Since the Korean War, the army had lost 500,000 men. The army was now ordered to cut an additional 130,000 men from its ranks. It had originally requested 925,000 men for FY 1959 as a base figure. The President personally reduced this total to 850,000. Another 20,000 men were added at the request of the JCS.[34] Conventional weapons procurement was de-emphasized. A $728 million request to modernize the army was slashed to $125 million. The army was pointedly refused permission to request any funds for these purposes in the FY 1958 supplemental.[35] Its renewed plea for more air lift went unabetted. Army requests totaled $8.9 billion.[36]

The navy's requests were treated more sympathetically insofar as its proposed programs increased the nation's strategic strike forces. The navy's request for $35 million for advanced planning on another nuclear powered carrier was granted. Top priority was assigned to the construction of two Polaris submarines. These were in addition to the three Polaris submarines included in the FY 1958 supplemental. The navy had originally requested nine submarines and appealed to Congress to make up the difference.[37] The active naval and air fleet was held to FY 1958 levels. Aircraft and ship procurement was slightly depressed. The navy added that it had attempted to secure $400 million to combat the growing Soviet submarine menace, but it had been permitted only $150 million.[38] Marine corps personnel was reduced to 175,000. While announced policy suggested that the administration was preparing for the possibility of limited war, operational policy as it was reflected in the administration's budgetary proposals indicated a diminishing capacity to engage in lesser forms of conflict.[39]

The air force was the principal beneficiary of the sputnik scare. The FY 1958 supplemental was keyed primarily to air force strategic operations. The air force estimated it would need $18.2 billion in new obligational authority or almost twice what the army or navy had received. To offset increases in expenditures for strategic forces and research and development,[40] the air force proposed to reduce its tactical fighter and airlift units. The air force estimated that it would maintain 105 wings in FY 1959, a decrease of twenty-two wings from the preceding year.[41] More funds were assigned for SAC, but considerably less than the air force wanted. General Curtis LeMay, commander of SAC, proposed fourteen B-52 wings. He received eleven, composed of thirty-nine B-52's instead of the previous forty-five per wing.[42] Tankers to refuel these bombers were likewise decreased.[43] Air Force Secretary James Douglas admitted that more funds had been requested for an acceleration of the Titan and Atlas ICBM programs than the administration had approved.

Congress joins the dissenters.—The members of the appropriations committees are proud of their role as watchdogs of the public purse. Both the public and a majority of legislators expect the appropriations committees to cut the requests of the executive branch. Members of the committees generally agree, too, that holding governmental spending to a minimum is their primary function. This sentiment is especially strong among members of the House Appropriations Committee. Notes one observer:

> Committee members state their goals in the essentially negative terms of guardianship—screening requests for money, checking against ill-advised expenditures, and protecting the taxpayer's dollar. In the language of the [House] Committee's official history, the job of each member is, 'constantly and courageously to protect the Federal Treasury against thousands of appeals and imperative demands for unnecessary, unwise, and excessive expenditures.' [44]

This basic value of protecting the public purse often comes into conflict, however, with the committees' not so clearly defined but important responsibility to provide adequate funds to carry on the government's necessary functions, especially those in defense, while it is searching for economies in spending. The conflict between these two general responsibilities—between economy and programmatic needs—can ordinarily be hidden in the complicated and sometimes deliberately misleading reports of the appropriations committees on the federal budget.[45] Sputnik drew the competition between these two values into public view. It forced a reordering of House and Senate responsibilities in favor of programmatic requirements. This shift could be detected in Representative George Mahon's subtly stated opening presentation to the House on the FY 1959 defense bill. He recognized that sufficient funds had not been provided in the preceding appropriations bill for FY 1958 to support a number of crucial programs:

> Last year, just prior to this time, we passed the annual defense appropriations bill. There was talk of economy, efficiency, and how to cope with service rivalries. Money aspects of defense

loomed large on the horizon. We said the defense budget was too fat, that it was unnecessarily big to finance the specific programs which had been submitted to Congress for funding in the President's budget. . . . In hindsight it is obvious that the budget submitted to us last year should have made more provision for rocketry and space age weapons.[46]

Mahon stated his point cleverly. Although he favored more defense spending in FY 1959, he was unwilling to have Congress assume principal responsibility for the recently discovered shortcomings in defense that were related to its action on preceding defense appropriations bills. As a member of the Democratic majority in control of the House Appropriations Committee, Mahon was particularly reluctant to accept responsibility for any lag in defense. The hearings, reports, and debates on the supplemental FY 1958 bill, particularly in the House, sought to absolve Congress and the defense appropriations subcommittee of responsibility for unpreparedness in defense. Mahon worked hard during the hearings and debates to demonstrate two points: (1) that the administration's supplemental requests were for new programs, and not to speed old programs to completion, and (2) that the $2.5 billion cut which Congress had made in 1957 had not affected Defense Department operations.

Mahon's first argument was designed to show that the administration was at fault for not having proposed an expansion of strategic forces sooner. Secretary of Defense Neil McElroy conceded that the programs in the FY 1958 supplemental were new.[47] It did not follow, as Mahon intended, that Congress was free of responsibility for past omissions. It had made little attempt to identify operational gaps in the American defense posture. It, too, shared responsibility for the setbacks in defense. Mahon's initial argument unwittingly implicated the Congress and his own subcommittee, a result that he had not anticipated.

Mahon's second gambit was less demonstrable. He argued on the floor of the House that the Defense Department had had sufficient

282

carry-over appropriations to accelerate any of its authorized programs. He pointed out further that it did not avail itself of much of the authority that it did possess.[48] Over $800 million in the air force's accounts for aircraft and missile procurement, for example, had allegedly not been utilized.[49] The Republicans on the subcommittee countered Mahon's argument. Representatives Richard Wigglesworth and Gerald Ford catalogued the reductions that Congress had affected in navy shipbuilding and air force construction projects.[50] The Republicans held the better of the argument.

Majorities of both parties, however they differed over which party was responsible for failures in defense, were agreed on the need for more defense spending. Mahon's questioning of McElroy suggested the mood of most legislators. Noting the increasing magnitude of the Soviet threat, Mahon wondered openly to McElroy about the administration's reluctance to step up defense spending. Its expenditure estimates did not depart significantly from the budgets of the two preceding years:

> We have discussed from time to time the fact that this [defense] budget is not very spectacular. It represents some advances over previous budgets in space age weaponry, in rocketry and otherwise, but certainly this budget does not go overboard in a big way for a vast new and different spending program for defense.
>
> The expenditures for fiscal year 1957 were in the area of $38 billion plus. It is going to be about $39 billion plus this year, and we are going up maybe to $40 billion or $41 billion plus. That is not very dramatic, I would say.[51]

A sense of urgency carried throughout the hearings on the defense bill. Outside witnesses appeared before both the House and Senate subcommittees to recommend a larger and more balanced defense establishment. Nelson Rockefeller was invited to appear before the House group to present the findings of the Rockefeller Brothers Fund study of national security.[52] Senator Henry Jackson of Washington made a special appearance before Senator Chavez' defense appropriations subcommittee to press for more Boeing B-52's, KC-135 refueling tankers, and long-range missiles.[53] Other legislators introduced newspaper and magazine articles into the proceedings of the hearings to support an enlargement of defense programs.[54]

Questioning was decidedly more policy oriented. The subcommittees role as the protector of the public purse was clearly, albeit temporarily, subordinated to its programmatic responsibilities. Again the House probed more deeply and over a greater range, but the efforts of Senator Stuart Symington on the Senate side matched the penetration of the House review. Each of the services was encouraged, more directly than in preceding years, to present its individual point of view and to take exception to the administration's defense recommendations. Subcommittee probes covered a wide array of topics— armed force personnel, strategic air lift, retaliatory power, missile and space progress, Soviet military capabilities and intentions, defense organization, and service rivalry. Secretary of Defense McElroy came under particularly close scrutiny during his appearance before the House group. He was asked to explain "what magic" there was in the force levels recommended by the Defense Department;[55] the slight increase in defense spending despite evidence of growing Russian military power;[56] the army's Nike-Zeus request that was largely rejected;[57] the slow progress toward an atomic powered airplane;[58] the lag in the Polaris program and the navy's insistence that production be almost doubled;[59] the slow pace of the nation's space program;[60] the meager financing of the air force's Minuteman, Atlas, and Titan programs;[61] the lack of air lift capabilities sufficient to air lift at least one division overseas;[62] the effect of personnel reductions on NATO operations;[63] and the impact of cutbacks of army reserve forces.[64]

The reports of the appropriations committees of both houses broke sharply with the administration's defense proposals. Both houses granted the President's supplemental request for FY 1958 and attached an additional $40 million in transfer authority for army missiles. There was general agreement between the two houses that programs aimed at increasing strategic forces or providing them with better protection should be emphasized. The House group made special mention of the Titan and Nike-Zeus antimissile missile, urging the Defense Department to speed them forward. The House granted the navy $638 million more for four additional Polaris submarines and three atomic-powered Regulus submarines. It also provided $90 million for the acceleration of the Minuteman missile and $48 million to equip all B-52's with Hounddog air-to-surface missiles.[65] The Senate concurred in the House action, replaced most of the cuts that the lower chamber had made, and subsequently added a number of its own increases. Almost $220 million was appended for 13 B-52 bombers and for 30 refueling tankers.[66] Both houses agreed that a $35 million navy request for a new nuclear powered carrier should be denied. Here House opposition prevailed.

Less agreement was marshaled within Congress on limited war capabilities. Opinion was divided, especially in the House where Mahon stood opposed to any sizable increase in personnel for army conventional forces. The House Appropriations Committee secured House consent to its proposal to override the administration and retain the marine corps at 200,000 men and the Army National Guard and Army Reserve at 400,000 and 300,000, respectively. Disagreement ensued among House subcommittee members over a similar increase for the army. Mahon vigorously opposed an amendment by Representative Sikes to keep the army at its FY 1959 strength of 900,000. Sikes' defense of his proposal followed essentially the same lines that he laid down in his initial and, in retrospect, prescient criticism of the New Look in 1954. Argued Sikes:

We may be approaching a stalemate in superweapons. We must consider that fact. We did reach a stalemate in gas warfare after World War I, and no nation since that time has used gas

285

warfare. Who can say that any nation in this modern age will actually undertake a nuclear war? If we are concentrating primarily on preparation for a nuclear war that no one will dare to risk, then what will be our defense position. . . . What would happen if [the Soviets] began a series of small wars—brush fire wars—or encouraged other people to begin them, as they did in Korea? Of what value would our arsenal of superweapons be under those circumstances? I recall that we had the equivalent of superweapons in our air superiority and our A-bombs at the time of Korea, but the ground forces were necessary to keep us from being driven completely off the peninsula. . . . How shall we resist conventional ground warfare if our capability is primarily and essentially for massive warfare? [67]

Sikes reasoning carried 108 to 78.[68]

These House increases in force levels were warmly received by the Senate where support for more conventional fighting power ran higher: "The scientist with the button," asserted Senator Dennis Chavez in presenting the defense bill to the upper house, "will never erase the need for the GI with the gun." [69] The Senate again went further than the House and wrote compulsory language into the FY 1959 appropriations measure to maintain military forces for the army and marine corps and the reserves at levels prescribed by the Congress. Pressure from the White House and Mahon's opposition to compulsory language secured deletion of the provisions for the army and marine corps. The floor under army reserve strength was kept. The conference committee on the defense measure agreed to the House increase of $42 million for army modernization and the Senate addition of $140 million for more air lift capacity. The Senate demand to add more B-52's and tankers to the air force inventory was temporarily shelved. The final bill approved by Congress granted the administration $39.6 billion for defense—$800 million more than it had requested. This increase was largely offset, however, by a $600 million reduction in mutual aid funds in a separate appropriations bill.

Congressional action on the FY 1959 defense bill showed Congress in its best light. Members of both parties who were assigned to the defense appropriations subcommittees made a sincere and, in comparison with preceding years, successful review of the administration's military program. They exercised considerable farsightedness in increasing appropriations for the Polaris, Hounddog, and Minuteman missiles. They dramatized the growing erosion of army strength and the serious deficiency of the nation's air lift capabilities. They brought into sharper focus the paucity of the United States limited war power. There was an increased awareness of the comprehensive character of the communist menace. "Our successes of the future in retaining world leadership," the House report commented, "will undoubtedly depend in considerable measure upon our accomplishments of what may be termed the spectacular; that is, doing those things that capture man's imagination. It is accomplishment of the spectacular that could help put us ahead and keep us ahead in the cold war." [70] Not by military power alone could the nation live, nor could it live without it.

CRISIS IN CONSENSUS: FY 1960

The President stands firm.—President Eisenhower's FY 1960 defense budget did not rise to the House's announced expectation. It produced no striking new directions in military policy. Despite Soviet achievements in space, increased pressures in West Berlin, and the recent experience of limited conflict in Lebanon and in the Formosa Straits, President Eisenhower recommended a defense budget that closely resembled his budget of a year before. Defense requests for new obligational authority were set at $40.85 billion, approximately $288 million less than the estimated appropriations for FY 1959. Projected Defense Department expenditures totaled $40.95 billion which was only $145 million more than in FY 1959. Most of the extra funds appropriated by Congress in FY 1959 were assigned to FY 1960 programs. Not only had the administration held the services to about the budgetary ceiling of the preceding year, but it also tied them again to the same percentage distribution of funding authority

287

that had prevailed since FY 1955. Of the total sum of defense, the air force received 46 per cent; the navy and marine corps, 28 per cent; and the army, about 23 per cent. Shifts in service programs were confined to this general pattern of defense spending authority among the services.[71]

The administration struggled to tailor its strategic concepts to its sparse budgetary cloth. Holding defense spending down had grown increasingly difficult as inflationary pressures in the economy and service demands for more funds grew. The administration, having run a $12.9 billion deficit in FY 1959, the largest of the postwar period, was determined to present a balanced budget to Congress. The strategic formula of the preceding six years was again applied. Strategic air power was favored at the expense of limited war forces. But, surprisingly enough, strategic bomber spending was stressed over ICBM procurement, research, and development. Sputnik and the prospect of an enlarged Soviet missile force had stirred the nation but had left the administration relatively unaffected in its basic response to these new forms of Soviet military power. Bomber forces, while not enlarged in organizational strength, were bolstered through increased deliveries of aircraft and missiles. Replacement of obsolescent bomber aircraft was accelerated. Eleven heavy bomber wings were planned for FY 1960, each with a full complement of forty-five B-52's. A twelfth wing was envisioned. Aircraft authorization was to inch upward from $5.9 billion to $6.2 billion, while new obligational authority for missiles, including strategic missiles, was to drop precipitously from $4.2 billion to $3.5 billion.[72] A strategic bomber force of forty-three wings, in combination with IRBM units to be stationed in Turkey, Italy, and the United Kingdom, was considered sufficient to deter Soviet military aggression. Matching Russian ICBM production, therefore, was thought to be unnecessary. Intelligence estimates which reported lessened Soviet activity in missile production were introduced before the defense appropriations subcommittees to support the administration's decision to concede what appeared to be long-

288

range missile superiority to the Russians.[73] The "manned bomber [was to remain]," said the House defense group, "the principal means of striking a decisive retaliatory blow."[74]

Army, navy, and marine corps forces were held to FY 1959 levels in spite of Congress' attempt a year earlier to raise personnel strength.[75] The air force was reduced by 5,000 men largely as a result of the deactivization of three air force tactical and air lift wings. Army modernization was retarded slightly, although the administration did allow $1.37 billion for this purpose. Army spokesmen noted that annual depreciation losses were $210 million greater than the amount permitted by the administration.[76] The navy, too, was checked in its effort to replace its rapidly deteriorating fleet. A new "Forrestal" carrier was approved, but over-all new shipbuilding requests were down almost $700 million from FY 1959.[77] Navy and air force aircraft inventories, particularly for support planes, were to be cut almost 3,000 below those in operation on June 30, 1958.[78]

Between limited and strategic war forces, air defense held middle priority in the Eisenhower budget. The bulk of the $1.7 billion military construction program for FY 1960 was earmarked for offensive strategic purposes. What was not spent on ICBM and long-range bomber sites was to be largely applied to air defense, including Nike-Hercules, Bomarc, and Hawk facilities as well as additional funds for early warning against enemy missiles and bombers. The effect of these enlarged expenditures on the army budget is noteworthy. Since air defense spending comprised a larger share of the army's essentially static budget, its expenditures for limited war necessarily had to suffer. General Maxwell Taylor, army chief of staff, pointedly told a California audience in December, 1958, in the midst of the President's final examination of his FY 1960 budget, that "expenditures for continental defense . . . do not contribute to our limited war effectiveness, notwithstanding their necessity for deterring or fighting a general war. The early warning systems, while justified by the requirements of general war, will have no use in lesser situations."[79]

Had the administration's defense proposals been made before sputnik, they would undoubtedly have been applauded as visionary. But in less than half a decade, the political, technological, and military conditions with which the defense budget had to deal had changed markedly. The President's defense proposals had not shifted accordingly. The dictates of a balanced budget constrained military spending and inhibited any sizable or imaginative departure from previous programs. Almost all of the President's $40 billion budget was already tied to established programs. What little maneuverability was gained within the budget was accomplished at the expense of non-nuclear fighting power. The administration found itself trapped between two irreconcilable forces. It could expend more funds for defense, but would have to sacrifice a balanced budget. It could, alternatively, balance the budget and face the ire of the increasingly larger and more clamorous body of supporters for an expanded defense effort. The administration chose, characteristically, a balanced budget.

Sensing that this decision would encounter widespread disapproval among the military services and within Congress, the administration moved to rally political support in Congress even before public presentation of the budget. A special conference lasting two and one-half hours was held at the White House for congressional leaders of both parties to preview the new budget and to elicit their adherence. In his State of the Union Message a week later, the President fused his enormous prestige to his defense policies which were soon to be announced for FY 1960. He asserted his conviction that "America can be sure of the strength and efficiency of her armed forces." He warned, too, against any departure from prevailing military policies:

> We must guard against feverish building of vast armaments to meet glibly predicted moments of so-called maximum peril. . . . We must avoid extremes, for vacillation between extremes is inefficient, costly, and destructive of morale. . . . The defense budget for the coming year has been planned on the basis of these principles and considerations. Over these many months I have *personally* participated in its development.[80]

President Eisenhower emphasized that the singular feature of the FY 1960 budget was that it was balanced for the first time in three years. The fact that it was also a positive budget linked to substantive programs was given fourth billing in a listing of its five distinguishing features.[81] The administration's determination to effect efficiency and economy in defense spending was mirrored, too, in its presentation of a new budgetary format for the military services. Budgetary categories that stressed the organizational identity of the services were abandoned in favor of cross-cutting functional groupings of personnel, operations and maintenance, procurement, and research and development. Service requests were grouped under these headings whereas they had been subordinated previously to the organizational distinctions of the military branches. The impression was created that service requests were measured against each other. Congressional hearings later proved otherwise. The allocation of resources among the services along previously established percentage guidelines belied the integrated appearance of the defense budget. To impress further upon Congress the need for more effective control of defense spending and to gain increased flexibility within the inhibiting confines of its own budgetary design, the administration went so far as to ask Congress to grant authority to the President to eliminate, if he chose, specific parts of the appropriations bills that would be presented to him. The President's extraordinary recommendation for an item veto, while doomed from the outset, did underscore the lengths to which the administration would go to keep government spending down.[82]

The capstone of the administration's effort to garner political support for its defense budget was still to be set in place. On January 19, the same day that the over-all budget was publicly announced, the Defense Department released a memorandum in which the Joint Chiefs of Staffs pledged their collective adherence to the FY 1960 military budget. "The Joint Chiefs of Staff," noted the document, "consider that the fiscal year 1960 proposed expenditure figure of $40,945 million is adequate to provide for the essential programs necessary for the defense of the Nation for the period under

291

consideration. They find no serious gaps in the key elements of the budget in its present form, but all have reservations with respect to the funding of some segments of their respective service programs." [83]

Breakdown in consensus: Executive phase.—But what reservations did the Chiefs have? The administration remained discreetly silent. So did the Joint Chiefs. Congress then seized the initiative on the defense budget to define their reservations more precisely. Relentless questioning of service officials before the armed services committees and especially before the defense appropriations groups uncovered deep and pervasive fissures in the policy consensus within the executive branch. The services were found to disagree among themselves; with the secretary of defense; and, while nominally bound to the President's budget, with the chief executive himself. Controversies raged over specific military programs, the level and composition of defense spending, and, most basic of all, the strategic policy that the nation should pursue.

Hearings in the House on the defense bill opened quickly, only four days after the President's formal presentation. The appropriations subcommittees pressed administration officials to defend their proposals in light of the enhanced communist military effort and heightened Soviet pressure on the Western position in West Berlin. The services were closely questioned with respect to their support of the President's defense recommendations. Behind the closed doors of the subcommittee room, a wave of resentment and criticism of the President's defense views slowly developed. The widespread nature of service dissent burst to the surface in early March. Responding to the request of Senator Lyndon Johnson in his capacity as chairman of the Senate preparedness subcommittee, the service chiefs composed a joint memorandum in which they spelled out in biting detail their reservations about the FY 1960 defense budget. The publication of the memorandum and special hearings, which were held to afford the Chiefs a forum to amplify and refine their remarks, undermined much of the administration's effort to paper over differences with the military services. The administration's January 19 memorandum that temporarily produced lame military support for its budgetary proposals was exposed as a heavy-handed, and even pathetic, failure to generate political consent within the executive branch.[84]

Feeding on almost four years of frustration, army chief, Maxwell Taylor, was most explicit and vigorous in stating his service's objections to the administration's position concerning four army responsibilities: (1) modernization; (2) Nike-Zeus; (3) personnel; and (4) surface-to-air missiles. According to the army, $2.8 billion was annually needed for a period of five years to advance the value of its inventory from $14 billion to a level of $20 billion, the value of the equipment which the army estimated that it would need "to meet early requirements of mobilization and combat."[85] The army was losing ground on its modernization program in the FY 1960 budget to the tune of almost $1.5 billion. Nike-Zeus requests had totaled over $1.0 billion, including funds for the production of long lead-time items, but the administration had restricted the program to research and development levels and cut army recommendations to $300 million.[86]

More serious, however, was the administration's sustained determination to hold army personnel strength down. General Taylor had requested a force of 925,000 men organized into fifteen divisions. He received 55,000 fewer personnel and suffered the loss of one division. The four division strategic reserve stationed in the United States was to be cut to three divisions, two of which were assigned training missions. To overcome personnel deficiencies in divisions stationed in Europe and Korea, army commanders were forced to incorporate thousands of foreign nationals into combat and support units. One-quarter of American divisional strength in Korea was composed of indigenous personnel. A proposed 10 per cent slash in reserve strength threatened further to weaken army preparedness as did the administration's decision to slow the introduction of surface-to-air missiles which were designed to defend ground personnel against enemy air attacks.[87]

Navy and marine corps discontent was also prominent and pointed. Admiral Arleigh Burke, chief of naval operations, expressed reservations about the maintenance and operations funds to sustain the fleet of 864 ships in FY 1960—approximately thirty ships below the levels operating two years earlier. The navy worried, too, about its future in the face of depressed funds for procurement of ships, aircraft, and missiles. Singled out for special attention were the antisubmarine and Polaris programs, which, complained the navy, were moving too slowly, and the lowered amounts allocated to navy research and development. Like the army, the marine corps grew increasingly alarmed at the diminishing size of its personnel strength—now at 175,000—the depreciating value of its weapons and equipment inventory, and the negative rate of its modernization program.[88] Six aircraft squadrons and six combat teams were scheduled to be deactivated. The navy confirmed what the army had already noted to a number of congressional bodies that personnel cuts in limited war forces had not occurred until after the Lebanese and Formosan crises had subsided.[89] The revelation disclosed the administration's intention to run the risk that such forces would not be needed in future conflict situations. In the midst of the congressional furor over the JCS memorandum, President Eisenhower suggested that fighting over West Berlin, would not be limited. Nuclear weapons, he hinted, would be used. In this context, the President saw little need for limited war forces for the defense of Berlin, the most likely area for a military confrontation to develop between the United States and the Soviet Union.[90]

The air force was more tempered in its criticisms, having again been favored in the FY 1960 budget. General Thomas White's comments on the budget, as air force chief of staff, strangely omitted mention of the nation's strategic missile program, the most actively discussed issue in Congress. Air force criticism centered on the administration's alleged failure to replace B-47 aircraft rapidly enough. Other air force reservations concerned the nuclear aircraft program, Bomarc, military construction, and operations and maintenance. Bombers, not missiles, were given priority status.[91]

The services insisted that their recommendations, if implemented, would not destroy the administration's ceiling on defense spending or unbalance the budget. Each of the service chiefs stressed, instead, that the percentage distribution of funds within the President's budgetary framework for defense might be rearranged.[92] In answer to a question by Senate Majority Leader Lyndon Johnson, General Taylor replied:

> Well, Senator, the problem of the Army Chief of Staff in recent years has been the rigidity of the percentage of the budget allocated to each service. . . . To me, this inevitable internal rigidity within the structure of our budget is wrong because it does not reflect the changing events in the world, the changing conditions of the military challenge that faces us. I would be happy if I thought that this budget [the President's defense budget] pattern deserved immortality. However I can't believe that it does. I think the logic of events will request it be changed.[93]

The specific budgetary and programmatic reservations of the services pointed to two, more fundamental, disagreements with the President's policies. While bowing politely, if not a little pietistically, before the idol of a balanced budget, the services were in actuality attacking the chief executive's over-all ceiling on defense spending. If all of the programs denied by the administration had been adopted, requests for new obligational authority would have jumped by about $7 billion—$3 billion for the army and $2 billion each for the navy and air force.[94] Increases this large were to become characteristic of the Kennedy, not the Eisenhower, administration. The budgetary struggles of FY 1959 through FY 1961 prepared the way for this budgetary break-through in defense policy.

The roots of service discontent lay still deeper than budgetary deprivation. The services also challenged the basic strategic concepts on which the administration's budget rested. In the late 1950's two conflicting strategies began to crystallize in interservice debates. The army and the navy gradually became identified with what was eventually labelled a finite deterrent strategy. The air force stood alone in its advocacy of a counterforce posture. Service thinking in all cases deviated from the Eisenhower administration's policy of massive retaliation.

The services disagreed on the nature of the military threats facing the nation, the deterrent requirements to forestall these threats, and the responses that should be employed if deterrence should fail. Army and navy spokesmen took issue with the air force's assessment that, according to General White, "the most *serious* and *immediate* military threat to the free world . . . continues to be strategic Soviet airpower." [95] The navy, like the army, was more concerned about limited war whereas before it had stressed its general war role. In defending its carrier program (now, ironically enough, on the ground that it was primarily useful for limited, not general war, purposes), the navy argued that limited military conflicts were more likely to occur than general war. "There has been no general war," the navy stated, "and general war is becoming less and less likely. But since World War II there have been many small wars and limited situations —nearly all involving naval forces. We expect this pattern to continue." [96] The army bolstered the navy position when it opened its own presentation of the budget with a chart listing the eighteen major limited wars that had occurred between 1945 and 1959.[97] Both services were agreed, too, that too much money was being spent for strategic forces to the detriment of limited war capabilities. Both asserted, as Army General Maxwell Taylor noted, that the United States had "an excess number of strategic weapons and weapon systems in the atomic retaliatory force." [98] A finite number of nuclear weapons and delivery systems were considered sufficient to build an adequate deterrent. The navy's Polaris submarine, almost invulnerable against enemy destruction, was designed to be the mainstay of a finite deterrent posture.[99] If deterrence failed, the primary targets marked for destruction were to be cities. The curious turnabout in the navy's position did not escape air force critics. The navy had argued a decade before that the air force's B-36 was useful to devastate cities, not military installations. Now it was pressing its Polaris weapon system to perform the same function.

The air force dissented from most of these views. Deterrence was not credible, air force spokesmen stated, if the consequences of its failure proved so paralyzing that the nation's nuclear forces would not be used for fear that American cities would be destroyed. Returning to more classical concepts of military strategy, the air force stressed the importance of attacking the enemy's military concentrations, and not cities, to minimize his capacity to do so if he should adopt such a course. More, not less, strategic forces—principally manned bomber forces—were needed "to prevail over an enemy should war occur." "The true measure of a successful offense in aerospace warfare," asserted General White, "is the ability to attack the heart of an enemy's military strength. This requires versatile striking power which can, selectively and decisively, destroy his military forces and war-making capacity."[100] Limited wars could be deterred by an enhanced strategic deterrent capability.

The air force maintained that ample limited war forces already existed. Army claims for its Nike-Zeus antimissile missile were similarly rejected. "The best defense is a good offense,"[101] retorted the air force. Funds saved by cutting expenditures in these two areas could well be applied to air force programs to expand its annual 46 per cent share of the military budget. The air force recommended, in addition, that operational control over the navy's Polaris system should be turned over to the Strategic Air Command to assure a controlled nuclear response to any military aggression. The army and navy charge that a counterforce strategy was too costly and, in the final analysis, impossible to achieve given increasing Soviet military capabilities was dismissed.

Breakdown in consensus: Congressional phase.—Before the services publicly broke with the administration, there were signs of legislative loss of confidence in the President's defense proposals.[102] Shortly after leaving the President's preview of his defense budget in January, Senate Majority Leader Lyndon Johnson told reporters that he was "deeply concerned and somewhat disappointed to observe that in the field of military preparations they [the administration] are programming as if we were living in a static world rather than an exploding and expanding and developing world."[103] Walter Lippmann sounded much of the principal anxiety in Congress about the President's defense proposals when he acidly remarked: "Assurances about our over-all strength are quite unconvincing. For nobody is prepared to believe that by a wonderfully lucky coincidence the money needed for national defense is just the amount of money we can afford to spend if the budget is to be balanced. . . . This initial error about the budget has forced Mr. McElroy into making the disastrous announcement that the United States has withdrawn from the missile race."[104] Commenting on President Eisenhower's State of the Union message that repeatedly stressed the superiority of American military power, Hanson Baldwin correctly predicted that "this opinion, once almost politically sacrosanct, will no longer satisfy either Congress or the public. The issue of the adequacy of our defense is likely to be a major one for a long time to come, and the opinions of the President, as Commander in Chief and one of the world's most famous soldiers will no longer suffice to quell criticism."[105]

The President and his chief defense aides, particularly those in the Budget Bureau and in the Office of the Secretary of Defense, were subjected to a constant drumfire of criticism from the Democratic-controlled Congress. Impressive Democratic gains in the 1958 congressional elections—forty-eight seats in the House and fifteen in the Senate—signaled public qualms about Republican leadership in defense and encouraged leading Democrats to seize the offensive against the President's defense proposals. This is not to imply that partisanship played the key or even a dominant role in congressional-executive differences over the FY 1960 defense bill. Yet the fact remains that, however sincere the motivations may have been of the Joint Chiefs in addressing their memorandum of dissent to Senator Lyndon Johnson, the memorandum could not be insulated from partisan implications despite the best efforts of the Chiefs or Senator Johnson. Johnson's position as Democratic majority leader of the Senate and his style of operation, which emphasized action and initiative even to the extent that the Senator issued his own annual legislative program for Congress, assured that the memorandum would become a part of the coinage of partisan debate. Johnson, indeed, was chairman of the Senate Preparedness Subcommittee and doubtless had a legitimate interest in securing the opinion of the Chiefs on the FY 1960 budget. Yet it was his broader political power and prestige that furnished sufficient encouragement to the Chiefs and afforded them some measure of political protection against immediate reprisal from the administration for having articulated their policy reservations. The depth and intensity of the Chiefs' reservations can be perceived by appreciating the enormous political risks that each ran in publicly criticizing the President's defense decisions. On the other hand, the administration's difficulty in securing the acquiescence, if not the consent, of the Chiefs should not be underestimated. Not only did the majority leader of the Senate stand between the President and his defense Chiefs, but so did the usually silent Democratic speaker of the house. On the same day that the memorandum of the Joint Chiefs was issued, Representative Sam Rayburn lent his powerful voice to the mounting criticism of the President's defense budget. He cautioned against balancing the budget at the cost of national defense. " 'We just cannot afford to take any risks,' Rayburn remarked. 'The times in which we are living are just too perilous to permit even the slightest let-up in our preparedness program.' " [106]

The special hearings held by the Johnson subcommittee and the revelations of the defense appropriations subcommittees of both houses seriously embarrassed the administration. Even some of the President's partisans took exception to his defense proposals.[107] The President's refusal to spend most of the extra funds appropriated by Congress in the FY 1959 defense bill rankled congressional sensibilities which are usually sensitive to any erosion in congressional power. The administration released funds for only one of the four Polaris submarines that Congress had approved in 1958. The other three were included in the President's FY 1960 program. No other procurement funds were assigned to the Polaris program.

The President's lecture to the Congress on economy and efficiency in his budget message gained him few friends, while irritating legislators on the appropriations committees who prided themselves on their faithful guardianship of the public purse. Nor did the President's new budgetary format for the Defense Department, suggesting an integrated approach to policy-making, win immediate or broad approval. Some, like Representative Carl Vinson, chairman of the influential House Armed Services Committee, saw in the change another presidential attempt to gain greater control over defense spending at the expense of Congress. In a letter addressed to the members of the House Appropriations Committee and to other House leaders, Vinson protested the division of the budget into categories that cut across service designations. "If the Congress surrenders its right and responsibility to raise and support armies and to provide for a navy, and to designate and provide for the personnel of each service," he wrote, then "we become a tax-raising body which simply appropriates money without any further voice as to how that money shall be expended." [108] Other legislators were simply confused by the new budget arrangements. They were alienated less by a disagreement over strategic policy than by the temporary breakdown in communications that the new budget produced.[109]

Congressional impatience and frustration with the executive branch did not stop at the presidential level. It went to the heart of the JCS. The JCS memorandum, while strengthening congressional attacks on the President's defense budget, had the backfiring effect of focusing attention on JCS organization and operations. Repeated attacks of one service on the position of the others during the appropriations hearings further eroded congressional confidence in the JCS as an institution. The subcommittees were surprised to discover that the JCS did not directly discuss nor decide such important cross-service questions as the size of the army—whether 870,000 or 900,000 men should be retained—the navy's carrier, or the size of the air force's strategic bomber program.[110] General Taylor was most illuminating in his testimony. He complained that the JCS never agreed upon any "standards of sufficiency" by which to determine over-all military requirements. Duplication, inefficiency, and even gaps in defense policy and preparedness consequently resulted. "We [the JCS] never look at the problem [of strategy and the budget] horizontally and determine whether each [military] function is properly supported by the appropriate forces of all contributing services."[111]

The House defense subcommittee was particularly disturbed by continued interservice rivalry. Its report on the FY 1960 defense measure bitterly criticized the JCS for its failure to provide a coherent strategic plan and consistent information and guidance to the Congress on defense policy. Its attack on the JCS, drawn heavily from General Taylor's testimony, implicitly took issue with the President and the secretary of defense for their inability to control the services and to produce a cohesive defense policy for the nation to which the military branches could repair. "Differences of opinion," said the report,

301

are natural and understandable, but the testimony clearly indicates that there is something wrong in our present military planning. It seems quite apparent that in this regard the Joint Chiefs of Staff, as a corporate body, is not providing the kind of advice and leadership which this country requires. . . . [T]here is . . . much confusion and duplication with resultant waste in the military establishment. The President, the Secretary of Defense, the Congress and the American people have a right to expect a better job from the Joint Chiefs of Staff in the way of military guidance. As a corporate body, the Joint Chiefs of Staff must set up plans for the guidance of the various commands and the respective services. Hard decisions are required, and the President, the Secretary of Defense and the Joint Chiefs must assume the major responsibility for tailoring military force requirements. . . . The Joint Chiefs of Staff should look at what is available for what purposes and attempt to match it with needs.[112]

As the hearings on the defense bill proceeded, the Congress and, in particular, the members of the defense appropriations subcommittees grew increasingly confused about "the standards of sufficiency," as Taylor had called them, that underlay the defense budget. The subcommittees found themselves whipped and lashed by a host of varying and competing claims with respect to defense policy. The administration expressed one view; each of the services, its own position. There was no conclusive guidance from any official or unofficial quarter as to the direction in which Congress should move. Simply passing more funds for defense made no sense. Service rivalry clearly evidenced large-scale waste and duplication in defense programs and operations. Providing the services with more funds held the prospect that more resources would be squandered without producing clearly tangible increases in defense preparedness. Meanwhile the national debt would grow in FY 1960 and contribute to the FY 1959 deficit. The Congress was hesitant to expand the defense budget and unbalance the budget since the President refused to adopt this course. On the other hand, legislators felt compelled to enlarge the nation's military base. Cross-pressured, legislators moved simultaneously in a number of different and sometimes conflicting directions. Many of the same controversies that had characterized executive deliberations and negotiations on the defense bill similarly divided the Congress. While differences can be found in the House and Senate debates on the bill, the main battles were fought in the hearings and in the final mark up of the bill in the executive meetings of the subcommittees. "Everything all during this debate [on the defense bill] would give . . . the impression," said Representative Daniel Flood, one of the most outspoken members of the House defense appropriations subcommittee, " . . . that this arrangement was a very ducky-wucky arrangement. Well, nothing could be further from the truth. We spent 5 days marking up this bill . . . and they had to practically call in the marines to get us off each other's neck. I want you to know that there were a lot of strong opinions both ways about this bill, and we hammered it out behind closed doors after great debate and hard work."[113]

Congress moves to decision.—Congress expressed itself on the defense bill in three broad areas: strategic defense, strategic offense, and limited war. These areas were, of course, intertwined but were, as in the past, not systematically treated in the hearings. The final decision on the defense bill came only after a long, eight-month process of sifting and sorting as well as constant haggling and bargaining among subcommittee members.

There was widespread agreement in both houses that the air defense program against enemy bombers needed improvement most. Service rivalry in this area, especially between the air force and army, had been most intense since the middle 1950's. The army pressed its Nike-Hercules system while the air force lauded the merits of its

Bomarc missile. Each system was based on a different concept of air defense. The Nike-Hercules was tailored to the army's point or local defense concept that emphasized air protection in the immediate vicinity of a potential military or civilian target. The air force's Bomarc, whose range capabilities were projected to be greater than the Nike-Hercules, rested on an area defense viewpoint. The two systems had been originally conceived as complementary air defense weapons. Gradually, however, the two began to compete with each other as the range differences between the two systems narrowed. The controversy between the army and air force was intensified by the fact that the future role of each service in air defense depended in great part on the success of each system. The struggle between the two services took specific shape, therefore, in the annual competition for funds for the two programs. Victory in the budgetary arena was tantamount to organizational survival in air defense.

The Congress was treated to an annual spectacle of a service scrap for more air defense funds. By the end of FY 1959 expenditures for Nike-Hercules and its predecessor, Nike-Ajax, totaled $3.9 billion. Bomarc was estimated to have cost $1.9 billion in the same period. Congress faced the prospect of having to appropriate another $1 billion for FY 1960 without much assurance that the secretary of defense would decide between the two systems before another year had passed. The Senate Armed Services Committee had urged Defense Secretary Neil McElroy to decide between Nike-Hercules and Bomarc. At the behest of the committee, Congress had authorized him to allocate funds between these two systems as he saw fit. Still nothing happened. Now it was Congress' turn to act to force the defense secretary out of his Hamlet role, to silence service squabbles, and to reduce waste and duplication. Congressional initiative was precipitated by the defense secretary himself. The following exchange between Secretary McElroy and Senator John Stennis, a member of both the Appropriations and the Armed Services committees, prompted congressional action:

304

Senator Stennis: . . . I am beginning to think that the Department of Defense itself would welcome a congressional decision on this matter [of air defense] and then you could move on into a more positive program.

Secretary McElroy: You certainly have touched us in a place that I would call vulnerable.

Senator Stennis: I do not want to embarrass you.

Secretary McElroy: You are not embarrassing us. This is one area where we have not done very well in making a decision. . . .

Senator Stennis: I appreciate your attitude tremendously, because I frankly think that is what has to be done, Mr. Secretary.[114]

Congressional help arrived, but with more devastating effect than either McElroy or the services could have anticipated. The Congress was in an angry mood. "In recent weeks some of our people in the Pentagon and the services have been more interested in a barrage of propaganda than they have been in barrages for the benefit of the air defense program," said Representative Gerald Ford, leading Republican spokesman on the defense appropriations subcommittee. "I am sick and tired of this bickering, and I think the public is likewise. I include the Air Force, the Army and the Navy, and others. If they would concentrate on doing the job rather than issuing press releases, we would all get a better job done with the money we make available."[115] Ford concurred in his committee's decision to cut $162.7 million from the Bomarc program "to focus attention upon the necessity for an early decision on the air defense missile controversy."[116] While the House group was slashing Bomarc, the Senate Armed Services Committee was vetoing the Nike-Hercules as a "virtually obsolete" system. The committee called upon the secretary of defense to develop a "master plan" for air defense.

Forced by Congress to make a decision, the Defense Department finally produced a "master plan" to save the air defense program

305

before it was completely destroyed. The plan reduced the amount that had been first scheduled to be spent for defense against bombers. A mix of Nike-Hercules and Bomarc missiles was recommended, with the emphasis to be placed on Nike-Hercules. The Nike-Zeus anti-missile system was upgraded as a mirrored response to the Soviet shift to long-range missiles. In keeping with these decisions, Congress provided $137 million more for the Nike-Zeus program than the administration had wanted. Bomarc was cut by $82 million, and, at the cost of retarding the construction of another navy carrier, $137 million more was assigned to antisubmarine warfare than had been requested.[117]

The one major anchor in congressional deliberations was nuclear preparedness. First priority was assigned to this objective. Disagreement arose, however, on what constituted an adequate nuclear deterrent. Many legislators appeared more sensitive to the complexities of the problem than the administration. Certainly congressional leaders in defense policy in both houses recognized the psychological and political significance of Soviet superiority in missile development. They were sensitive to the point that a large Soviet ICBM complex threatened the utility of the nation's exposed bomber bases. The sophistication of legislative understanding is suggested throughout the hearings. Two issues bear notice. The first dealt with the amount of nuclear power needed to absorb an enemy first strike and still be sufficient to launch a decisive retaliatory blow.[118] The discussion of this question led gradually to the more perplexing question of a pre-emptive strike in the face of an imminent enemy attack and the mutual devastation that a nuclear exchange would incur:

> Mr. Thompson: . . . Has this ICBM situation . . . revised military thinking to the point that you need superiority to be adequately prepared as a defender?
>
> General Twining: It always has been that way. . . .

Mr. Thompson: Again looking at it from the Russian stand-point, as a defender you need a sufficient retaliatory power to deter him from using his attacking force?

Mr. Flood: The new concept is a complete change. The concept is this: The true nuclear deterrent is what the other side thinks you will have left over after he strikes you with the first blow. . . .

Mr. Mahon: Do you take issue with that, General?

General Twining: No.

Mr. Mahon: . . . Are we not moving toward the time when if you were called upon to absorb an initial attack you will lose?

General Twining: Not necessarily.

Mr. Mahon: If you wait until they have delivered their blow you have about had it. The time can come when if you should wait until the blow is delivered then you have no capability of counterattack.[119]

A year later in its report on the FY 1961 defense bill, Mahon's subcommittee elaborated on its suggestion that the United States adopt a strategy of pre-emption in the face of impending enemy attack. The statement was given little attention when it was published, but it came very close to the position advocated by General Thomas Power, successor to General LeMay as head of sac, in a book that was banned by the Defense Department. The report was remarkable for its frankness, albeit cooly stated, considering the hazardous course that it advocated:

> In the final analysis, to effectively deter a would-be aggressor, we should maintain our armed forces in such a way and with such an understanding that should it ever become obvious that an attack upon us or our allies is imminent, we can launch an attack before the aggressor has hit either us or our allies. This

is an element of deterrence which the United States should not deny itself. No other form of deterrence can be fully relied upon.[120]

Congress was more willing to hedge its bets on deterrence than the administration. Both the House and the Senate agreed to increase air force missile funds by $172 million. Congress provided $85 million for eight more Atlas squadrons and $87 million to spur the Minuteman program. Atlas was viewed essentially as a stopgap measure since the missile was highly vulnerable to enemy destruction. The President was also authorized to incur a deficit in air force funds to maintain a continuous airborne alert if necessary.[121]

The requirements for limited war produced the most significant rift among legislators. In the House subcommittee, the air force strategic position held sway, although a strong minority led by Representatives Daniel Flood and Robert Sikes pressed the army position before the House.[122] The House report clearly indicated that the air force argument had been adopted by a majority of the subcommittee. The maintenance of a large retaliatory force was held to be a sufficiently effective deterrent to limited conflicts, a position that SAC chief, Curtis LeMay, had voiced a few years earlier[123] and that General Thomas White had reiterated in the hearings.

The House subcommittee gave no direct answer to the question of how the nation would react if a limited war should erupt. It spoke instead in parables. "If the fire department of a great city is able to put out a big fire in a 40-story building," noted Representative Mahon optimistically in presenting the defense bill to the House, "the chances are that it will be able to put out a little fire in a 1-story building. Our $40 billion defense program . . . might not be adequate to deal with the threat of global war, but it ought to be adequate to deal reasonably well with a limited war threat." [124]

The House agreed with Mahon. Amendments to increase funds to keep the army at 900,000 were defeated.[125] About $43 million was included for army modernization beyond the administration's request. The Senate, persuaded by the army's strategic viewpoint, added approximately $200 million to the House's grant. The Senate's position prevailed in conference, as did its increase to keep the marine corps at 200,000. Efforts to raise army personnel to 900,000 were stifled in the light of House and executive opposition. The national guard and the army reserve, however, were kept at levels of 400,000 and 300,000 men respectively, despite administration objections. Domestic political pressures succeeded in the case of the army's request for more reserve power where strategic analysis had failed. Through the intercession of congressional barons, the reserves reclaimed their annual tribute, a kind of twentieth-century Danegeld.[126]

The most extraordinary congressional outburst effecting limited war preparedness developed over the navy's carrier proposal. Since World War II the navy faced continued congressional opposition to its carrier fleet. Representative Clarence Cannon, chairman of the House Appropriations Committee, was the leading source of congressional resistance to further expansion of the navy's carrier program. Cannon's objections to more carrier forces predated the 1949 B-36 hearings. Cannon again launched a broadside against the navy in the House debates on the FY 1960 defense bill. He proffered the incredible argument that the bulk of the nation's military shortcomings were attributable to the carrier program. Said Cannon:

> We stand today exactly where Chamberlain stood when he met Hitler at Munich. Hitler had the planes. England was deficient in airpower. Today Khrushchev has the missiles and the submarines. We are deficient in both. We have frittered away on carriers the time and attention and money we should have devoted to the missile and the submarine. . . . Russia has been too wise to build a single carrier. They have copied every weapon we have devised except the carrier. That has been . . . the only difference in the military programs of the two nations. And as a result America has dropped every year in relative

military power and Russia has risen every year in world priority. There can be no other explanation. It is as simple as that. It is the carrier.[127]

Enough sentiment existed in the House to drop the navy carrier from the defense measure and to assign the bulk of its $280 million to antisubmarine warfare (ASW). The Senate refused to support the House move and instead added $100 million to the navy's request for a nuclear powered carrier. The issue was compromised in conference, the House position generally prevailing. The navy was given $35 million to begin work on a nuclear propelled ship, while half of its original request was transferred to ASW.

The final defense bill approved by Congress totaled $39.2 billion, a scant $19.9 million less than had been requested in the President's defense proposal. Military construction appropriations were handled separately. The many changes wrought by Congress in the defense measure obscured the larger and more significant point that the President's budgetary ceiling which had inhibited the development of a more balanced and effective military establishment in the first instance remained essentially intact. Congress forced a decision on air defense and spurred progress in missile and antimissile work, but it was unwilling to take the most decisive step of all. It held back from breaking the budgetary bond that principally fettered defense policy. Senator Lyndon Johnson spoke prematurely when he defended the Senate's $350 million increase in defense funds. Congress "had to add the money," said Johnson, "because the President and his advisers had moved too indecisively and too slowly." [128] The Senate's increase just about balanced the $400 million decrease of the House. The difference between the two houses was split in conference committee. That the Senate increase would be nullified in conference was never seriously in doubt. The pattern since World War II had generally been to divide in half increases and decreases between the houses. In order to pass a bill close to the President's spending mark,

310

the Senate's increase was vitally needed. The Senate had to run so that the Congress could stand still.

The battle over the FY 1961 defense budget approximated in general outline its two predecessors in the post-sputnik period. Once again it was Congress that pressed the chief executive, ironically enough, to assume his leadership responsibilities for an expanded defense effort. The military services kibitzed again from the sidelines, each with its own and often contradictory set of policy proposals and expenditure priorities. And the administration, resolute and steadfast, remained uncompromising in its opposition to an enlargement of military spending.

Turmoil in the executive branch continues.—President Eisenhower offered an almost carbon copy of his spending plan of FY 1960. Requests for new obligational authority for the Defense Department totaled $40.6 billion. Expenditures were set at $40.99 billion, a slight $40 million over FY 1960. The administration's defense program was a budgetary *tour de force*. Although all of the factors of the policy environment to which the defense budget was presumably a response were changing—political and military conditions abroad, the state of the economy at home, new technological findings, etc.—the administration's budgetary guidelines remained constant.

There were, accordingly, few noticeable changes in FY 1961 defense policies. The long-run trend to cut personnel and operating units continued, though at a reduced rate. Personnel for the services remained at about the levels of FY 1960. The navy was to lose 11,000 men; the air force, about twice as many. Both cutbacks were actually accomplished in the FY 1960 budgetary cycle. Air force wings were again reduced, including a decrease in the number of SAC wings from forty to thirty-eight. The administration called for the

311

operation of ninety-one combat wings, five below the previous year and fourteen below FY 1959. The fleet was diminished by another forty-three ships. The operating aircraft inventory of the air force and navy were cut by 1,000 planes. For the first time the army gained slightly in strength, adding one infantry battle group, one missile command and nine antiaircraft missile battalions. Research and development expenditures held about steady with FY 1960 at $3.9 billion.[129]

The administration's procurement schedule, an indicator of future trends, carried few surprises, although a discernible effort was made to accommodate previous congressional criticisms of defense policy. Long-range missile production was expanded as the administration announced a program of fourteen Titan and thirteen Atlas missile squadrons. These twenty-seven squadrons created an increase of seven squadrons over the preceding year which were to be furnished in part by the extra funds advanced by Congress in FY 1960 for this purpose. The administration had quietly incorporated these added appropriations into its planning. The Polaris program also received more attention. The administration requested the authorization of six additional submarines. In a special April message six more were added for a total of twenty-one. More funds were also advised for Atlas and Minuteman missiles. The President noted in his budget address that he had "authorized the Department of Defense to begin to acquire a standby airborne alert capability for heavy bombers."[130] As in the case of long-range missiles, Congress again had provided the President with standby authority to take such action.

The principal casualties of the administration's defense program including its April amendments, were Bomarc and its accompanying SAGE system and the B-70 bomber. The President recommended a cut of almost $600 million in the Bomarc and SAGE systems in his April revisions. The B-70, on the other hand, was restricted to a two-plane prototype program. Anticipating congressional hostility in cutting back the bomber, the President explained at considerable length the considerations that had entered into his determination.[131]

312

Congress was assured that the strategic mix of bombers and missiles which the administration advised was sufficient to deter the Soviets. The President studiously avoided any mention of a missile gap in his budget request. Secretary of Defense Thomas Gates, who had recently assumed the post after Neil McElroy's departure, explained to the House defense appropriations subcommittee that a new method of assessing Soviet missile production had led to the judgment that there would exist "no deterrent gap" in the early 1960's although he admitted that the Soviet Union's "superiority in ICBM's could be in the order of three to one in the period 1960–63." [132] The administration asserted that this spread was not likely to occur and, if it did, the American balanced deterrent of bombers and missiles would still be overwhelmingly more powerful than its Soviet counterpart. "Heretofore," summarized Secretary Gates,

> we have been giving you intelligence figures that dealt with the theoretical Soviet capability. This is the first time that we have had an intelligence estimate that says, 'This is what the Soviet Union probably will do.' Therefore, the great divergence [in ICBM's], based on figures that have been testified to in years past, narrows because we talked before about a different set of comparisons—ones that were based on Soviet capabilities.[133]

Assured by defense officials that the Soviets would not attempt a surprise attack against the United States, Congress was also informed that $650 million of the $922 million that it had applied to the FY 1960 budget had been released.[134] Most of the remaining $272 million was applied to the FY 1961 budget.[135]

Congressional action: Summary and critique.—Administration assurances did not assuage Congress. As Table 9 above notes,[136] both houses of Congress made a number of substantial changes in FY 1961 defense programs. The House increased funds in sixteen major defense areas and made reductions in eleven others. The House rearranged almost $4 billion in spending authority—or 10 per cent of the defense bill. The initial House bill, however, was only a slim $3 million over the President's total request. The Senate amended the House bill in its characteristic fashion. Restoring many of the specific program cuts which had been made, it also increased others of its own choosing. In presenting the defense bill to the upper chamber, Senator Dennis Chavez, chairman of the Senate defense appropriations subcommittee, boasted that ninety-seven separate program changes had been made.[137] Amendments by Senators Paul Douglas and Henry Jackson, which were accepted during the course of the debate, added $140 million more to the bill to maintain the marine corps at 200,000 and to provide more funds for army modernization. The Senate enlarged the President's defense recommendation by over $1 billion. In conference the two houses agreed to a final defense appropriation of just under $40.0 billion, $661.6 million over the administration's early budget estimates and $780.7 million over the President's revised request of April.

The principal prompting for these program changes, which are summarized in Table 9, is not difficult to find. The military services activated already conditioned congressional fears of military defeat at the hands of the Russians. They enlisted the support of various committees and members of Congress to sponsor and promote their pleas for more money and greater public recognition for their specific military programs. The air force, discouraged by the B-70 cutback and a slowdown in aircraft production, advanced arguments for more spending on missiles and, especially, on bombers and for improved protection of sac bases from enemy attack. Its appeal was addressed over the head of the President and the secretary of defense to Congress and the attentive public interested in defense issues. Air force charges helped stir the Senate Aeronautical and Space Committee and the Preparedness Subcommittee, both chaired by Senator Lyndon Johnson, to hold joint hearings on "the underlying principles and facts upon which the decisions governing our country's defense and space programs are based."[138] General Thomas Power set most of the stage for the hearings in two speeches that he delivered in January, 1960. Power told the influential Economics Club of New York on January 19 that the nation's strategic forces were threatened by nuclear annihilation. "According to released data on nuclear effects," Power said,

> it would take an average of three missiles, in their current state of development, to give an aggressor a mathematical probability of 95 percent that he can destroy one given soft target, some 5,000 miles away. This means that, with only some 300 ballistic missiles, the Soviet could virtually wipe out our entire nuclear strike capability within a span of 30 minutes. To further heighten this threat, only about half of these missiles would have to be ICBM's which are considerably less expensive and easier to produce.[139]

The speech was timely, having been delivered one day after the issuance of President Eisenhower's budget. A week later, on January 28, General Power delivered another address. Speaking before the American Legion on "The Role of Man in the Space Age," he pointedly told his audience that the air force expected the B-70 eventually "to take the place of the most modern bomber in SAC's inventory . . . the B-52."[140] The two speeches summarized the air force's public appeal for more manned, long-range aircraft and missiles, improved detection and dispersal facilities, and a rapid buildup in airborne capacity. The hearings of the Johnson preparedness group opened with an examination of General Power's public statements.

The other services found other effective, though less dramatic, ways to indicate their budgetary preferences. General Maxwell Taylor, recently retired from service, reiterated his already widely disseminated views on the inadequacies of the Eisenhower defense policies. His remarks before Congress in 1960 served primarily to sustain pressure on the administration. In the concluding section of his

315

prepared remarks before the Johnson unit, General Taylor asserted: "From about 1961 on, the tide will begin to turn against us—unless we take heroic measures now. To change the trend will require men, money, and sacrifice. The alternative is military inferiority—and there is no living long with communism as an inferior."[141] Other army spokesmen noted that army modernization funds were pegged just below full replacement rates on depreciation for the second successive year. They complained about unfilled airlift requirements, particularly for limited war. The army's case was strengthened when a joint army-air force exercise to ferry troops to Puerto Rico experienced numerous difficulties. A special House Armed Services Committee verified army complaints and reported serious shortages in airlift capacity. The House group also addressed a letter through its chairman, Representative Carl Vinson, to the House defense appropriations subcommittee calling for an almost $1 billion increase in army modernization funds above the President's recommendation.

The navy and marine corps were equally persuasive before Congress. General David Shoup, new marine corps commandant, repeated his service's need for more personnel. Admiral Arleigh Burke, while again pressing the navy's suit for another aircraft carrier before a reluctant Congress, also subtly upgraded the importance of the Polaris and, to a slightly greater extent than before, antisubmarine warfare capabilities. The appropriations committees were informed that the navy had requested to spend $19 billion for FY 1961 and had been allowed an expenditure program of $11.7 billion.[142]

Service criticism of Eisenhower security policies and operations were reinforced by attacks emanating from other segments of the executive branch and from influential private quarters. Senator Henry Jackson's subcommittee on national policy machinery harnessed much of the adverse commentary against the administration in its well-publicized hearings. It provided a forum where such important figures as Robert Lovett, former secretary of defense under President

Truman and a prominent Republican financier, could voice the need for a greater defense effort. "I think our past performance may have raised the hopes of the world excessively high," Lovett said in reply to a question posed by Senator Jackson. "But I feel, sir, that we are doing something short of our best in several fields. . . . "[143]

Against this backdrop of criticism and censure of the administration's defense policies, Congress made its many changes in the FY 1961 defense bill. But the significance of these shifts is greater than the political atmosphere in which they were wrought. There were a number of mixed and cross-cutting purposes behind Congress' reordering of defense priorities. These were reflected in the changes. Just as importantly, congressional attempts to reshape and redirect defense policy cast new light on the limits and opportunities of congressional capacity to influence and control defense policy and operations.

The increasing penchant in Congress to second-guess the administration and the military services demonstrated the alarming and continuing erosion of confidence in the administration's defense leadership among an enlarging body of congressional committees and legislators. Diminishing confidence in the administration's policies and the concomitant struggle that the enlarging void in consensus engendered hampered the entire defense effort. The administration appeared to be defending itself more against its friends at home than its enemies abroad. The top leadership of the services was dissipating itself in interservice maneuvering. Congress became another battleground for service warfare. By the last year of the Eisenhower administration, the magnitude of congressional-executive alienation over defense was approaching the dimensions of the rift that had characterized the final year of the Truman administration when sympathy for the Korean War was at its lowest ebb in Congress and among the public.

It is important to recognize, however, that the substantive issues which were widening the gap between administration defense policies

317

and congressional consent were almost the reverse of those during the Korean War. The Truman administration then had asked Congress and the country to assume more world-wide responsibilities than they were willing to discharge. Now the Eisenhower administration did not seem to be demanding enough. It was not leading the nation to accept greater sacrifices of its wealth and human resources to preserve the nation's security. On the issue of more defense, legislators who disagreed on other foreign and domestic problems could concur in the need for more defense spending. On this issue, otherwise quarreling Democrats like Senator Joseph Clark of Pennsylvania and Senator Richard Russell joined forces against the President. Similarly inclined, though obviously restrained somewhat by their party affiliation, were such Republicans as Senator Leverett Saltonstall of Massachusetts, Representative Gerald Ford of Michigan, and Governor Nelson Rockefeller of New York.

It is also clear that, without presidential assent and co-operation, Congress could not force its strategic views and their corresponding program requirements on the President. The Eighty-fifth and Eighty-sixth congresses never fully put themselves to the task of accomplishing these ends. Restrictive requirements were written into law only for the reserves. During this period Congress as such never really possessed an integrated and unambiguous strategic position. The defense appropriations subcommittees thought more along specific program lines. Even on this level, cohesive and continuing majorities did not form to underwrite defense programs. Air lift or Nike-Zeus would receive congressional attention one year and be forgotten the next. The general pattern of congressional support for defense programs was diffuse except in the area of air defense where congressional patience with slipshod Defense Department planning was exhausted or in House opposition to the navy's annual request for a carrier. Shifting coalitions of support or opposition for different programs were formed from issue to issue. Allies on one defense problem would become opponents on another. Pluralism was no less a characteristic of defense policy-making in each house than other aspects of public policy.

Coalitions also formed across chamber lines. House supporters of the navy's carriers, for example, pointedly avoided a floor fight on the House Appropriations Committee's decision to cut the carrier program out of the administration's FY 1961 request. They preferred instead to have the Senate reinstate the carrier and have its decision upheld in conference. An amendment offered on the floor in behalf of the carrier would almost certainly have been defeated in the House. Evading a showdown on the issue on the floor also avoided any formal recording of majority sentiment. If the full House had specifically rejected the carrier, the conference committee would have faced more difficulty in circumventing initial House opposition. House conferees would have been more rigidly bound to uphold their chamber's judgment.[144]

Generating political support for defined defense programs assumed in some instances the aspect of a lottery. Of the large number of military programs vying for congressional support at the opening of each session, it was never certain which would be given precedence over others, nor what considerations would finally determine the configuration of defense priorities adopted by Congress. Legislators themselves were never fully sure of the implications of their votes even after the President had signed the defense bill. Even in those instances in which Congress passed increased funds for a particular program, members did not always precisely know what the funds would buy or even how much was actually being added to Defense Department accounts. The army complained to the Senate that it would receive only $88 million of the $207.4 million that the House claimed it had voted for modernization. The lower chamber had included $120 million in its bill from other sources of army revenue which the army had already included in its original estimates.[145]

On the other hand, some lottery tickets stood a better chance of winning in the congressional sweepstakes than others. Tickets marked

"Army Reserves" were almost certain winners. Domestic politics weighted the reserve program out of proportion to its intrinsic strategic merit or its relation to other defense programs. Thanks to the assiduous cultivation of a fighting image that appealed to legislators and the presence of influential alumni in Congress, the marine corps similarly enjoyed wide popularity in the annual dispensation of funds by Congress. The Senate's commitment to a force of 200,000 men proved unflagging; the House's, while more volatile and unpredictable, was still sizable and perceptible. Senator Paul Douglas, an ex-marine hero of World War II, could always be relied upon, for example, to offer an amendment to increase marine corps personnel, although he otherwise interested himself in the economic and administrative aspects of defense policy.[146]

The ability of Congress to influence strategic policy depended critically on its willingness to oppose the President's defense spending ceilings and to generate public support for its collective views. An insufficient number of legislators or legislative leaders were prepared to undertake either task fully. Defense subcommittee chairman, Representative George Mahon, clearly felt constrained. "Except for budgetary considerations," he told General Thomas White, "there is strong indication that, to my mind, we would probably now have a Department of Defense budget of about $51 billion instead of about $41 billion; but the forces of Government and public opinion have been such that we have a military defense budget of about $41 billion."[147] Legislators hesitated to pursue policies that ran counter to their perceptions of "the forces of Government and public opinion," particularly in a presidential election year. Many cautiously waited for the trend in public opinion to become clearer. It is in this cramped political context that the House could effect program changes amounting to $4 billion and still pass a defense bill that was only $3.0 million over the President's January estimates. Some legislators, particularly those in the House, awaited, as did the proverbial Frenchman during the French Revolution, for the public to form in a mass protest before assuming the leadership of the movement.

The Senate's willingness to go beyond the House and the President and add $1 billion to the defense bill was not accidental. The Senate defense appropriations subcommittee, under the chairmanship of the well-meaning but ineffectual Senator Dennis Chavez, could successfully propose an expansion and an acceleration of various defense programs because it had already secured the active support, indeed the encouragement and impetus, of political leaders like Johnson whose prestige and influence were established not only in defense but in the larger and more decisive policy spheres of the Senate.

The Senate increase, while initially significant, did not shatter the President's over-all budget framework. The record of the Senate's examination of the defense bill suggests that no serious attempt was made to produce such a break-through. Senator Stuart Symington notes in the debates on the military measure that he was prepared to offer an amendment to increase the bill by $2.6 billion but was discouraged from presenting his proposal by the lack of support for it.[148] Since the House was already on record in favor of a balanced budget, there was again the almost certain prospect that it would cut the Senate figure to conform more closely with its own. The $661 million increase that was finally agreed upon tended, therefore, to create two favorable impressions: (1) that the Congress and its leadership were more aware and responsive to security problems than the chief executive and (2) that the increase in defense spending, while notable, would not seriously disrupt the President's fiscal policies so firmly tied to a balanced budget. For only a few more bucks, the public would receive a lot more bang.

Congress continued to be mindful of its interest in cutting waste in defense operations. The House took the lead and aimed the bulk of its $2 billion reduction at forcing efficiencies in administrative and maintenance operations and in procurement practices. The House proposed and eventually secured Senate acquiescence in a 3 per cent meat ax cut in all procurement funds for the Defense Department. Continued reports from the comptroller general that overpayments were being made prompted Congress to hack blindly at the appropriations for procurement. Its 3 per cent cut followed a similar 1 per cent across the board reduction in the FY 1960 bill. The ironic and self-defeating effects of this cut are immediately apparent. The industrious and efficient were penalized, while those who padded their estimates initially were able to absorb a congressional slash easily. The services were further encouraged, therefore, to inflate their estimates before Congress in the future.

The awkwardness of a number of congressional attempts to streamline Defense Department operations should not obscure the prescience and forward look of some of its views. Legislators were at least striving to conceptualize in defense program terms rather than solely in categories of financial management or spending ceilings. Even before the inauguration of a number of reforms in defense planning and policy-making by the Kennedy administration, the House appropriations defense group was groping its way toward these useful changes. Members of the House subcommittee recognized that financial controls were useless and misleading unless related to the projects and programs that they were designed to direct. The achievement of program objectives appeared "to be secondary to the restriction of expenditures within specified expenditure targets."[149] The House Appropriations Committee summarized most of its criticisms in its lengthy and at times biting report on the FY 1961 defense bill:

> Piecemeal financing resulting from conformity to fixed expenditure ceilings, coupled with the attempt to keep going as many as possible of the promising programs, has all too often resulted in weapon systems being advanced to the readiness-for-production stage much too late. . . .

Simply stated, the problem is merely one of taking into account the full implications of the entire financial burden over the life, involving a period of years, of each and every military development project at the earliest possible date. This has not been done in the past, and particularly at the highest levels in the Executive branch where control has tended in recent years to evolve to that of the single expenditure limitation. The expenditure limitation is such an easy method of establishing a control it can be exercised by a single person in a key decision-making position. This method of control, however, tends to ignore the detailed project evaluation of expert staff at lower levels, procedures for which have evolved over a period of many years.[150]

Persistent congressional pressure to reprogram funds or to increase funds for what it felt to be higher priority programs eventually did produce results. Congress' limited successes in FY 1959 and FY 1960 have already been noted. Its most significant impact on defense policy developed out of the FY 1961 bill. On August 1, 1960, Secretary of Defense Thomas Gates announced in a letter to Senator Lyndon Johnson that $476 million of $1.097 billion in previously frozen defense funds would be released for a variety of programs in which Congress was particularly interested. These programs included army reserves, modernization, air lift, airborne alert, the B-70 bomber, Samos, and Polaris. The largest beneficiary was Polaris. The Defense Department added $164 million to FY 1961 spending, and expanded the program from three fully funded and nine partially funded submarines to five fully funded and five partially funded vessels. Approximately $620 million was to remain permanently frozen, while an additional $979 million was to be placed in a temporary freeze until the Defense Department could review program requirements for FY 1961.[151] On October 1, the Defense Department released an additional $169 million for Polaris, Samos, and army modernization.[152] More funds were later apportioned for ASW and for the B-70. On October 26, the secretary of defense revealed that the B-70 would be upgraded from a prototype program and pursued as a complete weapons systems.[153] President Eisenhower carried forward this decision into his FY 1962 budget which asked for $358 million for the B-70. Secretary Gates remarked in the opening paragraphs of a long letter to Senator Johnson that the President, and not Congress, had taken the lead in fostering new defense programs.[154] President Eisenhower on August 8, in addressing Congress on its return for a special summer session before the November elections, also carefully underlined the actions which he had taken to accelerate the rate and broaden the base of defense preparedness.[155] The President's claim was not fully persuasive. Senator Lyndon Johnson, recently nominated as Democratic candidate for the vice-presidency, replied to President Eisenhower's message. His analysis of the Defense Department's release of funds, notwithstanding its partisan overtones, appeared closer to the actual significance of the defense speedup. "In his message to the Congress yesterday," said Johnson, "the President referred to actions he had taken to expand certain long-range defense programs. Although the President failed to mention it, the only reason he was able to take these actions was because the Congress had appropriated additional funds for these programs over the protests of the administration." [156]

On November 8, 1960, the Democratic presidential ticket of Senators John F. Kennedy and Lyndon B. Johnson scored a narrow election victory. Despite the slim margin of 100,000 votes by which the election was decided, the election of Kennedy and Johnson presaged a shift in all phases of defense strategy, weapons systems, and force levels and in the very process by which decisions would be reached in the Defense Department. Even before President Kennedy assumed office, majorities in both houses of Congress were prepared to receive the recommendations of the President for more defense spending and for a more balanced and flexible defense posture. President Kennedy's task was to harness congressional sentiment for the general policy changes to specific and identifiable military programs.

THE KENNEDY ADMINISTRATION AND THE EIGHTY-SEVENTH CONGRESS, 1961–1962

New Turns in Policy and Process

VII

The intellectual ferment and heated contentions in Congress of the post-sputnik period yielded no immediate overhaul in defense policies and operations. There were a few redirections in selected military programs, but certainly no major transformation of the nation's defense posture. Congress could raise some of the basic assumptions of strategic policy into question; it could challenge the military and political judgment of the chief executive; it could reorder the spending priorities of the defense establishment; and it could prepare itself and the public for an expansion of defense capabilities. But it could not by itself plan, organize, much less direct, an arms enlargement, however necessary, nor rationalize an increase of American armed might, both conventional and nuclear, into a coherent strategic doctrine. These were areas primarily of executive competence and responsibility.

The election of John F. Kennedy and, more pointedly, the appointment of Robert Strange McNamara to be the seventh secretary of defense opened the way for needed shifts in defense policy and operations. New and salutary turns were taken in the nation's substantive strategic policies, in its military force structure, deployment, and fighting preparedness, and in the organizational framework and process through which decisions on military policy and the defense budget were reached in the Defense Department. Not surprisingly, relations between Congress and the President in defense policy were also altered. The Eighty-seventh Congress marks a downturn in the number of congressional initiatives in defense policy and, correspondingly, a diminution of effective congressional influence. Three sets of factors generally explain much of the reduction of Congress' initiative and influence: (a) strong presidential leadership backed by firm and forceful civilian direction of the Department of Defense; (b) the sweeping policy and process changes set in motion by Secretary McNamara that received, by and large, broad congressional approval; and, to a lesser extent, (c) the changes in congressional handling of the defense budget, including both the authorization of spending programs and the appropriation of funds to implement them.

THE MC NAMARA INNOVATIONS[1]

Strategic policy and force structure.—The Eisenhower administration, notwithstanding its announced commitment to a balanced military structure composed of conventional and nuclear arms, confined itself to a narrow band of military options. Military planning contemplated the early and decisive introduction of nuclear weapons into any large-scale military conflict involving the United States. Conventional war with the Soviet Union in Europe was effectively ruled out, if for no other reason than that the receding size of the army and marine corps and the paucity of funds allocated to non-nuclear modernization and procurement, to air and sea lift, and to tactical air power, precluded such a confrontation beyond a limited probing action. Announced and operational strategy were at odds with each other. The introduction of tactical nuclear weapons into the American arsenal and their deployment abroad, even to forward areas in the NATO defense perimeter, mitigated, but did not significantly alter, the Eisenhower administration's heavy reliance on a massive retaliatory strategy to deter most forms of communist aggression.[2]

326

Growing Soviet strategic and tactical nuclear power undermined the credibility and the deterrent effect of the American nuclear arsenal. As the Soviets expanded their strategic strike forces, switched from bombers to long-range missiles, and reduced the vulnerability of these forces through dispersion, hardening, and concealment, the likelihood grew that the United States would risk its own self-destruction if it used its nuclear power against the Soviet Union. On the other hand, Soviet possession of large conventional forces posed a separate problem, especially in western Europe, given the perceived debilities of American nuclear might. While doubts developed in many quarters that the United States would have the will to employ its nuclear arsenal in response to a massive Soviet conventional attack on the Continent, others worried, indeed, that it would and thereby annihilate Europe. Premier Nikita Khrushchev's announcement in January, 1961, that the Soviet Union, while rejecting the notion of the alleged inevitability of thermonuclear war, was prepared to encourage and aid "wars of national liberation" further compounded the military-political problems facing the United States.

Secretary of Defense McNamara was keenly aware, as were his chief advisers, of the limited and, in light of enlarging Soviet nuclear capacity, the dwindling deterrent effect of American nuclear arms against communist expansionist probes. "Even at a time when our nuclear superiority was so great as to represent a monopoly," he told the House defense appropriations group,

> it did not deter Communist aggression in various parts of the world, as is illustrated by the Communist invasion of Korea, as is illustrated by the Communist pressure on Berlin in 1958, and as is illustrated by a series of other aggressive acts, political and military, by the Communists during the decade of the fifties.
>
> In any event, whatever the character of the deterrence provided by our nuclear superiority at a time when we had a monopoly on such nuclear weapons, it is quite clear, I believe, that deterrence can be expected to be less at a time when the

Soviet Union has sufficient nuclear power to damage severely this Nation. And under those circumstances, it seems essential to me that our foreign policy be based also upon other forms of deterrent power, other forms of deterrence to activities less violent than those which the Soviets might expect us to respond to with our nuclear power.[3]

To deter and, if necessary, to defend against these multiple communist threats, the Kennedy administration proposed not one or a limited number of military responses, but the development of a wide spectrum of military capabilities that would more closely correspond to the military challenge to be countered. Said President Kennedy in a special message to Congress in March, 1961: "Our defense posture must be both flexible and determined. Any potential aggressor contemplating an attack on any part of the free world with any kind of weapons . . . must know that our response will be suitable, selective, swift, and effective. . . . We must be able to make deliberate choices in weapons and strategy, shift the tempo of our production, and alter the direction of our forces to meet rapidly changing conditions or objectives at very short notice and under any circumstances."[4] A posture of flexible response was deemd to be more credible in support of American security interests and foreign policy objectives, because a clearer and closer correspondence could be struck between the military force that was to be applied by the President and the political stakes and the scope of the military conflict at issue between the United States and an enemy power. Administration planners did not believe that nuclear weapons were credible in a confrontation with the Soviet Union except in the most desperate situations, as proved to be the case in the 1962 Cuban crisis, which touched a central nerve of United States security and its hegemony in the North American hemisphere. The threat to use military force was viewed as credible only if a potential aggressor believed that the United States would actually implement its threat if its interests were challenged. Nuclear weapons were unable to meet this test, most Kennedy defense advisers felt, in terms of the conflict situations which the United States and its European allies were likely to confront. They concluded that an increase in the amount and variety of non-nuclear fighting capabilities offered a number of options to the President between capitulation and nuclear devastation in order to check limited communist incursions against the United States and the West. The Eisenhower administration and, in particular, Secretary of State John Foster Dulles had spoken, too, of shaping the military establishment so that the nation could "retaliate, instantly, by means and at places of [its] choosing" against communist aggression.[5] The Kennedy group argued, however, that the Eisenhower administration had failed to create the military instruments which would have given substantive operational effect of its announced policy view.

Kennedy administration officials foresaw the development of a wide number of contingencies around the world in which American and allied non-nuclear power could play an important, and perhaps, a decisive role in protecting Western interests and objectives.[6] There were, first of all, those situations in which large-scale conventional forces would be useful. Korea, Lebanon, and military action in the Formosa Straits seemed to provide important precedents for the future. Communist guerrilla activity encountered in Greece, the Philippines, Malaya, and Indo-China suggested still other forms which warfare might assume.

More immediately troubling was the exposed position of the West in Berlin where a Soviet takeover of the city might occur swiftly and unexpectedly. The reported presence of twenty-two divisions in East Germany and large Soviet reinforcements in eastern Europe and western Russia made such a quick thrust possible. The repeated threats of the Soviet Union to sign a separate peace treaty with East Germany and unilaterally to end allied rights in Berlin further deepened the anxiety of official Washington. The administration became convinced that NATO's conventional warfare capabilities were unable to deter or to defend against these military and diplomatic threats to American and allied interests. Few doubted that the defense of Berlin and Europe still rested principally on American nuclear power.

The administration determined in the early months of its office to de-emphasize what seemed to have been the previous administration's reliance on nuclear weapons. In his initial presentations to Congress, Secretary of Defense McNamara reversed the then popularly-conceived relation between nuclear and non-nuclear weaponry in the defense of Europe. While he called for the continued buildup of "forces required to deter an all-out nuclear war," he referred to these forces as a "shield" behind which the free world could repair "to cope successfully with lesser military aggression." Non-nuclear forces were to be the cutting edge—the sword—of American NATO power whereas the Eisenhower administration had viewed them largely as a means to maintain a temporary forward line of defense against a Soviet conventional aggression until United States nuclear might could be invoked.[7] Now the Kennedy administration proposed to meet a Soviet non-nuclear attack with adequate NATO conventional forces. An initially effective non-nuclear response gave promise in Europe of punishing military aggression, limiting damage, and denying territory to an enemy more successfully than early use of nuclear weapons.

While the nuclear threshold was to be raised, nuclear weapons were not to be abandoned. In its official pronouncements, many solicited by anxious European governments and most especially by West Germany, the administration repeatedly underscored its commitment to defend Europe, even with nuclear weapons if necessary. Administration spokesmen argued that larger conventional fighting power, apart from its military value in limited war engagements, was an addition to the American nuclear deterrent. Once American conventional forces were committed against the Soviets in Europe, the credibility of the United States nuclear guarantee would allegedly be established beyond doubt. In addition, their use would slow the escalation of the conflict which could prove disastrous for all antagonists. If the Soviets still refused to withdraw in the face of stiff non-nuclear opposition, then resort would be presumably made to tactical nuclear weapons and then upward along the scale of kiloton and megaton power.[8] However, a massive non-nuclear attack by the Soviet Union in Europe would be met by a nuclear response. The buildup of conventional forces, especially in the NATO area, was not viewed as a means to preclude such aggressive moves, but to deter and to check lesser non-nuclear actions, including those prompted by Soviet miscalculation of United States intentions or initiated accidentally. Stopping "an all-out surprise non-nuclear attack," observed Secretary McNamara in a major policy speech, ". . . is not in any case the contingency toward which the recent and future improvements in the mobility and capabilities of U.S. general purpose forces are primarily oriented."[9] Conventional forces would have a more circumscribed, yet a larger and more important, role to play in maximizing the military and political advantage of the West, while simultaneously reducing the benefits which a potential enemy might perceive in resorting to non-nuclear aggression. Said the defense secretary to Congress:

> We may well be faced with situations in Europe where it would not be to the advantage of ourselves or our allies to use even tactical nuclear weapons initially—provided we had the capability to deal with them through non-nuclear means. Nuclear weapons, even in the lower kiloton ranges, are extremely destructive devices and hardly the preferred weapons to defend such heavily populated areas as Europe. Furthermore, while it does not necessarily follow that the use of tactical nuclear weapons must inevitably escalate into global nuclear war, it does present a very definite threshold beyond where we enter a vast unknown.
> This does not mean that the NATO forces can or should do without tactical nuclear weapons. On the contrary, we must continue to strengthen and modernize our tactical nuclear capa-

bilities to deal with an attack where the opponent employs such weapons first, or any attack by conventional forces which puts Europe in danger of being overrun. We mean to defend Europe with every kind of weapon needed.

We must . . . increase our non-nuclear capabilities to foreclose to our opponent the freedom of action he would otherwise have, or believe he would have, in lesser military provocations. We must be in a position to confront him at any level of provocation with an appropriate military response. . . . The NATO powers have all the resources, the talents, and the skills needed to match our opponent at any level of effort in Europe.[10]

Under Secretary McNamara's leadership, new military requirements were established for the rapid expansion of the nation's and NATO's conventional forces. The goal of a thirty-division NATO force, honored more in the breech than in the observance, was reinstated. The Pentagon vigorously pressed reluctant NATO partners to increase their contributions to NATO's conventional capability. Interest in American non-nuclear forces was similarly pursued with novel vigor. Manpower levels for general purpose forces of all of the services were raised; army and marine corps divisions, strengthened; the rate of conventional weapons procurement and modernization, accelerated; air and sealift elements, expanded; outlays for tactical air power, stepped up; new organizational instruments, like STRICOM, fashioned to maximize the offensive capability of conventional air and ground units in battle; and the reserves of all of the services, more closely integrated into the operations and planning of the active forces.

The Kennedy administration was equally concerned about meeting communist subversion in the underdeveloped countries. Particularly disturbing were communist gains in Cuba and Latin America and in Southeast Asia. Communist penetration into Africa, as evidenced by the turmoil in the Congo, added to the administration's worries. Premier Khrushchev's January, 1961, speech rationalized the various instances of communist agitation around the world as a new phase of the East-West struggle. The Defense Department sought to develop capabilities to cope with counterinsurgency operations and thereby to secure the "internal stability" necessary for economic and social progress in the underdeveloped nations.

The South Vietnamese war increasingly occupied the attention of the administration. Some military advisers drew a parallel between the communist challenge in Indo-China and the Spanish Civil War before World War II in which Allied and Axis forces first met in a test of strength. Defense officials agreed that the United States would have to demonstrate that communist conquest by subversion could be resisted as effectively as direct aggression. New requirements were set, therefore, for special force personnel capable of organizing and training an indigenous population to protect itself against subversive elements and communist infiltration. Research and development funds were allocated in increased amounts not only for conventional weapons but also for the study of new techniques to combat guerrilla warfare. Military assistance was enlarged to areas vulnerable to communist agitation and was placed more directly under the control of the Defense Department.[11] New programs of civilian action to make the military forces of the underdeveloped nations the instruments of social and economic progress were begun. The army was assigned the major responsibility for counterinsurgency operations, and by early 1965 had earmarked its activities in this area as second only to its duties in nuclear and conventional warfare.[12]

The administration argued that an expansion of non-nuclear forces did not indicate a diminution of American determination to use nuclear weapons when necessary. "What is being proposed . . . " McNamara observed in one of his first congressional appearances as defense secretary, "is not a reversal of our existing national policy but an increase in our non-nuclear capabilities to provide a greater degree of versatility to our limited war forces."[13] What the administration sought was a clearer definition of those contingencies in which tactical and strategic nuclear weapons could play a useful and

333

credible deterrent and defense role. The administration had been presented with two rival theories of nuclear strategy. Navy and army circles pressed for a finite deterrent posture; the air force sought a combined counterforce and countervalue strategy which would permit an all-out attack against both cities and military targets.[14] After much argument and discussion within the Defense Department, lasting throughout most of the two years of the Eighty-seventh Congress, Secretary of Defense McNamara finally settled upon what might be termed a modified counterforce strategy. The secretary's choice rested on the assumption that, despite all efforts to forestall its development, a nuclear war might occur. It was important, therefore, to conduct such hostilities on terms which were, relatively speaking, favorable to the United States.[15]

First priority was placed on maintaining the superiority of American strategic nuclear weaponry. Concern about an alleged missile gap between the United States and the Soviet Union, a prominent campaign issue in 1960, dissolved shortly after the Kennedy administration assumed office. New intelligence data revealed that the United States held a commanding lead over the Soviet Union in the number and quality of its strategic and tactical nuclear arms and that the disparity between the two nations in these categories would increase if the United States expanded its production and dispersal of these weapons. Secretary McNamara viewed the prospect of American strategic superiority as an opportunity to broaden the base of his options approach to the use of military force. The superiority of American nuclear arms would afford the United States the option of holding in reserve its countervalue (or countercity) forces even after the nation had absorbed an enemy nuclear first strike. If the United States possessed enough nuclear-strike power to ride out an initial enemy attack, there would be no need for instantaneous and massive retaliation. An assessment could first be made to determine the size, scope, and significance of an enemy attack. Nuclear weapons would, therefore, be under continuously close and centralized political direction, even in the midst of a nuclear exchange. They would admit to a wider degree of discriminating use by the President than had hitherto been conceived or programmed. A spasmodic nuclear reflex to an enemy nuclear attack could be avoided; the danger of catalytic war reduced; and the inevitable pressures that would be built up during an international crisis minimized.

In the wake of a Soviet nuclear attack the United States would not immediately be forced to destroy Russian cities. "By building into our forces a flexible capability," Secretary McNamara told a House group, "we at least eliminate the prospect that we could strike back in only one way, against the entire Soviet target system including their cities. Such a prospect would give the Soviet Union no incentive to withhold attack against our cities in a first strike. We want to give them a better alternative." [16] A second-strike capability could limit damage to the nation's military forces and its cities. Sufficient reserve power would remain intact to attack strategic and conventional forces which had not yet been employed or to decimate enemy cities if such a course became necessary. The strategic superiority of the United States held the added hope that a nuclear war with the Soviet Union, if it should occur, could be terminated swiftly and on terms that were politically favorable to the West. American nuclear superiority increased its bargaining leverage both before and during a nuclear war.

On the other hand, complete protection against growing Soviet strategic might was dismissed as an infeasible goal in the foreseeable future. A doubling or tripling of the nation's strategic forces or even an expanded air and civil-defense effort would not prevent "casualties counted in the tens of millions." [17] Intelligence estimates indicated that the Soviets were increasing their strategic forces, dispersing and hardening them, and improving the size and effectiveness of their submarine-launched missiles. However, the projected size of this force in the first half of the 1960's was not thought sufficiently large or invulnerable to give the Soviet Union capability an incentive to confine itself to a nuclear strike solely against United States strategic forces and installations. In a revealing speech to the New York Economic Club in the fall of 1963, Secretary McNamara outlined the major elements of his strategic thinking in which he sketched the hazards and opportunities that it afforded:

> Deterrence of deliberate, calculated attack seems as well assured as it can be, and the damage-limiting capability of our numerically superior forces is, I believe, well worth its incremental cost. It is a superiority to which the smaller forces of the Soviet Union could not realistically aspire. That is one reason, among others, why I would not trade our strategic posture for that of the Soviets at any point during the coming decade.
>
> But given the kind of force that the Soviets are building . . . the damage which the Soviets could inflict on us and our allies, no matter what we do to limit it, remains extremely high. . . .
>
> That must, I suggest, be accepted as one of the determinants affecting policy. Another is that the same situation confronts the Soviet leaders, in a way that is even more intensely confining. In fact enormous increases in Soviet budgets would be required for them to achieve any significant degree of damage-limiting capability. The present Soviet leaders show no tendency to challenge the basis of the U.S. strategic deterrent posture by such expenditures.[18]

The requirements for McNamara's general war strategy as well as his advocacy for more non-nuclear forces were detailed in the annual and supplemental budget requests of the Defense Department. The number of strategic strike forces were increased. A number of actions were taken, too, to improve their invulnerability as well as their reaction time in responding to enemy attack. A shift in emphasis from bombers to missiles was initiated. Top priority was placed on the Minuteman and Polaris systems. The solid-fueled Minuteman could be fired more quickly than the competing land-based Atlas and Titan systems and could be hardened and dispersed more easily. The liquid-firing Atlas was deemed to be particularly vulnerable to

336

destruction by a surprise enemy nuclear attack. The solid-fueled Polaris, fired from hidden, deep-running submarines, was even less susceptible to detection and destruction than Minuteman, although less accurate and shorter ranged. Legislative authority and funds were secured to maintain one-half of the nation's long-range bomber forces on ground alert and one-eighth on air alert, when so directed by the secretary of defense. Research and development funds for an advanced antimissile system were approved. More effort was also concentrated on improving strategic intelligence techniques, partly through space satellites since the U-2 was no longer available for use over the Soviet Union.

A key aspect of the secretary's strategic design was to secure a reliable command and control network. Political direction of the nation's nuclear forces was impossible without such a system. New programs were inaugurated to produce "survivable, secure, redundant, and internetted command, control, and communication facilities." [19] Tightened security arrangements were instituted to preclude accidental or unauthorized use of nuclear weapons. Co-ordinated strategic targeting plans were formulated, a process already begun under the Eisenhower administration.[20]

Moves were made to discredit or to discourage the development of independent national nuclear forces outside of American control. "Limited nuclear capabilities, operating independently," Secretary McNamara told a University of Michigan audience in oblique reference to the French *force de frappe*, "are dangerous, expensive, prone to obsolescence, and lacking in credibility as a deterrent." [21] Alternatively, the United States stressed the indivisibility of American and European security and the corresponding need for a centralized, controlled, and discriminating response to Soviet aggression. The defense secretary in the same speech affirmed the American nuclear commitment to its European allies. "We are convinced," he said,

> that a general nuclear war target system is indivisible, and if, despite all our efforts, nuclear war should occur, our best hope

337

lies in conducting a centrally controlled campaign against all of the enemy's vital nuclear capabilities, while retaining reserve forces, all centrally controlled.

We know that the same forces which are targeted on ourselves are also targeted on our allies. Our own strategic retaliatory forces are prepared to respond against these forces, wherever they are and whatever their targets. This mission is assigned not only in fulfillment of our treaty commitments but also because the character of nuclear war compels it. . . . In short, we have undertaken the nuclear defense of NATO on a global basis.[22]

Additional assurances of American willingness to defend Europe were extended. More thorough briefings of American nuclear might were tendered to America's NATO allies by American military and political officials, including the secretary of defense. European nations were permitted increased access to American nuclear planning and targeting data. Expanding on the proposals of the previous administration, a multilateral nuclear force was proposed to enhance European participation in the nuclear defense of NATO.

Crucial to McNamara's strategic thinking was the need to disseminate sufficient information to the Soviet Union and other communist nations to apprise them of American strategic superiority and the kind of responses that they might expect if the United States were militarily or politically challenged. The Eisenhower administration had insisted on keeping the enemy guessing about American intentions and military capabilities. Most Kennedy advisers backed away from the brinkmanship stance which Secretary of State Dulles had assumed as a prominent feature of American foreign policy. They placed greater weight on the need to minimize the possibility of nuclear war or nuclear escalation as a result of accident, miscalculation, or misunderstanding. They reasoned, consequently, that potential enemies had to be notified in as much detail as possible about the superiority of American arms and the dimensions of American political intentions. In this connection, Secretary McNamara and his chief assistants lost few opportunities to publicly review United States military capabilities and security commitments. These pronouncements had the three-fold effect of assuaging allied anxieties and of warning enemies abroad and, incidentally, of informing congressional and public opinion at home.[23]

Integration of the executive defense process.—These shifts in policy could not be effected without important changes in the process by which decisions were reached and by which the political authority of the defense secretary and the President were asserted in military planning, programming, and budgeting.[24] The Eisenhower administration had tended to divide planning and programming activities from those of budgeting and resource allocation. These two streams of decision and action were annually brought together into temporary and uneasy alignment in order to present defense appropriations requests to Congress. A superficial unity of service views was achieved through the application of rigid expenditure ceilings for all defense programs.

Kennedy defense officials argued that the practice of controlling the budgetary and programming cycles through the exertion of rigid spending limits adversely affected the responsiveness of the nation's defense policies to its security and foreign policy imperatives and the adequacy of its military force structure. First of all, the plans and statement of requirements of each service either conflicted or were unrelated to each other. Army planning, Secretary McNamara discovered, was based on a long-war of attrition, while the air force envisioned a "short-war of nuclear bombardment to be measured in days, and not very many days at that."[25] The navy in its turn stressed the decisive nature of sea power.

Each service set its own requirements and the time phase in which they were to be reached. Serious program imbalances inevitably developed. Air force and navy air and sea lift capacity fell short of available ground troops that could be engaged in a large number of possible conflict situations. "We actually have more fight than we can ferry," remarked General David Shoup, marine corps commandant.[26] Military plans and programs were conceived independently of an over-all strategic view.[27] "I think the results can fairly be described as chaotic," Secretary of Defense McNamara noted in a public address. Assistant Secretary of Defense Charles J. Hitch added the testimony that "military planning was done essentially on a unilateral service basis, and, to a great extent, the order of priority of forces, weapons systems, and activities, was determined on the basis of the needs of the individual Military Department and not the needs of the Defense Establishment as a whole."[28]

Second, requirements and program plans generally bore little relation to the actual amount of resources which the administration was willing to spend for defense. "Enormous requirements existed on paper," observed the defense secretary, "often almost entirely disembodied from the actual size and nature of the procurement program."[29] On the other hand, gross errors in the stockpiling of equipment occurred. The army acquired almost three times as many 4.2 inch mortars and ten times as many 2.75 inch rockets as approved military plans required.[30] Research and development programs were often initiated without adequate review of the eventual cost and military utility of the weapon systems that they were likely to produce. Resources were wasted and other promising programs were hampered because of a lack of needed funds. A decoy missile, the Goose, was designed for use in conjunction with the B-52 to confuse enemy air defense. Eighty million was spent on the system before the decision was reached to cancel its development. It was finally realized that since the Goose could not be recalled once launched, it was incompatible with the B-52 which might have to be committed on ambiguous warnings.[31] Loosely applied financial and program controls under the Eisenhower administration were assigned the principal blame for these deficiencies.[32]

340

Third, military policy decisions were said to have been made on the basis of insufficient analysis of the comparative cost and effectiveness of forces and weapon systems designed to accomplish similar military missions. Navy and air force tactical aircraft requests, for example, were not assessed as part of an over-all strategic plan, nor were the air force's strategic atomic delivery systems against those of the navy's. Policy decisions about comparable military systems tended to be made in isolation from each other, and not on the basis of their corresponding cost and effectiveness in achieving defined military and political goals. Gaps developed in the acquisition of needed military capabilities, and resources were inefficiently applied across service lines to overlapping and duplicating programs.

Fourth, the Eisenhower administration was charged with having decided upon military force levels and weapon systems within too narrow a time frame. Their full developmental, investment, and operating costs were not carefully estimated. Since first-year costs were usually lower than the follow-on outlays, many programs were prematurely begun, only later to suffer excessive stretch outs or cancellation for lack of funds.[33]

Kennedy defense officials hinted further that the Eisenhower administration, including the President, had not exercised sufficiently strong leadership in pursuing many important aspects of defense policy. The military departments had filled the policy void. Service rivalry and, accordingly, the dilution of the capacity of elected and appointed political officials to define security and foreign policy goals were seen as the inevitable and unfortunate consequences. The Kennedy defense group under McNamara's forceful leadership determined early to assert its authority over the military and civilian bureaucracy and to assure its control over the formulation of defense policy. A strategy of flexible response could not tolerate, it was felt, large margins of error in the allocation of Defense Department resources or, more importantly, in the development of a force structure that could support varied and multiple security interests and

341

policy objectives. It demanded the active involvement of the political leadership corps of the executive branch in all major phases of the defense policy process, including planning, programming, and budgeting. It no less required the closest political direction of the deployment and use of military power, especially nuclear weapons. Even the setting of military requirements was judged to be too important a task to be left to the military. In the absence of precise and continuing political direction in these areas, those below in the administrative hierarchy, including the Joint Chiefs, would be unable to base their actions and decisions on a clear perception of the approved policy goals and procedural arrangements established by the politically responsible elements of the executive branch. Secretary McNamara indicated the principal factors underlying his innovations in defense procedures and organization to the House Armed Services Committee:

> We do have a basic management philosophy that we are trying to establish as a foundation for our day-to-day administration. It is a philosophy based on a decision pyramid and a system of administration in which all possible decisions are pushed to the bottom of that pyramid. But for intelligent decisions to be made at the bottom of the pyramid there must be a framework within which those decisions can be made. Basic policies must be established against which a decision-maker in the lower levels can compare his decision and gain some confidence that he is acting in accordance with a pattern of decisions elsewhere in the organization. This will lead to unity and strength, rather than an imbalance, which can only lead to weakness.
>
> And it is the establishment of these policies that can only be done at the top.
>
> The basic policy that we have established is a policy that shifts from a reliance on massive retaliation to the option response. . . . Now, this is a shift required, we believe, because of a change in the character of Soviet military forces in the world environment in which we find ourselves. . . . It is a shift, however, that requires a complete rebalancing of the military forces of this Nation, and *it is not something, therefore, that could be simply*

turned over to the services for them to decide unilaterally how they should proceed.

We must insure that the Army is balanced to the Air Force, that the Navy is balanced to the requirements of the Army, that the financial budget is balanced to the military force structure required as a foundation for our foreign policy.

It is this type of decision that comes up to my level and, until we translate this basic policy into a balanced force structure, I really know of no other way to follow. . . . through this transitional period.[34]

But how was political control to be reasserted and maintained? And, once asserted, what assurance was there that the decision of the secretary of defense was militarily sound, economically and administratively justifiable, and politically advantageous? Secretary McNamara faced much the same problem, in form at least, as his predecessors. If he was to lead his department rather than merely ratify the decisions reached elsewhere and brought to him for approval, he would have to accomplish two things: (1) he would have to have access to reliable military expertise and relevant military, economic, and political data to make strategic policy decisions, including the establishment of force level and weapon systems requirements for the services, from the point of view of the defense establishment as a whole; and (2) adequate political, administrative, and statutory authority to effect his decisions. These two sets of requirements were of course overlapping and reinforcing. To the extent that the secretary of defense could secure control over his department, he could, if he chose, secure the kind of information and expert judgment to make informed policy decisions. The reciprocal of this relation was similarly valid.

The secretary of defense approached the problems of expertise and control as interrelated. His most far-reaching innovation was the introduction of radically new budgetary and programming procedures.[35] The defense budget was reorganized into major program

343

packages. Nine such divisions were identified, for example, in the FY 1963 budget. These categories, such as Strategic Retaliatory Forces and General Purposes Forces,[36] cut across service lines and focused on the contributions that each of the services made to the missions assigned to the defense establishment. Each major program was divided into program elements. A program element "[was] defined as an integrated activity, a combination of men, equipment, and facilities which together constitute an identifiable military capability or support activity."[37] The program elements of Strategic Retaliatory Forces were aggregated into four subgroups: aircraft forces; missile forces, land based; missile forces, sea based; and command, control, communications, and support. The other major budgetary groupings were similarly subdivided. Each program element, in turn, could be reduced to the resource inputs—financial and non-financial— that comprised it. Resources categories might include men or materials such as fuel or equipment. Where heterogeneous items or activities were involved, dollar determinations were used. These resource inputs could then be translated into cost data that were uniformly collected and quantitatively expressed. These data could be subsequently related to existing appropriation and funding accounts.[38]

Military programs and their corresponding budgetary analogues were to be projected, moreover, for a five-year period. The program and budgetary plan for the Defense Department for the fiscal years 1963–67 was first devised by the Kennedy administration. It was presented to Congress along with the President's defense appropriations requests for FY 1963. "A 5-year period for both programs and costs was selected," noted Assistant Defense Secretary Charles Hitch, "as short enough to insure reasonably accurate estimates and long enough to provide a good approximation of the full cost [of any program]."[39] The five-year plan, since it encompassed all approved and operating programs, constituted a master plan for the defense establishment which could be centrally controlled by the Office of the Secretary of Defense (OSD) and, specifically, by the secretary himself.

A number of advantages were claimed for these budgetary procedures. They furnished planning standards and relevant operational data by which the cost-effectiveness of different and, in many instances, competing force levels and weapon systems could be evaluated at the secretarial level. Secretary McNamara explained the utility of these new arrangements to Congress.[40] The comparative advantages and disadvantages of the strategic retaliatory weapons available to the United States, for example, could be assessed in terms of their mission "to deter war by their capability to destroy the enemy's warmaking capabilities."[41] The major military factors that had to be weighed included the number and type of targets to be destroyed and the comparative capacity of the weapon delivery systems available to do the job. To determine the size and character of the forces which could most efficiently destroy the enemy's target system, each weapon delivery system was assessed in terms of the number and weight of its warhead capacity, enemy defense penetration capability, accuracy, reliability, and vulnerability. Since the cost of each system could be estimated with a considerable degree of precision, the combat effectiveness of each system per dollar outlay could thus be assessed. This form of analysis cut across service lines and centered the decision for military requirements for the defense establishment in the hands of the secretary of defense.

Through the five-year program-budgeting plan, the secretary of defense could maintain a balanced, yet changing, defense program which would continually relate the administration's strategic and foreign policies to the military capabilities and requirements needed to achieve them. Individual service programs could be tailored to complement and reinforce each other as parts of an over-all defense plan responsive to the political objectives determined by the leadership of the government. Tactical air power and air and sea lift capacity could be adjusted to the availability of ground troops that they were to support in battle. Service procurement could be closely tied to the availability of resources to preclude unrealistic or superfluous procurement planning. Deficiencies in inventory control or in unit readiness could presumably be corrected at the operating levels of the military establishment without clogging communication lines or burdening higher echelons with appeals for advice or authority before taking appropriate action. Planning would be centralized while operations would allegedly remain decentralized. At the secretarial level, the five-year plan appeared to provide a set of policy standards by which performance at the operating levels could be measured; at the working level, the plan furnished a detailed picture of the short- and long-term policies of the political leadership of the administration to guide decision and action.

The Kennedy defense group conceived of military planning, programming, and budgeting as a dynamic, on-going process, each element of which interacted with the other within a larger, rapidly changing technological, economic, and political environment. To assure defense establishment adaptability to these shifts within its sphere of action, elaborate provisions were made for changes at any time in defense programs and projects. Also established were periodic and comprehensive reviews of existing programs in May, August, and December to update them. These procedures for program adjustments were designed "to assure (1) that necessary changes are made in the [defense] program as required, (2) that these changes are made in an orderly way after thorough coordination within the Department of Defense, and (3) that all major changes are made only after approval by the Secretary of Defense."[42]

At the same time detailed precautions were taken to maintain tight secretarial control over the military establishment. Adapting the Defense Department to its environment was not to be accomplished at the expense of civil political control. The pervasive reach of the Office of the Secretary of Defense (OSD) and the secretary of defense is suggested by Mr. Hitch's description of the procedures governing program change for research and development. Under this heading, about three hundred and forty subactivities were identified for FY

346

1963. A shift in excess of two million dollars in any one of these sub-groups had to be specifically approved by OSD. Similar control arrangements were instituted for other major defense programs. From a theoretical viewpoint, fiscal control over the execution of both specific defense programs and their corresponding budget allotments could be achieved simultaneously within the framework of a single integrated system. Control would depend on the accuracy of the alignment of resource categories to program elements (military outputs) and appropriations accounts (financial inputs). Once an accurate alignment was achieved or closely approximated, control over major defense programs and program elements could be exercised through the manipulation of financial and non-financial resource inputs. Performance reports from the military departments to OSD would be presented in terms of program elements and resource categories, "combined with the determination of the more significant existing or expected deviations."[43] This "feedback" information generated by this control system would "'close the loop' in the planning-execution-control cycle."[44] The secretary of defense, therefore, would be freed to concentrate principally on policy problems involving the approval of program proposals, confident in the expectation that "significant deviations" would be reported to his office. Moreover, proposals for major changes in program or for the initiation of new programs would be projected over a sufficiently long period of time to assess their principal cost and their military effectiveness. Programs would not be initiated unless they would eventually serve a military use at a cost that compared favorably with other military capabilities that could perform the same function. Decisions about the merit of variously proposed innovations, particularly in research and development, would be made at an earlier stage of the decision process and largely on a determination rendered by OSD which would be independent of service dictation. An exchange between Defense Comptroller Charles Hitch and members of the House Government Operations Committee clarified these facets of the new program procedures:

347

Mr. Hitch: I think there is a systematic tendency to under-estimate costs.

Mr. Holifield: In order to get the foot in the door?

Mr. Hitch: In order to get the foot in the door.

Mr. Holifield: And they say, 'We are sorry, but we have to have more.'

Mr. Hitch: We just have to have the capability to smell out this sort of thing when it is happening.

. . . .

Mr. Roback: Do you get consistent understatements of costs of systems?

Mr. Hitch: I think there is certainly a tendency for costs to be understated in certain circumstances, and this is particularly true when the service or department or agency or contractor is trying to get his system or equipment accepted and approved. . . . This is why I think we have to have *an independent capability*.

Mr. Holifield: For evaluation?

Mr. Hitch: To evaluate the submissions.[45]

Furthermore, a continual updating of the five-year planning-programming-budgetary cycle facilitated the presentation of the annual defense budget to Congress. Each annual budget would be conceived as an increment to the approved five-year plan.[46] For any specified time period within the five-year cycle, testified Defense Secretary McNamara, a military budget could be "abstracted from the continually modified and continually adjusted military program." [47] In contrast to previous experience, suggested Defense Comptroller Hitch, the task of assembling the budget for congressional review would not have to be "crammed into a few weeks in the midst of the annual budget review." [48]

348

Improved budgetary procedures and financial controls, including "an independent capability" to evaluate cost data, could not by themselves secure secretarial control over the defense establishment. Control required more than the holding down of defense costs. President Kennedy had assigned his defense secretary two responsibilities. He was to "(1) develop the force structure necessary to meet . . . [the nation's] military requirements without regard to arbitrary budget ceilings, and (2) procure and operate this force at the lowest possible cost." [49] Tighter and more precise cost control over Defense Department operations would not necessarily produce a force structure relevant to the nation's foreign policies or security interests. Kennedy officials recognized that cost control ultimately depended on the determination of service force levels and weapons systems. This realization again posed the dual need of the defense secretary. He needed quick access to the data and expertise which were required to evaluate service proposals on a defense-wide basis and, equally important, he needed the authoritative approval of the Joint Chiefs for his decisions.[50] Armed with these elements, the defense secretary would then be in a most advantageous position to enlist strong presidential backing for his defense policies. The success of the secretary's presentations to Congress and the public critically hinged on the President's support.

These were not new problems for a defense secretary. They were endemic to the defense organization and inherent in the relation between the political leadership of the Pentagon and the administration, on the one hand, and the professional military corps, on the other. Secretary James Forrestal had experienced the same difficulties in his formulation of the FY 1950 budget.[51] Each of the services had presented budgetary claims twice as large as the administration was willing to spend for defense. Forrestal was unable to appeal to a military or civilian group to aid his independent evaluation of service-determined requirements. His improvised establishment of the

McNarney Board was not an adequate substitute for the authoritative military judgments and support that he sought, but failed, to secure through the Joint Chiefs of Staff. Forrestal's fight for a balanced force structure was lost in the struggle over the FY 1950 budget. His defeat was foreshadowed in his inability to produce agreement among the Joint Chiefs on service roles and missions at Key West and Newport in 1948. Forrestal reluctantly acceded to a budgetary compromise in which each service received an approximately equal share of the funds available to the defense establishment. A balanced force, related to a coherently articulated strategic view, was reduced to a balanced budget which was more responsive to autonomous service demands for separate but equal treatment within President Truman's $15 billion limit on military spending than to the nation's strategic and foreign policy imperatives.

The frustration experienced by Forrestal prompted his recommendation that the secretary of defense be granted more authority over the defense establishment. Many of his suggestions were incorporated into the 1949 amendments to the National Security Act of 1947. The 1949 changes downgraded the service departments and placed them under a single executive department. The secretary of defense was granted "direction, authority, and control over the Department of Defense." [52] A non-voting chairman of the Joint Chiefs of Staff was also created along with a deputy secretary and three assistant secretaries of defense. Under Title IV of the 1949 act, an assistant secretary was to head a newly established comptroller department for the Defense Department.

The 1949 reorganization was merely the first phase of a long evolutionary development in defense organization and procedures that has gradually increased the authority of the secretary of defense and increasingly assisted his access to the military information, expertise, and, accordingly, the political power to be derived from these sources, in order to define and adequately defend his military policies. The 1958 Defense Reorganization Act was particularly significant. The

Joint Staff was increased from 210 to 400 officers and placed more directly under the management of the chairman of the JCS who was granted the right to vote.[53] A director of research and engineering was also created with broad authority to supervise the research and development activities of the Defense Department. The secretary of defense was also authorized to "assign any weapon systems developed to such production and operation control as he may determine."[54] The secretary of defense, moreover, could combine common activities of the services and assign them to a separate organizational unit. His authority extended, too, to the designation of combat forces to unified and specified commands.

Drawing on these enlarged legislative authorizations and on the precedents of the defense secretaries who had served in office before him, Secretary McNamara developed a number of means by which he could assess service proposals and requirements and by which he could translate his policy decisions into operational results. McNamara indicated during his first months in office that he would make increasing use of the Joint Staff to supply him with information and advice to help him evaluate service recommendations on the basis of the over-all mission of the Defense Department. "The Joint Staff, being composed of experienced officers from all military services," McNamara told the Jackson subcommittee on national policy machinery, "has the potential of becoming a most valuable asset to the Department of Defense, *as a whole*. I am attempting to realize the potential by strengthening the participation of the Joint Staff in Department of Defense strategic deliberations."[55] Of the more than 100 special defense studies initiated by Secretary McNamara during 1961, approximately one-third were assigned to the Joint Staff.[56] The staff has steadily grown in response to the secretary's increased reliance upon it. While the Joint Staff has maintained a full complement of 400 officers, its statutory limit, another 1,170 military and civilian personnel work in close association with it through the Organization of the Joint Chiefs of Staff. These figures contrast with the

308 civilians and military personnel, including members of the Joint Staff, which comprised the JCS Organization in June, 1958. As of January, 1965, the Joint Staff included three lieutenant generals or vice admirals heading its principal sections or division and a lieutenant general who served as director.[57]

The JCS has been drawn more deeply than in the past into the preparation of the Defense Department budget. The trend toward military-economic decision-making which General Ridgway had resisted under the Eisenhower administration has nevertheless grown. The Kennedy defense group rejected both the Eisenhower view of permitting the military to set down its requirements within stated budgetary limits and Ridgway's conception of military professionalism that demanded exemption from the task of having to consider economic and political factors in deciding military policy.[58] Kennedy defense officials acted, in effect, on the assumption that the Eisenhower administration had not integrated the military and budgetary phases of the defense policy process either early or continuously enough or at a sufficiently high and sophisticated level of decision. The JCS reportedly held sixty-four meetings on the force requirements and budget estimates of the FY 1964 budget and 104 such sessions concerning the FY 1965 budget.[59] The JCS, according to General Earle G. Wheeler, its chairman, also participated actively in the discussion of major program and budget changes, such as the air force's RS-70 and its proposal for an "advanced manned strategic system" and the army's request for a new weapons helicopter.[60] Differences were expressed by each chief on these and other issues, and their varying views were made available, indeed solicited, by the secretary of defense for his final decision.[61] The increased use of the Joint Chiefs as a corporate body in deciding budgetary and program problems is suggested by General Maxwell Taylor's testimony before the House appropriations defense group on the increased workload of the JCS as a corporate entity, a development that Taylor's leadership of the JCS had encouraged:

Certainly . . . the Joint Chiefs of Staff participated more in this budget [FY 1964] than in any other budget I have been connected with in the past. I am speaking of the Joint Chiefs *as a corporate body.* . . . It has always been something of a question as to what extent the Joint Chiefs should get into the budget. . . . I find we can now get into it just about as much as we want to. By the program change device, all the program changes are available to the Chiefs for comment. We select only those of major importance for consideration, comment, and recommendations to the Secretary of Defense.

With regard to the budget this year, after October 1, [1962] when I became Chairman, there were a series of very important meetings held to comment on the Secretary's proposed position on several of the most important subjects. For example, we commented on the major force tabulations through the fiscal year 1967, the service and DOD proposals for modifying force levels and procurement rates in the 5-year program, the military assistance program, the logistics guidance and then on some of the major weapons programs such as the Skybolt, RS-70, and Nike-Zeus.[62]

An integral facet of Defense Secretary McNamara's mode of operation is to encourage different and conflicting points of view within the defense organization, while jealously reserving to himself the final resolution of policy disagreements. Service rivalry is used as a control mechanism by which the defense secretary can secure the opposing service opinions on the merit of each other's proposed requirements and recommendations for new weapons development.[63] McNamara has continued the practice of Defense Secretary Thomas Gates and meets frequently with the JCS to discuss a wide variety of defense and administration problems. He attended thirteen of the sixty-four meetings at which the JCS examined the FY 1964 defense budget. These meetings serve at least three important functions: (1) they expedite JCS decisions in that the defense secretary can more easily and quickly aid in resolving conflicting views or can negotiate an acceptable compromise; (2) they inform the defense secretary of JCS opinion at first hand; and (3) they indicate to the service chiefs the direction and scope of the secretary's thinking. A two-way flow of information and opinion is thus maintained.[64]

The door to the JCS is still that of its chairman. Secretary Forrestal's recommendation to Congress that the post of chairman be created was in great part conditioned by his inability to produce service harmony on strategic policy. From his sad experience in working with the JCS, and conscious of the precedent of Admiral William D. Leahy during World War II, Forrestal saw the need for a chairman who would continually present the defense secretary's viewpoint to the JCS, would inform the secretary about current JCS thinking, and would recommend his own course of action on strategic defense problems free from the competing pressures that must inevitably weigh in the decisions of the service chiefs.[65] Unlike them, the chairman would not be simultaneously a member of the JCS, a corporate agency designed to advise the secretary of defense on military questions, and the head of a military branch with its own perspective and material and human requirements. He would be primarily responsive to the needs of the defense secretary.

The importance of the chairman in defense policy formulation has steadily grown since Congress formally established the post in 1949. Its growth was given impetus by the tenure of Admiral Arthur Radford, who played a significant role in defense planning under the Eisenhower administration. The 1958 Defense Reorganization Act which granted the chairman the right to vote in JCS deliberations merely ratified and reinforced, rather than conferred, the pre-eminence of the chairman.[66] On twenty-three split decisions within the JCS between 1955 and 1959, the chairman's position, which was expressed on twenty-one of these issues, was supported by the secretary of defense on eighteen occasions, a total higher than that of any of the service chiefs who had participated in all of the controversies. Such support, as General Maxwell Taylor has suggested, is easy enough to understand. The chairman must be, first of all, personally acceptable to the defense secretary. Conflict between them would impair the position of the secretary of defense vis-à-vis either the President in whom his political authority must ultimately rest or the individual chiefs. Serious personal or policy rifts between the secretary of defense and the chairman present an intolerable situation for both. At such an impasse, one or the other must resign or be replaced.

As if to prophesy his own strong relation with Secretary of Defense McNamara, General Taylor has described the chairman's job as a kind of "party whip" for the secretary of defense and, by implication, the administration in fashioning service consensus on defense policy. The chairman must act in this capacity if he is to be responsive to the secretary's double need for military expertise and political support from within the military profession for his policy decisions. Said General Taylor:

> Certainly, it is important to the Secretary of Defense that the Chairman retain this predominant position.
>
> A Secretary of Defense needs a strong Chairman to direct the work of the Chiefs, to keep their noses to the grindstone, and to extract from them timely advice and recommendations—preferably of a kind which can be accepted and approved without embarrassment. Advice can be unpalatable and unwelcome, particularly if it runs afoul of political or economic considerations which the Administration holds in great store. A Secretary will look to the Chairman to prevent this kind of advice and to bring forth harmonious views on appropriate subjects which can then be used in support of the Department's programs. If the Chairman is to perform this function, obviously the Secretary must back him on the split issues. . . .
>
> Thus, the Chairman has come to be a sort of party whip, charged with conveying the official line to the Chiefs in the hope and expectation that they will be guided thereby in their actions. . . . Regardless of my disagreements with Admiral Radford, I always had a grudging admiration for his singleness

355

of purpose and his undeniable effectiveness in driving through the programs of the New Look.[67]

The chairman's presumed military knowledge and his close contact with the management of the Joint Staff, including his appointment of its director, provide important sources of power to the secretary of defense. Through them he can gain the military advice that he needs. Just as importantly, by enlisting the prestige and backing of the chairman, the secretary can influence jcs deliberations or can blunt service criticism of his actions.

McNamara, like his predecessors, has pursued a policy of promoting those military officers to higher command who, while they may differ with some of his policy positions, are willing to confine their disagreements to established Pentagon channels and are basically sympathetic to the secretary's method of reaching military-politico-economic decisions. It is no accident that General Taylor should have been made chairman of the Joint Chiefs of Staff after his brief tenure as the special military representative of President Kennedy. Many of the reforms in defense policy that Taylor advocated were implemented under McNamara's direction.

The defense secretary has also ignored precedent in securing presidential appointment of the chairman of the jcs and of individual service chiefs. A presumption had developed in some military quarters that the chairman's post would be shared on a rotating basis among the services. Until Taylor's appointment a cycle of rotation had been retained.[68] McNamara's departure from precedent to replace General Lyman Lemnitzer with another army general suggested his intention to obtain the appointment of a chairman who was sensitive to his strategic thinking and mode of operation. The appointment of Army General Earle Wheeler to succeed Taylor, who was sent as United States ambassador to South Vietnam, adds another thread to the McNamara pattern of officer appointment to the jcs. The surprise choice of Lieutenant General Harold Johnson as army chief of staff to succeed Wheeler in 1964, although he ranked forty-four on the army's list of general officers, further reflects the secretary's purpose to work with officers responsive to his point of view despite their lower standing on the service rolls of their armed branch.[69]

This pattern for which there was ample precedent in previous administrations is to be detected, too, in the reassignment or retirement of officers from the JCS who conflicted with the defense secretary not only on what policies should be adopted but also on how they should be handled. Admiral George Anderson was not reappointed to his post as chief of naval operations, but was sent instead to Portugal as the American ambassador. The partial reappointment of General Curtis LeMay for only a year's tenure—later extended for a few months—as air force chief of staff was conditioned in some part by his public disagreements with Secretary McNamara. Both Anderson and LeMay broke with McNamara on a number of vital issues. Admiral Anderson differed with McNamara on Defense Department carrier policy and the secretary's decision in the TFX contract dispute involving the development of a new tactical fighter. General LeMay was similarly unhappy with the TFX decision. Like Anderson, he preferred the development of separate fighter aircraft for the navy and air force instead of the single design decided upon by Secretary McNamara. General LeMay also vigorously objected to the secretary's refusal to advance the development of the B-70 or RS-70 bomber beyond a prototype program.[70] The appointment of General Lyman Lemnitzer as supreme allied commander in Europe for NATO forces has relevance in this context. Although General Lemnitzer was receptive to most of the substantive policy changes initiated by Secretary McNamara, he reportedly objected to some of the changes in the defense decision process, the short deadlines set by the defense secretary for JCS replies to his queries, and the bypassing of the military chiefs on a number of occasion.[71]

Reliance on the judgment of military officers has, of course, not been the sole means by which the secretary of defense has appealed for advice and information in forming defense policy. Secretary McNamara has strengthened his own office for these purposes. At the close of 1964, the Office of the Secretary of Defense contained sixteen presidential appointees of the rank of assistant secretary or higher. According to the estimate of Hanson Baldwin, the eleven deputy assistant secretaries of defense in 1962 approximately tripled in number two years later. The expenditures of the secretary's office have doubled between FY 1961 and FY 1963, climbing from $1.07 billion to $2.15 billion. The percentage increase in over-all defense expenditures meanwhile has been closer to 10 per cent.[72]

Of primary importance is the defense secretary's reliance on the Office of the Defense Comptroller and on the director of defense research and engineering. The enhanced role of the comptroller in cost analysis and control is obvious enough. What is not so clearly seen perhaps is the crucial importance of the director of research and engineering in influencing future defense policy. The determination whether proposed weapon systems, based on estimates of their technical feasibility and their military need, should be developed falls within the jurisdiction of the research director. The JCS and the military services still retain operating capabilities for weapons development and are provided channels through which they can present their views on weapons designs, but their proposals enjoy no necessary presumption of favor or validity. Cost analysis of new weapons proposals comes increasingly under the close scrutiny of the Comptroller's Office. Technical and scientific analysis of these proposals is correspondingly the responsibility of the director of research and engineering. Since modern weaponry is so expensive and depends so critically on scientific and technical knowledge and advancement, the advice and influence of military officers on weapons development has inevitably declined to the extent that scientific opinion and cost data must be taken increasingly into account. The greater reliance of the secretary of defense on scientific advisers who are outside the direct control of the military branches is both reflected and reinforced in

358

the directive of the defense secretary which made the Weapons System Evaluation Group, used by the Eisenhower administration to advise the JCS on strategic problems and weapons development, more responsive to the director of research and engineering.[73] The defense secretary is also in a stronger position to secure independent analysis of the evolving international environment and its impact on military requirements through the assistant secretary of defense for International Security Affairs (ISA) and the Defense Intelligence Agency (DIA), which now combines many of the separate and often overlapping intelligence activities once carried on by the individual services.[74]

Implications of process change.—The centralization of policy-making in the Office of the Secretary of Defense and in the person of the secretary himself has a number of significant implications both with respect to internal Defense Department decision-making and to relations with Congress. Service rivalry, while it still continues as it did under the Eisenhower administration, has gradually been transformed into a bilateral conflict between the services, either singly or in combination, and OSD or the defense secretary. This pattern recurs repeatedly in the defense conflicts that were fought on the congressional battleground during the Eighty-seventh Congress. In Congress' review of the FY 1962 and FY 1963 military budgets, the services can be seen to direct their criticism less at each other than at the secretary of defense. It is within OSD that the crucial decisions affecting service force levels and weapon systems—indeed the future—of each service are made. The JCS, as a corporate agency, still plays a role in defense decision-making despite the specialized relation of the chairman and the secretary of defense. Under McNamara's management of the defense establishment, it appears fair to argue that the JCS has participated directly in the determination of a larger number of important issues than under the Eisenhower administration. Its increased workload suggests its enlarged responsibilities in handling

359

planning, programming, and budgeting problems. Its integration into the new procedures for program change and clearance with the secretary of defense and OSD has widened its purview over policy questions. However, it would appear that its actual capacity to influence the determination of defense policy and military requirements has receded since the Eisenhower period. This curious turnabout stems not only from the growth of the secretary's power and his willingness to assert himself on policy issues but also from the fact that the JCS now operates within a larger decision framework that is composed of an expanding universe of assistant and deputy assistant secretaries and super-defense agencies,[75] each of which contributes its own perspective and expertise to strategic policy development.

The JCS suffers the same downgrading that most defense committees have experienced since McNamara's entry into office. For McNamara, committees should advise; they should not decide. "I feel that committees can serve a useful purpose," Secretary McNamara told the Jackson subcommittee on national policy machinery in 1961, "but they cannot be considered substitutes for creative leadership and personal responsibility for such leadership. Nor in my opinion should they be thought of as decision-making bodies, but rather, their function should be limited to that of a forum in which advice can be exchanged." [76] In a speech made two years later to newspaper editors, McNamara again confirmed his view that defense policy must rest in the hands of the secretary of defense, the principal political officer of the Defense Department:

> Although it is important to consider a variety of alternative policies, at the end we must have one defense policy, not three conflicting defense policies. And it is the job of the Secretary and his staff to make sure that this is the case. . . .
> There is nothing innately desirable about centralization. But the fact remains that when national security decisions affect broad interests they must be made from a central point, not from

subordinate points each specially concerned with one part of the forest—and not even by a committee made up of representatives of the different parts of the forest. For the nature of committees is to compromise their special interests, which is not the same as making the decision from the point of the national interest.[77]

Negotiation, bargaining, and controversy still proceed between the secretary of defense and the JCS, including separate confrontations between the secretary and a service chief. Defense Secretary McNamara has admitted, for example, that, at the request of the military services, he had reversed "about 60" of the 620 separate decisions that he had made on the FY 1963 budget, apart from major force structure decisions.[78] What is critical to recognize, however, is that these interactions between the secretary and the chiefs are not conducted on equal terms. The secretary of defense, by and large, defines the terms of bargaining and negotiation, and sets limits on what compromises can be reached.[79] Controversy over defense policy has certainly marked the Kennedy and Johnson administrations, but while the discussion and debate within the Defense Department have ranged over a broad number of problems, the actual political maneuverability of the services to change or modify decisions reached by the secretary of defense has been narrowed. End-runs to Congress to seek redress have continued to occur, most notably in the case of the TFX and the RS-70.[80] These and other attempts to secure congressional leverage to overturn the secretary's determinations have in large measure failed. Groups within Congress have disagreed with the defense secretary on a large number of issues, including military requirements for outer space, reserve policy, nuclear propulsion for ships and aircraft, Nike-Zeus, army modernization, civilian control over the military, and defense organization, but the position of the defense secretary has generally prevailed. As the secretary notches one victory after another in his confrontations with Congress, the incentives within the Pentagon to

361

circumvent his decisions outside established Defense Department channels for dissent are decreased. They are not likely to be eliminated so long as the services remain separately organized and their chiefs, while responsive to the secretary's need for military advice and counsel, continue to guard their own independent bases of authority. Nevertheless, each success of the secretary in the congressional area tends to strengthen his bargaining position with the services and before Congress.

Secretary McNamara's gathering of the reins of Defense Department control may be, as some have contended, a tribute more to his personal effort than to the organizational and procedural innovations that he has instituted. On this point the secretary has demurred.[81] McNamara and his chief associates argue that their reforms have not overtaxed them personally.[82] McNamara insists that he operates at his proper level, concentrating on the resolution of policy issues related to major Defense Department plans. Issues for decision are alleged to be sufficiently focused, yet comprehensive, in terms of their programmatic and budgetary implications to permit considered secretarial judgment. The number and difficulty of these issues is adequately controlled, with ample incentive and opportunity for decentralized decision and action, to preclude overloading at the osd level. Other defense secretaries, McNamara insists, can easily adjust to the institutional arrangements that he has introduced into the military establishment. The permanence that is intended for these innovations in the defense process and the importance that McNamara attaches to them is suggested in his testimony before the House defense appropriations group in 1964:

> Mr. Mahon: . . . It is said as long as you have Robert McNamara as Secretary of Defense, the Department of Defense will run well under the system, but when his term of office expires, it will be most unlikely that you will get a man of the capability and the background and experience and industry of McNamara, and that the system which he is building up may

prove in the long run to be a detriment rather than an advancement of the cause of national defense.

Secretary McNamara: I think quite the contrary. . . . The basic objective of the management system we are introducing and trying to operate, is to establish a rational foundation as opposed to an emotional foundation for the decisions as to what size force and what type of force this country will maintain. This rational structure, this intellectual foundation for determining the military forces we should build and support, is something that is laid out on paper. It is laid out first in the form of an analysis of the potential contingency war plans for a variety of situations and, then, a translation of those war plans into military forces. And finally, that force structure must be translated into programs and budgets. There is no reason in the world why this cannot be continued in the future. As matter of fact, I think it must be continued in the future, and I think, if the executive branch does not continue it, Congress itself can force a continuation of it.

Mr. Flood: Would you not consider that your greatest legacy? . . . .

Secretary McNamara: The answer is "Yes, indeed." The introduction of a rational foundation for military force planning, to be quite frank with you, is what we are trying to establish. . . . Once one has a rational foundation from which to begin, it is relatively easy to decide not to have a particular weapon system, the requirement for which cannot be found in the rationalization of the program.

Mr. Flood: I have always been concerned . . . that in your eagerness to do what you have done so well, that you are not Alexander the Great and break down and cry because there are no other hard decisions to make. . . .

Secretary McNamara: There are a few left I can think of. . . . [83]

The integration of planning, programming, and budgeting is the key to McNamara's successful centralization of power in his office.

The Eisenhower administration had permitted these facets of the decision process to remain fragmented and loosely co-ordinated. The consolidation process, including provision for continued readjustment in all these areas, has operationally had the effect of unifying the services in terms of a single defense plan. Notwithstanding the legal basis on which the three branches have maintained their independence, the secretary of defense is now armed with adequate statutory authority, which both Secretaries Gates and McNamara have shown little hesitancy in exercising, to transfer, co-ordinate, and consolidate service activities in terms of over-all Defense Department missions. The program-budgeting system utilized by McNamara acts as a substitute for formal service unification since the contributions of the services to the accomplishment of the purposes of the defense establishment can be evaluated comparatively on the basis of uniformly applied cost-effectiveness yardsticks to similar military service activities.[84] In the mind of Secretary McNamara, planning and budgeting (which in the McNamara scheme implies programming) are simply different facets of one integrative process of rational decision-making. "I equate planning and budgeting and consider the terms almost synonymous, the budget being simply a quantitative expression of the operating plans," he told the Jackson subcommittee.[85]

Eighty-seventh Congress and the Defense Policy Process

DIFFUSION OF THE LEGISLATIVE DEFENSE PROCESS

Background.—As if in counterpoint to the centralization of the Defense Department under Secretaries Gates and McNamara, the defense policy and budget process in Congress became more decentralized. With the major exception of military pay, construction, and assistance which required specific legislative authorizations before appropriations could be passed by Congress, the House and Senate defense appropriations groups had been the primary instruments by which Congress exercised its power of the purse over military policy. The defense appropriations bills which carried the bulk of the Defense Department's annual request for funding authority had been centrally reviewed by these subcommittees. Section 412(b) of the Military Construction Authorization Act of 1959 significantly modified this arrangement. It introduced the armed services committees once more into the center of the annual defense budgeting and programming process from which they had been effectively barred, largely as a result of their self-abdication of power and responsibility, since World War II. Section 412(b) provided that:

> No funds may be appropriated after December 31, 1960, to or for the use of any armed force of the United States for the procurement of aircraft, missiles, or naval vessels unless the appropriation of such funds has been authorized by legislation enacted after such date.[86]

The surface effect of Section 412(b) has been clear. Since 1961, Congress has essentially asserted its power of the purse in defense policy through four, not two, committees.

No one factor explains the introduction of this novel procedural layer into the congressional defense decision process.[87] Section 412(b) grows out of a tangle of historical circumstances and mixed committee and personal motives as well as divergent conceptions of the military requirements of strategic policy, both as to their cost and effectiveness, and of Congress' role and mode of action in determining them.

There is a sharp theoretical distinction made in Congress, though not always observed in practice, between authorizations and appropriations. Most governmental programs must first be authorized by an appropriate legislative committee before Congress can appropriate funds for their implementation. The relations between the legislative committees and the appropriations committees or, more precisely, the appropriations subcommittees which pass on the different parts of the President's budget, vary from one policy sector to another. In some areas, the legislative committees dominate the congressional policy process. Farm legislation represents one extreme. The basic price support formula established by the agriculture committees effectively controls the amount and distribution of appropriations which can be recommended by the corresponding farm appropriations groups. Until the passage of Section 412(b), the opposite situation obtained in the relations of the armed services and defense appropriations subcommittees. Legislative authorizations for the procurement of aircraft, missiles, and vessels, were cast in such vague legislative terms and the ceilings on their acquisition were set so high that they provided little or no operational guideline either for the Pentagon or for the appropriations committees in formulating policy in these areas.

Throughout the 1950's the legislation governing army and air force aircraft and missile procurement was the Army and Air Force Authorization and Composition Act of 1950.[88] The secretary of the air force was authorized to "procure guided missiles and 24,000 serviceable aircraft or 225,000 airframe tons of serviceable aircraft, whichever the secretary considers appropriate."[89] The number of missiles to be purchased was not specified, and those which were to be acquired were specifically exempt from the weight limitation on airframe procurement. The secretary of the army enjoyed similar latitude in procuring for army needs. He was authorized to "procure materials and facilities necessary to maintain and support the Army . . . including . . . guided missiles; modern standard items of equipment; equipment to replace obsolete and unserviceable equipment; necessary spare . . . materials, and parts; and such reserve of supplies as is needed to enable the Army to perform its mission."[90] The

366

air force and army were free to define their force levels and weapon systems within these broad gauged categories. These limits served the purpose more of preserving the legal authority of Congress and the jurisdictional prerogatives of the armed services committees to specify service procurement levels than of providing an operationally relevant and reliable means by which Congress could actively participate through its armed services committees in military and strategic policy.

The navy shared in Congress' liberal dispensations of procurement authority for its aircraft, missile, and ship construction programs. The secretary of the navy was granted blanket permission to "conduct research and development relating to guided missiles and [to] procure and construct guided missiles."[91] No checkrein on acquisition was provided. On behalf of the navy, the President was permitted to "acquire, construct, or manufacture naval airplanes, spare parts, and equipment necessary to provide and maintain 15,000 useful naval airplanes."[92] Whatever significance the 15,000 limit may have had was nullified by the added proviso that the navy secretary could ignore this ceiling "to meet the needs of the national defense."[93] The secretary's range of discretion was of dubious applicability since the aircraft program of the navy and marine corps never approached the limit set for it. Naval and marine corps *operating* aircraft on the eve of the Korean War totaled less than 5,000 planes. Despite the Korean hostilities and the increased aircraft attrition rates that were incurred, none of the services were forced to request additional procurement authorizations. The pre-Korean War determinations were sufficient.

Authorizations for naval vessels supplied an even more glaring example of loose legislative oversight by the armed services committees. The Vinson-Trammel Act of 1934, as amended, adequately fed not only most of the navy's voracious appetite for ships during World War II but also throughout the postwar period until the adoption of Section 412(b). By Representative Carl Vinson's estimate, the navy still possessed 2.5 million tons of vessel construction authority when Section 412(b) came into effect.[94]

Partly as a consequence of these extensive delegations of procurement authority, most of the important battles over air force, army, and navy force structure were fought within the arena of the defense appropriations subcommittees. The congressional-executive struggle over the size and composition of the air force, both before and after the Korean War, was centered in Congress' annual consideration of the defense appropriations bill. Dramatic entries into military policy by the armed services committees—in the carrier controversy of 1949, the Far East hearings of 1951, or the Symington air power investigation of 1956—placed in relief their loss of continuing impact on the direction and scope of defense policy. The primary channel for ongoing Pentagon-congressional contact occurred through the defense appropriations groups.

The armed services committees did maintain their prerogatives over military pay and personnel and military construction, while review responsibility for military assistance programs was granted to the foreign-affairs committees. The armed services committees gradually discovered, however, that their passage of pay and personnel legislation had little direct or significant effect on defense policy and on the nation's military strategic posture. Authorizations for personnel were established, like those for hardware procurement, with little regard to the operational needs of foreign and strategic policy. Army and air force strength, shortly before the North Korean attack, were set at 837,000 and 502,000, respectively.[95] Navy and marine corps enlisted personnel ceilings were defined, in turn, at 500,000 and 400,000 levels. Officers were to be procured at a fixed percentage of these totals.[96] These ceilings were suspended at the outbreak of Korean hostilities and have been subsequently extended on four other occasions.[97]

368

Even if these personnel ceilings had been more closely related to strategic requirements, they would still not have furnished Congress nor the armed services committees a sufficiently precise legislative tool with which to survey or to shape military policy. For the technological revolution in weaponry, ushered in by World War II, had rendered this legislative technique obsolete. Up to World War II, personnel totals were a crude index of a nation's military power. Advances in military mobility and fire power since the 1930's have depreciated the value of sheer numbers in open warfare. Modern armies, as the Communist Chinese discovered in Korea, depend on the quality and quantity of their arms and, by extension, on the productive capacity and scientific and technical skill of the nation which supplies them. Governmental policies for military procurement and the encouragement of research and development are, therefore, the blueprints from which the nation's immediate and future military prowess are constructed. To the extent that Congress influenced these plans and other aspects of military policy after World War II, the appropriations defense groups, not the armed services committees, must be considered the principal architects of the nation's military force structure.

The issue is posed.—Against this background of more than a decade and a half of the self-isolation of the armed services committees from the centers of defense policy, a number of congressional-executive clashes over defense reorganization and air-defense policy occurred that precipitated the drafting of Section 412(b). The issue of the proper role and jurisdictional prerogatives of the armed services committees was initially drawn in explicit terms in the Senate hearings on the Defense Reorganization Act of 1958. Ralph Flanders, long-time Republican Senator from Vermont, raised the problem when he complained that he had never been presented a comprehensive statement of the nation's defense policies and force structure either as a member of the armed services committee or as an ex officio member of the appropriations defense group. He said that he lacked any basis on which to evaluate the force and weapon system requirements presented by the Defense Department whether in relation to the military threats facing the nation or to the budgetary and manpower considerations that may have shaped them.[98] Senator Flanders reached the unsettling conclusion that he and his colleagues on the armed services committee had been derelict in carrying out their legislative duties. "I have felt," he told Defense Secretary Neil McElroy, "that I was unable to perform my constitutional responsibilities simply because I have not seen such a comprehensive approach to the structure of defense presented to me at any time. . . . It is the presentation of a defense structure and the examination of it by this committee which it seems to me would lead to a better carrying out of the duties that are làid upon us than we can do at the present time." [99] Flanders suggested a procedure by which the Defense Department would present an annual authorization bill which would set out service requirements in terms of their missions and would include "the manpower, armament, equipment, and construction program for each." [100] His view, while not detailed in the Senate defense reorganization hearings, was broad in scope. It would also have encompassed requirements for the reserves of the various armed services.[101] Flanders specifically denied that the annual appropriations process or the "scattered [defense] briefings taking place during the year" were a substitute for the authorization plan that he advocated.[102]

Flanders' remarks came at a critical point in congressional-executive relations. The administration's 1958 defense reorganization proposals were made in partial response to the sputnik launching and were conceived as a means of securing, through greater organizational unity, a harmony among the services on strategic policy, an end to service rivalry over weapon systems control and development, and a general speed up in Defense Department decision-making to enhance operational readiness and save money. The armed services committees, on the basis of their limited experience with the annual construction authorization bills, were acutely aware of the difficulty of securing these objectives and were dubious about the relevance of organizational solutions to substantive policy problems. They shared, too, a concern and anxiety, common to their colleagues throughout the Congress, that the United States was slipping behind the Soviet Union in military strength, particularly in long-range missiles, and that the administration was doing little to counteract this ominous development.

Democratic members of the Senate Armed Services Committee contested the defense secretary's need for more legislative authority to speed missile progress. They resisted the administration's insinuation in its request for a director of research and engineering that Congress had failed to provide adequate authority to the defense secretary to silence service squabbles, which were cited as a major cause of waste and duplication in defense operations and a primary obstacle to rapid Defense Department adjustment to expanding Soviet military power. They shied, too, at the imputation that they shared responsibility for the weaknesses of the defense program which the flight of sputnik dramatically revealed.[103] Committee members remembered that they had intervened in Defense Department weapon system controversies on a number of occasions because the secretary of defense had not acted quickly or decisively enough to resolve them. Senator Stennis offered as proof the fact that his armed services subcommittee on military construction had precipitated a timely decision in the air force–army clash over the Talos and Nike missiles. The subcommittee's action had prevented continued wasteful expenditures for the competing systems.[104] To settle the quarrel in the absence of secretarial initiative, the authorization group had struck the air force's Talos authorization requests from the FY 1957 air defense program. After some struggle, both with the House Armed Services Committee and the President, involving, in the latter instance, a veto of the first military construction bill, the authorization deletion for

Talos had been sustained. The demise of Talos had been formalized by Defense Secretary Charles Wilson in November, 1956, when he had assigned jurisdiction over the weapon to the army, which had favored Nike development. In the midst of the defense reorganization hearings, the military construction group had acted again to settle another army–air force fight over the merits of their respective Nike-Hercules and Bomarc A missiles. As a warning to the services and to the defense secretary, the authorization requests of both systems had been slashed by 20 per cent.[105]

Involvement in two cases of weapon systems competition between the services provided sparse evidence that the armed services committees had maintained a constant and comprehensive surveillance of defense policy or had consciously evaluated and independently judged the merit of its major facets on an ongoing basis. Senator Flanders' criticisms of the committee's exercise of its power were not entirely groundless. Flanders was not convinced by Senator Richard Russell's defense of the record of the armed services committees in authorizing legislation for the defense establishment.[106] The larger truth to which Flanders pointed, and which committee members gradually came to sense, was that the armed services committees were partly responsible for the shortcomings of the defense effort. Although the armed services committees had acted with what appeared to be salutary effect on two occasions, they had largely abdicated their duty—and collaterally their committee power—to pass on the over-all defense program. The massive pockets of waste, duplication, and indecision attendant to the air-defense program were likely to be dim reflections of even larger manifestations of these deficiencies in the annual appropriations bill which was more than twenty times the size of the yearly military construction authorization measure. Flanders forced his colleagues on the committee, including Senator Russell, to realize that they had permitted the appropriations defense subcommittees to fill, as best they could within the confined areas of their jurisdictional competence, the defense policy vacuum that the withdrawal of the armed services committees had created. As Senator Russell later admitted, the legislative tools at the disposal of the armed services group, comprising principally its control "over manpower legislation, military pay measures, and military construction authorizations," [107] were recognized as ill-suited to the tasks either of compelling the Defense Department to use funds more economically and efficiently or of inducing its leadership to adopt needed shifts in the direction and scope of defense policy. The committee had not even kept itself informed so as to be in a position to act on its knowledge. Senator Russell, as chairman of the Armed Services Committee, appeared mindful of the ramifications of the issue raised by Flanders. He asserted to Defense Secretary McElroy and the other members of the armed services group:

> I must say I am intrigued with, but not convinced by, the argument that the Congress ought to resolve all its troubles by just delegating all its powers to the executive branch of the Government, and by standing back to see how well the executive branch of the Government can legislate; and if it doesn't do it properly, the Congress will undertake, by some machinery, to come in and recapture the powers that it has delegated.
>
> We can't renounce our responsibility because the Department of Defense spends more money than any other department. If we do, it is just a confession that the Congress has outlived its usefulness.
>
> It is a millstone on the neck of the functioning of the Government, and we would best consider some more fundamental change in our system. . . .
>
> I cannot accept the basic argument that Congress, because it might be criticized for the manner of carrying out its constitutional responsibilities, ought to delegate all of them to any executive officer. . . . [108]

Senator Russell moves slowly.—The Senate Armed Services Committee, nevertheless, did not act immediately on Flanders' suggestion.

Initiative for any changes in the workload of the Armed Services Committee rested principally with its chairman, Senator Richard Russell, who was not prepared in 1958 to implement either his views or those of Flanders. The report of the Senate Armed Services Committee on the Defense Reorganization Act of 1958 did not recommend any enlargement of committee activities. It confined itself merely to a general statement of congressional duties in defense policy that gave small hint that Section 412(b) would soon be on the way. The report said:

> The committee recognizes military power as an instrument of national policy and the necessity for close cooperation between the executive and legislative branches in shaping that policy. If . . . Congress is to perform its constitutional responsibilities and give vitality to the fundamental doctrine of separation of powers, it must retain a meaningful measure of control over the combatant functions of the Armed Forces it creates. Otherwise . . . the legislative branch would thus abdicate its historic responsibility over the design and capabilities of our major instruments of military policy and would renounce its responsibility to provide for the common defense." [109]

Almost a year elapsed before Senator Flanders' remarks were resurrected for armed services committee action. Shortly before the 1959 Military Construction Authorization Bill was to emerge from the Senate Armed Services Committee, Senator Russell directed one of his principal staff members to translate Flanders' general recommendations into concrete legislative terms. The wording of Section 412(b) was hastily constructed just before the Senate committee markup of the authorization bill and was attached to it as an amendment, which was later to be known as the Russell Amendment.[110] Section 412(b) was not the product of long or careful staff study, nor of extended negotiations with the Defense Department. There was not time under the pressure of committee action on the authorization measure as well as on other pending business to conduct a searching review of armed services committee operations and relate them to its legislative responsibilities. It is no surprise, therefore, that the Senate report on the 1959 authorization measure was brief and cryptic about the motives and purposes underlying Section 412(b) and the implications of the change that it recommended in congressional oversight of defense policy. Less than a page was devoted to the amendment. In its original form the Russell amendment would have required "an annual authorization for the design, development, and procurement of aircraft and missiles." [111] Military procurement was identified as the key element in the defense program not only for its intrinsic importance—$9 billion of the Defense Department's FY 1960 appropriations request was earmarked for procurement—but also because it generated military requirements and spending for personnel, construction, and operations and maintenance.

The most interesting aspect of the Senate's version of 412(b) was what was excluded from it. Despite the committee's sweeping conception of the central importance of procurement, it limited itself to the authorization of aircraft and missiles. The surge of other committee business and the preoccupation of committee and staff members with other legislative duties precluded extended study and appraisal of other items that might have been logically included in the review process to assure a comprehensive and balanced review of military procurement and of over-all defense policy. The committee report was also strangely silent about the broad defense review suggested by Senator Flanders. His views were not given much weight in the actual Senate determination of 412(b), notwithstanding the fact that the military appropriations defense groups, especially the Mahon subcommittee in the House, were already manfully struggling, with mixed success, to conduct the kind of review that he had sketched.

In the conference discussion on the 1959 military construction bill between the two houses, naval vessels were added to the list of procurement items that might require previous authorization. This extension in committee purview was simultaneously narrowed by the added decision of the conferees that the words "design" and "development" be dropped. Some House members worried that the inclusion of these terms would over-extend the surveillance capacity of the armed services committees and would encourage Congress to dictate the specific details of each service's weapon systems.[112] Two years later, as an outgrowth of the heated exchange over the RS-70, these fears were quietly set aside. Unable to directly induce the Defense Department to develop the RS-70 bomber beyond a prototype program, the armed services committees recommended the amendment of Section 412(b) to include "research, development, test, or evaluation of aircraft, missiles, or naval vessels. . . . "[113] Armed with this enlarged interpretation of their mandate, the military committees successfully gained congressional consent to the addition of $320 million more in authorization for the RS-70 than the administration had requested for FY 1963. The research and development amendment was seen as a logical extension of the initial construction of Section 412(b).[114] The RS-70 controversy demonstrated to the armed services committees that research and development was as critical to the long-run structure of the defense establishment as procurement was to its more immediate composition and effectiveness. As procurement determined other elements of the defense programs, so also did research and development determine procurement. A kind of Mackinder's law of technology appeared to be operating in crude fashion: those who decided military research and development controlled the broad outline of procurement policy; those who controlled procurement policy determined the shape and character, though not necessarily the specific physical size, of the defense program. The expense and long lead-time of weapon systems development effectively precluded a wide number of choices at the procurement level of decision. At the procurement plateau of decision, choice narrowed to the quantitative determination of how many of a given order of available weapons to procure, not to the qualitative and, in the long run, more crucial question of what weapon systems or weapons mix should be designed and perhaps made operational.

The connection between research and development and procurement is perhaps obvious enough. What is not so clear are the purposes and motives underlying the original proposal of Section 412(b). The Senate report which recommended its adoption and the Senate and House debates which touched briefly on it offer scant guidance. The committees acted on the assumption that they were merely reasserting, although belatedly, their jurisdictional prerogatives. It must be said that, while the members of the defense appropriations subcommittees, especially those in the House group, expressed little enthusiasm for the measure, they considered the armed services committee move legitimate.[115] Their concern turned more on the practical wisdom of the action than on its propriety. There was basic agreement in Congress that the armed services committees had an uncontested right publicly to reclaim the authority that they already inherently possessed under prevailing congressional rules.[116]

Motives and effect.—Senator Russell's initiation of Section 412(b) presents somewhat of a puzzle. It would have been more logical to have expected Section 412(b) to have been proposed by the House and, specifically, by Representative Carl Vinson, chairman of the lower chamber's armed services committee. Russell saw defense policy both from the side of the armed services committee and the appropriations committee whereas Vinson was confined by the rules of the House to the military legislative group and had repeatedly disagreed with appropriations chairman, Representative Clarence Cannon, and the defense appropriations subcommittee over different phases of military policy. Russell, on the other hand, stood second in seniority to Senator Carl Hayden, chairman of the Senate Appropriations Committee, and could look forward with reasonable expectation in 1959, considering Hayden's advanced age, to succeeding him as chairman of that powerful committee. Section 412(b) would have had the effect of undercutting his position as a member of the appropriations group and as its future chairman.

These considerations are counterbalanced by the circumstance that the lassitude and ineffectiveness of the armed services committees were never more clearly revealed than in the post-sputnik period. A number of other committees, including the appropriations defense groups and the Senate preparedness subcommittee under Majority Leader Lyndon Johnson, were the most visible and energetic focal points of congressional activity in defense policy. Section 412(b) offered a means by which the armed services committees might again assume the leadership among congressional groups in their assigned domain of public policy. This purpose appeared uppermost in Russell's mind. A number of considerations prompt this view. Russell did not attach much importance to Flanders' criticisms insofar as they touched, not on the question of the power and responsibilities of the armed services committee, but on the ability of Congress as an institution to improve its oversight of defense policy and to enlarge its effective influence in this area. If Russell had been principally concerned about this latter problem, he would have displayed more anxiety about the fragmentary and illogical construction of Section 412(b). Russell acted, however, as if he were more troubled by the absence of the armed services committees from the main centers of defense policy-making. In this connection, the Senate report on the 1959 military construction bill stressed the failure of the armed services committee to authorize military procurement in specific detail as a guide for the appropriations committees. Passing reference was made to the need to reduce the costs of weapons procurement, but this factor, while a concern of Russell's, weighed more heavily in the minds of other members of the armed services committee, like Senator John Stennis, who on a number of occasions had urged the Defense Department and Secretaries Wilson and McElroy to end self-defeating service rivalry over weapons systems.[117] Members of the armed serv-

378

ices committees, through their authorization of military construction legislation, were cognizant of the failings of Defense Department planning, especially in air defense, and were actively in search of a more effective legislative device to influence defense policy and operations; to eliminate duplication and waste; and, after sputnik, to encourage the development of more effective military forces to counter Soviet advances. Committee members understood, too, that much of their effort in passing annual military construction authorization was meaningless since requirements for construction were derived from pre-existing determinations of military procurement needs. Major emphasis, nevertheless, was placed on the reassertion of the armed services committee's legislative authority to guide appropriations committee deliberations and decisions. "Lack of specificity in authorization for aircraft and missile procurement," concluded the 1959 report,

is in sharp contrast to the detailed annual authorizations for military construction which prescribe locations, categories, and amounts of construction authorization to be undertaken.

The committee has concluded that in the discharge of its legislative responsibilities an annual review of the aircraft and missile procurement programs is needed. A thorough examination of this area of activity may serve to reduce the enormous cost of defense and should assist the Committees on Appropriations in their consideration of the mammoth defense budget.[118]

Russell was, of course, solicitous about the apparent decline of American military strength in the late 1950's. He was aware also of the difficulties that Congress faced when it attempted to improve the nation's defense posture without the active support and cooperation of the President. But he tended, quite naturally, to interpret these problems in terms of the jurisdictional authority of his legislative committee. Russell became convinced that the annual Senate posture hearings did not probe deeply enough into the planning, operations, and costs of the military establishment. Just as importantly, he realized that, since they resulted in no specific legislation, the posture briefings were discounted in importance by committee members and other legislators. Section 412(b) was an obvious solution. Since it would necessitate authorizing legislation, it would lend substantive meaning and legal significance to armed services committee hearings.[119]

Chairman Carl Vinson of the House group also approached Section 412(b) from a committee viewpoint, although he initially drew different conclusions as to its feasibility and desirability. Vinson opposed the Russell amendment. Opinion differs about the precise reasons for his reluctance. Vinson did express doubt about the capacity of his committee and his staff to discharge the added responsibilities implicit in Section 412(b). Rumors circulated, too, that Vinson was not personally disposed, after many long and productive years of work in military affairs, to increase his already heavy workload in the final years of his legislative career. There was also the view that Vinson had prematurely acceded to Defense Department pleas to block the Russell amendment in conference. He generally preferred to have the military services decide their own procurement needs.[120] Vinson, however, relented before firm Senate committee support for 412(b) and before the mounting sentiment among members of his own committee who favored the shift.[121] The Russell amendment jogged many House committee members out of their legislative reverie. The Russell move quickened the awareness of many House members to the same opportunities for the assertion of committee power and responsibility that Flanders' criticism had originally opened to Russell. Ironically enough, as the Eighty-seventh Congress demonstrated, it was the House group rather than Russell's committee that exploited these possibilities to enhance the congressional and public esteem of the armed services committees.[122] Surprisingly, too, Vinson, whatever the motives or measure of his initial hesitancy, proved more forceful and enthusiastic than Russell in applying Section 412(b) against the Defense Department and the appropriations committees.

380

While members of the armed services committees in both houses were vitally interested in increasing Congress' review capacity and influence over defense policy and operations, the primary thrust of Section 412(b) was directed less at changing congressional-executive relations in defense policy in favor of the legislative branch than at assuring the ascendancy of the armed services committees as the principal spokesmen of Congress in defense policy. Devious motives need not be assigned either to Russell or Vinson or to the members of the armed services groups to understand why they acted as they did. This assertion of legislative committee prerogatives was quite normal—and even predictable—in spite of the long lapse of years since the armed services committees had played a central role in military affairs. The compelling incentives for such behavior lie, at least on the surface, in the committee system of Congress itself. Given the narrow jurisdictional divisions in Congress of committee authority, duties, and power and the attentiveness with which their territorial boundaries are usually guarded, it was only a matter of time and circumstance before the members of the armed services committees would reassert their right to pass on major elements of defense policy, a right that they had always enjoyed legally and logically, but which they had often neglected to exercise. The Defense Reorganization Act provided the convenient time to pose the question of the proper responsibilities of the armed services committees; the Military Construction Authorization Act of 1959, the expedient circumstance to crystallize inchoate and disparate member sentiment on the military service groups to pass Section 412(b) as an answer to it.

The chairman of every congressional committee, moreover, is under an obligation to himself and to his colleagues on the committee to be alert to opportunities to strengthen the prerogatives and privileges of his committee in the discharge of its circumscribed legislative responsibilities and to defeat moves that might weaken them. The personal and political success of legislators are in great part by-products of their committee's power and prestige. When Vinson momentarily faltered in these duties, the senior members of his committee urged him forward in much the same way that the Senate members of the foreign relations committee balked in March, 1965, at the suggestion of their chairman, Senator J. William Fulbright, to divide the foreign aid bill in two, a move that threatened to transfer the military assistance features of the bill to the armed services committee.[123]

Section 412(b) was implemented for the first time during the Eighty-seventh Congress. As the procurement authorization bills for 1961 and 1962 indicate, it has by and large been a disappointment in practice, however edified and legitimate may have been the original motives and purposes shaping its construction. The explanation did not exclusively lie in the fortunes and complexities of defense policy, nor in forceful presidential leadership in defense, nor in the increased exercise of secretarial power by Robert McNamara. The shortcomings of Section 412(b) were to be found primarily rooted in the diffuse committee arrangements of Congress and the decentralized power base that both yields and supports them. The implementation of Section 412(b) demonstrated that the power, prestige, and public image of the armed services committees could be enhanced without a substantial improvement in Congress' over-all understanding of defense policy and with a net decrease in its capacity to exert its influence in this area.

Eighty-seventh Congress and Defense Policy

YEAR OF TRANSITION: FY 1962

Changing view from the top.—The defense policy innovations inaugurated by the Kennedy administration were not presented to Congress for approval in an orderly fashion during 1961. When the new administration assumed office, it had not yet drawn up a detailed map of what defense course it would follow. Kennedy defense officials were initially more certain of their criticism of Eisenhower administration policies than they were agreed on a common approach to remedy past errors. Much of 1961 was needed to fashion the Kennedy defense program of flexible response. The New Look had required a similar incubation period. A new administration needs at least a year to gain control of the executive branch, appoint and instal hundreds of top personnel, and mold them into a working team responsive to the President's policy decisions. As the Kennedy administration grappled with these problems, it was confronted with the added difficulty of having to cope simultaneously with a series of immediate international crises.

The civil war in the Congo raised the possibility not only of increasing American commitment to the area but also the growing prospect of an American-Soviet confrontation in the heart of Africa. Southeast Asia was in a similar state of turmoil and confusion. Here, too, the United States and the Soviet Union appeared headed for a clash. The American-backed regime in Laos seemed on the verge of complete collapse in the face of mounting communist military successes. The Diem government in South Vietnam found itself under heavy internal pressure from the Communist Viet Cong and from the Hanoi regime in the North. It appealed to the new American government for increased economic and military assistance. The Cuban debacle of April 17–18, 1961, in which an American-supported invasion of anti-Castro forces was ignominiously defeated in the Bay of Pigs, added to the immediate cares of President Kennedy and his advisers. These emerging crises complicated the administration's effort to develop a set of long-run strategic policies.

However troubling and distracting these situations may have been, they paled before the ominous threat that the Soviet Union posed in Germany and West Berlin. On February 23, in a memorandum to the West German government, the Soviet Union resumed its previous hard line on Berlin and proposed a separate treaty. This action in connection with a number of preceding hostile moves by the Communist East German regime to limit Western access to Berlin signaled a new Russian offensive to gain its established objective of ousting the West from Berlin. The Western Allied Powers affirmed their rights in Berlin, and at the initiative of the United States conferred on the problem of developing an agreed position to counter the anticipated diplomatic, and perhaps even military, initiatives of the Soviet Union. To test Soviet intentions President Kennedy met with Premier Khrushchev in Vienna on June 3–4. At the conference the Soviet leader presented President Kennedy with an aide memoire which established a December 31, 1961, deadline for settlement of the German and Berlin questions. In the absence of a satisfactory East-West agreement, the Soviets threatened to sign a separate peace treaty with East Germany that would have terminated Western rights in Berlin and would have assigned control over access routes to the city to the East German government.[124]

The military response of the Kennedy administration to these developing crises in Europe and elsewhere assumed two major forms. On March 28, President Kennedy addressed a special message to Congress on his suggested revisions of President Eisenhower's defense program for FY 1962. The Republican administration had recommended a force structure and spending level for defense that closely resembled its proposals for FY 1961. President Eisenhower had sent to Congress a request for $41.8 billion in new obligational authority, $40.8 billion of which was included in his general appropriations bill. Total expenditures for the defense establishment were set at $42.9 billion.[125] President Kennedy added appropriations requests of $1.95 billion. His message had two main purposes: to strengthen and protect United States strategic strike forces and to augment its limited war capabilities. These proposals, while related in a general way to the administration's evolving strategic thinking and to the eroding international environment, were designed more as supplements to the

Eisenhower recommendations. They were "quick fixes" to mitigate a number of glaring weaknesses in the American force structure rather than parts of a fully articulated strategic plan of operations.

The Polaris program received an additional $1.34 billion, the bulk of the new appropriations request. Accelerated production of five Polaris submarines was ordered and ten more boats were proposed over the Eisenhower estimate of nineteen. Kennedy planners hoped to have twenty-nine Polaris submarines on station in about the same time that the Eisenhower administration had scheduled its nineteen-boat program. The substitution of three fixed for an equal number of mobile Minuteman squadrons was proposed at a cost of $96 million. Another $50 million was to be added to the Skybolt program. Extra precautions were outlined, too, to increase ground alert and to improve continental air defense, warning systems, and command and control equipment. These actions were to require $144 million. Research and development work on aircraft penetration aids, on reconnaissance, communication, and interceptor satellites, and on the Dyna-Soar, an experimental aerospace vehicle, was estimated at $226 million.[126] The solid-fueled Polaris and Minuteman missiles were assigned top priority. This shift gave the first hint of the new direction of the Kennedy administration's general war policies. The emphasis on strategic protection and warning was similarly connected to the President's desire for strategic forces which could survive an enemy first-strike and retaliate against targets of his choosing.

President Kennedy's changes in limited war capabilities were less notable, although administration leaders had spoken during the 1960 election campaign of the urgent need for conventional arms. In the March 28 proposals, 13,000 new personnel were to be added to President Eisenhower's planned FY 1962 force of 2.475 million. The army and marine corps received, in turn, 5,000 and 3,000 more troops. Navy additions of 3,000 were in connection with its Polaris program. The air force received the balance of 2,000 men. Most of the new funding requests for non-nuclear forces were aimed at providing hardware, not personnel, particularly for air and sea lift and for conventional weapons, including tactical aircraft and ammunition. Research and development for limited war was advanced by $122 million. Appropriations for these items totaled approximately $850 million. To offset these increases in future spending a number of defense programs were reduced or cancelled. The most significant decision concerned the restrictions of the B-70 to a prototype program.[127] Before leaving office, the Eisenhower administration had upgraded the B-70 to a weapons development level.

On May 25, shortly before his departure for Europe to meet with NATO leaders and Premier Khrushchev, President Kennedy addressed Congress again concerning so-called urgent national needs. Among these he included "reinforcement" of the nation's "capacity to deter or resist non-nuclear aggression" and civil defense.[128] The message, which recommended $237 million in new appropriations for conventional forces,[129] marked another modest administration instalment on its developing limited and general war strategy. The army's divisional structure was to be reorganized to speed its deployment and mobilization rates. These efforts were specifically aimed, moreover, at facilitating co-ordination with European forces and at strengthening the United States non-nuclear posture in the NATO area. New conventional equipment purchases were scheduled at a cost of $138 million. The marine corps was slated to be expanded to 190,000, and plans were laid for a fourth division which could be rapidly built in case of an emergency. Civil defense was upgraded as a defense function. The bulk of the civil defense program which the President outlined was assigned to the Defense Department.

Whatever value these shifts may have had in bolstering European confidence in the American military commitment to fulfil its NATO obligations, they apparently had little effect on the Soviet Premier. On his return from Vienna, President Kennedy made a sobering report to the nation on East-West relations. He observed that his "most somber talks" with Premier Khrushchev "were on the subject of Germany and Berlin." [130] Neither side had yielded in its demands. As a response to the mounting tensions over Berlin, the administration formulated yet another addition to the defense proposals which were pending before Congress.

On July 25, the President addressed the nation on the Berlin crisis and outlined a series of diplomatic and military initiatives to meet it. On the next day Congress received a request for $3.247 billion in new military appropriations. The President also requested and promptly received congressional authorization to order up to 250,000 members of the Ready Reserve to active duty for not more than one year and to extend enlistments and other military service obligations for the same length of time. These proposals had a twofold diplomatic and military importance. The announced buildup of armed forces was tantamount to a communication to the Soviet Union and to the European NATO powers that the United States would fight to maintain its war-won rights in Germany. The mobilization of reserve forces was of particular note since they were to be called up for the expressed intention of preventing the outbreak of hostilities, and not simply to engage in a conflict already begun. Congressional participation in these communications to the Soviets and to United States allies in Europe was obtained through the expedient of having that body pass an enabling resolution to grant the President authority to activate the reserves. The President already possessed legislative authority to call up one million reservists by declaring a national emergency. The administration deliberately chose not to exercise this authority out of fear that its use would accelerate already rapidly eroding relations between East and West. The reserve callup underscored the administration's resolve to limit as much as possible any foreseeable military confrontation in Europe to a non-nuclear base. As a hedge against the possibility of nuclear war, the administration requested $207 million for an expanded civil defense effort to survey and mark shelter spaces, to provide warning and detection equipment, and to conduct research and development on improving shelter systems.

The administration suffered no illusions that its July recommendations would be militarily relevant to the immediate Berlin situation. It nevertheless seized on the occasion as an opportunity to make a major instalment on its flexible response doctrine. The reserve callup was linked to a political decision to augment army divisional strength from fourteen to sixteen and to make three divisions of STRAF (Strategic Army Force), which were in training status, combat ready. The reserves would buy time while the new army divisions were being readied as permanent additions to the nation's non-nuclear force structure. The administration recommended the addition of 225,327 military personnel in its July proposals. Table 11 below summarizes the personnel increases requested by President Kennedy between March and July and compares them with the Eisenhower estimates for the same period as well as to the actual active duty total for June, 1960 and 1961. These increases along with previous proposals expanded the Eisenhower total by 250,000. Largest gainer in the July announcement was the army. Its active forces were to

TABLE 11*

ACTIVE FORCES MILITARY PERSONNEL
(In Thousands)

	June 30, 1960 (Actual)	June 30, 1961 (Actual)	Eisenhower FY 1962	Kennedy FY 1962
Army	872	859	870	1,008
Navy	618	627	625	657
Air Force	814	815	823	888
Marine Corps ..	171	171	175	190
Total	2,475	2,484	2,493	2,743

* Sources: S. Rept. 653, 87/1, 1961, p. 9; H. Doc. 155, 88/1, 1963, p. 167; B. B., *Budget of the United States, FY 1962,* p. 482.

jump from 875,000 to 1,008,000 by the close of FY 1962. The navy and the air force were to be expanded by 29,000 and 63,000, respectively. Non-nuclear procurement requests totaled $1.75 billion or one half of the July estimate. The balance was divided between military personnel and operations and maintenance accounts to support the troop buildup and to improve limited war readiness in air and sea lift, antisubmarine warfare, and tactical air power.[131] Steps were taken also to delay deactivation of B-47 bombers to sustain strategic strike power at maximum levels.

Congress supports the President.—Much of Congress' policy review of the Defense Department's FY 1962 budget proved irrelevant since the administration's March, May, and July supplements successively shifted the assumption on which its defense policies rested. The House and Senate had already acted on the first military procurement authorization bill and the House had passed the general appropriations bill before the July recommendations were made. Special hearings had to be hastily called in the House and Senate to afford the administration a formal setting in which to present its recommendations. The review was necessarily perfunctory as was the passage by Congress of a supplemental procurement authorization bill to underwrite the anticipated increases in the Defense Department's FY 1962 appropriations. In this confused atmosphere, it was difficult for the armed services committees and the defense appropriations groups to weigh the merit of the President's proposals. Legislators were aware of the larger international arena in which their action in passing on the President's defense recommendations were cast. They understood that their overwhelming support of the President's military buildup would strengthen his position in dealing with the Soviets over Berlin. The defense authorization and appropriations process was tied more closely than ever before to the movements of the executive branch in pursuing American interests abroad. Recognition of this connection,

TABLE 12*

CONGRESSIONAL ACTION ON FISCAL YEAR 1962 BUDGET REQUESTS BY APPROPRIATIONS TITLE
DEPARTMENT OF DEFENSE APPROPRIATIONS ACT, 1962
(In Millions of Dollars)

APPROPRIATIONS TITLE	BUDGET REQUEST					
	FY 1962 Budget Document	Budget Amendments, 3–28–61	Budget Amendments, 5–26–61	Budget Considered by the House	Budget Amendment, 7–26–61	Total Budget Request
	1	2	3	4	5	6
Title I—Military personnel	12,235	−252	12	11,995	751	12,746
Title II—Operations and maintenance	10,842	198	10	11,050	743	11,793
Title III—Procurement	13,378	1,591	138	15,107	1,753	16,860
Title IV—Research, development, test, and evaluation	4,349	376	65	4,790	....	4,790
Subtotal—Titles I–IV	40,804	1,913	225	42,942	3,247	46,189
Civil Defense	....	....	....	....	208	208
Grand total	40,804	1,913	225	42,942	3,455	46,397
Recapitulation:						
Army	10,171	50	100	10,321	1,441	11,762
Navy	12,036	1,473	60	13,569	1,052	14,621
Air Force	17,317	344	65	17,726	754	18,480
Office of the Secretary of Defense	1,280	46	....	1,326	208	1,534

TABLE 12—*Continued*

Appropriations Title	House Committee and House Floor Action		Department of Defense Reclama, 7–7–61	Budget Amendments, 7–26–61	Total DOD Requests for Senate Consideration
	Change from May 26 Budget†	Committee Report, 6–23–61; House Action, 6–28–61			
	7	8	9	10	11
Title I—Military personnel	+ 55	12,050	......	751	12,801
Title II—Operations and maintenance..	− 112	10,938	76	743	11,756
Title III—Procurement	− 226	14,881	......	1,753	16,643
Title IV—Research, development, test, and evaluation	+ 52	4,843	3	......	4,845
Subtotal—Titles I–IV	− 231	42,711	79	3,247	46,037
Civil Defense	......	......	......	208	208
Grand total	− 231	42,711	79	3,455	46,244
Recapitulation:					
Army	+ 39	10,359	27	1,441	11,827
Navy	− 111	13,458	17	1,052	14,527
Air Force	− 143	17,583	35	754	18,372
Office of the Secretary of Defense ...	− 16	1,310	......	208	1,518

* Source: SSAC, *Hearings, Department of Defense Appropriations*, FY 1962, 87/1, 1961, p. 1644.
† See column 4.

particularly after the July speech, gave impetus to Congress' approval of most of the President's requests. Protracted deliberation on his recommendations might have created the impression that Congress was divided over the President's stand on the German problem. Within a week after the President's July speech, the House and Senate Armed Services committees favorably reported a new authorization bill. On August 4 the Senate approved the Defense Department appropriations bill which, unlike the measure passed by the House in June, included all of the President's supplemental recommendations. Shortly thereafter the President was able to sign the bill into law.

The confusion attending Congress' review is suggested in Table 12. It displays the President's successive appropriations requests and indicates the staggered consideration given to them by Congress. The $40.8 billion appropriations request which the Eisenhower administration initially sent to Congress in the Defense Department Appropriation Bill for FY 1962 swelled to $46.4 billion or approximately 13 per cent in six months. After the eight lean Eisenhower years, most legislators welcomed these additions to the defense program, although in the rush of legislative passage of these requests they were not always certain of the specific implications of their action.

Section 412(b) tested.—The administration's opening presentation to Congress was embodied in its $11.9 billion procurement authorization bill for FY 1962. The measure marked the trial run of Section 412(b). The bewilderment engendered by the administration's changes in its defense proposals and by the turbulence of the international developments was compounded within the armed services committees. Neither was quite certain of the form which the new authorization bill would take. The House group continued to conduct its annual hearings on military posture, not fully mindful of the logical relation between this *tour d'horizon* and the procurement authorization bill. The bifurcation of the two hearings reflects the lack of preparedness among committee members for their new responsibilities and the uncertainty among them of the precise purpose of the procurement authorization proceedings.[132]

The armed services committees did reach agreement with the Defense Department on a number of fundamental procedural points. The authorization measure was to be largely identical in makeup to the appropriations bill. The armed services committees would pass the authorization measure by making lump sum grants under program headings, such as air force aircraft, that corresponded to existing appropriations categories. They would, moreover, receive the same detailed information as the defense appropriations groups on these programs.[133] Authorizations would be made annually. The military services obligated themselves to report to the armed services committees each year on the amount of existing authority that was still available in each category. They were also to be bound by the multiple sets of informal agreements that would be reached in the course of yearly hearings on the line item breakdown of major procurement programs.[134] Insofar as procurement items were involved, the military legislative committees were to be included in the reprogramming arrangements already in effect in Defense Department relations with the appropriations committees.[135] Both sets of committees would be similarly treated and both would have equal access to Defense Department data. The armed services committees would not acquire any new information. They would merely receive the material already disseminated to the defense appropriations subcommittees on procurement programs dealing with service aircraft and missiles and naval vessels.

The House and Senate hearings gave scattered attention to a number of important defense issues, including atomic propulsion systems for aircraft and vessels, Nike-Zeus, army modernization, and diminishing naval aircraft and ship procurement. Major interest on both sides of Capitol Hill centered, expectedly, on the future role of the manned bomber in the nation's strategic arsenal, a question that was to plague Congress and the executive branch throughout the Kennedy years and into the Johnson administration. The subtle Defense Department shift to ICBM's, which was thinly traced in the March amendments, and the belated discovery of American leadership in long-range missile development reactivated congressional attention in manned delivery systems after a three year lapse that began with the first Russian sputnik. The longer and more thorough House report joined the issue for the two armed services committees against the administration. While affirming its support of an expanded missile program, the House group questioned the reliability of missiles when compared with bombers, "a vehicle of known capability for the carrying of weapons of many kinds."[136] It noted that the bomber was a more flexible military instrument which, unlike the missile, had a "variety of modes" of action. It could be recalled or dispatched to new targets. The missile could only "go or not go." The report speculated, moreover, about the possibility of nuclear weapons being outlawed. It asked, rhetorically, "Would not at that time the nation who possesses a conventional capability be in a virtually absolute position with respect to his enemies?"[137] The Senate committee added the more sophisticated point that this situation might similarly obtain "if a condition of mutual strategic deterrence should be achieved."[138] It also referred optimistically to the availability of the Hounddog missile and the "promising possibility of a successful development of the Skybolt missile" to increase the life of the manned bomber.[139]

The House group recommended the addition of $393.2 million to the administration's $11.9 billion bill. In keeping with its support for the manned bomber, the committee asked the House to authorize $337 million more than the administration had requested in order to keep B-52 and B-58 production lines open. Kennedy officials had sustained the Eisenhower decision to stop production of these airplanes. Smaller sums were advised for special aircraft and jet engines. The committee expressed its interest in nuclear propulsion by redefining the navy's ship procurement program. It authorized the construction of six guided missile frigates, two of which were to be nuclear powered. The navy had asked for seven conventionally propelled ships. The committee action was encouraged by the remarks of Admiral Hyman Rickover, who testified that the navy was slow to accept nuclear propulsion and the higher costs that it entailed out of fear that the total number of its ship requests would be reduced.[140] The fear was hardly groundless in light of the committee's action. The Senate bill devoted itself to a $525 million increase in manned bomber authority, enough funds to keep production going and to allegedly furnish the air force another wing of strategic bombers.[141] The House had rejected this course. In its report to the full house the Senate committee also turned aside a request by Senator Strom Thurmond to add $169 million to the authorization measure for Nike-Zeus.[142]

The final measure passed by both houses carried the Senate figure of $525 million for bombers. The navy received authorization for seven frigates, including one to be nuclear propelled. Admiral Rickover and the navy were given a boost. Authorization was included for extra turbo-fan engines and cargo planes and for one, not three, special mission aircraft as the House had approved.

Both bills swept through their respective houses after brief debate and discussion. The Senate discussion covered less than six full pages of the *Congressional Record*.[143] House consideration, while similarly hasty, did focus briefly on two important defense issues concerning the adequacy of the administration's proposals for strategic missile forces and, to a lesser extent, on army preparedness. Floor discussion of these two issues, if read in connection with the House hearings, also casts important light on the tenuous power of the armed services committees to influence military policy in spite of Section 412(b). Representative Charles S. Gubser, abetted by the House Republican Policy Committee, offered an amendment on the floor to add $697.5 million to the authorization bill for the construction of six more Polaris submarines. Gubser referred to certain "top-ranking naval officers"—reportedly Chief of Navy Operations Arleigh Burke— who had recommended a forty-five–boat force.[144] Despite Gubser's grave warning of a "Polaris gap," his amendment lost by a vote of 105–58, having been previously beaten back in committee by the decisive margin of 25–3.[145] Although his amendment did not carry, Gubser's criticism of the administration's missile proposals fell within the proper sphere of his position as a minority member of the armed services committee. In its early months in office, the Kennedy administration was vulnerable to the charge that its force recommendations fell short of its own analysis of the nation's military needs. Gubser's view was vindicated less that a year later when the administration expanded the Polaris program to forty-one submarines.

The novel procedures under Section 412(b) facilitated Gubser's useful critique of the administration's policies. The procurement bill provided him a legislative context in which to cast his remarks. This situation added to their weight and legitimacy inasmuch as they were addressed to an approved congressional activity. On the other hand, Gubser's amendment, while it was aimed at a military problem, threatened to damage the fiscal and economic policies to which the administration still clung in early May before the Khrushchev-Kennedy meeting in Vienna and the July proposals in Congress. Gubser's demands stepped beyond the informal economic boundaries within which the armed services committee was expected to operate. Representative Carl Vinson was keenly aware of these limits on his committee's discretion in recommending military policies to the House. He was no more willing to carry a $700 million Polaris request to the House floor than he was willing to support a proposal made by another committee member to increase bomber authorizations by over $1 billion. "When I begin to realize about the realities of life [sic]," remonstrated Vinson,

I found the bombers were going to cost for one wing, $525 million, and then the other wing for the other bomber [B-58]

was $485 million. Now, do you think the House and the Appropriations Committee, with the position of the Department like it is, are going to make the money available? . . . I don't want to go to the floor of the House and be laughed off the floor and the committee laughed off.[146]

A compromise solution was found in the $337 million recommendation of the House group. It indicated the committee's interest in maintaining bomber production without challenging the fiscal assumptions which Vinson felt were presently accepted by a majority in Congress and by the administration.

Vinson was similarly sensitive to the limits of his committee's power in influencing military policy, an area in which its power was allegedly paramount. Section 412(b) regained for the armed services committees some of their lost prestige and notoriety by upstaging the defense appropriations groups through the annual routine of a procurement authorization, but the new procedure could not assure automatic compliance with military committee determinations. Committee influence was bounded not only by majority opinion in each house of Congress but, more particularly, by the potential opposition of the defense appropriations subcommittees and the Pentagon.

Vinson openly referred to these obstacles in his passing criticism of what he considered were the lagging efforts of the Kennedy administration to remedy army equipment and personnel deficiencies. He described his efforts in 1958 to enlist the backing of the House defense appropriations subcommittee in a concerted congressional move to pressure the Eisenhower administration into building the army to 925,000. Vinson recognized that the chief executive would not yield to scattered legislative criticism of his army policies unless sufficiently large majorities in both houses could be marshaled to oppose him. Representative George Mahon, while favoring an expansion of limited war capabilities, was convinced that congressional leverage should be applied first to other aspects of non-nuclear pre-

397

paredness. Mahon's resistance effectively sidetracked Vinson's efforts to generate congressional support for a larger army. A recalcitrant President could not be easily budged when congressional opinion was united in opposition to him on a defense policy issue. He could not be moved when Congress itself was divided. Vinson's behind-the-scenes moves to increase army strength in early 1961 were again thwarted by Mahon, who, although sympathetic to Vinson's proposals, felt that the new administration deserved more time to formulate its own course of action in meeting the growing limited war threat. Lacking solid congressional backing, Vinson was forced to retreat from further pursuit of the issue in his presentation of the military procurement authorization bill. He allowed himself only a passing shot during floor consideration of the measure. "It is the size of the Army, the weapons with which it is armed, and its mobility, that causes my continuing concern," observed Vinson,

> . . . On April 29, 1958, I expressed these facts . . . to the chairman of the Defense Subcommittee on Appropriations, the gentleman from Texas [Mr. Mahon], urging his assistance in holding the Army at a strength of 925,000. While that result was not accomplished, I want to very clearly say that I have no criticism whatsoever of Mr. Mahon.
>
> It is apparent to all of us that the Congress cannot unilaterally impose its will upon the executive branch in matters of this nature. We can authorize and appropriate to whatever extent we may wish, but the concurrence of the executive branch is an essential requirement to the accomplishment of the congressional decision of this nature. In that case the executive branch did not agree. So the Army went down to 870,000.[147]

The executive branch under President Kennedy also resisted additional personnel increases until it had reviewed existing policies in terms of its own assessment of the immediate and long-term ground-force needs of the nation. Section 412(b) proved of little use to

Vinson in his fight. Much of the thrust of Vinson's case for an army of 925,000 men lost legislative force since Section 412(b) did not extend to personnel levels.

Section 412(b), while it could underwrite an annual review of parts of the administration's military program, could not solve the larger problem of galvanizing a cohesive congressional majority on defense policy. An important effect of Section 412(b), on the contrary, has been to formalize committee relations and to place a higher premium on independent committee action to gain majority support on the floor of Congress for its policy positions. Attempts through bargaining and negotiation to seek informal agreements with other committees on defense issues of mutual interest were downgraded in favor of appeals to the majority opinion of each house. Whatever its ostensible purposes, Section 412(b) induced the members of the armed services committees, particularly those in the House where the Senate practice of overlapping membership of appropriations and armed service personnel was not employed, to stress the formal prerogatives of the committee rather than the over-all responsibilities of the Congress for defense. Members of the military groups tended to equate their circumscribed legislative powers and duties with the larger economic, military, and political obligations of Congress as a whole. Within this syndrome other committees appeared more as rivals than as potential allies. Much of the public deliberation of the House Armed Services Committee on the 1961 procurement bill was devoted to the task of writing authorizing legislation which would bind the appropriations committees to its determinations. The armed services group sought, moreover, to elicit favorable executive branch action on its legislative prescriptions. But as committee members probed the meaning of Section 412(b), they, like Vinson, grew progressively conscious of its limited political utility. An exchange between two leading Democratic members of the House committee during the markup of the authorization measure discloses the weak and vulnerable political position of the armed services committee when deciding on defense policy in isolation from other relevant congressional groups:

> Mr. Kilday: . . . We have been talking here about the Secretary of the Air Force, or the Chief of Staff, should have the determination [on bombers]. . . . The only question is whether this committee or the Appropriations Committee is going to make the recommendation for bombers, as to whether it is the 52 or 58, if we authorize either 52 or 58.
> Then it comes through the Appropriations Committee.

> Mr. Rivers: Absolutely.

> Mr. Kilday: And don't kid yourself: if the Appropriations Committee says 58's and the Department wants 52's, they are just not going to build 58's. There is no power in our Government to force them to buy it.[148]

The appropriations groups act.—Representative Kilday's apprehensions were well founded. The military committees could indicate those areas which they felt deserved appropriations support, but they could not dictate their positions to the appropriations subcommittees. Their leverage over them was, of course, greater than that of the President or the defense secretary since the appropriations groups could not ignore the position of the military committees on procurement policy once majorities in both houses passed on the annual authorization bill. On the other hand, the appropriations defense groups discovered that their discretion had not been as severely confined as was first imagined and that even within the limits established by Section 412(b), they still possessed some opportunity for independent action and maneuverability. Section 412(b), moreover, did not affect the scope or depth of the proceedings of the appropriations defense subcommittees. In contrast to the military legislative committees, they continued to review the bulk of the Defense Department's program, and not simply selected procurement

400

items; collected more military and economic data on these activities; and focused and discussed a greater number of defense issues, with greater and more penetrating detail, in the hearings and on the floors of both houses.

House and Senate members of the defense appropriations sub-committees openly criticized the administration's modest March and May increases for limited war.[149] The President's July proposals had not yet been formulated. Members castigated the administration on the small size of the army and the slow rate of army modernization.[150] They saw little practical difference between the new administration's recommendations and those of the preceding Eisenhower regime which the Democratic Eighty-sixth Congress had so bitterly attacked. The administration's decision to sustain its predecessor's cutback in army reserve strength by 70,000 men unsettled committee members who had expected stronger support with a change of leadership in the White House.[151] The navy's disgruntlement with the failure of the Pentagon leaders to approve a rate of aircraft and ship procurement replacement to keep pace with the rate of attrition in these categories was given extensive notice.[152] Exchanges between administration witnesses and committee members were often blunt and direct. Representative Daniel Flood, a stalwart advocate of greater army mobility, caustically observed at one point:

I have been concerned for a long time with airlift for the Army and Marines. . . . All the Chiefs of Staff and Joints of Staff [*sic*] and Secretaries and Assistant Secretaries have come up and sat in those chairs and they have told me year after year after year we had an adequate airlift.

Every statement they made was wrong. Not one of them was telling me the truth, or if they meant it they did not know what they were talking about. We have not had an airlift. We have not got one today. Happy New Year. This has been going on for years in this room. Generals and everybody have been saying that, and it has not been true. We have not had an adequate airlift. It is outrageous to tell us that here for years. [153]

Flood did not stand alone in his feelings. The House report singled out "the problem of mobility," and pointedly remarked that existing and proposed air and sea lift capabilities did not meet the nation's needs.[154] The entire limited war effort was deemed inadequate.

The House subcommittee stopped short of proposing its own recommendations. It encouraged the Defense Department to study the matter further. Representative George Mahon had already put the defense establishment on notice during the hearings that he expected an improved military plan for limited war capabilities. His candid remarks were tantamount to a threat that his committee might again assert itself as it had before and submit its own recommendations to the Congress. "I do not think the Army budget of the previous administration," said Mahon, "was by any means perfect, and I do not think the [Kennedy] amended budget of the Army is anything to wax lyrical about. You have not had too much time to work out a program . . . but I would like to feel that by the calendar year 1962 you would come up with a . . . Army program that would be the best ever."[155]

Representative Flood caught the spirit of the House defense subcommittee's feeling toward the administration's initial military proposals in his concluding remark before the full House during its June consideration of the defense bill. "I submit, Mr. Chairman, this is a good bill," asserted Flood. "Anything worth $42 billion is good, but it could be an awful lot better. Do not kid yourselves."[156] The House report issued on June 23 struck a more philosophical note of at least temporary reconciliation to the slow processes of governmental decision and action in defense. "It is most important to maintain an intelligent and objective attitude toward defense problems in the face of the growing and changing threat," remarked the report. "Under our open society, based as it is on a system of checks and balances, with the resulting spread in ultimate responsibility, often it takes considerable time for a new threat or problem to be understood by a sufficient number of people to generate action toward a solution. This is one of the prices we pay, and must continue to pay, for the democratic process so vital to the preservation of our way of life." [157]

The Democratic-controlled House and Senate defense appropriations groups, nonetheless, launched additional attacks on the administration's strategic force proposals. The House report recommended an increase of $448.8 million in increased appropriations to be applied by the defense secretary either for more B-52's and B-58's or for the rapid development of the B-70 program. [158] It expressed serious reservations about the slow pace of Nike-Zeus experimentation and the cancellation of the mobile Minuteman missile. [159] The committee was particularly anxious about what it felt to be the inadequate acceleration of the Polaris program to a 29-boat level. The committee attempted to circumvent the restrictions which the recently enacted authorization procurement bill implicitly placed on its recommendations. Since the armed services committees had provided for Polaris vessels through a lump sum grant that did not legally specify the number of ships to be acquired, the appropriations report suggested the swift enlargement of the Polaris fleet through the procurement of long lead-time components. "This could be accomplished," said the report, "under authorized reprogramming procedures." [160] The effect of the House committee's recommendations, if they had been applied, would have been to shift the struggle for more Polaris submarines from the House and Senate floor to informal bargaining between the armed services committees and the appropriations defense groups, on the one hand, and the Defense Department, on the other. Also urged was greater effort in antisubmarine warfare. "The Committee cannot stress too much the need to equip the Navy with modern ASW weapons in sufficient quantities to meet the ever menacing Soviet submarine threat," said the House report. [161]

The Senate defense appropriations subcommittee was similarly anxious about American strategic capabilities. The Senate group held special hearings on the closing of the production facilities for long-range bombers and on the $138 million cut in the Eisenhower administration's $358 million recommendation for the B-70. General Curtis LeMay, newly appointed air force chief of staff, advocated congressional increases of $525 million for an additional B-52 bomber wing and $488 million, the full House amount, for the B-70 program.[162] Defense Secretary McNamara rejected LeMay's estimates, claiming that the cost of another wing would exceed $525 million.[163] These conflicting cost estimates, important factors that had to be weighed in reaching a sound decision on the bomber program, had not been clearly delineated in the hearings of the armed services committees. The Senate appropriations group agreed that air force funds for the B-70 and B-52 should be increased, respectively, by $228 million and $525 million.

The appropriations bill was approved by Congress in final form in early August. It carried increases over administration estimates of $514.5 million for B-52 or B-58 production, $180 million for B-70 development, and $85.5 million for the Dyna-Soar program, the latter addition being a congressional prod to expand defense establishment exploration of the uses of outer space for military purposes. Appropriations were also included for the increased authorizations provided in the procurement authorization bill for selected military items. The bill approved all of the President's July requests. The defense appropriations groups were satisfied that, notwithstanding the differences between the President's order of spending priorities for defense and the priority list that they might have drawn up, the items that were proposed generally corresponded to those which had been repeatedly urged by them. A proviso, insisted upon by the House, was also added to the effect that all procurement appropriations were to be reduced by 2 per cent. The House demand, which was reluctantly acceded to by the Pentagon and by the Senate defense appropriations group, was aimed at compelling more efficient contracting practices.[164]

The administration was spared the task of exhaustively preparing Congress for the construction of a balanced force structure that could implement its flexible response doctrines. Despite the increased cost of defense and the heavier burden that would be placed on the nation's adverse balance of payments position, Congress was willing to underwrite the administration's defense buildup, if it could count on the commitment and leadership of the chief executive. The pre-July congressional appropriations review served the useful purpose of clarifying and crystallizing legislative sentiment for a broader and more powerful defense posture. It facilitated the President's decision to increase defense spending both to meet the immediate Berlin crisis and to inaugurate a renovation and expansion of the nation's military force structure.

THE TURN IS COMPLETED: FY 1963

A new force structure indicated.—President Kennedy's FY 1963 budget presented Congress with a Defense Department program that called for an expenditure of $49.7 billion and new obligational authority of $53.9 billion, including $1.5 billion for military assistance.[165] These expenditure increases carried defense spending to a new plateau upon which a larger force structure could rest. Table 13 compares force levels for 1961, 1963, and 1965. There is a marked contrast between the 1961 figures, the last military watermark of the Eisenhower administration, and the 1963 Kennedy totals, which form the basis for the 1965 force levels.

Changes in the size and mix of strategic forces are the most striking indicators of the difference between the Eisenhower and Kennedy force structures. The Eisenhower administration had been principally responsible for the thirteen Atlas and seven Titan missiles, as well as most of the bomber forces that are noted for June 30, 1963. Ground plans for the construction of these forces had been laid before the Kennedy takeover. The Kennedy group relied on

TABLE 13*

SUMMARY OF ACTIVE FORCES

Description	Actual, June 30, 1961	Actual, June 30, 1963	Estimated, June 30, 1965
Military personnel (in thousands):			
Army	858	975	963
Navy	627	664	674
Marine Corps	177	190	190
Air Force	820	869	829
Total, Department of Defense...	2,482	2,698	2,656
Selected military forces:			
Strategic retaliatory forces:			
Intercontinental ballistic missiles (squadrons):			
Minuteman	.....	2	16
Titan	.....	7	6
Atlas	4	13	.....
Polaris submarines	5	12	29
Strategic bombers (wings):			
B–52	13	14	14
B–58	1	2	2
B–47	20	13	5
Continental air and missile defense forces:			
Manned fighter interceptor squadrons	42	42	39
Interceptor missile squadrons (BOMARC)	77	8	6
Army air defense missile battalions†	49½	31½	23½
General purpose forces:			
Army divisions (combat ready)	11	16	16
Army surface-to-surface missile battalions	42½	48½	38½

TABLE 13—*Continued*

Description	Actual, June 30, 1961	Actual, June 30, 1963	Estimated, June 30, 1965
Army air defense missile battalions	26¾	31¾	32¾
Army special forces group	3	6	7
Warships:			
Attack carriers	15	15	15
Antisubmarine warfare	9	9	9
Nuclear attack submarines	13	16	23
Other	328	326	329
Amphibious assault ships	110	132	135
Carrier air groups (attack and ASW)	28	28	28
Marine Corps divisions/aircraft wings	3	3	3
Air Force tactical forces squadrons .	93	109	117
Airlift and sealift forces:			
Airlift aircraft (squadrons):			
C–130 through C–141	16	26	38
C–118 through C–124	35	31	19
Troopships, cargo ships, and tankers	99	101	99
Commissioned ships (all programs)	819	859‡	880

* Source: B.B., *U.S. Budget, FY 1964*, p. 67; *U.S. Budget, FY 1965*, p. 73; *U.S. Budget, FY 1965*, p. 70.
† Decreases reflect phaseout of Nike-Ajax and transfer of Nike-Hercules battalions to Army National Guard.
‡ Estimate.

these forces as a stop gap, while rapidly shifting to Minuteman and Polaris missiles systems which were less vulnerable to enemy destruction. What is of even more interest is the altered ratio between bombers and missiles. In January, 1962, the United States had nearly 1,700 intercontinental bombers—630 B-52's, 55 B-58's, and 1,000 B-47's. Its ICBM force was composed of eighty Polaris and less than seventy Atlas missiles. Four years later, while strategic aircraft inventories fell to below 1,000 planes with the phase-out of B-47's, land-based ICBM's increased to over 850 units. At sea 352 Polaris missiles were deployed in the bottoms of 22 nuclear submarines. The Atlas which had been the mainstay of Eisenhower planners was deactivated by the end of fiscal 1965. Meanwhile improvements were made in air and ground alert. Half of the bomber force was on ground alert in early 1965. The range, accuracy, and striking power of missiles were likewise enhanced.[166]

The most fundamental transformation occurred in non-nuclear fighting forces. Army and marine corps personnel increases leaped 127,000 in two years. During the Berlin crisis the army temporarily swelled to a force of over one million. By 1965 it had stabilized at a level of about 970,000 which was about 100,000 more than the Eisenhower-approved total and, not without significance, 45,000 more than army leaders had advocated. Defense Secretary McNamara and his advisers had set the requirements for the army. Combat divisions rose in the same two year period from eleven to sixteen, the rapid increase being assisted by the reserve callup. The expansion of air power support for ground operations is of special note. Tactical air wings increased by nineteen squadrons or approximately 20 per cent. Air lift capacity was augmented by the entry of eighteen squadrons of newer, faster, and more spacious aircraft as eight squadrons of older aircraft were dropped. The army's inventory of aircraft was permitted to grow from 5,564 to 6,338 small craft during the period.[167] The ranks of special forces, a crude indicator of United States involvement in countering communist subversion abroad, was enlarged from three to seven groups.

Congress adopts a new force structure.—Congress found it difficult to argue with its own success. Sentiment in both houses had been mounting since the flight of the first sputnik in favor of a military establishment with larger and more varied capabilities than had existed under the Eisenhower administration. The Kennedy FY 1963 defense budget proposed to Congress a force structure that in a sense was a response to already articulated congressional demands. The President had a ready market in Congress for his defense proposals. He experienced difficulty, not in selling his product, but in meeting existing demand, for most legislators were prepared to buy more military capabilities than the President was willing to offer for sale. Congress accepted the Defense Department's shopping list without fully analyzing whether the force structure outlined by Secretary McNamara did, indeed, contribute adequately to the realization of American interests and objectives. While congressional opinion on defense policy had slowly gained an appreciation for the utility of sufficient forces in being to support its diplomacy abroad, the tendency to view the acquisition of military forces as an end in itself rather than as linked to a larger strategic design still lingered on in influential legislative quarters.

The Kennedy force structure, whatever its merits as a remedy to past shortcomings in preparedness, raised a number of critical strategic problems of its own. One set of issues, for example, turned on the administration's general war strategy. Was it possible to fight a controlled nuclear war? If so, under what circumstances? Were the FY 1963 proposals for strategic nuclear forces capable of meeting these conditions? What would be the outcome of such a war? Was American nuclear superiority a meaningful military and political advantage? Were there any contingencies in which the second-strike doctrine might not apply? Secretary McNamara had suggested that a massive Soviet attack against Europe would be answered with nuclear weapons. What would constitute a massive attack?

Another set of issues revolved around the new accent on non-nuclear forces. The impact of this shift on NATO strategy and on cohesion within the alliance was especially acute. Some NATO powers, most pointedly France and West Germany, grew concerned that talk in American military circles about defending Europe with conventional weapons indicated a gradual withdrawal of the United States nuclear guarantee. In a nuclear confrontation between the United States and the Soviet Union, the President might abandon Europe to save the American homeland from atomic destruction. French President Charles de Gaulle suggested that the American doctrine of flexible response was proof of his argument that the United States sought to hedge its defense obligations to Europe. Pentagon insistence on the maintenance of the American nuclear monopoly heightened European fears about the sincerity of American intentions. The credibility of the American deterrent appeared diluted insofar as European security was at issue. While these doubts antedated the Kennedy administration, the rapid and sweeping change in the United States force structure added support to them.

These considerations, of course, did not exhaust the possible strategic implications of the Kennedy-McNamara force structure. They illustrate, nevertheless, the kind of questions that legislators might have legitimately pursued in their review of the Defense Department's authorization and appropriations bills. Instead, from the meandering stream of congressional questioning of the President's $12.48 billion procurement authorization bill and his $47.9 billion appropriations measure, two more narrowly defined defense issues were singled out by the military legislation and appropriations groups for special discussion and debate. The House Armed Services Committee staked all of its political power and prestige on the development of the RS-70 bomber as a complete weapon system. Its campaign for the RS-70 dominated congressional consideration of the administration's defense proposals. The appropriations defense groups, while necessarily attentive to the RS-70 controversy, lent their authoritative voices in defense policy to the army reserve program. The administration proposed a reduction in army reserve forces to 642,000 along with a realignment of the reserve organization. The appropriations subcommittees enlisted themselves again under the now slightly tattered banner of a 700,000 reserve force.

410

The RS-70 and reserve issues, while important in their own right, were essentially peripheral to the strategic implications of the Kennedy recommendations. The decision of the defense secretary and the President on the RS-70 and on reserve reduction and reorganization were parts of a larger strategic plan. The controversy engendered by the bomber and reserve questions obscured general congressional and public perception of this more inclusive design. The legislative and appropriations committees in defense preferred to argue the relative merits of manned delivery systems against ICBM's or to praise the contributions of the reserves to placate domestic interests. Bombers were dependable, proven, and—being manned—personal instruments of United States striking power. Their illustrious history was a part of the record of American military successes—points that the armed services committees were clear to emphasize. ICBM's were impersonal mechanisms of perhaps dubious practical value. The House Armed Services Committee conjectured that the "only knowledge of the actual workability of an ICBM fired in anger is in textbooks and in laboratories." Committee members were unanimously agreed that they would not "place the safety of [the] country in a purely academic attitude. . . . "[168] The reserve issue, moreover, had the advantage of constituent appeal. The National Guard Association was locally based in all of the fifty states and the Reserve Officers Association enjoyed national representation.[169] Votes could be pumped from the reserve controversy. Discussion of first- and second-strike capabilities were esoteric by comparison. Such concerns appeared to be of tenuous relevance to the hurly-burly of domestic politics or to the legislator's immediate problem of electoral survival.

The limits of Section 412(b) tested anew.—The House Armed Services Committee's report on the FY 1963 procurement authorization bill fell like a bombshell on Congress. The eighth line of the report carried the main charge of the explosion, which, on the surface, appeared harmless enough:

411

Page 1, line 10, strike '$3,135,000,000' and insert in lieu thereof '$3,626,000,000,' and add the following language: of which the Secretary of the Air Force is *directed* to utilize authorization in an amount not less than $491,000,000 during Fiscal Year 1963 to proceed with production planning and long lead-time procurement for an RS-70 weapon system.[170]

The committee left no doubt what it meant by "directed." "The RS-70 amendment means . . . exactly what it says; i.e., that the secretary of the air force . . . is directed, ordered, mandated, and required to utilize the full amount of the $491 million authorization granted. . . . "[171] observed the committee report. The committee had resorted to this extraordinary language in answer to Defense Secretary McNamara's October, 1961, announcement that he would not spend the extra funds voted by Congress in FY 1962 for the B-70 or for strategic bomber production.[172]

The administration had requested $171 million for the RS-70 system. The House group recommended an increase of $320 million. Its report quoted its previously stated arguments in support of more bombers.[173] To these it added others which spotlighted the special advantages of the RS-70's reconnaissance features. The committee envisioned four tasks for the RS-70. It would "observe and report the condition of the enemy during and after the initial strikes; increase assurance of destruction of priority targets; seek out and destroy unique targets—the extremely hard, the mobile, and the imprecisely located; and provide . . . precision, discrimination, and flexibility" for the nation's strategic strike forces.[174]

Secretary McNamara did not deny the value of these functions. His decision to restrict the RS-70 rested on his self-directed Defense Department analysis of the cost-effectiveness of the system. The defense study, supported by all of the Joint Chiefs except Air Force General Curtis LeMay, concluded that systems other than the RS-70 could perform the functions for which they were to be designed equally or more effectively and that, in light of these findings, the cost of the RS-70, which was estimated at $10 billion for a full weapons system, would be prohibitive. There was also no assurance that the bomber would fly or that the special equipment that it required—high resolution radar, automatic processing, display, and communications systems, and new air-launched missiles—could be easily developed.[175]

The subtle nuances of McNamara's cost-effectiveness analysis were blurred by the manner in which the House Armed Services Committee posed the policy problem of bombers versus missiles and the specific utility of the RS-70. The committee clouded the analysis of these problems by introducing the added constitutional issue whether Congress could compel an officer of the executive branch to act contrary to the directives of the President. "Is the function of the Congress solely a negative one in that it can withhold authority or funds and prevent something from being done?" asked the report. "Or can it exercise a positive authority and by affording the means require something to be done?"[176]

Quoting briefly from English and American legal precedents, the House committee drew the conclusion that "the President cannot by military orders evade the legislative regulations [sic] nor can Congress by rule and regulations impair the authority of the President as Commander in Chief."[177] Providing weapons for defense was deemed to fall within the meaning of a legislative regulation which Congress was constitutionally competent to issue. To demonstrate a pattern of executive "disregard of congressional will" the report cited fifteen instances between 1949 and 1961 in which the executive branch had refused to spend funds provided by Congress for defense purposes. To these legal findings, the committee added the point that experts themselves disagreed over the RS-70 and that after its "full and free discussion of [the] military matter" it felt itself to be "reasonably competent to form a judgment which warrants consideration."[178] But the committee wanted more than consideration. It wanted the full authority of Congress to be pledged in support of its recommendations not only on the RS-70 issue but also on the question of Congress' constitutional right to force presidential action in disagreements over defense policy issues. "When [the RS-70 increase] is backed by the vote of the whole House and the whole Congress," the report went on, "it is a mandate." [179]

The RS-70 issue would draw a halt to the allegedly deteriorating role of Congress "in determining national policy, defense or otherwise." [180] The report compared Congress to a doddering old man incapable of coping with the demands made upon him:

> More and more the role of the Congress has come to be that of a sometimes querulous but essentially kindly uncle who complains while furiously puffing on his pipe but who finally, as everyone expects, gives in and hands over the allowance, grants the permission, or raises his hand in blessing, and then returns to his rocking chair for another year of somnolence broken only by an occasional anxious glance down the avenue and a muttered doubt as to whether he had done the right thing.[181]

A fight on constitutional grounds, the report suggested, might restore Congress to its former state of vigor, much as the old man of the story might regain something of his lost vitality by expending his remaining energy on a paddling of his errant nephews and nieces.

The armed services committee adopted poor legislative tactics in its RS-70 fight, overextended its position, and underestimated the degree of congressional and presidential opposition that it would encounter. The Constitution was not a felicitous instrument by which to resolve a policy dispute that involved the weighing of technical data and the conflicting testimony of Defense Department witnesses. Many legislators understood that the political and technical differences over the RS-70 were complex enough without forcing them into a Procrustean bed of simplified and essentially misleading interpretations of Congress' constitutional role in defense policy. Moreover, the committee's arguments and the facts that it assembled did not accurately reflect the record of important contributions which Congress, through its initiative in the post-sputnik years, had made to defense policy. Overlooked by the committee report were the many instances in which Congress' recommendations had been adopted by the executive branch. Congress had intervened successfully in military policy for more than a decade and a half without resorting to cramped constitutional formulas to exert its influence.

Even if the likely view is accepted that Representative Vinson's committee had posed the constitutional issue to gain publicity and to galvanize majority opinion in Congress as political leverage over the chief executive on the RS-70 issue, it is apparent that the committee blundered. The Kennedy administration had taken long strides to improve the nation's defense posture. Defense Secretary McNamara enjoyed wide backing in Congress, even from among members of the armed services committees. Vinson himself had praised McNamara's grasp of defense problems and his handling of the Defense Department. Congressional members were not spoiling for a fight with a defense secretary whom they admired for his comprehensive understanding of defense problems and for his impressive direction of the military establishment. Besides, they generally supported his policies. Democratic legislators were reluctant, moreover, to contest a Democratic President who solidly backed his defense secretary. Only the Republicans could gain in the oncoming congressional elections from such a clash. For their part some Republicans did what they could to widen the split between congressional and executive Democrats, while they worked simultaneously to defeat the Vinson proposal. Representative Gerald Ford, leading minority member of the House defense appropriations group, spearheaded the Republican drive against Vinson. House Republican Leader Charles Halleck's aid was secured to oppose the Vinson move.[182] Ford personally delivered a three-pronged verbal attack on the House report.

He charged that it "invaded the responsibilities and the jurisdiction of . . . the President . . . usurped the appropriating authority of the committee on appropriations . . . [and] created inflexibility in the management of the RS-70 program. . . . "[183]

Ford's reference to the jurisdictional autonomy of the appropriations groups touched the most sensitive congressional nerve. Legislators might combine against the President on a policy issue, but they were not likely to do so at the expense of their power within Congress. Since their personal power depended so heavily on their committee assignments and on the prestige and influence of the committees, they were not disposed to sacrifice their respective committee's prerogatives, even in the assertion of Congress' alleged constitutional rights. In this respect Ford candidly stated his feelings on the House floor in the wake of an announcement that a compromise settlement between the armed services committee and the President had been reached on the RS-70:

> I think that the Congress would have been unwise to approve the language 'directs' because it would have caused trouble between two great committees, the Committee on Armed Services, and the Committee on Appropriations. . . . I am very jealous of the prerogatives of my committee, the Committee on Appropriations. I am very envious that the Committee on Armed Services exercise to the fullest its prerogatives. I do not want those of us who are members of the Committee on Appropriations drafting legislation on an authorization bill. . . . On the other hand, I do not think it is the prerogative of the Committee on Armed Services to invade the jurisdiction of the Committee on Appropriations. This language, if it had been approved . . . would have been an invasion of the authority of the Appropriations Committee.[184]

Democratic members of the defense appropriations subcommittees had already met with President Kennedy to join forces with him in opposition to Vinson. Adding to the weight of his position, President

Kennedy gained the support of the Democratic leadership of the House, including Speaker John McCormack and Majority Leader Carl Albert, to reach a compromise with Vinson or to challenge him if necessary.[185]

In a private meeting between Vinson and the President in the White House rose garden, a compromise agreement was reached which permitted Vinson to withdraw with a measure of grace despite his exposed political position. On the floor of the House, Vinson recommended the substitution of the word "authorized" for "directed" in granting funds to the secretary of the air force for RS-70 development. The secretary of defense on March 20 wrote a letter to Chairman Vinson in which he noted that he had initiated a "new study of the RS-70 program."[186] The house bill was then overwhelmingly passed and sent to the Senate where most of its provisions were accepted. Deleted only were House increases of $86.5 million for army aircraft and missiles and $10 million for air force missiles.[187] The Senate affirmed the $491 million authorization for the RS-70, without referring to the constitutional issue raised in the House report.

Appropriations bill passes.—In contrast to the procurement authorization measure, the defense appropriations bill slipped through Congress almost unnoticed, although it was the largest sum passed for defense since the Korean War. Floor attendance was sparse. At one point during the House presentation a head count produced only 31 legislators, including most of the defense subcommittee members.[188] At one important point in Senate consideration of the measure, a quorum was not present to vote on an important amendment by Senator William Proxmire.[189] Both the House and the Senate appropriations groups recommended adoption of the President's program.

The House increased administration requests by $699 million and made decreases totaling $766 million. The augmentations fell into two principal groups. The House rejected the administration request to reallocate $514.5 million which Congress had appropriated a year

417

before for strategic bombers. The House instead made another appropriation of this amount. The move had no effect on the defense program. The balance of the $182.3 million increase was largely divided among three programs: $52.9 million for RS-70 components; $42.0 million to accelerate Dyna-Soar; and $48.8 million to maintain the army national guard and the army reserve at 400,000 and 300,000, respectively. The small sum for the RS-70 was deceptive since the House provided $300 million in contingency funds to the secretary of defense from which to draw extra funds for the supersonic bomber at his discretion.[190] The Senate concurred in these decisions, but added appropriations of $491 million for the RS-70. Also included was mandatory language to keep the reserves at 700,000.[191]

The final bill compromised on an RS-70 appropriation of $326.6 million. A number of legislative restrictions on administrative action were also written into the bill. The most important of these concerned work in navy shipyards and payments on Defense Department research contracts. The final bill totaled $48.14 billion or approximately $250 million over the administration's requests.[192]

Aside from the RS-70 program, the other major disagreement between the defense appropriations groups and the Pentagon centered on the reduction and reorganization of army reserves. The Defense Department had activated approximately 120,000 army reservists during the Berlin crisis as well as about 28,000 air force and navy personnel. Throughout the fall and winter of 1961–62, congressional offices were flooded with complaints from the reservists and "filler" personnel who had been activated. They asked congressional intercession to be released from duty or to secure legislative remedy for a host of real and imagined injuries that they had undergone during the callup. Morale among some reservists fell so low that the Defense Department was compelled to issue a pamphlet to explain the reasons for the activation. The difficulties that had arisen in shaping the reserve units into fighting teams prompted the Defense

418

Department to devise a realignment of reserve forces leading to the deactivation of eight national guard and army reserve divisions and a diminution of reserve strength to 642,000. This action prompted Congress to repair to the old standard of 700,000 army reservists in paid status.[193]

A compromise favorable to the defense secretary's position was finally reached. The House group objected to the Senate's mandatory language for many of the same reasons that it had opposed a directed proviso for the RS-70. The Senate's version of the appropriations bill was softened to a statement of legislative interest in the maintenance of existing reserve units "insofar as practical." The extent of the defense secretary's victory is indicated, furthermore, by his letter to Senator A. Willis Robertson, chairman of the Senate defense appropriations group. In lieu of the restrictive language proposed by the Senate, the defense secretary agreed to keep the reserves at 700,000 provided that all units maintained qualified personnel at 90 per cent levels, applied the same recruiting standards as the active army, and stayed within their authorized strength. These cleverly constructed administrative reservations made it impossible for the army guard and the army reserves to reach a 700,000 manning plateau. On June 30, 1963, the Defense Department reported an army guard force of 360,714 and an army reserve of 284,896 for a total of 645,610. The figure closely corresponded to Secretary McNamara's recommended level of 642,000.

Decline of Congressional Influence

Relevant factors.—What accounts for the decrease in the number and impact of congressional initiatives and innovations in defense policy during the Eighty-seventh Congress? The most significant factor was the more forceful leadership of President Kennedy in strategic

419

and foreign policy. The President steadfastly supported the policies and actions of Defense Secretary McNamara before Congress. Majority sentiment in Congress, moreover, generally favored most of the policy and process innovations that McNamara introduced. For his part, McNamara personally gained widespread congressional confidence in his management of the sprawling and diverse military establishment. He was both respected and admired and, equally important, feared by legislators who were not eager to engage the defense secretary in open conflict and risk defeat in much the same way as Vinson did on the RS-70 issue. McNamara's record in legislative infighting was impressive during his first two years in office. His victories buttressed his already ascendant position in the Defense Department.

The centralization of power in the hands of the secretary of defense also diminished public displays of service rivalry and blocked or impeded service end-runs to Congress. There was little incentive for service officials to appeal to Congress for remedy of an adverse decision by the defense secretary if their political exposure was not likely to have an appreciable effect on the secretary's policy determinations. It should be noted, too, that thanks to McNamara's policies, the services received considerably more human and material resources than under the Eisenhower administration. Budgetary affluence, while it did not silence service complaints entirely, blunted much of their point. In a number of cases, the army offering the most prominent example, Secretary McNamara revised service requirements upward. Hitherto, conflicts among the services or between them and the political leadership of the Pentagon and the administration provided the opening wedges for congressional opinion to assert itself and for its influence to be felt in defense policy. As these internal opportunities for the exercise of congressional power gradually diminished, so also did external stimulants to congressional action in defense affairs temporarily decline. Traumatic shocks of the scale and impact of the Korean War and sputnik did not occur. While there were moments of acute international tension as in the Berlin crisis of 1961 and the Cuban confrontation of 1962, the favorable outcomes of these embroglios for American interests served to reinforce, not erode, congressional confidence in United States military superiority. There was little sense and less domestic political mileage to be gained in attacking the President or his defense secretary in those areas where their policies yielded the most satisfactory results. The incentives for restrained criticism from Congress since the inception of the Eighty-seventh Congress were enhanced, though obviously not precluded as Representative Vinson demonstrated, by single party control of both branches of the government.

While the trend since the inception of the Eighty-seventh Congress has tended in the direction of a diminution of congressional initiative and innovation in defense policy, it is by no means irreversible. Under different international conditions, with a change in the leadership in the executive branch and with different personnel in the Defense Department, Congress might well return to the pattern that it established during the Eighty-sixth Congress. Even during the Eighty-seventh Congress, congressional intervention was encouraged in those areas where experts disagreed among themselves, as on the RS-70 and nuclear propulsion. The history of congressional-executive relations since World War II indicates wide oscillations in the range of the role that legislators and the legislative branch have played in strategic and foreign policy. This process of expansion and contraction is likely to continue. In the first half of the 1960's, the slope of the line of Congress' impact on defense policy was decidedly downward.

Section 412(b) reviewed.—Section 412(b) contributed to this declining trend. The review conducted by the armed services committees did not provide Congress with additional information or insight by which to analyze and evaluate the military proposals and strategic policies of the administration. Nor did it excel the probing investigations of the defense appropriations subcommittees, particularly on the House side. The principal benefit of Section 412(b) was the greater awareness among armed services committee members of the diversity and complexity of the defense effort. There was some basis for Senator Russell's view, therefore, that Section 412(b) "affords a much broader base of information and understanding in Congress." This knowledge did not produce any extensive changes in administration programs other than marginal reductions in scattered programs and some shifts of emphasis. These results were already a common feature of the appropriations review. Section 412(b) added little to it. Senator Russell conceded this point in his presentation of the FY 1963 authorization procurement bill to the Senate when he confessed "that the results of this procedure to date" were not "earth shaking in their significance." [194] Russell, moreover, underlined again the major purpose of Section 412(b). "It affords," he said, "the appropriate legislative committees an opportunity to express their judgment in areas for which they have responsibility." [195]

Not without relevance, the RS-70 bomber, the major issue pressed by the armed services committees, progressively lost the endorsement of the air force, its chief supporter. A follow-on bomber remained an important air force interest, but by 1965 technological progress had overtaken the RS-70 and other manned delivery systems were being given higher priority attention.[196] The FY 1967 defense budget carried funds for the development and production of a supersonic bomber to replace the B-52. The reluctance of the House appropriations group to grant larger appropriations for the RS-70 than the administration had requested and the refusal of the defense secretary to spend more on the RS-70 system were by and large vindicated.

The major defect of Section 412(b), however, was not informational. It was political. Section 412(b) emphasized existing divisions in Congress along committee lines at the expense of over-all congressional power in defense policy. By stressing committee prerogatives and the question of what committee should make decisions, not what decisions should be made, Section 412(b) weakened congressional cohesion which is a prerequisite for the effective assertion of

Congress' authority, especially in the face of growing centralization in the executive branch. The diffusion and dissipation of congressional power and authority were more pronounced in the House, where the armed services committee and the appropriations defense group drifted progressively apart. As a consequence, an already strong defense secretary strengthened his position before Congress. The armed services committees increased their prestige and influence over security affairs relative to the defense appropriations subcommittees since the inception of Section 412(b), but Congress' political power in these areas decreased vis-à-vis the President and the Secretary of Defense.

This unforeseen effect of Section 412(b) was given deepened significance by the fact that it grew out of the Senate hearings on the Department of Defense Reorganization Act of 1958 which paved the way for the unprecedented centralization of the defense establishment under the Kennedy and Johnson administrations. As Defense Secretary McNamara was rapidly establishing the primacy of his office over the military services, Congress, through the implementation of Section 412(b), was accelerating the centrifugal tendencies of its committee and leadership arrangements. Even as the secretary of defense was consolidating his position through the integration of defense planning, programming, and budgeting, Congress was increasingly emphasizing these distinctions. The armed services committees stressed in effect their hegemony over defense planning and programming—and then only over limited aspects of these areas confined to aircraft, missiles, and naval vessels—and tacitly advised the appropriations committees to focus on budgetary and administrative considerations. This result was all the more curious since Senator Flanders, as a member of both the Senate Armed Services Committee and the defense appropriations subcommittee, initially inspired Section 412 (b). It was as if Flanders were dividing himself in two.

The divisive effect of Section 412(b) in Congress can be seen more clearly through an analysis of Flanders' statement of the problem of Congress' role in defense policy and his solution to it. Flanders recognized the need for a congressional review of the defense program that included all of its major component parts, each related to the other, and linked to the nation's security interests and foreign policy goals. Part of Flanders' problem, therefore, was to devise means by which Congress could conduct such a review which he felt was lacking in the operations of the armed services and appropriations committees. He was aware that Congress needed accurate and comprehensive program and budgetary data concerning the principal parts of the administration's defense program which was, in turn, presented as one element of the government's foreign and domestic policies. Congress also needed access to the competing arguments and proposals that various segments of the military establishment had advanced before the administration finally defined its own policy positions with respect to its defense program. Only through a knowledge of these rival points of view would Congress ultimately be in a position to evaluate the merits of the administration's recommendations and make its influence felt. Lacking such access to technical expertise and professional judgment, it would be making its policy determinations in an informational vacuum.

The other part of Flanders' problem was to achieve a wider and more inclusive review of defense policy *through* the existing institutional organization of Congress. For Flanders the bridge between the requirements of a fully effective and continuing review of defense policy and the process requirements intrinsic to Congress' decentralization of power and responsibility was an annual authorizing bill for the entire defense program which would be passed upon by the armed services committees. Such a procedure seemed to be logically related to the jurisdictional authority of the armed services committees accepted by most legislators and defined by the Legislative Reorganization Act of 1946. It also appeared sufficiently comprehensive to embrace a review and analysis of the major factors which Congress would have to weigh if it were to reach an independent evaluation of the defense proposals of the executive branch.

424

Flanders had unfortunately set himself an impossible task. The authorizing scheme that he tentatively proposed demanded a review of all relevant planning, programming, and budgetary factors that had shaped the administration's defense proposals and not, in Flanders' own words, "bits and pieces of . . . appropriations" which are glued "together with some imagination . . . [to] arrive at an overall defense program." [197] To be fully effective a congressional review of the administration's defense recommendations would have required not only an analysis of defense policies and proposed expenditures to implement them but an understanding of the connections between the military and non-military parts of the nation's strategic posture and, finally, an integrated grasp of the relations and interactions of domestic and foreign policy. Flanders' suggested authorization procedure did not ostensibly envisage so comprehensive a review of the administration's policies and programs. Rather than pose this larger issue squarely, he struggled to fashion a legislative instrument that would yield more adequate congressional surveillance and influence over defense policy by exhausting the possibilities of the legislative mandate already possessed by the armed services committees. The problem that Flanders defined for himself was inherently insoluble. The jurisdictional competence of the armed services groups furnished too shaky and confining a base on which to conduct the kind of broad gauged review of strategic policy that his proposal implied.

Even if Flanders' terms of reference had been accepted, an effective policy review would have required a congressional capacity to marshal a unified position in order to assert its collective authority and power in those areas where it disagreed with the administration's defense package, the substantive merits of the policy issue notwithstanding. To have asserted its will with some expectation that it would solicit a satisfactory executive branch response, Congress would have had to be in a position to co-ordinate the divergent viewpoints of its committees and hammer out a position that would have commanded wide legislative support. The fragmentation of committee power and responsibility impeded the task of building and sustaining a viable consensus in the face of continued executive opposition. The major effect of Section 412(b) was to unduly burden already outdated legislative machinery for harnessing and focusing majority sentiment in Congress on those aspects of strategic policy where it could be most effective and efficient. Seen in a reverse light, Section 412(b) can be interpreted not so much as another factor contributing to the breakdown of the legislative process but as a product of the process itself.

Flanders' dilemma is all the more poignant when it is recalled that his imaginative sketch for a defense review was discarded by the Senate Armed Services Committee. Section 412(b) did not exploit the potentialities of the military group's legitimate sphere of authority. As it is presently constructed, Section 412(b) emphasizes a congressional focus on specific military hardware items that deflects attention from strategic policy questions. The congressional-executive skirmishes that have been fought on the battlefield of the armed services committees have reflected this bias. There is no doubt, as some individuals close to the legislative defense process have argued, that Congress can only exert its influence on a selected number of concrete defense issues. For reasons which are made more explicit in Part III below, it cannot equal the President and the executive branch in strategic policy. Nevertheless, the question remains that legislators cannot be certain that the priorities that they set for military spending correspond to the defense needs of the nation, unless they possess a comprehensive grasp of strategic policy. The armed services committees still review only a part of the defense program and continue to segregate their review of the administration's military procurement and military construction authorizations bills. This anomaly has been partially overcome in the Senate where joint hearings on the procurement authorization and selected parts of the general appropriations bills have been held since 1964 between the armed services committee and the defense appropriations group. This integration of activity has occurred in great part through the chance circumstance that Senator Russell, as a consequence of the fortuitous workings of the seniority system, became chairman of both committees. There is no assurance that this arrangement will continue when the chairmanships of the two committees are again held by different senators.

Congressional machinery for dealing with the requirements of security and foreign policy are outmoded. They cut across committee lines. No one committee of Congress is responsible for review and action upon all of these diverse economic, military, and political requirements. That at least some legislators are conscious of this difficulty is indicated in an exchange between the members of the Jackson subcommittee on national policy machinery during the questioning of Mr. Charles Hitch, defense comptroller, over Kennedy administration innovations in defense budgeting and programming:

> Senator Javits: What I had in mind, Mr. Chairman, is that if we are going to be . . . raising the problems which are inherent in this new approach of the [Defense] Department, we should also revise the organizational structure of the Congress to deal with them.
>
> Senator Jackson: I agree with you completely. When the administration presents the kind of package up here that will not fit our committee system, then I think we will move in response. It usually is initiated from the Executive side, or at least, it has been in the past, and we will be forced to do something about our committee structure.[198]

The major change in Congress' committee structure in national security and foreign policy has been Section 412(b). Considering its roots in the Defense Department Reorganization Act of 1958, it was a response to the anticipated centralization of the defense establishment. It has not, however, been proportionate to the sweeping changes that the executive branch has undergone in the past decade. Section 412(b) has not proved to be any more a solution to the problem of congressional oversight and influence than the arrangements that were operative before its adoption. To the degree that it has hampered the work of the appropriations defense groups, particularly on the House side, it has diluted their effectiveness and reduced the value of Congress' potential contribution to military policy.

Epilogue.—The evolution of United States strategic problems did not halt, of course, with the Eighty-seventh Congress. The closing months of the Eighty-seventh Congress found the United States and the Soviet Union at loggerheads over Soviet implacement of long-range missiles on Cuban soil, while at the end of the first third of the Eighty-eighth Congress, the United States and the Soviet Union, in a dramatic turnabout, entered into serious negotiations leading to a limited nuclear test ban agreement. The Cuban confrontation and the signing of the test ban treaty mark a fork in the road, indicating the divergent routes that Soviet-American relations could take in the the divergent routes that Soviet-American relations could take in the 1960's and beyond. It was not at all certain in 1965 down which path the super powers would move. Continuing disagreement over Berlin and Germany and sustained hostilities in Southeast Asia, involving, by the winter of 1965, 200,000 American military personnel in the South Vietnam war, menaced further advance toward a viable *détente*. The inability of the United States and Communist China to settle their differences also threatened the outbreak of a war that might engulf not only Asia but the rest of the globe. That the United States would successfully cope with these and other international problems in the future could not be predicted with certainty. The inept handling of the Santo Domingo crisis in 1965

428

further increased doubts about the United States successful management of its foreign affairs in the future. Whether the United States would develop an effective strategic policy, including military and non-military elements, for the remainder of the twentieth century would continue to depend in large measure on the enlightenment and resolution of its people, the vitality of its governmental institutions, and the foresight and will of its leaders. How much can Congress be expected to do? Part III attempts to supply an answer.

PART III

STRATEGIC POLICY, DEFENSE BUDGETS, AND CONGRESS

Guidelines for the Future and an Evaluation of the Past

VIII

What role should Congress play in strategic policy through its power of the purse? The role that it has actually played since World War II offers some guide. It indicates the range of Congress' potential contribution. Drawing on this experience, the component parts of its role in defense policy can be delineated and its record in passing on the President's defense proposals can be assessed. Thus, the criteria that should guide Congress' participation in defense policy through its funding power are explicitly stated below and simultaneously applied to Congress' handling of the major defense appropriations bills in Congress in the period 1945-1962—the Seventy-ninth through the Eighty-seventh congresses. These guidelines for Congress' role in defense policy are implicit in the running description and analysis of the congressional defense budgetary process of Part II.

Congress will be used in two senses. Most generally Congress will refer to both houses considered as a whole which share responsibility for the common defense and for the support of United States foreign policy. This sense of Congress is inherent in the question of what role it can, and should, play in future defense policy development. Within this meaning Congress is viewed as more than the sum of its parts which are composed of individual congressmen and committees. However, in evaluating the actual past actions and decisions of Congress insofar as they concern the defense budgetary process, the praise and blame which is assigned to Congress refers principally to the work of the defense appropriations subcommittees and the armed services committees. Relevant roles played by other committees and legislators will be noted. These distinctions between the two senses of Congress can perhaps best be grasped if it is understood that, although the members of the appropriations groups and military service committees are presently the protagonists of the annual defense budget drama, their activities do not necessarily exhaust the intellectual and political tasks and duties which Congress as a whole possesses in strategic policy through its control of federal funds.

CONSTRAINTS ON CONGRESS [1]

Paradoxically enough, the role which Congress cannot play in shaping military strategic policy through its power of the purse indicates the role that it can assume. To recognize the major constraints under which Congress operates in defense matters is to define its capabilities in these areas and, consequently, the expectations that may be entertained with respect to its utility as a political institution. An appreciation of these limitations guards against asking too much or too little of Congress; and, more importantly, directs attention to the necessary functions which Congress should principally perform in maintaining popular government and in achieving the nation's objectives in strategic policy.

The constitutional authority of Congress supplies only the most general guide for congressional action. In exercising its appropriations power for the support of the military establishment, Congress acts in a particular kind of technological, military, administrative, and domestic political setting which defines the scope and nature of its actual or potential discretion to influence military policy. It is in terms of the actual or potential discretion which Congress can feasibly exercise in defense policy formulation that a judgment of its behavior is rendered possible, notwithstanding the broad language

434

of the Constitution with regard to Congress' authority. The setting in which Congress can exercise some measure of independent choice in defense policy is delimited by three general factors: (1) the present complex, technical character of military power and the high degree of scientific and military professionalism required to relate military force to the achievement of national goals; (2) the inherent executive nature of foreign policy and military affairs, especially under conditions of modern warfare; and (3) the expectations and moods which the public has toward military and foreign policy and toward its representatives in Congress.

The first two factors are largely opposite sides of the same coin. Huge, well-organized, technically competent bureaucratic structures are needed to fulfil the requirements of military policy and administration. The dominant feature of a bureaucracy is its executive arrangements of decision-making based on a hierarchical division of functions and authority. Congress' task is not to eliminate expertise and executive initiative in security and foreign affairs as obstacles to its assertion of power and authority. It could do so only at the expense of the nation's efforts in these areas, for the effective formulation and implementation of security and foreign policy imply the continuous operation of these elements. No security or foreign policy is possible without them since they are, in effect, instrumentalities that must be responsive to the variety of military threats to American security and foreign policy interests and objectives. These threats are external to Congress. By itself, it has little power to influence them directly except through its reliance on expertise and executive leadership. As the discussion below indicates, however, reliance does not necessarily imply slavish subordination. Rather, Congress must come to terms with expert judgment and executive leadership and fashion a role for itself that both supplements and encourages their efficient and responsible organization and operation.

The third factor is qualitatively different. It is susceptible to wide interpretation, expansion, and refinement over time. It is a function

435

of the political maturity of the American people; of their perception of the material, intellectual, and emotional requirements of military and foreign policy and the role of government in these areas; and of the quality of leadership manifested by the President and Congress. These elements are subject to constant and continuing change and reformulation. Since World War II congressional participation in defense policy has fluctuated markedly. In the Eighty-sixth Congress, its contribution was significant. In other periods legislators have been unduly swayed by their perceptions of public sentiment or have been timid or negligent in asserting their views, particularly in the face of strong executive resistance.

1. Military policy and expertise.—In 1789 a reasonable expectation existed that Congress could effectively exercise its military powers without much outside assistance or guidance. Through its own investigations, it could be expected to determine the kinds of armed forces required for the nation's defense and its foreign policy objectives. Even lower-level questions of supply and logistics, involving food, forage, horse cavalry, and muskets were conceivably within its grasp. At the time of the Constitutional Convention, legislatures were generally able to deal with a large share of the military issues facing the nation. Properly motivated, they were potentially capable of resolving the nation's strategic problems. Specialized military, scientific, and technical knowledge and training were not so critical as they are today. Thus Trevelyan could write of parliamentary government in England: "The Great French War—alike in the first phase in the time of Pitt and Nelson, and in its last in the time of Castlereagh and Wellington—was fought by the House of Commons. The comparison of the Roman Senate fighting Hannibal was in the mind of every educated man." [2] Many of the Framers could maintain this same degree of assurance in congressional competence in strategic matters.

436

The same certainty is no longer possible. The relatively slow pace and simple problems of eighteenth and nineteenth century life have been irrevocably transformed. The Industrial Revolution, scientific discovery, technological innovations, the awakening of the great masses of the world to political independence, social equality, and material advancement, and the incessant clash of irreconcilable political ideologies—all of these processes of change have overtaken Congress. It cannot rely on its own knowledge and resources to make the proper political decisions that can deal with the manifold and interrelated problems arising from them.[3] It must depend for advice and guidance on a host of experts, ranging from economists, political area analysts, and military officers to civilian scientists and technicians, specializing in such varied fields as agronomy, nuclear energy, and missile propulsion systems. Contemporary military technology has completely bypassed the primitive weapon systems of the past. Mechanized mass armies, employing tanks, guided missiles, and atomic field weapons, have replaced the poorly equipped and largely immobile forces of the past. Missile-firing submarines and "Forrestal" supercarriers have supplanted the wooden man-of-war. The strategic bomber similarly may find its days numbered, to be largely replaced perhaps by a complicated and generally invulnerable system of hardened and mobile intercontinental ballistic missiles. Accordingly, this technological revolution in weaponry has resulted, and will continue to result, in corresponding changes in military strategy which must be integrated with other power resources in constructing an over-all national strategy.

The ongoing flux in weapons development alone, apart from other factors, renders many of Congress' traditional procedures and organizational methods obsolete. This is clearly revealed in the Senate hearings on the Kennedy administration's proposals for a test ban treaty with the United Kingdom and the Soviet Union. Ostensibly, the final decision rested with the Senate, and in an important political sense this was true. But this political decision was so hedged about by scientific and technical considerations that, in effect, a fundamental part of the judgment as to the advisability of the test ban treaty was transferred from Congress to the military establishment on the one hand and to the scientific community and the prevailing opinion within it on the other. This shift occurred because the decision to accept or reject the test ban agreement hinged critically on an assessment of the impact which it would have on the then existing and future military research and development programs of the United States and the Soviet Union. Only those military officers, scientists, and administrators connected with military preparedness, nuclear physics, and the related fields in chemistry and biology could answer this question.[4] Without their guidance and advice, Congress could not have made a final determination that was mindful of the possible and probable consequences of the test ban treaty for the United States strategic position. The test ban hearings provide but one dramatic example of Congress' dependence on the expertise of the executive branch, now a routine, largely unnoticed, feature of its annual defense appropriations and authorizations hearings.

2. *Military policy and executive initiative.*—These evolving facets of the military, scientific, and technological environment have been paralleled by enormous changes within the executive branch of the federal government leading to its increasing dominance over most areas of public policy, especially those concerning military policy.[5] Initiative in security and foreign policy reside in the President and the complex of executive departments and agencies that he heads. There has been nothing sinister about this increase in executive power. The sources of this expansion are implicit in Hamilton's incisive remark that "it is of the nature of war to increase the executive at the expense of the legislative authority."[6] The threat of war produces the same effect, especially in the nuclear age when military conflict among the great powers carries the seeds of swift atomic devastation.

438

Developing a coherent military strategy is properly an executive function. The component parts of a strategic plan require executive initiative in their formulation and executive control in their implementation. Through its vast intelligence resources, the executive branch possesses the nation's most complete picture of the enemy's political intentions and military capabilities, knowledge which for security reasons must remain secret and unavailable to many legislators. Only the executive branch commands the needed scientific, technical, and military expertise to formulate the proper responses to enemy threats and to determine the military requirements needed to support them. Only it has the personnel, administrative experience, and complicated bureaucratic structure to administer a world-wide military organization; only it can potentially operate with the efficiency of a unity of command; and only it can move with energy, secrecy, and dispatch—qualities which are absent, quite legitimately, from the slow and open deliberations of a democratic legislature. Although not always successful, only the President and the executive agencies under his direction have the capacity to orchestrate the many complicated and controlled moves, as during the Cuban crisis of 1962, which are implicit in a successful marriage of military planning and operations and diplomatic maneuvering. The foresight of the Framers, who refused to define in restrictive detail how the war power might be exercised by the President and by Congress, has made possible the rapid growth of the executive branch in response to military and strategic imperatives without forcing one word to be changed in the Constitution.[7] It has also permitted the expanding power of the federal government to be lodged in the executive branch where it can be more effectively exercised.

Congress cannot oversee in detail the immense and sprawling military establishment which presently directs the energies of almost four million civilian and military personnel and exercises varying controls over an additional five million non-governmental personnel engaged in defense contract work. Congress' appropriations power, in particular, is not put to its most effective use if it is solely directed

439

toward specific control and management of Defense Department administration.[8] These burdensome tasks are too heavy for any legislator, committee, or even the entire Congress to carry. The Hoover Commission estimated that the Defense Department spends about $30 million yearly simply to prepare its budget.[9] It would be an exhaustive task to review only this one, small aspect of Defense Department operations which in itself does not directly raise any military policy questions.

The Hoover Commission figure, which is doubtless well below the actual cost today of producing the annual Defense Department budget, does suggest the magnitude of Congress' problems, should it attempt too close an examination of defense activities. Once embarked on such a course, it would be quickly ensnared in an intricate web of minute facts. Its energies would be quickly sapped, and its attention deflected from the policy considerations presumably underlying administrative action. As fact upon fact would be compiled, a grave risk would be run that congressional understanding of the varying importance of different military policy proposals would be obscured. Quite possibly lost in the sea of budgetary numbers and administrative minutiae would be the objectives to be served by the defense establishment and the political costs and benefits which might result from using different kinds and combinations of physical force as a response to foreign political and military challenges. Congress would have traded the substance of governmental power for the trappings of it. It would have relinquished its ability to keep pace with the rapid movement of international events and to influence the direction of national policy in light of these changes. And a confused and troubled public would have to look elsewhere, as indeed it often has, for guidance and security.

3. *Electorate expectations and moods.*—In the broadest sense, expectations refer to all those desirable political ends which citizens,

440

including most especially the voting public, seek to achieve through the political process and their conception of the proper means, including institutional mechanisms, which should be employed to attain these ends.[10] The electorate has certain expectations of Congress as a whole and of the behavior of individual legislators that place both under constraints. These include the political objectives about which Congress makes decisions and the prestige and status of Congress as a governmental institution. Voters expect Congress and the President to provide for defense against enemy attack and to define and secure basic foreign policy goals. But they also hope for more—often a great deal more. They may desire lower taxes or assorted tax privileges. Or, they may demand increased governmental spending for a variety of programs—social security, health, education, highways, public transportation, agricultural surpluses, full employment, urban redevelopment—all of which may compete with spending proposals of the defense establishment for the nation's limited human and material resources. Or, they may resist conscription laws, restrictions on private spending and investment, and economic controls which may be necessary for an effective strategic position. To the extent that Congress is compelled to pursue these competing objectives, its discretion will be restricted in the kinds of force levels and weapons systems that it can provide the Defense Department.

Voters may also narrowly constrict congressional discretion in how military power, once organized, may be utilized. From a political standpoint, Congress may be unable to furnish the executive branch with sufficient flexibility to meet specific military contingencies, such as limited or guerrilla warfare situations; or it may be precluded from taking advantage of arms control and disarmament arrangements with foreign powers which might be useful in advancing the nation's interests and objectives through non-violent means; or it may be checked in its capacity to supplement and co-ordinate military power with other national power resources, such as foreign aid, to influence the behavior of foreign powers. Expectations may exceed the nation's

441

ability to realize them, whatever the magnitude of its effort. Struggles over foreign policy since 1940 in the United States can be interpreted as a process of bringing public expectations into line with what could be feasibly achieved through the exercise of American power. Whether or not "victory," defined as capitulation of the enemy to American will, is possible in the cold war is only the current manifestation of this evolutionary process. It is still difficult for many Americans to understand or to accept emotionally the fact that "victory" in the World War II sense of the word of unconditional surrender is no longer possible in an age in which antagonists possess nuclear weapons.[11]

Equally important for an understanding of congressional action are the vacillating moods of the electorate toward military and foreign policy problems. In contrast to expectations, which suggest some form of conceptualization of political means and ends, moods "lack intellectual structure and factual content."[12] They are, as Professor Gabriel Almold observes, "superficial psychic states [that] are bound to be unstable since they are not anchored in a set of explicit value and means calculations or traditional compulsions."[13] It is precisely *because* the moods of the public often undergo rapid and radical permutations that significant limits are placed on the discretion of governmental officials in military and foreign policy. Long-range planning and swift adjustment to the vicissitudes of novel international conditions are seriously impeded. Fluctuating and unpredictable, the changing emotive responses of the public are not likely to be congruent with the short- and long-term needs of security and foreign policy. They are important operational factors that Congress cannot overlook in reaching policy decisions.

The American approach to military conflict and foreign policy since World War II has been marked by the volatile and oscillating moods of the populace. The demobilization immediately after World War II was prompted largely by popular sentiment. Little public enthusiasm could be marshaled between 1945 and 1947 for the maintenance of a large military establishment, the continuation of the draft, or the introduction of universal military training. Public optimism after the war gradually eroded as big power harmony collapsed. A rearmament effort briefly gained public favor after the Czech coup d'état in 1948. When the February crisis passed without menacing communist activity elsewhere, the public, lacking adequate leadership from the executive and legislative branches, lapsed again into complacency. The Berlin Blockade and air lift (July, 1948–May, 1949), while prompting anxiety in official circles, did not stir the nation to rearm for possible military conflict with the Soviet Union in Europe or elsewhere. The Korean War compelled partial mobilization and thenceforward forced the United States to support a large defense effort. Sentiment to sustain the Korean struggle was, nevertheless, soon withdrawn. Again the public mood tired of the conflict which it did not fully comprehend. During the elections of 1952 public attitudes alternated radically between fits of frustration over the stalemate in Korea and clarion calls for a "roll back" of the Iron Curtain or the liberation of captive territories. Public sentiment toward the cold war stabilized for a short time after the end of hostilities in Korea. Massive retaliation provided a measure of comfort from the daily anxieties of the cold war. Sputnik in 1957, however, rekindled national fears, and a new preparedness movement was galvanized. The mutability of public sentiment lends evidence to de Tocqueville's prescient observation that

> democracy appears . . . better adapted for the conduct of society in times of peace, or for a sudden effort of remarkable vigor, than for the prolonged endurance of the great storms that beset the political existence of nations. . . . Clear perception of the future, founded upon judgment and experience . . . is frequently wanting in democracies. The people are more apt to feel than to reason; and if their present sufferings are great, it is to be feared that the still greater sufferings attendant upon defeat will be forgotten.[14]

While congressional decisions have been affected by these shifts in public mood, it is too much to argue that Congress has been helpless before public moods and expectations or that it has failed since World War II to inform and direct them. Legislators do exercise some independence in approving defense appropriations. Their behavior cannot be fully explained through an analysis of social forces operating in their respective constituencies. Any standards which are applied to congressional action in military policy must take into account some degree of congressional discretion in its response to security and foreign policy problems. Such a view can be adopted without losing sight of the many conflicting and overlapping pressures which influence the decisions of individual legislators and, ultimately, of Congress itself.

Congress is a dynamic organization. It acts and *reacts*. What it says and does has an effect on the power which it, the President, and the federal government can exercise. Congress and congressmen influence the groups and individuals which seek to influence them. The relationship is reciprocal. Congress is armed, moreover, with a power that is denied to the lobbyist. It can legitimate public policy; the lobbyist is largely restricted to influencing it. Only Congress can pass defense appropriations. It is not simply another lobby agency, although its participation in the defense policy process can be cast in this light.[15] That Congress seeks to influence, modify, and change the President's military proposals derives ultimately from the powers and responsibilities with which it is charged under the Constitution. A complete interpretation of its action—or inaction—in security and foreign policy matters must in great part be conceived as a function of its institutional duties.

The standards for congressional action outlined below imply a congressional obligation to expand the scope and relevance of Congress' present role in defense policy in those areas where it can make a useful contribution. It has a duty to itself, the President, and the public to minimize the number and importance of those constraints which hamper its capacity to act as a vehicle of popular government. The criteria which are applied below to congressional decision and action are not static and inflexible. They are designed to be interpreted in terms of the shifting historical conditions under which Congress operates and with which it must cope. They must be re-evaluated in light of new elements of domestic and international life. Congress must be partially judged, accordingly, by its willingness and capacity to re-evaluate its organization and modes of operation.

The technical, constitutional, political, and administrative restraints on Congress' discretion obviously place limits on its role in strategic military policy. These constraints do not nullify Congress' role; they bring it instead into sharper focus.

Congress does not act in isolation in passing authorizations and appropriations for defense spending. It responds in terms of two general political and constitutional relations: the President and the public. In relating the nation's military power to its foreign policy objectives, Congress, like the voting public, must initially follow the President's lead. It is (and ought to be) primarily a consent-granting institution. Congress' duties, however, are greater than the electorate's, for it is obliged, as an institution of government, to evaluate the President's leadership and the merit of his defense policies on a continuing basis. Passage of the annual defense authorization and appropriations bills in Congress provides the occasion for such an ongoing evaluation. Congress' relation to the President is basically instrumental. It is characterized by a congressional concern with the military means to be employed by the nation.

Congress' relation to the public in strategic matters is inherently different, though it is intimately related to its responsibilities vis-à-vis the President. With respect to the public, Congress must be principally concerned with the virtue of the political and moral ends to be served by strategic policy and the military power needed to

445

achieve them. Like the President, Congress has important leadership responsibilities. In discharging these duties as a coequal branch of the government, its relation to the President is one of co-operation, not subordination.

CONGRESS AND THE PRESIDENT

The leverage which Congress' power of the purse provides over security policies is both positive and negative. The latter is well known and is generally accepted as Congress' principal means to control the executive branch. Its role in defense policy formation is conceived in terms of the negative exercise of its authorization and appropriations powers. By simply denying funds to the executive branch, Congress exercises a veto control over Defense Department activities; its acts, as many have pointed out, "as a check on an irresponsible [executive] government." [16] While important, this negative power may still not produce the military plans and programs which are needed to answer the security imperatives confronting the nation. It prevents the President from acting; it does not inspire nor direct him to act wisely.

What is needed is an exercise of Congress' consent power that will encourage the formulation of military policies in the executive branch which can meet the exigencies of national security. At least six separate functions can be identified that define Congress' positive use of its consent power through its control of the federal purse. These include a responsibility (1) to define the political objectives underlying the defense budget; (2) to test the military feasibility of these objectives, including the contingency plans to effect them; (3) to relate these plans to the nation's military forces and weapons system; (4) to assess the economic and fiscal feasibility and operational efficiency of defense policy; (5) to generate alternatives to the President's defense proposals when they prove defective; and (6) to oppose the President in order to effect its legislative determinations.

These functions, while conceptually distinguishable, are of course intermingled and overlapping in the actual process of congressional decision and action on the defense budget. They are isolated here for purposes of analysis and evaluation. Their discharge assures Congress an important and respected place in strategic policy-making. Their neglect or abandonment undermines the effectiveness and relevance of the nation's strategic policies based on the assumption of popular and congressional consent. The intellectual functions which are discussed below are not inexorably bound to a particular strategic policy, although what appear to be the shortcomings of certain defense policies are noted. Within the same time frame divergent policies could conceivably be adopted by Congress even though the same rational steps were executed in reaching a policy position.

1. Probing political objectives.—Congress must first define for itself the full range of the nation's strategic imperatives if it is to utilize its consent power in anything but a negative way. This would initially entail a congressional understanding of the foreign policy objectives of the United States. These goals must be explicitly stated in meaningful detail at some point in the congressional budgetary process. Unless Congress understands the nation's foreign policy goals underpinning the President's defense budget, it will overlook the major reasons shaping the administration's military proposals. It will be legislating within a political vacuum. It will have deprived itself of the measures it needs to evaluate the President's recommendations. Unguided or only vaguely disciplined by political objectives, it will be unable to determine whether it has equipped the executive branch with enough military power to conduct a successful security or foreign policy. The grave risk will be run that military policies will become increasingly unrelated to the nation's foreign policy objectives or possibly in serious conflict with them.

In its review, Congress should also probe for political objectives other than those implied by military requirements that may have influenced the total amount and the component parts of the administration's defense funding bills. A variety of domestic economic factors, for example, may have had a significant impact on the size and composition of the defense budget: a desire for a balanced budget, for full utilization of economic resources, for constraints on inflationary pressures, or for the relief of depressed areas. Congress should bring such considerations to the surface to expose whether they have had a determining effect on the formulation of security policies reflected in the Defense Department budget. It should establish whether, and to what extent, the administration's military strategy has been decided upon in an inverted manner; that is, by establishing a budgetary ceiling for the support of the armed forces and by subsequently devising a military posture, including defined force levels and weapons systems, to conform to that money limitation. Or, the defense budget might reflect expedient compromises among opposing strategic doctrines, force levels, and weapons system proposals of the military services. Under such circumstances, Congress would be obliged to specify—at least for itself—these compromises so as to prevent waste and costly duplication of effort and to preclude careless oversight in strategic planning and operations.

The history of Congress' handling of the defense appropriations bills since World War II can be conceived as an evolutionary process in which the defense appropriations subcommittees have become increasingly aware of the foreign and domestic policy dimensions of defense policy. There is a perceptible difference between the questions raised in the defense appropriations review today and in the past. Policy questions appear in the 1960's in increasing number whereas in the late 1940's they were almost totally absent. The enlargement and deepening of legislative understanding of the foreign and domestic implications of defense policy has been the product of approximately twenty years of experience. The pace and movement have not been direct and linear, but halting and circuitous. The gap between defense policy and other policy objectives has been progressively narrowed. While divergencies still persist, they are not as open and glaring as before. The defense appropriations groups have demonstrated an increasing sensitivity to the conceptual unity of defense policy with other segments of governmental policy. However, given the political constraints under which they operate within Congress, they are often unable to act on the enlarging clarity of their intellectual grasp.[17]

The demobilization effort after World War II, as General George C. Marshall complained, was not directed by any clearly defined international objectives. A national mood to retrench rather than a rational set of foreign policy objectives dictated the pell-mell dismantling of the armed forces. The direction and speed of the demobilization was guided less by a consideration of foreign policy requirements than by the logistics capacity of the armed services and the size of the administrative staff to complete the program. The political vacuum of the war years continued into the postwar period. Lacking any clear perception of the international conditions and objectives that they sought through the war; lacking, too, the will and enlightenment to define what those objectives might be after the end of hostilities, a majority of legislators saw little need for a large military establishment. The functions of the military services were viewed as narrowly confined to occupying enemy territories until peace treaties could be signed, to maintaining civil order, and to providing funds for the relief and rehabilitation of war-ravaged areas. Bereft of political guidelines or clearly defined foreign-policy objectives on which to rest requirements for strong armed forces in being, Congress easily capitulated to domestic pressures for demobilization, and spurred the effort to a swift conclusion.

The quality of Congress' policy review of the defense bill did not improve significantly in the late 1940's. The political and military implications of the Truman administration's containment strategy were given perfunctory examination. A containment strategy, as George Kennan suggested, called for "the adroit and vigilant application of counter-force at a series of constantly shifting geographical and political points, corresponding to the shifts and maneuvers of Soviet policy. . . . "[18] Containment was to prevent further Soviet expansion. Checked by the direct or implied assertion of United States power, the ruling elite of the Soviet Union would gradually become convinced of the futility of pursuing an imperialistic foreign policy. It was felt that, as Soviet cognizance of American strength and resolution grew, the iron hold of the Stalinist regime on the Russian people would gradually loosen and the hostile attitude of the Soviet government toward the West would mellow.

In its examination of defense appropriations, Congress never seriously questioned how much time or sacrifice might be necessary to curb Soviet aggrandizement until the Russian regime softened or capitulated to the West. The military appropriations groups studiously avoided analyzing American policy interests abroad or determining precisely what Soviet political aspirations and likely military and non-military initiatives that containment was actually supposed *to contain*. Efforts to discuss United States policy toward Germany were stifled in the FY 1947 review of the War Department appropriations bill. The status of Germany was considered a policy question beyond the appropriations subcommittee's formal jurisdiction or area of concern. The naval appropriations group similarly sidestepped policy issues. The House report on the Navy Department bill for FY 1949 expressed the empty hope that "the world situation" would soon stabilize. The political conditions acceptable to the United States as a basis for this stabilization were not elaborated.

The Korean War did not immediately produce a heightened political grasp of the military dimensions of the cold war struggle. That the American commitment of troops was logically related to the nation's implicit pursuit of a containment strategy was not fully understood. The administration itself was tentative about its strategic policies. Congress in its turn did not approach the defense budgets of the early 1950's as annual instalments on an over-all strategic plan. The inflated budgets of the Korean War were seen more as an emergency response to an imminent military threat or, to those who disapproved of American involvement in Korea, as simply an unnecessary burden on national resources. Throughout the Korean conflict, many legislators worried more about the impact of defense spending on economic prosperity than about the political stakes of the armed struggle, both in Asia and in Europe.

Initial congressional enthusiasm for the New Look inhibited, though it did not fully preclude, the further definition of the nation's political objectives within the defense appropriations process. The New Look initially offered Congress an inviting and plausible formula by which the nation's military forces could be disengaged, the sacrifices of defense preparedness lessened, and the political influence of the United States increased. Through massive retaliation, the decisive military element of the New Look, a cheap and convenient method seemed to have been devised to freeze indefinitely the political relations of the world in favor of the United States under the aegis of a kind of nuclear Pax Americana. The New Look substituted a strategy for a political design. Its political obtuseness became evident only gradually to most legislators and to the members of the defense appropriations groups. A number of incidents slowly compelled many congressmen to face and accept what had otherwise been only a suppressed and inchoate fear: that the status quo of the early 1950's could not be indefinitely preserved. Continuing adjustments in American political objectives, policies, and attitudes toward the communist and neutralist world would be necessary. So also the United States would have to be prepared to exert a broader range of military capabilities than thermonuclear weapons, if its military power was to prove effective and credible under a wide variety of political circumstances. An accumulation of international crises had a mounting effect on congressional thinking. Among these, the most important were the French defeat in Indo-China in 1954, the tension in the Formosa Straits in 1955, the Suez and Hungarian outbreaks in 1956, as well

451

as the Iraqi coup d'état, the threat of hostilities in Lebanon, and renewed Chinese Communist bombardment of Nationalist-held islands in 1958. The defense hearings of the late 1950's reflected an enlarging interest in the evolution of potentially dangerous political conditions abroad and their relation to American military policy. Successful Soviet ICBM tests and the flight of sputnik prompted further the defense subcommittees to review more critically not only the political relevance of the nation's military preparedness but also to engage themselves, albeit tentatively, in the broader dialogue of defining the purposes of national life, and, just as importantly, the proper military and non-military means to achieve them.

The defense appropriations subcommittees still do not approach the defense budget from a distinctly foreign policy perspective. The slow growth of legislative sensitivity to the objectives of defense policy since World War II has not overcome the still apparent hesitancy of the appropriations subcommittees and military services committees to raise foreign policy issues publicly in their review of the defense authorization and appropriations bill. Developing relations between the United States and the Soviet Union or with the communist world are treated perfunctorily compared with the time and effort that are expended on the budgetary and detailed administrative aspects of the defense bill. American relations with China or American presence in Southeast Asia in the 1960's are given cursory examination. Taboos still surround the discussion of United States–Cuban relations. Military requirements, including the size, structure, composition, and deployment of military forces, tend to be evaluated in isolation from these policy areas. The defense funding process remains uncomfortably insulated from troubling foreign policy problems which Congress and the nation must somehow resolve.

2. *Feasibility of political objectives and contingency planning.*— Simultaneously with its probe of policy objectives, Congress should test the feasibility of the administration's proposed objectives against

452

the actual and potential military threats blocking their achievement. The strength and importance of these military obstacles must be properly assessed in light of current estimates of enemy capabilities and intentions. Congress must keep itself informed about these estimates, critically analyze their validity, and correlate them with the military policies reflected in the defense budget. Following its evaluation, Congress must receive a clear description of the range of possible contingencies in which force might have to be used, the likelihood of each, and the plans which have been developed to respond to these eventualities.

In the absence of such knowledge, the choice of political objectives may become increasingly detached from world-wide power realities. Armed with such information, Congress and the executive branch are mutually disciplined: the former by being made more aware of the difficulties involved in using military power to reach political objectives; the latter by being forced to defend its policies before a coequal branch of the government. Although an appreciation by Congress and the President of the power realities of the international environment cannot guarantee success in foreign relations, it is an indispensable ingredient of military planning which is itself only a part of over-all national strategy.

Congress has too often overlooked the connection between the nation's political objectives and the military power needed under variously defined circumstances to support them. The failure of the legislature to plumb the policy goals of United States actions abroad has impeded congressional understanding of the critical link between announced or tacitly stated policies and military planning. Without a firm perception and conscious agreement on the purposes of defense policy, congressmen have little incentive to identify or analyze the contingencies under which American power might have to be employed. American aid to Greece and Turkey in 1947 exemplifies the separation between policy goals and contingency planning. Through the initiative of Secretary of the Navy James Forrestal, the navy assembled a special force to demonstrate American support for the governments of Greece and Turkey in their efforts after World War II to withstand the demands of the Soviet Union and the pressures of the satellite powers in eastern Europe. As early as April 10, 1946, the United States had dispatched the "USS Missouri" to the Mediterranean. The presence of the battleship, which symbolized American victory over Japan, indicated the resolve of the United States to assert its military influence to safeguard a free Greece and Turkey. " 'With the *Missouri* treated as a symbol of our power and intent,' wrote Walter Lippmann at the time, 'we can make it unmistakably clear in Moscow just where we believe the outer limits of their expansion are.' " [19] While the executive branch was committing American sea power in the Mediterranean and while Congress itself was passing an unprecedentedly large assistance bill for Greece and Turkey, Congress cut the naval defense appropriations bill for FY 1948 and FY 1949. The review of the navy appropriations bills in the Eightieth Congress bore little relevance to the activities of the United States in the Mediterranean. Even the heated debate over the FY 1947 naval funding measure in the last session of the Seventy-ninth Congress was not related to maturing American efforts to stabilize the nations of southern Europe and the Middle East and to preserve their pro-Western orientation.

Containment implied a military establishment flexible enough to apply military force of subtly shaded degrees to secure differently valued political objectives under various geographic conditions. It assumed, too, the pre-existence of American military capabilities which could be activated immediately to stem Soviet or communist aggressive probes around the world. It required forces in being which could both deter and defend. The Truman administration shrank from spelling out these requirements to Congress. Congress, however, did not force the administration to confront the defense implications of its own strategy. Congressional pressure focused more on cutting taxes or on identifying niggling economies in defense spending than

454

on suggesting new military programs which were responsive to United States strategic needs. The air-power debates before Korea were no exception. They were not conducted within the framework of a fully articulated national strategy or a political design. Congress voted increased funds for strategic air power primarily as a terror device. In case of war, the homeland of the Soviet Union would be destroyed. The political outcome of such a conflict was largely cast in the vision of a devastated Soviet Union. The question of how nuclear weapons would thereafter achieve a more stable or viable international environment was not pursued.

Reports in the late 1940's from General Hodges' command in Korea that his forces were exposed and vulnerable to attack were discounted. The fall of China provoked no congressional analysis of the military and foreign policy implications of the Nationalist defeat. The Soviet detonation of an atomic device was given equally little attention. In the FY 1951 review of the defense budget that followed the Soviet nuclear success, Congress manifested a strange complacency about the eroding international position of the United States. The discussion of the pre-Korean War budgets disclosed the congressional expectancy that war would begin with another Pearl Harbor–like attack on the United States. Preoccupied with this one overriding military contingency, the legislative branch was unprepared for the Korean War. Only days before the North Korean attack, the House approved a smaller military budget than the year before. It is true that Congress, through the action of the foreign relations committees, did furnish billions of dollars in economic aid during this period to Europe and Asia. These actions, while notable and commendable, did not deal directly with the growing military requirements of a world-wide containment posture. As these requirements expanded, the American military establishment shrank.

The impact which different levels of defense spending might have on political conditions abroad or on American security interests was never adequately discussed in Congress' review of the annual defense budget before the Korean War. The struggle over the FY 1950 budget, to which Defense Secretary James Forrestal devoted so much of his attention, yielded a number of conflicting budgetary proposals. The military services succesively recommended budgets of $30 billion and $23.6 billion. Representative Carl Vinson, chairman of the House Armed Services Committee, pressed for a $16.9 billion budget. The administration after considerable internal quarrel finally submitted a $14.2 billion proposal. Congress did not seize on the opportunity to project the different military capabilities that each budget would purchase, nor did it assess the utility of each of these alternative levels of preparedness to anticipate or to meet different conflict situations in which American political goals were at stake. What kind of military operations could be sustained by each budget? What kind of military confrontations or engagements might each prevent? What were the probable and possible military and political consequences of maintaining a forty-eight, fifty-nine, or seventy-group air force? Without answers to these questions Congress could not reasonably decide the viability of any of the alternative budgets which were recommended. Its decisions to approve the President's budget and to add nearly $800 million for more strategic air power rested, therefore, on incomplete and unduly fragmentary information. The Korean War exposed the weaknesses of American military power and, by implication, the imperfections of the defense decision process in Congress and in the executive branch.

Congress moved slowly in the wake of the Korean War to enlarge the scope and deepen the penetration of its annual defense review in terms of the military capabilities needed to effect strategic plans. Congress accepted the partial mobilization at the start of the Korean conflict as a temporary expedient. Many legislators, as well as segments of the administration, envisioned the early termination of the Korean War. The Truman administration's supplemental appropriations request to underwrite the Korean buildup was cast in this light. Only gradually did the appropriations groups and a majority of legislators accept and adjust to the long-term need for a higher defense spending plateau and for larger forces in being. The New Look policies adopted in 1954, approximately a year after the end of hostilities in Korea, finally formalized congressional consent to a new expenditure level for defense that hovered between $35 and $40 billion annually during the remainder of the 1950's.

Congress moved slowly to adopt military policies that were grounded in the experience of the Korean War. The New Look which Congress approved ignored the novel constraints on warfare that the Korean fighting had introduced. Instead, the pre-Korean military strategy of the Truman administration was reaffirmed. The major difference between the pre- and post-Korean nuclear deterrent postures turned on the size and operational status of the nuclear strike forces to be maintained, and not on an assessment of the contingencies in which non-nuclear forces might have to be used. The predominant source of disagreement between Congress and the chief executive during the Eisenhower period centered on the requirements for an effective and credible nuclear deterrent. The Eisenhower cutback of 23 wings from the goals of a 143-wing air force set by the Truman administration was carefully reviewed during the FY 1953 defense hearings, and air force complaints were fully aired. Congress prodded the administration for the remainder of the decade to increase air power expenditures. When informal appeals failed, it appropriated extra funds. The Symington airpower hearings of 1956 precipitated a $900 million add-on for strategic bombers for FY 1957. Between FY 1959 and FY 1961 billions of additional funds were appropriated for strategic bombers and missiles as well as for facilities to protect and alert the nation's strategic forces.

Congress found the notion of defending foreign areas or American interests against Soviet or communist aggression, if the nuclear deterrent were to fail, less inviting. Building a consensus in Congress that was prepared to support a more varied and flexible military stance required the remainder of the Eisenhower period. Except for its approval of a higher expenditure level for defense, Congress did not support a progressive re-evaluation of American military doctrine that assimilated the experience of the Korean War. It is not surprising, therefore, that the New Look policies proved bankrupt even as they received Congress's stamp of approval. Slow to consent to larger expenditures for defense, Congress was even slower to perceive the impotence of the defense policies that it had approved.

The French debacle at Dienbienphu in 1954 and the subsequent withdrawal of France from Indo-China initially exposed many of the defects of the New Look. Without the commitment of large numbers of American ground troops, the French position was militarily untenable in Southeast Asia. A decision by the United States to intervene, on the other hand, would have necessitated a fundamental revision of the New Look since American troop strength was to be reduced, conventional weapons inventories slimmed, and Army modernization throttled. Nuclear weapons, as an army field report from Indo-China concluded, could not be substituted for ground forces in a jungle war. The political considerations barring the use of nuclear weapons were equally compelling. The adverse psychological impact of atomic bombings in Asia would have seriously damaged the political position of the United States in the East. British and other allied opposition to enlarged Western military involvement in Southeast Asia, possibly leading to the use of nuclear weapons, chilled administration enthusiasm for any intervention scheme. What is extraordinary is that key legislative leaders meeting with President Eisenhower to discuss the Indo-China crisis rejected the proposal of an American military commitment largely on these same grounds.[20] The flash of insight into the debilities of the New Look unfortunately did not preclude a congressional blessing for the FY 1955 defense bill that inaugurated and legitimized the Eisenhower administration's defense policies.

Criticism of the administration's defense proposals did, of course, develop in some isolated congressional quarters. A dissident group of younger senators voiced objections, but they failed in their attempt to improve army preparedness. In the House, Representative Robert Sikes led a one-man assault on the New Look. He offered a trenchant analysis of its shortcomings in the hearings and in the floor discussion of the FY 1955 defense bill. He perceptively forecast the imminent development of a balance of terror between the Soviet Union and the United States which would mutually deter both from initiating a nuclear war. These instances of congressional opposition and prescience were rare and isolated in the middle 1940's.

There was no concerted congressional attempt until the post-sputnik period to relate the strategic plans and military capabilities proposed by the administration to the nation's alliance obligations. As the nation reduced its conventional forces and militarily disengaged itself from Asia in the middle 1950's, it increased its political commitments in that area through the SEATO and ANZUS pact and in bilateral agreements with Japan, the Philippines, South Korea, and Nationalist China. In Europe, the United States and its allies abandoned the Lisbon goal of close to 100 divisions, which was designed to underwrite NATO's forward strategy, almost as soon as it was adopted. A forward posture, implying the determination of the NATO powers to defend Europe and to minimize the possibility of its nuclear incineration in a general war with the Soviet Union, was devalued before it could be properly implemented. Announced and operational policies contradicted each other. These gaps between political objectives and commitments, on the one hand, and the military capability to reach them, on the other, became issues in Congress only after a series of outside events shocked a majority of legislators to face the deficiencies of the nation's heavy reliance on nuclear armaments. The succession of limited conflicts involving American arms in the second half of the 1950's and the Soviet Union's possession of impressive long-range bomber and missile strike forces pointed as much to the shortcomings of the nation's foreign policy objectives as to the inadequacy of massive retaliation as a politically or militarily relevant solution to the nation's expanding strategic problems. To its credit, congressional leadership in the post-sputnik period slowly directed Congress to reassess its support of the Eisenhower defense policies.

The consensus that crystallized during the first Kennedy Congress on conventional forces and on a broader military posture indicated a new and encouraging awareness in Congress of the functions and limits of military power and of the utility of adequate preparedness. The Kennedy buildup of 1961 was undertaken to prevent a general global conflict from developing. It marks one of the few instances in which Congress, led by an energetic chief executive, has acted to influence and control the emergence of political and military contingencies that might necessitate the actual application of the nation's military power at a cost considerably greater than that incurred by the expansion itself. Congress' previous assents to an expansion of armaments had been largely reactions to already perilous international circumstances involving American security interests. Congress now acted on the previously inarticulated and tentatively held realization that prompt and adequate assertion of military power could preclude the development of situations that would require the actual application of military might, with all of the attendant risks that such a commitment of force might entail, especially against a nuclear power like the Soviet Union. The military defense bill was viewed, moreover, in a new light. It was seen more clearly not only as a statement of military capabilities but as a means of bargaining and communicating with potential enemies. The defense budget and Congress' understanding and consent to it were related more closely than ever before to the ongoing diplomatic and strategic maneuvers of the nation.

3. *Force levels, weapons systems, and political objectives.*—Gauging the relative urgency of the nation's strategic problems and the merit of the planned responses to resolve them represents only a partial contribution of Congress to military policy-making. Congressional

follow-through is just as important. Congress must assure itself that the specific force levels and weapons systems reflected in the defense budget are appropriate to the administration's planned military responses and the nation's political objectives. At this stage military means, planning goals, and policy ends must be fused. The anticipated consequences of using one form of military power must be weighed against those of another in terms of the military and political objectives which are sought.

If the executive branch is reluctant to furnish a candid appraisal of the force levels and weapons systems which it has proposed, Congress must be prepared to search carefully and persistently for possible gaps or duplications in the nation's military capabilities. Some general determination must be made at the congressional level that the use of some weapons such as tactical nuclear missiles, will not produce more adverse political effects than the political gains which may be secured through their use. If funds are to be appropriated for one weapons system instead of another—say for more H-bombs and icbm's rather than for another armored division—the possible objectives to be advanced by such spending should be stated as clearly as available research data will permit. Failure to conduct such an analysis, or to prod the executive branch into such an examination, may contribute to the subordination of political values to the dictates of weapons technology and production, inverting the proper relations with possibly disastrous ramifications. To forestall this danger, Congress must project the kinds of possible political consequences which might result from using different weapons systems to secure stated goals under the constantly changing conditions of international relations. Its task is complicated by the present need for long lead times in weapons systems development. Badly conceived decisions, undirected by political goals, may place the nation in a vulnerable position in future years. It may find itself equipped with military weapons and forces which are unrelated to new political imperatives and to its policy objectives.

461

To be sure, choosing among a proliferation of feasible weapons systems is an enormously demanding task. Technical choices must still be left to the military and civilian experts of the executive branch and of the defense industry. Congress cannot be expected to decide the proper techniques of antisubmarine warfare and the type of military equipment needed to prevail in such operations. Neither can it decide which model tank is needed to counteract enemy armored strength nor the speed and range requirements of fighter aircraft. Quite properly, these decisions should remain in the hands of Defense Department personnel who are technically equipped to make them. Estimating the intrinsic military value of various weapon systems admittedly falls in large part outside the scope of congressional competence.

But the political purposes for which these weapons are designed and the manner in which they will be used by the executive branch are proper objects of congressional concern. The Eisenhower New Look policies with their heavy reliance on long-range nuclear striking power, should have been closely examined by Congress. No less should the new defense shift of the Kennedy and Johnson administrations toward conventional forces and missile forces be open to continuing scrutiny to assess its political implications, both at home and abroad. Because the problem of choice in military weaponry has been so vastly complicated, it is essential that Congress, as a political institution par excellence, be interested in the political effects of defense policies. Its deliberative processes are admirably adapted to this function. If discharged, Congress would be doing what it can do best.

In approving the raising and use of military forces, Congress' deliberations should be guided by what might be termed a doctrine of proportionality. In operation, this doctrine would act as a guideline for the joining of military and foreign policy-making with the nation's political and ethical goals. Congress should determine that military forces be made available which are capable of meeting a wide variety of conflict situations from guerrilla warfare to nuclear attack. In sum, it should provide the President with military forces that can be employed, if he chooses, in such measured and graduated amounts that at least a crude correspondence can be struck between the military force that is to be used or threatened and (a) the military force that is to be met; (b) the geographical scope and character of the conflict; and, most critical of all, (c) the political stakes at issue.[21]

The threatened nuclear war over Cuba in 1962 illustrates, in effect, the doctrine of proportionality in operation.[22] The political ramifications of Russian missiles in Cuba were of the most elemental importance. If the Soviet flanking action had proved successful, United States hegemony in the Western Hemisphere and, by implication, its influence throughout the world would have been seriously impaired. The American threat of nuclear war, while raising the ominous specter of vast human and material devastation, was proportional to the gravity of the Russian challenge. But it is important to recall that the administration initially framed its threat to the Soviet Union in terms of a quarantine to offset the menacing character of its action, although the actual effect of the air and naval operation in the Caribbean was tantamount to a selected embargo of Cuba. An air strike against the missile sites or an invasion of Cuba were ruled out in the first stages of the crisis. The embargo not only proved successful but it also bought time to negotiate the peaceful withdrawal of the missiles. An air strike would have almost certainly resulted in the death or wounding of some of the reportedly 15,000 to 20,000 Russian personnel stationed in Cuba, quite possibly precipitating an enlargement of the military conflict beyond Cuba. The embargo localized the military action to the waters around Cuba, as it simultaneously communicated to the Soviet government the depth of American determination to remove the missile threat off its shores. Political consultations were commenced on this understanding and the missiles were returned to the Soviet Union.[23] A form of brinkmanship had been played out by the United States, but its strategic superiority was placed *within* the context of a broader framework of military responses. An appeal upward on a scale of increasing military force was resisted until lesser forms of military power had been exhausted as a means of seeking an appropriate political remedy. Had the embargo failed, an air bombardment and, quite possibly, an invasion of Cuba would very likely have been launched.

What is important to recognize is that the military forces and weapons systems that were employed in the North Vietnamese and Cuban situations existed in being *before* the contingency requiring their use arose. Had not Congress made provision for such forces, the United States would have been helpless in responding to the challenges against its interests or it might have been compelled to employ more military force than was necessary, increasing the risk of escalating the conflict, with all its attendant dangers. It is not enough that Congress furnish the chief executive with overwhelming military power, as in the case of thermonuclear weapons. It is more politically and ethically relevant that he be provided with usable military power in adequate quantities to meet different military contingencies, simultaneously if necessary, to protect and advance United States interests and objectives.

The notion that it is important to maintain a wide spectrum of military capabilities in being to meet a broad range of political and military contingencies has only recently taken root in Congress and particularly in the armed services and defense appropriations groups. Since World War II, with minor fluctuations from year to year, Congress has favored more strategic air power capacity than the administration in power, whether Democratic or Republican, has proposed. Until sputnik, strategic air power maintained an almost exclusive hold on congressional thinking. Before Korea Congress, like the Truman administration, placed its faith in nuclear weaponry. Congressional increases for military power, to the limited extent that they occurred before 1950, were aimed at providing more nuclear striking power. Congressional fascination with the destructive capacity of nuclear weapons is partially suggested in its cool support of naval air power. The navy's carrier based aircraft could deliver nuclear weapons to enemy targets, but not in the large kiloton quantities of air force bombers. The navy argued that its delivery systems were more discriminating. In dealing with the question of nuclear annihilation, Congress indicated little interest in, or understanding of, the subtleties of the navy position.

The New Look revived congressional hopes in the omnicompetence of air power. Congressional efforts in military policy focused rigidly on the size of the air force's bomber and gradually on strategic missiles as reports suggested Soviet progress in this area. Sputnik reinforced congressional demands for more long-range nuclear delivery capacity. In each congress since sputnik—the Eighty-fifth through the Eighty-eighth—Congress has pressed more funds on the administration to expand either the nation's strategic bomber or missile capabilities. These increases, however, have been cast in a more intelligent and mature light than previous congressional air power demands. The Soviet Union's achievements in space and in long-range missile development, together with its enlarging stock of nuclear weapons, impressed a majority of legislators for the first time that nuclear warfare was reciprocal. The United States, too, faced devastation in an atomic exchange with the Soviet Union. The Cuban crisis of 1962 deepened this understanding. While Congress has not retreated in its support for nuclear weapons since sputnik, it tends to view them less as a means to resolve the nation's strategic problems than as a precondition for the use of other, less cataclysmic military and non-military forms of national power. This process of enlightenment, begun at the end of World War II, is still unfolding. Minority segments of congressional membership still speak and act as if nuclear weapons were only larger forms of conventional fire power.

There is a remarkable fixation in Congress on specific quantities of military hardware or levels of manpower. Advocates of different forms of military power have been adept at seizing upon slogans

465

that center around some magic number of force levels or weapons systems to generate majority support for their interests. Air power enthusiasts have shown noticeable aptitude in capsulizing the congressional discussion of strategic problems in simple and misleading catch phrases. Before Korea, the seventy-group air force was the flag around which Congress was induced to rally. The 143 wing standard was then raised during the Korean conflict and sympathy for this goal spilled over into the Eisenhower administration. In the 1960's, air force supporters, reacting to the stress of the Kennedy and Johnson administration on ICBM's, emphasized instead man's role in strategic bombing, first through the B-70 and RS-70 and later, when advances in technology had overtaken these manned delivery systems, through proposals for a follow-on bomber. Other shorthand slogans during the last three years of the Eisenhower administration included a 900,000-man army and a 200,000-man marine corps. Those pressing for more air lift fixed upon the objective of enough air lift capacity to transport one division to any part of the world.

Congressional penchant for military hardware has led to the associated phenomena of its concentration on matching Soviet and communist military capabilities on almost an item-by-item basis. While communist superiority in manpower has been generally conceded by Congress, it has sought, primarily through increases in air power, to compensate for this disparity in troop strength by at least equaling the communists in the quantity and quality of American strategic forces. The military and political dimensions of the cold war have often been misguidedly reduced to a probem of American capacity to keep abreast of the Soviets bomber for bomber and missile for missile. The Eisenhower administration was partially correct in its insistence that the number of nuclear delivery vehicles available to each nation meant little by itself. Congress was not quick to grasp the kernel of logic in the administration's counter slogan of "no deterrent gap" despite a perceived "missile gap" in the late 1940's. In the initial two years after sputnik, Congress often found it easier to calculate the differences between United States and Russian missile production than to penetrate the sometimes rarified atmosphere of deterrent eschatology and weapons mixes.

Despite congressional obsession with the concrete and the specific, it has not always been clear, ironically enough, what military capabilities it was actually buying through its many increases in military funds since World War II. The $822 million increase in air funds in the defense supplement of FY 1948 was nullified by Congress' own hand when it permitted the President to spend the funds over so long a span of time that the potential effect of the increase was effectively compromised. The more significant FY 1950 add-on for air power indicated further congressional misunderstanding about what it was specifically accomplishing through its revision of the President's defense budget. Most legislators, including the chairman of the House Appropriations Committee, were convinced that the increases which they were voting would buy more long-range bombers. The air force had already provided for these aircraft in its budget and planned to utilize the extra funds, if the President had released them, for tactical and transport units. Congress' increase in army modernization funds for FY 1961 similarly bought little extra army preparedness, notwithstanding congressional claims to the contrary. In its increase Congress relied on funds in army accounts that had already been committed to modernization.

Whatever the defects of Congress' use of its appropriations power, it must be credited with having inspired a number of specific, yet beneficial, changes in the nation's defense establishment. Congressional threats to deny funds both for Nike-Hercules and Bomarc prompted a reluctant Defense Department to formulate a more effective plan for air defense. Congressional initiative prevented hundreds of millions of dollars in unnecessary duplication and assisted the development of a more reliable air-defense network. As Part II has described at length, Congress has successfully induced the administration on numerous occasions to spend more money on nuclear and conventional armaments when they were needed. During the period between 1958 and 1961 congressional activity in defense policy reached its peak. Congress' record during these years outdistanced the importance and merit of its contribution to defense policy of the preceding decade. The cumulative effect of its specific responses of support for separate and identifiable military programs was to expose indirectly many of the weaknesses of the Eisenhower administration's strategic policies and to cast doubt on the practice of restricting the size and direction of defense policy within rigid budgetary categories.

4. *Military capabilities, economic feasibility, and fiscal policy.*— Before consenting to the President's defense measures, Congress must finally submit them to the test of economic feasibility. The resources at the disposal of the federal government are inherently limited. Funds are not available for every military and non-military proposal which is introduced into Congress for its review and approval. Priorities must be set. A determination must be made as to whether new defense and non-defense programs should be adopted; whether they should not be integrated into existing ones; or whether old ones should be continued at variously defined levels or simply dropped. The budget helps to establish priorities by reducing the cost of competing programs into a common monetary denominator. Dollar comparisons can then be made between programs on the basis of their initial cost and their sustained maintenance. Although such quantitative statements of cost cannot provide all the standards needed to accept or reject a program, they supply useful guidelines in making a choice.[24] They furnish some measures, however crude, for comparing defense programs with each other and with other aspects of the government's budget. While this process of decision will not assure that a balance will be struck between the nation's military power-in-being and its foreign policy goals, it indicates an approach by which the many claims on the public treasury can be systematically examined and decided upon. In this way, defense issues will at least

468

receive a fair airing, and military and non-military programs will be forced to compete against each other.

By relating military and non-military programs to each other, available resources tend to be used more effectively and efficiently. Each program is forced to prove its merit. Initially, military budgetary proposals would have to be compared by Congress with other aspects of strategic planning. Congress would have to be convinced that the President's defense program admits the minimum cost in human and material resources and that its intended objectives could not be accomplished more easily and at less expense by other means, such as economic assistance, propaganda, or diplomatic maneuvering. If this analysis is carried to its logical conclusion, security policies would ultimately have to be interwoven with all of the government's foreign and domestic programs. Through such a procedure, Congress would be in a better position to evaluate how much would be lost or gained when it expanded an old program, adopted a new one, or generally raised or lowered governmental expenditures for selected items.

If Congress bases its decision on a calculation of gain and loss, it will be in a position to determine more accurately whether the nation can afford more defense spending. Distributing national resources on a comparative basis will direct congressional attention to the proper questions which it should ask in making military strategy. The effect that more taxation or controls would have on the free economy or the impact that decreased expenditures for non-defense programs would have on the nation's welfare would be weighed against the alleged need for defense outlays. Through this balancing process, Congress would be consciously deciding not only the level and character of the defense budget but also the entire range of federal expenditures and revenues to which the size and shape of the defense budget are inextricably bound. Congress would not be answering the false question of what are our military needs regardless of the political costs; neither would it disregard the harmful effects which increased spending might have on the economy or other essential governmental

469

programs and objectives. Nor would it be narrowly preoccupied with an arbitrary budgetary limit beyond which it refuses to push federal expenditures, to the detriment of defense preparedness.[25] The government's budget would be viewed as a whole composed of financial inputs and outputs required by various defense and non-defense programs. It would not be simply (and falsely) accepted as the sum total of a dozen or more separate and largely unrelated appropriations bills passed at each session of Congress.

If the military and non-military budgets are seen as aspects of a seamless fabric which is tightly woven from the existing governmental pattern of taxation and borrowing, a proper congressional settlement of security policy must inevitably lead to the formulation of a coherent fiscal policy which is functionally related to the nation's strategic military plans. This follows from the proposition that federal expenditures must be viewed always in relation to actual or anticipated revenues, which depend in the final analysis on the ability of the economy's productivity and the political willingness of the public to grant the necessary funds for various levels of federal spending. Successful military policies depend, consequently, on the funds available for their implementation. Unless Congress consents to a fiscal policy which is intimately related to defined military objectives, the accomplishment of the latter may fail for want of a solid financial foundation on which a large, complicated military establishment must rest.

The budgetary categories that Congress relies upon inhibit its ability to review the defense budget in terms of the military capabilities and the political objectives that it is designed to secure. The defense bill is presently divided into four major titles: military personnel; maintenance and operations; procurement; and research, development, test, and evaluation. A fifth title, military construction, is considered in a separate appropriations measure. The Defense Department and the services present their respective appropriation requests within these major titles and the corresponding sub-categories and sub-sub-categories of each. The hearings focus largely on these budgetary classifications. Until recently there was no clear way to relate these budgetary divisions to the program goals and the military and political objectives of defense policy. The policy statements of the secretary of defense and the Joint Chiefs of Staff were presented at one level of analysis; the budgetary data that was submitted to Congress, at another level. Like two parallel canals, they moved in the same direction but remained unconnected with each other. Here and there in the hearings a spur would be built to unite the two budgetary waterways for a brief instant, yet it was impossible to determine on the basis of the budgetary categories that were employed how one affected the other. The cost of competing bomber and missile systems, for example, was not presented as a regular part of the budgetary review. Nor was it possible to determine the respective amounts to be expended for comparable army and marine corps units. Cost figures for Nike-Hercules and Bomarc were often in controversy because the services utilized different methods of estimation. Even if Congress had wished to weigh the cost of training and equipping troops of allied nations against expenditures for corresponding American troop strength, cost figures were not readily available to make a comparison. The budget simply was not presented in terms of the force levels and weapons systems that it proposed to purchase. Congress often bought military programs blindly since many of them did not carry identifiable price tags.

Under Secretary of Defense Robert McNamara, budgetary procedures and categories have been developed which translate military programs, such as strategic retaliatory forces or general purpose forces, into budgetary figures which indicate more accurately the long- and short-term costs of each as well as the contribution that each makes to different facets of strategic policy. These budgetary innovations cut across the functional categories of military personnel, maintenance

471

and operations, and the like. They provide a means by which the secretary of defense can identify duplications in service activities or gaps in operational capabilities.

Congress, nevertheless, clings to the old budgetary forms, although the appropriations defense units had initially taken a lead in the 1950's in advocating a basic overhaul of defense budgeting. By relying on existing functional categories, such as personnel and operations and maintenance, as well as on the innumerable subclassifications into which each major heading is divided, legislators are encouraged to focus on detailed budgetary and administrative data largely disconnected from program content. A close relation appears, therefore, between congressional fascination with military hardware items and the multiple budgetary categories of the defense bill. Many congressmen act as if they are convinced that they are controlling defense policy through these elements. What are generally lost to them are the broader political and military ramifications of the inventory statistics on military capabilities or of proposed budgetary expenditures. Each year the appropriations committees move, in almost ritualistic form, through the confusing labyrinth of budgetary classifications. In examining the army budget for FY 1955, the Senate defense appropriations subcommittee discovered that the Atlanta General Depot was financed by thirteen different appropriation accounts which were channeled through fifteen operating agencies of the army. One of the accounts for maintenance and operations was subsequently broken down into fifteen additional budgetary programs. Funds for nine of these programs were funneled into the Atlanta General Depot only after being divided into forty-five budget projects at the army comptroller level. Allocations were made from these forty-five budget projects to six operating agencies of the army which made funds available to the depot through a total of thirteen allotment accounts. The Senate subcommittee dispatched staff members to assemble and analyze these data. It did not see fit to examine the New Look policies as carefully as it reviewed the administration of the Atlanta depot.

Certainly its limited staff resources were not committed to a policy evaluation. The subcommittee and the Senate approved the New Look on the basis of only meager knowledge of its military and foreign policy implications.

To compensate for the absence of military and political criteria on which to rest their decisions, the appropriations committees appeal to a number of seemingly antiseptic standards that, while lacking relation to defined defense objectives, suggest universal applicability. Prominent among these is the appeal to the past. Congressional reviews of the defense budget often lean heavily upon expenditure and appropriations data of the preceding two fiscal years to the fiscal year under examination. The past then becomes prologue to the future. Many decisions of Congress are partially or wholly reached on the basis of the budgetary information of previous outlays. The merit of each budgetary category tends to be assessed on its own terms disengaged from the goals that it is intended to achieve. In an age of rapid technological and political change, the budgetary past is a feeble and misleading guide to the military and political future.

Meat-axe cuts are another favorite control device that generally proves self-defeating. The procurement reductions of FY 1960, FY 1961, and FY 1962, instigated largely by the House defense appropriations group, cut across various military programs and projects. The efficient were penalized for their industry and productivity since they were directed to absorb the same percentage reduction as their more wasteful peers. Administrators were encouraged to inflate their estimates in future budget preparations. Congress thus undermined its own purpose which is to check unnecessary and duplicatory service activities. It never knows, moreover, what effect these across-the-board cuts will have on military programs. Similarly misleading is congressional reliance on inapplicable ratios that abstract from the program goals from which they are derived. Officer-enlisted personnel ratios have been used by Congress in the past to control the number and rate of promotions in the services. The effect of such controls

473

on morale, re-enlistment rates, or program requirements have been rarely or only superficially explored.

While Congress shows great weakness in consolidating and co-ordinating the military programs within the defense budget, it manifests greater inability in comparative evaluation of the military and non-military parts of the federal budget. Each agency budget is considered in a separate appropriations bill isolated from the others without cross-reference.

Even bills which are closely associated with American foreign policy move through Congress largely unrelated to each other. Before the defense establishment was organized into a single department, Representative Albert Engel, chairman of the House War Department Appropriations Subcommittee, complained that his group never knew what its navy counterpart was doing.[26] From the broader perspective of national security, a similar criticism may be leveled at the handling of authorization and appropriations measures today. The House Armed Services Committee and the House Subcommittee on Department of Defense Appropriations are not kept informed on a continuing basis of the findings and decisions of the authorization and appropriations groups which pass on the administration's military and economic assistance programs. Along with military power, military and economic aid are instruments of United States strategic and foreign policy. The effective use of each implies the preceding mutual relation of all within a common strategic plan. Only isolated, fragmentary, and informal efforts are made within Congress to conduct such a co-ordinated review. In addition, the State Department budget, which includes United States contributions to international organizations, proceeds through Congress in separate authorization and appropriations bills. Their connection with the defense and economic assistance bills remains obscure. Such questions as whether more economic aid can be substituted for military preparedness or whether military requirements are affected by economic assistance or the

474

extent of American participation in international peace-keeping activities are not uniformly and systematically discussed.

The most serious defect of Congress' review of the defense bill is its failure to relate defense spending and fiscal policy. In most of the years since World War II, particularly until the flight of sputnik, strategic imperatives have been subordinated to vague and changing conceptions of what military expenditures the economy could bear. Congress has usually supported, often more adamantly than the President, the imposition of budgetary ceilings on defense spending. In the first decade after World War II, congressional concern centered more often on the alleged threat of the cold war to the nation's economy than on the military menace to its political objectives and even independent existence. Congressional preoccupation with economic factors might have been justified if it had rested on a clear and coherent perception of the actual and potential economic capacity. It did not. Congress acted on the crude rule of thumb that balancing governmental revenues and expenditures was a primary national objective. Consequently, the level of military spending that Congress would approve, despite the strategic risks involved, was largely determined by revenue laws and fixed charges and governmental commitments that were outgrowths of the past. Many of these obligations to the past were set by legal and moral imperatives. The most important of these included interest on the national debt, social security payments, or retirement claims of former civilian and military personnel. Others, while more susceptible to legislative revision, hindered the expansion of the military establishment. These encompassed such programs as farm price supports, federal contributions to highway, irrigation, conservation, and social welfare programs, and veterans' benefits. Since a balanced budget was of overriding importance during most of the years since World War II, these already established programs in the federal budget inhibited increases in defense spending. Revenue bills designed to stimulate economic growth and productive capacity might have been developed to enlarge the size of governmental revenue without necessarily impairing non-military programs or restricting the purchasing power of businesses and individuals. The revenue decreases proposed in Congress in the late 1940's were not cast in these broader economic terms. They were conceived more simply and misguidedly as the most direct method to increase private spending and consumption, not to meet public needs. In the 1960's, ironically enough, the massive amount of defense spending which has been finally accepted, hampers the development of governmental programs responsive to other national problems, both foreign and domestic.

A major impediment to the emergence of a more flexible and adaptable congressional approach to public policy is still Congress' reluctance to base its appropriations decisions and program support on an articulated fiscal policy that reflects a more sophisticated economic understanding than the questionable goal of a balanced budget. The executive branch under Presidents Kennedy and Johnson has pursued more tenable economic policies. The Trade Expansion Act of 1962 and the revenue reduction bill of 1963 suggest the new and enlightened directions of economic policy formulation in the Presidency and executive branch. Many of the vestigial artifacts of discredited economic notions linger on, however, in congressional thinking.

Congress has also concentrated too narrowly and heavily on the material costs of the defense budget rather than on the political gains to be derived from defense preparedness and the controlled assertion of United States military power. The domestic political gains temporarily obtained through decreased military expenditures in the late 1940's were outweighed by the adverse foreign military and political consequences arising from the nation's unpreparedness for the Korean War. Penny-pinching confined American diplomatic maneuverability through the New Look period. It slowed United States progress in space and missile development. After each blow to American military power and international position and prestige, defense expenditures had to increase at a faster rate than would have been otherwise necessary, in order to regain lost ground. These rapid expansions of neglected military programs proved economically wasteful and inflationary. The motives underlying the establishment of budgetary limits of defense spending not only incurred disheartening political liabilities but also failed to achieve their primary aim of holding military expenditures to minimal levels. The congressional review of the defense budget has been unduly influenced by short-term economic considerations rather than directed by long-term economic and political objectives. In responding to these pressures too quickly in past examinations of the defense bills, Congress mortgaged much of its flexibility and discretion in succeeding reviews of defense spending.

5. *Generating alternatives.*—To be useful, congressional questioning and probing must go beyond the presentations of the administration's official representatives. If Congress relied exclusively on them for advice and counsel, its continued independence as a political institution and its utility as a body for shaping military strategic policy would be jeopardized. It must assure itself that alternatives to administration proposals are not more politically beneficial, technically feasible, and economically efficient. Through a ventilation of opposing policy and program positions, Congress can clarify differences over political objectives and diverse military policies, the general consequences of variously proposed policies, and the range of policies which the nations can adopt and the public will support. In generating alternative viewpoints, a traditional legislative function, Congress informs itself about the issues underlying strategic policy and the different routes by which they may be approached and resolved. Congress' ability to control or influence military policy ultimately depends on the number and significance of the alternatives that it can raise. The

importance of its role hinges on its capacity to develop spending choices beyond those of a simple acceptance or rejection of administration budgetary proposals.

Legislators can initially rely on their own knowledge of military affairs to weigh the virtues of the administration's recommendations and the alternatives to them. Many of the leading members of the defense appropriation subcommittees of both houses have concerned themselves with problems of military affairs longer than many of their counterparts in the defense establishment.[27] For example, Representative George Mahon, chairman of the House defense appropriations group, has served on a military appropriations committee since World War II. But the personal resources of the individual legislator are hardly sufficient to overcome the limitations of Congress in defense policy. Legislators need outside assistance if they are to make an independent evaluation of the administration's money requests for defense.

Generally, congressmen can turn to three sources for help in deciding whether the Defense Department's estimates are adequate to achieve the proposed objectives stated by the administration and whether those military policies themselves are capable of protecting and promoting the nation's interests. First of all, civilian and military defense officials are among the most important springs of congressional information on military questions. This is not as ironic as it may appear. It has long been recognized that the executive departments, no less than Congress or the nation, are divided by differences among top officials or between "indians" and "chiefs" within the same agency. Legislators can bring these submerged disagreements of opinion within the administration to the surface in hearings on the defense budget bill. The divergent statements of administration witnesses offer Congress a window, so to speak, through which it can examine the many considerations guiding the formation and execution of the defense budget. The formal channel of communication which hearings provide may also be, and to a degree is, supplemented by a system of

478

informal contacts between Congress and the Pentagon. It must be recognized, too, that rumors and "leaks" reaching interested and influential congressmen can sometimes perform a salutary function, despite the harmful effects they often have on maintaining administrative morale and unity.[28]

Second, consultation with outside experts can broaden the horizon of Congress' knowledge about strategic affairs and allow it to consent to the annual defense budget on a more enlightened basis. Advice from these quarters helps legislators to formulate a proper understanding of strategic problems. Legislators are supplied useful questions to ask administration officials as well as effective counterarguments to existing military and strategic policies. In this respect, for example, Governor Nelson Rockefeller presented the House Subcommittee on Defense Department Appropriations with a perceptive criticism of the Eisenhower administration's defense program when he appeared before it in 1958.[29] His testimony provided subcommittee members with a different and valuable viewpoint based on an intensive study of the Rockefeller Brothers Fund.[30] Governor Rockefeller's testimony enabled Congress to argue with some validity that its modification of some of the President's defense recommendations for FY 1959 were partially guided by policy alternatives which were superior to those put forward by administration advocates.

Finally, Congress can turn to its own staff, including the Legislative Reference Service, for aid in gathering information to improve the decision-making process within its control. Congressional staffs can prepare questions for the defense hearings, assist in writing reports, act as a continuing link to the Defense Department, and, generally, perform hundreds of minor duties to relieve legislators for more important policy matters. They can be especially useful when they assist congressmen in anticipating future military problems—a legitimate staff function—or in discouraging new defense proposals which, if implemented, might dilute the effectiveness of existing policies or even nullify them.[31]

479

In the absence of these sources of information, Congress is seriously impeded in its attempts to analyze the defense budget. They provide the needed guidance to uncover flaws in the administration's recommendations and to suggest workable alternatives to them. Since Congress' effectiveness in defense policy depends on these diverse avenues of information, it must have a policy toward them that will support its over-all approach to the defense budget. It presently does not.

Congress has been slow to raise opposing policy views in its examination of the annual defense bills. In the first decade after World War II, all of the services experienced difficulty in their attempts to secure a congressional hearing of their disagreements with the administration over the defense budget. Only the air force proved moderately successful in its congressional campaign for a force of seventy groups. It, too, was finally rebuffed in the FY 1951 defense bill. The navy's case against the administration and the air force was effectively blocked in the defense appropriations subcommittees. The House Armed Services Committee reluctantly conducted an investigation of naval charges, but it had no appreciable effect on the defense appropriations groups.

Broader appropriations subcommittee interest in developing different policy positions from those held among the services and the administration took firmer shape at the close of the Korean War. In 1953, the House and Senate groups provided a forum for air force criticism of the Eisenhower "Interim Look." During the next two years of the Eisenhower administration, Congress resisted mounting service pressures to present their policy differences to the public. Congress reasserted itself in 1956. The House Defense Appropriations Subcommittee focused criticism on the low state of army and air force preparedness and on the nation's lagging development of a long-range missile program. Except for a $900 million increase in air power funds, principally for bombers, Congress took no action to meet the criticisms of defense policy that its investigations divulged.

Sputnik prompted Congress to plug obvious gaps in military policy and administration. Its most notable successes, as the discussion above indicates, were achieved in the post-sputnik period. The services were given ample opportunity to present their cases within a public forum. Congress weighed the conflicting testimony that was offered and reshaped parts of the administration's policies accordingly. The trends in defense spending that Congress helped set into motion in the latter 1950's were reinforced and elaborated by the Kennedy administration.

Since 1961, Congress has sustained an interest in flushing Defense Department differences into the open and in fashioning alternatives to the administration's recommendations on either economic or military grounds. Unfortunately recent congressional participation in defense policy has given sign of narrowing again from its peak of the immediate post-sputnik period. The Eighty-seventh and Eighty-eighth congresses have concentrated on the future of long-range manned delivery systems. Other important aspects of military defense, such as special warfare forces or the American sponsored proposal for a multilateral nuclear force in NATO, have been slighted or have received cursory treatment.

Neither of the defense appropriations subcommittees provides enough staff members who are experienced or trained in the substantive issues of defense policy. During the Eighty-sixth Congress, the House defense subcommittee retained six full-time staff members; the Senate, four. Their duties were general and diffuse and their efforts were thinly spread over the entire defense budget. They were not specifically charged to analyze critically the merit of the administration's defense proposals. The staffs were so small that a thorough policy review would have been impossible even if they had been directed to concentrate their attention on major strategic issues. Staff shortages, now painfully evident, were even more acute a decade before. In the debate on the FY 1952 defense bill, Representative Errett Scrivner, ranking Republican member of the House defense

481

appropriations unit, complained that his subcommittee relied on only two assistants, while the heads of the military departments were usually aided by as many as seventeen assistants in presenting their estimates to Congress.[32] The situation in the Senate was admitted to be worse in 1951. The Senate military appropriations subcommittee employed only one full-time staff member to handle a $60 billion appropriations bill.

The subcommittees do engage outside experts who are usually trained in the areas of budgeting, accounting, or administrative management. They are retained on a temporary basis and are in most instances "lent" for short periods of time by federal agencies other than the Defense Department. The House and Senate defense subcommittees secure a large number of their short-term work force from the Federal Bureau of Investigation and the General Accounting Office.[33] While the competence and professional skill of these personnel are high within their fields of specialization, they are not trained or temperamentally or professionally inclined to criticize the administration's defense proposals from a policy standpoint. Their attention is drawn to questions of budgetary integrity and administrative efficiency, and not to military preparedness and foreign policy.

The subcommittees resist hiring more staff. Many members are concerned that a large staff would merely turn itself into another bureaucracy and further complicate the task of acquiring information from the administrative departments. Senator Richard Russell, who in 1965 was chairman of the Senate defense appropriations subcommittee, was reputed to be a "small staff man" for much these same reasons.[34] Outside experts are rarely employed from business, the academic community, or respected semipublic institutions like RAND or the Navy's Center for Naval Analysis.

Within its own ranks Congress makes poor and inadequate use of the Legislative Reference Service, which it created in the Legislative Reorganization Act of 1946. The service initially gave promise of evolving into a kind of Budget Bureau for Congress, serving as a

482

high-powered, professional staff agency on domestic and military and foreign policy for the guidance and assistance of individual legislators and committees. After almost twenty years of experience, the prospects of this development now are not great. The service is starved for funds, and the congressional groups which pass on its budget are insensitive to the needs of the service and the professional staff requirements of Congress. The service, moreover, is not likely to expand or to improve markedly so long as it is bound to the conservative and cautious direction of the Librarian of Congress. The service cannot be responsive to policy problems when it is rooted to the institutional framework and mentality of a library. Fact finding and gathering are inevitably stressed at the expense of policy analysis and evaluation. Personnel policies regarding the hiring of professional staff are shaped accordingly.

The service's small professional staff is often saddled by trivial assignments to write speeches for the commemoration of national guard armories or to praise diverse nationality groups, conservation organizations, boy scout troops, and the like in statements that are inserted with tired regularity in the *Congressional Record*. Except for senior specialists, top-grade experts on various domestic and foreign-policy issues who operate independently of the seven divisions of the service,[35] and a handful of division analysts who by their own initiative or demonstrated competence have developed close ties with individual congressional offices and committees, the service's limited personnel resources are increasingly devoted at congressional behest to the trifling and the petty. A vicious circle thus obtains. To the extent that the service's image in the minds of legislators is shaped by its handling of constituent requests rather than by its capacity to contribute to the substantive policy problems facing Congress, the service is less likely to be used as a professional staff agency. As its professional functions are subordinated to the discharge of routine and banal tasks, the leadership of the service encounters greater difficulty in justifying appropriations requests for the support of expanded professional aid to congressional offices and committees. The upshot is that Congress deprives itself of a potentially valuable instrument for the analysis and assessment of domestic and foreign policy problems.[36]

The Foreign Affairs Division of the Legislative Reference Service, one of its seven operating units, presently carries two defense analysts on its table of organization and a scattering of area specialists. In addition, two senior specialists outside of the Foreign Affairs Division concentrate on military and space policy problems. These staff resources are slim and overtaxed when related to the work that needs to be done on the defense budget if Congress is, through its appropriations and military service groups, to gain sufficient control of the defense budget to suggest alternative courses of action when and where they appear desirable.

6. *Opposing the President.*—Although Congress may discover flaws in the President's defense recommendations as well as feasible alternatives to correct them, it cannot easily induce or compel the President to adopt its views. Presidents Truman, Eisenhower, and Kennedy all refused to spend appropriations for defense purposes which went beyond their respective requests to Congress. They all interpreted congressional appropriations—in the words of President Kennedy— as "only a ceiling, not a mandate to spend." [37]

Congress has had to resort to extraordinary legislative action to force the President to pursue policies that he opposed. In 1958, 1959, and 1960, for example, Congress forbade the President to commit any funds for army national guard personnel unless it was kept at a level of 400,000 men.[38] Despite the indisputable constitutionality of these legislative directives, they seriously interfere, if used casually or too often, with the flexible adjustments of approved defense policies and administrative procedures to changes in the international and domestic environment. Except in cases of extreme presidential laxity and ineptitude, they cannot provide a substitute for swift and energetic executive action in military affairs. The extent and variety of national exigencies, as Alexander Hamilton understood clearly two centuries ago, cannot be fully predicted or defined; nor can the corresponding military responses needed to satisfy them. Executive action must be adapted to each novel situation.

If it appears that Congress can seldom do much to overcome manifest weaknesses in defense policy in the face of presidential intransigence or without simultaneously diminishing the effectiveness of executive branch initiative and operations, why then should it trouble to determine whether the administration's strategic proposals are militarily, economically, and politically sound? The answer is inherent in Congress as a goal-directing institution. By articulating its own alternatives to official strategic defense policies and by appropriating funds to carry them out along with the remainder of the President's program, Congress establishes criteria by which the administration's activities can be judged. Exercised with restraint and with a minimum of partisanship, fully cognizant of its inability to replace the President as planner and executor of an enormously complicated military enterprise, Congress' reordering of military priorities and policies may force a lackadaisical or misdirected executive branch into building and supporting an adequate defense force to pursue more salutary strategic policies.[39] Although the President may still fail to implement Congress' changes in the defense budget, the issue between these two coequal branches of the government will have been joined for public discussion and debate. Congress will have demonstrated its indispensability as an instrument of popular government and of successful defense policy.

Congress has often been sharply attacked for having reversed or altered Defense Department priorities for force levels and weapon systems. Congress' duty to survey defense policy is usually conceded,[40] but the opinion is commonly expressed that "'this surveillance must not be broadened to an extent where Congress can dictate the weapons of defense.'"[41] This standard for congressional action, while

485

widely accepted, is unnecessarily rigid and confining. Its effect, if exclusively applied by Congress, would be to weaken further its role in defense policy. This standard overlooks, too, the credible record of accomplishment of Congress in defense policy since World War II.

Restricting Congress to a surveillance function is tantamount to undermining eventually the utility of that function. Its effective discharge by Congress depends on the possibility that Congress can directly correct deficiencies in the adequacy and economy of national defense. Unless there is a pay-off in policy terms, Congress is given little incentive to conduct a searching review of the defense budget on policy grounds or to instruct public opinion. In the absence of this incentive, legislators are encouraged to train their energies and attention on the annual budgetary expedition to expose pockets of waste, inefficiency, or corruption in defense management. Pork barrel considerations rise to ascendancy. There are at least domestic political gains to be made from such traditional assaults on the chief executive's budget.

Congress by and large has sparingly used its power over military appropriations to legislate defense policy directly. Only in the peculiar area of army reserve policy has it specifically compelled the administration to spend additional funds to maintain the national guard and the army reserves at congressionally determined levels. Otherwise it has provided additional funds to the executive branch for defense on a basis that has preserved presidential initiative, flexibility, and discretion. Even in the area of reserve policy, Congress has shown unexpected adaptability. Since 1961 it has increasingly albeit reluctantly permitted the secretary of defense to formulate reserve policy in terms of strategic requirements, and less as a response to domestic political pressures. In those instances in which the President has released the extra funds voted by Congress for specific defense programs or has anticipated congressional criticisms and has initiated shifts in defense policy to meet or blunt them, the results have generally been salutary. Except for the Korean War, Congress has made its most beneficial contribution to defense policy during periods of intense controversy with the President and the executive branch. There is little to fear from more active, informed, and direct participation by Congress in defense policy so long as Congress acts on a perception of its limits and potentialities as a consent-granting institution.

The need for congressional initiative in defense policy will obviously vary, accordion-like, with the President in office. It will be potentially greatest when the President is weak, distracted, and ineffective. It will be less when the President is strong, active, and alert to strategic and foreign policy problems. Congress' record indicates, however, that it has been better disposed in its organization and procedures, and in its collective intellectual grasp of strategic problems to respond to executive initiative than to mitigate the deficiencies of executive branch leadership by its own forceful and enlightened entry into defense policy. Congress has been slow to propose policies which compensated for shortcomings and oversights in those offered by the executive branch. Its institutional arrangements have been, and still are, more responsive to direct, massive, and immediate strategic threats than to the anticipation and prevention of their emergence. The defense policy initiatives of the Eighty-sixth Congress, the high point of congressional intervention in defense policy, were no exception. They were prompted by the flight of sputnik and by reports of successful Soviet ICBM tests. Fortunately, too, congressional leaders, like Representative George Mahon, Senate Majority Leader Lyndon Johnson, and House Speaker Sam Rayburn—fortuitously all Texans and political bedfellows in state politics—were available to mold and direct the inchoate majorities favoring a greater defense effort which were galvanized by these outside shocks. Even these leadership efforts were circumscribed in their immediate effect. Although Congress successfully shifted some defense spending priorities and encouraged a number of new and beneficial developments in military programming, it fell short of transforming the economic and fiscal policies that underlay the New Look.

In its review of the defense budget, Congress' duties vis-à-vis the President mix and gradually merge with its responsibilities vis-à-vis the public. Three distinct functions can, nevertheless, be isolated that define its unique relation to the public. As an instrument of popular rule, Congress has at least three crucial leadership functions: (1) It should inform and instruct the public about the political purposes underlying strategic policies and the human and material requirements to achieve them. (2) It should clarify and define the fundamental ethical values which the nation seeks through military force. (3) It should aid the President in marshaling public support for the nation's foreign policy goals and military policies.

Informing and instructing the public.—In a democracy public support for the government's defense policies will not be sustained for long, especially if they are burdensome, unless the public understands and accepts the purposes underlying them. Knowledge of the political purposes of the defense effort stabilizes public moods and expectations about foreign policy. The human and material sacrifices that the public must make can be justified in terms of these purposes. It is important, therefore, that these purposes be sufficiently defined to provide a guide for public action and the benefits to be derived from them. World Wars I and II were fought on such vague and idealized political grounds that public disillusionment with the outcome of both wars was almost inevitable. In this connection, the public must be apprised of the perils and opportunities of strategic policies so that temporary reversals or defeats can be absorbed without necessitating disruptive interruptions in sound strategic policies.

Congress has not always followed these guidelines. Before President Eisenhower assumed office, he suggested in a number of speeches that he would adopt a more aggressive strategic position than con-

488

tainment. The hint of a liberation strategy attracted wide public and legislative pronouncements of support. Once in power, the Eisenhower administration reverted to many of the previous administration's more circumscribed, announced goals. Public expectations, however, were inflated beyond any reasonable prospect of fulfilment. Large segments of the public then had to be re-educated to accept the Eisenhower restatement of containment whereas otherwise they could have been reinforced in their initial commitment to containment and its admittedly onerous military and non-military requirements. Congress and, most particularly, the Democratic minority of the Eighty-third Congress lost an opportunity to clarify the considerations that required the abandonment of liberation proposals and the continued maintenance of a containment posture.

Alternatively, the public will grasp the need for measured changes in defense policies only when it has been schooled in the basic elements of contemporary strategic problems. Only an instructed public can appreciate the need for rapid adjustments in defense and foreign policy to meet new international conditions. In the absence of such instruction, large segments of the public are likely to become exasperated by the government's policies as they are seemingly drawn in first one direction and then another. Vacillating public moods will tend to replace stable expectations about the nation's foreign policies. The government's flexibility abroad will be undermined by unpredictable oscillations and divisions in public sentiment. Public support for the government's strategic policies under these circumstances must necessarily be tenuous. The nation's bargaining power with its enemies will be correspondingly decreased. Political compromises may then have to be reached that serve only to reinforce the public's skepticism and disdain of foreign policy and military involvement abroad.

Confidence in the Truman administration's conduct of the Korean War, for example, was partially lost because the public was not adequately informed about the political stakes of the war, the exposed military position of the nation, and the risks of general war if the fighting in Korea had been escalated through the introduction of nuclear weapons or through the bombing of Chinese military bases. Many interpreted the war as a military defeat rather than as a successful blockage of communist efforts to overrun South Korea and to undermine the United States position throughout the Far East. The new rules of limited military conflict ushered in by nuclear weapons had still not seeped down to the public. Congress must bear some responsibility for muddled public understanding of the Korean War. Senator Richard Russell's Far East hearings after the dismissal of General Douglas MacArthur provided some guidance and exposed some of the hazards of pursuing a policy of "victory" or unconditional surrender in a nuclear age. They were not bolstered by a similarly enlightened approach in Congress' review of the annual defense budgets during this period.

The task of informing the public is never done since the nation must constantly reshape its defense policies to fit new modalities of international life. The defense budget review, therefore, provides a periodic occasion for Congress to restate the importance of current policies or to publicize the need for new ones. A careful examination of the President's defense budget can be a useful teaching device. If Congress discharges the tasks already indicated above in reviewing the President's defense proposals, even to the extent of challenging his recommendations, the public will be made aware of its responsibilities in strategic planning and operations. It will know what sacrifices it will have to make and what shifts will be necessary in its thinking and responses to foreign affairs. The continued exercise of Congress' educative function will alert the small, yet influential, attentive public to the implications of the government's strategic proposals.

The educative function of the defense budget has not been fully perceived or acted upon. The defense bill has been treated too

490

narrowly and routinely as just another appropriations measure to be handled like all the rest—a technical chore for experts in the area, the province of a small group in the legislature. As defense policy has slipped out of the hands of Congress and even largely out of the control or influence of the committees and subcommittees concerned with defense issues, the knowledge and interest of legislators in defense issues has correspondingly diminished. Similarly, the public's grasp of defense problems has often been cloudy, confused, and fragmentary.

Clarifying and defining values and assumptions.—A democracy, if it is to remain consistent with its ethical ideals, has a distinct obligation to justify the use of force and to limit and discipline its use to defined political purposes which themselves are morally justifiable. Operationally, the controlling ideal of democratic rule is the replacement of coercion by persuasion in the domestic governing of the nation. While these two principles are mixed in all democratic regimes, there is no doubt as to which is preferred. Democracy, based on the rule of the many, requires that national objectives and policies rest on a broad, popular consensus.[42]

A majority may turn to coercion to exercise its will, as it did in passing the Civil Rights Bill of 1964. But even as it compelled the integration of public accommodations and the protection of Negro voting rights, coercion was invoked hesitantly. The reluctance to expose the coercive elements of the civil rights measure is embodied in the establishment of the Community Relations Service, whose principal task is to obtain voluntary compliance with the law. Nor is it without significance that the first head of the service should be a distinguished Southern governor who had once been publicly committed to segregation and who would, therefore, presumably be persuasive, yet understanding and sympathetic, in his dealings with segregationists. The American democracy, if it is to bring conformity

491

between its actions and ethical goals, must be similarly guided by the principle of persuasion over coercion in the formulation and execution of its military and foreign policies.

When force must be employed, it must be justified in terms of the political and moral ends sought by the nation. Congress, as an instrument of popular rule, is obliged to clarify and define these purposes and the assumptions on which strategic policy is conducted. Unless there is a continuing re-examination and re-evaluation of the purposes guiding the nation's military efforts, there is the danger, already suggested, that strategic policy and defense preparedness will become substitutes for the very objectives that they are allegedly designed to support.

When violence is invoked in settling differences among nations, it is an admission that the construction of a mutually acceptable political and legal relation between antagonists has failed. Military force fills the vacuum where human purpose and adaptability have proved defective. The application of violence involving the destruction of life and property may be necessary to avoid a greater evil such as capitulation to a rival state whose regime is base and depraved or to prevent the overthrow of a legitimately constituted government. Force may also be justified to dispose another state to negotiate differences. The policy of the United States to build a situation of strength in Europe during the Berlin crisis of 1961 before negotiating with the Soviet Union offers a case in point. Force provides the framework within which bona fide political talks can take place and within which persuasion with an exchange of rival viewpoints can have maximum play, once a level of military stabilization has been reached. In the absence of conventional buildup of military power, the Soviet Union might have used its superior ground forces to unduly influence the outcome of the negotiations over Berlin during the crisis period. The United States show of force and allied solidarity in Europe blunted Soviet pressures on the city, and gradually tensions were again relaxed.

492

Force may be necessary, but it is not to be preferred. The lesser use of force in international conflict is to be preferred to the greater use, if the former is capable of producing the legitimate policy objects that are sought. The lesser the military force that is applied or threatened, the closer, by and large, is the principle of persuasion over coercion approached. Indeed, the latter is most clearly guarded in those instances in which the nation strives to achieve its legitimate foreign and strategic goals through non-coercive means, such as economic and technical aid programs and even political concessions to its antagonists.

Congress must be credited with having on some occasions risen to the task of consciously redefining American attitudes and political objectives. The Senate's decisive passage of the test ban treaty in 1963 suggests that Congress is capable of re-examining the fundamental bases of the nation's strategic policy and of reshaping them to conform to new realities of international life. Although a majority of legislators remained convinced that the Soviet Union had not abandoned its transnational goals of domination, they were willing to enter into a limited test ban agreement to end atomic pollution of the atmosphere and to arrest the diffusion of nuclear weapons. For the first time Congress was willing to approve an arms control agreement with the nation's principal rival. The emotional difficulties and domestic political objections to be overcome in consenting to the treaty should not be minimized despite the element of mutual national self-interest that underlies the treaty. Since the breakup of the big power harmony of World War II, most congressmen and the general public have assumed that the Soviet Union would neither keep international agreements nor enter into them unless it would secure the preponderant advantage. In entering into an arms control agreement, Congress indicated a deeper appreciation of the political dilemmas posed by the use of nuclear weapons than it had manifested in the past. The House defense appropriations group, for example, came very close to advocating a modified pre-emptive strike strategy in the FY 1960 and FY 1961 defense bills. The test ban treaty suggests, however, that Congress, as a partial outgrowth of the Cuban confrontation of 1962, had become more sharply aware of the limits of military force as a means of achievirg or approximating the nation's political and moral goals. An attempt was made to achieve a *rapprochement* with the Soviet Union to mitigate, if not necessarily to end, the possibility of a mutually destructive nuclear war. Accommodation and compromise, the instruments of persuasion, were employed to resolve issues of mutual national interest.

The Senate's achievement in the test ban treaty contrasts sharply with its record and that of the House's in defining the ethical value of the nation's political and military policies and in evaluating the ethical dimensions of using different forms of military power under variously defined contingencies. The annual defense bills are certainly never approached in these terms. Nor is the defect solely attributable to the defense appropriations subcommittees. In the B-36 and strategy hearings of 1949–1950, the navy had attacked the air force's strategic bombing concepts as morally reprehensible and offered its carrier bombing forces as a more militarily discriminating and morally justifiable tool to destroy enemy targets. The issues raised by Admiral Ralph A. Ofstie were never pursued by the House Armed Services Committee. The FY 1951 defense bill, although reviewed during the course of the strategy hearings, similarly took no apparent cognizance of the navy's arguments.[43] Instead Congress, acting on the recommendations of the appropriations committees, cut defense spending and further reduced the over-all military preparedness of the nation. Congress committed the nation more heavily than before to its nuclear strike forces without sufficiently examining the political or moral implications of its decision. Not without irony, it failed to appropriate sufficient funds to prevent the diminution of nuclear-strike forces.

Congress bypassed another opportunity during the Korean conflict to re-examine the need for more and varied forms of military power.

494

Its debates on the defense bills, to the extent that they occurred, concentrated on narrow questions of economy and efficiency in military spending. The FY 1953 defense bill passed through Congress as if it has been staged by some "absurd" dramatist. From the point of view of the foreign and strategic imperatives facing the nation, congressional preoccupation with the Smith amendment calling for a limit on defense expenditures was senseless and self-defeating.[44] As men died and the world trembled before the prospect of global conflict, Congress through its appropriations groups fiddled with accounting forms and budgetary estimates.

Marshaling public opinion.—Congress must decide strategic policies in terms of the nation's strategic and foreign policy requirements, even if its decisions initially meet with wide popular resentment. This aspect of its leadership role is inherent in its constitutional authority to legitimate the nation's strategic policies in appropriating funds for defense. Congress and each legislator must be prepared to increase taxes, institute economic controls, or tighten conscription laws if the nation's interests and policy goals demand such action. Decisions to cut back arms production or to disengage the nation's military power from certain areas of the world may have to be supported to stabilize or improve relations with rival states. No democracy can long survive, especially when challenged abroad, unless its elected officials are willing to risk defeat at the polls by pursuing policies that, while temporarily unpopular, resolve the nation's strategic problems. Victory in elections or the conciliation of disaffected domestic groups cannot be overriding considerations; threshold strategic imperatives must take precedence. The leadership of a democracy cannot any more escape this order of priority than it can avoid the competing and paradoxical requirement that its defense policies must rest on broad popular consent.

Congress acts for the public as a whole and must be judged accordingly. Although each congressman is elected locally to represent local interests, his decisions as a legislator have national implications for which he must be held responsible. In security and foreign policy matters, Congress and each congressman must be judged, in the final analysis, on the basis of their responsiveness to the more encompassing interests and objectives of the wider public. The public in whose behalf Congress acts is a larger body than the American electorate. It includes all those who are alive today and all those who have preceded and who will succeed them in the future. Congress does not make decisions for a moment. Its decisions affect past commitments and promises and also shape the future. It has a responsibility to those who have come before and those who have yet to share a part of the future that congressional decision and action aid in forming. The electorate is only the politically activated part of the public that makes its influence felt in periodic elections.[45]

Each legislator's responsibility and the responsibility of Congress to national security and to a democratic foreign policy transcend a strict accounting to a contingent majority of voters. Edmund Burke's perceptive understanding of the normative duties of public office and the principles that should guide the relations between the elected official and his constituency are still applicable. Indeed, the applicability is greater since the problems of government are greater and are becoming progressively more complicated and confusing. The public must rely heavily and, in such situations as the Cuban crisis of 1962, decisively on the judgments and evaluations of elected officials.

It can be granted that governmental policies that do not enjoy widespread electoral support will be ultimately abandoned or revised. The implementation of unpopular policies can only be a temporary expedient to meet immediate strategic imperatives. President Truman could not call for a national referendum to commit American troops in Korea. His first responsibility was to cope with the crisis and only afterward could he attempt to win popular support for his action. His administration's efforts to reconcile the electorate obviously failed. Its policies were repudiated in the 1952 elections. The President,

496

nevertheless, must be disposed to risk loss of electoral confidence in order to maximize the long-run interests of the nation. A majority of legislators in Congress must be similarly prepared to support the administration. Measured by its handling of defense appropriations during the Korean War, Congress did not provide as much support to the administration as it was able.

Congress, of course, cannot be arbitrarily singled out for criticism, and all of the blame for past failures in defense policy heaped at its doors. The public shares responsibility for these defects, too. Under these circumstances, where a fissure exists between the terms of public consensus and what may be considered a desirable strategic posture, criticism leveled against Congress for its failure to support certain types of strategic policies must pass beyond it and center on the American electorate and on the elite leadership within it. If the voting public is unwilling to make the sacrifices needed for strategic operations or to recast some of its political expectations and attitudes to facilitate the construction and maintenance of a strong strategic position, Congress and the President can do little despite their best efforts. This is simply to recognize again that the success of strategic planning depends, in the final analysis, on the populace and that democratic constraints and processes are often in conflict with the requirements of military and foreign policy. On the other hand, in the absence of firm and energetic political leadership, a democratic people cannot survive in a hostile world. Congress has a responsibility to bridge the often conflicting requirements of effective strategic policies and the dictates of popular consent. Discharging its leadership functions is a key factor in the successful execution of this bridging process.

That Congress has not always discharged its leadership responsibilities is clear enough. The test ban treaty offers an exception. The efforts of some legislators to increase defense spending and inform public opinion during the final years of the Eisenhower administration provide additional encouragement. These instances of congressional statesmanship have not been frequent or sustained. Congress' inhibiting effect on the conduct of the Korean War and its collective refusal to understand the significance of that conflict have already been noted. Revealing, too, is congressional hypersensitivity to constituent pressures for decreased governmental spending and balanced budgets during most of the years since World War II, especially up to 1958. Congress has always carefully waited for the chief executive to define both the political and economic limits of the defense budget. Except for tentative and indirect attacks on the President's spending limits in the immediate post-sputnik years, legislators usually have avoided departures from conventional budgetary wisdom. Political expediency has been hidden behind a façade of crude economic maxims and slogans. A spending ceiling of $15 billion was first set on defense spending. Then $30 billion briefly became the symbol of budgetary orthodoxy. Later $38 billion and $40 billion were considered the upper limits that the nation could afford. After a long struggle, defense budgets of $50 billion or more a year were finally accepted under the Kennedy and Johnson administrations. Congress has now become so accustomed to passing large defense measures that a recently developed counterresistance threatens to memorialize this level of defense expenditure.

Congress has been, on occasion, an obstacle to the development of an enlightened public opinion. After the Czech coup d'état in 1948, the House War and Navy Department appropriations subcommittees were in a position to spur Defense Secretary James Forrestal's recommendation for a modest program of military rearmament. The breakdown in Soviet-American negotiations after World War II, the piece-meal communist takeover of eastern Europe, Soviet agitation in the Mediterranean and the Middle East, including Greece, Turkey, and Iran, prepared the public for an increase in defense readiness. Yet Forrestal made little headway with Congress and the President. Political leadership, as Forrestal was acutely aware, was lacking in the executive and legislative branches to sustain public awareness and harness its support for more and varied military capabilities. Congress shares responsibility with the chief executive for the breakdowns in leadership.

Tools of information, instruction, and leadership.—The hearings, reports, and debates on the defense appropriations bills are potentially important mediums by which Congress can inform, instruct, and lead the public. While the hearings have perceptibly improved since 1945 in their increasing attention to policy issues, they still remain defective education vehicles. Until Robert McNamara became secretary of defense, the hearings provided sparse discussion of defense strategy. Where policy matters were raised, they were usually buried, irretrievably, in the heaps of indigestible data diligently collected by the defense subcommittees in the thousands of pages of closely packed testimony from administration witnesses. The appropriations hearings of both houses on the FY 1963 budget exceeded 5,000 pages. If the procurement and construction authorization hearings are added along with the construction appropriations hearings of both houses, total testimony exceeds 9,500 pages. No legislator can absorb, much less understand, what the mountain of facts and figures assembled in the hearings signify. Even before the hearings grew so large and cumbersome, congressmen, like Senator Brien McMahon during the debates on the FY 1947 navy bill, complained that the hearings provided him with little guidance in casting his vote for the defense bill.[46] The problem has been aggravated by the growing complexity of defense issues and the parallel growth in size of the annual defense hearings.

Subcommittee members nevertheless pride themselves on the length of the hearings and on the bulk of the testimony that is taken. Debates on the defense bill are often prefaced by statements from appropriations committee members that praise the bulky measurements of the published hearings.[47] A presumption is suggested that because the defense appropriations group has worked long and hard to gather an immense, albeit unmanageable, body of information, it has somehow comprehended and resolved the major problems of defense policy. The size of the hearings becomes then a kind of club that committee members can wield to blunt the criticism of their colleagues who have not gone through the painful and exhausting exercise of gathering the confusing array of administration testimony on defense policy. There is little time, a week or only a few days in some instances, between the time that all of the hearings are published and floor consideration of the defense bill. Some of the hearings, like those of the House Armed Services Committee on procurement, are not indexed. The reader confronts a blur of almost a thousand pages of closely packed print. The hearings of the House defense appropriations subcommittee, closed largely on grounds of security and as a means of resisting lobbying pressures, frustrate further the flow of information to House members and to the public. Legislators who are not members of the appropriations committees are thus placed at a distinct disadvantage in raising objections to the defense bill on the floor. Defense policy tends to become the private preserve of the ascetic few who have labored long hours in the budgetary vineyard.

The presentations of Secretary of Defense McNamara have been a welcome departure. They are comprehensive, yet precise and clear, in their delineation of the major policy dimensions of the administration's strategic policies. The defense secretary initiated the change. Congress did not prompt it. Despite this innovation, questioning of administration witnesses continues to flit from issue to issue. The desultory, unsystematic movement of the questioning vexes and bewilders the reader. What is recorded finally is a long, disorderly catalogue of specific military, political, economic, administrative, and budgetary problems. The relative importance of each problem, however, is not indicated. Mesmerized by the seemingly endless flow of detail canalized in the hearings, the reader is tempted to perceive the problems which are discussed as being of equal significance. The hearings do not indicate the priority of importance of the nation's defense issues. The executive sessions of the defense appropriations subcommittees do set priorities when they finally mark up the defense funding bill for presentation to the full chambers of each house of Congress, but these sessions are secret and offer no guidance to legislative members. The House Armed Services Committee, on the other hand, publishes parts of its executive sessions in marking up the annual defense procurement authorization bill. This useful practice has been offset by the length and desultory flow of subcommittee discussion. The printed hearings have not been carefully prepared to be usable for most legislators who can devote only a limited portion of their hard-pressed time and energy resources to defense questions.

Attempts have been made in the House to present an orderly list of strategic policy questions to administration officials during hearings on the defense appropriations bill. This heartening procedure has been diluted in its effectiveness. The subcommittee chairman has experienced difficulty in controlling the questioning of administration officials by the individual members of his group. Representative George Mahon, chairman of the House subcommittee, has remarked that he has often had difficulty in encouraging some subcommittee members beyond "fifth-grade arithmetic." [48] The fancy of each legislator determines too much of the quality and direction of the subcommittee's questioning. Moreover, when a witness is asked to comment on policy issues, such as the size of the military budget and its adequacy, the intent of the question is often less to analyze the merit of the answer than to solicit an authoritative opinion that the subcommittee can cite to justify its recommendations. The hearings of the armed services committees on the annual procurement authorizations bill have not been perceptibly more informative than those of the appropriations committees.

The same care for budgetary and administrative detail continues into the House and Senate reports on the defense appropriations bills. The House report is invariably longer, sometimes exceeding 100 pages. Under Representative George Mahon's direction the reports

501

have included some discussion of major defense issues, but the bulk of the report still focuses on matters of departmental administration and on the allocation of funds, which are assigned in lump sums of hundreds of millions of dollars to functionally defined defense activities. The Senate report is exclusively directed toward the budgetary categories of the budget. Broad policy issues are not raised. The bill is collapsed into the hardware and personnel items that it provides. The report becomes little more than a brief inventory of the defense capabilities of the fiscal year under consideration. It is impossible to determine from the Senate report and from much of the House report what the various proposed appropriations for maintenance and operations, procurement, research and development, and personnel signify with respect to the nation's policy objectives or the spectrum of foreign military threats that face it. The reports of the armed services committees on the procurement authorization bill follow a similar pattern.

The reports on the defense bill could be easily transformed into "White Papers" on national defense. They could become instruments by which the Congress could inform itself and, in turn, the public on defense policy. They could be shaped into more effective vehicles for the coherent assertion of congressional will. They are neither of these things now. In the absence of such instruction the public can hardly be expected to respond enthusiastically to the government demands made upon it.

The conference reports are especially cryptic. Only specific amendments indicating the sums of money in dispute between the two houses are listed, after which the compromise figure agreed to by the conferees is noted. Even the misleading functional budgetary categories that possess at least some program content are not mentioned. Legislators must wait until the floor presentation of the conference measure before receiving an explanation of the report. Differences between the two houses are shrouded behind a smoke screen of almost meaningless figures, often totaling billions of dollars.

The obfuscation is not without import. The conference committees often decide important program changes such as the inclusion or deletion of a navy carrier or an air force fighter squadron.

As instruments of public information and instruction, the debates and discussions on the defense bill on the floor of each legislative chamber have not compensated for the defects of the reports and hearings. They have reinforced them. Rarely have they stimulated interest or produced enlightenment among legislators or the public. They are generally too short to attract public attention. Tens of billions of dollars have been approved after only one day of debate. Attendance on the floor is often poor. Legislators presenting the defense bill to their respective houses have often remarked on the absence of a quorum.[49] The lack of broad congressional participation on the military funding bill, representing half of the federal government's annual budget, is a crude index of the failure of the floor debates as an educative tool.

While the summaries of the defense bill made by subcommittee members are factual and informative, they relate only vaguely to the foreign policy goals of the nation. Members are told that x-billions of dollars are required to deter communist aggression or to purchase variously defined levels of military hardware. The array of strategic problems which the defense bill is presumably designed to resolve is not specifically differentiated or related to various foreign policy contingencies. Defense budgets of $50 billion are incomprehensible when presented in such lump sums. The justifications offered on the floor can be equally employed to support military budgets of $50 billion or half that amount.

Congress segregates the defense bill from other aspects of federal activity in floor debate. The relation of defense spending to other actual or proposed federal programs is seldom raised. Objections to the level or composition of defense spending, especially insofar as it inhibits other domestic or foreign policy programs, is discouraged. Open legislative controversy is happily minimized but often at the

503

expense of other policy goals that remain unarticulated. The floor debates provide little insight into the foreign policy dimensions of military policy. They furnish almost no key to its domestic implications. Does the defense budget reduce the capacity of the federal government to promote education, social welfare, or economic stability? Does it constrain the level of federal participation in programs to improve and develop the nation's human resources? Do the short-run requirements of military defense seriously affect, perhaps needlessly, the long-run development of an educated and informed populace capable of copying with future security and foreign policy problems? Such questions go begging in the floor examinations of the defense bills. Many legislators hold tenaciously to the comfortable assumption, lately acquired, that large defense budgets by their very size and awesome complexity produce national safety and success in foreign policy. The act of passing the measure is a form of public catharsis absolving the individual legislator from facing the controversial domestic and foreign policy problems implicit in the defense budget. Bills are passed overwhelmingly each year. Often no opposition is registered. Given the inherently limited resources of governmental revenues, the priorities of national policy tend to be set elsewhere, especially by the Defense Department bureaucracy, without adequate exposure to the counterclaims of alternative domestic and foreign program needs. "To the extent that the American people and Congress shrink from questioning the size and cost of our Defense Establishment," as Senator William Fulbright has observed,

> they are permitting military men, with their highly specialized viewpoints, to make political judgments of the greatest importance regarding the priorities of public policy and the allocation of public funds.
>
> The abnegation of responsibility by the Congress in this field is strikingly illustrated by its debates or, more accurately, nondebates, on the defense budget. When, for example, Senator McGovern . . . suggested last September [1963] that defense

spending might be reduced by 5 percent, the Senate, with virtually no discussion, moved to enact the whole Defense appropriation bill. . . . Again this year, the Congress is speeding the enactment of the Defense budget with splendid indifference to its size and content.[50]

When criticism is registered, it tends to be closely tied to the special interests of individual congressmen. Much debate time is devoted to such questions of local interest as the size of the national guard, the use of locally produced milk in Alaska, time study analyses in navy shipyards, or the transfer or deactivation of military installations and hospitals. These problems are considered legitimate contributions to the defense debate. Small sums of money are haggled over, while billions are approved mechanically. All sense of political proportion is lost.

Congress must consciously act as it was intended—as an instrument of government. The principles of action set down here, while not definitive, indicate those elements of congressional calculation, decision, and action that should be emphasized in its deliberations. Congress is elected to legislate public policy. It must be allowed, and should allow itself, to act according to its assessment of the strategic needs of the nation and to defend its action in public debate and discussion. An important test of congressional action in defense policy is how it exercises its power of the purse. In using its power, Congress' failures have unfortunately too often outweighed its achievements.

DEFENSE POLICY PROCESS:
CRITIQUE AND PRESCRIPTIONS

IX

CRITIQUE

Introduction.—Defense policy is made in Congress through both a decision and a consensus process.[1] While these two aspects of the defense policy process are simultaneous in their operation and are inextricably joined in actual practice, the requirements of one differ, and often conflict, with those of the other. Inequalities arise between the kinds of policies which are needed to underwrite the nation's policy goals and security interests abroad and what a majority of legislators will accept. By themselves, the intellectual, technical, and administrative constraints affecting Congress cannot wholly explain the shortcomings of its handling of the defense budget or of its grasp of strategic policy. The defects of congressional decision and action in defense policy are in large part functions of the consensus process that operates between Congress and the executive branch and, particularly, within Congress itself.

Were Congress to be given more staff, information, or more meaningful budgetary categories, it would still be hampered in developing a larger and more effective role for itself in defense policy. Congress is ensnared in a political process, partly of its own fabrication, that frustrates its analysis of the defense budget in terms of the political objectives and contingency plans to implement them. The existing consensus process discourages the evaluation of force levels and weapon systems in light of these elements. It daunts legislative efforts to generate alternatives to the President's proposals or to galvanize majority support to change outmoded policies or to oppose the President's recommendations when they prove defective. It dilutes congressional capacity to lead public opinion.

The diffuse policy process in Congress creates a complicated and largely intangible system of reinforcing incentives that encourage individual legislators and congressional committees to neglect and, in many instances, to abandon the institutional responsibilities charged to Congress as a whole in defense policy. These incentives motivate members of Congress to emphasize, even against their own predilections, their personal interests and narrow viewpoints at the expense of executing Congress' institutional duties. They encourage legislators to avoid conflicts over fundamental and long-range strategic issues that are not likely to result in an immediate personal or political gain and to stress concrete, marginal and often self-defeating objectives that appear to be more easily and feasibly reached in the short run. That Congress has operated as well as it has since World War II is a tribute to the independent efforts, energy, and foresight of individual legislators rather than a response in many instances to the incentives afforded them by the decentralized distribution of power and responsibility in Congress.

Legislators are torn between two generally conflicting compulsions in passing on defense appropriations. They are whipsawed, on the one hand, by their perceived need to discharge the duties of their office and, by extension, the defense responsibilities of Congress and, on the other, by their need to participate visibly and effectively in making public policy. A dual rationality thus confronts each legislator and each congressional committee concerned with defense policy: one is cast in intellectual and moral terms; the other, in the rubrics of political power. Actions that may appear rational to a legislator in light of a dispassionate appraisal of strategic imperatives may simultaneously appear irrational in light of the policies that a sizable

507

majority in Congress and in the nation will accept at the moment. Legislators and legislative committees are drawn, therefore, to advance policies which, while perhaps seriously defective, give promise of being adopted. The consensus requirements of defense policy in Congress create a new set of considerations for legislative assessment. Since World War II, the consensus process has strained, sometimes gravely, Congress' ability to discharge its defense responsibilities. While individual congressmen and committees have from time to time participated visibly and effectively in defense policy development, Congress as an institution has fallen short of achieving the possibilities of its potentially elevated role in defense and strategic policy.

How does the consensus process between Congress and the executive branch and within Congress itself inhibit Congress' role in military policy? The answer depends upon an understanding of how the consensus process generates a system of personal and committee incentives, which discourage a policy review of the defense budget, and upon Congress' full assumption of its leadership responsibilities. The experience of the defense appropriations groups provides a guide for analysis.

Executive-congressional constraints.—The defense budget is part of the President's over-all budget. What success the budget, including those segments devoted to defense, achieves in Congress is tantamount to the President's personal success. His power, prestige, and position are tied firmly to it. If the budget is amended or revised against his will, his status and stature, depending on the political importance of the change, are correspondingly diminished. The President's budget is, in the final analysis, a political document. It summarizes his political and program recommendations and the weight that he attaches to each of them. To oppose the President's defense budget is to oppose the President and, potentially, to challenge the gamut of his policy recommendations. A strong President, therefore, will generally resist assaults on parts of his budgetary proposals not only on their own merits but also insofar as they effect his over-all economic and fiscal policies as well as other substantive program recommendations. Signs of presidential weakness at one point in the annual budgetary battle before Congress may prompt administration opponents to risk attack against what appear to be other vulnerable sections of the budget. The Presdent must create the impression of firm resolution in support of his budget, even as he is forced to accept various compromises and defeats at the hands of different congressional groups.

Congress, as a body, faces impressive difficulties in effectively opposing specific parts of the President's budget, even in those instances when a majority can be arrayed against him. The task of successfully challenging the President is more complicated and arduous for a subcommittee, such as the House or Senate appropriations subcommittees. The defense groups are understandably inclined to avoid direct clashes with the President and to concede to him the benefit of any doubts that they might have concerning the adequacy or appropriateness of defense policies. Since doubts are intrinsic to defense policy, given the innumerable imponderables with which it must deal, the President's defense proposals and his political position in defending them have been, on the whole, sufficiently strong and compelling to resist most subcommittee attacks.

Since World War II Presidents have generally expected their executive departments to support their budgets before Congress. While each President has manifested a different level of tolerance for end runs to Congress to circumvent his policy determinations, each has assumed, except for a momentary lapse by President Eisenhower in 1957,[2] final responsibility for his budget. Congressional expectations are similarly oriented. Legislators accept the budget as the President's, and not as their own creation, and assume that he will publicly defend it. Members of the defense appropriations subcommittees share this attitude. Moreover, in passing on the military phase of the budget, they recognize that candid answers to probing ques-

509

tions about various controversial segments of defense policy may expose an administration witness to a crossfire between the President and Congress. This awareness, combined with an initial deference to the President's budgetary proposals, subtly restrains legislators from pursuing a line of questioning that, while embarrassing to the administration, may hazard executive branch reprisal against the witness. The effectiveness and gravity of this constraint varies, of course, with the temper and prestige of the witness and the specific issue under examination. It is, nevertheless, an ever-present factor in congressional hearings on the defense appropriations bill.

Even when criticisms of the administration's defense policies are presented in the hearings, congressional partisans of the President are almost always on hand to attack outspoken witnesses on grounds of substantive policy or of disloyalty to the President. The impact of any defection from the President's defense budgetary proposals tends to be softened under these conditions. If a witness is too forthright and affirmative in his censure of the administration, he runs the risk of losing even the little support that he can garner in Congress for his position because of legislative expectations concerning the President's budgetary prerogatives or legislative fears about presidential counter-opposition. Congress' own expectations, when linked to these fears, provide reinforced leverage for the President by which he can exercise greater control over executive branch personnel and by which, accordingly, he can blunt congressional assaults on his spending proposals. These congressional expectations become marginal additions to the President's power largely because he already possesses formidable power and prestige and acts from a position of strength in presenting his budget.

Administration witnesses appearing before appropriations groups are acutely conscious of their vulnerable positions.[3] Except in rare, but notable, instances, the overwhelming majority of administration representatives who testify on the President's budget view themselves as his agents. For every Admiral Hyman Rickover or Admiral Arthur

510

Radford, who successfully defied service or administration pressure, there are the more numerous counterbalancing examples of Admirals Louis Denfeld and George Anderson and of Generals Matthew Ridgway and James Gavin. Each was either politically isolated or ostracized after he had openly criticized administration policies. The chief executive, therefore, generally enjoys an initial advantage in presenting his proposals to Congress. Mock congressional hearings which are conducted within the Defense Department and the Budget Bureau also sharpen the wit and responses of administration witnesses, while presumably strengthening their loyalty to the President's defense policies. The elaborate Defense Department displays, charts, movies, and seemingly inexhaustible supply of data which are presented during the hearings can easily overwhelm a committee. "I'll bet they laugh up their sleeves when they get back to the Pentagon after a session down here," said a congressional appropriations staff member. "We don't give them much of a run for their money." [4]

Congressional reluctance to oppose the President is further buttressed during periods when the same party controls the legislative and executive branches of the government. Under these circumstances the members of the defense appropriations subcommittees and armed services committees are restrained in their opposition to the President not only by his impressive political power but by considerations of party loyalty, cohesion, and mutual political benefit. There have been of course numerous instances where congressional members and the President, although of the same party, have been in sharp conflict. Representative Carl Vinson's insistence on authorizing funds for the RS-70 in FY 1963 and Representative George Mahon's vigorous support for more air power in FY 1950 are prominent examples. But there is more than an accidental relation between the increasing tempo and intensity of congressional criticism of the Eisenhower administration's defense policies and the Democratic control of Congress between 1955 and 1961—the Eighty-fourth through the Eighty-sixth congresses. Alternatively, as the adoption of President Eisenhower's New Look policies by the Republican Eighty-third Congress indicates, party leadership enhances a President's power to define his defense policies and tempers congressional criticism and opposition.

Congress' relations with the executive branch, beyond the President's immediate office, also cramp its capacity to analyze the defense budget critically and comprehensively. The annual defense budget is not a *tabula rasa* on which Congress can freely scrawl its policy decisions. It is in large measure a product of past decisions and compromises with countless elements of the executive branch. Past policy determinations have been reached only after long, tedious, and complicated negotiation and bargaining. The economic, political, and status interests of thousands of civilian and military officials and their corresponding outside supporters are closely tied to these decisions. Defense policies which are reached only after exhaustive effort and which rest on a delicate balance of mutually reinforcing interests are not easily questioned or quickly discarded. Attempts to overturn entrenched, though outdated, defense policies necessarily provoke opposition in administration ranks. Even unaffected elements, foreseeing future challenges to their own positions, are encouraged to aid in a logrolling effort to impede any significant transformation of existing defense programs. Simply reaffirming what has already been agreed upon in previous go-arounds of the defense budget generally carries few risks and stirs little controversy. There is no assurance, moreover, that efforts to contravene accepted policies will be successful and, if successful, will yield any direct political benefit to an individual legislator or to a committee.

Congressional-executive struggles over defense policy in the middle-Eisenhower years pointedly illustrate the many political power impediments that blocked large-scale departures from New Look programs or the Eisenhower administration's spending ceilings. Any move by the defense appropriations groups to improve army preparedness at the expense of the air force, given the restrictions on defense spending, would have been defeated even if the subcommittees had made a strong and concerted effort to rearrange spending priorities in favor of conventional forces. Air power advocates, including members of the defense subcommittees, were clearly in the ascendancy in Congress. Air force supporters were generally agreed that if extra funds for defense were provided, they should be earmarked for more strategic air power, and not for limited warfare capabilities. The navy, too, placed itself in temporary league with the air force and acquiesced in continued decreases in army strength.

Even if air power advocates could have been reconciled to an increase in conventional forces without diminishing air force nuclear striking power, other groups would still have fought against the enlargement of any military program, including army expansion, or an increase in the defense budget or both. Secretary of the Treasury George Humphrey, for example, sharply criticized the President's budget for FY 1958. He charged that governmental expenditures, including by implication those for defense, were inflated and would have to be cut to circumvent a depression. His rebuke came hard on the heels of the Symington air power hearings in 1956 and Congress' $900 million increase to the FY 1957 defense budget for strategic delivery systems. Spurred by Humphrey's claims and by pressures that he helped to activate within Congress to reduce governmental expenditures, the defense appropriations subcommittees were again induced to search for economies in the President's defense budget rather than to review its programmatic merit or to suggest areas where additional defense programs might be speeded to completion, expanded, or initiated to attain policy goals. Until sputnik, attempts within Congress to increase army spending failed decisively. A $46 million increase for more marine corps personnel in the FY 1956 defense budget represented the sole congressional redirection of the New Look. This limited victory, too, was quickly undone when the chief executive impounded most of the extra funds which were provided.

Congressional constraints.—Within the area of its potential discretion, Congress itself is the major source of its own frustration in

513

defense policy. Devising a national strategy requires the integration of the nation's power resources, both military and non-military, to meet a host of threats to the nation's policy goals and security objectives. It demands the allocation of inherently limited resources among a variety of competing military and non-military programs. It necessitates choices according to some hierarchical statement of coherent and rationally determined ends. But the political process in Congress of which the defense budget process is one aspect does not operate so logically or systematically. Strategic issues, each encompassing a variety of military and non-military elements, are broken down in Congress and treated piecemeal as if they were independent of each other. Various and sundry facets of national and military strategy are distributed haphazardly through almost every sphere of congressional committee activity. Questions of treaty obligations or authorizations for foreign economic aid are directed to the foreign affairs committees; questions of military policy are sent to the armed services committees; the military applications of space technology are reviewed by the space committees; organizational questions are examined by the government operations committees; questions of nuclear policy are addressed to the Joint Atomic Energy Committee; other questions dealing with foreign commerce, agriculture, labor, and educational programs—all of which bear on national strategy—are apportioned among the remaining legislative committees of Congress. Moreover, since 1961 the armed services committees have asserted their right to authorize procurement of military hardware and, since 1962, research and development programs.

Funding the many programs approved by these legislative committees is a concern of the appropriations committees. Over-all strategic questions are fragmented further within them. One appropriations subcommittee reviews the Atomic Energy Commission budget; another, the Defense Department; a third, military construction; a fourth, economic aid and foreign loan grants; a fifth, the State Department; a sixth, the deficiency requests coming from all of these

514

sources. The President's budget, correspondingly, is carved into twelve to seventeen appropriations bills in each legislative session. These funding bills are treated often as if they did not affect or influence each other. The defense bill is only the biggest and brightest star in a larger constellation of appropriation bills. The close relation of strategic and non-strategic programs in the allocation of the government's funds is ignored in Congress and, accordingly, it is obscured in the minds of the public. The revenue bills underlying appropriation measures are handled by yet another group of committees—the House Ways and Means and the Senate Finance committees.

While strategic problems are dismantled in Congress for investigation, they are not subsequently rebuilt for over-all discussion and policy determination. Policy-making in Congress is dispersed. No congressional group or individual legislator is responsible for passing on the nation's strategic design. The defense appropriations subcommittees and the armed services committees have jurisdiction over only a part of the President's budget. They have no control and little influence over the other parts of the administration's proposals, although decisions in other areas of the chief executive's budget place limits on military expenditures and on the flexibility and adaptability of defense policies. Nor can subcommittees propose changes in tax laws or extend governmental regulation of the economy if more military spending is required for national security. Comparisons between the military construction, defense, and mutual security programs are almost nonexistent. Comparisons between military and non-military programs are all but foreclosed. What integration exists is forged in the executive branch, principally by the secretary of defense and the Budget Bureau.

If one of the defense appropriations subcommittees seeks to revise the President's defense proposals, it must work through the decentralized policy process in Congress. As a general rule the broader the scope and the larger the magnitude of their proposed departure from the President's spending and program proposals, the more difficulty

515

the subcommittee will face in building a viable coalition of congressional support. As a subcommittee's proposals for change enlarge, more and more groups, in and out of the government, are aroused in opposition to the suggested changes. Being only one subcommittee of a major legislative committee which, in turn, is part of a larger galaxy of semi-autonomous congressional groups and diverse informal power centers, the subcommittee is discouraged from frontally assaulting the President's position or challenging existing defense policies. Prospects of success in overturning fiscal and economic policies on which defense policies rest are likewise dim. Pressures applied at any point to change defense policies potentially activate a chain of antagonistic comment and reaction all along the defense policy process. Presidential hostility, supplemented by resistance from divergent executive, congressional, and non-governmental sources, dissuades the defense groups from undertaking the sizable job of piecing together what must necessarily be a loose and fragile coalition.

The task of the subcommittee is complicated further by the fact that since World War II it has rarely been sufficient simply to build a temporary coalition in order to induce the President or the executive department to adopt the subcommittee's policy recommendations. The coalition must be sustained over time. Passing increased appropriations for one or a set of military programs over the President's recommendations in any one year has usually failed to force the chief executive to capitulate to congressional or subcommittee preferences. Support for a basic reformulation or redirection of defense policy may take a number of years to effect, as the experience of the post-sputnik years suggests. Holding a coalition together for more than one year in the face of continued, perhaps mounting, presidential resistance has proven to be an almost impossible task for the defense appropriations groups to perform. They do not command a sufficiently large enough power base in Congress. Members of the defense subcommittees themselves have often become disheartened after a heated clash with the President or with congressional groups opposed to changes in defense policy or budgetary priorities. Representative George Mahon, for example, who spearheaded the air power increases in the FY 1949 and FY 1950 budgets, completely reversed his position a year later and allied himself with the chief executive to block moves afoot in Congress to expand air power spending.[5]

The success of the defense appropriations groups in the last years of the Eisenhower administration was due in large part to the active support and stimulus that they received from congressional leaders, like Majority Leader Lyndon Johnson and Speaker Sam Rayburn, who were influential within a larger sphere of congressional action. In the absence of access to these more inclusive centers of congressional influence, the defense appropriations subcommittees are inclined to avoid attempts at broadly redefining defense policy, notwithstanding fundamental disagreements with it. They have but a small piece of power to play within the defense policy process and within the even larger political process that operates between Congress and the executive branch and within Congress. Since the introduction of Section 412(b), the power base of the defense appropriations groups has further receded. On procurement and research and development projects for missiles, ships, and aircraft, the appropriations subcommittees must abide by the authorizations ceilings set by the armed services committees. The difficulties attendant to the construction of a new consensus on defense policy in the face of potentially massive opposition or indifference or a mixture of both, induce the subcommittees to use their limited power resources frugally and conservatively. They tend to expend what little influence they have on programs and policies that give promise of gaining sustained support in Congress and in the executive branch.

The incentives of limited power.—The decentralization and diffusion of power and responsibility in Congress create a set of incentives that orient individual congressmen and the defense appropriations subcommittees away from a full programmatic review of the defense budget. Unable to influence over-all defense policy significantly by his own efforts, each legislator is led to adopt one of three broadly defined legislative styles as a member of the appropriations group. These styles persist over time, although an individual legislator may not necessarily assume the same style of action from year to year, nor restrict himself to a single style in any one year.

Most members are induced, first of all, to choose the time-honored role of watchdog of the public purse. Tradition and habit conspire with the decentralized configuration of power relations in Congress to deflect the individual congressman's attention from the policy issues underlying the defense budget. He can gain prestige among his colleagues and reknown among his constituents by creating the image of himself as a tireless defender of the public treasury. He can enhance the value of his slim power resources simply by conforming to prevailing legislative expectations of his proper role as a member of an appropriations subcommittee.

Confused, too, by the complexity of the defense bill and the strategic issues that it raises and faced by the likelihood of failure if he should agitate to change defense policy significantly, the legislator can relieve these frustrations by repeated, if somewhat arbitrary, jabs each year at different sections of the defense budget in the hope of striking soft spots that can be conveniently cut. If he is fortunate, he may uncover segments of administrative mismanagement, inefficiency, and even corruption. These discoveries, however circumscribed they may appear from the point of view of strategic policy, rationalize the legislator's impotence in light of his broader legislative responsibilities in defense policy formulation. These successes are familiar and visible marks of his legislative achievement. They can be quickly understood and praised by other legislators and the public alike without subtle and tortuous reflection on the goals of defense policy or the diverse military means needed to secure them. The legislative maxim that half a loaf is better than none is thus revised. Members of the defense appropriations groups are tempted to content themselves with a few crumbs.

Legislators may assume a second style of action that focuses on specific and narrowly defined programmatic goals. The program style divides itself into two aspects. Some legislators identify themselves closely with the interests and perspectives of one of the services. Representatives Daniel Flood and Robert Sikes have consistently stressed army programs. Except for the Republican Eighty-third Congress, Representative Sikes was the subcommittee chairman of the army phase of the defense appropriations bill when the bill was reviewed from 1951 to 1957 on a service basis. Other legislators, like Representative George Mahon and Senator Leverett Saltonstall, adopt a more eclectic program posture. Over the years they have pressed for a variety of military programs from among the individual services.

The emphasis that a program receives tends to depend on the degree of general interest and support that can be marshaled in Congress. Air lift capabilities may be urged during one legislative session, more Polaris submarines during a second, or increased naval aircraft inventories during a third. In any event only a few program changes are usually advanced in any year whether by service advocates or by their more eclectic-minded colleagues. Legislators are wary of committing their power resources to any wholesale changes in defense policy, however salutary they might appear to be. The risks of being defeated are greater as more shifts are proposed. Priorities must be set each year as to which programs will receive primary or secondary emphasis in the negotiations and bargaining, whether tacit or explicit, with other legislators and legislative committees.

Legislators, of course, have on numerous occasions gone beyond the advocacy of one or two programs and have attempted to mount broader and more inclusive attacks on the defective policies of the administration. These assaults, however, often have been principally inspired by personal rather than institutional considerations. Repre-

519

sentative Robert Sikes's one-man critique of the New Look in the hearings and in the floor debates on the FY 1955 defense bill is relevant. Sikes trenchantly analyzed the shortcomings of the New Look and correctly forecast the imminent development of a balance of terror between the Soviet Union and the United States which would mutually deter both from initiating a nuclear war. He likewise foresaw the emergence of increasing instances of non-nuclear conflict in the peripheral areas of the world.[6]

Sikes's example of prescient and constructive opposition, so rare and isolated in the middle 1950's, was more a projection of his individual insight than an expression of institutional clairvoyance and compulsion. His *tour de force* may be at least partially explained as an outgrowth of his close association with the army as a reserve general rather than as a response elicited by his legislative office. Inner-legislative pressures hindered efforts to analyze President Eisenhower's recommendations in terms of their effectiveness in supporting American interests abroad at politically and economically acceptable levels of cost. Indeed, Sikes had to contravene legislative presumptions that were subtly inducing him to concur in his subcommittee's decision to approve the New Look force levels and lowered spending ceilings for defense. To launch his incisive attack he had to surmount the normal expectations of his legislative role as a member of the House Appropriations Committee. It is instructive to note that his efforts, while exposing him to the criticisms and opposition of his colleagues, secured no immediate gains for the army or any noticeably for Sikes. His floor amendments in the early years of the New Look to increase army preparedness failed by wide margins.

A third style of operation is simply to avoid as much conflict with outside administration and congressional groups as possible. This posture also takes on two modes which contrast sharply with each other. In the first expression of this conciliatory style, the legislator withdraws from active participation in committee hearings and deliberations and emphasizes other committee assignments, as in the

Senate where members have multiple committee responsibilities, or concentrates on serving constituent interests, mending political fences, and generally protecting his legislative seat. Neither the goal of economy and efficiency nor the standard of military utility is avidly pursued. Almost by default the legislator molds his actions and decisions to his perception of prevailing congressional opinion.

On the other hand, a legislator may actively and seriously engage himself in his subcommittee's review of the defense budget, but adopt the role of mediator and compromiser of differences, seeking thereby to evade a confrontation with the executive branch or other centers of congressional opinion and influence. The chairmen of the House and Senate defense appropriations subcommittees have often cast themselves in this role. They have usually tried to conciliate actual and potential controversies within their subcommittees and between their subcommittees and the administration on military policy. The search for mutual agreement and broad consensus becomes the uppermost concern.

This conciliatory style is linked, moreover, to the attempt of the subcommittee chairmen and their subcommittees to minimize their responsibility for the defense appropriations measure. It is no accident that the chairmen of the defense appropriations groups generally introduce the defense appropriations bill to their respective chambers with the prefatory statement that the measure being presented is "the best possible compromise that could be achieved." Other subcommittee members normally confirm the need for compromise and consensus. Arguments are posed that the President's lead must be followed or that public and congressional opinion is unwilling to support innovations in defense policy. By noting these constraints on their discretion and by relying on what is made to appear as a sort of chimerical collective responsibility that rests on a series of tacit and formal legislative and executive branch agreements, the chairmen and the members of the appropriations subcommittees attempt to disengage themselves partially from full responsibility for any unfortunate consequences that may develop in the wake of the bill's passage. This hedge against an unknown and possibly adverse future is certainly understandable since neither the chairmen nor their subcommittees exercise great power to determine the makeup of the defense appropriations bill or the nation's strategic policies. In this connection, a deeper significance can be attached to Representative Albert Engel's handling of the FY 1947 War Department bill in which he pressed the Truman administration to assume greater responsibility for the appropriations measure.[7] Similarly, Senator Elmer Thomas, in opposing a congressional increase in funds for strategic air power in FY 1950, affirmed his trust in the chief executive's judgment to hold defense spending within $15 billion.[8] A decade later, Representative George Mahon, in presenting the FY 1959 defense bill to the House, absolved himself and his subcommittee of responsibility for the setback engendered by sputnik during the preceding fiscal year, for the small size of the FY 1958 defense bill, and for the subsequent congressional cuts which were made in it. Mahon indicated that "talk of economy, efficiency and how to cope with service rivalries" had led his subcommittee to cut defense appropriations. He shifted the major share of blame for the political, psychological, and technical defeat administered by sputnik to the President and the executive branch. "Congress is not always right," Mahon remarked, "but Congress was, I believe, right . . . last year [FY 1958]. . . . In general, we approved the [administration's] programs, but said they could be financed with less money. We gave every dollar requested for space age weaponry. In hindsight, it is obvious that *the budget submitted to us* last year should have made more provision for rocketry and space age weapons."[9]

Since these individual legislative styles of operation are essentially expressed within the larger framework of the defense appropriations subcommittees, it is no surprise that the decisions and actions of the subcommittees, considered as collective bodies, are similarly conditioned by the decentralization of power and the diffusion of responsibility in Congress. The defects of the subcommittees' handling of the defense appropriations bills can be explicated in no small part in these terms.

Lacking power to transform defense policy without large and sustained outside administration and congressional support, the defense appropriations subcommittees have little incentive to review the defense budget in light of its military or economic feasibility. The effective scope of their influence is necessarily confined to a narrow band of choice. The subcommittees are encouraged, therefore, to limit their energies and attention to the constricted sphere of their immediate influence and control. They are drawn initially to direct themselves to the administrative and budgetary facets of the defense bill apart from its security and foreign-policy implications. Within this area their jurisdictional autonomy, while narrow, is beyond question.

If drawn, nevertheless, into examining policy questions when the administration's proposals appear too glaringly deficient, the subcommittees usually focus on specific force levels and weapon systems. They are able to build support for marginal and minimal adjustments in defense policy and capabilities more easily than for a major transformation of the nation's strategic posture. Questioning in the hearings is directed toward military personnel figures and hardware items. Recommended changes in administration proposals are cast in these narrower, concrete terms in the subcommittees' reports. Over-all discussion of strategic policy is generally avoided. A wider or more elevated focus of interest is likely to have little effective or visible political payoff in Congress. Proposals for a specific number of bomber wings or marine corps personnel, which do not seriously affect a broad cross-section of executive or congressional interests, are likely to succeed whereas a full-scale attack on prevailing policies, however defective, would fail.

Each defense group is only one tiny kingdom in a congressional universe composed of a host of other kingdoms, all of varying power and prestige, none of which is able to dominate the policy process.

Each military subcommittee is in ceaseless quest, therefore, of outside support for its policy determinations which, willy-nilly, affect this larger universe. This burdensome task is lightened if the subcommittee merely annexes to itself the already committed power of the President to his budget or aligns itself with prevailing conventional wisdom in Congress. By upholding the President's recommendations, the subcommittee gains a powerful friend rather than creates a formidable foe. It is in this connection that the opinions of administration witnesses are solicited, not for purposes of analysis or criticism but with an eye toward their utility in gaining congressional approval for the defense bill that the subcommittees finally report to their respective chambers. The subcommittees have always respected the President's over-all budgetary spending levels even when they have proposed specific shifts in defense expenditures and program priorities. They have repeatedly advanced recommendations for marginal changes in the President's proposals on the grounds that federal spending would still remain within the limits set by the chief executive. Disagreement with the President and the executive branch could then be confined to bargaining within the budget and not broadened to include the economic and political justification of the framework itself.

The small and tenuous power base on which the subcommittee must rest its decisions contributes to other, already described, shortcomings in Congress' review of the defense bill. There is little need for a large staff of experts trained in military and foreign policy if the subcommittees are not disposed to act on the policy, planning, and program information that they assemble. Nor is there a compelling need for an elaborate agenda for the hearings which is geared to these policy considerations if the subcommittees do not feel inclined to utilize the data that it uncovers. The subcommittees are induced to collect only those pieces and fragments of information that are immediately relevant to the limited number of power calculations that bear on the achievement of the pinched and attenuated program goals that they must normally set for themselves.

524

Even to maximize these marginal objectives, it is essential that the defense subcommittees present a united front to the outside world. Pressures are strong within the subcommittee to effect a consenus before the presentation of the final defense bill to the full appropriations committee or to the floors of either legislative chamber. Since World War II there has not been a single instance of a split position within an appropriations committee report of either house on the defense bill. Subcommittee members have disagreed on the floor, but these differences are not reflected in the reports themselves. The penchant for internal subcommittee unity is a mark of all of the appropriations subcommittees. Between 1947 and 1957, only nine minority positions have been filed out of 141 appropriations reports that have been tendered.[10] Members who oppose the bill on the floor are placed in an embarrassing position since they have seemingly agreed to the measure in executive session. Legislators generally uphold the committee report. Floor debate on the defense measure, in turn, tends to be robbed of any significant value beyond personal and constituent interest, since little can be changed in the defense bill at this late bargaining stage.

Having little power, the defense appropriations subcommittees are provided little incentive to inform themselves about the major strategic issues facing the nation. They have even less incentive to formulate and press for broad and sweeping alternatives to the administration's defense proposals, although they may appear necessary. The upshot is that Congress, as an institution, is deprived of the information and alternatives that it needs if it is to exert any control or influence over defense policy. More importantly, it is deprived of the guidance that it needs to discipline the policy recommendations and operations of the executive branch and to discipline its own understanding and approach to strategic policy. The principal fault for these deprivations does not lie essentially in the subcommittees. It rests more heavily on the system of incentives that arises from the decentralization of power and diffusion of responsibility within Congress itself.

The policy process in Congress emphasizes past policy decisions and agreements too heavily to the detriment of adapting the nation to new strategic conditions. It places too great a premium on the stability and continuity of existing policies. In other words, the consensus process in Congress hampers the development of policies which are relevant and effective in advancing the nation's foreign policy objectives and security interests. The marginal, incremental approach of Congress to the military appropriations bill and, correspondingly, to defense policy has increasingly found itself out of joint with the requirements of policy that are attuned to the nation's strategic imperatives. Congress has been slow to perceive the rapid social, political, economic, and technological changes occurring in the world. It has been even more ponderous and lethargic in developing policies that can cope with them. Moving in their separate orbits are, on the one hand, the policy process and the pragmatic, issue-by-issue settlement of strategic problems that it induces and, on the other, the revolutionary conditions of international life. National policies, painstakingly pieced together and supported by bits and pieces of power, fall progressively behind the march of the events and circumstances that they are designed to influence and shape. Outside shocks, such as the Korean War or the flight of sputnik, traumatically wrench the policy process into temporary alignment with the objective conditions of the outside environment. But once the emergency has passed, the policy process again resumes its desultory course.

The policy process, as it is presently constituted, does not lend itself to resolving or even fully discussing international problems as handily as it disposes of domestic conflict. True to Madison's design, factions and individuals within Congress barter and trade their parcels of political power for narrowly defined political objectives. Buyers and sellers constantly interchange their positions. Opposing majorities comprised of clusters of factions hold for one issue; dissolve on another; and reappear with slightly changed emphasis and supporting personnel on a third. Party lines are repeatedly blurred and broken.

526

Issues are continually compromised. Large-scale departures from existing policies are usually blocked. The domestic order is stabilized and preserved. In settling public questions in Congress there is a great deal of verbal conflict, clever electoral posturing, and continuous effort to build temporary coalitions, but no violence.

Strategic policy emerges from Congress in important part as a residual element of the struggle among changing factions and shifting alliances. Since no group in Congress is responsible for the over-all character of national strategy, pressures are weak within Congress for an over-all definition of strategic problems or for a disciplining of domestic interests to conform to international realities. Like the proverbial blind men and the elephant, legislators seize at different parts of the strategic imperatives confronting the nation and misinterpret their full nature. The thrust of the congressional policy process is in the direction of drift and irresolution; of fits and starts in long-range policy formulation; of uncertain, unreflective reactions to sudden emergencies. Congress neither prepares itself nor the public for the emerging crises endangering the nation's security and foreign objectives. Bewildered, Congress stumbles from crisis to crisis. Unable to define the nation's strategic problems, it is also unable to understand its faulty judgments and the frailties of its decision and consensus processes. Domestic and foreign policy problems tend still to be too insulated from each other. The policy process does not mesh the two. Congressional energy, time, and attention are directed below the horizon of the rapid changes occurring in the international environment. The proclivities of the policy process are inclined inward, toward domestic affairs, for guidance and direction.

The struggle for power in Congress that is the motive force of the policy process has not yet fully comprehended or adequately adjusted to the new dimensions and modalities of life created by the nuclear age. The incrementalism fostered and abetted by the policy process does not necessarily produce defense and foreign policies that meet the nation's policy objectives or security interests. One can perhaps

527

find comfort in a market place theory of the policy process that produces beneficial national policies as a natural by-product of the clash of competing interests which compromise their narrow goals for mutual advantage. But the record of Congress since 1945 belies such optimism. The policy process does not automatically yield salutary national policies that simultaneously conciliate domestic interests and secure national objectives abroad. Keynesian analysis and sad experience have repudiated the notion of a self-regulatory market economy which can produce full employment. The hidden hand of Adam Smith could not be found. Analysis of the policy process should similarly dispose of the notion of a hidden hand or a manifest destiny that providentially guides the actions and decisions of the policy process in Congress or of the larger domestic order.

PRESCRIPTIONS

Caveats.—Analysis of Congress' participation in defense policy through its power of the purse since World War II indicates the need for a fundamental reform of its policy process. The call for congressional reform is, of course, not novel. The congressional reform movement has been a part of the American political scene for many years. The Legislative Reorganization Act of 1946 blunted criticisms of Congress for a short time, but the failure of the act to accomplish its purposes has again stirred reform efforts. The movement in the last decade has grown progressively larger and more vocal. Every session of Congress is now characterized by a battle over rules as well as the membership ratios and responsibilities of congressional committees. A number of noteworthy changes have been effected. These include an increase in the size of the rules committee to make it more responsive to party leadership in the Eighty-seventh Congress, the Senate's introduction of a modest rule of germaneness in the Eighty-eighth Congress, and the reintroduction of the twenty-one-day rule in the House in the Eighty-ninth Congress.

Proposals for reform are voluminous, covering every aspect of congressional action and decision.[11] In one way or another all of these discussions of reform are relevant to any examination of how Congress might be reconstituted to handle security policy more effectively or efficiently in order to maximize its contribution to the construction of sound strategic policies and operations. Security policy affects every important phase of American life; alternatively, legislative activity in any area of public policy, including more especially Congress' passage of the federal government's annual budget, has some direct or indirect impact on strategic policy. While a complete discussion of the changes that might be made to improve congressional organization and operations in security policy would have to include a broader analysis of all aspects of congressional reform, it is more reasonable to focus the discussion of prescriptions on Congress' handling of strategic issues and thus to link it more immediately to the discussion above. These broader considerations of congressional reform should be kept in mind, nevertheless, since any shifts in internal congressional relations to cope with strategic policy must necessarily have an impact on other aspects of congressional activity. The over-all character of public policy will likely be changed as modifications are introduced into congressional institutional arrangements. If they are not to mislead, reform proposals must ultimately be cast in political policy and power terms. Reformers, although often aware of the relation of the institutional change and public policy, have not always been careful to explicate the connection precisely.

Within the context of national security, congressional reform should prepare Congress to assume its defense responsibilities. To recapitulate, reform should accomplish the following objectives:

1. It should lead to a redistribution of power and responsibility in Congress that will create a system of incentive which will encourage a review and determination of the defense budget in terms (a) of the policy goals that it seeks to achieve, (b) of its military and economic feasibility, (c) of its fiscal implications, and (d) of its relation to other strategic and non-strategic programs.

2. It should encourage Congress to collect, assemble, and evaluate the data that are needed to review the budget in these comprehensive terms and to develop alternative points of view to administration proposals that prove inadequate.

3. It should permit both houses of Congress to act quickly and decisively on their respective understanding of defense and foreign-policy requirements.

If these objectives are achieved, the two principal defects of Congress' handling of the defense budget and of defense policy will be largely overcome. Congress would come to a clearer, more incisive, and more inclusive understanding of the scope and implications of national strategic policy, and it would be able to act on its knowledge with greater dispatch and certainty. The existing consensus process and the claims that it makes often conflict with the requirements of policies capable of meeting the nation's long-run strategic imperatives. The task then is to minimize the tension between these two sets of requirements. The struggle for individual and group power and advantage within Congress, while allowed to proceed, must be harnessed within a broader policy process that encourages Congress as a whole to assume its institutional responsibilities in defense policy.

Instrumentalities must be devised which can provide a focal point for the expression of national interests in public policy, particularly legislation dealing with defense, without necessarily destroying the capacity of local and special interests to present their claims within the policy process. These conflicting values can be reconciled in appreciable degree if a distinction is made between congressional *vehicles* for the presentation of multiple viewpoints and interests and congressional *agencies* for the control and determination of public policy. Presently, the two tend to be the same. Power in Congress is distributed among its many committees and subcommittees. They are simultaneously vehicles for special and local pleading and agencies by which public policy is predominantly controlled and directed

530

within Congress. Narrow interests, working through these committee arrangements, can gain hold of segments of congressional power and utilize their gains to force tacit or explicit concessions from what majority opinion would otherwise have adopted as public policy. Or, they may prevent Congress from acting at all. None of these committees is responsible for over-all national policy. None assumes a distinctly national point of view. None certainly speaks for Congress in national strategic policy. The upshot of the decentralization of power and the diffusion of responsibility in Congress is that local and special interests are emphasized at the expense of a national perspective and at the cost of an effective national strategic posture that, while stable, is rapidly adaptable to changing international conditions. Institutional mechanisms must be fashioned which can drive a wedge between the capacity of the committees and subcommittees of Congress to act both as vehicles for the presentation of special interests and as almost exclusive agencies for the determination of policies that often depreciate and discount overriding national needs. In other words, the institutional processes of decision and action in Congress should give precedence to national interests in security and foreign-policy development rather than to purely domestic and local concerns as they do today. The awesome implications of modern warfare indicate the need for this shift in emphasis. The future of domestic politics hinges on the resolution of this larger problem as well as on the success that the United States achieves in exerting its influence abroad to the advantage of the nation's security, interests, and objectives.

What follows is a set of proposals which indicates the direction that congressional reform should take in security and foreign policy. The likelihood that Congress and the nation will adopt some or all of the proposals which are suggested below is not great.[12] Less extensive recommendations have been repeatedly rejected in the past. The immediate feasibility of the proposals which are noted is, however, beside the point. There is merit in pursuing the logical and likely political consequences of a reform scheme that seeks to correct the defects of Congress' handling of defense policy through its appropriations power. The dimensions of the problem posed by the existing congressional policy process and the kinds of policies that are likely to emerge from its retention are thus revealed in bolder relief. The principal source of difficulty stems from the decentralization and diffusion of power and responsibility in Congress, formally embodied in the overlapping jurisdictional divisions of the standing committees. Obviously this condition of decentralization and diffusion is the chief stumbling block to congressional reform. Any modernization of Congress that purports to adapt it to the contemporary world, nevertheless, must grapple with this problem.

National policy committees.—The establishment of a National Policy Committee in each house of Congress provides a model or guide for congressional reform. The national policy committees would be responsible for the following functions:

1. They would survey and review over-all security policies, both military and non-military, to assure that they are compatible with, and capable of supporting, American security interests and foreign policy objectives.

2. They would provide guidelines for the federal budget, specifying what the government's fiscal and economic policies should be in terms of its annual revenues and expenditures in order to integrate and co-ordinate the decisions and actions of other committees and subcommittees of Congress.

3. They would sponsor all public bills on the floor of Congress.

4. And consistent with the traditions of each house, they would define the rules that should govern each house as well as establish the legislative agenda of each, including the length of time that bills would be reviewed and debated.

Each house would have its own National Policy Committee, composed of the majority and minority leaders and the ranking committee members of each party from all of the standing committees of each respective chamber. Party ratios would be set for the National Policy Committee to assure the majority party a clearcut majority on the committee. The party caucus of the majority party would, by secret ballot, elect such other members of the committee at large from among its membership as to secure a majority on the committee. These at large members would be chosen on a geographic basis to assure broad national representation of the party. The chairman of the National Policy Committee in each chamber would be the majority leader in the Senate and the speaker in the House, each, also, elected by secret ballot. Committee chairmen and ranking minority members, while ex officio members of the National Policy Committee of their respective chambers, would, in turn, be chosen in party caucuses by secret ballot from slates composed of the top three members in seniority on each committee.

The committees would be staffed with enough professional personnel to carry out their broad responsibilities. Staff members would be trained and experienced in military and economic analysis. They would normally continue in their assignments despite changes in party control, much like the staff of the Senate Foreign Relations Committee. The professional staffs under the control of the chairman of the committee would be expected to work for both parties, but would be responsible only to whoever was the chairman of the committee. All work assignments would have to be approved by him subject to majority veto of the entire committee. The chairman might also appoint additional staff aides principally for liaison work with the other committees of Congress. They would be used primarily to smooth relations between the National Policy Committee and the legislative committees of each chamber which would be reporting their bills to the policy committee for sponsorship on the floor. The minority leaders of the House and Senate policy committees, who would sit as the ranking members of the National Policy Committee of their respective chambers, would be allocated funds for the maintenance of a small staff, partisan in orientation, under their direction.

The staff would organize the agenda and suggest questions for hearings on the broad questions of foreign policy, national security, and economic and fiscal affairs. Leading administration spokesmen, including the secretaries of state, defense, and treasury and the director of the Budget Bureau would outline the policies of their departments, describe new programs being initiated, and assess the value of already existing programs. The policy committee would have an opportunity during these hearings to question the relation of departmental policies and programs and the over-all activities of the federal government.

The staffs would prepare periodic reports under the direction of the chairman which would set out the fiscal and economic guidelines adopted by the policy committee to direct the activities of the other committees of each house of Congress, especially the appropriations and revenue committees and those legislative committees which pass on authorization bills. In this connection the staff would prepare memorandums analyzing the legislation reported by the committees to assess its compatibility with existing policy committee guidelines. If conflicts were detected, then either the legislation or the guidelines would be revised to maintain a moving harmony between them.

The staff would also be expected to conduct special analyses of strategic, fiscal, and economic problems of general significance. These studies would focus on issues of longer-range congressional interest and importance. The ongoing examination and study of future military, economic, and foreign policy problems would be institutionalized within congressional operations. The work of the staffs in these fields would be supplemental to the work already being conducted by the other legislative committees like the armed services groups or the

Joint Economic Committee. Areas for study, such as the proposal for a multilateral nuclear force for NATO, a foreign policy problem like so many today which cut across existing committee arrangements, might well be suggested during the hearings.

Part of the staff would be devoted primarily to the task of studying and proposing ways in which the federal budget and the individual departmental budgets might be made more comprehensible and amenable to congressional influence and control at policy levels. Emphasis would be placed on collecting program data which would cut across departmental lines and on devising budget categories that would reflect the functions carried on by the federal government. The principal difficulty in developing coherent and concise budgetary data and categories lies in the fact that programs are often multidimensional and are simultaneously administered by different executive agencies. Water programs, for example, fall within the domain of a number of governmental agencies and, correspondingly, each agency activity accomplishes a number of purposes, including irrigation, conservation, and recreation. The problem of developing meaningful budgetary data and categories, while difficult, is not beyond improvement, as the Defense Department's introduction of program budgeting indicates. Assembling comparative budget data would furnish Congress and the national policy committees the information needed to assess the relative political, economic, and social benefits of various strategic and non-strategic programs against their respective costs in human and material resources. Generating alternatives in Congress the essence of political influence and control, hinges on the development of such data.

The staffs of the national policy committees would maintain a running account of the status of the President's budget in Congress. Periodic reports could be issued to apprise the policy committees and other interested legislators and congressional groups of such information as the progress of bills before the appropriations subcommittees, the actions being contemplated on these measures, and the proposed changes in revenue legislation that might affect governmental fiscal policies. There is presently no central clearing house in Congress where such data can be secured.

The creation of national policy committees in each house of Congress would obviously result in a major transformation of congressional power relations, organization, and procedures. The decisive nature of military and foreign policy to the nation's life and the compelling need for greater and more effective congressional participation in their development prompt the proposal for a basic change in the congressional policy process. Without reform Congress will be unable to increase the value of its contribution to strategic policy and the significance of its institutional stature. A new system of incentives must be created that can encourage individual legislators to assume the responsibilities for defense policy that Congress can, and should, discharge. The national policy committees, possessing general power of legislation yet responsible to majority opinion in each chamber, would provide an agency of legislative control that not only would reconstitute congressional power relations but would also create wholly new and inviting incentives that would promote improvements in Congress' handling of defense policy, without simultaneously destroying the pluralistic quality of the congressional policy process.

The national policy committees would discharge vitally needed functions now neglected in Congress and would possess sufficient power and, correspondingly, sufficient incentive to assume their responsibilities. These groups, devoted to the integration and co-ordination of national policy, would be induced to adopt a perspective necessarily broader than the existing narrower viewpoints of the individual committees of Congress, each with a confined set of functions to perform and in possession of only a circumscribed amount of power to effect its will. The national policy committees would be drawn to collect, organize, and evaluate data of public policy significance from a national point of view. Legislation emerg-

536

ing from the other committees of Congress would be funneled through the national policy committees and would have to be justified in relation to other proposed and existing public policies and in relation to the benefits to be derived by the nation as a whole. Public bills and the issues they raise would not remain insulated from each other or from broader national purposes. A larger number of interests would have to be taken into account. Domestic and foreign policy making would proceed more as a unity, and not as separate and unrelated areas of national concern and action. The narrower, but important, goals of economy and efficiency would also be better served as governmental programs, forced to compete against each other for scarce revenue resources, would tend to be rationalized and simplified through the review process of the national policy committees. Duplications could be more effectively identified and eliminated. Program gaps could be more quickly pinpointed as related governmental activities were brought together within a central arena.

If the national policy committees were effectively to review security policy and to co-ordinate and integrate it with over-all public policy, including the government's fiscal and economic policies, they would have to be given the powers of sponsoring legislation and setting the agenda and, subject to the Senate's tradition of free debate, the legislative rules governing debate on the floor of each chamber. Lacking defined legislative powers, the committees' larger review and advisory responsibilities would be quickly negated. The committees would suffer the same fate as the Joint Committee on the Legislative Budget which was established by the Legislative Reorganization Act. The joint committee was charged with the duty of reporting a legislative budget by February 15 of each legislative session. The budget was to set out estimated federal receipts and expenditures for the fiscal year and carry with it a concurrent resolution placing a ceiling on appropriations. The February 15 date was unrealistic since work on the specific parts of the President's budgetary requests were then barely underway in the appropriations subcommittees. The determinations of the joint committee were outside the framework of the congressional process. The laying down of appropriations ceilings and guidelines for fiscal and economic policy was separated from the actual legislation being shaped in the committees of Congress and took no account of the legislative schedule of Congress. The national policy committees, which would sponsor legislation on the floors of each house and determine their agendas would largely overcome these shortcomings.

It is also advisable to avoid the practice of passing congressional resolutions that state the expenditure and appropriation limits of the government or that attempt specifically to legislate strategic, economic, or fiscal policy along the rigid lines of a Soviet five-year plan. In a free democracy—especially one like the United States that is characterized by a great and bewildering diversity of interests—strategic, economic, or fiscal policies cannot realistically be minutely legislated, although they often depend on some form of basic legislative authorization. Policy-making in a democracy is an ongoing process of adjustment and compromise. Hardened ceilings and rigid target goals hinder and preclude the myriad of adaptations that are necessary and intrinsic to the requirements of a popularly determined consensus. They cannot be easily shaped to meet new strategic developments or made responsive to the legitimate claims of divergent domestic interests. This is not to say that the guidelines which are issued by the national policy committees would be meaningless. Their findings and recommendations would not be ignored by the other committees of Congress as are those of the Joint Economic Committee. The national policy committees would assure agreement between their guidelines and the legislation reported to them by the other committees of Congress since they would sponsor all legislation on the floors of their respective chambers.

On the other hand, the powers of the national policy committees would not be as sweeping as they may appear on the surface. The ranking committee members of each party from the standing committees of Congress would compose the bulk of their memberships. The committee system below the national policy committees would still be preserved. The committees would still normally exert the dominant influence in shaping congressional legislation that fell within their respective jurisdictions. They would remain the courts of original jurisdiction, so to speak. In presenting their legislative recommendations to the national policy committees for sponsorship, the legislative, appropriations, and revenue committees of Congress would possess the natural advantage of experience and information, values which will likely continue to be rated highly by other legislators and committees in Congress. Committee chairmen would wear two hats. They would represent their committee's interests and views in the national policy committees, and, alternatively, the viewpoint of the policy committees in the deliberations of their committees.

Since the national policy committees, like other committees of Congress, would be bipartisan, the pluralistic, cross-party system of compromise and accommodation that characterizes the contemporary congressional process would not be destroyed. It would merely be tempered and tuned to yield more comprehensive and informed legislation more quickly and decisively. Logrolling would, and should, continue among the committees of Congress. Trading favors is a necessary function of the diversity of American life and the multiplicity of interests that it encompasses. Logrolling would also mark the actions and decisions of the national policy committees. But whereas logrolling proceeded largely in terms of the specific favors which were swapped with little or no concern for national implications of such policy determinations, the national policy committees would be disposed to examine the possible consequences of such manipulations. The leaders and membership of the policy committees would be unable to absolve themselves of responsibility for short-sighted policies that would have a deleterious effect on national security or on the nation's economic and fiscal strength and stability. They could not pretend that they lacked power, responsibility, or adequate professional assistance to pass needed national legislation. National policy, deriving initially from the standing committees of Congress, would be informed by the needs of special and geographical interests, while these interests would be disciplined by the need to justify their objectives in terms of their contribution to larger national goals. The committees of Congress would be maintained as vehicles for the presentation of diverse and rival interests, but they would have to transfer some of their existing capacity to control legislation to the policy committees.

The favorable impact which the national policy committees are likely to make on internal committee operations should not be ignored. The defense appropriations groups are presently discouraged from reviewing the defense budget from the point of view of generating alternative policy proposals to those advised by the executive branch. The exacting consensus requirements of the congressional policy process offers little prospect that alternatives, once developed, will actually be adopted. The defense appropriations subcommittees do not have ready access to the diffuse centers of power in Congress to negotiate and bargain for large-scale changes in defense policy. The national policy committees would focus sufficient power and responsibility and would provide the necessary machinery for securing prompt support for needed changes, however large, in defense policy. The bits and pieces of consent that would have to be gathered could be fitted together quickly within the national policy committees. Their memberships would be sufficiently representative on the basis of population and geography that the committees would increasingly become *vehicles* for majority opinion in each house and *agencies* for majority party control and responsibility. The committees would not necessarily be losing power. They would likely gain some. Improved political cohesion and decision machinery in Congress would enhance their over-all capacity to assert themselves within a larger sphere of public policy. The committees would share in this enlargement of congressional influence. Their individual influence would be expanded in absolute terms, although it would be less within Congress relative to the national policy committees.

There is the fact, too, that the seniority rule would be modified to include the election of committee chairmen by party caucus from among the top three members in seniority on each committee. Committee chairmen are likely to be more responsive to majority opinion and to party direction when their position both within their committees and on the national policy committee depends on them. On the other hand, the redeeming aspects of the seniority system—its predictability and its emphasis on stability and experience—would be largely preserved because the choice of candidates for the post of chairman would be confined to the leading members of each committee in years of service. A healthy competition within each committee is then likely to occur as the second and third men in seniority perceive the possibility of becoming chairman if they demonstrate a more amenable disposition to party policies and majority sentiment. They would be encouraged to adopt legislative styles that posture beyond the cramped mores and ruling procedures of internal committee operations. They would be encouraged to develop a national viewpoint within the committee and to emphasize broader policy questions. The most attractive legislative rewards would lie beyond the conditioned confines of the standing committees and would reside in the national policy committees. Power, prestige, and position would be functions of membership on the national policy committees. In seeking membership on the national committees, the individual congressman would harness his personal ambitions and talents to national interests.

The establishment of national policy committees would elicit more party competition in Congress thus having a beneficial effect on the discharge of Congress' leadership functions. Since the responsibility for legislation would be largely centered in the national policy committees, party members on the committees would necessarily have to weigh more carefully their support or rejection of proposed legislation.

Public visibility of party responsibility would be sharpened. The minority party would be induced to search for defects in the administration's policy proposals and for malpractices in bureaucratic operations. The hearings of the national policy committees—and conceivably those of the other committees of Congress—would be likely to take on more the aspect of adversary proceedings as administration witnesses were questioned more critically. Party advantage would be placed in the service of national policy, much as it was in the later years of the Eisenhower administration. The opinions of witnesses would not be used simply as grist for the committee's argument on the floor, but as subjects of contention between the parties. Split reports would probably become more frequent and chamber debates more interesting to other legislators and the public alike. The upshot of increased party conflict would be two-fold. The public would be better informed about public policies, including matters of security and foreign affairs. Congress, moreover, would pose more policy choices to itself for its collective determination. Bipartisanship in strategic policy formation has its limits. The nation's political values and institutions are informed by the proposition that governmental policies are likely to be sounder and sturdier in the long run if they are the products of a sharp competition of ideas in public debate. The parties are appropriate and convenient mechanisms through which rival and divergent strategic points of view can be responsibly presented.

Other changes.—The proposed powers of the national policy committees over legislative scheduling and floor debate need clarification. Time is a precious legislative commodity. It is inherently scarce. Given, too, the increasing number of issues on which Congress must pass, the availability of time is progressively diminishing. The policy committees, subject to majority opinion in their respective chambers, could schedule legislation and regulate floor action in accord with the demands being placed on Congress. The Senate's tradition of free debate, always an obstacle to improved legislative scheduling, need not be discarded. The Senate National Policy Committee would still be forced to lead by consensus, and the rules of procedure that it would propose would be controlled by majority opinion in the upper chamber. The cloture rule might be amended, as many have proposed, to require only three-fifths, not two-thirds, of the Senate to cut off debate. The stringency of the Senate's morning hour, its weak rule of germaneness in debate, and its prohibition against committee meetings while the Senate is in full session might also be revised to maximize the time resources of the Senate.

Minority rights would be adequately protected. The principles of the separation of power and federalism would not be abandoned. They would, indeed, be strengthened if Congress' influence were to grow and its contribution to public policy were to be more effective and noteworthy. The federal government would continue to operate through the action of four majorities, including the majorities in the House, the Senate, the Presidency, and the Supreme Court whose membership, while chosen for life, must still be nominated to office by the President and confirmed by the Senate. These majorities differ in composition, in the time when they are formed, and in the specific bases of their legitimacy.[13] The protection of individual liberty and minority rights would still depend on the checks and balances that developed among these four majorities working through separate institutional bodies. The toilsome task of building a coalition of majority support would remain in light of the diversity of interests in American life and the multiple governmental bodies through which they express themselves. The checks and balances system would work adequately enough without supplementing it with onerous rules that frustrate majority action and the government's ability to adapt the nation to the revolutionary conditions of modern life. Simple majorities operating in each governmental institution would gradually supplant the concurrent majority system now operating through Congress. These consensus requirements are too high a price to pay for union when that union faces an accelerating number of foreign and security problems. The Constitution, ironically enough, would operate as it was originally intended.

The House National Policy Committee would absorb the functions of the rules committee although separate arrangements might be made to handle private bills. Legislative scheduling would again become principally a party responsibility. To utilize legislative time more efficiently electric voting might be introduced. Year-round sessions would help, too. They would provide a predictable schedule for individual congressmen and committees to follow. Congress could recess in the summer and return refreshed through the fall in non-election years or otherwise adjourn just before elections to avoid a lame duck Congress. House members might usefully be placed on a four-year footing to relieve them of the burdens of almost constant campaigning while in office. This change, unlike the others which have been proposed, would require a constitutional amendment. Ombudsman procedures, such as those inaugurated in some of the Scandinavian countries, might also be created to aid individual congressman with their constituency chores and free them for their committee assignments.[14]

A word should also be addressed to the appropriations and authorization process. This subject is treated in other studies at considerable length. No attempt will be made to reproduce these discussions.[15] Two points bear notice. First of all, the defense policy responsibilities of the armed services committees and the defense appropriations sub-committees should be more sharply defined to preclude both duplication and gaps in the congressional review process. The armed services committees now annually authorize major procurement and research and development programs. The appropriations groups cover the same ground as well as the remaining segments of the defense budget. It would be advisable for the armed services committees to broaden the scope of their authorization review to include the entire defense program and to cast their authorizations in terms of these programs rather than in procurement and research and development categories that reflect only part of the over-all defense program. The use of procurement and research and development categories correspond to their employment in the appropriations bills. Both authorization and appropriations bills should be revised to conform to the program data which the Defense Department can now supply. If the armed services committees were prepared to conduct an annual, comprehensive review of defense policy in programmatic terms, then the appropriations subcommittees could legitimately concentrate their attention on administrative detail. Any move in this direction should rest on the firm assurance that the program review functions now being exercised by the defense appropriations groups, particularly the House unit, be performed by some congressional body. The practice of passing separate authorization and appropriations bills for military construction should be abolished. Military construction projects are logical parts of other more encompassing military programs.

In any case, closer co-operation between the armed services committees and the defense appropriations subcommittees should be encouraged. The Senate's recent practice of holding joint hearings on the defense authorization and appropriations bills should be introduced into the House. Not only would the time of administration officials be used more efficiently, but members of the two committees would learn to work with each other rather than at cross purposes. Joint hearings would preclude the mean competition for headlines that has implicitly characterized some congressional hearings. A congressional committee can obtain notable publicity if it can persuade or arrange for prominent administration leaders to appear before it. Until the implementation of Section 412(b), the appropriations defense units reaped an annual windfall of publicity as a result of the appearance of the secretary of defense before them to defend his department's appropriations requests. Now the defense secretary must appear first before the armed services committees to testify in support of the annual procurement authorization measure. Section 412(b),

545

as some congressional staff members contend, was partially instituted to produce precisely this dubious result. Joint hearings would distribute more equitably the prestige and publicity benefits that are to be derived from the congressional appearances of the secretary of defense, his principal civilian assistants and advisers, and the Joint Chiefs of Staff on the annual defense budget. Both the appropriations and military service groups would share in these legislative spoils and could then concentrate their attention and energies on the substantive elements of the defense budget. In the absence of an agreement on joint hearings in the House, the Senate's custom of appointing ex officio members of the legislative committees to their counterpart appropriations subcommittees might be adopted.

Much of the point of these status considerations would be effectively reduced if the national policy committees were established. Their hearings, being wider ranging and more inclusive, would tend to become the publicity centers of each congressional session. More important, the establishment of national policy committees would necessarily induce a long overdue reassessment of the authorization-appropriation distinction not only in defense policy but over the gamut of congressional policy interests with the intent of reducing the waste of time, duplication, personal animosities, and artificial policy divisions which the institutional embodiment of this distinction in two sets of legislative committees and appropriations subcommittees tends to generate. The committee chairmen who would be members of the national policy committees can be expected to fight to preserve their committee's jurisdictional autonomy. The national policy committees, nevertheless, would provide a forum within which these jurisdictional divisions could be continually challenged, re-evaluated and rationalized to adapt them to the nation's substantive policy problems, both domestic and foreign. The current legislative habit of splintering policy problems to conform to the cramped pigeonholes of Congress' division of labor, which are set out in the Legislative Reorganization Act of 1946, would be partially checked. The national policy committees would, at a minimum, facilitate the resolution of committee conflicts. In particular, the gulf between the armed services committees and the appropriations groups, especially on the House side, could be ameliorated. Dissension within the ranks of Congress on defense policy exposes the warring legislative factions to manipulation by outside interests, the executive departments, and, as the 1962 controversy over the RS-70 suggests, by the secretary of defense. The national policy committees, possessing greater powers than other congressional groups and resting their decisions and actions on a broader congressional consensus, could insulate other committees from these forms of manipulation.

Second, the omnibus appropriations bill should be reintroduced. It has never received a fair test in Congress. The omnibus measure would permit Congress an opportunity for an over-all review of the budget and would allow comparisons within the budget between strategic and non-strategic programs. The creation of the national policy committees, charged with the responsibility for economic and fiscal policy, presupposes the adoption of an omnibus bill. The determination of fiscal and economic policies and their integration with security and foreign policy considerations requires a consolidation of proposed federal spending in one document. Only in this way can the closely related elements of defense strategy, military requirements, and resource capabilities be comprehensively studied and evaluated by Congress. The passage of the annual omnibus budget would be high point of each legislative session and the focus for public attention. The public's understanding of the interrelations of domestic and foreign policy programs would be enhanced and its perception of the fiscal and economic implications of defense policy and of the federal budget as a whole deepened.

The criticisms of the omnibus proposal are multiple, though not completely persuasive.[16] They rely on defects in other aspects of congressional operations to deny the validity of the omnibus approach. The scheduling difficulties experienced in passage of the FY 1951

Omnibus Appropriations Bill are surmountable. Better legislative scheduling and floor direction through party leadership via the national policy committees would overcome many previous drawbacks. Deadlines could be set for the reports of the appropriations sub-committees. The consolidated bill could then be presented to the national policy committees by May 1. Floor presentation of the bill could then be made after a review by the national policy committees. Two to three weeks of debate could be scheduled in the House followed by Senate action on the bill during the month of June. The bill need not be hastily rushed through each legislative chamber, as critics maintain, if Congress gains increased control over its time resources. One reform hinges on the other. Certainly an omnibus bill would not be slower than the existing procedures for handling appropriations bills. In 1963 only four out of twelve appropriations bills had passed Congress by December 1, five months after the start of the fiscal year. Between June 30 and December 1, Congress was forced to pass three extensions of the previous year's spending levels.

To assure that administrative operations conform to congressional intent, the General Accounting Office might be furnished additional staff and financial assistance to conduct expenditure analyses of each agency. Section 206 of the Legislative Reference Act of 1946 authorizes such reviews, but Congress has failed to appropriate funds to carry out this function. The appropriations subcommittees conduct extensive expenditure reviews of agency operations and, consequently, dissipate their energies and limited time on administrative control rather than on policy direction. To be sure the two are linked, for programs authorized by Congress may be undermined or ignored in practice by the agency. But the complexities of policy-making today require a diminution of congressional committee and subcommittee attention to strictly administrative considerations. A strengthened GAO staff, capable of analyzing program data as well as financial and administrative management and of relating both to congressionally approved policy goals, would secure two valuable objectives: the

548

congressional committees would be relieved for more important policy tasks and the quality of Congress' discharge of its traditional surveillance responsibilities would be enhanced.[17]

Concluding remarks.—The proposals for reform which have been indicated are not exhaustive. They concentrate on the overriding importance of strategic and foreign policy considerations. Other proposed changes depend on an analysis of the requirements of other areas of public policy and interest which fall outside the boundaries of this study. In the final analysis only Congress can reform itself. At a minimum, therefore, it should establish a representative committee or commission to review and evaluate its organization, procedures, and committee arrangements and to suggest changes in its operations and existing system of power and responsibility. In the absence of self-analysis and of large-scale changes in Congress' handling of its affairs, including use of its limited time resources and the level at which it focuses its attention, it will be unable to assert its voice effectively in public policy determinations.

What is needed in Congress is a policy process that encourages improved strategic and foreign policies and that, while preserving multiple access points for the presentation of rival points of view, focuses party responsibility and secures majority direction in congressional deliberations and decisions. Only some form of legislative centralization of power and responsibility will accomplish these ends. An institutional reform of this nature will not guarantee the adoption of salutary public policies, but it is a precondition to their development and implementation.

Political institutions that cannot accommodate themselves to new political conditions are either bypassed by other governmental agencies or trampled over by outside force. The history of France since 1940 is testimony to these unhappy consequences. Foreign invasion destroyed the Third Republic; the Algerian question, the Fourth Republic. In both cases the legislative processes of the government

549

were unable to deal with critical foreign and domestic crises. To correct these failures the Fifth Republic now centers political power in the hands of a powerful, popularly elected President. The national legislature has been eclipsed, perhaps irretrievably, in power and prestige. Popular government in France has been dealt a serious blow.

Congress need not suffer a similar ignominious demise. It can play an important part in public policy and, in particular, in defense policy. But if Congress is to make a contribution to national life that is consistent with its elevated Constitutional position, it must accept the responsibilities that are intrinsic to its power. To be sure, Congress has grown in maturity and foresight as an institution since World War II. But the problems of strategic and foreign policy, not to mention those of domestic policy, have multiplied in number and complexity, too.

We are thus brought full round to the question posed rhetorically by Alexander Hamilton at the beginning of the *Federalist Papers*: "It has been frequently remarked," said Hamilton, "that it seems to have been reserved to the people of this country, by their conduct and example, to decide the important question, whether societies of men are really capable or not of establishing good government from reflection and choice or whether they are forever destined to depend for their political institutions on accident and force."[18] Congress has not fully exerted its collective power or mental acumen in this great enterprise. The friends of popular government hope that it will.

APPENDIXES

APPENDIX A

MAJOR BILLS REVIEWED BY THE STUDY*

1. Military Appropriations Act, 1947
2. Navy Department Appropriations Act, 1947
3. Military Appropriations Act, 1948
4. Navy Department Appropriations Act, 1948
5. Supplemental National Defense Appropriations Act, 1948
6. National Military Establishment, Military Functions Appropriations Act, 1949
7. National Military Establishment, Navy Department Appropriations Act, 1949
8. National Military Establishment Appropriations Act, 1950
9. General Appropriations Act, 1951, Chapter X, Defense Appropriations
10. Supplemental Appropriations Act, 1951
11. Second Supplemental Appropriations Act, 1951
12. Fourth Supplemental Appropriations Act, 1951
13. Department of Defense Appropriations Act, 1952
14. Second Supplemental Appropriations Act, 1952
15. Urgent Deficiency Appropriations Act, 1952
16. Department of Defense Appropriations Act, 1953
17. Department of Defense Appropriations Act, 1954
18. Department of Defense Appropriations Act, 1955
19. Department of Defense Appropriations Act, 1956

* A number of other bills besides the annual appropriations bill for the Department of Defense carry appropriations for military purposes. These include bills for military construction, foreign aid, atomic energy, and space. The budget of the Central Intelligence Agency is also hidden throughout the budget measures of Congress.

20. Department of Defense Appropriations Act, 1957
21. Department of Defense Appropriations Act, 1958
22. Supplemental Defense Appropriations Act, 1958
23. Department of Defense Appropriations Act, 1959
24. Department of Defense Appropriations Act, 1960
25. Department of Defense Appropriations Act, 1961
26. Department of Defense Appropriations Act, 1962
27. Department of Defense Appropriations Act, 1963
28. Act to Authorize Appropriations for Aircraft, Missiles, and Naval Vessels, 1961†
29. Act to Authorize Additional Appropriations for Aircraft, Missiles, and Naval Vessels, 1961†
30. Act to Authorize Appropriations during Fiscal Year 1963 for Aircraft, Missiles, and Naval Vessels, 1962†

† Authorization bills are listed by chronological year; appropriations bills, by fiscal year.

APPENDIX B: HOUSE MEMBERS OF SUBCOMMITTEE ON DEPARTMENT OF DEFENSE APPROPRIATIONS,‡ 1949-1964*

(Eighty-first Congress, First Session, through Eighty-eighth Congress, Second Session)

| Congress: | 81/1 | 81/2 | 82/1 | 82/2 | 83/1 | 83/2 | 84/1 | 84/2 | 85/1 | 85/2 | 86/1 | 86/2 | 87/1 | 87/2 | 88/1 | 88/2 |
Year:	1949	1950	1951	1952	1953	1954	1955	1956	1957	1958	1959	1960	1961	1962	1963	1964
George H. Mahon (Texas)	C	C	C	C	M	M	C	C	C	C	C	C	C	C	C	C
Harry R. Sheppard (California)	M	M	M	M	M	M	M	M	M	M	M	M	M	M	M	M
Robert L. F. Sikes (Florida)	M	M	M	M	M	M	M	M	M	M	M	M	M	M	M	M
†Albert J. Engel (Michigan)	M	M														
†Charles A. Plumley (Vermont)	M	M														
John J. Riley (South Carolina)			M	M	M	M	M	M	M	M	M	M	M			
†John Taber (New York)			M	M												
†Richard B. Wigglesworth (Massachusetts)			M	M	C	C	M	M	M	M						

*Key: C=chairman; M=member. In 1949, the Military and Naval Appropriations committees were combined in the House and Senate to form House and Senate subcommittees on Armed Services Appropriations. These subcommittees were renamed in 1950 the subcommittees on Department of Defense Appropriations.

† Indicates Republican members all others are Democrats.

‡ Appendixes B and C follow the tables indicating membership on the military appropriations subcommittees of the House and the Senate in the period 1933–1950 that are to be found in Elias Huzar, *The Purse and the Sword* (New York: Cornell University Press, 1950), pp. 33–35.

APPENDIX B—*Continued*

	81/1 1949	81/2 1950	82/1 1951	82/2 1952	83/1 1953	83/2 1954	84/1 1955	84/2 1956	85/1 1957	85/2 1958	86/1 1959	86/2 1960	87/1 1961	87/2 1962	88/1 1963	88/2 1964
†Errett P. Scrivner (Kansas)	M	M	M	M	M	M	M	M	M	M						
Albert Gore (Tennessee)				M												
Antonio M. Fernandez (New Mexico)				M												
Daniel J. Flood (Pennsylvania)				M			M	M	M	M	M	M	M	M	M	M
Foster Furcolo (Massachusetts)				M												
†Glen Davis (Wisconsin)				M		M	M	M								
†Gerald R. Ford, Jr. (Michigan)					M	M	M	M	M	M	M	M	M	M	M	M
†Edward T. Miller (Maryland)					M	M	M	M	M	M						
†Harold C. Ostertag (New York)					M	M	M	M	M	M	M	M	M	M	M	M
†Roman L. Hruska (Nebraska)					M	M										
W. F. Norrell (Arkansas)							M	M	M	M	M	M				

APPENDIX B—*Continued*

	81/1 1949	81/2 1950	82/1 1951	82/2 1952	83/1 1953	83/2 1954	84/1 1955	84/2 1956	85/1 1957	85/2 1958	86/1 1959	86/2 1960	87/1 1961	87/2 1962	88/1 1963	88/2 1964
Jamie L. Whitten (Mississippi)							M	M	M	M	M	M	M	M	M	M
George W. Andrews (Alabama)							M	M	M	M	M	M	M	M	M	M
Charles B. Deane (North Carolina)							M	M								
Albert Thomas (Texas)										M	M	M	M	M	M	M
Charles Boyle (Illinois)										M	M					
†Hamer H. Budge (Idaho)										M						
†Melvin Laird (Wisconsin)										M	M	M	M	M	M	M
†Glenard P. Lipscomb (California)											M	M	M	M	M	M
†Phil Weaver (Nebraska)											M	M	M	M		
†William E. Minshall (Ohio)											M	M	M	M	M	M
†Keith Thompson (Wyoming)											M	M				

APPENDIX C: SENATE SUBCOMMITTEE ON DEPARTMENT OF DEFENSE APPROPRIATIONS, 1949-1964*

(Eighty-first Congress, First Session, through Eighty-eighth Congress, Second Session)‡

Congress:	81/1	81/2	82/1	82/2	83/1	83/2	84/1	84/2	85/1	85/2	86/1	86/2	87/1	87/2	88/1	88/2
Year:	1949	1950	1951	1952	1953	1954	1955	1956	1957	1958	1959	1960	1961	1962	1963	1964
Elmer Thomas (Oklahoma)	C	C														
Carl Hayden (Arizona)	M	M	M	M	M	M	M	M	M	M	M	M	M	M	M	M
Richard B. Russell (Georgia)	M	M	M	M	M	M	M	M	M	M	M	M	M	M	C	C
Joseph C. O'Mahoney (Wyoming)	M	M	C	C												
Dennis Chavez (New Mexico)	M	M	M	M	M	M	C	C	C	C	C	C	C	C		
Pat McCarran (Nevada)	M	M	M	M	M	M										

* Key: C=chairman; M=member; and X=ex officio member. In 1949, the Military and Naval Appropriations committees were combined in the House and Senate to form House and Senate subcommittees on Armed Services Appropriations. These subcommittees were renamed in 1950 the subcommittees on Department of Defense Appropriations.
† Indicates Republican members; all others are Democrats.
‡ In 1964, the Senate Committee on Armed Services and the Senate Subcommittee on Department of Defense Appropriations held joint hearings on the authorization and appropriations bill for the Department of Defense. Ex officio members on the appropriations subcommittee from the Senate Committee on Armed Services are, therefore, not listed for 1964. The House (see Appendix B) does not follow the practice of appointing members of the House Armed Services Committee to the House Subcommittee on Department of Defense Appropriations.

APPENDIX C—Continued

	81/1	81/2	82/1	82/2	83/1	83/2	84/1	84/2	85/1	85/2	86/1	86/2	87/1	87/2	88/1	88/2
Congress / Year:	1949	1950	1951	1952	1953	1954	1955	1956	1957	1958	1959	1960	1961	1962	1963	1964
Burnet R. Maybank (South Carolina)	M	M	M	M	M	M										
Lister Hill (Alabama)	M	M	M	M	M	M	M	M	M	M	M	M	M	M	M	M
John L. McClellan (Arkansas)	M	M	M	M	M	M	M	M	M	M	M	M	M	M	M	M
A. Willis Robertson (Virginia)	M	M					M	M	M	M	M	M	M	M	M	M
†Chan Gurney (South Dakota)	M	M														
†Styles Bridges (New Hampshire)	M	M	M	M	M	M	M	M	M	M	M	M	M			
†Clyde M. Reed (Kansas)	M															
†Homer Ferguson (Michigan)	M	M	M	M	C	C										
†Kenneth Wherry (Nebraska)	M	M	M													
†Guy Gordon (Oregon)	M	M			M	M										
†Leverett Saltonstall (Massachusetts)	M	M	M	M	M	M	M	M	M	M	M	M	M	M	M	M
Millard Tydings (Maryland)	X	X														

APPENDIX C—Continued

Congress:	81/1	81/2	82/1	82/2	83/1	83/2	84/1	84/2	85/1	85/2	86/1	86/2	87/1	87/2	88/1	88/2
Year:	1949	1950	1951	1952	1953	1954	1955	1956	1957	1958	1959	1960	1961	1962	1963	1964
Harry F. Byrd (Virginia)	X	X	X	X	X	X	X	X	X	X	X	X	X	X	X	
†Wayne Morse § (Oregon)	X	X	X	X												
†William Knowland (California)		M	M	M	M	M	M	M	M	M						
†Milton R. Young (North Dakota)			M	M	M	M	M	M	M	M	M	M	M	M	M	M
†Edward J. Thye (Minnesota)			M	M	M	M	M	M	M	M						
Lyndon B. Johnson (Texas)			X	X			X	X			M	M				
†Joseph R. McCarthy (Wisconsin)				M												
†Margaret Chase Smith (Maine)					M	M	M	M	M	M	M	M	M	M	M	M
†Ralph E. Flanders (Vermont)					X	X	X	X	X	X						
†Robert C. Hendrickson (New Jersey)					X	X										
Allen Ellender (Louisiana)							M	M	M	M	M	M	M	M	M	M
John Stennis (Mississippi)							M	M	M	M	M	M	M	M	M	M

§ At the time indicated Senator Morse was a Republican; subsequently he became a Democrat.

APPENDIX C—*Continued*

	81/1 1949	81/2 1950	82/1 1951	82/2 1952	83/1 1953	83/2 1954	84/1 1955	84/2 1956	85/1 1957	85/2 1958	86/1 1959	86/2 1960	87/1 1961	87/2 1962	88/1 1963	88/2 1964
†Henry C. Dworshak (Idaho)							M	M	M	M	M	M	M	M		
Stuart Symington (Missouri)									X	X	X	X	X	X	X	
John O. Pastore (Rhode Island)											M	M	M	M	M	M
†Francis Case (South Dakota)											X	X	X	X		
†Karl E. Mundt (South Dakota)											M	M	M	M	M	M
Estes Kefauver (Tennessee)													M	M		
†Gordon Allott (Colorado)														M	M	M
A. S. Mike Monroney (Oklahoma)															M	M
Michael J. Mansfield (Montana)															M	M
†Thomas H. Kuchel (California)															M	M
†Barry Goldwater (Arizona)															X	
Warren G. Magnuson (Washington)																M

NOTES

NOTES

A NOTE ON NOTES

Since this study is largely based on public documents, a simplified system of handling these materials was devised to reduce citations to manageable proportions. The abbreviations listed below indicate sources of congressional or executive-agency documents or the nature of the material which was employed. Insofar as public materials are concerned, the citations of each chapter form an integral unit. Within each chapter a full statement is made of any public document, report, hearing, etc., when it is initially cited. Thereafter, each additional reference to the citation within a chapter appears in a shortened version. Congressonal references list the Congress, the session, and the year from which a citation is drawn. Thus, for example, the reference HSAC, *Hearings, Department of Defense Appropriations, FY 1962,* 87/1, 1961, refers to a publication which was issued by a House Subcommittee of the Committee on Appropriations dealing with defense appropriations during the 87th Congress, 1st Session, 1961. References to the *Congressional Record* are drawn both from the daily edition and the bound volumes. In the latter instance, the initial reference in each chapter carries the Congress, session, year, volume, part, and page, as in the example, C. R., 79/2, 1946, XCII, Part 6, 7323. Thereafter, only the volume, part, and page of the bound volume are furnished.

A slightly different form of handling was advised for books, articles, pamphlets, and the like, which in some cases are noted repeatedly. A full citation is made when the work is first introduced; thereafter, the author's name only appears. However, if it is necessary for the sake of clarity or if more than one work of an author is cited, a short title also is furnished.

Abbreviations

B.B.—Budget Bureau
C.R.—Congressional Record
DOD—Department of Defense
HCMA—House Committee on Military Affairs
HCA—House Committee on Appropriations

HCAS—House Committee on Armed Services
H. Doc.—House Document
H. Rept.—House Report
HSAC—House Subcommittee of the Appropriations Committee
P. L.—Public Law
SCAS—Senate Committee on Armed Services
SCFR—Senate Committee on Foreign Relations
SCGO—Senate Committee on Government Operations
S. Doc.—Senate Document
SNPM—Subcommittee on National Policy Machinery, Senate Committee on Government Operations
S. Rept.—Senate Report
SSAC—Senate Subcommittee of the Appropriations Committee
Stat.—United States Statutes
U.S.C.—United States Code

CHAPTER I

1. Sir Henry S. Maine, *Popular Government* (New York: Henry Holt, 1886), pp. 60–61. The quotation from Maine is slightly inverted, but his essential meaning is not affected.

2. The terms *democracy, popular government,* and *representative government* will be used interchangeably. All refer to a political regime in which the highest government officials are held responsible for their actions and policies at periodic elections. The elections, which provide for universal suffrage, must offer alternative choices of policies and of candidates for public office. Communist elections, which do not allow such choices to the voter, obviously fall outside the limits of this definition.

3. See, for example, Walter Lippmann, *Essays in the Public Philosophy* (Boston: Little, Brown, 1955); Hans J. Morgenthau, *Politics in the Twentieth Century* (3 vols.; Chicago: University of Chicago Press, 1962), *passim;* Gabriel A. Almond, *The American People and Foreign Policy* (New York: Praeger, 1960); and Harry Howe Ransom, *Can American Democracy Survive Cold War?* (New York: Doubleday, 1963).

4. Edward Mead Earle (ed.), *The Federalist* (New York: Modern Library, n.d.), p. 337.

5. The President's powers implied by his functions as commander in chief, as chief executive, and as the principal representative of the United States in foreign policy were combined by Lincoln to form the broad and undefined war powers which he exercised during the Civil War in carrying out his oath of office "to preserve, protect, and defend the Constitution. . . ." Presidents Woodrow Wilson, Franklin D. Roosevelt, and Harry S Truman also relied on these far-reaching war powers for much of their authority during, respectively, World Wars I and II and

the Korean conflict. Presidential exercise of broad governmental powers during the nation's four most costly wars helped a great deal to shift the locus of power over questions of military policy from the legislative to the executive branch of the federal government, notwithstanding the original intention of most of the Founding Fathers, who hoped to make Congress pre-eminent within this area of policy-making. It took the genius of Lincoln to formulate an interpretation of the Constitution which made it possible for him to circumvent Congress' more extensive constitutional powers over military matters. The following represent some of the more relevant and important works which deal with the growth and scope of the President's military powers: Edward S. Corwin, *The President: Office and Powers, 1787–1957* (4th ed.; New York: New York University Press, 1957); Edward S. Corwin and Louis W. Koenig, *The Presidency Today* (New York: New York University Press, 1956); Clinton L. Rossiter, *The Supreme Court and the Commander in Chief* (Ithaca: Cornell University Press, 1951); Clarence A. Berdahl, *War Powers of the Chief Executive in the United States* (Urbana, Ill.: University of Illinois Press, 1921). See also Richard E. Neustadt, *Presidential Power: The Politics of Leadership* (New York: Wiley, 1960); and Ernest R. May, *The Ultimate Decision: The President as Commander-in-Chief* (New York: Braziller, 1960).

6. The trend toward increasing federal control of the reserves began with the Dick Act in 1903 which provided for dual federal and state direction of the militia in peacetime. The trend has grown apace ever since, aided and abetted by two world wars which necessitated the close integration of reserve and active armed force units. The expanding power of the federal government in this area culminated in the sweeping reorganization of the national guard under Secretary of Defense McNamara over the strong protests of the National Guard Association and many state officials who are responsible for reserve activities. See Eilene Galloway, *History of United States Military Policy on Reserve Forces 1775–1957*, prepared for HCAS, February, 1957; HCAS, *Military Reserve Posture Hearings*, 87/2, 1962; HCAS, *Report of Subcommittee No. 3 on Military Reserve Posture*, August 17, 1962; HSAC, *Hearings, Defense Appropriations for 1964*, 88/1, 1963, Part 1, pp. 134–36. See also George Fielding Eliot, *Reserve Forces and the Kennedy Strategy* (Harrisburg, Pa.: Stackpole, 1962).

7. Samuel P. Huntington, *The Soldier and the State* (Cambridge: Belknap, Harvard University Press, 1957), pp. 169–77; Martha Derthick, "Militia Lobby in the Missile Age: The Politics of the National Guard," in Samuel P. Huntington (ed.), *Changing Patterns of Military Politics* (New York: Free Press, 1962), pp. 190–235; Derthick, *The National Guard in Politics* (Cambridge: Harvard University Press, 1965); and D. W. Brogan, "The United States: Civilian and Military Power," in Michael Howard (ed.), *Soldiers and Governments* (London: Eyre and Spottiswoode, 1957), pp. 167–85.

8. The published papers of Senator Arthur Vandenberg and those of James Forrestal provide a rich storehouse of information and insight into the intricacies and frustrations of congressional-executive collaboration in military and foreign policy. See Arthur H. Vandenberg, Jr. (ed.), *The Private Papers of Senator Vandenberg* (New York: Houghton Mifflin, 1952); James Forrestal, *The Forrestal Diaries*, ed. Walter Millis (New York: Viking, 1951).

567

9. Interpreting the American voter has now become a highly complicated and technical enterprise. Yet the most distinguishing feature of the writing in this area is its controversial and often inconclusive character. See, for example, Eugene Burdick and Arthur Brodbeck (eds.), *American Voting Behavior* (Glencoe, Ill.: Free Press, 1959); Walter Berns, *Essays in the Scientific Study of Politics*, ed. Herbert Storing (New York: Holt, 1962), pp. 1–62; and August Campbell, *et al.*, *The American Voter* (New York: Wiley, 1960). Consult also the citations noted in these works.

10. Earle (ed.), *The Federalist*, p. 337.

11. Max Farrand (ed.), *The Records of the Federal Convention of 1787* (4 vols.; New Haven: Yale University Press, 1911–37), II, 329–30.

12. Earle (ed.), *The Federalist*, p. 142.

13. *Ibid.*, p. 190.

14. See Farrand (ed.), *The Records of the Federal Convention of 1787*, II, proceedings of August 6, 17, 18, 21, 23, and September 5, 12, 14, 17. Louis Smith, *American Democracy and Military Power* (Chicago: University of Chicago Press, 1951), pp. 17–36, discusses the considerations that were weighed by the Philadelphia Convention in its deliberations on the military clauses of the Constitution.

15. Earle (ed.), *The Federalist*, pp. 226–63.

16. Smith, *American Democracy and Military Power*, pp. 17–36.

17. For two conflicting views, see Huntington, *The Soldier and the State*, pp. 163–92; and Smith, *American Democracy and Military Power*, pp. 24–36. The point of view in the present volume differs from both these works in that its major concern is with the response of the United States to military strategic problems, and not with the derivative problems of civil-military relations. This latter question is seen as a part of the greater problem of controlling the government which is invested with military powers. Civilian officials may pose a greater threat to the liberties of a people than a standing army. A uniform by any other name might conceivably be as oppressive.

18. Farrand (ed.), *The Records of the Federal Convention of 1787*, II, Proceedings of August 6, 18, 21, 23, and September 12, 14, 17.

19. Robert E. Osgood, *Limited War* (Chicago: University of Chicago Press, 1956), pp. 41–43. An excellent interpretation of the effect which America's historical experience has had on the attitude of the American people toward war and foreign relations may be found in Reinhold Niebuhr's *The Irony of American History* (New York: Scribner, 1952), pp. 1–42, 65–68. See also George Kennan, *American Diplomacy, 1900–1950* (New York: New American Library, 1952 printing), pp. 55–90; and Hans Morgenthau, *In Defense of the National Interest* (New York: Knopf, 1951), pp. 3–33.

20. The military ideas of Hamilton are summarized in Edward Mead Earle's "Adam Smith, Alexander Hamilton, Friedrich List: The Economic Foundations of Military Powers," in *Makers of Modern Strategy*, (ed.), Edward Mead Earle (Princeton: Princeton University Press, 1952), pp. 128–38.

21. Earle (ed.), *The Federalist*, p. 165.

22. *Ibid.*, p. 266.

23. Leonard D. White, *The Jacksonians* (New York: Macmillan, 1954), p. 188; *idem, The Republicans* (New York: Macmillan, 1956), pp. 134–35.

24. White, *The Jacksonians*, p. 189.

25. Huntington, *The Soldier and the State*, pp. 226–30. Professor Huntington's book should also be consulted for an over-all discussion of the relations of the military establishment to civil authority in the United States from 1789 to 1940, pp. 193–312. Examine also Russell F. Weigley, *Towards an American Army* (New York: Columbia University Press, 1962).

26. Morris Janowitz, *The Professional Soldier* (Glencoe, Ill.: Free Press, 1960). On p. 204, Professor Janowitz writes: "Despite its increased size, and its elaborate organizational alliances with other civilian leadership groups, the military profession and its elite members are not effectively integrated, on a social basis, with other leadership groups. There is little evidence to support the argument that the military forms an integral part of a compact social group which constitutes the power elite. Rather, in fact, the contrary seems to be the case: namely, the political behavior of the military in the United States is still deeply conditioned by its social isolation."

27. H. Doc. 227, 86/1, 1959, p. 126.

28. Professor Harold D. Lasswell has been the most prominent exponent of the "garrison state" thesis, and coined the term itself. His viewpoint is scattered over a number of articles and books. The following are representative: (1) Harold D. Lasswell, *National Security and Individual Freedom* (New York: McGraw-Hill, 1950), pp. 23–49; (2) *idem,* "The Garrison State," *American Journal of Sociology,* XLVI, No. 4 (January, 1941), 455–68; (3) *idem,* "Sino-Japanese Crisis: The Garrison State versus the Civilian State," *China Quarterly,* XI (1937), 643–49; and (4) *idem,* "The Garrison State Hypothesis Today," in *Changing Patterns of Military Politics,* ed. Samuel P. Huntington (Glencoe, Ill.: Free Press, 1962), pp. 51–70. Perhaps the most extensive attack on Professor Lasswell's position may be found in Huntington, *The Soldier and the State*, pp. 346–50. These pages can be read with profit in conjunction with Lasswell's writings in order to provide some balance to the latter's point of view.

29. C. Wright Mills, *The Power Elite* (New York: Oxford University Press, 1956), *passim.,* but especially pp. 198–297. Again, see Janowitz, *The Professional Soldier,* pp. 204–11, as well as Daniel Bell, *The Age of Ideology* (New York: Collier Books, 1961), pp. 47–74, for a contrary view.

30. Fred J. Cook, *The Warfare State* (New York: Macmillan, 1962), p. 351. For similar views, see Henry M. Christman, *Peace and Arms: Report from the Nation* (New York: Sheed & Ward, 1964); Tristram Coffin, *The Passion of the Hawks* (New York: Macmillan, 1964); and John Swomley, *The Military Establishment* (Boston: Beacon, 1964).

31. Cook, *The Warfare State,* p. 350.

32. Janowitz, *The Professional Soldier,* pp. 355–56.

33. C. R., 80/1, 1947, XCIII, Part 7, 8308.

34. See SCAS, *National Security Act of 1947*, as amended, Committee Print, 85/2, 1959.

35. Commission on Organization of the Executive Branch of the Government, *The National Security Organization*, A Report to the Congress, February, 1949, pp. 2–3.

36. Farewell Address of President Dwight D. Eisenhower. *New York Times,* January 18, 1961, p. 22.

37. For an elaboration of this theme, see William Anderson, "Intention of the Framers: A Note on Constitutional Interpretation," *American Political Science Review,* XLIX, No. 2 (June, 1955), 340-52.

38. The definition of the component parts of military and national strategic policy are drawn in great part, though in amended form, from Osgood, *Limited War,* p. 7; and *idem, NATO: The Entangling Alliance* (Chicago: University of Chicago Press, 1962), pp. 7–9. Citation must also be made of Karl von Clausewitz, *On War,* trans. O. J. Matthijs (Washington: Combat Forces, 1953), especially Books I and VIII.

39. Although the definition of Congress employed in this study stresses Congress' institutional responsibility for defense, it is not intended to obscure the manifold interactions of legislators among themselves and with the outside world, nor to obfuscate the complicated power relations existing between the subcommittees and the full committees of the House and Senate Appropriations and Armed Services committees. For a treatment of inner-congressional relations, especially as they bear on foreign relations, consult the following general works: George B. Galloway, *The Legislative Process in Congress* (New York: Crowell, 1953); James MacGregor Burns, *Congress on Trial* (New York: Harper, 1949); Ernest Griffith, *Congress: Its Contemporary Role* (3d ed.; New York: New York University Press, 1961); James Burnham, *Congress and the American Tradition* (Chicago: Regnery, 1959); Roland Young, *This Is Congress* (New York: Knopf, 1943); *idem, The American Congress* (New York: Harper, 1958); Bertram Gross, *The Legislative Struggle* (New York: McGraw-Hill, 1953); Holbert Carroll, *The House of Representatives and Foreign Affairs* (Pittsburgh: Pittsburgh University Press, 1958); James Robinson, *Congress and Foreign Policy-Making* (Homewood, Ill.: Dorsey, 1962); Robert A. Dahl, *Congress and Foreign Policy* (New York: Harcourt, Brace, 1950); Daniel S. Cheever and H. Field Haviland, Jr., *American Foreign Policy and the Separation of Powers* (Cambridge: Harvard University Press, 1952); and Warner Schilling (ed.), *Strategy, Politics, and Defense Budgets* (New York: Columbia University Press, 1962), pp. 1–266.

40. For example, Bertram Gross argues in his *The Legislative Struggle,* pp. 7–8: "If the entire process of government can be described as one of group struggle for power, how does the legislative process differ from the administrative process and the judicial process? When viewed at a high enough level of abstraction, there is little or no difference. Both the contestants in the struggle and their objectives are generally the same. At a more specific level of description, however, the difference is that the legislative struggle is fought on a different battlefield. This calls for a more specialized use of general weapons and a development of specialized strategy,

tactics, rules, procedures, and organizational forms." See also Earl Latham, "The Group Basis of Politics: Notes for a Theory," *American Political Science Review,* XLVI, No. 2 (June, 1952), 376–97. Also pertinent is David B. Truman, *The Governmental Process* (New York: Knopf, 1951). For a critique of the "group theory of politics" see the essay by Leo Weinstein in *Essays in the Scientific Study of Politics,* ed. Herbert Storing (New York: Holt, 1962).

41. A great deal has been written about the military mind—or the absence of one. See Burton M. Sapin and Richard C. Snyder, *The Role of the Military in American Foreign Policy* (Garden City: Doubleday, 1954), p. 79, n. 12, for a number of useful citations to other articles on this subject. Professor Huntington, *The Soldier and the State,* pp. 59–79, also deals extensively with the alleged existence of a "military mind." See also the extensive bibliography which he presents on civil-military relations in foreign countries in his *Changing Patterns of Military Politics,* pp. 235–66. Examine also the publication of the Committee on Civil-Military Relations Research of the Social Science Research Council entitled *Civil-Military Relations: An Annotated Bibliography, 1940–1952* (New York: Columbia University Press, 1954). A more recent and, in some ways, the most notable attempt to handle the illusive concept of the "military mind" may be found in Professor Janowitz' study, *The Professional Soldier.*

42. See, for example, Edgar S. Furniss, Jr., *De Gaulle and the French Army* (New York: Twentieth Century Fund, 1964); James H. Meisel, *The Fall of the Republic* (Ann Arbor: University of Michigan Press, 1962).

43. See Huntington, *Changing Patterns of Military Politics,* pp. 261–66, and works cited therein; John J. Johnson (ed.), *The Role of the Military in Underdeveloped Countries* (Princeton: Princeton University Press, 1962); and *idem, The Military and Society in Latin America* (Stanford: Stanford University Press, 1964); and Morris Janowitz, *The Military in the Political Development of New Nations* (Chicago: University of Chicago Press, 1964).

44. B.B., *U.S. Budget, FY 1965,* pp. 72, 112.

45. There is growing evidence that a "new civil-military relation" has been evolving since 1940 which is sophisticated and intricate enough to resolve many of the difficulties created at these different levels of the civil-military problem in the United States. The Senate Subcommittee on National Security Staffing and Operations has prepared a group of readings which elaborate on this theme. See the committee print entitled *Administration of National Security, Selected Papers,* 87/2, 1962, especially pp. 8–16, 102–16, 137–48, 153–71, 190–201. Most relevant is the article by Gene M. Lyons on pp. 102–16 which is reproduced from his "The New Civil-Military Relations," *American Political Science Review,* LV, No. 1 (March, 1961), 53–63.

An excellent example of the close working relations which now must be developed between civilian and military bureaucrats and between these groups and elected and appointed political leaders may be seen in the Senate hearings which reviewed the Kennedy administration's test ban agreement with the Soviet Union and the United Kingdom. All these officials, including interested and knowledgeable people from private and semi-private organizations, are joined together in a discussion of the implications of the test ban treaty. Public policy on important strategic questions of such far-reaching implications requires that all of these individuals and groups be consulted and their approval elicited before a position can be legitimately and effectively adopted. See SCFR, *Hearings, Nuclear Test Ban Treaty*, 88/1, 1963. These hearings are unique in that three Senate committees held joint hearings on the treaty agreement, including the Committee on Foreign Relations, the Committee on Armed Services, and the Senate members of the Joint Committee on Atomic Energy.

46. HCAS, *Hearings on Military Posture and H. R. 9751*, 87/2, 1962, p. 3206.

CHAPTER II

1. Harry S Truman, *Memoirs* (Garden City: Doubleday, 1957, I, 507. For general materials dealing with American military demobilization, see the following: John Sparrow, *History of Personnel Demobilization in the United States Army* (Washington: Department of the Army, 1952); George E. Allen, *The Liquidation of Federal War Agencies* (Washington, 1945); HCMA, *Hearings on Demobilization*, 79/1, 1946; and annual reports of the secretary of war and the navy, 1945–47.

2. H. Doc. 227, 86/1, 1959, p. 123.

3. S. Doc. 90, 79/1, 1945, p. 1.

4. It is no accident that the bulk of Elias Huzar's *The Purse and the Sword* (Ithaca: Cornell University Press, 1950) deals with congressional oversight of the army's budgetary and administrative practices rather than military policy. Congress was predominantly concerned with the accuracy of departmental estimates and the efficiency of administration. See especially, pp. 62–131, 207–374.

5. The War Department budget included $700 million for non-military functions; the navy estimates included a request to transfer $500 million from the naval stock fund.

6. B.B., *U.S. Budget, FY 1947*, p. xxx.

7. HSAC, *Hearings, Military Appropriations, FY 1947*, 79/2, 1946, pp. 401–2.

8. There were, of course, governmental officials who were deeply concerned about the growing Soviet threat to the United States and about the slow response of the United States to meet it. James Forrestal, President Truman's secretary of the navy is the most prominent example. See his *Diaries*, ed. Walter Millis (New York: Viking, 1951). For an excellent and authoritative discussion of this period, see Stephen G. Xydis, *Greece and the Great Powers, 1944–1947* (Thessaloniki: Balkan Studies, 1963), especially pp. 156–59, 505–56. Also useful is Arnold A. Rogow, *James Forrestal: A Study of Personality, Politics, and Policy* (New York: Macmillan, 1963).

9. HSAC, *Military Appropriations, FY 1947*, p. 18.

10. *Ibid.*, p. 26.

11. *Ibid.*, p. 44. Emphasis added.

12. Compare H. Rept. 2311, 79/2, 1946; and HSAC, *Military Appropriations, FY 1947*, pp. 101–26, especially pp. 105–16.

13. H. Rept. 2311, 79/2, 1946, pp. 3–7.

14. *Ibid.*, pp. 4–5.

15. *Ibid.*, pp. 3–7.

16. C.R., 79/2, 1946, XCII, Part 6, 7323–55.

17. SSAC, *Hearings, Military Appropriations, FY 1947*, 79/2, 1946, and S. Rept. 1590, 79/2, 1946. Emphasis added.

18. C.R., XCII, Part 6, 7875–78.

19. Comparisons between plans 1-A and 2 may be found in the following documents: HSAC, *Hearings, Navy Department Appropriations, FY 1947*, 79/2, 1946, pp. 31–35, 47–49; H. Rept. 2085, 79/2, 1946, pp. 1–5.
Some discrepancy may be discerned between the statement of Mr. McNeil, fiscal director of the Navy Department (Navy *Hearings*, pp. 48–49), and the report of the House Appropriations Committee over the funding of Plan 1-A. The House report was accepted as the standard to follow because it was written after the hearings on naval appropriations were held and, presumably, after all information bearing on financing Plan 1-A was brought to the House committee's attention.

20. H. Rept. 2085, 79/2, 1946, pp. 1-2.

21. HSAC, *Navy Department Appropriations, FY 1947*, 79/2, 1946, p. 8.

22. *Ibid.*

23. *Ibid.*, p. 33. Emphasis added.

24. See HSAC, *Navy Department Appropriations, FY 1947*, pp. 24–25, 37, 46–47, 386–87, 545, 573–74, 578–79, 593, 1280–81, 1415–19, 1420–21, 1479, 1984–85.

25. HSAC, *Military Appropriations, FY 1947*, pp. 18–19.

26. H. Rept. 2085, 79/2, 1946, p. 4.

27. *Ibid.*

28. *Ibid.*, p. 7.

29. *Ibid.*, p. 15 and C.R., XCII, Part 5, 5535–39.

30. *Ibid.*, p. 7. See also C.R., XCII, Part 5, 5533.

31. H. Rept. 2085, 79/2, 1946, p. 19.

32. C.R., 79/1, 1945, XCI, Part 8, 10206.

33. *Ibid.*, XCII, Part 5, 5542.

34. *Ibid.*, XCII, Part 5, 5550.

35. *Ibid.*, XCII, Part 5, 5553.

36. SSAC, *Hearings, Navy Department Appropriations, FY 1947*, 79/2, 1946.

37. *Ibid.*, pp. 146–48.

38. S. Rept. 1435, 79/2, 1946.

39. C.R., XCII, Part 6, 7268–78.

40. *Ibid.*, XCII, Part 6, 7278 ff.

41. *Ibid.*, XCII, Part 6, 7285.

42. *State of the Union*, H. Doc. 1, 80/1, 1947, p. 9.

43. *Ibid.*, p. 10.

44. *Ibid.*, p. 11.

45. B.B., *U.S. Budget, FY 1948*, pp. M17–M63.

46. HSAC, *Hearings, Military Establishment Appropriations, FY 1948*, 80/1, 1947, p. 5.

47. *Ibid.*, p. 176.

48. *Ibid.*, p. 1241.

49. *Ibid.*, p. 601.

50. *Ibid.*, p. 602.

51. William Reitzel, *et al.*, *United States Foreign Policy, 1945–1955* (Washington, D.C.: Brookings, 1956), p. 91.

52. H. Rept. 495, 80/1, 1947, p. 8–9; HSAC, *Military Establishment Appropriations, FY 1948*, pp. 613–16.

53. SSAC, *Hearings, Military Establishment Appropriations, FY 1948*, 80/1, 1947, p. 3.

54. C.R., 80/1, 1947, XCIII, Part 7, 8605.

55. H. Rept. 495, 80/1, 1947, p. 8.

56. *HSAC Military Establishment Appropriations, FY 1948*, p. 648.

57. *Ibid.*, p. 177.

58. SSAC, *Military Establishment Appropriations, FY 1948*, p. 293.

59. HSAC, *Military Establishment Appropriations, FY 1948*, p. 628.

60. C.R. 80/1, 1947, XCIII, Part 5, 6277.

61. H. Rept. 495, 80/1, 1947, p. 3.

62. *Ibid.*, pp. 4–5.

63. Truman, *Memoirs, I*, 522–23, 548–52, 593–96.

64. C.R., XCIII, Part 5, 6277.

65. *Loc. cit.*

66. *Ibid.*, 6358.

67. *Ibid.*, 6471.

68. S. Rept. 465, 80/1, 1947, p. 15.

69. C.R., XCIII, Part 7, 8605–14, 8884–88.

70. *Ibid.*, Part 8, 10234.

71. *Loc. cit.*

72. Lloyd Mallon, *Peace Is a Three-Edged Sword* (Englewood, N.J., Prentice-Hall, 1964), pp. 107–8.

73. See Samuel P. Huntington, *The Common Defense* (New York: Columbia University Press, 1961) for a brief, but useful, summary of the revenue position of the Truman administration before the Korean War, pp. 41-43.

74. See S. Doc., *Appropriations, Budget Estimates, Etc.*, 79/2 through 81/2, 1946–50, *passim*.

75. Paul Y. Hammond, "Super Carriers and B-36 Bombers: Appropriations, Strategy, and Policies," *American Civil-Military Decisions*, ed. Harold Stein (Birmingham: University of Alabama Press, 1963), pp. 468–69.

76. HSAC, *Hearings, Navy Department Appropriations Bill, FY 1948*, 80/1, 1947, p. 1346.

77. *Ibid.*

78. *Ibid.*, p. 1397.

79. *Ibid.*, pp. 1358-59.

80. *Ibid.*, p. 83.

81. HSAC, *Supplemental Hearings, Navy Department Appropriations Bill, FY 1948*, 80/1, 1947, pp. 12–18.

82. HSAC, *Navy Department Appropriations, FY 1948*, p. 112; H. Rept. 390, 80/1, 1947, p. 3.

83. *Ibid.*, pp. 854–55.

84. HSAC, *Navy Department Appropriations, FY 1947*, p. 1.

85. *Ibid.*

86. HSAC, *Navy Department Appropriations, FY 1948*, pp. 2–3.

87. Stephen G. Xydis, "The Genesis of the Sixth Fleet," *U. S. Institutes*, LXXXIV, No. 8 (August, 1958), 41–50.

88. H. Rept. 390, 80/1, pp. 18–23.

89. C.R., XCIII, Part 4, 5540.

90. *Ibid.*, p. 5545.

91. *Ibid.*, p. 5549–52.

92. SSAC, *Navy Department Appropriations, FY 1948*, 80/1, 1947, pp. 98, 133, 163 ff.

93. *Ibid.*; S. Rept. 338, 80/1, 1947; C.R., XCIII, Part 6, 7586 ff.

94. H. Rept. 2385, 80/1, 1947.

CHAPTER III

1. See Forrestal, *Diaries, passim;* and Reitzel *et al.* pp. 83–96.

2. "Mr. X," "The Sources of Soviet Conduct," *Foreign Affairs,* XXV, No. 4 (July, 1947), 466–82.

3. H. Doc. 569, 80/2, 1948, pp. 1–2.

4. *Ibid.,* p. 2.

5. *Ibid.,* pp. 3–4.

6. Forrestal, *Diaries,* p. 397.

7. H. Doc. 569, 80/2, 1948, p. 4.

8. Forrestal, *Diaries,* pp. 397–98; Paul Y. Hammond, "Super Carriers and B-36 Bombers: Appropriations, Strategy, and Politics," pp. 475–76.

9. "Mr. X," *Foreign Affairs,* XXV, 576.

10. Louis Halle suggests that Point Four was an improvised policy position, too. Louis J. Halle, "On Teaching International Relations," *Virginia Quarterly Review,* XL, No. 1 (Winter, 1964), 11–25.

11. Hammond, "Super Carriers and B-36 Bombers," p. 504.

12. SCAS, *Hearings, Universal Military Training,* 80/2, 1948, pp. 30, 330–31.

13. *Ibid.,* pp. 330 ff.

14. HSAC, *Hearings, Supplemental National Defense Appropriations Bill, FY 1948,* 80/2, 1948, p. 4.

15. SSAC, *Hearings, Supplemental National Defense Appropriations Bill, FY 1948,* 80/2, 1948, pp. 73–80 and 91.

16. *Ibid.,* p. 3. See also Forrestal, *Diaries,* pp. 412–14.

17. SCAS, *Universal Military Training,* 80/1, 1948, pp. 392 ff.

18. SSAC, *Supplemental National Defense Appropriations Bill, FY 1948,* p. 34.

19. *Ibid.,* p. 60. The air force's appeal to the Congress for support prompted *New York Times* analyst Hanson Baldwin to remark that " 'unification' becomes a joke when the Secretary of the Air Force goes over the head of the Secretary of Defense and of the President himself." *New York Times,* April 15, 1948, p. 16.

20. U.S., President's Air Policy Commission, *Survival in the Air Age* (Washington, D.C.: Government Printing Office, 1948), p. 25.

21. *Ibid.,* p. 14.

22. S. Rept. 949, 80/2, 1948, p. 4.

23. Forrestal, *Diaries,* p. 413.

24. C.R., 80/2, 1948, XCIV, Part 4, 4448.

25. *Ibid.,* 4452.

26. *Ibid.*, 4456 ff.

27. *Ibid.*, 4530.

28. *Ibid.*, 4548.

29. S. Rept. 1223, 80/2, 1948.

30. C.R., XCIV, Part 4, 4536.

31. *Loc. cit.*

32. Forrestal, *Diaries*, pp. 416–17.

33. *Ibid.*, p. 438.

34. HSAC, *Hearings, Military Functions, National Military Establishment Appropriations, FY 1949*, 80/2, 1948, Part 3, p. 18.

35. *Ibid.*, pp. 25, 818.

36. *Ibid.*, Part 2, p. 170.

37. H. Rept. 2135, 80/2, 1948, Part 3, pp. 24–25.

38. *Ibid.*, p. 10.

39. *Ibid.*

40. HSAC, *Hearings, Military Functions, National Military Establishment Appropriations, FY 1948*, Part 3, p. 18.

41. H. Rept. 2135, 80/2, 1948, p. 10.

42. SSAC, *Hearings, Military Functions, National Military Establishment Appropriations Bill, FY 1949*, 80/2, 1948, pp. 2–3, 55.

43. H. Rept. 2430, 80/2, 1948.

44. HSAC, *Hearings, Navy Department Appropriations, FY 1949*, 80/2, 1948, p. 3.

45. *Ibid.*, pp. 131–32.

46. Hammond, "Super Carriers and B-36 Bombers," pp. 465–569, describes the navy's postwar carrier program. See also letter of resignation of Secretary of the Navy John Sullivan to Secretary of Defense Louis Johnson which is printed in full in HCAS, *Hearings, The National Defense Program—Unification and Strategy*, 81/1, 1949, pp. 622–23. Sullivan outlines the navy's cutback of its over-all shipbuilding program to secure an enlarged carrier force.

47. HSAC, *Hearings, Supplemental to Navy Appropriations, FY 1949*, 80/2, 1948, pp. 15, 97, 102.

48. *Ibid.*, p. 15.

49. *Ibid.*, pp. 56–57.

50. H. Rept. 2136, 80/2, 1948, p. 27.

51. HSAC, *Navy Department Appropriations, FY 1949* and *Supplemental to Navy Appropriations, FY 1949*.

52. H. Rept. 2136, 80/2, 1948, p. 3.

53. C.R., XCIV, Part 6, 7081–82.

54. Ibid., 7082.

55. SSAC, Hearings, Navy Department Appropriations, FY 1949, 80/2, 1948.

56. S. Rept. 1621, 80/2, 1948.

57. Forrestal, Diaries, p. 437.

58. Ibid.

59. There are three excellent accounts of the executive-congressional phases of the FY 1950 defense budget. No other defense budget has ever received so thorough a treatment. The discussion here does not pretend to match or surpass them. It is principally interested in the congressional phase of the budget as a part of Congress' handling of the defense budget since World War II. For other accounts see Warner Schilling (ed.), Strategy, Politics, and Defense Budgets (New York: Columbia University Press, 1962), pp. 1–266; Huzar, pp. 184–206; and Forrestal, Diaries, pp. 492–530. The most comprehensive and useful is Schilling's analysis.

60. B.B., U.S. Budget, FY 1950, p. M19.

61. H. Rept. 417, 81/1, 1949, p. 2.

62. Forrestal, Diaries, p. 505. Lieutenant General Alfred Gruenther was officially director of the joint staff and Forrestal's primary link to the Joint Chiefs of Staff. Gruenther's duties were eventually assigned to the chairman of the JCS, a post created by the 1949 Defense Reorganization Act.

63. Ibid., pp. 492–537.

64. Huzar, p. 185. See Schilling, Strategy, Politics, and Defense Budgets, pp. 95–134, for a detailed discussion of what Schilling calls the "climate of opinion" in Congress which had settled on a military spending limit of $15 billion a year.

65. HSAC, Hearings, Military Establishment Appropriations Bill, FY 1950, 81/1, 1949, Part 1, p. 12.

66. Ibid., p. 16.

67. Ibid., p. 17.

68. B.B., U.S. Budget, FY 1950, pp. M19–M22.

69. HSAC, Military Establishment Appropriations Bill, FY 1950, Part 2, pp. 103–5.

70. Ibid., Part 4, p. 567.

71. Ibid., Part 4, pp. 567–70. There were indications in the postwar period that the army and air force looked to the diminution of the navy. General Alfred Gruenther told Forrestal in December, 1947, that "there was a general impression throughout the Army and Air Force, but particularly in the latter, that the amount of money provided for the Navy was disproportionate to the tasks of the Navy and its use in a future war. The Air people made the point . . . that the plant, weapons and ships of the Navy were far out of line with the existing material strength of the Air Force." Forrestal, Diaries, p. 352.

72. HSAC, *Military Establishment Appropriations Bill, FY 1950*, Part 2, p. 439.

73. *Ibid.*, Part 2.

74. *Ibid.*, Part 3, p. 30.

75. *Ibid.*

76. *Ibid.*, Part 4, pp. 80–83.

77. *Ibid.*, p. 19.

78. *Ibid.*, Part 2, p. 439.

79. *Ibid.*, p. 135.

80. *Ibid.*, Part 3, pp. 603–4.

81. HCAS, *The National Defense Program—Unification and Strategy*, p. 623.

82. HSAC, *Military Establishment Appropriations Bill, FY 1950*, Part 3, pp. 613–19, 635.

83. *Ibid.*, p. 5.

84. See, for example, *ibid.*, Part 2, pp. 15–17, 98–103, and Part 3, pp. 1–3, 39–45.

85. *Ibid.*, Part 1, p. 207. Emphasis added.

86. *Ibid.*, p. 215.

87. *Ibid.*, pp. 206–7.

88. Schilling, *Strategy, Politics, and Defense Budgets*, pp. 54–134, provides a thorough criticism of Vinson's presentation and of Mahon's subcommittee. He suggests that the "climate of opinion" in 1949 hindered the Congress in raising questions about the validity of the President's $15 billion ceiling. The analysis here, while agreeing essentially with most of Schilling's observations, assigns more weight to the merit of what at least some congressmen, like Vinson and Mahon, were trying to do in analyzing the President's defense proposals. The significance of Mahon's departure and, relatedly, his enhanced prestige, within the House in the 1950's and 1960's as an authority on military affairs, did produce important and salutary changes in defense policy and military preparedness. This was particularly evident in the immediate post-sputnik period. See Chapter VI, below. Under Mahon's leadership the House Appropriations Subcommittee did become progressively interested and expert in military policy.

89. *Ibid.*, p. 60.

90. H. Rept. 417, 81/1, 1949, p. 12.

91. *Ibid.*, p. 31.

92. It is well to remember that the report of the defense appropriations subcommittee is usually accepted by the full appropriations committee. Mahon was summarizing the appropriations committee report which was essentially his subcommittee's report.

93. C.R., 81/1, 1949, XCV, Part 5, 4429.

94. HSAC, *Military Establishment Appropriations Bill, FY 1950,* Part 1, p. 235.

95. *Ibid.,* p. 236.

96. C.R., XCV, Part 4, 4500–4501.

97. *New York Times,* October 30, 1949, pp. 1, 3. For commentary and criticism of the President's decision to impound the extra air force funds, see HSAC, *Military Establishment Appropriations Bill, FY 1950;* and H. Rept. 1797, 81/2, 1950.

98. C.R., XCV, Part 4, 4430.

99. *Ibid.,* 4499; also 4435, 4527–28.

100. *Ibid.,* 4529.

101. *Ibid.,* 4500–4501.

102. *Ibid.,* 4527–28.

103. *Ibid.,* 4546.

104. S. Rept. 746, 81/1, 1949, p. 5.

105. See SSAC, *National Military Appropriations Bill, FY 1950,* 81/1, 1949.

106. *Ibid.,* p. 32.

107. S. Rept. 746, 81/1, 1949, p. 6.

108. C.R., XCV, Part 9, 12315.

109. *Ibid.,* 12308.

110. *Ibid.,* 14355.

111. H. Rept. 1454 and H. Rept. 1386, 81/1, 1949.

112. Hammond, "NSC 68: Prologue to Rearmament," *Strategy, Politics, and Defense Budgets,* ed. Warner Schilling, p. 319.

113. HCAS, *The National Defense Program—Unification and Strategy,* pp. 622–23.

114. HCAS, *Investigation of the B-36 Bomber Program,* 81/1, 1949. Especially see the testimony of Mr. Cedric R. Worth, pp. 524 ff.

115. HCAS, *The National Defense Program—Unification and Strategy,* p. 51. The most authoritative account of the B-36 and the unification controversies may be found in Hammond, "Super Carriers and B-36 Bombers," pp. 465–567. See also Millis, pp. 238–50 and the series of articles written by Hanson Baldwin in the *New York Times* from October 6 through October 26, 1949, *passim.*

116. HCAS, *The National Defense Program—Unification and Strategy,* p. 52. See testimony of Radford and the experts that he assembled, *ibid.,* pp. 39–183.

117. *Ibid.,* p. 185.

118. *Ibid.,* p. 189.

119. *Ibid.,* p. 186.

120. *Ibid.*

121. *Ibid.*

122. HSAC, *Department of Defense Appropriations, FY 1951*, 81/1, 1950, Part 5, pp. 2631–33, Part 2, p. 301.

123. Noted Vinson in the House Armed Services Unification and Strategy hearings: "Here, during this week we are fighting for what the departments say the Nation needs and the departments have justified every item. Then Mr. Johnson, to make his record of saving $800,000,000, says Congress is giving more money than he needs and he lets Congress go along and do it and then he says: 'I will cut it out and it will reflect credit on my great ability to save the taxpayers' money.' [applause]

"We are going to have a lot to say about this in these hearings. . . . Congress is not going to be led into a position of appropriating money and then have some bureaucrat . . . say, 'I won't do that. I want to make a record of my own. I want to show up the Congress.'" HCAS, *The National Defense Program–Unification and Strategy*, p. 307.

124. H. Doc. 227, 86/1, 1960, p. 123.

125. B.B., *U.S. Budget, FY 1951*, pp. M26–M27.

126. HSAC, *Defense Appropriations, FY 1951*, Part 2, pp. 214–15.

127. SSAC, *Department of Defense Appropriations, FY 1951*, 81/2, 1950, pp. 15–16.

128. *Ibid.*, p. 15.

129. HSAC, *Defense Appropriations, FY 1951*, Part 4, p. 1990.

130. *Ibid.*, Part 3, pp. 1315–16, 1326. See all of Part 3 for a full statement of the air force program.

131. *Ibid.*, Part 5, p. 2659.

132. *Ibid.*, p. 2661.

133. Compare *ibid.*, Part 5, pp. 2630 ff and *ibid.*, Part 1, pp. 42–80.

134. See *ibid.*, Part 2, pp. 203, 213–15, 249–50, 380–83; Part 3, pp. 1315–17; and Part 4, pp. 1749–54, 1895–96, 1947, 2608.

135. *Ibid.*, Part 2, p. 249.

136. H. Rept. 1797, 81/2, 1950, p. 281.

137. *Ibid.*, p. 312.

138. C.R., 81/2, 1950, XCVI, Part 5, 6749.

139. HSAC, *Defense Appropriations, FY 1951*, Part 2, p. 250.

140. See pp. 105–6 above.

141. H. Rept. 2135, 80/2, 1948, pp. 24–25.

142. C.R., XCVI, Part 4, 4681.

143. *Ibid.*, Part 5, 6177.

144. *Ibid.*, Part 4, 4681–82.

145. *Ibid.*, p. 4680–91; *ibid.*, XCVI, Part 5, 6175–88.

146. *Ibid.*, Part 4, 4685

147. See pp. 100–101 above.

148. HSAC, *Additional Supplemental Hearings, Defense Appropriations, FY 1951*, 81/2, 1950.

149. C.R., XCVI, Part 5, 6745, 6750.

150. *Ibid.*, p. 6846.

151. H. Rept. 2991, 81/2, 1950.

CHAPTER IV

1. *New York Times*, July 20, 1950, p. 14.

2. H. Doc. 432, 86/2, 1960, p. 124.

3. See pp. 165–66 below.

4. *New York Times*, July 20, 1950, p. 14.

5. Laurence W. Martin, "The American Decision to Rearm Germany," *American Civil-Military Decisions*, ed. Harold Stein (Birmingham: University of Alabama Press, 1963), pp. 656–57.

6. Paul Y. Hammond, "NSC 68: Prologue to Rearmament," *Strategy, Politics, and Defense Budgets*, ed. Warner Schilling, pp. 356–57.

7. *New York Times*, July 20, 1950, p. 14.

8. HSAC, *Hearings, Supplemental Appropriations Bill for FY 1951*, 81/2, 1950, p. 20.

9. See Millis, *Arms and the State* (New York: Twentieth Century Fund, 1958), p. 342, for a contrary view. Mr. Millis creates the impression that the Second Supplemental Bill was formulated in response to the Chinese attack. This interpretation credits the Truman administration for swifter action in a crisis situation than was actually the case. See House Special Subcommittee on National Defense Appropriations, *Hearings, Second Supplemental Appropriation Bill for 1951*, 81/2, 1950, Part 1, p. 77.

10. Quoted in Millis, *Arms and the State*, p. 253.

11. Omar N. Bradley, "This Way Lies Peace," *Saturday Evening Post*, October 15, 1949, p. 33.

12. Hammond, "NSC: Prologue to Rearmament," p. 348.

13. HSAC, *Second Supplemental Appropriations, FY 1951*, Part 1, p. 20. Emphasis added. Even economy-directed Louis Johnson, before he left office, was compelled by the seriousness of the Korean struggle to place military needs above short-run economic solvency; see HSAC, *Supplemental Appropriations Bill, FY 1951*, p. 4, where Johnson noted: "One month ago the Republic of Korea was

invaded. The action of the United Nations, supported by the United States, called for the use of troops, ships, and aircraft to repel this criminal aggression which threatened the peace of the world and the security of our own country. In the light of the actual fighting that is now in progress, we have reached the point where the military considerations clearly outweigh the fiscal considerations."

14. HSAC, *Second Supplemental Appropriation Bill, FY 1951*, Part 1, p. 2. General George Marshall opened the Senate hearings with this statement: "Now, our ardent hope is, of course, that we do not become involved in a World War, but of necessity we have got to be ready for such an eventuality. There are two ways of approaching the matter. One is a tremendous build-up here immediately; and the other is, I think much the sounder—establish, through a medium of this interim proposal . . . a high level base from which we can make the most rapid progress effectively, and much more economically than otherwise."

15. *Ibid.*, Part 1, p. 21.

16. The Army ordnance program is pieced together from various sources. See HSAC, *Supplemental Appropriation Bill, FY 1951*, pp. 29, 45; HSAC, *Second Supplemental Bill, FY 1951*, Part 3, pp. 6–13, 22, 144; HSAC, *Hearings, Supplemental Appropriation, FY 1951*, 82/1, 1951, pp. 33, 37, 239–41.

17. HSAC, *Supplemental Appropriation Bill, FY 1951*, pp. 103, 176; HSAC, *Second Supplemental Appropriation Bill, FY 1951*, Part 1, p. 76; and HSAC, *Fourth Supplemental Appropriation Bill, FY 1951*, p. 624.

18. HSAC, *Supplemental Appropriation Bill, FY 1951*, pp. 251, 270–73, 388; HSAC, *Second Supplemental Appropriation Bill, FY 1951*, Part 1, p. 138; and HSAC, *Department of Defense Appropriations, FY 1952*, 82/1, 1951, Part 1, p. 72.

19. See, for example, C.R., 81/2, 1950, XCVI, Part 12, 16650–64.

20. *Ibid.*, 16889.

21. HSAC, *Supplemental Appropriation Bill, FY 1951*, pp. 10–15, 21–22, 231–32.

22. C.R., XCVI, Part 10, 13508.

23. *Loc. cit.*

24. See Chapter II, pp. 67–68 above.

25. H. Rept. 2987, 81/2, 1950, p. 39.

26. B.B., *U. S. Budget, FY 1952*, pp. M8, M14–M15.

27. HSAC, *Hearings, Department of Defense Appropriations, FY 1952*, 82/1, 1951, Part 1, pp. 3, 16.

28. SSAC, *Hearings, Department of Defense Appropriations, FY 1952*, 82/1, 1951, pp. 2–3.

29. See, for example, HSAC, *Defense Appropriation, FY 1952*, Part 3, p. 28.

30. Truman's decision to send troops to Europe touched off what was to be later termed "The Great Debate." Senator Robert A. Taft, a strong contender for the Republican presidential nomination of 1952, focused on President Truman's

583

action and unleashed one of his bitterest attacks on the Democratic administration. On January 5, 1951, Senator Taft openly broke with the Truman administration over the question of sending troops abroad. He shattered the Truman-Vandenberg attempt to construct a bipartisan foreign policy. Argued Taft: "There has been no real bipartisan policy . . . since the 1948 election. It is a proper ideal . . . We [the Republicans] certainly would be prepared to make concessions, but certainly the policy of concessions should not be a one way street. . . . Certainly the Republican minority cannot be attacked for failure to agree on policies on which they have not even been consulted, or on policies which they regard as detrimental to the welfare of the Nation.

.   .   .   .

"We see now the beginning of an agreement to send a specified number of American troops to Europe without that question ever having been discussed in the Congress of the United States. . . . A new policy is being formulated without consulting the Congress or the people." (C.R., 82/, 1951, XCVII, Part 1, 55).

31. HSAC, *Defense Appropriations, FY 1952*, Part 2, p. 1239.

32. *Ibid.*, Part 3, p. 427.

33. *Ibid.*, p. 131.

34. *Ibid.*, pp. 768–69, 779–80.

35. DOD, *Semiannual Report, January-June, 1952*, p. 190.

36. *Ibid.*, p. 191.

37. HSAC, *Defense Appropriations, FY 1952*, Part 4, p. 10.

38. *Ibid.*, pp. 10–11.

39. *Ibid.*, pp. 69, 619.

40. Compare H. Rept. 790, 82/1, 1951, p. 2, and HSAC, *Defense Appropriations, FY 1952*, Part 1, p. 204.

41. S. Rept. 730, 82/1, 1951.

42. S. Doc. 88, 82/1, pp. 556–57.

43. See, for example, SSAC, *Defense Appropriations, FY 1952*, pp. 1511–21.

44. C.R., XCVII, Part 7, 9543.

45. *Ibid.*, 9721.

46. *Ibid.*, Part 8, 11085.

47. *Ibid.*, Part 7, 11135.

48. *Ibid.*, 9558.

49. *Ibid.*, 9546.

50. HSAC, *Defense Appropriations, FY 1952*, Part 2, pp. 50–59, 580–81, 1180; Part 3, pp. 136, 167, 210–27, 228–29, 247, 872–73, 1235.

51. C.R., XCVII, Part 7, 9746.

52. H. Rept. 790, 82/1, 1951, p. 4.

53. C.R., XCVII, Part 8, 11085–90, 11096–97, 11187, 11189, 11893–96; Part 9, 11220–21, 11127–28, 11229–32.

54. *Ibid.*, Part 9, 11237, and H. Rept. 1097, 82/1, 1951.

55. C.R., XCVII, Part 8, 11134–35.

56. To be precise an air force group is a subdivision of a wing. Usually four groups comprise a wing, composed of a primary mission group and three supporting groups. In the previous air force requests for seventy and then ninety-five groups, it was assumed that Congress would also provide the necessary supporting elements. Thus, there is no major difference between the air force requests for combat groups before the Korean War and for combat wings in 1952.

57. B.B., *U. S. Budget, FY 1953*, p. M2.

58. *Ibid.*, p. M13.

59. HSAC, *Hearings, Department of Defense Appropriations, FY 1953*, 82/2, 1952, pp. 87–88.

60. *Ibid.*, p. 144.

61. *Ibid.*, p. 89.

62. HSAC, *Hearings, Department of the Army Appropriations, FY 1953*, 82/1, 1952, pp. 9, 119–20.

63. *Ibid.*, p. 776.

64. *Ibid.*, p. 230.

65. HCA, *Department of Defense Appropriation Bill for 1953*, Committee print to accompany H. R. 7391, 82/2, 1952, p. 35.

66. *Ibid.*, p. 3; HSAC, *Hearings, Department of the Navy Appropriations, FY 1953*, 82/2, 1952, Part 1, p. 528.

67. *Ibid.*, p. 175. The semiannual report of the secretary of the navy from January 1 to June 30, 1953, lists 409 active combatant ships. They were divided along the following lines: 247 destroyers; 110 submarines; 19 cruisers; 4 battleships; 15 light aircraft carriers. DOD, *Semiannual Report of the Secretary of Defense, January 1 to June 30, 1953*, p. 174. See also the following for a discussion of the navy's stress on naval air power: SSAC, *Defense Appropriations, FY 1953*, pp. 317, 1027–29, 1030–36; and HSAC, *Navy Appropriations, FY 1953*, Part 1, pp. 14, 504 ff., 517. During the hearings, Navy Secretary Dave Kimball flatly stated that, "as to airpower," he could not "agree with [Air Force] Secretary [Thomas] Finletter that the Air Force is the only deterrent to war that we have." SSAC, *Hearings, Department of Defense Appropriations, FY 1953*, 82/2, 1952, p. 317. Consult, too, the testimony of Admiral William Fechteler, *ibid.*, pp. 1030 ff., for a defense of the navy's role and the critical importance of naval air power which would "carry the war to the enemy in its initial stages. . . . knock out its coastal bases. . . . prevent him from receiving any outside help, and . . . put him on the defensive. . . . " *Ibid.*, p. 1032.

68. HSAC, *Navy Appropriations, FY 1953*, Part 1, pp. 334–35.

69. H. Rept. 1685, 82/2, 1952, p. 11.

70. HSAC, *Hearings, Department of Air Force Appropriations, FY 1953*, 82/2, 1952, pp. 210, 250.

71. *Ibid.*, pp. 25–26.

72. *Ibid.*, p. 39.

73. *Ibid.*, p. 284.

74. See, for example, SSAC, *Defense Appropriations, FY 1953*, pp. 230–31, 344, 375; Samuel Lubell, *The Future of American Politics* (New York: Harper, 1952).

75. HSAC, *Defense Appropriations, FY 1953*, p. 90.

76. SCAS, *Hearings, Military Situation in the Far East*, 82/1, 1951.

77. President Herbert Hoover's speech is reproduced in the *Congressional Record*. See C.R., 82/1, 1951, XCVII, Part 2, A773-75.

78. Senate, SCAS and SCFR, *Hearings, Assignment of Ground Forces of United States to Duty in European Area*, 82/1, 1951.

79. H. Rept. 1685, 82/2, 1952, pp. 81 ff.

80. HCA, Committee Print to Accompany H.R. 7391, 82/2, 1952, p. 7. See also C.R., 82/2, 1952, XCVIII, Part 3, 3624.

81. HCA, Committee Print to Accompany H.R. 7391, 82/2, 1952, p. 22.

82. *Ibid.*, p. 37.

83. *Ibid.*, p. 35.

84. See pp. 103–4 above.

85. HCA, Committee Print to Accompany H.R. 7391, 82/2, 1952, p. 49.

86. *Ibid.*, p. 71.

87. *Ibid.*, p. 49.

88. C.R., XCVIII, Part 3, 3630 ff.

89. *Ibid.*, 3620–21.

90. *Ibid.*, 3896–3902.

91. *Ibid.*, 3905.

92. SSAC, *Defense Appropriations, FY 1953*, pp. 214–15, 231–32, 235, 249–51, 290–92, 383–86, 575, 594–95.

93. See Robert Wallace, *Congressional Control of Federal Spending* (Detroit: Wayne State University Press, 1960), pp. 79–81, for a discussion of the final FY 1953 defense appropriations bill.

94. SSAC, *Defense Appropriations, FY 1953*, p. 221.

95. *Ibid.*, p. 227.

96. *Ibid.*, pp. 222–27.

97. *Ibid.*, p. 221.

98. Compare *ibid.*, pp. 538–86, and HCA, Committee Print to Accompany H.R. 7391, 82/2, 1952, p. 71.

99. SSAC, *Defense Appropriations, FY 1953*, p. 227.

100. *Ibid.*, pp. 776–826.

101. HCA, Committee Print to Accompany H.R. 7391, 82/2, 1952, p. 22.

102. S. Rept. 1861, 82/2, 1952, p. 25.

103. *Ibid.*, p. 7.

104. The Senate subcommittee granted the air force $150 million above its initial requests for personnel purposes, but did not extend the same benefits to the army and navy, explaining "that the cost of the military pay raise (Public Law 346) during *Fiscal Year* 1953 can be absorbed by the Department of Defense within the amounts of the appropriations recommended herein." *Ibid.*, p. 10. The same reasoning was not applied to the air force.

105. C.R., XCVIII, Part 7, 5435.

106. *Ibid.*, 8852.

107. *Ibid.*, 8613.

108. SSAC, *Defense Appropriations, FY 1953*, p. 344.

109. *Ibid.*, p. 884.

110. See the following pages which point up the economic orientation of the Senate subcommittee in its approach to the Defense Department's annual budget: *ibid.*, pp. 1, 21–22, 180, 196, 232–33, 324, 884, and C.R., XCVIII, Part 7, 8426.

111. HSAC, *Hearings, Department of the Air Force Appropriations, FY 1954*, 83/1, 1953, p. 958. News release of President Eisenhower reproduced in full.

112. *Ibid.*

113. *Ibid.*, p. 231. Speech of President published in part.

114. *Ibid.*, p. 230.

115. *Ibid.*, p. 229.

116. *Ibid.*, p. 252.

117. *Ibid.*, p. 310.

118. The Truman program called for a military force at the end of FY 1954 of 3,647,612; the Eisenhower recommendations were set at a level of 3,356,087. See HSAC, *Defense Appropriations, FY 1954*, p. 435.

119. HSAC, *Hearings, Department of the Army Appropriations, FY 1954*, 83/1, 1953, p. 59–68.

120. *Ibid.*, pp. 123, 33–34.

121. HSAC, *Hearings, Department of the Navy Appropriations, FY 1954*, 83/1, 1953, p. 252.

122. *Ibid.*, pp. 252, 371.

123. *Ibid.,* pp. 600–601, 1078.

124. *Ibid.,* pp. 756–57.

125. HSAC, *Defense Appropriations, FY 1954,* Part 1, p. 6.

126. SSAC, *Hearings, Defense Appropriations, FY 1594,* 83/1, 1953, Part 1, pp. 6–7.

127. HSAC, *Air Force Appropriations, FY 1954,* p. 958.

128. *Ibid.,* pp. 959–60.

129. SSAC, *Defense Appropriations, FY 1954,* Part 1, p. 277.

130. *Ibid.,* Emphasis added.

131. SSAC, *Defense Appropriations, FY 1954,* Part 1, p. 572.

132. HSAC, *Defense Appropriations, FY 1954,* p. 309.

133. SSAC, *Defense Appropriations, FY 1954,* Part 1, p. 35.

134. *Ibid.,* p. 566; HSAC, *Air Force Appropriations, FY 1954,* pp. 232–33.

135. *Ibid.,* p. 888; SSAC, *Defense Appropriations, FY 1954,* Part 1, p. 61.

136. *Ibid.,* pp. 531–32, 439.

137. *Ibid.,* p. 39.

138. *Ibid.,* p. 573.

139. C.R. 83/1, 1953, XCIX, Part 6, 7803, 7932; *ibid.,* XCIX, Part 7, 9394, 9452, 9480, 9494, 9499, 9580, 9585, 9603, 9616.

140. S. Rept. 601, 83/1, 1953; and H. Rept. 580, 83/1, 1953.

141. C.R., XCIX, Part 6, 7817.

142. Representative Mahon attempted to absolve the President from responsibility for the air force reductions. *Ibid.,* p. 7810.

143. *Ibid.,* Part 7, 9459.

144. *Ibid.,* Part 6, 7970; and *ibid.,* Part 7, pp. 9603, 9614.

145. H. Rept. 1015, 83/1, 1953; S. Doc. 77, 83/1, 1953, pp. 444–45.

146. H. Rept. 680, 83/1, 1953, p. 45.

CHAPTER V

1. For a more detailed description and analysis of the more than year-long process over which the New Look was formulated, see Glenn H. Snyder, "The New Look of 1953," *Strategy, Politics, and Defense Budgets,* ed. Warner Schilling, pp. 383–524. See also the various articles on the Eisenhower defense strategy published by *Fortune* during the 1950's and written by Charles J. V. Murphy. See especially the three-part article that appeared in the January, February, and March numbers of *Fortune* in 1956. They sketch the genesis of the New Look: "The

Eisenhower Shift, Part I." *Fortune,* LIII (January, 1956). 82–87+; Part II, *ibid.,* LIII (February, 1956). 110+; Part III. *ibid.,* LIII (March, 1956). 110+.

2. Emmet John Hughes, *The Ordeal of Power* (New York: Atheneum, 1963), p. 49.

3. Robert J. Donovan, *Eisenhower: The Inside Story* (New York, Harper, 1956), p. 17.

4. Opinion differs widely on the significance of the "Helena" voyage. Two accounts place great importance on this meeting. These include Donovan's *Eisenhower: The Inside Story* and Murphy, *Fortune,* LIII (March, 1956). Two participants at the conference—Admiral Arthur W. Radford and Emmet John Hughes —deny that the "Helena" trip produced, in the words of Mr. Hughes, "portentous 'strategic decisions.'" Hughes, p. 49; letter from Admiral Arthur W. Radford to the author, December 17, 1964. In his letter, Admiral Radford specifically denies Donovan's attribution that he had argued on the "Helena" that United States military power was "dangerously overextended" and that "too large a fraction of the U. S. power in being had been drawn . . . into exposed positions where it could be too easily pinned down." Donovan, p. 18. The discussion above is largely based on the views of Hughes and Radford.

5. Senator Robert Taft broke with the Truman administration and President Truman's JCS team on a number of key defense and foreign policy issues. See, for example, the Senate hearings on sending troops to Europe in 1951; SCFR and SCAS, *Hearings, Assignment of Ground Forces of the United States to Duty in the European Area,* 82/1, 1951. Testimony of General Bradley is found on pp. 126–52; Taft's, on pp. 603–66.

6. Matthew B. Ridgway, *Soldier* (New York: Harper, 1956), p. 267.

7. Snyder, "The New Look of 1953," p. 414.

8. *Ibid.,* pp. 415–18.

9. Murphy, "Defense and Strategy," *Fortune,* XLVIII (December, 1953), 78; Snyder, "The New Look of 1953," pp. 423–25.

10. Murphy, "Defense and Strategy," *Fortune* XLVIII, 78; Snyder, "The New Look of 1953," 424–25.

11. *Ibid.,* p. 437.

12. Murphy, "Defense and Strategy," *Fortune,* XLVIII, 78 ff; Snyder, "The New Look of 1953," pp. 429–42.

13. Taylor, *The Uncertain Trumpet,* p. 21.

14. B.B., *U.S. Budget, FY 1955,* p. M39.

15. HSAC, *Hearings, Department of the Navy Appropriations, FY 1955,* 83/2, 1954, pp. 17, 41.

16. HSAC, *Hearings, Department of Defense Appropriations, FY 1955,* 83/2, 1954, p. 116.

17. H. Doc. 436, 85/2, 1958, p. 121. Expenditures totaled $1.7 billion in FY 1952; $1.8 billion in FY 1953; and $1.9 billion in FY 1954.

18. B.B., *U.S. Budget, FY 1955*, p. M47.

19. The increase in army strength from 1,164,000 to 1,172,700 is accounted for by the addition of ROTC graduates who otherwise would not have had billets.

20. B.B., *U.S. Budget, FY 1955*, p. M43.

21. For a general summary of how the decision was reached in the executive branch to increase continental defense, see Huntington, *The Common Defense*, pp. 326–41. See also Snyder, "The New Look of 1953," pp. 420–22.

22. B.B., *U.S. Budget, FY 1955*, p. M5; HSAC, *Hearings, Department of the Army Appropriations, FY 1955*, 83/2, 1954, pp. 2–3.

23. SCAS, *Hearings, A National Reserve Plan*, 84/1, 1955, p. 304.

24. SSAC, *Hearings, Department of Defense Appropriations, FY 1955*, 83/2, 1954, p. 83.

25. Ridgway, *Soldier*, p. 289.

26. B.B., *U.S. Budget, FY 1955*, p. M39.

27. *Ibid.*

28. C.R., 83/2, 1954, C, Part 6, 8324.

29. B.B., *U.S. Budget, FY 1955*, p. M38.

30. H. Doc. 1, 83/2, 1954, p. 2.

31. John Foster Dulles, "The Evolution of Foreign Policy," *Department of State Bulletin*, XXX, No. 761 (January 25, 1954), 108. Italics are Dulles'.

32. *Ibid.*

33. *Ibid.*

34. HSAC, *Army Appropriations, FY 1955*, p. 54.

35. *Ibid.*, p. 42.

36. Edward L. Katzenbach, Jr., "How Congress Strains at Gnats, Then Swallows Military Budgets," *The Reporter*, XI, No. 2 (July 20, 1954), 35.

37. HSAC, *Army Appropriations, FY 1955*, p. 43. Emphasis added.

38. *Ibid.*, p. 57.

39. *Ibid.*, p. 43.

40. *Ibid.*, p. 54.

41. See testimony of Ridgway, HSAC, *Hearings, Department of the Army Appropriations, FY 1956*, 84/1, 1955, pp. 10–116, especially pp. 23–24.

42. Ibid., pp. 41 ff: Ridgway, *Soldier*, pp. 286–94; and Matthew B. Ridgway, "My Battles in War and Peace: Conflict in the Pentagon," *Saturday Evening Post*, CCXXVIII, No. 30 (January 21, 1956), 46 ff.

43. HSAC, *Army Appropriations, FY 1955*, p. 44.

44. SSAC, *Hearing, Department of Defense Appropriations, FY 1955*, 82/2, 1954, p. 476.

45. *Ibid.,* p. 44.

46. C.R., C, Part 6, 8341.

47. H. Rept. 1545, 83/2, 1954, p. 3.

48. S. Rept. 1582, 83/2, 1954, p. 2.

49. H. Rept. 1917, 83/2, 1954.

50. C.R., C, Part 4, 5669, 5678, 5682–84.

51. *Ibid.,* 5675; *ibid.,* C, Part 5, 5749, 5760–61.

52. *Ibid.,* Part 4, 5675–78.

53. *Ibid.,* 5682.

54. *Ibid.,* Part 5, 5751.

55. *Ibid.,* 5758.

56. *Ibid.,* 5760.

57. *Ibid.,* 5771–80. In the spring of 1954, in the midst of Congress' review of the New Look budget, the French position in Indo-China rapidly deteriorated with the fall of Dien Bien Phu to communist forces. A meeting was held at the State Department of April 10 for congressional leaders, informing them of administration plans to intervene with American arms to save the French position. Under sharp congressional questioning, Secretary of State John Foster Dulles and JCS Chairman Admiral Arthur Radford admitted that the Joint Chiefs of Staff had not approved the venture and that the United States had not secured the support of its major allies, the United Kingdom and France, to intervene. Congressmen attending the secret meeting rejected Radford's recommendation to enter the fighting in Indo-China on these two grounds. General Ridgway's resistance to the idea of intervention was the most clearly defined of the Joint Chiefs. He is reported to have estimated that the United States would have to commit 500,000 men a year and accept casualties of 25,000 a month if it intervened in Indo-China. See Ridgway, *Soldier,* pp. 274–78 and the revealing article of Chalmers Roberts, "The Day We Didn't Go to War," *Reporter,* XI (September 14, 1954), 31–32; also Charles J. V. Murphy, "America's New Strategic Situation," *Fortune,* L (August, 1954), 70–74.

58. C.R., C, Part 5, 5777.

59. *Ibid.,* 5780.

60. *Ibid.,* Part 4, 5684.

61. *Ibid.,* 5685.

62. *Ibid.,* 5674.

63. *Ibid.,* 5684.

64. *Ibid.,* 5685.

65. *Ibid.,* Part 6, 8324–27.

66. *Ibid.,* 8433.

67. *Ibid.,* Part 6, 8324.

68. *Loc. cit.* In some sense, it would be more precise to say that the New Look emphasis on atomic weapons and its de-emphasis on ground forces tended to follow the already established British shift in this direction. Even before the Eisenhower administration took office, British defense officials held talks with the Truman JCS in an attempt to persuade the United States to cutback ground forces for NATO and to concentrate on building atomic delivery forces as the British had decided to do. See Charles J. V. Murphy, "Defense and Strategy," *Fortune*, XLVIII (December, 1953), pp. 82 ff.

69. C.R., C., Part 6, 8442.

70. Ridgway, *Soldier*, p. 277.

71. *Ibid.*

72. C.R., 84/1, 1955, CI, Part 1, 600.

73. *Ibid.*

74. B.B., *U.S. Budget, FY 1956*, p. M29.

75. Said Admiral Radford: "Our planning does not subscribe to the thinking that the ability to deliver massive atomic retaliation is, by itself, adequate to meet all our security needs. It is correct to say we are relying exclusively on one weapon, or one service, or that we are anticipating one kind of war. I believe that this nation could be a prisoner of its own military posture if it had no capability, other than one to deliver a massive atomic attack." Quoted in H. Doc. 100, 85/1, 1957, p. 41.

76. HSAC, *Hearings, Department of the Army Appropriations, FY 1956*, 84/1 1955, pp. 23–26. H. Rept. 493, 84/1, 1955, p. 10.

77. *Ibid.*, p. 31.

78. B.B., *U.S. Budget, FY 1956*, p. M18–M19. Also H. Rept. 493, 84/1, 1955, p. 61.

79. HSAC, *Army Appropriations, FY 1956*, p. 27.

80. H. Rept. 493, 84/1, 1955, pp. 58–61.

81. HSAC, *Hearings, Department of Defense Appropriations, FY 1956*, 84/1, 1955, p. 74.

82. *Ibid.*, pp. 70–74.

83. SSAC, *Hearings, Department of Defense Appropriations, FY 1956*, 84/1, 1955, p. 59.

84. *Ibid.*, p. 71.

85. See *Ibid.*, pp. 58–59, 91, 118, 125, 157–60, 198–202, 215–22; HSAC, *Defense Appropriations, FY 1956*, pp. 1–171; and HSAC, *Army Appropriations, FY 1956*, pp. 10–117. The more acute congressional awareness of the policy issues that were raised by the FY 1956 budget are suggested in the citations noted herein.

86. HSAC, *Defense Appropriations, FY 1956*, pp. 31–32, 66–67, 109, 183, 222, 252, and 493.

87. See Samuel P. Huntington, *Soldier and the State*, pp. 169–177; Martha Derthick, "Military Lobby in the Missile Age: The Politics of the National Guard,"

Changing Patterns of Military Politics, ed. Samuel P. Huntington (New York: Free Press, 1962), pp. 190–235; *idem, The National Guard in Politics* (Cambridge: Harvard University Press, 1965).

88. SASC, *Hearings, A National Reserve Plan,* 84/1, 1955.

89. HSAC, *Defense Appropriations, FY 1956,* pp. 24, 33, 75, 109, 168.

90. *Ibid.,* pp. 23, 29, 109, 154.

91. *Ibid.,* p. 165.

92. HSAC, *Army Appropriations, FY 1956,* p. 45. Gordon L. Craig, "Germany and NATO: The Rearmament Debate, 1950–58," *NATO and American Security,* ed. Klaus Knorr (Princeton: Princeton University Press, 1959), pp. 236–59.

93. HSAC, *Army Appropriations, FY 1956,* p. 648a.

94. H. Rept. 493, 84/1, 1955, p. 3.

95. *Ibid.,* pp. 3–4.

96. *Ibid.,* pp. 56–61; S. Rept. 545, 84/1, 1955, pp. 10–15.

97. C.R., CI, Part 6, 6228–36.

98. *Ibid.,* Part 7, 8682, 8705.

99. S. Doc. 88, 84/1, 1955, pp. 596–97.

100. B.B., *U.S. Budget, FY 1957.*

101. HSAC, *Hearings, Department of Defense Appropriations, FY 1957,* 84/2, 1956, p. 2.

102. S. Doc. 146, 84/2, 1956, pp. 768–69.

103. See Ridgway, *Soldier;* and *idem, Saturday Evening Post,* CCXXVIII, 17–19, 46–48.

104. HSAC, *Defense Appropriations, FY 1957,* p. 110.

105. *Ibid.,* pp. 126–30.

106. *Ibid.,* pp. 564–75.

107. *Ibid.,* pp. 40–41.

108. H. Rept. 2104, 84/2, 1956, p. 40.

109. HSAC, *Defense Appropriations, FY 1957, passim.* These hearings should not be confused with those held separately for the army, navy, and air force. See n. 16, above.

110. Compare SSAC, *Hearings, Department of Defense Appropriations, FY 1957,* 84/2, 1956, with the following: (1) HSAC, *Defense Appropriations, FY 1957;* (2) HSAC, *Defense Appropriations, FY 1957,* 84/2, 1956; (3) HSAC, *Hearings, Department of the Navy Appropriations, FY 1957,* 84/2, 1956; (4) HSAC, *Hearings, Department of the Air Force Appropriations, FY 1957,* 84/2, 1956.

111. SCAS, *Hearings, Study of Air Power,* 84/2, 1956. Also, SCAS, *Airpower, Report of the Subcommittee on the Air Force.* Committee Print, 85/1, 1957.

112. HSAC, *Defense Appropriations, FY 1957*, pp. 433–34. The army argument and budgetary proposals which are summarized above are based on the testimony of Generals Taylor and Ridgway before the House Subcommittee on Defense Department Appropriations. See *ibid.*, pp. 432–558, 559–641. A useful summary of the army's position may be found in Taylor, *The Uncertain Trumpet*, pp. 32–46, 92 ff.

113. Charles J. V. Murphy, "The New Air Situation," *Fortune*, LII (September, 1955), 87.

114. *Washington Post*, August 21, 1955, p. E5.

115. "Red Rocket Know-how Matches Ours," *Nation's Business*, Vol., XLIII, February, 1955.

116. *Washington Star*, February 12, 1956, p. A25. Emphasis added.

117. Charles J. V. Murphy, *Fortune*, LII, 87.

118. SCAS, *Airpower Report*, p. 10.

119. *Ibid.*

120. SSAC, *Defense Appropriations, FY 1957*, p. 1225.

121. See LeMay's testimony, *ibid.*, pp. 1221–50.

122. HSAC, *Defense Appropriations, FY 1957*, p. 2. See also the following pages for further House commentary on the missile progrom: pp. 51–54, 84–86, 290–91, 445–67, 470–71, 512, 515, 574, 673, 710–12, 738–39, 743, 786–817, 869–908, 928, 932–33, 937–39, 949–51, 960–61, 1130–31, 1211–36.

123. *Ibid.*, p. 872.

124. *Ibid.*, p. 879.

125. Trevor Gardner, "Our Guided Missile Crisis," *Look*, XX (May 15, 1956), 46. Examine, too, his "Must Our Air Force Be Second Best?" *Look*, XX (May 1, 1956), 77–83.

126. S. Rept. 2260, 84/2, 1956, pp. 5–6, 14; S. Doc. 146, 84/2, 1956, pp. 768–69.

127. SCAS, *Airpower Hearings*, 84/2, 1956, Part 21, pp. 1587–88; H. Rept. 2104, 84/2, 1956, p. 40.

128. C.R., CIII, Part 1, 402; SCAS, *Airpower Hearings*, Part 21, pp. 1556–58, 1587–88; S. Rept. 545, 84/1, 1955, p. 6.

129. S. Doc. 146, 84/2, 1956, pp. 768–69.

130. *Ibid.*

131. *Ibid.*

132. *Ibid.*, p. 843.

133. Gordon Harrison, "Wanted: More Politics in Defense," *Harper's Magazine*, CCXIII, No. 1276 (September, 1956), 55.

134. B.B., *U.S. Budget, FY 1958*, pp. M27–M29.

135. SCAS, *Airpower Report*, p. 10.

136. HSAC, *Hearings, Department of Defense Appropriations, FY 1958,* 85/1, 1957, p. 411. Emphasis added.

137. *Ibid.,* p. 558.

138. *Ibid.,* p. 568.

139. H. Rept. 471, 85/1, 1957, p. 44.

140. *Ibid.,* pp. 43–44.

141. HSAC, *Defense Appropriations, FY 1958,* pp. 904–905.

142. *Ibid.*

143. HSAC, *Hearings, Department of the Air Force Appropriations, FY 1958,* 85/1, 1957, pp. 230–31.

144. H. Doc. 1, 85/1, 1957, p. 3.

145. HCA, *Hearings, The Budget for 1958,* 85/1, 1957, p. 5.

146. *Ibid.*

147. C.R., 85/1, 1957, CIII, Part 1, 1374.

148. HSAC, *Defense Appropriations, FY 1958,* p. 943.

149. HCA, *The Budget for 1958, pp.* 43–44.

150. C.R., CIII, Part 6, 7605.

151. *Ibid.,* 7894.

152. S. Doc. 67, 85/1, 1957, pp. 430–31.

153. *Ibid.*

154. H. Rept. 471, 85/1, 1957; S. Rept. 543, 85/1, 1957.

155. The efforts of some legislators who criticized the dominance of fiscal consideration in the defense budget proved unavailing. See remarks of Senator Stuart Symington, C.R., CIII, Part 8, 10621.

156. HSAC, *Defense Appropriations, FY 1958,* p. 419.

157. *Ibid.,* pp. 419–20.

158. Taylor, *The Uncertain Trumpet,* pp. 181–97.

159. HSAC, *Defense Appropriations, FY 1958,* p. 2066.

160. *Ibid.,* p. 124.

161. H. Rept. 471, 85/1, 1957, p. 6.

162. See HSAC, *Defense Appropriations, FY 1958,* pp. 20–23, 124–26, 299, 418–20, 425, 2065. The Senate largely passed over the question of atomic weapons. For a discussion of the possible consequences resulting from the use of atomic weapons in limited war situations which appeared during the late 1950's, see Osgood, *Limited War,* pp. 251 ff. For a different view, see Henry A. Kissinger, *Nuclear Weapons and Foreign Policy* (New York: Harper, 1957), pp. 174–232. Professor Kissinger subsequently revised his views in his *The Necessity for Choice* (New York: Harper, 1961). For a briefer statement of Professor Kissinger's later views

on nuclear weaponry which parallel those of Osgood's, see *idem*, "Limited War: Nuclear or Conventional?—A Reappraisal." *Arms Control, Disarmament, and National Security,* ed. Donald G. Brennan (New York: Braziller, 1961), pp. 138–52.

163. C.R., CIII, Part 6, 7619.

164. HSAC, *Defense Appropriations, FY 1958,* p. 2049.

165. *Ibid.,* p. 425.

166. *Ibid.,* pp. 1135, 2029.

167. H. Rept. 471, 85/1, p. 6.

168. Ibid., pp. 94–107. See also, HSAC, *Defense Appropriations, FY 1958,* pp. 1289–92.

169. H. Rept. 471, 85/1, 1957, p. 20.

170. HSAC, *Defense Appropriations, FY 1958,* pp. 13–17.

CHAPTER VI

1. James Gavin, *War and Peace in the Space Age* (New York: Harper, 1958), p. 19. General Gavin cites a figure of $700 million. The precise sum quoted here is furnished through the courtesy of Colonel Charles H. Donnelly, senior specialist, Legislative Reference Service.

2. Herman Kahn, *On Thermonuclear War* (Princeton: Princeton University Press, 1960), pp. 311 ff.

3. Department of Defense Release, No. 344–60, April 4, 1960.

4. H. Doc. 335, 88/2, 1964, pp. 156–57.

5. John Stoessinger, *Financing The United Nations System* (Washington: Brookings, 1964).

6. Noted a Gallup Poll release of March 2, 1960: "A growing number of Americans in recent months have come to believe that the No. 1 problem facing the country today is the state of our military defenses. Just last fall—before the advent of the debate on the issue now raging in Washington—only one person in a hundred interviewed by the Gallup Poll cited our lagging behind Russia in missiles, rockets and other aspects of military preparedness as what he felt is American's No. 1 problem.

"Today, fifteen in every hundred . . . single out the 'missile lag' or other areas in our defense setup where they feel the U. S. trails Russia. . . .

"But the fact that an increased number cite our military defense specifically does indicate that the Washington debate is having some impact on the 'grass roots'— and this has particular election-year significance."

7. See Chapter VIII for a discussion of these functions.

8. H. Doc. 100, 85/1, 1957, pp. 39–41.

9. C.R., 85/2, 1958, CIV, Part 13, 16515–16; *ibid,* Part 14, 19524–29; H. Rept. 1830, 85/2, 1958, pp. 64–65; S. Rept. 1937, 85/2, 1958, p. 13; H. Rept. 462,

87/1, 1961, pp. 3–5; H. Rept. 1607, 87/1, 1961, p. 61; H. Rept. 873, 87/1, 1961, pp. 6–7; S. Rept. 653, 87/1, 1961, pp. 31–32.

10. S. Rept. 1937, 85/2, 1958, p. 6; S. Rept. 476, 86/1, 1959, p. 17; C.R., 1958, CIV, Part 13, 16515; *ibid.* 1959, CV, Part 12, 15072; *ibid.* 1960, CVI, Part 14, 19527–29.

11. See H. Doc. 335, 88/2, 1964, p. 158.

12. C.R., CIV, Part 14, 17701.

13. *Loc. cit.*

14. *Loc. cit.*

15. S. Rept. 1982, 85/2, 1958, p. 4.

16. For a discussion of the intervention of the armed services committees, particularly the Senate Armed Services Committee, into defense policy, examine Raymond H. Dawson, "Congressional Innovation and Intervention in Defense Policy: Legislative Authorization of Weapon Systems," *American Political Science Review*, LVI, No. 1 (March, 1962), 42–57; and Bernard Gordon, "The Military Budget: Congressional Phase," *Journal of Politics*, XXIII, No. 3 (August, 1961), 689–710; and H. Rept. 1406, 87/2, pp. 1–9.

17. SNPM, *Hearings, Organizing for National Security*, 1961, 3 vols.

18. Henry Rowen, *National Security and the American Economy in the 1960's*, Study Paper No. 18 for the Joint Economic Committee, 86/2, 1960.

19. HCGO, *Hearings, Civil Defense*, 85/2, 1958.

20. HCGO, *Hearings, Organization and Management of Missile Programs*, 86/1, 1959.

21. *Washington Post*, March 8, 1959, p. A1; *Washington Star*, February 14, 1960, p. C1; *New York Times*, February 9, 1960, pp. 1, 8; SSAC, *Hearings, Department of Defense Appropriations, FY 1960*, 86/1, 1959, p. 33.

22. Evidence of voter concern in 1958 over defense and foreign policy is to be found in Roger Hilsman, "The Foreign Policy Consensus," *Journal of Conflict Resolution* (December, 1959), especially p. 372.

23. SSAC, *Hearings, Department of Defense Appropriations, FY 1960*, 86/1, 1959, p. 33.

24. Maxwell Taylor, *The Uncertain Trumpet* (New York: Harper, 1959); John Medaris, *Countdown for Decision* (New York: Putnam, 1960); and n. 1, above.

25. *Washington Post*, December 20, 1957, pp. A1, A19.

26. Rockefeller Brothers Fund, *International Security: The Military Aspect*, especially pp. 62–64.

27. H. Doc. 1, *State of the Union Message*, 85/2, 1958, p. 2.

28. *Ibid.*, p. 5.

29. BB, *Budget, FY 1959*, p. M8.

30. H. Doc. 364, 85/2, 1958.

31. S. Doc. 103, 85/2, 1958.

32. B.B., *U.S. Budget, FY 1959*, p. M8.

33. *Ibid.*, p. M5.

34. C. R., CIV, Part 12, 10186.

35. HSAC, *Hearings, Supplemental Defense Appropriations for 1958*, 85/2, 1958, pp. 282 ff.

36. C.R., CIV, Part 13, 16551.

37. HSAC, *Hearings Department of Defense Appropriations, FY 1959*, 85/2, 1958, Part 1, pp. 515–20.

38. *Ibid.*, p. 593.

39. H. Rept. 1830, 85/2, 1958, pp. 46–53.

40. HSAC, *Defense Appropriations, FY 1959*, Part 1, p. 130.

41. *Ibid.*, pp. 122, 130, 157, 189–92, 210.

42. HSAC, *Supplemental Defense Appropriations, FY 1958*, pp. 81 ff.

43. HSAC, *Defense Appropriations, FY 1959*, Part 1, pp. 831–48.

44. Quoted from Richard F. Fenno, Jr., *The House Appropriations Committee as a Political System: The Problem of Integration*, paper delivered at the annual meeting of the American Political Science Association, September 6–9, 1961, p. 4.

45. Wallace, especially pp. 65–127, describes the various devices employed by the appropriations committees to create the impression that they have economized without having actually affected basic government programs.

46. C.R., CIV, Part 8, 10016. See also similar remarks of the ranking Republican of the House subcommittee. *Ibid.*, CIV, Part 8, 10020–21.

47. HSAC, *Hearings, Supplemental Defense Appropriations, FY 1958*, pp. 1–25; H. Rept. 1288, 85/2, 1958, pp. 1–3.

48. C.R., CIV, Part 1, 714–45, 914–16.

49. *Ibid.*, 714–45.

50. *Ibid.*, 914–16.

51. HSAC, *Defense Appropriations, FY 1959*, Part 1, p. 353.

52. *Ibid.*, pp. 44–107.

53. SSAC, *Hearings, Department of Defense Appropriations, FY 1959*, 85/2, 1958, pp. 832–48.

54. See, for example, HSAC, *Defense Appropriations, FY 1959*, Part 1, pp. 341–45.

55. *Ibid.*, p. 364.

56. *Ibid.*, p. 353.

57. *Ibid.*, p. 356.

58. *Ibid.*, p. 357.

59. *Ibid.*, p. 358.

60. *Ibid.*, p. 359.

61. *Ibid.*, p. 361.

62. *Ibid.*, pp. 387–89.

63. *Ibid.*, pp. 490–91.

64. *Ibid.*, pp. 491–94.

65. H. Rept. 1830, 85/2, 1958, p. 9.

66. S. Rept. 1937, 85/2, 1958, p. 13.

67. C.R., CIV, Part 8, 10180.

68. *Ibid.*, 10190.

69. *Ibid.*, Part 12, 15583.

70. H. Rept. 1830, 85/2, 1958, p. 4.

71. B.B., *U.S. Budget, FY 1960*, p. M27. See also *New York Times*, January 25, 1959, p. E5; Taylor, *The Uncertain Trumpet*, pp. 65–66.

72. B.B., *U.S. Budget, FY 1960*, pp. M30, 445–49.

73. HSAC, *Hearings, Department of Defense Appropriations, FY 1960*, 86/1, 1959, Part 1, pp. 18, 43.

74. H. Rept. 408, 86/1, 1959, p. 12.

75. See Table 10 above.

76. HSAC, *Defense Appropriations, FY 1960*, Part 1, p. 365.

77. B.B., *U.S. Budget, FY 1960*, p. 445.

78. *Ibid.*, p. 447.

79. HSAC, *Defense Appropriations, FY 1960*, Part 1, p. 98. Taylor's speech is herein reprinted.

80. H. Doc. 1, *State of the Union*, 86/1, 1959, pp. 3–4. Emphasis added.

81. B.B., *U.S. Budget, FY 1960*, p. M5.

82. *Ibid.*, M22–M23. President Eisenhower's request for an item veto had a long history. Presidents Grant, Hayes, Arthur, Wilson, and Franklin Roosevelt had made similar overtures to Congress and had been similarly turned down.

83. SSAC, *Hearings, Department of Defense Appropriations FY 1960*, 86/1, 1960, p. 102.

84. SCAS, Preparedness Subcommittee, *Hearings, Major Defense Matters*, 86/1, 1959, Parts 1–2. The memorandum of the Joint Chiefs is published in the *New York Times*, March 9, 1959, p. 14.

85. *Ibid.*

86. HSAC, *Defense Appropriations, FY 1960*, Part 1, pp. 374–75; SCAS, Preparedness Subcommittee, *Major Defense Matters*, Part 1, pp. 45–46.

87. See testimony of General Maxwell Taylor, *ibid.*, pp. 296 ff., and of General Lyman L. Lemnitzer, SSAC, *Defense Appropriations, FY 1960*, pp. 67 ff.

88. *New York Times*, March 9, 1959, p. 14; HSAC, *Defense Appropriations, FY 1960*, Part 1, pp. 471 ff., especially pp. 471–517.

89. *Ibid.*, p. 491.

90. *New York Times*, March 15, 1959, p. E3; William W. Kaufmann, *The McNamara Strategy*, (New York: Harper, 1964), p. 26.

91. *Ibid.*, March 9, 1959, p. 14; HSAC, *Defense Appropriations, FY 1960*, Part 1, pp. 785–986; SCAS, Preparedness Subcommittee, *Major Defense Matters*, Part 1, pp. 81–82.

92. See for example, HSAC, *Defense Appropriations, FY 1960*, Part 1, p. 330.

93. SCAS, Preparedness Subcommittee, *Major Defense Matters*, Part 1, pp. 44–45.

94. *Ibid.*, p. 138; HSAC, *Defense Appropriations, FY 1960*, Part 1, pp. 44–45.

95. SSAC, *Defense Appropriations, FY 1960*, p. 253.

96. HSAC, *Defense Appropriations, FY 1960*, Part 1, p. 518.

97. *Ibid.*, p. 296.

98. *Ibid.*, p. 330.

99. *Ibid.*

100. SSAC, *Defense Appropriation, FY 1960*, p. 254.

101. *Ibid.*

102. For a general commentary on the defense policy process during this period of ferment, see Morton Halperin, "The Gaither Committee and the Policy Process," *World Politics*, XIII, No. 3 (April, 1961), 360-84.

103. *New York Times*, January 6, 1959, pp. 1, 4.

104. Quoted in C.R., February 5, 1959, p. 1715, Daily Edition.

105. *New York Times*, January 11, 1959, p. 14.

106. Quoted from the *Washington Post*, March 8, 1959, p. Al.

107. *Washington Post*, January 5, 1959, p. Al; *ibid.*, March 12, 1959, p. Al.

108. *New York Times*, January 30, 1959, p. 3.

109. Interview with staff personnel, Senate defense appropriations subcommittee, December 9, 1959.

110. HSAC, *Defense Appropriations, FY 1960*, Part 1, pp. 78, 131, 331–36, 343, 430–33, 827.

111. *Ibid.*, p. 334.

112. H. Rept. 408, 86/1, 1959, pp. 10–11. See also comments in Senate. C.R., July 13, 1959, pp. 12002–4, Daily Edition.

113. C.R., June 3, 1959, p. 8741, Daily Edition.

114. SSAC, *Defense Appropriations, FY 1960*, p. 33.

115. C.R., June 2, 1959, p. 8649, Daily Edition.

116. H. Rept. 408, 86/1, 1959, p. 16.

117. C.R., September 1, 1960, p. 1959, Daily Edition. For discussions of the air defense problem in Congress, see Dawson, *American Political Science Review*, LVI, 42–57; H. Doc. 432, 86/2, 1960, pp. 25–26, 41–47; S. Rept. 296, 86/1, 1959; and particularly, S. Rept. 434, 86/1, 1959.

118. Albert Wohlstetter had already raised many of these issues in his very influential article in *Foreign Affairs* of a few months before. Albert Wohlstetter, "The Delicate Balance of Terror," *Foreign Affairs*, XXXVII, No. 2 (January, 1959), 211–35.

119. HSAC, *Defense Appropriations*, Part 1, pp. 72–73.

120. H. Rept. 1561, 86/2, 1960, p. 8.

121. H. Rept. 408, 86/1, 1959, pp. 12–14, 16–17.

122. C.R., June 2, 1959, pp. 8645–54; *ibid.*, June 3, pp. 8741–56, *passim.* Daily Edition.

123. See pp. 233–34 above.

124. C.R., June 2, 1959, p. 8643, Daily Edition.

125. *Ibid.*, June 3, 1959, p. 8756, Daily Edition.

126. *Ibid.*, August 4, 1959, p. 13791, Daily Edition.

127. *Ibid.*, p. 13795, Daily Edition.

128. *Washington Post*, July 14, 1959, p. A5. For other Democratic criticism of President Eisenhower, see *ibid.*, May 21, 1959, p. A10.

129. B.B., *U.S. Budget, FY 1961*, pp. M1–M27, 435–42. *New York Times*, January 19, 1960, pp. 17–22, reproduces the President's budget message.

130. *Ibid.*, p. 18.

131. *Ibid.*

132. HSAC, *Hearings, Department of Defense Appropriations, FY 1961*, 86/2, 1960, Part 1, p. 25.

133. *Ibid.*, p. 23.

134. A distinction should be kept in mind between the total funds actually appropriated by Congress vis-à-vis the administration's requests and the shifts in program funds which Congress makes within the total figures that it appropriates. In the FY 1961 budget, Congress passed a defense bill that closely approximated the administration's request, but, within this sum, it made total additions and subtractions of $4 billion that canceled each other out.

135. HSAC, *Defense Appropriations, FY 1961*, Part 1, p. 56; SSAC, *Hearings, Department of Defense Appropriations, FY 1961*, 86/2, 1960, Part 1, p. 14.

136. See p. 265 above.

137. C.R., 86/2, 1960, CVI, Part 8, 12789.

138. Senate, Preparedness Investigating Subcommittee of the Senate Armed Services Committee and Committee on Aeronautical and Space Sciences, *Hearings, Missiles, Space, and Other Major Defense Matters*, 86/2, 1960, p. 1.

139. Quoted in *ibid.*, p. 4.

140. Quoted in *ibid.*, p. 11.

141. *Ibid.*, p. 187.

142. HSAC, *Defense Appropriations, FY 1961*, Part 2, p. 72.

143. SNPM, *Hearings, Organizing for National Security*, 1961, I, 20–21.

144. Interview with a member of the House defense appropriations subcommittee, May, 1960.

145. SSAC, *Defense Appropriations, FY 1961*, Part 2, p. 1574.

146. See Chapter IV, pp. 147, 151 above.

147. HSAC, *Defense Appropriations, FY 1961*, Part 2, p. 243.

148. C.R., CVI, Part 8, 12822.

149. H. Rept. 1561, 86/2, 1960, p. 24.

150. *Ibid.*, p. 25.

151. C.R., CVI, Part 12, 16026–37, 16387–88.

152. *Washington Star*, October 1, 1960, p. A1.

153. *Ibid.*, October 26, 1960, p. A20.

154. C.R., CVI, Part 12, 16027.

155. *New York Times*, August 9, 1960, p. 14.

156. C.R., CVI, Part 12, 16037.

CHAPTER VII

1. Aside from primary sources, a number of secondary sources which deal with the policy and process changes inaugurated by Secretary of Defense Robert McNamara have been consulted. Of these the most useful have been William W. Kaufman, *The McNamara Strategy* (New York: Harper, 1964) and the excellent yearly summaries of defense policy that are prepared by Colonel H. Donnelly, senior specialist of the Legislative Reference Service. Colonel Donnelly's studies include exhaustive bibliographies of defense materials that have appeared during the year. Colonel Donnelly's studies between 1961 and 1963 may be found under the following headings: H. Doc. 502, 87/2, 1962; H. Doc. 155, 88/1, 1963; and H. Doc. 335, 88/2, 1964.

2. General Maxwell Taylor makes this point in his *The Uncertain Trumpet*. He restated his criticism of massive retaliation in testimony before the House Subcommittee on Department of Defense Appropriations in his capacity as chairman

of the Joint Chiefs of Staff: "It seems to me the more balanced approach to our requirements, whereby we provide amply for the strategic deterrent, for conventional forces and for this new factor, counterinsurgency forces, gives much greater strength to our national posture. Our negotiators—our President, our Secretary of State—can do many things, backed by this kind of flexible force, which they never could have done in the days when massive retaliation was virtually the sole military response." HSAC, *Hearings, Department of Defense Appropriations, FY 1964,* 88/1, 1963, Part 1, pp. 227–28.

3. *Ibid.,* Part 1, pp. 228, 111. See also speech of Defense Secretary Robert McNamara to the American Society of Newspaper Editors, April 20, 1963.

4. H. Doc. 123, 87/1, 1961, p. 4.

5. See pp. 198–99 above.

6. See, for example, HSAC, *Hearings, Department of Defense Appropriations, FY 1962,* 87/1, 1961, Part 3, pp. 18–20, 150–67; *idem, Defense Appropriations, FY 1964,* Part 1, pp. 90–106.

7. HCAS, *Hearings, Authorizing Appropriations for Aircraft, Missiles, and Naval Vessels for the Armed Forces,* 87/1, 1961, p. 1249. In its report the House Armed Services Committee refers also to strategic nuclear forces as the shield, not the sword, of Western deterrence and defense. H. Rept. 380, 87/1, 1961, p. 25. Professor Henry Kissinger states the relation between NATO "shield" and "sword" forces during the Eisenhower administration: "To understand the European reaction to . . . [flexible response] it is important to compare them with what has heretofore been traditional NATO doctrine. Until the advent of the Kennedy administration the ground forces in Central Europe had been considered the 'shield' and the nuclear forces the 'sword.' It was part of NATO doctrine that a massive attack on Central Europe would be met with some form of nuclear retaliation practically from the outset; the conventional forces were to deal only with minor probes. It was never considered that a full-scale conventional defense of Europe should be attempted." The case against the administration is overstated. The departure from "traditional NATO doctrine" under the Kennedy administration, while significant, was not as great as Kissinger suggests. See Chapters V and VI above. The quote is drawn from p. 23 of Henry A. Kissinger, "NATO's Nuclear Dilemma," *The Reporter,* XXVIII, No. 7 (March 28, 1963), 22–37.

8. Kaufmann, *The McNamara Strategy,* pp. 66–67.

9. Speech of Defense Secretary Robert McNamara to the Economics Club of New York, November 18, 1963.

10. HSAC, *Defense Appropriations, FY 1964,* Part 1, pp. 101–2.

11. SCFR, *Hearings, Foreign Assistance Act of 1962,* 87/2, 1962, pp. 55 ff.

12. *Army Times,* February 5, 1965, p. 5. That President Kennedy was personally concerned about the problem of American preparedness to combat communist subversion and guerrilla warfare is suggested in Hugh Sidey's biography. Hugh Sidey, *John F. Kennedy: President* (New York: Crest, 1964), pp. 74–86, 150.

13. SSAC, *Hearings, Department of Defense Appropriations, FY 1962,* 87/1, 1961, p. 26.

14. See pp. 296–98 above.

15. For a general discussion of Defense Secretary McNamara's thinking about nuclear war, see Kaufmann, *The McNamara Strategy,* especially pp. 47–134, 300–313; and Harold B. Moulton, "The McNamara General War Strategy," *Orbis,* VIII, No. 2 (Summer, 1964), 238–54. For a critique of McNamara's earlier views, see Michael Brower, "Controlled Nuclear War," *New Republic,* CXLVII, No. 4 (July 30, 1962), 9–15; *idem,* "Nuclear Strategy of the Kennedy Administration," *Bulletin of the Atomic Scientists,* XVIII, No. 8 (October, 1962), 34–41. For a general critique of Kennedy administration defense policies, especially as they affect NATO strategy, see the following articles by Henry A. Kissinger: "Strains on the Alliance," *Foreign Affairs,* XLI, No. 2, (January, 1963), 261–85; "Coalition Diplomacy in a Nuclear Age," *ibid.,* XLII, No. 4 (July, 1964), 525–45. See also n. 7, above, and S. Doc. 21, *Problems and Trends in Atlantic Partnership, II,* 88/1, 1963.

16. HSAC, *Defense Appropriation, FY 1964,* Part 1, p. 111.

17. *Ibid.* For the most recent statement of Secretary McNamara's position on civil defense, see his published presentation before the Senate Armed Services Committee and the Senate Subcommittee on Department of Defense Appropriations, Office of Secretary of Defense, FY 1966, pp. 63–69.

18. Speech of Defense Secretary McNamara, November 18, 1963.

19. Address of Alain C. Enthoven, deputy assistant secretary of defense, to the Loyola University Forum for National Affairs, Los Angeles, February 10, 1963,

20. B.B., *U.S. Budget, FY 1962,* p. M24.

21. Speech of Defense Secretary Robert McNamara at the University of Michigan, June 16, 1962.

22. *Ibid.*

23. One compilation of Defense Secretary McNamara's public statements, including week-long presentations before Congress, totaled 163 separate items between January, 1961, and November 8, 1963. During this same period Deputy Secretary of Defense Roswell Gilpatric made seventy-eight appearances. The bulk of these presentations dealt with American military capabilities and foreign policy intentions. Data, courtesy of Mr. Louis Higgs.

24. The organizational and procedural changes instituted by Secretary of Defense McNamara were in a very real sense made possible by the legislative and administrative innovations which his predecessors in office had already initiated and which Congress supported. The changes wrought by Secretary McNamara must be viewed against this larger historical backdrop to be fully understood. In this connection read especially Paul Y. Hammond, *Organizing for Defense* (Princeton: Princeton University Press, 1961). Useful, though more partisan and less thorough, is Thomas Ries, *The Management of Defense* (Baltimore: Johns Hopkins Press, 1964). Both works contain extensive bibliographical references. See also Harry Howe Ramson, *Can American Democracy Survive Cold War?*

25. Speech of Defense Secretary McNamara, April 20, 1963.

26. HCAS, *Hearings, Military Posture Briefings*, 87/1, 1961, p. 987.

27. Speech of Defense Secretary McNamara, April 20, 1963.

28. HCGO, *Hearings, Systems Development and Management*, 87/2, 1962, Part 2, p. 514.

29. Speech of Defense Secretary McNamara, April 20, 1963.

30. *Ibid.*

31. *Ibid.*

32. Defense Comptroller Charles Hitch discusses these shortcomings in relation to research and development in HCGO, *Systems Development Hearings*, Part 2, pp. 531–34, 543–46.

33. Kaufmann, *The McNamara Strategy*, pp. 170–71.

34. HCAS, *Hearings on Military Posture*, 88/1, 1963, pp. 373–74.

35. The most thorough and authoritative discussion of these programming and budgetary changes are discussed by Charles J. Hitch, assistant secretary of defense (comptroller), in HCGO, *Systems Development, Hearings*, Part 2, pp. 513–47. Particularly useful are the appendixes to these hearings which reproduce Defense Department directives dealing with programming and budgetary procedures. See Part 2, pp. 641 ff. Consult also Charles J. Hitch and Roland McKeon, *The Economics of Defense in The Nuclear Age* (Cambridge: Harvard University Press, 1960). Useful are the hearings of the Senate Subcommittee on National Policy Machinery. See SNPM, *Hearings, Organizing for National Security*, 1961, I, 1004–56, 1183–1228. For a critical analysis of Defense Department programming, see James R. Schlesinger, "Quantitative Analysis and National Security," *World Politics*, XV, No. 2 (January, 1963), 295–315. See also n. 15, Chapter IX.

36. The others included Continental Air and Missile Defense Forces, Airlift and Sealift Forces, Reserve and Guard Forces, Research and Development, General Support, Civil Defense, and Military Assistance Program HCGO *Systems Development, Hearings*, Part 2, p. 652.

37. *Ibid.*, p. 651.

38. Some of the problems connected with the programing system of the Defense Department may be found in *Study Report—Programming System for the Office of Secretary of Defense*, June 25, 1962. This document is reproduced in *ibid.*, Part 2, pp. 645–752.

39. *Ibid.*, p. 524. Hitch also observed that in the case of long leadtime items, an eight year projection is used.

40. HSAC, *Hearings, Department of Defense Appropriations, FY 1963*, 87/2, 1962, Part 2, pp. 4–15.

41. *Ibid.*, p. 13.

42. HCGO, *Systems Development, Hearings*, Part 2, p. 528.

43. *Ibid.*, p. 662.

44. *Ibid.*

45. *Ibid.*, pp. 544–45. Emphasis added.

46. SNPM, *Organizing for National Security*, I, 1009.

47. *Ibid.*, p. 1194.

48. *Ibid.*, p. 1009.

49. HSAC, *Defense Appropriations, FY 1964*, Part 1, p. 89. Secretary Mc-Namara had previously stated this mandate in his presentations of the defense budgets for FY 1962 and FY 1963.

50. Kaufmann, *The McNamara Strategy*, pp. 20–21, indicates that Defense Secretary McNamara fully understood the importance of access to adequate military data and expertise "on which to assess [on an independent basis] what the Services were demanding."

51. See pp. 89 ff. above.

52. The 1947, 1949, and 1958 military establishment reorganization acts appear in a committee print of the Senate Committee on Armed Services, December 18, 1958. See Committee Print, p. 70.

53. *Ibid.*, p. 89.

54. *Ibid.*, p. 93.

55. SNPM, *Organizing for National Security*, I, 1187. Emphasis added.

56. *Ibid.* Also, H. Doc. 502, 87/2, 1962, p. 77.

57. Hanson Baldwin, "Slow-down in the Pentagon," *Foreign Affairs*, XLIII, No. 2 (January, 1965), 271–72; SCAS, *Hearings, Department of Defense Reorganization Act of 1958*, 85/2, 1958, pp. 295–96.

58. The Ridgway view still commands adherents within professional military ranks. See, for example, the article by Colonel Robert N. Ginsburgh, "The Challenge to Military Professionalism," *Foreign Affairs*, XLII, No. 2 (January, 1964), 255–68. On the other hand, in an early 1964 speech, while General Maxwell Taylor was still chairman of the Joint Chiefs of Staff, he said: "I do not share the view that each advisor should be a specialist bringing to the table a narrow specialized view of the problem derived from the interests of the agency of government which he represents. President Kennedy resolved any doubt in the minds of the Joint Chiefs of Staff as to his views on the subject when in April 1961 he wrote to them as follows: 'While I look to the Chiefs to present the military factor without reserve or hesitation, I regard them to be more than military men and expect their help in fitting military requirements into the over-all context of any situation, recognizing that the most difficult problem in Government is to combine all assets in a unified, effective patterns.'" Speech of General Taylor at the Annual Meeting of the Fellows of the American Bar Association, February 16, 1964.

59. HSAC, *Defense Appropriations, FY 1964*, Part 1, p. 343; *idem, Hearings, Department of Defense Appropriations, FY 1965*, 88/2, 1965, Part 4, p. 307.

60. *Ibid.*, Part 4, pp. 598–600. General Wheeler made these remarks as army chief of staff.

61. Opinion differs over the role which the military have played in deciding defense policy. See the testimony of General Curtis LeMay on the FY 1964 defense

budget, *ibid.*, Part 4, pp. 511–14. However, on another occasion General Maxwell Taylor remarked: "As for the corporate body of the Joint Chiefs of Staff, I can certainly testify that it has not been by-passed during my tenure of office as Chairman. Indeed, we have received so many new functions, particularly those relating to the budget, that there is some danger that the Joint Chiefs of Staff Organization will be overloaded to the detriment of the discharge of its broad strategic responsibilities." Speech of General Taylor, February 15, 1964.

62. HSAC, *Defense Appropriations, FY 1964,* Part 1, pp. 343–44. Emphasis added.

63. Speech of Defense Secretary McNamara, April 20, 1963; SNPM, *Organizing for Defense,* I, 1196–97.

64. In the opinion of some military leaders, these values are not to be discounted. See Maxwell Taylor, *The Uncertain Trumpet,* pp. 120–21, where he states "that it is possible for the Secretary of Defense to make the existing machinery work better than it has. For one thing, he can get much closer to the Chiefs than has either Secretary Wilson or Secretary McElroy. Only once in my experience did Mr. Wilson ever sit down with the Chiefs for an extended period to try to understand their difficulties. . . . Although I suggested informal conferences with Mr. McElroy, beginning shortly after he came into office, he never gave the Chiefs any real opportunity as a body for serious discussion of basic issues. . . . Meanwhile, the President held aloof from the internal issues of the Chiefs, depending on the Secretary of Defense to adjust the differences."

65. Ries, *The Management of Defense,* p. 134, criticizes Forrestal's recommendation that the post of chairman of the JCS be created. Ries accuses Forrestal of "articulating one of the common myths of organization folklore [that] there is a single, consistent plan to accomplish every policy goal." This judgment is too harsh. Forrestal possessed a considerably more subtle conception of the requirements of strategic and foreign policy and had few illusions about organizational solutions to policy problems. See n. 8, Chapter 2.

66. Taylor, *The Uncertain Trumpet,* pp. 106–11.

67. *Ibid.,* pp. 109–10.

68. The chairmen of the Joint Chiefs of Staff are as follows, with their service affiliation and the months and year of their respective assumption of office: (1) Omar N. Bradley (army, August, 1949); (2) Arthur W. Radford (navy, August, 1953); (3) Nathan F. Twining (air force, August, 1957); (4) Lyman L. Lemnitzer (army, October, 1960); (5) Maxwell D. Taylor (army, October, 1962); (6) Earle G. Wheeler (army, July, 1964).

69. *New York Times,* June 25, 1964, p. 16.

70. SCGO, *Hearings, TFX Contract Investigation,* 88/1, 1963, Parts 1–10.

71. Interviews, March, 1965.

72. H. Doc. 335, 88/2, 1964, p. 158. Also Baldwin, *Foreign Affairs,* XLIII, 271. A distinction must be made between rank and legislative post. The 1958 Defense Reorganization Act, the most recent defense reorganization measure, creates seven assistant secretaries and a director of research and engineering.

73. *New York Times,* July 27, 1962, p. 1.

74. The defense secretary's presentations to Congress now include extensive discussion of the international setting in which military policies and programs are formulated. See statement of Defense Secretary Robert McNamara before a joint session of the Senate Armed Services Committee and the Senate Subcommittee on Department of Defense Appropriations, FY 1966, pp. 3–30.

75. The super agencies of the Defense Department include the following: Defense Atomic Support Agency (1959); National Security Agency (1952); Defense Communications Agency (1960); Defense Intelligence Agency (1961); Defense Supply Agency (1961). Parentheses indicate dates of establishment.

76. SNPM, *Organizing for National Security,* I, 1190. During Defense Secretary McNamara's first six months in office, 600 of 3,000 existing committees were abolished.

77. Speech of Defense Secretary McNamara, April 20, 1963.

78. SCAS, *Hearings, Military Procurement Authorization, FY 1963,* 87/2, 1962, p. 29.

79. For a different view of the defense decision process as it operates in the executive branch, see Samuel P. Huntington, *The Common Defense,* pp. 146–74. Huntington's analysis appeared too early to take account of the changes instituted by Secretary McNamara.

80. H. Doc. 335, 88/2, 1964, pp. 83–84; see pp. 411–17 below for a discussion of the RS-70 controversy.

81. HSAC, *Department of Defense Appropriations, FY 1965,* 88/2, Part 4, pp. 302–304.

82. Former Deputy Defense Secretary Roswell Gilpatrick under McNamara has noted: "The major decision-making involved in the management of the military establishment requires perhaps a thousand decisions in the course of a year, most of which are of a character that are susceptible of adequate consideration at the executive level at the average rate of several per day for the individual executive involved. Looking at the Department of Defense decision-making process in these terms, I am not aware, after two years on the job, of any crushing or unmanageable burden resting upon the office of the Secretary of Defense as a result of the present system of centralization. On the contrary, I believe the present system not only is preferable in theory but works in practice and does not require super men to make it function." Speech of Deputy Defense Secretary Roswell Gilpatrick before the National Defense Committee of the National Association of Manufacturers, January 23, 1963.

Opinion is seriously divided on the effect of the organizational and procedural changes instituted by Defense Secretary McNamara. Criticisms are raised that OSD has become an operating department, that it is overloaded and not only stifles action and decision today but will very likely break down in a serious future crisis; and that the civilian leadership of the Pentagon is ignoring the advice and experience of military services. See the arguments of Ries and Baldwin as well as the views expressed in HCAS, *Report of Special Subcommittee on Defense Agencies,* 87/2, 1962.

83. HSAC, *Defense Appropriations, FY 1965,* Part 4, pp. 303–4.

84. SNPM, *Organizing for National Security,* I, 1192. Defense Department activities are, of course, being continually reorganized. Secretary McNamara has directed the establishment of the Defense Intelligence, the Defense Supply Agency, and STRICOM, a new command which integrates ground and air forces. The discussions of Defense Department organization by Colonel Charles Donnelly provide detailed information, including bibliographical entries. See n. 1, and n. 24, above.

85. *Ibid.,* I, 1197.

86. P.L. 86–149. 72 *Stat.* 322.

87. For two conflicting view points, see Raymond H. Dawson, "Congressional Innovation and Intervention in Defense Policy: Legislative Authorization of Weapon Systems," *American Political Science Review,* LVI, No. 1 (March, 1962), pp. 43–57; and Bernard K. Gordon, "The Military Budget: Congressional Phase," *Journal of Politics,* XXIII, No. 3 (August, 1961), pp. 689–710.

88. 64 *Stat.* 321.

89. 10 U.S.C. 8062, 9531.

90. 10 U.S.C., 4331.

91. 10 U. S. C., 7201.

92. 10 U. S. C., 7341.

93. 10 U. S. C., 7341.

94. HCAS, *Military Posture Briefing,* 87/1, 1961, p. 929.

95. 10 U.S.C. 3201, 8202.

96. 10 U. S. C., 5401. Authorized naval officer levels call for a force of line officers not larger than 7 per cent of authorized enlisted strength. The percentages set for the supply corps and civil engineering are 12 and 3 per cent respectively. Marine corps office levels are also defined at a level of 7 per cent of enlisted personnel. 10 U.S.C. 5403, 5404, 5405.

97. 10 U.S.C. 3201. The latest suspension, in effect until July 1, 1967, was signed into law on March 28, 1963.

98. SCAS, *Defense Reorganization Act of 1958,* pp. 31–32, 67–69, 312–17.

99. *Ibid.,* pp. 314–15.

100. *Ibid.,* p. 314.

101. *Ibid.,* p. 317.

102. *Ibid.* See also, p. 32. Senator Flanders was obviously not persuaded by the observations of Senator Richard Russell, chairman of the Senate Armed Services Committee, that the committee did pass on the important aspects of defense policy. Senator Russell was apparently not persuaded by his own initial remarks and later became the chief sponsor of Section 412(b). Senator Russell credits Senator Flanders with having been the first to suggest an annual review of defense policy by the armed services committees that passed on the "fundamental requirements involved." Letter to the author, February 19, 1965.

103. SCAS, *Defense Reorganization Act of 1958*, especially pp. 14–36, 317–21. "You might be interested ot know, you were not here at the time," Senator Richard Russell pointedly informed Defense Secretary McElroy, "that several members of this committee, time and again, urged your predecessor [Charles Wilson] to take some action to coordinate and correlate the missile development, to avoid this very waste that is now being charged to the Congress. We do not feel that we could sit here in committee and pass a law that would say one man down in one of the Departments should have charge of the missile development. We thought that was an administrative matter. . . ." *Ibid.*, p. 16.

104. *Ibid.*, pp. 37–55, especially pp. 37–41, 51–55.

105. Dawson, *American Political Science Review*, LVI, 49–50.

106. SCAS, *Defense Reorganization Act of 1958*, p. 32.

107. C.R., April 11, 1962, p. 5807, Daily Edition.

108. SCAS, *Defense Reorganization Act of 1958*, p. 68.

109. S. Rept. 1765, 85/2, 1958, p. 40.

110. Interviews, March, 1965.

111. S. Rept. 296, 86/1, 1959, p. 15.

112. Interviews, March, 1965.

113. The wider language was the Senate's. The original House version was restricted to the research, development, or procurement of the RS–70.. H. Rept. 1406, 87/2, 1962, p. 32; S. Rept. 1315, 87–2, 1962, p. 18.

114. Letters from members of the House and Senate Armed Services committees.

115. Letters from members of the House and Senate Armed Services Appropriations committees.

116. Interviews, March 1965.

117. See Chapter VI, pp. 304–6, and n. 103 above.

118. S. Rept., 296, 86/1, 1959, p. 16; C.R., 86/1, 1959, CV, Part 11, 14719; *ibid.*, 14764.

119. Interviews, March, 1965. There is some doubt whether Senator Russell himself took the posture hearings very seriously. He was not always sure what they contained, although he certainly was aware of their limitations even as a technique for gathering information about defense policy. In defending the record of the Armed Services Committee to Senator Flanders, Senator Russell said: "We [the Armed Services Committee] do get, in general terms, the defense picture, in almost every instance—*I don't believe we did it this year*—by a briefing early in the session by the Department of Defense. . . . They come in with graphs and charts and show how many divisions they are going to have of infantry. . . . and so forth. But, of course, when they go before the Appropriations Committee for the money it is broken down in a little more detail." SCAS, *Department of Defense Reorganization Act of 1958*, p. 32. Emphasis added.

120. Interviews, March, 1965. Dawson, *American Political Science Review*, LVI, 52–53.

121. Interviews, March, 1965.

122. Guiding the actions of the appropriations committee looms important in the deliberations of the House Armed Services Committee. See HCAS, *Authorizing Hearings*, 87/1, 1961, pp. 1679–1721.

123. Interviews, March, 1965. *New York Times*, March 31, 1965, pp. 1, 8.

124. Joseph G. Whelan, "Berlin: A Chronological Summary with an Analytical Commentary, July, 1959, to December, 1961," Legislative Reference Service, Library of Congress, mimeo.

125. B.B., *Budget of the United States, FY 1962*, p. M20; SSAC, *Hearings, Department of Defense, FY 1962*, 87/1. 1961, p. 1647, insert p. 2.

126. H. Doc. 123, 87/1, p. 13.

127. *Ibid.* Also see SCAS, *Hearings, Military Procurement Authorization, FY 1962*, 87/1, 1961, pp. 1–46, wherein Defense Secretary McNamara makes a detailed presentation of the President's March 28 recommendations.

128. *Urgent National Needs, A Special Message to Congress by President Kennedy*, May 25, 1961, pp. 17–24.

129. H. Doc. 179, 87/1, 1961, p. 5.

130. *New York Times*, June 7, 1961, p. 16.

131. *The Berlin Crisis, Report to the Nation by President Kennedy*, July 25, 1961, and S. Rept. 653, 87/1, 1961, p. 3.

132. HCAS, *Authorizing Hearings* 87/1, 1961; *idem, Military Posture Briefings*, 87/1, 1961. The House did integrate its posture and authorization hearings in 1963.

133. SCAS, *Authorizing Hearings*, 87/1, 1961, pp. 25–27; HCAS, *Authorizing Hearings*, 87/1, 1961, p. 1258–60.

134. *Ibid.*, pp. 1532–36.

135. See latest Defense Department directives on reprogramming, DOD Directives 7250.5, 7250.10, dated, respectively, March 4 and March 5, 1963.

136. H. Rept. 380, 87/1, 1961, p. 3.

137. *Ibid.*

138. S. Rept. 253, 87/1, 1961, p. 4.

139. *Ibid.*

140. HCAS, *Authorizing Hearings*, 87/1, 1961, pp. 1599–1617.

141. S. Rept. 253, 87/1, 1961.

142. C.R., May 15, 1961, p. 7412, Daily Edition.

143. *Ibid.*, pp. 7407–12.

144. H. Rept. 380, 87/1, 1961, p. 67.

145. C.R., May 24, 1961, p. 8321, Daily Edition.

146. HCAS, *Authorizing Hearings*, 87/1, 1961, pp. 1683–84.

147. C.R., May 24, 1961, p. 8219, Daily Edition. Vinson apparently had better luck with the Senate defense appropriations group which printed his letter advocating a stepup in army preparedness in its hearings. SSAC, *Defense Hearings, FY 1962*, p. 1150.

148. HCAS, *Authorization Hearings*, 87/1, 1961, p. 1701.

149. The problem of limited preparedness was not confined to any one part of the House or Senate hearings or floor presentations. See, for example, HSAC, *Defense Appropriations, FY 1962*, Part 3, especially pp. 150-245, 289, 315-16, 346-54; and SSAC, *Defense Appropriations, FY 1962*, pp. 66, 77, 123, 158, 294, 628-29, 1150-51, 1176, 1388-89. See also Senator Willis Robertson's discussion of his attempts to gain administration backing for more limited war preparedness. C.R., August 3, 1961, p. 13472-73, Daily Edition.

150. C.R., June 27, 1961, pp. 10635-38, Daily Edition.

151. SSAC, *Defense Appropriations, FY 1962*, pp. 359-78; HSAC, *Defense Appropriations, FY 1962*, Part 3, p. 189.

152. *Ibid.*, pp. 289, 315-16, 346-47; SSAC, *Defense Appropriations, FY 1962*, pp. 161, 629.

153. HSAC, *Defense Appropriations, FY 1962*, p. 353.

154. H. Rept. 574, 87/1, 1961, pp. 11-12.

155. HSAC, *Defense Appropriations, FY 1962*, Part 3, p. 177.

156. C.R., June 27, 1961, p. 10637, Daily Edition.

157. H. Rept. 574, 87/1, 1961, pp. 4-5.

158. *Ibid.*, p. 7.

159. *Ibid.*, pp. 6-7, 9.

160. *Ibid.*, p. 9.

161. *Ibid.*, p. 49.

162. SSAC, *Defense Appropriations, FY 1962*, p. 1551.

163. *Ibid.*, p. 1679.

164. The Senate was strongly opposed to the House meat ax cut, but relented before House insistence. SSAC, *Defense Appropriations, FY 1962*, pp. 1677-78.

165. B.B., *Budget of the United States, FY 1966*, pp. 70-72.

166. *New York Times*, January 19, 1965, p. 16.

167. B.B., *Budget of the United States, FY 1966*, p. 70.

168. H. Rept. 1406, 87/2, 1962, p. 4.

169. See n. 87, Chapter V above.

170. H. Rept. 1406, 87/2, 1962, p. 1. Emphasis added.

171. *Ibid.*, p. 9.

172. H. Doc. 502, 87/2, 1962, p. 160.

173. See above, pp. 393-94.

174. H. Rept. 1406, 87/2, 1962, p. 9.

175. The House Armed Services Committee clash with the Pentagon raged throughout March and the first part of April, 1962. See, for example, the following issues of the *Washington Post*: March 7, p. A15; March 8, pp. A1, A20; March 15, p. A15; March 16, pp. A1, A2; and March 22, p. A1, A17. A fuller discussion of Defense Secretary McNamara's position, issued on March 15, 1962, may be found in Kaufmann, *The McNamara Strategy*, pp. 220–28.

176. H. Rept. 1406, 87/2, 1962, p. 8.

177. *Ibid.*, p. 7.

178. *Ibid.*, p. 8.

179. *Ibid.*

180. *Ibid.*, p. 7.

181. *Ibid.*

182. Interviews. *Washington Post*, March 22, 1962, pp. A1, A17.

183. C.R., March 21, 1962, pp. 4329–30, Daily Edition.

184. *Ibid.*, p. 4330, Daily Edition.

185. Interviews. *Washington Post*, March 22, 1962, p. A17.

186. C.R., March 21, 1962, p. 4309, Daily Edition.

187. S. Rept. 1315, 87/2, 1962, pp. 3–4.

188. C.R., April 17, 1962, p. 6327, Daily Edition.

189. *Ibid.*, June 13, 1962, p. 9599, Daily Edition.

190. H. Rept. 1607, 87/2, 1962, pp. 3–4.

191. S. Rept. 1578, 87/2, 1962, pp. 3–7.

192. S. Doc. 162, 87/2, pp. 704-5.

193. HSAC, *Defense Appropriations, FY 1963,* Part 1, pp. 112, 193, 340–41.

194. C.R., August 1, 1962, p. 14243–44, Daily Edition.

195. *Ibid.*

196. SSAC, *Hearings, Department of Defense Appropriations, FY 1965,* 88/2, 1964, Part 1, pp. 735–36.

197. SCAS, *Defense Reorganization Act of 1958,* p. 32.

198. SNPM, *Organizing for National Security,* I, 1028.

CHAPTER VIII

1. Some of the theoretical conceptions of government underlying this chapter were influenced in varying degrees of importance by the following works: John Stuart Mill, *Considerations on Representative Government* (Indianapolis: Bobbs-

Merrill, 1958); *The Federalist Papers*, particularly Nos. 10 and 51; Walter Lippmann, *The Public Philosophy* (New York: New American Library, 1955); L. S. Amery, *Thoughts on the Constitution* (2d ed.; London: Oxford University Press, 1953); and Yves R. Simon, *Philosophy of Democratic Government* (Chicago: University of Chicago Press, 1951), especially pp. 99–143.

2. G. M. Trevelyan, *History of England* (New York: Doubleday Anchor Books, 1952), III, 73.

3. It should be noted that a serious question can even be raised about Congress' ability to control and direct the military establishment during the nation's formative years. The broad grants of appropriations authority given to the War and Navy departments in the early days of the republic evidence Congress' heavy reliance on the executive branch. See Leonard D. White, *The Federalists* (New York: Macmillan, 1948), pp. 327-28; *idem, The Jeffersonians* (New York: Macmillan, 1951), pp. 109–12.

4. SCFR, *Hearings, Nuclear Test Ban Treaty*, 88/2, 1963. See also the editorial comment of Walter Lippmann, *Washington Post*, August 22, 1963.

5. Most of the works cited in n. 39, Chapter I, above, touch in one way or another on the diminution of congressional influence within the federal government.

6. Earle (ed.), *The Federalist*, p. 43.

7. Perhaps a major exception to this conclusion is the Sixteenth Amendment, which granted the federal government the authority to tax personal income.

8. The hazards facing Congress when it employs its appropriations power as a tool of administrative direction are perceptively discussed, for example, in Lucius Wilmerding's *The Spending Power* (New Haven: Yale University Press, 1943). Elias Huzar's *The Purse and the Sword*, pp. 62–373, deals specifically with Congress and military appropriations as does Edward L. Katzenbach's "How Congress Strains at Gnats, then Swallows Military Budgets," *Reporter*, XI (July 20, 1954), 31–35. For a more recent study, see Robert A. Wallace, *Congressional Control of Federal Spending*, pp. 65–127.

9. U.S., Commission on Organization of the Executive Branch of the Government, *Budget and Accounting, A Report to the Congress*, June, 1955, p. ix.

10. The term "electorate" is used here because it refers more specifically to that part of the over-all population that can affect governmental policies through the exercise of its right to vote.

11. See, for example, SCAS, Special Preparedness Subcommittee, *Hearings, Military Cold War Education and Speech Review Policies*, 87/2, 1962, Parts 1–8.

12. Gabriel A. Almond, *The American People and Foreign Policy* (New York: Praeger, 1960), p. 69.

13. *Ibid.*

14. Alexis de Tocqueville, *Democracy in America*, Reeve text, ed., Phillips Bradley (New York: Vintage Books, 1955), I, 237.

15. Professor Samuel P. Huntington notes: "The most prominent congressional role is that of prodder or goad of the Executive on behalf of specific programs or

activities. With the Executive as the decision-maker, Congress has become the lobbyist. Congressional groups engage in sustained campaigns of pressure and persuasion to produce the desired strategic decisions on the part of the Executive, just as in other areas the Administration uses pressure and persuasion to move its legislation through Congress." ("Strategic Planning and the Political Process," *Foreign Affairs*, XXXVIII, No. 2 [January, 1960], 287).

16. Irving Kristol, "Democracy and Babel," *Columbia University Forum*, III (Fall, 1960), 17.

17. See Chapter IX below.

18. George F. Kennan, *American Diplomacy*. 1900–1950 (New York: New American Library, 1952), pp. 113–14.

19. Quoted by Stephen G. Xydis, *US Naval Institute Proceedings*, LXXXIV, 41.

20. See Chapter V, n. 57. above.

21. These conditions are suggested by Osgood, *Limited War*, pp. 237–50.

22. For a European view that parallels this analysis of the Cuban crisis, see Alfred Grosser, *La Politique Extérieure de la Cinquième République* (Paris: Seuil, 1965), pp. 131 ff. The doctrine of proportionality is not meant as a definitive rule for the determination of military operations. It is merely a shorthand statement of those factors which must be weighed in reaching a decision on the military means that a nation should employ to gain its political objectives. What assessment a policy-maker reaches of the enemy's military forces, the geographic scope of the conflict, or the political stakes at issue will vary from one situation to another and will depend on the information, intellectual capacity, values and resolution of those in positions of power.

23. There appears little doubt that the Kennedy administration carefully weighed each of its military moves in the Cuban confrontation of 1962. Dr. Alain C. Enthoven, one of Secretary of Defense McNamara's most influential aides, notes: "Each military move was, in effect, a carefully formulated message from the President to Khrushchev, intended to convince him that the United States would use military force to the extent necessary to achieve removal of the offensive weapons. But each move was also intended to convince him that he could withdraw without armed conflict, if he would withdraw." Address to the Loyola University Forum for National Affairs, Los Angeles, February 10, 1963.

24. A treatment of budgetary theory that still provides some perceptive insights may be found in V. O. Key's "The Lack of Budgetary Theory," *American Political Science Review*, XXXIV, No. 4 (December, 1940), 1137–44. For a more extensive treatment of governmental budgeting, see Jesse Burkhead, *Government Budgeting* (New York: John Wiley, 1956). With special reference to defense economics and budgeting, consult Arthur Smithies, *The Budgetary Process in the United States* (New York: McGraw-Hill, 1955), pp. 229–328; Frederick Mosher, *Program Budgeting* (Chicago: Public Administration Service, 1954). See also Chapter VII, n. 35 above.

25. These points are forcefully made by Bernard Brodie, *Strategy in the Missile Age* (Princeton: Princeton University Press, 1959), pp. 362–65; and Hitch and McKeon, pp. 46–48.

26. See pp. 48–50 above.

27. See Appendixes B and C for a listing of House and Senate Defense Appropriations Subcommittee members who have served since 1949, when the subcommittees were created. See Huzar, pp. 33–35.

28. Samuel P. Huntington, in his "Strategic Planning and Political Process," *Foreign Affairs*, XXXVIII, No. 2 (January, 1960), 285–99, describes the policy-making procedures in the executive branch as a "legislative process." A more extensive treatment of the conflict-consensus process of the Defense Department is found in Huntington's *The Common Defense*. Interestingly enough, Maxwell D. Taylor wrote with some seriousness that the experiences which had been most helpful to him as a member of the Joint Chiefs of Staff were those that he had acquired during his "membership in the Northeast High School Society of Debate in his pre–West Point days in Kansas City." Maxwell D. Taylor, *The Uncertain Trumpet*, p. xiv.

29. HSAC, *Hearings, Department of Defense Appropriations Bill, 1959*, 85/2, 1958, pp. 44–107.

30. Rockefeller Brothers Fund, *International Security: The Military Aspect* (New York: Doubleday, 1958).

31. During the Eighty-sixth Congress, the House and Senate engaged on the average a total of slightly more than nine hundred employees on their permanent committee staffs for varying periods. The House maintained a force of slightly more than five hundred workers; the Senate, about four hundred and twenty. (Source: Legislative Reference Service. For opposing views as to the utility of congressional staffs, see Ernest Griffith, pp. 47–48, 58–59, 70–75, 114 ff: and Bertram Gross, pp. 280–83, 421–23).

32. C.R. 82/1, 1951, XCVII, Part 9, 9555.

33. Interview with Mr. Samuel Crosby, then clerk to the House Defense Appropriations Subcommittee, and now a special assistant to the secretary of defense.

34. Interview with Senate staff member, February 8, 1960.

35. The operating divisions of the Legislative Reference Service (LRS) include American law, economics, education and public welfare, foreign affairs, government and general research, natural resources, and science policy research. In FY 1963, LRS carried 215 budgeted positions, including clerical and administrative help; 228 positions were indicated for FY 1965. SSAC, *Hearings, Legislative Branch Appropriations*, 1965, 88/2, 1964, p. 276, p. 2.

36. Based on personal experience of the author as an analyst in national security, 1961–62, and on numerous informal interviews since then.

37. *Washington Post*, October 27, 1961, p. A8.

38. 72 *U.S. Stat.* 715, (1958); 72 *ibid.* 367 (1959); 74 *ibid.* 340 (1960).

39. This conclusion is suggested by Hans J. Morgenthau's seminal article in the *New Republic*, "The Last Years of Our Greatness," CXXXIX (December 29, 1958), 11–16.

40. See, for example, "Congress on Defense," *ibid.*, June 15, 1959, p. 2, and the *New York Times*, May 30, 1959, pp. 1, 2 which describes the position of the *Army, Navy, Air Force Journal* with respect to Congress' role in defense policy.

41. *Ibid.*, p. 1. The quotation reflects the position of the *Army, Navy, Air Force Journal*. See also the view of Hanson Baldwin, *New York Times*, May 28, 1959, p. 13.

42. Simon, *Philosophy of Democratic Government*, pp. 99–143.

43. See pp. 109–12 above.

44. See pp. 106 ff.

45. Lippmann, *The Public Philosophy*, pp. 32–38.

46. See pp. 55–56 above.

47. Said Representative William E. Minshall during House floor consideration of the Defense Appropriations Bill for FY 1962: "I am particularly fortunate to serve on the Defense Department Appropriations Subcommittee. I think it is one of the most important committees of the House. Certainly, we meet longer hours than any other committee of the House. We meet daily, for long hours. . . . One thing I should like to mention is the fact that last year we had in our subcommittee over 8,000 pages of testimony. There would have been much more than that if there had been added to the record of the testimony those pages that had been deleted for security purposes." (C.R., April 18, 1962, p. 6360, *Daily Edition*).

48. Interview with Representative George Mahon.

49. See p. 417 above.

50. C.R., Vol. CX, April 7, 1964. Release issued by the Office of Senator J. William Fulbright.

CHAPTER IX

1. Professor Warner Schilling deals extensively with this problem in his previously cited case study of the FY 1950 defense budget. See Schilling, (ed.), *Strategy, Politics, and Defense Budgets*, pp. 1–266. The analysis here differs from Schilling's in two important and seemingly paradoxical senses. First, it attributes greater success to Congress than Schilling does in its efforts to influence and, at times, to improve defense policy since World War II. Schilling's case study does not cover a sufficiently long time-span to evaluate the evolution of Congress' response to, and impact on, strategic policy. Second, this study argues that Congress can potentially play a greater and more salutary role in defense policy than Schilling and others admit. It is in terms of this larger, potential role, sketched in Chapter VIII, that the conclusion is drawn that Congress has done poorly. This view does not contradict the initial point that Congress has done a better job in strategic policy than many recognize. The point of view and the standards of evaluation here are different. In sum, this study sets higher and more exacting standards to

test congressional action in strategic policy than appears to be currently acceptable and judges Congress accordingly. It attempts, simultaneously, to present a balanced picture of congressional behavior, indicating both the commendable and the questionable aspects of Congress' influence on strategic policy since 1945 through its appropriations power.

2. See pp. 238–43 above.

3. See Taylor, *Uncertain Trumpet*, pp. 111–14; Gavin, *War and Peace in the Space Age*, pp. 165–72.

4. Interview, March, 1965.

5. See pp. 100–101, 121–22 above.

6. See pp. 204–8, 211–12 above.

7. See pp. 120, 238–43 above.

8. See pp. 105–7 above.

9. C.R., 82/2, 1958, CIV, Part 8, 10016. See also above, pp. 281–83.

10. Richard F. Fenno, Jr., The House Appropriations Committee as a Political System: The Problem of Integration, paper delivered at the annual meeting of the American Political Science Association, September 6–9, 1961, p. 13.

11. The literature of congressional reform is large enough to warrant separate study. A useful and extensive bibliography may be found in the following work: Senate, Committee on Rules and Administration, *Hearings, Senate Rules and Procedures*, 88/1, 1963, pp. 221–24. Not listed are a number of recent publications of relevance. These include Joseph Clark, *Congress: The Sapless Branch* (New York: Harper, 1963); *idem, The Senate Establishment* (New York: Hill & Wang, 1963); Charles Clapp, *The Congressman* (Washington, D.C.: Brookings Institution, 1964); Robert Bendiner, *Obstacle Course on Capitol Hill* (New York: McGraw-Hill, 1964); Daniel M. Berman, *In Congress Assembled* (New York: Macmillan, 1964); and the Arden House publication, *The Congress and America's Future*, Report of the Twenty-sixth American Assembly, 1964. See also, n. 15 below.

12. Roger H. Davidson, *et al.*, found in an opinion poll of legislators that 61 per cent were opposed to changes in the structure and procedure of the House of Representatives. The poll catalogued the average reaction of eighty congressmen to thirty-two proposals for change. (Paper delivered at Public Affairs Center, Dartmouth College, March 7–8, 1964).

13. See Chapter I where these relationships are discussed at greater length.

14. The Ombudsman technique is discussed in Senate, Committee on Rules and Administration, *Hearings, Senate Rules and Procedures*, pp. 111–24.

15. A number of works which deal specifically with the budgetary process in Congress include Joseph P. Harris, *Congressional Control of Administration* (Washington, D.C.: Brookings Institution, 1964), especially pp. 104–217; Arthur Smithies, *The Budgetary Process*, especially pp. 175–97; Robert Ash Wallace,

Congressional Control of Federal Spending; and John S. Saloma, *The Responsible Use of Power* (Washington, D.C.: American Enterprise Institute, 1964). Especially useful is Aaron Wildavsky, *The Politics of the Budgetary Process* (Boston: Little, Brown, 1964). Professor Wildavsky's work offers the best available description and analysis of the politics of the budgetary process in Congress. Although this study generally agrees with his factual findings, it differs sharply from his evaluation of the policy implications of the existing budgetary process in Congress, particularly with respect to strategic and foreign policy. See also n. 24, Chapter VIII.

16. A summary of the criticisms that have been made against the omnibus bill procedure may be found in Robert Ash Wallace, "Congressional Control of the Budget," *Midwest Journal of Political Science*, III (May, 1959), 160–62.

17. The proposal for the implementation of Section 206 is drawn largely from Robert Wallace's discussion, *ibid.*, Ill. 163–67, and *idem*, *Congressional Control of Federal Spending*, pp. 155–67.

18. *The Federalist*, p. 3.

INDEX

INDEX

Acheson, Dean, 191

"Admirals' Revolt" (1949), 87, 229

Africa: communist penetration into, 332

Agency for International Development, 29

Air Force, U.S.: appropriation requests for FY 1947, 40, 44; appropriations for FY 1952, 136, 137; average strength for FY 1949, 82; Bomarc, 304, 306, 312, 372; budget for FY 1947, 44; budget for FY 1951, 116; budget estimate for FY 1958, 279; budget requests for FY 1959, 280; comparison of groups, 102; 58-group force, 101, 102; requirements for FY 1950, 93, 94; 70-group force, 37, 40, 74; status in FY 1947, 39–41; "stretch-out" drive of FY 1953, 155; Talos authorization, 371

Air lift, 249

Air Policy Board (congressional), 78, 79

Air Policy Commission (Finletter Commission), 78

Air power: approval by Congress, 79–83; debate during 1956 presidential campaign, 238

Albert, Carl, 417

Alsop, Joseph, 232

Anderson, George, 357, 511

Andrews, George W., 215; amendment, 224

Andrews, Walter, 79

Arms Control and Disarmament Agency, 29

Army, U.S.: average strength for FY 1949, 82; budget for FY 1951, 114; budget for FY 1958, 239; Nike-Ajax system, 304; Nike-Hercules system, 303, 304, 306, 372; presentations for FY 1949, 81–85; requirements for FY 1950, 93, 94; standing, 18; "stretch-out" drive, FY 1953, 154

Army and Air Force Authorization and Composition Act (1950), 366

Atlas missile system, 336, 408

Atomic bomb, 59; U.S.S.R. possession of, 79

Baldwin, Hanson, 298, 358

Berlin crisis, 387–89

Bombers: B–29, 59; B–36, 59, 109, 110; B–52, 236; B–70, 312

Bombing, strategic, 39

Bradley, Omar, 94, 131, 132, 138, 144, 182, 183

Brinkmanship diplomacy, 227

Brown, Clarence, 146

Budget proposals: defense, for research, development, and testing, 28

Bureaucracy: civil-military relations and, 28

Burke, Arleigh, 294

627